EUROPEAN COMPARATIVE COMPANY LAW

Recent attempts to harmonise company law within the EU have led to major European company law reforms. This examination of European company law uses seven European countries as case studies: the United Kingdom, France, Germany, Italy, Spain, Belgium and the Netherlands. Taking into account recent company law reform within these jurisdictions and the extensive action plan adopted by the European Commission, the authors consider EU Company Law Directives, the case law of the Court of Justice on the directives and the right to free movement and establishment in the Treaty of Rome. Attention is also given to the European Economic Interest Grouping (EEIG) and the European Company (SE). At a time when both EU and national company laws are undergoing significant change and reform, this book will aid understanding of an emerging discipline.

Professor Mads Andenas is a Professor at the University of Oslo and the University of Leicester, the Director of the Centre of Corporate and Financial Law, Institute of Advanced Legal Studies, University of London, and a Visiting Senior Research Fellow, Institute of European and Comparative Law, University of Oxford.

Professor Frank Wooldridge is a former Professorial Fellow of the British Institute of International and Comparative Law, London and the former Law Society Senior Research Fellow, Institute of Advanced Legal Studies, University of London. Both authors have been members of the Company Law Committee of the Law Society of England and Wales.

EUROPEAN COMPARATIVE COMPANY LAW

MADS ANDENAS

and

FRANK WOOLDRIDGE

CAMBRIDGE
UNIVERSITY PRESS

CAMBRIDGE UNIVERSITY PRESS
Cambridge, New York, Melbourne, Madrid, Cape Town,
Singapore, São Paulo, Delhi, Mexico City

Cambridge University Press
The Edinburgh Building, Cambridge CB2 8RU, UK

Published in the United States of America by
Cambridge University Press, New York

www.cambridge.org
Information on this title: www.cambridge.org/9781107407640

First published 2009
First paperback edition 2012

A catalogue record for this publication is available from the British Library

Library of Congress Cataloguing in Publication data
Andenaes, Mads Toennesson, 1957–
European comparative company law / Mads Andenas and Frank Wooldridge.
p. cm.
ISBN 978-0-521-84219-8
1. Business enterprises – Law and legislation – Europe.
2. Corporation law – Europe. I. Wooldridge, Frank. II. Title.
KJC2432.A93 2009
346.24′066–dc22
2008054122

ISBN 978-0-521-84219-8 Hardback
ISBN 978-1-107-40764-0 Paperback

CONTENTS

Preface *page* xiii
Table of Cases xvi
Table of Legislation xxi

1. Introduction 1
   I. The new European company law 1
   II. An outline of this book 3

2. European and comparative company law 7
   I. Harmonisation and free movement 7
      A. Treaty provisions 7
      B. Free movement and the fundamental freedoms: the right of establishment 10
      C. Free movement of capital 14
      D. The harmonising directives in the field of company law 20
      E. Draft legislation 28
      F. Methodological problems concerning company law harmonisation 33
   II. Comparative company law 41
      A. Introductory remarks 41
      B. Comparative law and the harmonisation of company law 42
   III. Comparative company law and national legal reforms 49
      A. Continental reforms 49
      B. UK Company law reform and comparative law – DTI's strategic framework 50

3. Formation of companies 52
   I. Introduction 52
   II. Formation of private and public companies in the United Kingdom 53
      A. Process of formation 53
      B. Special rules applicable to public companies 54

C. The memorandum and articles (constitution) of the company 55
D. Constructive notice 58
E. Pre-incorporation contracts 59
F. Transfer proposals in the consultation document 'Completing the structure' 60
III. Formation of private and public companies in France 61
A. The *société à responsabilité limitée* (SARL) 62
B. The *société anonyme* (SA) 64
IV. Formation of private and public companies in Germany 67
A. Formation of private companies 67
B. Special rules applicable to one-man companies 70
C. Liabilities in respect of pre-registration activities 70
D. Formation of an AG 72
E. Special rules relating to the one-man AG 77
F. Liability in respect of pre-incorporation transactions 77
V. Formation of public and private companies in Italy 78
A. Formation of public companies 78
B. Formation of private companies in Italy 82
VI. Formation of private and public companies in Spain 83
A. Formation of private companies in Spain 83
B. Single member private companies 85
C. Liabilities in respect of pre-incorporation transactions 86
D. Simplification of incorporation procedures 86
E. Formation of public companies in Spain 87
F. Liabilities in respect of pre-incorporation transactions 89
VII. Formation of private and public companies in Belgium 90
A. Formation 90
B. Liability in respect of pre-incorporation transactions 92
VIII. Formation of private and public companies in the Netherlands 92
A. Liabilities in respect of pre-incorporation transactions 94
B. Dutch legislation on pro-forma companies 95

4. The types of business organisation 99
I. Introduction 99
II. Public limited liability companies 103
A. The French SAS 105
B. Limited partnerships with shares 107
III. Private companies 109
A. Private companies in the United Kingdom 109
B. Private companies in France 111
C. Private companies in Germany 115

D. Private companies in Italy 119
E. Private companies in Spain 122
F. Private companies in Belgium 124
G. Private companies in the Netherlands 128
H. Proposals for the European Private Company 129
IV. Partnerships 130
A. Civil partnerships 131
B. Silent partnerships and other forms of partnership without legal personality 132
C. General partnerships 135
D. General partnerships in some other European countries 137
E. Limited partnerships 152
F. Special type of limited partnership in Germany and France 159

5. Share (or equity) capital and loan capital 168
I. Equity securities issued by United Kingdom companies 170
II. Equity securities issued by French companies 171
A. Preference shares (*actions de préférence*) 173
B. Securities giving rights of conversion into shares (*titres donnant accès à terme au capital*) 174
III. Equity securities issued by German companies 175
A. Private companies 175
B. Public companies: the provisions of Articles 139–141 of the German *Aktiengesetz* (AktG) 176
IV. Equity securities issued by Italian companies 180
V. Equity securities issued by Spanish companies 185
VI. Equity securities issued by Belgian companies 186
A. Belgian provisions concerning preference shares 187
B. Private companies 187
C. Public companies 188
VII. Equity securities issued by Dutch companies 189
A. Preference shares 190
B. Priority shares 191
C. Warrants 191
VIII. Increase and reduction of capital 192
A. Applicable legal rules in the United Kingdom 192
B. Applicable legal rules in France 195
C. Applicable rules of law in Germany 202
D. Applicable legal rules in Italy 211
E. Applicable legal rules in Spain 218
F. Applicable legal rules in Belgium 222
G. Applicable legal rules in the Netherlands 226

IX. Acquisition, purchase, and redemption by a company of its own shares 230
A. Applicable legal rules in the United Kingdom 230
B. Applicable legal rules in France 233
C. Applicable legal rules in Germany 235
D. Applicable legal rules in Italy 237
E. Applicable legal rules in Spain 239
F. Applicable legal rules in Belgium 241
G. Applicable legal rules in the Netherlands 244
X. Financial assistance for the acquisition of shares 246
A. Loan capital 248
B. The position in the United Kingdom 249
C. The position in France 250
D. The position in Germany 253
E. The position in Italy 256
F. The position in Spain 259
G. The position in Belgium 261
H. The position in the Netherlands 264

6. Management and control of companies 265
I. Introduction 265
II. The position in the United Kingdom 267
A. General considerations 267
B. The appointment, vacation of office and removal of directors 268
C. Powers of directors 269
D. Duties of directors 271
E. The general meeting 275
F. Minority protection 278
III. The position in France 283
A. Managers of an SARL; their powers and duties 283
B. Control over the managers of an SARL 284
C. Position of the members of an SARL 285
D. Different management structures in an SA 286
E. The single board system 287
F. The dual board system 290
G. Directors' liability 293
H. The position of the shareholders 295
IV. The position in Germany 297
A. The management and control of a GmbH 297
B. The management and control of an AG 307

V. The position in Italy 320
A. Public companies 320
B. Private companies 346
VI. The position in Spain 352
A. Private companies (SRLs) 352
B. Public companies (SAs) 357
VII. The position in Belgium 361
A. Patterns of management and control 361
B. Public companies 361
C. Private companies 367
VIII. The position in the Netherlands 368
A. Management structures 368
B. The regime applicable to 'large' companies 369
C. Powers and duties of the management board 371
D. The general meeting 373
E. Rights of minority shareholders 374

7. Business entities governed by Community law 377
I. European Economic Interest Grouping 377
A. History and scope 377
B. Profits of the grouping 380
C. Prohibitions 380
D. Limitation on membership 381
E. Formation and publicity 381
F. Transfer of the official address 383
G. Structure and functioning of the grouping 384
H. Winding up and dissolution 387
I. Legal regime applicable to the grouping 389
J. Implementation 391
II. The European Company 391
A. Introductory remarks 391
B. Capital, shares and bonds 395
C. Principal organs 395
D. Annual accounts and consolidated accounts 400
E. Winding up and other insolvency procedures 401
F. Entry into force 402
G. Employee involvement 402
H. Concluding remarks 410
III. European Cooperative Society 412
IV. The European Private Company 414

8. Employee participation 417

I. Introduction 417
II. The position in the United Kingdom 419
III. The position in France 419
A. Works council 420
B. Personnel representatives 422
C. Trade union delegations 422
D. Purpose of the different institutions 422
E. Employee representatives on the boards of public companies 423
IV. The position in Germany 424
A. Works councils 424
B. Functions of the unions 427
C. Employee representation on the supervisory board 427
D. Codetermination in the coal, iron and steel industry 428
E. Codetermination in certain holding companies 429
F. Codetermination under the Works Councils Act 1952 429
G. Codetermination under the Act of 2004 430
H. Codetermination under the 1976 Act 431
I. Constitutionality of the Codetermination Act 1976 433
V. The position in Italy 435
VI. The position in Spain 436
A. Works councils 436
B. Employees' meetings 437
C. Trade union section 437
VII. The position in Belgium 437
VIII. The position in the Netherlands 438
A. Works councils 438
B. Employee participation on the supervisory board 440
IX. Community law and employee participation 440
A. Collective redundancy 440
B. Transfer of undertakings 441
C. European Works Councils Directive 442
D. Directive on a general framework for informing and consulting employees in the EC 445
E. Models for employee participation in the draft Fifth Directive 446

9. Groups of companies 448

I. Introduction 448
II. The preliminary draft Ninth Directive 449
III. European Community legislation on groups 450

IV. German *Konzernrecht* 451
A. Connected companies 452
B. Integration 457
C. De facto groups 458
D. Contractual groups involving private companies 461
V. The new provisions of Italian law concerning groups of companies 467
VI. Definition of groups of companies and related concepts 470
A. The position in the United Kingdom 470
B. The position in France 472
C. The position in Germany 473
D. The position in Italy 473
E. The position in Spain 474
F. The position in Belgium 476
G. The position in the Netherlands 478
VII. Group liability 480
A. Special provisions protecting creditors 484
B. Minority shareholder protection 485

10. Cross-border mergers and acquisitions 491
I. Introduction 491
II. Cross-border mergers 492
A. Influence of the Third Directive 492
B. History and legal basis 493
C. Advantages over the European Company Statute 493
D. Scope 493
E. Cash and shares components of merger consideration 494
F. Relevance of national law 495
G. Requirements governing formation and disclosure 495
H. Location of the registered office: the real seat doctrine 496
I. Independent expert reports 496
J. The protection of shareholders and creditors 497
K. Opposition on public policy grounds 497
L. Scrutiny and publicity 497
M. Consequences of the merger 498
N. Employee participation 499
O. Concluding remarks on the Tenth Directive 504
III. Takeovers 504
A. Introductory remarks 504
B. The Thirteenth Directive on Takeovers 506

11. Investor protection 516

I. Introduction 516
II. Insider dealing 519
III. Disclosure 521
IV. Market manipulation 524
V. Standard of communication 526
VI. Safe harbour 527
VII. Preventive measures 529
VIII. Supervisory authority and sanctions 530
IX. Implementation in the Member States 531
X. Implementation in the United Kingdom 532
XI. Implementation in Germany 534

Index 536

PREFACE

This book is a contribution to the emerging discipline of comparative European company law. The new discipline remains rooted in the company laws of the different Member States. European Union directives provide a framework and more and more detail. Free movement is important: the directives and regulations adopted by the EU gives effect to the right of establishment and the free movement of capital. The further internationalisation of capital markets is another important factor. Academic scholarship has provided insights that contribute to the reform process. In parallel, the transformation to a market economic system in former communist countries has provided a rich field for scholarship. Knowledge about other Member States' company laws has a central role here. Knowledge may be necessary in order to understand provisions of an EU directive, or the functioning of a feature of one's own or another country's company law.

New features of company law in the EU include incorporation in one Member State under another Member State's laws, cross border mergers and new EU company forms. EU law and more than one Member State jurisdiction are involved at the same time. Also here, knowledge of the laws of the other Member States is required, both in policy making, law reform, corporate planning and transactions.

This knowledge is also often required even if the matter is a purely internal one to one Member State. The treaty freedoms and directives can often not be correctly understood and applied if the analysis is limited to the relationship between one's own jurisdiction and EU law. It is necessary also for this reason, to look to the laws of other Member States.

Company law is undergoing fundamental change in Europe. All European countries have undertaken extensive reform of their company legislation which remains in a state of permanent reform. Domestic company law reform has traditionally been driven by initiatives to remedy weaknesses that have come to light in larger corporate failures or scandals. Initiatives to make corporate governance more effective is one such feature of recent European company law reform. Company law reform has at the same time been taken in the opposite direction by the wish to simplify and lessen the burdens, in particular on smaller and mediumsized businesses (SMEs). The new Member States have gone through even more fundamental reform to facilitate a modern market economy and then to implement the *acquis communautaire* in company law. The prospect of regulatory competition increasing the number of domestic businesses incorporating abroad has, for instance, strengthened the pressure to reduce capital requirements in national company laws. The case law of the European Court of Justice on the right of establishment and to provide services, and the free movement of capital, has in the recent years been brought to bear on national company law and corporate practice. National company law rules have been set aside as restricting the free movement of companies or restricting the exercise of the fundamental freedoms in other ways. As European Union law gradually opens up the choice of country of incorporation for businesses in Europe, the competition between national company laws is increasing further.

The harmonisation of European company law through EU legislation (directives and regulations) has also been given a new impetus by the case law of the Court of Justice and different initiatives by the European Commission. This requires transposition in national company legislation. New EU legislation gives further effect to the free movement of companies, which again opens up for regulatory competition. National company legislation cannot now be applied without regard to the case law of the European Court of Justice on the fundamental freedoms in the EC Treaty on the right of establishment and to provide services and the free movement of capital. Many provisions of the national legislation require the active use of the directives they transpose.

In case of conflict, EU law requires that it is the rule of the directive that is applied. More generally, the EU company law legislation in directives and regulations constitutes a system which is the basic framework for national company law, and often the natural starting point when company law matters are to be resolved. Neither can EU company law legislation in directives and regulations be applied without regard to the fundamental freedoms in the EC Treaty and the case law of the European Court of Justice. EU company legislation itself has to be interpreted and applied so that it complies with in the EC Treaty on the right of establishment and to provide services, and the free movement of capital. In case of conflict here, the Treaty prevails.

Comparative law is not of any less importance in this new context. The application of the fundamental freedoms in the EC Treaty in the review of national company law, can be assisted by analysis of the company laws of other Member States. That is even more so the case for the transposition or subsequent interpretation of EU directives. Concepts and rules often originate in a national system, and even if they may change when they are imported into a directive, knowing about their original meaning may provide assistance. Also, the way that directives have been transposed in other Member States may assist when a directive is to be given effect in the application of national company legislation.

Company law has traditionally been a fruitful field for comparative study. There is an increasing need for knowledge about the core features of the different national systems. The practitioner, judge, law reformer and scholar share this need. EU law and comparative law are disciplines with their own methodology. Our focus in this book is limited to the normative system of national company laws within the framework of EU law. Our ambition has not been to provide an analysis of the economic or social contexts which are important for the understanding of how the different company law rules function in the different jurisdictions.

We have collaborated on this project for some years and share responsibility for the outcome to which we have contributed in equal measure.

Mads Andenas and Frank Wooldridge
London, January 2008

TABLE OF CASES

ECJ Cases

Arjomari-Prioux/Wiggins Teape [1991] 4 CMLR 854 451

CaixaBank France, C-442/02 [2004] ECR I-8961 12
Cartesio, C-210/06 OJ 2006 C165 13–14, 56
Centros Ltd v. Erhvervs- og Selskabsstyrelsen, C-212/97 [1999] ECR I-1459 4, 11–13, 34, 36, 95, 96–8
Commission v. Belgium, C-503/99 [2002] ECR I-4809 14, 15–16
Commission v. Germany, C-112/05 19
Commission v. Italy, C-174/04 [2005] ECR I-4933 19
Commission v. Netherlands, C-282/283/04 [2006] ECR I-9141 19
Commission v. Portugal, C-367/98 [2002] ECR I-4731 14, 15–17
Commission v. Spain, C-463/00 [2003] ECR I-4581 17–18
Commission v. United Kingdom, C-98/01 [2003] ECR I-4641 17
Cooperative Rabobank, C-104/97 [1997] ECR I-7211 43

Daihatsu, C-97/96 [1997] ECR I-6843 8
Daily Mail, R v. Treasury ex p, Case 81/87 [1988] ECR 5483 13, 14, 30–1, 56, 496
De Lasteyrie du Saillant, C-9/02 [2004] ECR I-2409 12

Elf-Aquitaine, Commission v. France (Elf-Aquitaine), C-483/99 [2002] ECR I-4781 14, 15–16

Gebhardt, Case 55/94 [1995] ECR I-4165 11, 12

Kamer van Koophandel en Fabrieken voor Amsterdam v. Inspire Art Ltd, C-167/01, [2003] ECR I-10155 4, 97
Katsikas, C-132/91, C-138/91 and C-139/91 [1992] ECR I-6577 442
Keck and Mithouard, C-267/268/91 [1993] ECR I-6097 17
Konle, C-302/97 [1999] ECR I-3099 14
Kraus, Case 19/92 [1993] ECR I-1689 11

Mac Quen, C-108/96 [2001] ECR I-837 12
Marks & Spencer, C-62/00 [2002] ECR I-6325 10
Metallgesellschaft Ltd and others v. IRC and another and Hoechst AG and Another v. Same, C-397/98 and C-410/98 [2001] ECR I-1727 11

Ny Mölle Kro, Case 287/86 [1987] ECR 5465 442

Pfeiffer, C-255/97 [1999] ECR I-2835 11

Reyners v. Belgium, Case 2/74 [1974] ECR 631 11

Saldanna and MTS Securities Corporation v. Hiross Holding, C-122/96 [1977] ECR I-5325 8
Sevic Systems AG v. Amtsgericht Neuwiel, C-411/03 [2005] ECR I-10805; [2006] 1 CMLR 45; [2006] 4 All ER 1072 4, 11–12, 26, 493, 496
Spikers v. Benedik, Case 24/85 [1986] ECR 1119 442
Suzen, C-13/95 [1997] ECR I-259 442

Thieffry, Case 71/76 [1977] ECR 765 11
Tomberger, C-234/94 [1996] ECR I-3145 40

Überseering BV v. Nordic Construction Company Baumanagement GmbH , C-208/00 [2002] ECR I-9919 4, 11, 30–1, 36, 98, 378, 392

Wendelboe, Case 19/83 [1985] ECR 457 442

X and Y, C-436/00 [2002] ECR I-10829 12

Domestic Cases

Belgium

Pasicrise [1994] Ghent Commercial Tribunal 348 364

France

Cour de Cassation
20 November 1922, *Société Lambourn v. Varounis* DS-1926, I-305 481
Société Immobilière et Financière du Parc v. Bitsch, Gaz Pal 1958/1, 150 481
12 November 1962, *Pilon v. SA Philippe Pain et Vermorel*, RD 1962, 648 481
24 January 1995, *Revue des Sociétés* 1995 46 166
Com, 3 May 2001 113

Germany

Bundesgerichtshof (Supreme Court)
[1975] NJW 212 317
[1994] ZIP 1103 302
[1995] NJW 398 302
[1995] NJW 1359 300
[1997] NJW 1923 166
[1998] NJW 1645 71
[2000] NJW 2983 300
[2001] NJW 1042 71
BGHZ 9, 157 117
BGHZ 13, 179 143
BGHZ 14, 25 117
BGHZ 14, 264 117
BGHZ 60, 324 165
BGHZ 65, 15 *ITT* 462, 482
BGHZ 65, 378 72
BGHZ 69, 334 *Veba Gelsenberg* 452
BGHZ 70, 132 77
BGHZ 71, 296 143
BGHZ 72, 45 72
BGHZ 75, 334 203
BGHZ 76, 335 203
BGHZ 80, 69 *Süssen* 462, 482
BGHZ 80, 129 69, 72, 77
BGHZ 80, 182 72
BGHZ 83, 122 *(Holzmüller)* 166, 313, 314
BGHZ 85, 293 47
BGHZ 89, 162 *Hermann/Ogilvy* 462, 482
BGHZ 90, 378 203
BGHZ 92, 253 *Siemens* 461
BGHZ 94, 324 301
BGHZ 95, 330 *Autokran* 462, 463, 482
BGHZ 97, 269 30
BGHZ 103, 184 *Linotype* 487
BGHZ 105, 324 *Supermarkt* 461
BGHZ 107, 7 *Trefbau* 463
BGHZ 110, 342 165
BGHZ 111, 224 117
BGHZ 115, 187 *Video* 452, 463
BGHZ 122, 123 *TBB* 463

BGHZ 126, 181 302
BGHZ 129, 136 *Girmes* 487
BGHZ 134, 333 72
BGHZ 134, 392 166
BGHZ 146, 341 101, 132
BGHZ 149, 10 *Bremer Vulkan* 464
BGHZ 151, 181 *KBV* 464, 466
BGHZ 154, 370 132
II ZR 3/04, *Trihotel* 118, 466
II ZR 206/02 *Autohändler* [2005] ZIP 117 465
II ZR 256/02 *Unterschlagen* [2005] ZIP 250 465
Bundesverfassungsgericht (Constitutional Court)
BVerfGE 50, 290 433
BVerfGE 99, 367 429
Oberlandesgericht (OLG) (Court of Appeal)
Munich [1995] Die AG 232, 233 *(EKATT/Riedinger)* 313
Reichsfinanzhof
decision of 18 February 1933, RStBI 375 159
Reichsgericht
RGZ 105, 101 103
RGZ 125, 356 317
RGZ 128, 1 117
RGZ 166, 129 117

Netherlands

19 February 1988, HR 1988, NJ No.487 481
18 November 1994, HR 1995, NJ No.170 482

United Kingdom

Adams v. Cape Industries [1990] Ch 433 481
Allen v. Gold Reefs of West Africa (1900) Ch 656 179
Bell v. Lever Bros [1932] AC 161 480
Birch v. Cropper (1889) 14 App Cor 529 170
Brady v. Brady [1989] AC 755 247, 272
Canadian Safeway v. Thompson [1951] 3 DLR 295 272
City Equitable Fire Insurance, Re [1925] Ch 407 275
Clark v. Cutland [2003] EWCA 810 280
Cook v. Deeks [1916] 1 AC 554 272
Daniels v. Daniels [1978] Ch 406 278
D'Jan of London, Re [1993] BCC 646 271, 275

Ebrahimi v. Westbourne Galleries Ltd [1973] AC 360 281
Eley v. Positive Government Secretary Life Assurance Co. [1875] 1 Ex D 20 58
Ernest v. Nicholls (1853) 6 HL 401 59
Foss v. Harbottle (1843) 2 Hare 461 276, 281
Gamlestaden Fastigheter AB v. Baltic Partners Ltd & Ors (Jersey) [2007] UKPC 26; [2007] 4 All ER 164; [2007] BCC 272; [2008] 1 BCLC 468 280
Gordon v. Holland (1913) 108 LT 385 136
Guinness plc v. Saunders [1990] 2 AC 663 269
Hely-Hutchinson v. Brayhead Ltd [1968] 1 QB 549 273
Henry v. Great Northern Railway Co. (1957) 1 De G & J 1606 170
Hickman v. Kent and Romney Marsh Sheep-Breeders Association [1915] Ch 881 58
House of Fraser plc v. ACGE Investments [1987] AC 387 195
Howard Smith v. Ampol Petroleum Co. Ltd [1974] AC 821 (PC) 272
Hydrodam (Corby) Ltd, Re [1994] 2 BCLC 180 483
Kelner v. Baxter (1866) 2CP 174 59, 60
Levy v. Abercorris Slate and Slab Co. (1887) 37 Ch D 260 249
Lindgren v. L and Pe Estates [1968] Ch 572 480
Mosely v. Koffyfontein Mines [1904] 2 Ch 108 250
Newborne v. Sensolid (GB) Ltd (1954) 1 QB 45 60
Norman v. Theodore Goddard [1991] BCLC 1028 271, 275
North West Transportation Co. v. Beatty [1887] 12 AC 589 (PC) 276
Oakbank Oil Co. v. Crum [1882] 8 App Cases 65 58
O'Neill v. Phillips [1999] 2 BCLC 1 281, 282, 283
Pavlides v. Jensen [1956] Ch 565 278
Peso Silver Mines Ltd v. Cropper (1996) 58 DLR (2d) 1 273
Phonogram v. Lane (1982) QB 938 60
Queensland Mines Ltd v. Hudson (1978) 52 AJLR 399 (PC) 273
Regal (Hastings) Ltd v. Gulliver [1967] 2 AC 134 272
Royal British Bank v. Turquand (1855) 5 E and B 248 270
Scottish Insurance Capital Corp. v. Wilson and Clyde Canal Company [1949] AC 462 171, 195
SH & Co. (Realisations) 1990 Ltd, Re [1993] BCC 60; [1993] BCLC 1309 249
Smith and Fawcett Ltd, Re [1942] Ch 304 271
Smith v. Croft (No.2) [1988] Ch 144; [1986] 1 WLR 580 276, 280
Wallensteiner v. Moir (No.2) [1975] QB 373 280
Williams v. Natural Life Foods [1998] 1 WLR 830 102

TABLE OF LEGISLATION

EC Law

Treaties

Amsterdam Treaty OJ 1997 C340
Protocol 36
EC Treaty
Art. 3(g) 24
Art. 28 17
Art. 43 7, 12–14, 15, 97, 392
Art. 43(2) 10
Arts. 43–48 10
Art. 44 493
Art. 44(2)(g) 7, 8, 36
Art. 44(3)(a) 391
Art. 46 97
Art. 47(2) 8
Art. 48 12–14, 21, 97, 375, 392, 413
Art. 48(1) 10
Art. 48(2) 7, 9, 377, 394
Art. 54 28, 45
Art. 54(3)(f) 395
Art. 54(3)(g) 23, 24, 25, 26
Art. 56 15
Art. 56(1) 14
Arts. 56–69 10
Art. 58 15
Art. 65(b) 35
Art. 81 491
Art. 95 7, 9
Art. 95(1) 8, 9
Art. 226 517, 532
Art. 234 13, 415
Art. 249(2) 9

Art. 249(3) 36
Art. 251 8, 493, 518
Art. 293 9, 10, 493
Art. 293(3) 9
Art. 308 9
Rome Convention on Contractual Obligations 1969 48
Art. 6(2) 48

Regulations

2137/85 on the European Economic Interest Grouping, OJ 1985 L199/1 9, 99, 167, 377
Preamble
recital 11 390
recital 14 390
recital 15 390
recital 16 380–1, 390
recital 17 390
Art. 2 390
Art. 2(1) 385
Art. 2(2) 382
Art. 3(1) 378, 380
Art. 3(2) 380–1
Art. 4 378, 381
Art. 4(1) 387
Art. 4(2) 388
Art. 4(3) 381
Art. 4(4) 381
Art. 5 382
Art. 6 381
Art. 7 382
Art. 8 382, 386
Art. 9 382–3, 390
Art. 9(2) 382
Art. 10 381, 382
Art. 11 383
Art. 12 378, 383, 388
Art. 13 383
Art. 14 383
Art. 14(1) 383
Art. 17 384
Art. 17(3) 390

Art. 19 384
Art. 20 378, 379
Art. 20(1) 385
Art. 20(2) 385
Art. 21 380
Art. 21(2) 385, 386, 390
Art. 22 385–6
Art. 22(2) 386
Art. 24(1) 386
Art. 24(2) 386
Art. 26 386
Art. 27(1) 387, 390
Art. 27(2) 387
Art. 28(1) 387
Art. 29 387
Art. 30 387
Art. 31 387–8, 389
Art. 32 387, 388
Art. 32(1) 388
Art. 33 387
Art. 34 386
Art. 35 387
Art. 35(1) 388
Art. 36 388
Art. 37 387
Art. 37(1) 386
Art. 39(1) 381
Art. 40 379, 380
4064/89 OJ 1989 L395/1 451
Art. 3(1) 451
1310/97 OJ 1997 L180/1 451
1346/2000 Bankruptcy Regulation, OJ 2000 33
2157/2001 on the Statute for a European company, OJ 2001 L294/1 9, 26, 99, 377, 391
Preamble
recital 9 402
recital 15 393
recital 20 393
recital 22 402
Art. 2(1) 393
Art. 2(2) 393
Art. 2(3) 394
Art. 2(4) 394

Art. 3(2) 394
Art. 5 395
Art. 6 392, 393
Art. 7 392, 401
Art. 8 376, 392–3
Art. 8(4) 399
Art. 8(10) 393
Art. 8(13) 393
Art. 9 376, 392, 413
Art. 10 392
Art. 11 392
Art. 12(1) 392
Art. 12(2) 392
Art. 13 395
Art. 14(1) 395
Art. 23(1) 399
Art. 25 497
Art. 26 497
Art. 32 395
Art. 32(6) 399
Art. 33 395
Art. 34 395
Art. 35 395
Art. 36 395
Art. 37 395
Art. 38 396
Art. 39(1) 396, 397
Art. 39(2) 396
Art. 39(3) 396
Art. 39(4) 397
Art. 39(5) 396
Art. 40(1) 396
Art. 40(2) 399
Art. 41 397
Art. 41(1) 396
Art. 42(2) 397
Art. 43(3) 399
Art. 43(4) 396, 397
Art. 46 398
Art. 47(1) 398
Art. 48(1) 398
Art. 48(2) 398

Art. 49 398
Art. 50(1) 398
Art. 50(3) 398
Art. 52 399
Art. 53 399
Art. 54(1) 399
Art. 55 399
Art. 56 399–400
Art. 57 400
Art. 59 399
Art. 59(1) 400
Art. 61 400
Art. 62 400
Art. 63 401
Art. 64(1) 401
Art. 64(2) 401
Art. 64(3) 401–2
Art. 66(b) 399
Art. 69 392
Art. 70 495
1606/2002 on the application of international accounting standards, OJ 2002 L243/1 25, 400
1435/2003 on the European Cooperative Society, OJ 2003 R2007/1 413
Art. 7 413
Art. 8 413
Art. 59 413
2273/2003 implementing Directive 2003/6/EC as regards exemptions for buy-back programmes and stabilisation of financial instruments OJ 2003 L336/33 522, 528
Art. 3 529
Art. 4(4) 530
Art. 6(1) 529
Art. 6(2) 529
Art. 6(3) 529
139/2004 on the control of concentration between undertakings OJ 2004 L24/1 491

Directives

68/151/EEC on co-ordination of safeguards which, for the protection of the interests of members and others, are required by Member States of companies within the meaning of the second paragraph of Art. 58 of the Treaty, with a view to making such safeguards equivalent throughout the Community OJ 1968 L65/8 (1st Company Directive) 21, 22, 23, 52, 395

Art. 1 45, 494
Art. 2 57
Art. 3(5) 390
Art. 3(7) 390
Art. 7 60
Art. 9 39
Art. 9(1) 42–3, 385
Art. 9(2) 39, 42
77/91/EEC on co-ordination of safeguards which, for the protection of the interests of members and others, are required by Member States of companies within the meaning of the second paragraph of Art. 58 of the Treaty, in respect of the formation of public limited liability companies and the maintenance and alteration of their capital with a view to making such safeguards equivalent OJ 1977 L26/1 (2nd Company Directive) 3–4, 21, 22, 23, 37, 52, 104
Art. 9 39
Art. 10(4) 450
Art. 10b(6) 37
Art. 15(1)(a) 38
Art. 15(1)(b) 38
Arts. 18–24 37
Art. 19 528
Art. 19(1) 231, 232, 239
Art. 23 37–8, 192, 246
Art. 23(1) 37
Arts. 23–39 43–4
Art. 24a 37
Art. 25 169
Art. 29 37–9
Art. 29(1) 37–8
Art. 29(4) 38–9
Art. 32 194
Art. 42 487
77/187 on transfers of undertakings OJ 1977 L61/26 418, 441
78/660/EEC on annual accounts of certain types of companies, OJ 1978 L221/11 (4th Company Directive) 21, 24, 25, 37, 40, 44–5, 96, 130, 164, 400, 479
Art. 57 480
78/855/EEC on mergers of public limited companies, OJ 1878 L295/36 (3rd Company Directive) 21, 23, 26, 393, 395, 492–3
Art. 4(1) 494
Art. 5 495
Art. 7 496

Art. 7(1)(3) 495
Art. 8 495
Art. 8(c) 495
Art. 9 496
Art. 19 498
Art. 25(c) 495
Art. 27 495
Art. 29 451
80/723/EEC on the transparency of financial relations between public enterprises and the state OJ 1980 L195/35 451
82/89 on the division of public limited liability companies, OJ 1982 L378/47 (6th Company Directive) 20, 21, 23
83/349/EEC on consolidated accounts, OJ 1983 L193/1 (7th Company Directive) 21, 24, 25, 32–3, 37, 40, 96, 164, 400, 479, 480
Art. 1 45, 450, 474
Art. 1(1)(d) 475
Art. 20(1) 44–5
84/253/EEC on the approval of persons responsible for carrying out the statutory audits of accounting documents, OJ 1984 L126/20 (8th Company Directive) 25, 37, 400
85/611/EEC 28
86/635/EEC 24
88/627/EEC on the information to be published when a major holding in a listed company is acquired or disposed of, OJ 1988 L348/62 28
89/592/EEC on insider dealing OJ 1989 L334/30 6, 21, 28, 518, 519, 521
Art. 2 521
Art. 2(4) 519
Art. 3(a) 523
Art. 3(b) 523
Art. 7 521
89/666/EEC on disclosure requirements in respect of branches opened in a Member State by certain types of companies governed by the law of another State, OJ 1989 L395/36 (11th Company Directive) 21, 25–6
89/667/EEC on single-member private limited liability companies, OJ 1989 L395/4082 (12th Company Directive) 26, 42
90/435 on the common system of taxation of parent companies and subsidiaries in different members states 451
90/604/EEC amending Directive 78/660/EEC and Directive 83/349/EEC as concerns the exemptions for small and medium sized companies and the publication of accounts in ecus, OJ 1990 L317/57 24

90/605/EEC amending Directive 78/660/EEC and Directive 93/349/EEC as regards the scope of those directives, OJ 1990 L317/60 24, 130, 164
91/674/EEC on the annual accounts and consolidated accounts of insurance undertakings, OJ 1991 L374/7 24, 401
92/22/EEC on investment services in the securities field, OJ 1993 L141/27 28
Art. 7(13) 519
92/101/EEC amending Directive 77/91/EEC on the formation of public limited companies and the maintenance of and alteration of their capital, OJ 1992 L374/64 37
93/6/EEC 28
93/22/EEC on investment services in the securities field, OJ 1993 L141/27 28
94/45/EC on the establishment of a European Works Council or a procedure in Community-scale undertakings and Community-scale groups of undertakings for the purposes of informing and consulting employees, OJ 1994 L254/64 28, 410, 418, 442, 504, 513
Art. 2(1)(b) 443
Art. 3 443
Art. 4 445
Art. 4(1) 443
Art. 5(5) 404, 444
Art. 6 443
Art. 6(2) 443
Art. 7 444
Art. 8 418, 446
Art. 8(1) 444
Art. 8(2) 444
Art. 10 444, 446
Art. 11(4) 444
97/74/EC OJ 1998 L10/2 410, 442, 504
98/59/EC on collective redundancies, OJ 1998 L225/16 440, 503, 513
Art. 2(1) 441
Art. 2(3) 441
Art. 3(1) 441
Art. 4(1) 441
2000/12/EC on the taking up and pursuit of the business of credit institutions, OJ 2000 L126/1 28, 401
2001/23/EC on transfers of undertakings OJ 2001 L82/16 418, 440, 441, 503
Art. 1(1) 441
Art. 5 441
Art. 7 442

2001/34/EC on the admission of securities to official stock exchange listing and on information to be published on those securities, OJ 2001 L184/1 28
2001/51 OJ 2003 L 179/16 400
2001/65/EC amending Directives 78/660/EEC, 83/349/EEC and 86/635/EEC as regards the valuation rules for the annual and consolidated accounts of certain types of companies as well as of banks and other financial institutions, OJ 2001 L283/28 24
2001/86/EC supplementing the Statute of the European Company with regard to the involvement of employees, OJ 2001 L294/22 26, 99, 377, 391, 397, 398, 399, 499, 513
Preamble
recital 3 402
recital 4 402
Art. 1(1) 402
Art. 1(2) 402
Art. 2(d) 403
Art. 2(k) 404
Art. 3 402
Art. 3(1) 403
Art. 3(2) 403
Art. 3(3) 403
Art. 3(4) 404, 502
Art. 3(5) 404
Art. 3(6) 403, 404, 406, 410
Art. 3(7) 404
Art. 3(a)(1) 501
Art. 4 402
Art. 4(1) 405
Art. 4(2)(b) 409
Art. 4(3) 405
Art. 4(4) 405
Art. 5 402, 405, 406
Art. 6 402, 405
Art. 7 402
Art. 7(1) 501
Art. 7(2)(b) 406, 503
Art. 7(3) 405–6
Art. 8(2) 408
Art. 8(4) 409
Art. 10 409
Art. 12 409
Art. 13 409–10
Art. 14 410

Art. 15 410
Art. 16 410
2002/14/EC establishing a general framework for informing and consulting employees in the European Community OJ 2002 L80/29 47, 504
2003/6/EC on market abuse OJ 2003 L96/16 3, 6, 28, 516
Preamble
recital 15 518
recital 16 520
recital 17 520
recital 22 525
recital 24 529–30
recital 26 530
recital 31 520
recital 36 531
recital 44 525
Art. 1 518
Art. 1(1) 520, 521
Art. 1(2) 516, 524–6
Art. 1(3) 519, 533
Art. 1(4) 519
Art. 2 521
Art. 2(1) 520
Art. 3 522
Art. 4 521
Art. 6 522
Art. 6(1) 521
Art. 6(2) 528, 529
Art. 6(3) 519, 523–4, 530
Art. 6(4) 530
Art. 6(5) 526
Art. 6(6) 530
Art. 6(9) 524
Art. 7 519
Art. 8 528, 529
Art. 10 533
Art. 10(1) 533
Art. 11 530
Art. 12 531, 535
Art. 13 531
Art. 14(1) 531
Art. 16 535
Art. 20 518

2003/38/EC amending Directive 78/660/EEC as regards amounts expressed in euros, OJ 2003 L120/22 24
2003/51/EC amending Directives 78/660/EEC, 83/349/EEC, 86/635/EEC and 91/674/EEC, OJ 2003 L178/16 24, 401
2003/58/EC, OJ L220/13 22
2003/124/EC Definition and Disclosure Directive, OJ 2003, L339/70 518, 522
Art. 3(1)(9) 523
2003/125/EC on the fair representation of investment recommendations and the disclosure of conflicts of interest OJ 2003 L339/73–7 522, 525
Art. 2 526
Art. 3 526
Art. 4(1) 527
Art. 5 526
Art. 6(3) 527
Art. 6(4) 527
Art. 7 527
Art. 8 527–8
Art. 9 527
2004/25/EC on takeover bids (13th Company Directive), OJ 2004 L142/12 3, 491, 506–15
Art. 3 508, 513, 514
Art. 3(1) 505
Art. 4 513
Art. 4(2) 505
Art. 4(5) 514
Art. 5 490, 505, 512
Art. 6 505, 513
Art. 6(10) 509
Art. 7 505, 513
Art. 7(1) 508
Art. 8 505, 513
Art. 9 505, 506, 507, 508
Art. 9(2) 27, 508
Art. 9(3) 27, 508
Art. 10 506
Art. 11 506, 507, 510
Art. 11(4) 508, 509
Art. 12 509
Art. 12(3) 506–7, 514
Art. 12(5) 509
Art. 13 505
Art. 13(3) 507

Art. 14 513
Art. 15 27, 511
Art. 16 27, 490, 512
Art. 17 514
Art. 20 515
2004/72/EC on accepted market practices 518
2005/56/EC on cross-border mergers of limited liability companies, OJ 2005 L310/1 (10th Company Directive) 3, 6, 10, 26, 395, 491, 492–3
Preamble
recital 3 497
recital 12 503
Art. 1 493–4
Art. 2 494
Art. 2(1)(4) 494
Art. 3(1) 494
Art. 4(1)(a) 494
Art. 4(1)(b) 495, 497
Art. 4(2) 495, 497
Art. 5 495
Art. 6 495, 495–6
Art. 8 496
Art. 8(1) 496
Art. 8(2) 497
Art. 8(4) 497
Art. 10 497–8
Art. 11 497–8
Art. 11(1) 498
Art. 11(2) 498
Art. 13 498
Art. 14 498
Art. 16 498, 499–503
Art. 19 504
2006/43 on statutory audit of annual accounts and consoldiated accounts, amending Directives 78/660 and 83/349 and repealing Directive 84/253, OJ 2006 L257/87 25, 400
2006/68/EC amending Council Directive 77/91/EEC as regards the formation of public limited liability companies and the maintenance and alteration of their capital OJ 2006 L264/32 4, 23, 38, 104, 528
Art. 1(4) 169–70, 232
Art. 10b(6) 38
2006/69/EC, OJ L264/32 37
2007/46, OJ 2006 L224/1 24

National Legislation

Belgium

Civil Code
Art. 1690 127
Code des Sociétés (Companies Code)
Art. 2 151
Art. 3(2) 100
Art. 5 244
Art. 5(1) 476
Art. 5(2) 477
Art. 5(3) 477
Art. 7(1) 477
Art. 10(1) 478
Art. 12 478
Art. 13 478
Arts. 46–54 134
Art. 50 134
Art. 51 134
Art. 52 134
Art. 53 134
Art. 54 134
Art. 60 92
Art. 65(2) 92
Art. 66 91, 151
Art. 67 91
Art. 68 91
Art. 69 92, 151, 158
Art. 72 158
Art. 73 91, 158
Art. 109 477
Art. 110 477
Art. 111 478
Art. 112 477
Art. 113 477
Art. 168 487
Art. 169 487
Art. 201 150
Art. 203 151, 158
Art. 204 151
Art. 206(2) 158

Art. 207 158
Art. 207(1) 158
Art. 208 158
Arts. 210–349 124
Art. 211 90
Art. 212 124
Art. 213 125
Art. 214 90, 125
Art. 215 90, 125
Art. 216 125
Art. 218 91
Art. 219 90, 91, 125
Art. 223 91, 125
Art. 224 91
Art. 226 92
Art. 229 125
Art. 229(1) 90
Art. 232 125
Art. 233 125
Art. 238 125, 187
Art. 239 125, 187
Art. 240 187
Art. 240(1) 187
Art. 240(2) 187, 189
Art. 241 187, 188, 189
Art. 242 241–2
Art. 243 125, 261
Art. 245 261
Art. 246 261
Art. 248 261
Art. 249 126
Art. 249(2) 224
Art. 250 126
Art. 251 126
Art. 252 126
Art. 253 126, 261
Art. 255 127, 367
Art. 256 127, 367
Art. 257 367
Art. 257(1) 127
Art. 257(2) 127
Art. 257(3) 127

Art. 258 127
Art. 259 367
Art. 263 127
Art. 265 368, 483
Art. 265(1) 127–8
Art. 286 188, 222, 224
Art. 288 222
Art. 290 368
Art. 291 368
Art. 292 262
Arts. 292–301 261–2
Art. 293 262
Art. 295 261
Art. 297 262
Art. 298 263
Art. 302 222
Art. 303 223
Art. 305 223
Art. 306 223
Art. 307 223
Art. 308 223
Art. 309(1) 223
Art. 309(2) 224
Art. 310(3) 224
Art. 311 224
Art. 312 224
Art. 313 224
Art. 316 225
Art. 317 225
Art. 318 225, 226
Art. 321 242
Art. 321(1) 243
Art. 322 243
Art. 322(1) 243
Art. 325 243
Art. 325(2) 243
Art. 326 243
Art. 329 246
Art. 331 242
Arts. 334–339 488
Art. 340 489
Art. 341 489

Art. 394 91
Art. 395 90, 91
Art. 397 91
Art. 399 91
Art. 439 90
Art. 440 90
Art. 450 91
Art. 451 92
Art. 452 92
Art. 453 92
Art. 456(1) 90
Art. 480 188
Art. 481 189
Art. 482 189
Art. 483 186
Art. 484 186
Art. 489 263
Art. 490 263
Art. 491 263
Art. 499 263
Art. 501 263
Art. 503 242
Art. 503(1) 187
Art. 508 186
Art. 509 186
Art. 513 489
Art. 518 361
Art. 519(1) 361
Art. 521 362
Art. 522(1) 361, 365
Art. 522(2) 362, 367
Art. 523 362–3, 367
Art. 524 363–4
Art. 525 362
Art. 526 362
Art. 527 364
Art. 528 364
Art. 528(2) 363
Art. 529 363
Art. 529(2) 364
Art. 530 365, 483
Art. 531 365

Art. 532 365
Art. 542 367
Art. 544 367
Art. 547 367
Art. 548 367
Art. 549 367
Art. 554 366
Art. 556 365
Art. 557 365
Art. 558 222, 224, 366
Art. 559 242, 366
Art. 560 222, 367
Art. 561 364
Art. 562 365, 368
Art. 567 365
Art. 568 262
Arts. 568–580 262
Art. 569 262
Art. 571 261
Art. 574 262
Art. 575 263
Art. 581 222, 366
Art. 582 223
Art. 583 223, 263
Art. 584 223
Art. 586 223
Art. 588 223
Art. 589 223
Art. 592 263
Art. 592(1) 223
Art. 592(2) 224
Art. 595 224
Art. 596 224, 263
Art. 601 224
Art. 602 224
Art. 603 222, 263
Art. 605 222
Art. 606 222
Art. 612 225, 366
Art. 613 225
Art. 614 225, 226
Art. 615 242

Art. 620 244
Art. 620(1) 242, 243
Art. 621 244
Art. 622 244
Art. 622(2) 243
Art. 623 243, 244
Art. 626 242
Art. 627 243–4
Art. 629 246
Art. 635 489
Arts. 636–641 488
Art. 642 489
Art. 643 489
Art. 645 366
Art. 646 90
Arts. 654–660 109
Laws and Decrees
12 July 1989 391
19 July 1989 391
27 July 1989 391
8 November 1989
Art. 41 490

France

Code Civil (Civil Code)
Art. 1690 113, 173
Art. 1832 167
Art. 1842 131
Art. 1844–1 140
Art. 1844–7 140
Art. 1857 61
Art. 1871–1 132, 133
Art. 1871–3 132
Art. 1872–1 132
Code du Commerce (Commercial Code)
Art. L210-1 100
Art. L210-2 62, 65
Art. L210-6 138
Art. L221-1 137
Art. L221-2 138
Art. L221-3 138, 162

Art. L221-4 139
Art. L221-5 139
Art. L221-6 139
Art. L221-7 139
Art. L221-8 140
Art. L221-9 140
Art. L221-12 138
Art. L221-13 138
Art. L221-14 113
Art. L221-15 140
Art. L221-16 140
Art. L221-17 113
Art. L222-1 154
Art. L222-2 153, 162
Art. L222-6 154, 162
Art. L222-8 154
Art. L222-10 163
Art. L223-1 62
Arts. L223-1–L223-43 111
Art. L223-2 62
Art. L223-3 62, 112
Art. L223-6 62
Art. L223-7 196
Art. L223-9 63, 196
Art. L223-11 172, 251
Art. L223-12 113, 172–3
Art. L223-13 115
Art. L223-14 114, 200
Art. L223-15 115
Art. L223-16 114
Art. L223-17 113
Art. L223-18 163, 283
Art. L223–18(6) 284
Art. L223–19 284
Art. L223–21 284
Art. L223-22 285
Art. L223–25 283
Art. L223-26 284, 285
Art. L223-27 285
Art. L223-28 113, 286
Art. L223-29 283, 286
Art. L223-29(1) 163

Art. L223-30 195, 196, 285
Art. L223-30(1) 286
Art. L223-30(2) 286
Art. L223-31 195
Art. L223-32 196
Art. L223-34 200, 201, 233
Art. L223-35 251
Art. L223-37 487
Art. L223-43 285
Art. L223-231 487
Art. L224-2 64
Art. L225-1 65
Art. L225-2 64
Art. L225-8 174, 251
Art. L225-10 251
Art. L225-14 174
Art. L225-16 287
Art. L225-17 287
Arts. L225-17–L225-56 290
Arts. L225-17–L225-126 105
Art. L225-18 287, 288
Art. L225-19 288
Art. L225-21 289
Art. L225-22 288
Art. L225-23 163, 424
Art. L225-25 287
Art. L225-27 288, 423
Art. L225-28 423
Art. L225-29 423
Art. L225-30 424
Art. L225-32 424
Art. L225-33 424
Art. L225-35 289, 290
Art. L225-35(4) 289
Art. L225-38 289, 293
Art. L225-40 294
Art. L225-40(4) 294
Art. L225-41(1) 294
Art. L225-43 293
Art. L225-45 288
Art. L225-46 288
Art. L225-47 289, 290

Art. L225-48 200, 290
Art. L225-52 46
Art. L225-53 289, 290
Art. L225-55 290
Art. L225-56 290
Art. L225-56(2) 290
Art. L225-57 286, 290
Art. L225-58 291
Art. L225-61 291
Art. L225-62 291
Art. L225-64 291
Art. L225-66 291, 292
Art. L225-67 291
Art. L225-68 291, 292
Art. L225-68(3) 292–3
Art. L225-68(6) 293
Art. L225-69 292
Art. L225-71 163, 424
Art. L225-75 292
Art. L225-77 292
Art. L225-79 424
Art. L225-79(2) 292
Art. L225-79(3) 292
Art. L225-80 424
Art. L225-81 292
Art. L225-82 292
Art. L225-86 293
Art. L225-88 294
Art. L225-88(4) 294
Art. L225-89(1) 294
Art. L225-91 293
Art. L225-96 173, 197, 296
Art. L225-96(2) 174
Art. L225-98 197, 296
Art. L225-100 198, 287, 292, 295
Art. L225-103 289, 296, 486
Art. L225-105 296
Art. L225-115 297
Art. L225-116 297
Art. L225-117 297
Art. L225-118 297
Art. L225-120 297

Art. L225-123 296
Art. L225-124 296
Art. L225-127 197
Art. L225-128 197
Art. L225-129 197, 198
Art. L225-129-1 198
Art. L225-129-2 198
Art. L225-129-4 198
Art. L225-130 197
Art. L225-131 197
Art. L225-132 199
Art. L225-133 199
Art. L225-134 199
Art. L225-135 199
Art. L225-147 174, 199
Art. L225-148 174
Art. L225-198 233
Art. L225-204 201
Art. L225-205 201
Art. L225-206 233
Art. L225-208 234
Art. L225-209 234, 235
Art. L225-210 234
Art. L225-215 236
Art. L225-231 421
Art. L225-231(1) 297
Art. L225-231(2) 297
Art. L225-243 105
Art. L225-248 202
Art. L225-252 295
Art. L225-253 295
Art. L226-2 165
Art. L227-1 105, 115
Arts. L227-1–L227-20 105
Art. L227-5 106, 115
Art. L227-6 106
Art. L227-8 106
Art. L227-9 115
Art. L228-11 173
Art. L228-35 188, 189
Art. L228-36 248
Art. L228-39 251

Art. L228-40 252
Art. L228-43 251
Art. L228-46 252
Art. L228-47 252
Art. L228-49 253
Art. L228-51 251
Art. L228-53 253
Art. L228-54 253
Art. L228-58 252
Art. L228-59 252
Art. L228-65 253
Art. L228-68 253
Art. L228-72 253
Art. L228-73 253
Art. L228-91 174, 252
Art. L228-92 252
Art. L228-97 248
Art. L228-98 174
Art. L229-95 174
Art. L230-7 133
Art. L232 133
Art. L232-1 289
Art. L232-12 287, 295
Art. L233 133
Art. L233-1 472
Art. L233-2 472
Art. L233-3(1) 472
Art. L233-16 289, 472
Code du Travail (Labour Code)
Art. L422-1 422
Art. L422-2 422
Art. L422-5 422
Art. L431-1 420
Art. L431-1-1 422
Art. L432-1 421
Art. L432-4 421
Art. L432-5 421
Art. L432-6 163, 420–1, 421
Art. L439-1 420, 444
Art. L439-6 444
Art. L439-24 444

Art. L461-1 420
Art. L483-1 418
Code Monétaire et Financier (Financial Code)
Art. L4465-1 517
Laws and Decrees
Ordonnance of 23 September 1967 166
Decree 67–236 of 23 March 1967
Art. 2 62
Art. 12 115, 140, 284
Art. 20 62
Art. 26(1) 62
Art. 26(2) 63
Art. 26(3) 63
Art. 33 285
Art. 36(1) 285
Art. 40 286
Art. 43 115
Art. 44 284
Art. 55 65
Arts. 58–71 64
Art. 73 66
Art. 74(2) 66
Art. 74(3) 66
Art. 180 201
Art. 181 201
Art. 182 201
Art. 183 201
Art. 184 202
Art. 185(3) 201
Art. 200 46, 295
Art. 201 295
Art. 285 66
Law 67–833 517
Law 78–9 167
Law 85–98 5 January 1985
Art. 180 483
Law 1985–697 11 July 1985 112
Law 86–897 112
Law 89–377 13 June 1989 166, 391
Law 89–432, 28 June 1989 391
Law 94–1 105
Law 96–385 444

Law 99-587
Art. 3 105
Law 2001-420, 15 May 2001 105
Law 2003-706, 1 August 2003 66-7
Order of 24 June 2004 171-2, 173
Ordinance 2004-274
Art. 12 250
Ordinance 2004-604 252
Law 2004, 24 June 2004 173, 196, 197-8
Law 2005-882 286
Réglement Général de l'Autorité des Marchés Financiers
Art. 622-1 517
Art. 622-2 517
Art. 633-1 517
Art. 633-4 517

Germany

Abgabenordnung (AO) (General Tax Code)
§ 69 303
Aktiengesetz (Public Limited Liability Companies Act) 49-50
§ 1(1) 76
§ 2 72, 73
§ 4 73
§ 5(2) 73
§ 6 73
§ 7 73
§ 8(1) 73
§ 11 175
§ 12(1) 175
§ 12(2) 175
§ 15 453
§§ 15-19 448, 452
§ 17 453
§ 18(1) 431, 453, 454, 470
§ 21 315
§ 23(1) 73, 315
§ 23(3) 73, 210
§ 23(5) 74
§ 25 74
§ 26 74, 76
§ 27 72, 74

§ 30 74
§ 32 75
§ 32(2) 75
§ 33(2) 75
§ 34 75
§ 34(1) 75
§ 36(2) 76, 77
§ 36a(1) 74
§ 36a(2) 75
§ 37(4) 76
§ 41(1) 73, 76, 77
§ 41(2) 76, 77, 78
§ 41(3) 78
§ 41(4) 72
§ 42 76, 77
§ 50 318
§ 53 318
§ 56(1) 235
§ 56(3) 235
§ 57 204
§ 58(1) 315
§ 58(2) 315
§ 64(1) 303
§ 68(2) 104
§ 71 236
§§ 71–71d 230
§§ 71–71e 528
§ 71a 236, 246
§ 71b 236
§ 71c(2) 236
§ 71e 236
§ 76(1) 307, 427
§ 76(2) 307
§ 76(3) 299, 308
§ 77(1) 308
§ 77(2) 308
§ 78 319, 427
§ 78(2) 308
§ 78(3) 308
§ 80 310
§ 80(1) 309

§ 81 310
§ 83 310
§ 84(1) 307
§ 84(3) 308, 312
§ 85 308
§ 87 309
§ 88 310
§ 88(1) 309
§ 89 309
§ 90 309, 312
§ 90(3) 304
§ 90(4) 304
§ 91(2) 310
§ 92 310
§ 92(1) 309
§ 92(2) 310
§ 93 47, 267, 271, 305, 313
§ 93(1) 305, 310
§ 93(2) 310, 311
§ 93(4) 311, 318
§ 93(5) 311
§ 95 311
§ 96(1) 307
§§ 96–99 311
§ 100(1) 311
§ 100(2) 312
§ 101(1) 311
§ 101(2) 311
§ 102 312
§ 103(1) 312
§ 103(2) 312
§ 103(3) 312, 318
§ 103(4) 312
§ 105(1) 308
§ 105(2) 308
§ 111 304, 427
§ 111(2) 312
§ 111(4) 309, 313, 398
§ 112 304, 312, 319, 427
§ 116 305, 313, 318
§ 117 318

§ 117(4) 318
§ 118(2) 314
§ 119(1) 311, 314
§ 121 316
§ 121(2) 309
§ 122(1) 310, 318
§ 122(2) 314, 318
§ 122(3) 310, 314
§ 123(2) 315
§ 124 316
§ 128 317
§ 130(1) 317
§ 130(5) 318
§ 131 316, 318
§ 131(3) 409
§ 132(2) 409
§ 133(1) 317
§ 134(1) 316
§ 134(2) 316
§ 134(3) 316
§ 135 317
§ 139 175
§ 139(1) 176
§ 139(2) 176
§§ 139–41 316
§ 140 175, 177
§ 140(2) 177, 178
§ 141 175, 178
§ 141(1) 178, 179
§ 141(2) 178, 179
§ 142(1) 320
§ 142(2) 320
§§ 142–6 487
§ 147 318
§ 147(4) 319
§ 148 319
§ 150(2) 315
§ 161 310
§ 170 427
§ 170(1) 313
§ 170(2) 313, 314
§ 170(3) 314

§ 171 313, 427
§ 172 313
§ 173(1) 313
§ 174(1) 313, 314
§ 175(1) 314
§ 175(2) 316
§ 175(3) 316
§ 176(2) 314
§ 179 317
§ 182 205, 255
§ 182(1) 317
§ 183 205
§ 184 205
§ 186 255
§ 186(1) 205
§ 186(3) 205
§ 186(4) 206
§ 188 205
§ 188(1) 206
§ 188(2) 206
§ 189 206
§ 192(1) 206, 255
§ 192(2) 206, 255
§ 192(3) 206, 255
§§ 194–200 206
§ 202 256
§ 202(1) 206
§ 202(2) 206
§ 202(3) 206, 256
§ 202(4) 206
§§ 203–206 206
§ 204(1) 206
§ 207 207
§§ 207–220 206
§ 212 207
§ 214 207
§ 221(1) 255
§ 221(2) 255
§ 221(3) 255
§ 221(4) 255
§ 222(1) 209, 317
§ 222(2) 209

§ 222(4) 209
§§ 222–228 209
§ 224 210
§ 225 210
§ 229(1) 210
§ 229(2) 210
§ 233(2) 208, 210
§ 234 210
§ 235 210
§ 237(3) 211
§§ 237–239 211
§ 243 463
§ 277 108
§ 278(1) 108
§ 278(2) 108
§ 279(2) 166
§§ 279–290 108
§ 291 453, 454
§§ 291–328 448, 452, 453
§ 292 454
§ 293(2) 455
§ 293(3) 455
§ 293a 455
§ 293b 455
§ 294(2) 455
§ 302 456, 463
§§ 302–305 454
§ 303 456, 463
§ 304 456, 461
§ 305 456, 461, 488
§ 306 488
§ 308 309, 455
§ 309 455
§ 309(1) 455
§ 309(2) 455
§ 309(3) 318
§ 310 455
§ 310(4) 318
§ 311 309, 458, 459
§§ 311–318 449, 454, 458
§ 312(1) 459
§ 313 459

§ 314 459
§ 315 459
§ 317 459
§ 317(1) 458
§ 317(2) 460
§ 317(4) 318
§ 318 458
§ 318(4) 318
§ 319 453, 457
§§ 319–327 452
§ 320 457
§ 320b 488
§ 321(1) 457
§ 322(1) 457
§ 323 309, 457
§ 323(1) 318
§ 324(1) 458
§§ 327a–327f 511
§ 399 313
§§ 399–403 311
§ 400 313
§ 404 311, 313
§ 405 313
Anlegerschutzverbesserungsgesetz (Investor Protection Act) 2004
§ 1 534
Bausparkassengesetz (Building Society Act)
§ 2(1) 116
Betriebsverfassungsgesetz (BetrVG) (Works Council Act) 1952 5, 163, 298, 424
§ 76(1) 298, 307, 429
§ 76(2) 430
§ 77 298, 429
§ 111 407–8
Betriebsverfassungsgesetz (BetrVG) (Works Council Act) 1972 424
§ 1 425
§ 2 425
§ 5(1) 425
§ 5(3) 426
§ 7 425
§ 8 425
§ 9 425
§ 14 425
§ 14a 425

§ 15 426
§ 21 425
§ 47 425
§ 54 425
§ 76 426
§ 80(2) 426
§ 87 426
§ 106(2) 426
§ 106(3) 426
§ 111 426
§ 112 426
§ 112(4) 427
§ 112a 426
§ 113 426
Betriebsverfassungsgesetz (BetrVG) (Works Council Act) 1988
§ 28 426
§ 28a 426
§ 37(2) 426
§ 106 426
Betriebsverfassungsgesetz (BetrVG) (Works Council Act) 2001 424
BGB (Civil Code)
§ 179 71
§§ 705–740 131, 142
§ 717 143
§ 736 143
§§ 737–740 143
§ 793 254
§ 826 118, 466
BGBI 1994 I.744 144
§ 7(1) 145
§ 7(3) 145
BGBI 1994 I.1961 307
BGBI 1998 I.1878 144
BGBI 2001 I.2267 5
BGBI 2004 I.2633–2639 5
Bundesrechtsanwaltsordnung (BRAO) (Federal Lawyers Act)
§ 51(a)(1) 146
§ 59c 144
Civil Procedure Code
§ 829 462, 482
§ 835 462, 482

Constitution
§ 3(1) 429
§ 5(1) 430
Art. 9(3) 433–4
Art. 14 433
Art. 14(1) 434
Art. 14(2) 434
Drittelbeteilungsgesetz (DrittelbG) (One-Third Participation Act) 2004 (BGBI 2004 I.974) 117, 163, 298, 299, 379, 430
§ 1 298, 304, 430–1
EWIV-Ausführungsgesetz 1988 (BGBI 1988 514) 391
FGG (Voluntary Jurisdiction Act)
§ 144b 70
GmbHG (Private Limited Liability Companies Act)
§ 1 67, 116
§ 2(1) 67
§ 3 67
§ 3(2) 175
§ 4 67
§ 4a(1) 67
§ 5 117
§ 5(1) 68, 117
§ 5(2) 68, 117
§ 5(4) 68, 205
§ 6 68
§ 6(2) 299
§ 6(3) 117, 299
§ 6(5) 163
§ 7(2) 68, 70, 77
§ 7(3) 68
§ 8 68, 69
§ 9(1) 69
§ 9c 69
§ 10 70
§ 13 116
§ 13(2) 464
§ 15(3) 118, 175
§ 15(4) 118, 175
§ 16 118
§ 19(4) 70
§ 19(5) 205
§ 27 306

§ 30 119, 203, 204, 208, 464, 465–6
§ 30(1) 204, 235, 462, 465
§ 31 119, 203, 204, 208, 464, 465–6
§ 31(1) 208
§ 31(2) 208, 465
§ 32a 203, 204, 208, 254, 462, 470, 481
§ 32a(1) 203, 208, 209
§ 32a(2) 209
§ 32a(3) 209
§ 32b 203, 204, 208, 209, 254, 462, 470, 481
§ 34 235
§ 34(2) 235
§ 34(3) 235
§ 35(1) 427
§ 35(2) 301
§ 35(4) 301
§ 37(1) 301, 461
§ 37(2) 301
§ 38(1) 300
§ 38(2) 300
§ 42a(1) 304
§ 43 267
§ 43(1) 117, 301
§ 43(2) 301
§ 43(3) 301
§ 43a 301
§ 45(1) 305, 306
§ 45(2) 305
§ 46 305
§ 46(5) 68, 161, 299, 300
§ 47(1) 300, 306
§ 47(2) 306
§ 47(4) 161, 301, 306
§ 48 305
§ 48(1) 306
§ 48(2) 306
§ 48(3) 307
§ 50(1) 486
§ 51a 462, 486
§ 51b 462, 486
§ 52 427
§ 52(1) 299, 304, 427

§ 52(2) 69
§ 53 207, 208
§ 53(1) 118, 306
§ 53(2) 202, 306
§ 53(3) 118
§ 54 202, 208
§ 54(3) 207
§ 55 202
§ 55(1) 306
§ 56 203
§ 57c–57o 203
§ 58 208
§ 58(1) 207
§ 58a 207
§ 58d(1) 210
§ 58d(2) 208
§ 58e 210
§ 60(1) 306
§ 64 302
§ 66 306
§ 78 68
§ 84 302
§ 84(3) 300
§ 85 302
§ 85f 210
§ 122 486
§ 179(2) 178
§ 319 468
§ 320 468
§ 322 468
§ 826 119
HGB (Commercial Code)
§ 1(2) 141
§ 2 142
§ 10 70
§ 11 70
§ 15 144
§ 18 73
§ 32a 165
§ 32b 165
§ 49 308
§ 50 308

§ 54(1) 309
§ 105 71, 141, 144
§ 105(3) 142, 143
§ 106 142
§ 112 143
§ 115 142
§ 116(1) 142
§ 118 463
§ 124 142
§ 125 143, 145
§ 125(1) 142, 143
§ 126 142, 145
§ 126(2) 143
§ 127 145
§ 128 71, 143
§ 129 145
§ 130 143, 145
§ 131(3) 163
§§ 131–135 144
§§ 131–144 146
§ 140 144
§ 160(1) 143
§ 161 108, 154, 155, 163
§ 161(1) 155
§ 162 155
§§ 162–177a 155
§ 164 155
§ 166 155
§ 170 155
§ 171 154
§ 172(6) 161
§ 172a 165
§ 176 155
§ 177 163
§ 181 301
§§ 230–7 133
§ 264(2) 40
§ 272(2) 315
§ 290 448, 473
Hypothekenbankgesetz (Mortgage Bank Act)
§ 2(1) 116

Insolvenzordnung (Insolvency Act) 1998
§ 39 203
§ 39(1) 209
§ 174(3) 209
Kapitalgesellschaften-und Co.Richtliniengesetz (KapCoRiLiG) 2000 164
Mitbestimmungsgesetz (Codetermination Act) 1951 117, 311
§ 1(2) 428
§ 4 428
§ 6 428
§ 8 428
§ 8(1) 432
§ 9 428
§ 13(1) 428
§ 15(1) 432
§ 16 432
§ 18 432
Mitbestimmungsgesetz (Codetermination Act) 1976 117, 298, 300, 311, 417, 431, 499
§ 1(1) 307
§ 2 431
§ 4(1) 163
§ 5(1) 431
§ 6 117
§ 7 432
§ 7(1) 299, 431
§ 7(2) 299, 431
§ 9(1) 432
§ 15(1) 431
§ 15(3) 432
§ 25(1) 304
§ 27 433
§ 27(2) 434
§ 29 433
§ 29(2) 299, 434
§ 31 299
§ 31(2) 433
Montan-Mitbestimmungsgesetz (Montan-MitBestG) (Coal, Iron and Steel Codetermination Act) 1956 298–9, 300
§ 3(2) 304, 429
§ 4(1) 307
§ 9 429
§ 12 299

Partnerschaftsgesellschaftgesetz (PartGG)
§ 1 144
§ 6 144
§ 8 145
§ 8(1) 145
§ 8(2) 145
§ 8(3) 145
§ 9(1) 146
§ 9(4) 146
Publizitätsgesetz (Company Disclosure Act) 1969 448, 452
Schiffsbankgesetz (Ship Mortgage Bank Act)
§ 2(1) 116
Supplementary Coal and Steel Codetermination Act 1956 300
Takeover Act 2002
§ 33 509
§ 33a 509
§ 37 512
§ 39a 511
§ 39c 511
UMAG, BGBI (2006) 1 315
Umwandlungsgesetz (UmwG) (Conversion Act) 1994
§ 226 160
Versicherungsaufsichtsgesetz (VAG) (Insurance Control Act)
§ 7(1) 116
Viertes Finanzförderungsgesetz (4th Financial Market Promotion Act) 2002 6, 534
VolkswagenGesetz (VW Act) 1960 19–20
Wertpapierhandelsgesetz (Securities Markets Act)
§ 10 534
§ 14 534
§ 20a(1) 534

Italy

Civil Code 119
Art. 2257 122, 347
Art. 2257(1) 147
Art. 2258 122, 347
Art. 2266(2) 147
Art. 2267(2) 147
Art. 2270(1) 148
Art. 2270(2) 148
Art. 2272 148

Art. 2289 148
Art. 2291(1) 147
Art. 2291(2) 147
Art. 2293 156
Art. 2295 147
Art. 2296(1) 147
Art. 2297(2) 147
Art. 2298(1) 147
Art. 2299 82
Art. 2304 148
Art. 2305 148
Art. 2307 148
Art. 2313 156
Art. 2314 156
Art. 2314(2) 156
Art. 2315 156
Art. 2317(1) 157
Art. 2318(1) 157
Art. 2320(1) 156
Art. 2320(3) 156
Art. 2325 *bis* 78
Art. 2327 215
Art. 2328 79
Art. 2328(1) 80
Art. 2329 82, 83
Art. 2329(1) 80
Art. 2330 81, 82
Art. 2330(1) 81
Art. 2330(2) 82
Art. 2330(3) 82
Art. 2331 82
Art. 2333 79, 80
Art. 2334 79, 80
Art. 2335 79, 80
Art. 2336 79, 80–1
Art. 2341 83
Art. 2341 *bis* 341
Art. 2341 *ter* 341
Art. 2342 81
Art. 2343 81, 212
Art. 2343(1) 83
Art. 2343(4) 217

Art. 2344 217, 218
Art. 2346 81, 181
Art. 2346(2) 181
Art. 2346(3) 181
Art. 2346(6) 181
Art. 2347 181
Art. 2348 339
Art. 2348(1) 182
Art. 2349 184
Art. 2349(1) 184
Art. 2350 184
Art. 2350(2) 340
Art. 2351 183, 339
Art. 2351(2) 182, 183, 340
Art. 2351(3) 182
Art. 2351(4) 182
Art. 2353 184, 237
Art. 2354(2) 81
Art. 2356 81
Art. 2357 237, 238
Art. 2357 *bis* 237, 238
Art. 2357 *ter*(2) 238, 340
Art. 2357 *quater* 237
Art. 2358 238
Art. 2359 344, 467, 473–4
Art. 2359(1) 473–4
Art. 2359 *bis* 238
Art. 2359 *ter*(2) 239
Art. 2364 332
Art. 2364 *bis* 333
Art. 2365 333
Art. 2366(3) 334
Art. 2366(4) 334
Art. 2367 333–4, 345, 486
Art. 2368(1) 337
Art. 2368(3) 337, 338
Art. 2368(4) 338
Art. 2369 338–9
Art. 2370(4) 335
Art. 2372 335, 336
Art. 2373 340
Art. 2374(2) 335

Art. 2376 184, 185, 343
Art. 2377 340, 341, 342
Art. 2379 340
Art. 2380 321
Art. 2380 *bis* 321
Art. 2380 *bis*(5) 321
Art. 2381 322
Art. 2382 321
Art. 2383(1) 321
Art. 2383(2) 321
Art. 2383(3) 321
Art. 2384 322, 333
Art. 2389 322
Art. 2390 323
Art. 2391 323, 347
Art. 2392 323
Art. 2393 345
Art. 2393(5) 324
Art. 2393 *bis* 324, 345, 346
Art. 2394 324
Art. 2395 324
Art. 2397 325, 327
Arts. 2397–2409 324
Art. 2398 327
Art. 2399 259, 325, 326, 327
Art. 2399(1) 331–2
Art. 2400(1) 325
Art. 2402 327
Art. 2403 325, 327
Art. 2403(1) 326, 331
Art. 2403 *bis* 326, 327
Art. 2404 327
Art. 2405(1) 326, 327
Art. 2406 327, 334
Art. 2407 327
Art. 2408 327
Art. 2408(1) 334
Art. 2408(2) 326
Art. 2409 327, 345, 348
Art. 2409 *quater*(3) 345
Art. 2409 *nonies* 331
Art. 2409 *duodecies* 331

Art. 2409 *terdecies*(1) 331
Art. 2409 *septiesdecies* 331
Art. 2409 *noviesdecies*(1) 332
Art. 24092 *bis*(1) 344
Art. 24092 *bis*(3) 325, 331, 344, 345
Art. 2410 257
Art. 2410(2) 257
Art. 2411 257
Art. 2411(2) 257
Art. 2412 257
Art. 2412(1) 257, 258
Art. 2412(4) 257
Art. 2413 215, 257
Art. 2415(1) 258
Art. 2415(2) 258
Art. 2415(3) 258
Art. 2418 259
Art. 2419 259
Art. 2420 *bis* 259
Art. 2420 *bis*(2) 259
Art. 2420 *bis*(4) 259
Art. 2423(1) 343
Art. 2423(4) 344
Art. 2426 327
Art. 2427(16) 322
Art. 2428 469
Art. 2428 *ter* 322
Art. 2429(1) 344
Art. 2429(2) 326, 327, 344
Art. 2429(3) 344
Art. 2433(3) 216
Art. 2435 *bis* 122
Art. 2436 212, 214, 257
Art. 2437 217, 342, 343
Art. 2437 *bis* 342
Art. 2437 *ter* 342
Art. 2438 212
Art. 2439 212
Art. 2439(1) 212
Art. 2440 212
Art. 2441 213

Art. 2441(6) 327
Art. 2441(8) 184, 213
Art. 2442 212, 213, 345
Art. 2443 322
Art. 2443(2) 121
Art. 2444 212, 214
Art. 2445(1) 214
Art. 2445(3) 215
Art. 2445(4) 215
Art. 2446 216, 322
Art. 2446(3) 217
Art. 2446(5) 217
Art. 2447 216, 217, 322
Art. 2447 *bis* 258
Art. 2447 *ter* 258
Art. 2447 *decies* 258
Art. 2462(2) 121
Art. 2463(1) 119, 215
Art. 2463(2) 82, 83
Art. 2463(3) 83
Art. 2464 83
Art. 2464(4) 83, 180
Art. 2465 83, 212
Art. 2465(1) 83
Art. 2466(3) 218
Art. 2466(6) 180
Art. 2467 469
Art. 2468(1) 83, 120, 181
Art. 2468(2) 83, 119, 120, 121
Art. 2468(3) 180
Art. 2469(1) 120
Art. 2469(2) 120
Art. 2469(3) 180
Art. 2469(4) 180
Art. 2470(2) 120
Art. 2470(4) 121
Art. 2472 121
Art. 2473 121, 217
Art. 2473(1) 121, 351
Art. 2473 *bis* 351–2
Art. 2474 237, 350

Art. 2475 122, 347
Art. 2475 *bis* 122
Art. 2475 *bis*(1) 347
Art. 2475 *ter* 347
Art. 2476 347, 348
Art. 2476(3) 351
Art. 2476(4) 351
Art. 2476(6) 351
Art. 2477(1) 122
Art. 2477(2) 122, 348
Art. 2477(3) 122, 348
Art. 2477(4) 122
Art. 2478 *bis* (1) 351
Art. 2478 *bis* (5) 216
Art. 2479 349
Art. 2479 (4) 346
Art. 2479 (5) 346
Art. 2479 *bis* (2) 350
Art. 2479 *bis* (3) 212, 350
Art. 2479 *ter* 350–1
Art. 2480 214
Art. 2481 212
Art. 2481(2) 212
Art. 2481 *bis* 212
Art. 2481 *bis* (6) 214
Art. 2481 *ter* 214
Art. 2482 214
Art. 2482(2) 215
Art. 2482(3) 215
Art. 2482 *bis* 214, 216, 217
Art. 2482 *ter* 214, 216, 217
Art. 2482 *quater* 214
Art. 2483 122, 256
Art. 2483(1) 256
Art. 2483(3) 256
Art. 2497(1) 467, 468
Art. 2497(2) 468
Art. 2497(4) 468
Art. 2497 *bis* 468–9
Art. 2497 *ter* 469
Art. 2497 *quater* 342, 469

Art. 2497 *quinquies* 469
Art. 2497 *sexies* 467
Art. 2497 *septies* 467
Art. 2501 *ter* 322
Art. 2506 *bis* 322
Commercial Code 119
laws and decrees
300/1970 on workers' rights 435
216/1974
Art. 17 322
127/1991
Art. 25 474
Art. 26 474
88/1992 324
385/1993
Art. 14 79
Art. 106 79
58/1998 256, 320
Art. 93 474
Art. 106 490
Art. 108 489
Art. 122 340–1
Art. 123 341
Art. 125 333–4, 345
Art. 126(1) 338
Art. 126(2) 338
Art. 126(3) 339
Art. 126(4) 338
Art. 128 326
Art. 129 345–6
Art. 131 343
Art. 132(1) 238
Art. 132(2) 238, 239
Art. 132(3) 238
Art. 136(1)(b) 336
Art. 136(1)(c) 336
Art. 136(1)(e) 336
Arts. 136–144 335, 337
Art. 137(1) 335, 336
Art. 138(1) 336
Art. 138(2) 336

Art. 139(1) 336
Art. 140 336
Art. 141 336
Art. 142 336–7
Art. 143 337
Art. 144 337
Art. 145 182, 340
Art. 145(1) 183
Art. 145(2) 183
Art. 145(3) 183
Art. 145(5) 183
Art. 145(7) 183
Art. 146 182, 183
Art. 147 182
Art. 147(3) 183
Art. 148(1) 328
Art. 148(2) 328
Art. 148(3) 325, 328, 329
Arts. 148–154 327
Art. 149(1) 328
Art. 149(2) 328
Art. 149(3) 328–9
Art. 150(1) 329
Art. 151 329
Art. 151(2) 334
Art. 151 *bis* 329–30
Art. 151 *bis*(3) 334
Art. 151 *ter* 330
Art. 152 327, 330
Art. 153 330, 344
Art. 153(1) 326
Art. 154 327, 330
Art. 156(4) 345
Art. 157(1) 345
Art. 159 345
Art. 159(1) 325, 345
1998 law of 24 Feb
Art. 111 488
6/2003 320
16/2003 119
37/2004 182, 327
Art. 9.77 328

Netherlands

Burgerlijk Wetboek (Civil Code)
Arts. 1655–1688 101
Art. 1679 152
Art. II.9 372
Art. II.10 372
Art. II.17 93
Art. II.18 373
Art. II.24a-1 479
Art. II.24b 245, 479
Art. II.24c 479
Art. II.66(1) 93
Art. II.66(2) 93
Art. II.67 226
Art. II.67(1) 93
Art. II.67(2) 93, 129
Art. II.67(5) 93
Art. II.68(2) 93, 226
Art. II.69(1) 94
Art. II.69(2) 94
Art. II.72 373
Art. II.79(2) 226
Art. II.80(1) 93, 226
Art. II.80b(1) 94
Art. II.92(1) 189
Art. II.92a 488
Art. II.93(1) 94
Art. II.93(2) 95
Art. II.94a 94
Art. II.94a(1) 94
Art. II.94a(2) 94
Art. II.94b 94
Art. II.94b(2) 94
Art. II.95(1) 244
Art. II.96(1) 190, 226
Art. II.96(2) 190, 226
Art. II.96(3) 226
Art. II.96a 264
Art. II.96a(1) 227
Art. II.96a(2) 227, 264
Art. II.96a(6) 227

Art. II.96a(7) 227
Art. II.98(1) 244
Art. II.98(2)(a) 244
Art. II.98(2)(b) 129, 228, 244
Art. II.98(3) 245
Art. II.98(4) 230, 245
Art. II.98(5) 245
Art. II.98(9) 244
Art. II.98c 246, 248
Art. II.98c(1) 129, 247
Art. II.98d 245
Art. II.98d(1) 246
Art. II.99(2) 228
Art. II.99(3) 228
Art. II.99(4) 228
Art. II.100(1) 229
Art. II.100(2) 229
Art. II.100(3) 229
Art. II.100(5) 229
Art. II.100(6) 229
Art. II.101(3) 372
Art. II.102(1) 375
Art. II.105(1) 190, 373
Art. II.108(1) 373
Art. II.108(2) 373
Art. II.109 374
Art. II.110 374, 486
Art. II.111 374, 486
Art. II.112 374, 486
Art. II.113(1) 374
Art. II.114(1) 374
Art. II.117(2) 374
Art. II.118 189
Art. II.129 369, 371
Art. II.130 369, 371
Art. II.132 368
Art. II.133(2) 191, 369
Art. II.134(1) 368
Art. II.134(2) 191
Art. II.134(4) 93
Art. II.138 372, 483
Art. II.138(2) 372

Art. II.140(2) 369
Art. II.142(1) 369
Art. II.146 372
Art. II.149 372
Art. II.152 370, 479
Art. II.153 129
Art. II.153(2) 191, 369
Art. II.153(3) 371
Art. II.155 191
Art. II.155(1) 371
Art. II.157(1) 368
Art. II.158 370
Art. II.161(2) 370
Art. II.161(3) 370
Art. II.161a 440
Art. II.162 368, 371
Art. II.164 371
Art. II.172 371
Art. II.177(1) 93
Art. II.177(2) 93
Art. II.178(1) 93
Art. II.178(2) 93, 129
Art. II.178(4) 226
Art. II.178(5) 93
Art. II.179(2) 93
Art. II.180(1) 94
Art. II.180(2) 94
Art. II.183 373
Art. II.191(1) 93
Art. II.191b(1) 94
Art. II.195 128
Art. II.201(1) 189
Art. II.201a 488
Art. II.202 129
Art. II.203(1) 94
Art. II.203(2) 95
Art. II.204a 94
Art. II.204a(1) 94
Art. II.204a(2) 94
Art. II.204b 94
Art. II.204b(2) 94
Art. II.205 244

Art. II.206(1) 190, 226
Art. II.206a 264
Art. II.206a(1) 227, 228
Art. II.206a(2) 227, 264
Art. II.206a(3) 227
Art. II.207(2) 229
Art. II.207(2)(a) 244
Art. II.207(2)(b) 129, 228, 244
Art. II.207(2)(c) 230, 245
Art. II.207(2)(d) 230, 245
Art. II.207(3) 245
Art. II.207(5) 244
Art. II.207(c) 129
Art. II.207(d)(1) 246
Art. II.207c 246, 248
Art. II.207c(1) 247
Art. II.207d 245, 246
Art. II.208(2) 228
Art. II.208(3) 228
Art. II.208(4) 228
Art. II.209 229
Art. II.209(1) 229
Art. II.209(2) 229
Art. II.209(3) 229
Art. II.209(5) 229
Art. II.209(6) 229
Art. II.210(3) 372
Art. II.212 375
Art. II.216(1) 190, 373
Art. II.216(3) 372
Art. II.218(1) 373
Art. II.218(2) 373
Art. II.219 374
Art. II.220 374, 486
Art. II.221 374, 486
Art. II.222 374, 486
Art. II.223(1) 374
Art. II.224(1) 374
Art. II.227(2) 374
Art. II.228(5) 189
Art. II.239 369, 371
Art. II.240 369, 371

Art. II.242 368
Art. II.243(2) 191, 369
Art. II.244(1) 368
Art. II.244(2) 191
Art. II.244(4) 93
Art. II.245(1) 368
Art. II.248 372, 483
Art. II.248(2) 372
Art. II.250(2) 369
Art. II.252(1) 369
Art. II.256 372
Art. II.259 372
Art. II.262 370, 479
Art. II.263(2) 129, 191, 369
Art. II.263(3) 371
Art. II.265 191
Art. II.265(1) 371
Art. II.267(1) 368
Art. II.268 370
Arts. II.268–274 129
Art. II.271(2) 370
Art. II.271(3) 370
Art. II.272 368
Art. II.272a 440
Art. II.274 371
Art. II.343(1) 375
Art. II.343(4) 375
Art. II.344 374
Arts. II.344–359 487
Art. II.346(b) 374
Art. II.349a 374
Art. II.393(2) 373
Art. II.393(4) 373
Art. II.393(5) 373
Art. II.394 372
Art. II.1295 128
Commercial Code
Arts. 15–35 101
Art. 16 134, 151
Art. 18 152
Art. 19 159

Art. 23 151, 152
Art. 31 152
Commercial Registry Law (Handelsregisterwet)
Art. 7 159
Pro-Forma Foreign Companies Act 1998
s. 1 95
s. 2 95
ss. 2–6 96
s. 4 96
s. 4(4) 96
s. 5 96
s. 6 96
s. 7 96
Works Council Act 1971 (Wet op de Ondernemingsraad) (WOR) 371
Art. 2 438
Art. 3(1) 439
Art. 3(2) 439
Art. 6(1) 438
Art. 9(2) 438
Art. 16 438
Art. 17 438
Art. 18 438
Art. 21 438
Art. 25(1) 417, 439
Art. 26(4) 418
Art. 26(5) 418, 439
Art. 27(1) 440
Art. 27(3) 440
Art. 27(5) 418, 440
Art. 31–31c 439
Art. 33 439
Art. 35b 438

Spain

Civil Code
Art. 1689 149
Art. 1690 149
Art. 1691 149
Commercial Code
Art. 42 474–6
Art. 82 476

Art. 119 149
Art. 122 148
Art. 125 148
Art. 126 149
Art. 127 149
Art. 128 150
Art. 132 150
Art. 133 149
Art. 136 150
Art. 139 149
Art. 140 149
Art. 143 149
Art. 144 149
Arts. 145–150 157
Art. 148(4) 157
Art. 150(2) 157
Arts. 151–157 108, 157
Art. 170 149
Art. 171 149
Art. 218(4) 149
Laws
1953 Law of 17 July 84
8/80 on works councils 436
11/85 on trade union representation 436
24/1988 Securities Market Act
Art. 4 475, 476
Art. 60 490
Art. 112 360
Art. 113 360
Art. 114 360
Art. 116 360
Art. 117 360
19/1989 (Public Companies Act) 84
Art. 2 88
Art. 7(1) 87
Art. 11 88
Art. 11(1) 88
Arts. 14–18 89
Art. 15 86, 89
Art. 16 86
Art. 17(2) 89
Art. 18 89

Art. 31 89
Art. 38 85, 89
Art. 39(1) 85
Art. 39(2) 85
Art. 42 240
Art. 74(1) 239
Art. 75 239–40
Art. 76(1) 241
Art. 77 241
Art. 78 241
Art. 79(1) 241
Art. 79(3) 240
Art. 87 239, 474–6
Art. 95 358
Art. 96 358
Art. 97 359
Art. 98 359
Art. 99 360
Art. 100 359
Art. 101 359
Art. 102 359
Art. 103 220, 260, 359
Art. 105(1) 359
Art. 123 358
Art. 123(2) 357
Art. 124 357
Art. 125 357
Art. 126 357
Art. 127 358
Art. 127 *bis* 358
Art. 127 *quater* 358
Art. 127 *ter* 358
Art. 128 357
Art. 129 357, 358
Art. 130 357
Art. 131 357, 358
Art. 132 357
Art. 133 354
Art. 133(1) 354
Art. 134 358
Art. 134(5) 354
Art. 135 358

Art. 137 357
Art. 141 358
Art. 144 358
Art. 151 220
Art. 151(1) 218
Art. 152 220
Art. 152(2) 218
Art. 153 220
Art. 155(1) 218
Art. 155(2) 220
Art. 156 220
Art. 156(1) 218
Art. 157(2) 218
Art. 158 219
Art. 159 219
Art. 160 220
Art. 162(1) 219
Art. 162(2) 219
Art. 163 220, 239
Art. 163(1) 221
Art. 163(2) 222
Art. 164(2) 222
Art. 165 221
Art. 166 221
Art. 167 221
Art. 168(1) 221
Art. 168(2) 221
Art. 169 222
Art. 171 353
Art. 282(1) 260
Art. 283(2) 260
Art. 284(1) 260
Art. 284(2) 260
Art. 285 260
Art. 286(1) 260
Art. 291 260
Art. 292(1) 260
Art. 292(2) 261
Art. 294(1) 261
Art. 294(3) 261
Art. 327 396
Arts. 329–336 396

116/1992 of 14 February 1992 260
2/1995 (Private Companies Act) 84, 122
Art. 3 100
Art. 4 85, 87, 122
Art. 5 87
Art. 5(1) 185
Art. 5(2) 122
Art. 9 259–60
Art. 10(1) 476
Art. 10(2) 474, 475
Art. 11(1) 85
Art. 11(3) 86
Art. 12(2) 84
Art. 13 85
Art. 18(2) 85
Art. 19(2) 85
Art. 20(2) 85
Art. 21 85
Art. 26 122
Art. 27 122
Art. 29(2) 123
Arts. 29–34 122
Art. 30(1) 123
Art. 30(3) 123
Art. 34 123
Art. 39(1) 239
Art. 39(2) 239
Art. 40 240
Art. 40(1) 240, 241
Art. 43 123
Art. 44(1) 354
Art. 44(2) 352, 354
Art. 45 355
Art. 46 355
Art. 46(1) 123
Art. 46(2) 123
Art. 47 355
Art. 48 355
Art. 49 355
Art. 50(1) 185
Art. 50(2) 185
Art. 51 355

Art. 52 124
Art. 52(1) 355
Art. 53 356
Art. 53(2) 218
Art. 53(3) 218
Art. 56 356
Art. 57(1) 123, 352
Art. 57(2) 123, 352
Art. 58(1) 353
Art. 58(2) 353
Art. 58(3) 353
Art. 60(1) 353
Art. 61 353
Art. 62 353
Art. 62(2)(d) 353
Art. 63 353
Art. 65 353
Art. 66 353
Art. 69(1) 354
Art. 69(2) 354
Art. 70 354
Art. 73(1) 218
Art. 74(1) 218
Art. 74(2) 218
Art. 74(3) 218
Art. 74(4) 218
Arts. 74–76 241
Art. 75 219
Art. 76 219
Art. 78(1) 219
Art. 78(3) 219
Art. 79 220
Art. 79(1) 220–1
Art. 79(2) 219
Art. 81 221
Art. 82(1) 221
Art. 82(2) 221
Art. 83 222
Art. 84 353
Art. 85 185
Art. 90 185
Art. 91 185

Art. 91(2) 185
Art. 92(1) 186
Art. 92(3) 186
Art. 95(1) 124
Art. 96 124
Art. 98 124
Art. 126(1) 86
Arts. 130–144 86–7
Art. 131 87
Art. 132 87
Art. 135 87
Art. 136 87
Art. 139 87
5/1995 on the legal arrangements for disposal of public shareholdings in certain undertakings 18
37/1998 219
50/1998 219
44/2002 219, 360
1/2003
Art. 14 124
Art. 141 124
4/2003 86
7/2003 (sociedad limitadad de nueva empresa) (2 April) 84, 86, 354
26/2003 360
432/2003 490
19/2005 396
16/2007 474
47/2007 475

United Kingdom

Airports Act 1986 17
Companies Act 1985 102
s. 2 55
ss. 10–12 52
s. 13 52
s. 14(1) 58
s. 35 56
s. 35A 39, 56, 270
s. 35A(1) 270
s. 35B 56
s. 36C 60

s. 74(2) 273, 483
s. 80 192, 193
s. 80A 192
s. 89 193
s. 89(1) 193
s. 91 193
s. 94(2) 168, 171, 193
s. 94(5) 193
s. 95(1) 193
s. 101 54
s. 103 54
s. 106 54
s. 108 44
s. 112 54
s. 118 54
s. 121 192
s. 131 44
s. 135 194
s. 135(2) 194
ss. 135–141 194
s. 136 194
ss. 151–158 110
s. 153(1)(a) 247
s. 159 171, 230
s. 160(4) 195
s. 162 171
s. 162(2) 195
ss. 162–170 230
s. 163 231
s. 163(3) 230, 231
s. 164 231
s. 166(1) 232
s. 166(3) 232
s. 171 232
s. 258 448
s. 258(2)(c) 45, 448
s. 258(4) 45, 448
s. 282 267
s. 291 268
s. 303 269
s. 309 272
s. 317 273

s. 322A 56
s. 366 276
s. 370A 277
s. 379A 275
s. 381A 275
s. 381B 275
s. 427A 492
ss. 431–453 487
s. 459 111, 280, 281
ss. 459–461 282
s. 460 111
s. 461 111
s. 711A(1) 59
Sch. 48
para. 10 44
para. 11 44
Table A
Art. 70 270
Art. 71 270
Art. 72 270
Art. 73 269
Art. 75 268
Art. 81 269
Art. 82 268
Art. 84 270
Companies Act 2006 230
s. 3(1) 57
s. 4(1) 110
s. 7(1) 57
s. 9 55–6
ss. 9–13 52
s. 17 57
s. 19 268
s. 19(1) 57
s. 20(1) 57
s. 29 57
ss. 29–41 56
s. 33(1) 57–8
s. 40 39, 270
s. 40(1) 59, 270
s. 40(2) 59
s. 51 60

s. 91 54
s. 151 267
s. 168(1) 269
ss. 171–177 271, 274
s. 172 267, 271, 272
s. 172(1) 267
s. 174 271
s. 174(2) 275
s. 175 273
s. 177 273
s. 178 274
s. 180 57
ss. 190–196 274
ss. 197–214 274
ss. 215–222 274
s. 223 274
s. 239 279
s. 239(7) 279
s. 251(1) 273
s. 260(1) 279
s. 260(2) 279
s. 260(3) 279
s. 261 279
s. 262 279
s. 262(3)(c) 280
s. 262(3)(d) 280
s. 262(3)(f) 280
s. 263 279
s. 263(2) 279
ss. 265–269 280
s. 268(2)(c) 280
s. 268(2)(d) 280
s. 270 111
s. 282 277
s. 283 277
s. 288(1) 275
s. 288(2) 275, 277, 278
ss. 288–300 110
s. 303 276, 486
s. 303(3) 277
s. 304(1) 277
s. 307 277

s. 312(1) 277–8
s. 318(2) 277
s. 336 110, 275, 277, 278
s. 336(1) 276
s. 357 277
s. 405 471
s. 423 110
s. 430A 513
s. 430B 513
s. 430C 513
s. 437 110
s. 479 488
s. 495 110
s. 548 169, 193
s. 550 193
s. 551 193
s. 560 168, 169, 171
s. 561 193
s. 564 193
s. 565 193
s. 566 193
s. 567 193
s. 568 193
ss. 569–573 193
s. 584 54
ss. 584–587 54
s. 585 54
s. 586 54
s. 588 54–5
s. 593 54
ss. 593–597 54
s. 630(2) 510
s. 641 194
ss. 641–657 194
s. 642 194
s. 643 194
s. 644 194
ss. 677–680 110
s. 678(1) 246
s. 678(2) 247
s. 682(1) 247
s. 684(2) 231

s. 684(3) 231
ss. 684–689 171
s. 686(1) 231
s. 687(2)(a) 232
s. 688 231
s. 690 171
ss. 690–708 195, 231
s. 692(2)(a) 232
s. 693(2) 231
s. 693(2)(b) 231
s. 693(4) 231
s. 694(3) 231
s. 694(5) 231
s. 695(3) 231
s. 701(1) 231–2
s. 701(3) 232
ss. 709–712 232
s. 712(2) 232
s. 712(7) 232
s. 714 232
s. 716(1) 232
s. 719 233
s. 721 233
s. 723 233
s. 724(2) 230
s. 733 232
s. 738 249
ss. 743–746 250
s. 755 110
s. 756 110
s. 900 492
ss. 904–918 492
s. 943 505, 508
s. 943(1) 513
s. 966 510
s. 966(5) 510
s. 968(2) 510
s. 968(6) 510
s. 969(1) 510, 511
s. 979 511
ss. 983–985 513

s. 994 111, 279, 280, 281, 282, 485
s. 995 111, 282, 485
s. 996 111, 282
s. 996(2) 282
s. 1159 470–1
s. 1161(5) 471
s. 1162 448, 470–1
s. 1167 56
Sch. 6 471
para. 2 471
Sch. 7
para. 2 471
para. 3(1) 471
Company Director Disqualification Act 1986 269
s. 1 269
s. 2 269
Contracts (Rights of Third Parties) Act 1999 60
Criminal Justice Act 1993 21, 521
Enterprise Act 2002 258
European Communities Act 1972
s. 4(3) 59
s. 9 39
s. 9(4) 59
Sch. 2 para. 1 507
Financial Services and Markets Act 2000
s. 11 519
s. 91 534
s. 96A 533
s. 118 532–3
s. 118B 532
s. 118C 532
s. 143 514
Insolvency Act 1986 102, 484
219 485
435 485
s. 122(1) 281
s. 123 485
s. 213 274, 389, 482
s. 214 274, 275, 389, 482, 483
s. 214(4) 275
s. 221(4) 389
s. 221(5) 389

s. 221(7) 389
s. 238 485
s. 239 485
s. 240(2) 485
Limited Liability Partnerships Act 2000 102, 137
Limited Partnerships Act 1907 152
s. 4(2) 102
s. 6 153
s. 8 153
Partnership Act 1890 135
s. 2 135
s. 5 136
s. 9 136
s. 17(1) 386
s. 20(1) 136
s. 24 135
s. 26 135
s. 28 135, 136
s. 29 135
Value Added Tax Act 1994
s. 45 135
Statutory Instruments
Companies (Single Member Private Limited Companies) Regulations 1992, SI 1992/1699 277
European Economic Interest Grouping (Northern Ireland) Regulations, SI 1989/191 391
European Economic Interest Grouping Regulations, SI 1989/638 379, 382, 386
Reg. 5 384
Reg. 8 388–9
Reg. 19 389
Reg. 20 384
European Public Limited Liability Regulations, SI 2004/2326 396
Financial Services and Markets Act 2000 (Market Abuse) Regulation 2005, SI 2005/381 532
s. 10(2) 533
s. 22 533
Sch. 1 533–4
Sch. 2 532
Prescribed Markets and Qualified Investments Order 2001, SI 2001/ 996 532, 533
Regulatory Reform (Removal of 20 Member Limit in Partnerships) Order 2002 101

Takeover Directive (Interim Implementation) Regulations 2006, SI 2006 507
Transnational Information and Consultation of Employees Regulations, SI 1999/3323 418, 444

United States

Securities Exchange Act 1934
s. 10(b) 519–20

1

Introduction

I. The new European company law

Company law is undergoing fundamental change in Europe. All European countries have undertaken extensive reform of their company legislation. Domestic company law reform has traditionally been driven by initiatives to remedy weaknesses that have come to light in larger corporate failures or scandals. Initiatives to make corporate governance more effective is one such feature of recent European company law reform. In parallel, company law reform has been taken in the opposite direction by the wish to simplify and lessen the burdens in particular on smaller and medium-sized businesses (SMEs). The new Member States have gone through even more fundamental reform to facilitate a modern market economy and then to implement the *acquis communautaire* in company law. The prospect of regulatory competition increasing the number of domestic businesses incorporating abroad, has increased the pressure to reduce capital requirements.

The case law of the European Court of Justice on the right of establishment and to provide services and the free movement of capital, has in recent years been brought to bear on national company law and corporate practice. National company law has been set aside as restricting the free movement of companies or restricting the exercise of the fundamental freedoms in other ways. As European Union law gradually opens up the choice of country of incorporation for businesses in Europe, the competition between national company laws is increasing.

The harmonisation of European company law through EU legislation (directives and regulations), has also been given a new impetus by the case law of the Court of Justice and different initiatives by the European Commission. This requires transposition in national company legislation. New EU legislation gives further effect to the free movement of companies, which again opens up for regulatory competition.

National company legislation cannot now be applied without regard to the case law of the European Court of Justice on the fundamental freedoms in the EC Treaty on the right of establishment and to provide services and the free movement of capital. Many provisions of the national legislation require the active use of the directives they transpose. In case of conflict, EU law requires that it is the rule of the directive that is applied. More generally, the EU company law legislation in directives and regulations constitutes a system which is the basic framework for national company law, and often the natural starting point when company law matters are to be resolved. Neither can EU company law legislation in directives and regulations be applied without regard to the fundamental freedoms in the EC Treaty and the case law of the European Court of Justice. EU company legislation itself has to be interpreted and applied so that it complies with the EC Treaty on the right of establishment and to provide services and the free movement of capital. In case of conflict, the Treaty prevails.

Comparative law is not of any less importance in this new context. The application of the fundamental freedoms in the EC Treaty in the review of national company law, can be assisted by analysis of the company laws of other Member States. That is even more so the case for the transposition or subsequent interpretation of EU directives. Concepts and rules often originate in a national system, and even if they may change when they are imported into a directive, knowing about their original meaning may provide assistance. Also the way that directives have been transposed in other Member States, may assist when a directive is to be given effect in the application of national company legislation.

Comparative law is of great importance also when company lawyers are to apply the company laws of other Member States. This is increasingly necessary as a consequence of the Internal Market integration. Contracts with companies of other Member States, investments in their securities and cross-border mergers are just some of the many transactions which require such knowledge.

The company with business in one Member State and incorporation in another, is a further field where comparative company law is required. At the upper end of the market, it is often not enough to have company lawyers of the different jurisdictions working together. There is a growing need for company lawyers with extensive comparative law expertise. At the lower end, where one cannot afford legal advice from experts from different jurisdictions, the company lawyer must just deal with the comparative law issues that occur.

This provides a considerable challenge to scholarship and teaching. This book is intended as one contribution to the emerging discipline of comparative European company law.

II. An outline of this book

The present work examines certain important aspects of the company laws of seven European countries, namely the United Kingdom, France, Germany, Italy, Spain, Belgium, and the Netherlands. Whenever relevant and possible, reference has been made to the situations in these countries. However, the work does not limit itself to the national company laws of these seven countries, but also examines certain bodies subject to a mixed legal regime, such as the European Economic Interest Grouping (EEIG) and the European Company (SE). The emergent discipline of European company law is considered in the following chapter of the present work, in the light of the harmonisation of company law by the European Union and company law reforms in the different national jurisdictions. The relevant harmonising directives and certain draft instruments also receive consideration in Chapter 2. It has also been found necessary to consider harmonising directives in Chapter 8 on employee participation; Chapter 10 on takeovers and mergers deals with the Thirteenth Directive on takeovers;[1] Chapter 11, which is the final one, deals with the Directive on market abuse (insider dealing and market manipulation).[2] As is pointed out in Chapter 2, the harmonising process may have certain defects; it is sometimes very protracted. Directives may become outdated or otherwise in need of reform: both the SLIM Group[3] and the High Level Group of Company Law Experts[4] recognised that the Second Company Law Directive needed certain reforms. One outcome of this was the amendments in a 2006 revision

[1] Directive 2004/25/EC of 21 April 2004 on takeover bids, OJ 2004 L142/12–23. See for the history of the Directive, Commission Communication of 2 October 2002 on the proposal for a Directive of the European Parliament and Council on takeover bids. The chapter also considers the Tenth Directive, Directive 2005/56/EC on cross-border mergers of limited liability companies, OJ 2005 L310/1.

[2] Directive 2003/6/EC on market abuse (including insider dealing and market manipulation), which replaces Directive 592/89 on Insider Dealing.

[3] SLIM stands for Simpler Legislation for the Internal Market, see the 1996 report, COM (96) 204.

[4] As a result of the blockage of the Takeover Directive in the European Parliament, the Commission set up a High Level Group of Company Law Experts under the chairmanship of Jaap Winter to provide advice on key priorities for modernising company law in the European Union. It produced two major reports, see Report of the High Level Group of Company Law Experts on Issues related to Takeover Bids of 10 January 2002, http://ec.europa.eu/internal_market/company/docs/takeoverbids/2002-01-hlg-report_en.pdf; Report of the High Level Group of Company Law Experts of 4 November 2002, http://ec.europa.eu/internal_market/company/docs/modern/report_en.pdf.

directive.[5] The second chapter also deals briefly with the relevance of the comparative law method to the harmonisation of company law both at the European and national level.

Chapter 3 considers the methods of formation of public and private companies in the Member States under consideration. Because of their topicality and relevance it also deals, inter alia, with the important questions of the transfer of the head offices of companies from one Member State to another, and the recognition of foreign companies. Similar problems have been encountered in the jurisprudence of the European Court of Justice in such recent cases as *Centros*,[6] *Überseering*,[7] *Kamer van Koophandel*[8] and *Sevic*.[9]

Chapter 4 is concerned with the various types of business organisation which exist in the relevant Member States. In addition to considering public and private companies, and partnerships, it also deals with hybrid forms of entity such as the French SAS and the various kinds of German GmbH & Co KG, some of which, like the French SAS, are of considerable practical importance. This chapter also briefly considers the private proposal for the introduction of a European Private Company (EPC); the High Level Panel of Company Law Experts recommended a feasibility study to assess the practical need for the introduction of an EPC, and this was followed up in the EU Commission's Communication *Modernising Company Law and Enhancing Corporate Governance in the European Union – A Plan to Move Forward*.[10]

The following two chapters, which are lengthy, deal with matters of cardinal importance to the understanding of company law, namely share

[5] Directive 2006/68/EC of 6 September 2006 amending Council Directive 77/91/EEC as regards the formation of public limited liability companies and the maintenance and alteration of their capital.

[6] Case C-212/97 *Centros Ltd* v. *Erhvervs- og Selskabsstyrelsen* [1999] ECR I-1459.

[7] Case C-208/00 *Überseering BV* v. *Nordic Construction Company Baumanagement GmbH* [2002] ECR I-9919.

[8] Case C-167/01 *Kamer van Koophandel en Fabrieken voor Amsterdam* v. *Inspire Art Ltd* [2003] *ECR* I-10155. This case concerned whether the Netherlands courts could invoke Arts. 1–5 of the law of 1997 governing proforma foreign companies against the Dutch branch of a company incorporated in the United Kingdom, which carried on all or nearly all its business through a branch in the Netherlands. *Alber AG* (following *Centros*) held this to be impossible and the Court agreed generally with his approach.

[9] Case C-411/03 *Sevic Systems AG* v. *Amtsgericht Neuwied* [2005] ECR I-10805; [2006] 1 CMLR 45; [2006] 4 All ER 1072.

[10] *Communication from the Commission to the Council and the European Parliament – Modernising Company Law and Enhancing Corporate Governance in the European Union – A Plan to Move Forward*, COM (2003) 284.

and loan capital, and management and control. The length of these chapters is explained by the number of topics involved, and the diversity of ways in which certain such topics are regulated in the different Member States. Thus, for example, in France and Germany, many different types of company securities exist, and this is discussed in Chapter 5 on share (or equity) capital and loan capital. The German double board system and its optional French counterpart are considered in detail in Chapter 6, which does not however attempt to deal in detail with questions of corporate governance.

In Chapter 7, the legal regimes governing the EEIG and SE are examined in some detail. Attention is also paid to the Statute for a European Cooperative Society.[11] The succeeding chapter deals with employee participation, on which there has been recent legislation in Germany,[12] as well as an important Community directive on a general framework for informing and consulting employees,[13] which has required implementation in the United Kingdom and the other Member States. Chapter 8 deals with employee representation on the supervisory or executive boards of French, German and Dutch companies.

The topic dealt with in Chapter 9 consists of the regulation of groups of companies. This matter has given rise to a number of problems and one may postulate that it is now unlikely that detailed proposals comparable to those enshrined in the abortive draft Ninth Directive on the conduct of groups would now be acceptable to the Member States. The High Level Panel of Company Law Experts did not recommend the enactment of a body of law applicable to groups of companies. However as it suggested some regulation of particular problems relating to groups appears necessary.

This was recognised by the *Forum Europaeum Konzernrecht* which reported on this matter in 1998, as well as by the High Level Panel. Thus the latter body recommended that Member States should be required to provide for a framework rule for groups that allow those concerned with the management of a group company to adopt and implement a coordinated group policy provided that the interests of the group's

[11] OJ 2003 L207. The object of this statute is to provide cooperatives with adequate legal instruments to facilitate their cross-border and transnational activities. The new Statute parallels the SE Statute but has been tailored to the specific characteristics of cooperative societies.

[12] See *Betriebsverfassungsgesetz* 2001 (BGBl 2001, I.2267) and *Drittbeteiligungsgesetz* of 18 May 2004 (BGBl 2004, I.2633–2639) replacing *Betriebsverfassungsgesetz* 1952.

[13] OJ 2002 L80/29.

creditors are protected, and that there is a balance of burdens and advantages over time for the shareholders. This proposal may owe something to French law, but it may be of too general a character to have much influence on the conduct of groups. Although they have certain defects the provision of German *Konzernrecht* have been thought to merit detailed discussion in this chapter. They have had a considerable influence outside Germany, for example in Portugal, Brazil, Slovenia and Croatia.

The penultimate chapter deals with takeovers and mergers. As well as examining the Thirteenth Directive on takeovers, it examines in outline the rules of law of certain of the relevant Member States concerning mandatory bids and defences to takeovers. The impact of the Cross-Border Mergers Directive is considered in this chapter.[14] A more comprehensive examination of the law governing takeovers would exceed the limits of the present work. This chapter also briefly, considers mergers, and the rules of competition law which applies to them.

The work concludes with an account of the Market Abuse Directive (covering insider dealing and market manipulation),[15] which has the effect of repealing the Insider Dealing Directive of 1989, which was implemented in rather different ways in all the Member States. This is the first Directive under which the Commission submitted comitology proposals for secondary legislation under the Lamfalussy procedure. The creation of a satisfactory legal framework for dealing with market manipulation has taken some time and has now moved on to the national level of transposing the EU directive and secondary legislation. Much comparative material is available on the transposition of the Insider Dealing Directive, which has been repealed but where the legislation that implemented it in some countries remains in place (such as with the UK insider dealing legislation). The transposition in Germany has required amendment of the law relating to market manipulation which is contained in the Fourth Financial Market Promotion Act of 2002.

[14] Directive 2005/56/EC of 26 October 2005 on cross-border mergers of limited liability companies OJ 2005 L310/1.

[15] Directive 2003/6/EC on insider dealing and market abuse OJ 2003 L96/16.

2

European and comparative company law

I. Harmonisation and free movement

A. *Treaty provisions*

It is now recognised generally that although there is no question of the total approximation or harmonisation of the company laws of the Member States, a considerable body of European company law has been brought into existence.[1] This has come about mainly through the enactment of directives under Articles 44(2)(g) and 95 EC (former Articles 54(3)(g), 100a EC). The first mentioned Article is set out in Chapter 2, 'Right of establishment of Title II EC, "free movement of persons, services and capital"'. It provides:

> The Council and the Commission shall carry out the duties devolving on them under the preceding provisions,[2] in particular (g) by coordinating to the necessary extent the safeguards which for the protection of the interests of members and others, are required by Member States of companies within the meaning of Article 48(2)[3] with a view to making such safeguards equivalent throughout the community.

[1] See for instance E. Werlauff, *EU Company Law. Common Business Law for 28 States*, 2nd edn (Copenhagen: DJØF Publishing, 2003) who argues in his introduction that 'the company law of these many states is not uniform – nor it is required to be so – but all the main company rules will, or shall, be reflected in the company law of each individual state.' He continues: 'In the "old" days European law accounts of company law necessarily had to be comparative … the emphasis was on the differences in the company law of the states. Now the emphasis will be on the common, cross border features of company law.' He sets out a systematic treatment of EU company law with less emphasis on transposition of directives or national law concepts. See the very important book by S. Grundmann, *Europäisches Gesellschaftsrecht* (Heidelberg: C. F. Müller, 2003) and also V. Edwards, *EC Company Law* (Oxford: Clarendon Press, 1999), whose treatment generally follows the directives in their order of adoption.

[2] These provisions are those of Art. 43 EC, which prohibits restrictions on the setting up of agencies, branches or subsidiaries by nationals of any Member State in the territory of another Member State. This prohibition is applicable to restrictions on the setting up of agencies, branches or subsidiaries by nationals of any Member State in the territory of any Member State.

[3] This provision stipulates that 'companies or firms' means companies or firms constituted under civil or commercial law including cooperative societies and other legal persons governed by private or public law, save for those which are not profit making.

Article 44(2)(g) EC is the basis for nearly all enacted directives in European company law. Despite its position in Chapter 2 of the Treaty, the Community institutions pursue a broad interpretation which is orientated towards the aims of the Treaty.[4] In that view also measures with the purpose of approximating the prevailing conditions of company law can be based on it as long as they have beneficial effect on cross-border transactions.[5] A broad construction of Article 44(2)(g) EC may now be justified, but there must be a link between the legislation adopted under this provision and the fostering of a company's right of establishment.[6] Previously, there was considerable support for an interpretation according to which Article 44(2)(g) EC is restricted to rules which promote the right of establishment.[7] Article 44(2)(g) EC merely gives the competence to issue directives, not regulations.

Article 95(1) EC provides for a different procedure for the adoption of measures for the approximation of the provisions laid down by law, regulation or administrative action in the Member States which have as their object the establishment and functioning of the internal market. Such measures must be adopted by means of the rather long and complex co-decision procedure set out in Article 251 EC, which gives the European parliament the ultimate power of vetoing the relevant draft legislation. In European company law Article 95(1) EC has in practice only been significant as the basis for directives on capital market law.[8] It has been regarded as *lex generalis* in relation to Article 44(2)(g) EC.[9] The Community legislator regularly uses both. Article 44(2)(g) and Article 95(1) EC as legal bases to enact these directives.[10] Article 95(1) EC also

[4] See Case C-97/96, *Daihatsu* [1997] ECR I-6843, 6864.

[5] R. Houin, 'Le régime juridique des sociétés dans la Communauté Economique Européenne' [1965] RTDE 11, 16; see also Edwards, *EC Company Law*, pp. 5–9 and M. Habersack, *Europäisches Gesellschaftsrecht* (Munich: Beck, 1999), para. 20.

[6] See Case C-122/96, *Saldanna and MTS Securities Corporation* v. *Hiross Holdings* [1977] ECR I-5325.

[7] See e.g. Rodière, 'L'harmonisation des legislations européennes dans le cadre de la C.E.E.' [1965] RTDE 336, 342–50; Y. Scholten, 'Company Law in Europe' [1967] 4 CMLR 377, 382; see for the discussion also: P. van Ommeslaghe, 'La première directive du Conseil du 9 mars 1968 en matière de sociétés' [1969] CDE 495, 502–16; P. Sanders, 'Review of Recent Literature on Corporation Law' [1967] 4 CMLR 113, 119 ff; E. Stein, Harmonization of European Company Laws (1971) 174–182.

[8] S. Heinze, *Europäisches Kapitalmarktrecht* (Munich: Beck, 1999), p. 12; E. Wymeersch, 'Company Law in Europe and European Company Law' [2001] 6 *Working Paper Series*, Universiteit Gent 3.

[9] Following the broad interpretation of Art. 44(2)(g) EC.

[10] But other articles have also been invoked, for instance Art. 47(2) EC for the UCITS Directive, the former Art. 54(2) EC for the Directive on Mutual Recognition of Listing Particulars.

entitles the Community legislator to enact regulations.[11] Nevertheless, Community regulations in Company Law have not yet been based upon Article 95(1) EC. Both the Council Regulation 2137/85 on the European Economic Interest Grouping (EEIG)[12] as well as the Council Regulation 2157/2001 on the Statute for a European company (SE)[13] were based on Article 308 EC.[14] Article 308 EC provides that the Council may, acting unanimously on a proposal from the Commission and after consulting the European Parliament, take the necessary measures, if action by the Community should prove necessary to attain in the course of the operations of the common market one of the objectives of the Community, and the Treaty has not provided the necessary powers. The European Economic Interest Grouping is a fiscally transparent entity having some of the characteristics of a company and some of an unincorporated body. The European Company is able to operate across borders. It is subject to a rather complex legal regime, consisting partly of rules of European law. The European Company is described more fully in the succeeding chapter.

Article 293 EC is another source for Community measures in European company law. It provides that the Member States shall enter into negotiations with each other with a view to securing for the benefit of their nationals: the mutual recognition of companies or firms within the meaning of the second paragraph of Article 48, the retention of legal personality in the event of transfer of their seat from one country to another, and the possibility of mergers between companies or firms governed by the laws of different countries. On this basis, in 1968 the six original Member States signed the Convention on Mutual

[11] Article 249(3) EC provides that 'a directive shall be binding as to the result to be achieved, upon each Member States to which it is addressed, but shall leave to the national authorities the choice of form and methods'. Article 249(2) EC provides that 'a regulation shall have general application. It shall be binding in its entirety and directly applicable in all Member States.'

[12] Council Regulation 2137/85 EEC of 25 July 1985 on the European Economic Interest grouping, OJ L199 of 31 July 1985, 1.

[13] Council Regulation (EC) 2157/2001 of 8 October 2001 on the Statute for a European company (SE), OJ 2001 L294/1.

[14] The Commission and the European Parliament preferred Art. 95. See the draft proposal of 16 October 1989, OJ C263/41 and OJ 1991 C176/1 and for the discussion: H. W. Neye, 'Kein neuer Stolperstein für die Europäische Aktiengesellschaft' [2002] *Zeitschrift für Gesellschaftsrecht* 377 f; Wiesner [2001] GmbH-Rundschau, R 461; G. F. Thoma and D. Leuering, 'Die Europäische Aktiengesellschaft – Societas Europaea' [2000] *Neue Juristische Wochenschrift* 1449; M. Lutter, 'Europäische Aktiengesellschaft – Rechtfigur mit Zukunft?' [2002] *Betriebsberater* 1, 3.

Recognition of Companies and Legal Persons.[15] It however never came into force as it was not ratified by the Netherlands.[16] The implementation of this provision would have required an international treaty, and the unanimous consent of the Member States and of their parliaments would have been necessary. Also negotiations for a Convention on cross-border mergers failed.[17] The issue is now governed by the Tenth Directive.[18] Treaties between the Member States did not develop to a useful instrument for the approximation of national company laws.

B. Free movement and the fundamental freedoms: the right of establishment

The Treaty provisions mentioned above concern the application of the right of establishment to companies and the harmonisation of the laws of the Member States. The four freedoms, especially the right of establishment (Articles 43–48 EC) and the free movement of capital (Articles 56–69 EC) provide the foundations of European company law. They also generate the precondition for a free and economical choice of location. For instance, the application of the right of establishment and to provide services has ended certain discriminatory taxation laws.[19]

The right of establishment can be regarded as the cornerstone of European company law. Articles 43(2) and 48(1) EC provide that companies established in the EC may create secondary establishments in other Member States and thus set up agencies, branches or subsidiaries

[15] See for the text: [1968] *Revue trimestrielle de droit européen* 400; for the English version: [1969] EC Bull Supp 2 and E. Stein, *Harmonization of European Company Laws* (1971), p. 525. A Convention under Art. 293 EC is not technically a Community Act, but a Treaty between the Member States. See for more details: Edwards, *EC Company Law*, pp. 384–6; B. Goldman, 'The Convention between the Member States of the European Economic Community on the Mutual Recognition of Companies and Legal Persons' [1968–69] 6 CMLR 104.

[16] E. Werlauff, *EC Company Law* (Copenhagen: Jurist- og Økonomforbundets, 1993), pp. 15–17.

[17] See for the preliminary draft of the Convention of 1967: *Comité des experts de l'article 220 alinéa 3 du Traité CEE, 'Droit des sociétés – Fusions internationales, Avant-projet de convention relatif à la fusion internationale des sociétés anonymes', Document de travail* no. 4, 16.082/IV/67-F. See for the draft convention of 1972 EC Bull Supp 13/73 and B. Goldman '*La fusion des sociétés et le projet de convention sur la fusion internationale des sociétés anonymes*' [1981] 17 CDE 4.

[18] The Tenth Council Directive on cross-border mergers, [2005] OJ L310/1. See for the legislative history and background, P. Farmer 'Removing legal obstacles to cross-border mergers: EEC proposal for a tenth directive' [1987] *Business Law Review* 35 f., 53.

[19] See case C-62/00 *Marks & Spencer* [2002] ECR I-6325.

there. There is a considerable body of decisions of the ECJ in which the non-discriminatory exercise of this right of secondary establishment has been emphasised[20] and elaborated. This has contributed to the considerable body of European company law, which otherwise owes its existence to the recognition of certain general principles of law, secondary legislation, and decisions of the ECJ concerning such legislation, provisions of which have sometimes been held to be directly effective.

It is a matter of debate whether following the decisions of the ECJ in *Centros*[21] and *Überseering* line of cases,[22] it is now the case that a company is given the right of primary establishment under Community law (as opposed to national law) to transfer its statutory seat from one Member State to another.[23] This problem with its link to the question of mutual recognition of companies will be discussed more fully in the succeeding chapter.

The ECJ held in *Sevic*,[24] decided a few weeks after the enactment of the Tenth Directive on Cross-Border Mergers, that a Luxembourg company had the right to merge with a German company, despite contrary rules of German law. Refusal to permit a merger would be a restriction in the

[20] Note the account of certain of these cases in J. Usher, *The Law of Money and Financial Services in the European Community* (Oxford: EC Law Library, 2000), pp. 91–6. In Joined Cases C-397/98 and C-410/98, *Metallgesellschaft Ltd and others* v. *IRC and Another* and *Hoechst AG and Another* v. *Same*, [2001] ECR I-1727; Case 19/92 *Kraus* [1993] ECR I-1689, 1697 para. 32; Case 55/94, *Gebhardt* [1995] ECR I-4165, 4197 para. 37; Case C-212/97, *Centros* [1999] ECR I-1459, 1491 para. 20 ff.; Case C-255/97 *Pfeiffer* [1999] ECR I-2835, 2860, para. 19. First, the ECJ held that Art. 43 only prohibits discriminatory restrictions. See, e.g.: Case 2/74 *Reyners* v. *Belgium* [1974] ECR 631, 651 para. 16/20; Case 71/76 *Thieffry* [1977] Case 765, 777 f.

[21] Case C-212/97, *Centros* [1999] ECR I-1459. See for more details: J. P. Hansen, 'A new look at Centros – from a Danish point of view' [2002] 13 EBLR 85.

[22] Case C-208/00, *Überseering* [2002] ECR I-9919; F. Wooldridge 'Überseering: Freedom of Establishment of Companies Affirmed' [2003] 14 EBLR 227; W. Roth, 'From Centros to Überseering: Free Movement of Companies Private International Law and Community Law' [2003] 52 ICLQ 192; E. Wymeersch, 'The Transfer of the Companies Seat in European Company Law' [2003] 40 CMLR 661; M. Andenas, 'Free Movement of Companies' [2003] 119 LQR 221.

[23] It does not seem that the Court recognised such a right of primary establishment in *Centros*: see the discussion of the case in St Rammeloo, *Corporations in Private International Law – a European perspective* (Oxford University Press: 2001), pp. 72–85: note especially the literature mentioned in footnote 233 on p. 72. In *Überseering*, which is discussed in the chapter on the formation of companies, the court has at least recognised the right to transfer the actual centre of administration from one Member State to another: note in particular para. 64 of its judgment. See also M. Andenas, 'Free Movement of Companies' [2003] 119 LQR 221.

[24] Case C-411/03 *Sevic Systems AG* [2005] ECR I-10805.

meaning of Articles 43 and 48 EC and could only be justified if it pursued a legitimate objective under the Treaty and justified by imperative grounds in the public interest. The ECJ regarded the treatment of the Luxembourg company as an instance of discrimination. In para. 22 of the judgment it stated that:

> In so far as, under national rules, recourse to such a means of company transformation is not possible where one of the companies is established in a Member State other than the Federal Republic of Germany, German law establishes a difference in treatment between companies according to the internal or cross-border nature of the merger, which is likely to deter the exercise of the freedom of establishment laid down by the Treaty.

It follows from *Centros*[25] that non-discriminatory measures which form obstacles or hindrances to access to market also requires justification on public interest grounds. One reading of this and the line of cases discussed here is that anything which makes cross-border establishment less attractive constitutes a restriction under Articles 43 and 48 EC. Such a wide restrictions concept goes much beyond the discrimination found in the present cases, and its consequences for company legislation in Member States are potentially far-reaching.

The ECJ addresses justifications in para. 23 of *Sevic*:

> Such a difference in treatment constitutes a restriction within the meaning of Articles 43 EC and 48 EC, which is contrary to the right of establishment and can be permitted only if it pursues a legitimate objective compatible with the Treaty and is justified by imperative reasons in the public interest. It is further necessary, in such a case, that its application must be appropriate to ensuring the attainment of the objective thus pursued and must not go beyond what is necessary to attain it (see Case C-436/00 *X and Y* [2002] ECR I-10829, paragraph 49; Case C-9/02 *De Lasteyrie du Saillant* [2004] ECR I-2409, paragraph 49).

The intensity of the review of the proportionality of national company law constituting a restriction under the wide test now developed becomes of great importance.

[25] Case C-212/97 *Centros Ltd* v. *Erhvervs- og Selskabsstyrelsen* [1999] ECR I-1459. See also Case C-55/94 *Gebhard* [1995] ECR I-4165, para. 37; Case C-108/96 *Mac Quen* [2001] ECR I-837, para. 26; Case C-442/02 *CaixaBank France* [2004] ECR I-8961, para. 11. In the latter case the ECJ gave 'market access' a wide scope. The ECJ extended the *Gebhard* formula to measures which prohibit, impede or make less attractive the freedom of establishment.

One remaining question is the application of the *Centros* line of cases to companies leaving a jurisdiction. The cases have dealt with discrimination by host state authorities against a company from another Member State. The question is if the same wide restrictions concept can be applied to regulation by the country of incorporation or seat when the company wants to leave the jurisdiction. Here the case of *Daily Mail*[26] still casts its shadow over the area. The well known distinction between export and import restrictions has been used to limit the recent ECJ case law on free movement of companies. The cases can be cast as dealing with discrimination against foreign companies. But restrictions on the exit of companies from one jurisdiction, entering another, either remaining a foreign company there or as a company incorporated in the new jurisdiction, constitutes a major obstacle to free movement and the functioning of the Internal Market. It is suggested that the *Daily Mail* case has no clear *ratio*, and the approach to exit restrictions is inconsistent with that taken to such restrictions in the case law on free movement. The facts of the *Daily Mail* case did not give rise to adding questions of the structure of the legal personality of the company, and the transfer of its residence to Netherlands for tax purposes was not relevant as a company law matter. Both the United Kingdom and the Netherlands accept the incorporation doctrine.

In the cases where the ECJ has had to refer to *Daily Mail*, it has done so in a manner that perhaps could leave the impression that it is still good law, supporting exit restrictions. However, the ECJ has not had any opportunity to reconsider and overturn *Daily Mail*, and the references made to the case does not develop a new *ratio* for the case or support that the ECJ would treat entry of companies ('export restrictions') any differently from exit ('import restrictions'). However, the ECJ may soon have to address the exit issues directly. A Hungarian Court of Appeal has referred several questions[27] to the European Court (ECJ) in the case of *Cartesio*.[28] The Hungarian court asks the following questions on the free movement of companies:

> May a Hungarian company request transfer of its registered office to another Member State of the European Union relying directly on community law (Articles 43 and 48 of the Treaty of Rome)? If the answer is affirmative, may the transfer of the registered office be made subject to any

[26] Case 81/87 *R* v. *Treasury ex p Daily Mail* [1988] ECR 5483.
[27] Under the Art. 234 EC Treaty procedure.
[28] (Case C-210/06). OJ C165, of 15 July 2006, 17.

> kind of condition or authorisation by the Member State of origin or the host Member State?
>
> May Articles 43 and 48 of the Treaty of Rome be interpreted as meaning that national rules or national practices which differentiate between commercial companies with respect to the exercise of their rights, according to the Member State in which their registered office is situated, is incompatible with Community law?

The important part of the questions to the ECJ is the reference to conditions imposed on the company leaving the jurisdiction. In its ruling on the questions in *Cartesio* the ECJ has an opportunity to overrule *Daily Mail*, or make very clear that *Daily Mail* is limited to its facts in a legal and factual context which is very different today.

C. *Free movement of capital*

The free movement of capital has in a number of cases provided the grounds for review of national company legislation and practice. The free movement of capital has become an important precondition for the establishment of companies and the European company law. The internal market can only be established if capital transactions can be made without any non-discriminatory restrictions.[29] Article 56(1) EC provides that all restrictions on the movement of capital between Member States and between Member States and third countries shall be prohibited.[30] The ECJ held in its *Elf Aquitaine* decision 2002[31] that any restriction on investment or on the exercise of control in European companies, like 'Golden Shares',[32] is in breach of the principle of the free movement of capital The ECJ held that:

[29] Case C-483/99 *Commission* v. *France (Elf-Aquitaine)* [2002] ECR I-4781; Case C-302/97 *Konle* [1999] I-3099, para. 44.

[30] For a closer look see Moloney, *EC Securities Regulation*, 45.

[31] Cases C-367/98 *Commission* v. *Portugal* [2002] ECR I-4731; C-483/99 *Commission* v. *France* (*Elf-Aquitaine*) [2002] ECR I-4781 and C-503/99 *Commission* v. *Belgium* [2002] ECR I-4809.

[32] So-called 'Golden Shares' guarantee certain voting rights or blocking power. They could for instance confer the right to outvote other shareholders at general meetings, or to veto certain decisions of the company, such as the sale of core assets. Other rights of Golden Shares could follow from provisions in the company's articles or shareholder agreements intended to ensure that no shareholder is beneficially entitled to an interest in more than a fixed proportion of voting shares. A third variant enables the government to nominate some of the directors. In some jurisdictions, golden shares have been created under existing company legislation, in others new legislation has been required to introduce State prerogatives in privatised companies.

> the free movement of capital, as a fundamental principle of the Treaty, may be restricted only by national rules which are justified by reasons referred to in Article 58 of the Treaty or by overriding requirements of the general interest and which are applicable to all persons and undertakings pursuing an activity in the territory of the host Member State. Furthermore, in order to be so justified, the national legislation must be suitable for securing the objective which it pursues and must not go beyond what is necessary in order to attain it, so as to accord with the principle of proportionality.

In the *Golden Share* cases the restrictions primarily originated with Member State authorities wishing to influence the decision making process within a privatised company or its shareholder structure. There are other cases where the restriction follows primarily from a decision of the company, its management or its shareholders.

In the first round, the European Commission brought three actions for infringement of Articles 56 EC Treaty (free movement of capital) and 43 EC Treaty (freedom of establishment) against Belgium, France and Portugal.[33] The 2002 cases concerned control procedures such as the rules on prior authorisation and rights of veto in companies that had been privatised. This was a way of securing a certain level of state control after privatisation. The case against Portugal concerned limitations on participation by non-nationals and a procedure for the grant of prior authorisation by the Minister of Finance once the interest of a person acquiring shares in a privatised company exceeds a ceiling of 10 per cent. The companies concerned were undertakings in the banking, insurance, energy and transport sectors.

In the case against France, the Commission complained that a Decree of 1993 vested in the State a 'golden share' in Société Nationale Elf-Aquitaine. The Minister for Economic Affairs is required, first, to approve in advance any acquisition of shares or rights which exceeds established limits on the holding of capital and, second, may oppose decisions to transfer shares or use them as security.

The case against Belgium concerned two Royal Decrees from 1994 vesting in the State 'golden shares' in Société Nationale de Transport par

[33] Cases C-367/98 *Commission* v. *Portugal* [2002] ECR I-4731; C-483/99 *Commission* v. *France* [2002] ECR I-4781 and C-503/99 *Commission* v. *Belgium* [2002] ECR I-4809. It did not follow the opinion of its Advocate General, but basically agreed with the Commission's complaint that 'golden shares' can, depending on the circumstances, infringe the free movement of capital and the freedom of establishment. Dismissing the complaint against Belgium, it upheld the applications against France and Portugal.

Canalisations and in Distrigaz. The Minister for Energy might oppose any transfer of technical installations and any specific management decisions taken from time to time concerning the companies' shares which may jeopardise national supplies of natural gas.

The Court considered that the 'golden shares' held by each of these three countries were restrictions. The legislation was liable to impede the acquisition of shares in the undertakings concerned. It could dissuade investors in other Member States from investing in those undertakings. The Court focused:

(1) on the prohibition (in Portugal) on the acquisition by nationals of another Member State of more than a given number of shares;
(2) the requirement (in France and Portugal) that prior authorisation or notification is to be given where a limit on the number of shares or voting rights held is exceeded; and
(3) the right (in France and Belgium) to oppose, *ex post facto*, decisions concerning transfers of shares.

The Court then considered the grounds put forward by way of justification for the restrictions. They were based on the need to maintain a controlling interest in undertakings operating in areas involving matters of general or strategic interest. The Court first held that, concerning the objective pursued by France (to guarantee supplies of petroleum products in the event of a crisis), it fell within the ambit of a legitimate general interest. But the Court considered the measures went beyond what is necessary in order to attain the objective indicated. The provisions did not indicate the specific, objective circumstances in which prior authorisation or a right of opposition ex post facto will be granted or refused, and were contrary to the principle of legal certainty. The Court was unable to accept such a lack of precision and such a wide discretionary power, which constitutes a serious impairment of the fundamental principle of the free movement of capital.

The Court did however accept the justification put forward by Belgium (to maintain minimum supplies of gas in the event of a real and serious threat). Here, no prior approval is required. Intervention by the Belgian public authorities in the context of a transfer of installations and the pursuit of management policy was subject to strict time limits, in accordance with a specific procedure involving a formal statement of reasons and subject to an effective review by the courts.

The need to safeguard the financial interests of the Portuguese Republic did not pass the test. The Court referred to the settled case law to the effect that such economic grounds, which were put forward in support of a prior authorisation procedure, can never serve as justification for restrictions on freedom of movement.

In 2003, the ECJ handed down decisions in two further actions by the European Commission, this time against Spain and the UK.[34]

The UK case followed the privatisation of the British Airport Authority (BAA) in the late 1980s. The articles of association of this company made provision for a special share to be held by the Secretary of State allowing a veto of winding up or a disposal of one of the UK airports. In addition to that, the articles prohibited any shareholder from holding more than 15 per cent of the BAA shares. Concerning the veto, the judgment endorsed the broad scope of capital movement and establishment as in the 2002 cases: the EC Treaty prohibits all restrictions on the movement of capital between Member States and between Member States and third countries and direct investments in the form of participation in an undertaking by means of shareholding or the acquisition of securities on the capital market constitute capital movements. Regarding the 15 per cent restriction, the UK had argued in essence that the alleged 'restrictions' were in fact rules defining the company itself and applicable by mechanisms of private company law only. The Court held that the restrictions at issue do not arise as the result of the normal operation of company law. The articles of association were to be approved by the Secretary of State pursuant to the Airports Act 1986 and that was what actually occurred. In those circumstances, the Member State acted in this instance in its capacity as a public authority.

Finally, the Court also rejected the UK argument that the BAA provisions were to be considered as 'selling arrangements' under the *Keck* case law on Article 28 EC.[35] The UK argued that its case did not entail a restriction on the free movement of capital as access to the market was not affected. This could be an important ruling, closing the door for

[34] Case C-463/00 *Commission* v. *Spain* [2003] ECR I-4581, and Case C-98/01 *Commission* v. *United Kingdom* [2003] ECR I-4641.

[35] Case C-267/268/91 *Keck and Mithouard* [1993] ECR I-6097. As long as they are not discriminatory, 'selling arrangements' (distinguished from 'product requirements'), are not considered to be restrictions under Art. 28 EC on the free movement of goods. *Keck* is one outcome of the Sunday trading litigation of the early 1990s where the argument was that regulation of the opening hours of shops (such as a ban on Sunday trading) could constitute a restriction on the free movement of goods. After *Keck*, a ban on Sunday trading would typically be a 'selling restriction' and Art. 28 EC would not be engaged.

holding that a broad category of potential restrictions should go clear of the free movement of capital as long as they are not discriminatory.

The Spanish provisions that were challenged constituted a system of prior administrative approval in several privatised companies[36] introduced by the Spanish legislation extending to major decisions relating to the winding up, demerger, merger, or change of corporate object of certain undertakings, or to the disposal of certain assets of those undertakings.[37] The ECJ[38] held this system to constitute a restriction on the free movement of capital and also addressed possible justifications for a restriction. A justification could not be excluded for reasons of public interest, but the Court quickly rejected the justification offered in the Spanish case, mainly on grounds that the concerned undertakings could not qualify as undertakings whose objective was to provide public services. 'Public security' could be relied on only if there is a genuine and sufficiently serious threat to a fundamental interest of society which was not present in this case.[39]

[36] The undertakings were Repsol, Telefónica, Argentaria, Tabacalera and Endesa, dealing with a wide range of business activities.

The Spanish Law 5/1995 on 'the legal arrangements for disposal of public shareholdings in certain undertakings' which governs the conditions on which several Spanish public-sector undertakings were privatised introduced a system of prior administrative approval. Major decisions relating to the winding-up, demerger, merger or change of corporate object of certain undertakings or to the disposal of certain assets of, or shareholdings in, those undertakings needed to be approved.

[37] The Spanish Law 5/1995 on 'the legal arrangements for disposal of public shareholdings in certain undertakings' which governs the conditions on which several Spanish public-sector undertakings were privatised.

[38] The Spanish rules had been held to be justified by Advocate General Colomer in his Opinion and the court did not follow the Advocate General.

[39] The ECJ did not accept that, in the case of *Tabacalera* (tobacco) and *Argentaria* (commercial banking group operating in the traditional banking sector), that the legislation could be justified by general interest reasons linked to strategic requirements and the need to ensure continuity in public services. Those undertakings are not undertakings whose objective is to provide public services. In the case of *Repsol* (petroleum), *Endesa* (electricity) and *Telefónica* (telecommunications), the Court acknowledged that obstacles to the free movement of capital could be justified by a public-security reason. However, the Court held that the proportionality requirements were not satisfied for the following reasons:

(1) the administration had too broad discretion, exercise of which is not subject to any condition;
(2) investors were not appraised of the specific, objective circumstances in which prior approval will be granted or withheld;
(3) the system incorporates a requirement of prior approval;

A further judgment from 2005 reaffirms the principles developed in the previous cases.[40] The case concerned an Italian rule providing for an automatic suspension of the voting rights attached to shareholdings exceeding 2 per cent of the capital of companies in the electricity and gas sectors, where those holdings are acquired by public undertakings not quoted on regulated financial markets and enjoying a dominant position in their own domestic markets. The ECJ ruled that the suspension of voting rights prevents effective participation by investors in the management and control of undertakings operating in the electricity and gas markets. That the provision only affects public undertakings holding a dominant position in their domestic markets does not detract from that finding. A general strengthening of the competitive structure of the market in question did not constitute a valid justification for restricting the free movement of capital.[41]

In 2006, the ECJ again ruled on 'golden shares', this time in two Dutch telecommunications companies Koninklijke KPN NV (KPN) and TNT Post Groep NV (TPG).[42] When these companies were partly privatised in the 1990s, the statutes of KPN and TPG contained a special share held by the Netherlands State, conferring special rights to approve certain management decisions of the organs of those companies. The ECJ held that these special rights were not limited to cases where the intervention of that state was necessary for overriding reasons in the general interest recognised in the case law. The ECJ considered that the special rights in the Dutch case discouraged not only direct investors but also portfolio investors.

In 2007, the ECJ ruled on the Commission action against Germany over the 1960 Volkswagen-Gesetz (VW Act).[43] This legislation is based on a 1959 agreement between the Federal Republic (Bund) and the Federal State (Land)

(4) the operations contemplated are decisions fundamental to the life of an undertaking; and finally, although it appears possible to bring legal proceedings, the Spanish legislation did not provide the national courts with sufficiently precise criteria to review the way in which the administrative authority exercises its discretion.

40 Case C-174/04 *Commission* v. *Italian Republic* [2005] ECR I-4933.

41 Italy adopted a provision after the judgment, which amended the law in question. However, the Commission did not consider that the changes introduced fully implemented the ruling of the Court and consequently on 13 October 2005 reminded Italy of its obligation to comply.

42 Cases C-282/04 and 283/04 *Commission* v. *Kingdom of the Netherlands* [2006] ECR I-9141.

43 Case C-112/05 *Commission* v. *Germany* [2007] ECR I-8995.

of Lower Saxony, and reserves some special rights to the Land of Lower Saxony which has been the biggest single shareholder of the German carmaker. The special rights include that of the ten members representing shareholders in the supervisory board, four will represent public authorities. The maximum limit on the voting rights of a single shareholder to 20 per cent coincides with shareholding of the federal and state governments at the time the law was adopted. The ECJ held that the law dissuades those wishing to acquire a larger shareholding, and constitutes a restriction on the free movement of capital.

The free movement of capital judgments discussed here are in cases brought by the European Commission in cases against Member States. The case law is extending an intense review of state practice relating to the exercise of rights as a shareholder, and it is clear that the state cannot operate with the same freedom as a private shareholder.

At the same time, there is the question of the consequences of this case law on restrictions imposed in company articles and in agreements between private shareholders. The direct effect of the fundamental freedoms where both parties are private (not Member States or emanations of Member States), is much discussed. The free movement of capital is generally considered to be capable of direct effect not only where one of the parties is the state ('vertical direct effect) but also where there are only private parties involved ('horizontal direct effect').

National company laws and practice will be subject to a gradual review through the case law, and the ECJ's jurisprudence on the free movement of capital will give new impetus to the harmonisation effort in EU legislation. The basic foundation is now laid in the cases discussed above but the actual impact and speed of this process is another matter.

D. The harmonising directives in the field of company law

The Company Law Directives cover a number of disparate areas of law and with the exception of the Sixth Directive[44] (which only had to be implemented in Member States where divisions as defined in the Directive, were permitted) have all required implementation by Member States. The impact of the company law directives, together with that of certain other directives in the field of securities law, has been extensive in

[44] Sixth Council Directive of 17 December 1982 based on Art. 54(3)(g) of the Treaty, concerning the division of public limited liability companies (82/891/EEC), OJ 1982 L378/47.

all the Member States. These directives have had considerable influence on the United Kingdom Companies Acts 1980, 1981, 1989, and 2006 as well as on certain other United Kingdom primary and secondary legislation.[45]

Although Article 48 EC is applicable to all forms of companies or firms, the secondary European company law covers primarily companies limited by shares or otherwise having limited liability. According to the considerations of these directives the coordination of these provisions was especially important since the activities of such companies often extend beyond the frontiers of national territories.[46] It has also been argued that these entities in contrast to partnerships and their equivalents in other Member States share more similarities and can therefore be harmonized more easily.[47]

Amongst the companies limited by shares the law of public companies is regulated more intensively. While the First, the Fourth, the Seventh and the Eleventh directives are applicable both to public and private companies, the Second, Third, Sixth directives apply only to the public limited company.[48] In the view of the European legislator the distinction is made because their activities predominate in the economy of the Member States.[49] This concept has often been criticised because the use of the different company forms is divergent between the Member States.[50] For that reason the distinction between companies of different size and economic importance is more significant.[51] In addition to that, some Member States who only had a single form of limited company

[45] E.g., Council Directive (EEC) 89/592 of 13 December 1989, OJ 1989, L334/30 on insider dealing was implemented in the UK by Part V of the Criminal Justice Act 1993.

[46] Recital 1 of the First and Second Directive.

[47] G. C. Schwarz, *Europäisches Gesellschaftsrecht* (Baden-Baden: Nomos, 2000), para. 14, 293.

[48] E. Wymeersch, 'Company Law in Europe and European Company Law' [2001] 6 *Working Paper Series, Universiteit Gent* 6.

[49] See consideration 1 of the Second Directive and consideration 3 of the draft Fifth Directive.

[50] See also E. Wymeersch, 'Company Law in Europe and European Company Law' [2001] 6 *Working Paper Series, Universiteit Gent* 5; See for a comparative overview: G. C. Schwarz, *Europäisches Gesellschaftsrecht* (Baden-Baden: Nomos, 2000), para. 15, 530 ff.; E. Wymeersch, 'A Status Report in Corporate Governance Rules and Practices in Some Continental European States', in K. Hopt, H. Kanda, M. Roe, E. Wymeersch and St Prigge (eds), *Comparative Corporate Governance* (Oxford: Clarendon Press, 1998), pp. 1045, 1049.

[51] E. Wymeersch, 'Company Law in Europe and European Company Law' [2001] 6 Working Paper Series Universiteit Gent, 6; K. Hopt 'Europäisches Gesellschaftsrecht – Krise und neue Anläufe' [1988] *Zeitschrift für Wirtschaftsrecht* (ZIP) 96, 103.

introduced a private company form for smaller companies, a more useful form, in the process of the implementation of the Directives.[52]

The First Directive[53] is concerned with the disclosure and publicity requirements of companies, the validity of pre-incorporation and *ultra vires* transactions entered into by companies, and the nullity of companies.

The Second Directive[54] provides for minimum requirements for the formation of public companies and the maintenance, increase and reduction of their capital.[55]

Both the First and the Second Directive have been subject to proposals for revisions undergoing a process of simplification. In 1999 the Company Law SLIM Working Group issued a Report on the simplification of the First and Second Company Law Directive.[56] The Commission supported these recommendations relating to the First Directive and issued a proposal for its amendment.[57] The main object of the proposal

[52] M. Lutter, '*Die Entwicklung der GmbH in Europa und in der Welt*', in M. Lutter (ed), *Festschrift 100 Jahre GmbH-Gesetz* (Baden-Baden: Nomos, 1992), pp. 49–55 (Denmark, the Netherlands).

[53] First Council Directive of 9 March 1968 on coordination of safeguards which, for the protection of the interests of members and others, are required by Member States of companies within the meaning of the second paragraph of Art. 58 of the Treaty, with a view to making such safeguards equivalent throughout the Community (68/151/EEC), OJ 1968 L65/8.

[54] Second Council Directive of 13 December 1976 on coordination of safeguards which, for the protection of the interests of members and others, are required by Member States of companies within the meaning of the second paragraph of Art. 58 of the Treaty, in respect of the formation of public limited liability companies and the maintenance and alteration of their capital, with a view to making such safeguards equivalent (77/91/EEC), OJ 1977 L26/1, on which see C. M. Schmitthoff, 'The Second Directive on Company Law' (1978) 15 CMLR 43; G. Morse, 'The Second Directive – raising and maintenance of capital' [1977] *European Law Review* 126.

[55] See for the implementation in the different Member States: F. Wooldridge, *Company Law in the United Kingdom and the European Community* (London: Athlone Press, 1991), pp. 25 ff.

[56] See Report from the Commission to the European Parliament and the Council – Results of the fourth phase of SLIM, 4 February 2000, COM (2000) 56 final; E. Wymeersch, 'Company Law in the Twenty-First Century' [2000] 1 *International and Comparative Corporate Law Journal* 331, 332–5; E. Wymeersch, 'European Company Law: The Simpler Legislation for the Internal Market (SLIM) Initiative of the EU Commission' [2000] 9 *Working Paper Series, Universiteit Gent.*

[57] Proposal for a Directive of the European Parliament and the Council amending Council Directive 68/151/EEC, as regards disclosure requirements in respect of certain types of companies, 3 June 2002, COM (2002) 279 final. The Directive was amended by Directive 2003/58/EC [2003] OJ L220/13.

was to accelerate the filing and disclosure of company documents and particulars by the use of modern technology, and to improve the cross-border access to company information by allowing voluntary registration of company documents and particulars in additional languages. It was also decided to update the First Directive where necessary, namely with regard to the types of companies covered and the references to the Accounting Directives. In respect of the Second Directive the High Level Group of Company Experts suggested in its Report of 2002 a two-step approach a short-term reform of the Directive and a creation of an alternative capital regime in the long run.[58] Directive 2006/68/EC of the European Parliament and of the Council of 6 September 2006 has since been enacted, amending Council Directive 77/91/EEC as regards the formation of public limited liability companies and the maintenance and alteration of their capital.[59] This instrument permits the relaxation of the valuation requirement for contributors in kind in some circumstances. It also contains new provisions governing the giving of financial assistance for acquisition of shares. The relevant provisions are very detailed.

The Third[60] and Sixth Directives are respectively concerned with mergers and divisions of public companies; the former instrument has no application to takeover bids, but to the type of operation known in the United Kingdom as reconstructions.

[58] See Report of the High Level Group of Company Law Experts of 4 November 2002, 78–93 http://europa.eu.int/comm/internal_market/en/company/company/index.htm. Some of the main governance reforms proposed were as follows:

(1) the minimum capital requirement should not be removed, nor increased;
(2) the introduction of no par value shares is widely demanded;
(3) the valuation requirement for contributions in kind should be relaxed in certain cases;
(4) the conditions under which listed companies can restrict or withdraw preemption rights when they issue new shares should be simplified;
(5) more flexible requirements should be established at least for unlisted companies for the acquisition of own shares;
(6) the prohibition of financial assistance should be relaxed; and
(7) squeeze-out and sell-out rights should be introduced generally.

[59] Directive 2006/68/EC of 6 September 2006 amending Council Directive 77/91/EEC as regards the formation of public limited liability companies and the maintenance and alteration of their capital, [2006] OJ 264/32.

[60] Third Council Directive of 9 October 1978 based on Art. 54(3)(g) of the Treaty concerning mergers of public limited liability companies (78/855/EEC), OJ 1978 L295/36.

The Fourth Directive[61] is concerned with the accounts of public and private limited liability companies, whilst the Seventh Directive[62] is concerned with the consolidated accounts of such companies. Both these directives make provision for a number of options and are influenced by Anglo-Dutch as well as by French and German accounting principles. The Fourth and Seventh Directive were frequently amended.[63] They were modified by two directives of 8 November 1990 which dealt respectively with exemptions for small and medium-sized companies (SMEs) and the publication of accounts in ECUs, and the scope of these two accounts Directives.[64] Recently, the European Council adopted a Directive of 13 May 2003 which amends the Fourth Directive in respect to the possible exemptions of small and medium-sized enterprises (SMEs) from certain accounting requirements.[65] In addition to that, the Directive of 18 June 2003 brings existing accounting rules into line with current best practice.[66] It complements the International Accounting Standards (IAS) Regulation as the amendments allow Member States which do

[61] Fourth Council Directive of 25 July 1978 based on Art. (3)(g) of the Treaty on annual accounts of certain types of companies (78/660/EEC), OJ 1978 L221/11.

[62] Seventh Council Directive of 13 June 1983 based on Art. 54(3)(g) of the Treaty on consolidated accounts (83/349/EEC), OJ L193/1: see F. Wooldridge, 'The EEC Council Directive on Consolidated Accounts' [1988] 37 ICLQ 714. Amendments were made to the Fourth and Seventh Directives by Directive 2006/46 of 14 June 2006 OJ 2006 L224/1.

[63] See, e.g. Directive 2001/65/EC of the European Parliament and of the Council of 27 September 2001 amending Directives 78/660/EEC, 83/349/EEC and 86/635/EEC as regards the valuation rules for the annual and consolidated accounts of certain types of companies as well as of banks and other financial institutions, OJ 2001 L283/28 or Council Directive 91/674/EEC of 19 December 1991 on the annual accounts and consolidated accounts of insurance undertakings, OJ 1991 L374/7.

[64] Council Directive of 8 November 1990 amending Directive 78/660/EEC on annual accounts and Directive 83/349/EEC on consolidated accounts as concerns the exemptions for small and medium sized companies and the publication of accounts in ecus (90/604/EEC), OJ 1990 L317/57 and Council Directive of 8 November 1990 amending Directive 78/660/EEC on annual accounts and Directive 83/349/EEC on consolidated accounts as regards the scope of those directives (90/605/EEC), OJ 1990 L317/60.

[65] Council Directive 2003/38/EC of 13 May 2003 amending Directive 78/660/EEC on the annual accounts of certain types of companies as regards amounts expressed in euro, OJ 2003 L120/22. The Directive raises the thresholds for turnover and balance sheet total under which Member States can apply the exemptions. The Council's move follows a Commission proposal in January 2003. See the Proposal for a Council Directive amending Directive 78/660/EEC as regards amounts expressed in euro of 24 January 2003, COM (2003) 29 final.

[66] Directive 2003/51/EC of 18 June 2003 amending Directives 78/660/EEC, 83/349/EEC, 86/635/EEC and 91/674/EEC on the annual and consolidated accounts of certain types of companies, banks and other financial institutions and insurance undertakings, OJ 2003 L178/16.

not apply IAS to all companies to move towards similar, high quality financial reporting. Besides, it provides for appropriate accounting for special purpose vehicles, improves the disclosure of risks and uncertainties and increases the consistency of audit reports across the EU.

The International Accounting Standards (IAS) or International Reporting Standards Regulation, adopted in June 2002 requires all EU companies listed on a regulated market to use IAS from 2005 onwards and allows Member States to extend this requirement to all companies.[67] It is the aim of the IAS Regulation to help eliminate barriers to cross-border trading in securities by ensuring that company accounts throughout the EU are more reliable and transparent and that they can be more easily compared.[68]

The Eighth Directive[69] deals with the approval of the auditors of the annual and consolidated accounts of public and private limited liability companies. Differences between accounts and auditing regimes and rules concerning the independence of auditors make it difficult to make meaningful comparisons of financial statements audited in different countries.[70] Important alterations were made to the Eight Directive by Directive 15 May 2006 on statutory audit of annual accounts and consolidated accounts amending Council Directives 78/660 (the Fourth Company Law Directive) and Directive 83/349 (the Seventh Directive) and repealing Directive 84/253.[71]

The Eleventh Directive[72] governs the coordination of Company Law concerning disclosure requirements in respect of branches opened in a Member State by specified kinds of companies governed by the law of

[67] Regulation (EC) 1606/2002 of 19 July 2002 on the application of international accounting standards, OJ 2002 L243/1.

[68] See also the Proposal for a Regulation on the application of international accounting standards, Brussels of 13 February 2001, COM (2001) 80 final.

[69] Eighth Council Directive of 10 April 1984 based on Art. 54(3)(g) of the Treaty on the approval of persons responsible for carrying out the statutory audits of accounting documents, (84/253/EEC), OJ 1984 L126/20.

[70] The Eighth Directive contains no guidance on the independence of auditors, which has been the subject matter of a consultation by the Commission. See the Commissions Recommendation of 15 November 2000 on quality assurance for the statutory audit in the European Union: minimum requirements, OJ 2001 L91/91. The new Statutory Audit Directive 2006/43/EC supplements the Fourth and Seventh Directives by laying down requirements of professional qualifications and independence of persons entrusted with the task of auditing accounts. It also supplements the IAS Regulation.

[71] OJ 2006, L257/87.

[72] Eleventh Council Directive of 21 December 1989 concerning disclosure requirements in respect of branches opened in a Member State by certain types of companies governed by the law of another State (89/666/EEC), OJ 1989 L395/36.

another Member State. Single member private limited liability companies are governed by the Twelfth Directive.[73]

The Tenth Directive[74] on Cross-Border Mergers of public limited companies supplements the Third Directive on national mergers of such companies. Germany feared that international mergers may be used for the purpose of circumventing codetermination laws, and this long delayed the adoption of this proposal.[75] The High Level Group of Company Experts recommended that the Commission should urgently bring forward this proposal.[76] It was argued that the Directive supplementing the Statute for a European company[77] could be a model for resolving the difficulties relating to the board structure and employee participation. The SE Statute has also had an impact as a means of effecting cross-border mergers and of the ECJ ruling in *Sevic*[78] will have an impact in this field.

The Proposal for a Thirteenth Directive on the coordination of company law concerning take-over bids of 1997 was rejected by the European Parliament on 4 July 2001 (273 votes for and 273 votes against).[79] The European Parliament's decision was motivated by three main political considerations:

(1) rejection of the principle whereby, in order to take defensive measures in the face of a bid, the board of the offeree company must first

[73] Twelfth Company Law Directive of 21 December 1989 on single-member private limitedliability companies (89/667/EEC), OJ 1989 L395/4082.

[74] Directive 2005/56/EC of 26 October 2005 on cross-border mergers of limited liability companies, OJ 2005 L310/1. This generally adopted the mechanisms of the original Proposal of 14 January 1985 for a Tenth Council Directive based on Art. 54(3)(g) of the Treaty concerning cross-border mergers of public limited companies (COM (84) 727 final), OJ 1985 C23/11.

[75] V. Edwards, *EC Company Law*, pp. 391–3.

[76] See Report of the High Level Group of Company Law Experts of 4 November 2002 http://europa.eu.int/comm/internal_market/en/company/company/index.htm, 101.

[77] Council Directive 2001/86/EC of October 2001 supplementing the Statute of the European Company with regard to the involvement of employees, OJ 2001 L294/22.

[78] Case C-411/03 *SEVIC Systems* [2005] ECR I-10805.

[79] For the Commission's amended proposal, see COM(97) 565 final, 10 November 1997, 1997 OJ C378/10. The text rejected had – after long negotiations – previously been agreed by the delegations of the Parliament and the European Council in a Conciliation Committee meeting on 6 June 2001. See for the text the Report of the High Level Group of Company Experts on Issues related to Takeover Bids of 10 January 2002 http://europa.eu.int/comm/internal_market/en/company/company/index.htm. See for the discussion, especially for the influence of the Directive on the self-regulation of takeovers in the UK: B. Pettet, 'Private versus Public Regulation in the fields of Takeovers: The Future under the Directive' [2000] 11 *European Business Law Review* 381; M. Andenas, 'European take-over regulation and the City Code' [1996] 17 Co Law 150; M. Andenas, 'European Takeover Directive and the City' [1997] 18 Co Law 101.

obtain the approval of shareholders once the bid has been made, until such time as a level playing field was created for European companies facing a takeover bid;

(2) regret that the protection which the directive would afford employees of companies involved in a takeover bid was insufficient;

(3) the failure of the proposal to achieve a level playing field with the United States.

The Commission therefore set up a High-Level Group of Company Law Experts under the chairmanship of Professor Jaap Winter with the task of presenting suggestions for resolving the matters raised by the European Parliament.[80] Taking into account the recommendations made by the Group the Commission presented a new Proposal for a Thirteenth Directive in 2002.[81] The new proposal pursued the same objectives as its predecessor. First, it set out to strengthen the legal certainty of cross-border takeover bids in the interests of all concerned and to ensure protection for minority shareholders in the course of such transactions. It furthermore tried to establish a framework for action by Member States by laying down certain principles and a limited number of general requirements. Nevertheless, the Commission tried to supplement it in such a way as to incorporate the amendments adopted by the European Parliament to the previous proposals and to follow the recommendations of the Winter Report as regards a common definition of 'equitable price' (Article 5) and the introduction of a squeeze-out right (Article 14) and a sell-out right (Article 15) following a takeover bid.[82] In line with the recommendations of the Winter Report, the new proposal retained the principle (in Article 9) that it is for shareholders to decide on defensive measures once a bid has been made public and proposed greater transparency of the defensive structures and mechanisms in the companies affected by the proposal (Article 10). Furthermore, the Proposal stipulated that restrictions on transfers of securities and restrictions on voting rights should be rendered unenforceable against the offeror or cease to have effect once a bid has been made public (Article 11). However, Article 12 of the Takeover Directive permits Member States not to apply this break-through mechanism, or the provisions of Article 9(2) and (3) of the Directive.

80 Report of the High Level Group of Company Experts on Issues related to Takeover Bids of 10 January 2002 http://europa.eu.int/comm/internal_market/en/company/company/index.htm.

81 Proposal for a Directive on takeover bids, 2 October 2002, COM (2002) 534 final.

82 In the finalised version of the Directive, the squeeze-out right was included in Art. 15 and the sell out right in Art. 16. Otherwise, the numbering contained in the proposal remained unaltered.

Other directives govern the information which must be published when major shareholdings in a listed company are acquired and disposed of,[83] the protection of investors by supervising investment firms,[84] and the establishment of a European Works Council.[85] Important is also the new Directive on insider dealing and market abuse.[86] The amendments were necessary to ensure consistency with legislation against market manipulation. A new Directive was also needed to avoid loopholes in Community legislation which could be used for wrongful conduct and which would undermine public confidence and therefore prejudice the smooth functioning of the markets.

E. Draft legislation

There are several company law instruments which have not been adopted yet. The proposed Fifth Directive[87] on the structure and functioning of the organs of public limited companies[88] has not yet been enacted and seems unlikely to be, at least in its present form, even though it is one of the first projects in European company law.[89] Its initial

[83] Council Directive 88/627/EEC of 12 December 1988 on the information to be published when a major holding in a listed company is acquired or disposed of, OJ 1988, L348/62 which has been integrated into Directive 2001/34/EC of 28 May 2001 on the admission of securities to official stock exchange listing and on information to be published on those securities, OJ 2001 L184/1.

[84] Council Directive 93/22/EEC of 10 May 1993 on investment services in the securities field, OJ 1993 L141/27. See also the new Proposal for a Directive on Investment Services and Regulated Markets and amending Council Directives 85/611/EEC, Council Directive 93/6/EEC and Directive 2000/12/EC, COM (2002) 625.

[85] Council Directive 94/45/EC of 22 September 1994 on the establishment of a European Works Council or a procedure in Community-scale undertakings and Community-scale groups of undertakings for the purposes of informing and consulting employees, OJ 1994 L254/64.

[86] Directive 2003/6/EC of 28 January 2003 on insider dealing and market manipulation (market abuse), OJ 2003 L96/16 which replaced the Council Directive 89/592/EEC of 13 November 1989 coordinating regulations on insider dealing, OJ 1989 L334/30.

[87] Amended Proposal of 20 November 1991 for a Fifth Directive based on Art. 54 of the EEC Treaty concerning the structure of public limited companies and the powers and obligations of their organs, COM (91) 372 final).

[88] For a useful account of this proposal, see Edwards, *EC Company Law*, pp. 387–90.

[89] See for more details Boyle, 'Draft Fifth Directive – Implications for Directors' Duties, Board Structure and Employee Participation' [1992] 13 *The Company Lawyer* 6; Conlon, 'Industrial Democracy and EEC Company Law – a Review of the Draft Fifth Directive' [1975] 24 ICLQ 348; Du Plessis/Dine, 'The Fate of the Draft Fifth Directive on Company Law – Accomodation Instead of Harmonisation' [1997] *Journal of Business Law* 23; Keutgen, 'La proposition de directive européenne sur la structure des sociétés anonymes', [1973] 72 *Revue pratique des*

proposals on board structure and employee participation which were stigmatised as being too rigid, were subsequently made more flexible, but have still remained unacceptable, although they may have some influence on further work on corporate governance. The Report of the High Level Group of Company Experts of 4 November 2002 focuses on several issues the Fifth Directive was meant to deal with.[90] The recommendations cover in particular shareholder rights relating to the participation in general meetings, cross-border voting, board structure (choice between one-tier/two-tier) and the role of non-executive and supervisory directors. In a Communication on shareholder rights[91] the Commission set out its ideas for a Directive on shareholder rights. The principal issue appears to be the exercise of shareholders' voting rights, especially where shareholders invest in shares through shares held by intermediaries. There may well be a consensus in the Council of the proposed directive in the near future, and also on one share – one vote initiatives which remain controversial.

Finally, a proposal exists for a Fourteenth Directive on the transfer of the registered office or the de facto head office of companies[92] from one Member State to another.[93] Certain countries use the place of incorporation theory to govern the affairs of companies where a foreign element is involved, whilst others employ the real seat theory (*siège réel* doctrine) for this purpose.[94] The real seat is the place where a company's head

Sociétés 1; Kolvenbach 'Die Fünfte EG-Richtlinie über die Struktur der Aktiengesellschaft (Strukturrichtlinie)' [1983] *Der Betrieb* 2235; Temple Lang, 'The Fifth EEC Directive on the Harmonization of Company Law – Some Comments from the Viewpoint of Irish and British Law on the EEC Draft for a Fifth Directive Concerning Management Structure and Worker Participation' [1975] 12 CMLR 155 and 345; Welch, 'The Fifth Draft Directive – a False Dawn?' [1983] 8 ELR 83.

90 See Report of the High Level Group of Company Law Experts of 4 November 2002 http://europa.eu.int/comm/internal_market/en/company/company/index.htm.

91 Commission proposal for a directive on the exercise of shareholders' voting rights (COM (2005) 685).

92 The Directive is applicable to all companies or firms. This is in accordance with Arts. 43, 48 EC. See in detail, S. Grundmann, *Europäisches Gesellschaftsrecht* (Heidelberg: C. F. Müller, 2003), para. 895; Others request the restriction of the scope of the Fourteenth Directive to companies limited by share because this would more appropriate in respect to the scope of other company law directives. See, for instance, G. di Marco, 'Der Vorschlag der Kommission für eine 14. Richtlinie – *Stand und Perspektiven*' [1999] *Zeitschrift für Gesellschaftsrecht* 3, 7.

93 DOCXV/6002/97-EN of 20 April 1997. See for the German text [1999] *Zeitschrift für Gesellschaftsrecht*, 157.

94 This, of course, is a very imprecise differentiation. See in detail, S. Grundmann, *Europäisches Gesellschaftsrecht*, para. 295 ff; for a comparative overview, see Edwards, *EC Company Law*, p. 335; H. Merkt, 'Das Europäische Gesellschaftsrecht und die Idee des

office, or central management or control is located.[95] The transfer of the registered office (place of incorporation) from one Member State which recognises the place of incorporation theory to another such state does not seem possible at present. Furthermore, the transfer of the real seat of a company from one Member State which recognises the real seat doctrine to another such state may be impossible or difficult. Thus the transfer of the real seat of a company out of Germany has been held to entail the dissolution of that company in Germany, and hence its liquidation. If this view were to be upheld, it would have burdensome tax consequences,[96] but it is doubtful whether the European Court of Justice would uphold the German approach, despite its controversial decision in *Daily Mail*[97] which was distinguished in *Überseering*.[98]

The draft Fourteenth Directive attempts to circumvent the above difficulties, but still awaits adoption. A revised proposal, based on the Commission's consultation on the transfer of a company's registered office from one Member State to another may be anticipated. Further measures governing the matter of the de facto head office are unlikely in the immediate future. However, it is anticipated that a future such proposal would aim to facilitate the freedom of companies to forum shop within the EU Member States whose domestic legislation best suits the company. Furthermore, the freedom of establishment of companies seems to assume a right of transfer of the seat. For that

"*Wettbewerbs der Gesetzgeber*"' [1995] 59 RabelsZ, 545; 560; J. Wouters 'European Company Law: Quo vadis?' [2000] 37 CMLR 257, 284 and also Lutter, 'The Cross-Border Transfer of a Company's Seat in Europe' [2000] *Europarättslig Tidskrift* 60; J. Wouters and H. Schneider (eds), *Current Issues of Cross-Border Establishment of Companies in the European Union* (Antwerp: Apeldoorn, 1995); J. P. Hansen 'A new look at Centros – from a Danish point of view' [2002] 13 *European Business Law Review* 85, 86.

95 For the German law: *Bundesgerichtshof* in BGHZ 97, 269; 272; even after the *Überseering* decision of the ECJ: *Bundesgerichtshof* [2002], *Recht der Internationalen Wirtschaft*, 877; See for the different definitions of the real seat: Drury, 'Migrating Companies' [1999] ELR 354, 362.

96 For the positon in the UK: F. Wooldridge, *Company Law in the United Kingdom and the European Community* (London: Athlone Press, 1991), p. 8; for Germany: J. Thiel, 'Die grenzüberschreitende Umstrukturierung von Kapitalgesellschaften im Ertragssteuerrecht' [1994] *GmbH Rundschau* 277, 278; H. F. Hügel, 'Steuerrechtliche Hindernisse bei der internationalen Sitzverlegung' [1999] ZGR 71, 98; for France: M. Menjucq, *Droit européen des sociétés* (Paris: Montchrestien, 2001) pp. 301 f., 309 f.: and for Italy: H. Bruhn, *Niederlassungsfreundliche Sitzverlegung und Verschmelzung über die Grenze nach italienischem Recht – eine rechtsvergleichende Untersuchung unter Berücksichtigung der europäischen Niederlassungsfreiheit* (Bonn: Diss, 2002) pp. 142–97 and 197–234.

97 Case 81/87 *R* v. *Treasury ex p Daily Mail* [1988] ECR, 5483.

98 Case C-208/00 *Überseering BV* v. *Nordic Construction Company Baumanagement GmbH* [2002] ECR, I-9919.

reason the High Level Group of Company Experts recommended that the Commission should move forwards with this directive.[99] In *Überseering*, the ECJ held that when a company transferred its seat from the United Kingdom to Germany, the latter country could not deny it legal capacity and the capacity to bring legal proceedings. It is unclear whether the ECJ would now adopt the same approach as in the *Daily Mail* case to the situation where the home state restricts the transfer of the central administration of a company incorporated under its laws to another Member State. *Überseering*, which is discussed further in the following chapter leaves certain matters unsettled.[100] The differentiation made between exit and entry restrictions undertaken by some through an interpretation of this case, finds no base in the relevant law on the right of establishment and to provide services and the free movement of capital. The differentiation was not mentioned in the ECJ's judgment in the *Daily Mail* case. However, in particular some German writers and courts have used this decision to permit exit restrictions upon German companies.

The draft Fourteenth Directive has seemed to be of importance because the concept of a 'common market for companies' would appear to involve the possibility of the alteration of a company's head office or primary establishment from one Member State to another. The implementation of the draft Directive may give rise to certain tax problems which require resolution before it is enacted.[101] It is thought that the transfer should be tax neutral, and should produce the same effect as a cross-border merger. This would require amendments of Directive 9/434/EC. It may also give rise to prejudice for creditors situated in the state from which the company has migrated, who discover that the security given to them in accordance with the proposed directive is

[99] See Report of the High Level Group of Company Law Experts of 4 November 2002 http://europa.eu.int/comm/internal_market/en/company/company/index.htm 101. For the difficulties relating to the board structure and employee participation the Directive supplementing the Statute for a European company could be a model.

[100] See also F. Wooldridge, 'Freedom of Establishment of Companies Affirmed' [2003] 14 EBLR 227, 234; M. Andenas, 'Free Movement of Companies' [2003] 119 LQR 221.

[101] R. A. Deininger, *Grenzüberschreitende Verlegung des Hauptverwaltungssitzes und der Geschäftsleitung von Kapitalgesellschaften – eine Betrachtung unter europarechtlichen, gesellschaftsrechtlichen und steuerrechtlichen Gesichtspunkten* (Herdecke: GCA, 2001); C. Ebenroth and T. Auer, 'Die Vereinbarkeit der Sitztheorie mit europäischem Recht – Zivil- und steuerrechtliche Aspekte im deutschen Recht' [1994] *GmbH Rundschau* 16.

inadequate. It was also contended that the provisions of the proposed Coordinating Directive on employee participation are unsatisfactory. It has been proposed that employee participation rights should be governed by legislation of the host Member States, but where they are more firmly enshrined in the home Member State, they should be maintained or registered.

Although drafts of a proposed Ninth Directive on Groups of Undertakings have been circulated in the past,[102] no further work on this proposed instrument, which would have applied to subsidiaries taking the form of a public company (the form of the parent undertaking would have been immaterial) since 1984. The apparent abandonment of work on groups of undertakings seems regrettable. As is contended in the section which follows, the proposal was probably too much influenced by German law to prove widely acceptable. However, recent proposals on a Corporate Law Group for Europe have been made by a private body consisting of academics, the *Forum Europaeum Konzernrecht.*[103] These proposals were published in Stockholm by the Corporate Governance Forum. The Group of Company Law Experts set up by the Commission failed to recommend the enactment of a coherent body of law dealing with groups of companies.[104] Nevertheless, it made suggestions for a better financial disclosure of group structure in respect to the Seventh

[102] See for the proposal of 1984 Doc III/1639/84-E. The German text can be found in [1985] *Zeitschrift für Gesellschaftsrecht* 444, the French text in Commission Droit et Vie d'Affaires, [1986] *Modes de rapprochement structurel des enterprises.* See also: V. Edwards, *EC Company Law*, p. 390 f.; U. Immenga, *'L'harmonisation de droit de groupes de sociétés – La proposition d'une directive de la Commission de la C.E.E.'* [1986] 14 *Giurisprudenza Commerciale* 846 and Hommelhoff, 'Zum revidierten Vorschlag für eine EG-Konzernrichtlinie', in Reinhard Goedeler (ed), *Festschrift Fleck* (Berlin: de Gruyter, 1988), p. 125.

[103] This was funded by a German Foundation, the Fritz Thyssen Stiftung. See the publication of their proposals in Forum Europaeum Konzernrecht Konzernrecht für Europa [1998] *Zeitschrift für Gesellschaftsrecht*, 672; Manóvil, *Forum Europaeum sobre derecho de grupos – algunas de sus propuestas vistas desde la perspective sudamericana* in: J. Basedow (ed), *Aufbruch nach Europa, Festschrift 75 Jahre Max-Planck-Institut für Privatrecht* (Tübingen: Mohr Siebeck, 2001), p. 215; J. Lübking, *Ein einheitliches Konzernrecht für Europa* (Baden-Baden: Nomos, 2000); D. Sugarman and G. Teubner (eds), *Regulating Corporate Groups in Europe* (Baden-Baden: Nomos, 1990); C. Windbichler, '"Corporate Group Law for Europe" – Comments on the Forum Europaeum's Principles and Proposals for a European Corporate Group Law' [2000] 1 EBOR 265; E. Wymeersch, *'Harmoniser le droit des groupes de sociétés en Europe?'*, in O. Due (ed), *Festschrift Everling* (Baden-Baden: Nomos, 1995), p. 1699.

[104] See Report of the High Level Group of Company Law Experts of 4 November 2002 http://europa.eu.int/comm/internal_market/en/company/company/index.htm, 94.

Company Law Directive and consistency with International Accounting Standards. Another recommendation is to require national authorities, responsible for the admission to trading on regulated markets, not to admit holding companies whose sole or main assets are their shareholding in another listed company, unless the economic value of such admission is clearly demonstrated.

Finally, in 1987 the Commission introduced a preliminary draft for a directive on the liquidation of companies[105] which has not been developed further in the following years. The EU Bankruptcy Regulation was adopted as Regulation 1346/2000; its provisions represent a compromise between the universal and territorial principles. The main insolvency proceedings must take place in the state of domicile of the debtors while insolvency proceedings may be commenced in states in which the debtor has a place of business.

F. *Methodological problems concerning company law harmonisation*

It is sometimes contended that there is no need for such an extensive programme of company law harmonisation. It is thus argued that better results might be obtained by means of regulatory competition.[106] According to this idea legislators can be compared with producers of other goods and therefore regulated by the market.[107] Another aspect is that competition can be used as a discovery process which leads to more efficient solutions.[108] Many point to the fifty state legal orders available

[105] See for the text: draft Proposal DOC XV/43/87-EN; and for comments: E. Werlauff, *EC Company Law* (Copenhagen: Jurist- og Økonomforbundets Forlag, 1993), 408 ff. E. Werlauff, *EU Company Law*, 2nd edn (Copenhagen: Jurist- og Økonomforbundets Forlag, 2003).

[106] Basis for this theory were the ideas of Tiebout, 'A Pure Theory of Local Expenditures' [1956] 64 *Journal of Political Economy* 416 ff. (Exit-Option).

[107] D. C. Esty and D. Geradin, 'Regulatory Co-operation' [2000] *Journal of International Economic Law* 235, 238 f; K. Gatsios and P. Holmes, 'Regulatory Competition', in P. Newman (ed.), *The New Palgrave of Economics and the Law*, vol. 1 (London, 1998), p. 271.

[108] J. A. Schumpeter, *The Theory of Economic Development – An Inquiry into Profits, Capital, Credit, Interest and the Business Cycle* (Cambridge, 1934); F. A. Hayek, 'Competition as a Discovery Procedure' in: F. A. Hayek (ed), *New Studies in Philosophy, Politics, Economics and the History of Ideas* (Chicago: University Press, 1985), pp. 179 ff; see also W. Kerber, 'Rechtseinheitlichkeit und Rechtsvielfalt aus ökonomischer Sicht,' in S. Grundmann (ed), *Systembildung und Systemlücken in Kerngebieten des Europäischen Privatrechts, Gesellschaftsrecht, Arbeitsrecht, Schuldvertragsrecht* (Tübingen: Mohr Siebeck, 2000), pp. 67, 68; V. Vanberg and

to companies in the United States.[109] However, American company law may be less concerned with the protection of investors, creditors and employees than is European company law. Investors are thus protected through the medium of Federal securities regulations whilst creditors receive protection through the medium of federal bankruptcy legislation and the Uniform Commercial Code.

S. Deakin contrasts two models of regulatory competition. One based on a US pattern of 'competitive federalism', the other a European conception of reflexive harmonisation. In the European context, he contends, harmonisation of corporate and labour law, contrary to its critics, has been a force for the preservation of diversity, and of an approach to regulatory interaction based on mutual learning between nation states. It is thus paradoxical, and arguably antithetical to the goal of European integration, that this approach is in danger of being undermined by attempts, following the *Centros* case, to introduce a Delaware-type form of inter-jurisdictional competition into European company law.[110]

Further, there are several reasons why a legislative competition in the European Union cannot be as effective as in United States.[111] Traditionally, competition between the laws of Member States has not been regarded as an appropriate paradigm for the law of the European Community.[112] Further, of the 27 states which are at present members of the EU, broadly speaking, it appears that only six (the United Kingdom,

W. Kerber, 'Institutional Competition among Jurisdictions: An Evolutionary Approach' [1994] 5 *Constitutional Political Economy* 193, 198.

109 See J. Wouters, 'European Company Law: Quo Vadis', (2000) 37 CmLRev 256, 282–9. See for the development in United States: L. A. Bebchuk, 'Federalism and the Corporation: The Desirable Limits on State Competition in Corporate Law' [1992] 105 *Harvard Law Review* 1435, 1444–8; Alva, 'Delaware and the Market for Corporate Charters – History and Agency' [1990] 15 *Delaware Journal of Corporate Law* 885 ff.; R. M. Buxbaum and K. Hopt, *Legal Harmonization and the Business Enterprise – Corporate and Capital Market Law Harmonization Policy in Europe and the U.S.A.* (de Gruyter Berlin/New York 1988) pp. 25 ff.; Romano, *The Genius of American Corporate Law* (Washington, 1993), pp. 14 ff.; Butler, 'Nineteenth Century Jurisdictional Competition in the Granting of Corporate Privileges' [1985] 14 *Journal of Legal Studies* 129 ff.; Conard, 'An Overview of the Laws of Corporations' [1973] 71 *Michigan Law Review* 623 ff.

110 S. Deakin, 'Legal Diversity and Regulatory Competition: Which Model for Europe?' (2006) 12 *European Law Journal* 440.

111 H. Merkt, '*Das Europäische Gesellschaftsrecht und die Idee des "Wettbewerbs der Gesetzgeber"*' [1995] 59 *RabelsZ* 545, 560; Wouters, 'European Company Law: Quo vadis?' [2000] 37 CMLR 257, 284.

112 W. Kolvenbach, 'EEC Company Law Harmonization and Worker Participation' [1990] 11 U.Pa.J.Int.Bus.L. 709; 711 ff.; expressly C. M. Schmitthoff, 'The Future of the European Company Law Scene', in C. M. Schmitthoff (ed), *The Harmonization of European Company Law* (UK: National Committee of Comparative Law, 1973) 3, 9

Ireland, Denmark, Netherlands, Finland and Sweden) accept the incorporation theory, according to which a company is governed by the law in accordance with which it is duly established.[113] The other EC countries treat the law governing the internal affairs of a company as that of the place where it has its real seat (management and control centre). There is however, some doubt as to whether France still makes the real seat the principal connecting factor.[114] The use of the real seat theory makes it difficult for competition to occur between jurisdictions in the field of company law: according to this theory companies have to be incorporated, or reincorporated in the country in which they have their real seat. In addition to that, there are several tax barriers which may make a legislative competition more difficult.[115] The more pluralistic orientation of many European company laws (for instance towards employee representation) does not permit a simple choice between the different national laws which would be necessary for an effective competition.[116] Finally, there is no comparable incentive for European legislators to compete since incorporation fees have not much importance for the budget of the different Member States.[117] It may of course ultimately prove possible to simplify the exercise of the right of primary establishment of companies through the enactment of the proposed Fourteenth Directive, which has been mentioned above,[118] or possibly through the decisions of the European Court of Justice.

('the Community cannot tolerate the establishment of a Delaware in its territory. This would lead to a distortion of the market by artificial legal technicalities').

[113] See the account of the incorporation theory in S. Rammeloo, *Corporations in Private International Law* (Oxford: Oxford University Press, 2001), pp. 116–20.

[114] Note in this context, M. Menjucq, *Droit international et européen des sociétés* (Paris: Montchrestien, 2001). pp. 90–95.

[115] W. F. Ebke, '*Unternehmensrecht und Binnenmarkt – E pluribus unum?*' [1998] 62 RabelsZ 195, 208; R. Romano, 'Explaining the American Exceptionalism in Corporate Law', in W. Bratton, J. McCahery, S. Piccioto and C. Scott (eds), *International Regulatory Competition and Coordination – Perspectives on Economic Regulation in Europe and the United States* (Oxford: Clarendon Press, 1996), pp. 127, 141.

[116] H. Merkt, '*Das Europäische Gesellschaftsrecht*', 59 RabelsZ 545, 554–560; K. Gatsios and P. Holmes, 'Regulatory Competition', 271, 274.

[117] R. Romano, *The Genius of American Corporate Law* (Washington, 1993), p. 133; D. Carney, 'Competition among Jurisdictions in Formulating Corporate law rules: An American Perspective on the "Race to the Bottom" in the European Communities' [1991] 32 *Harvard International Law Journal* 423, 447.

[118] Furthermore, Article 65(b) EC enables measures in the field of judicial cooperation in civil matters having cross-border implications to be taken insofar as necessary for the proper functioning of the internal market.

After the decisions *Centros* and *Überseering* one might take a more positive view. They can be understood as decisions towards more freedom of choice.[119] The principle of mutual recognition as a foundation for the Free Movement in the EU might be a functional instrument.[120] Even if the Freedom of Establishment can be restricted by national law for reasons of general interest the national law of the host Member State cannot be applied if the home Member State delivers equivalent protection. This gives a certain room for competition between the different national legislators.

The concepts of subsidiarity and proportionality, which are contained in a Protocol annexed to the Amsterdam Treaty,[121] may have some inhibiting effect on further harmonisation of company law, although the existence of these concepts does not seem to have had an inhibiting effect in the fields of consumer and environmental law.[122] Harmonisation through the medium of model laws, as in the United States, would seem to have the disadvantage that considerable delays may occur in taking any action, and there may well be significant disparities in the extent to which particular features of the relevant model are adopted in particular states.

It will be remembered that according to Article 249(3) EC directives leave Member States a choice of form and method and may be compared in this respect to model laws. However, certain of the provisions of the

[119] S. Grundmann, 'Wettbewerb der Regelgeber im Europäischen Gesellschaftsrecht – jedes Marktsegment hat seine Struktur' [2001] *Zeitschrift für Gesellschaftsrecht* 783; E. Wymeersch, 'Company Law in the Twenty-First Century' [2000] 1 *International and Comparative Corporate Law Journal* 331, 339.

[120] S. Grundmann, 'Das Thema Systembildung und Systemlücken', in S. Grundmann (ed), *Systembildung und Systemlücken in Kerngebieten des Europäischen Privatrechts, Gesellschaftsrecht, Arbeitsrecht, Schuldvertragsrecht* (Tübingen: Mohr Siebeck, 2000), pp. 1, 16. See for more details: E. Lomnicka, 'The Home Country Control Principle in the Financial Service Directives and the Case Law', in M. Andenas and W-H. Roth, *Services and Free Movement in EU Law* (Oxford: Oxford University Press, 2002), pp. 295, 315.

[121] Treaty of Amsterdam amending the Treaty on European Union, the Treaties establishing the European Communities and related Acts, OJ 1997 C340. See also J. P. Gonzalez, 'The Principle of Subsidiarity (a Guide for Lawyers with a Particular Community Orientation' [1995] *European Law Review* 355; A. K. Toth, 'The Principle of Subsidiarity in the Maastricht Treaty' [1992] 29 CMLR 1079.

[122] Not only as a consequence of the wording in Art. 44(2)(g) EC ('coordinating to the necessary extent') it has been doubted if the principle of subsidiarity can have a further restricting effect. See summary: K. J. Hopt, 'Company Law in the European Union: Harmonization and/or Subsidiarity' [1999] 1 *International and Comparative Corporate Law Journal* 41, 48.

company law Directives contain detailed and highly specific rules: this is true, for example, of certain provisions of the Second Directive. On the other hand, certain directives, in particular the Fourth and Seventh Directive, contain a considerable number of options and alternatives. This is necessary given differences in accountancy practice in the Member States.[123]

It is sometimes suggested that legislation by directives gives rise to the risk of petrification of the laws as directives cannot be amended very easily. The risk seems to be exaggerated: certain of the directives provide for the establishment of Contact Committees to make recommendations for their amendment: this is true of the Fourth, Seventh and the Eighth Directives. Certain directives have been amended. Thus quite frequent amendments have been made to the Fourth Directive on Company Accounts. Articles 18–24 of the Second Directive on the formation of public companies and the maintenance and alteration of their capital, which are concerned with the subscription and acquisition by a company of its own shares was extended to transactions of this kind through the medium of controlled companies by Article 24a of the Directive which was incorporated by Council Directive (EEC) 92/10 of 23 November 1992.[124]

However, it has been contended that certain of the provisions of the Second Directive, for example those of Article 23 prohibiting (with certain exceptions) a company advancing funds, making loans or providing security with a view to acquisition of its own shares by a third party, and those of Article 29(1) concerning pre-emptive rights on an increase of capital, may well not be entirely satisfactory.[125] The Law Society's Standing Committee on Company Law criticised Article 23 on the ground that instead of the absolute prohibition now enshrined therein, financial assistance should be prohibited unless the transaction concerned had been approved by a shareholders' resolution.[126] Article 29(1) has been criticised by Rodière on the

[123] Edwards, *EC Company Law*, p. 117.

[124] Council Directive 92/101/EEC of 23 November 1992 amending Directive 77/91/EEC on the formation of public limited companies and the maintenance and alteration of their capital, OJ 1992 L374/64.

[125] Although Art. 23 Second Directive was modelled on existing United Kingdom legislation. See Edwards, *EC Company Law*, 51. Art. 23(1) has now been replaced by the new provisions of Art. 10b(6) incorporated in the Second Directive by Directive 2006/69/EC l, OJ 2006, L264/32.

[126] Memorandum No. 346, p. 78.

ground that it imposes only one method of protecting existing shareholders against the dilution of their holding to the exclusion of others, and may be regarded as going beyond harmonisation.[127] The High Level Group of Company Experts in its Report of 4 November 2002 took up a similar position as they suggested that acquisition of own shares should be allowed within the limits of the distributable reserves, and not of an entirely arbitrary percentage of legal capital like the 10 per cent limit of the current Directive.[128] The Company Law Slim Working Group already in 1999 considered that current prohibitions on financial assistance in Article 23 should be reduced to a practical minimum and recommended to limit financial assistance to that part of the assets to which creditors cannot assert any claim (to the amount of distributable net assets[129] and to the subscription of new shares).[130] In respect of Article 29, the High Level Group held, as the SLIM Group already had suggested, that for listed companies it would be appropriate to allow the general meeting to empower the board to restrict or withdraw pre-emption rights without having to comply with the formalities imposed by Article 29(4), but only where the issue price is at the market

[127] Rodière, '*L'harmonisation des legislations européennes dans le cadre de la CEE*' [1965] RTDE 336, 353 ff. For recent proposals for amendment of the Directive by the Group of Company Law Experts, see 24 Co Law (2003), 52. No such amendment has been made by Directive 2006/68/EC, OJ 2006 L264/32 which covers only a limited number of topics. Further amendments may be made in the future.

[128] The same should apply to the taking of own shares as security. It should be possible to establish flexible requirements at least for unlisted companies. See Report of the High Level Group of Company Law Experts of 4 November 2002 http://europa.eu.int/comm/internal_market/en/company/company/index.htm, 84.

[129] This standard is also followed in certain Member States with regard to financial assistance granted by private limited companies, which are not subject to the directive. The new provisions contained in Art. 10b(6) of Directive 2006/68/EC stipulates, inter alia, that the aggregate financial assistance granted to a third party shall at no time permit the reduction of the net assets below the amounts specified in Art. 15(1)(a) and (b) of the Second Directive. Thus, except in the cases of reduction of subscribed capital, no redistribution to shareholders may be made when on the closing date of the last financial year, the net assets as set out in the company's approved accounts are, or following such a distribution would become, lower than the amount of the subscribed capital plus those reserves which may not be distributed under the law or the statutes. The Second Directive only applies to public listed companies.

[130] See Report from the Commission to the European Parliament and the Council – Results of the fourth phase of Slim, 4 February 2000, COM (2000) 56 final; E. Wymeersch, 'Company Law in the Twenty-First Century' [2000] 1 *International and Comparative Corporate Law Journals* 331, 332–5; E. Wymeersch, *European Company Law: The Simpler Legislation for the Internal Market (SLIM) Initiative of the EU Commission*, [2000] 9 *Working Paper Series, Universiteit Gent.*

price of the securities immediately before the issue or where a small discount to that market price is applied.[131]

The harmonisation of company law has encountered the difficulty that certain legal concepts may be familiar in one Member State, but unfamiliar and hard to understand in another. The most obvious example of this is the concept of the organs of a company, which is used in the First Directive in relation to *ultra vires* transactions. This concept is familiar in Germany and in some other Member States (such as France and the Netherlands) but is not familiar in the United Kingdom or Ireland.[132] This unfamiliarity and differences between German and other concepts of corporate representation[133] help to explain the difficulties encountered by the United Kingdom in implementing Article 9 of the First Directive.[134] A third attempt at such implementation which departs to some extent from section 35A of the Companies Act 1985,[135] which itself replaced section 9 of the European Communities Act 1972, has taken place with the enactment of section 40 of the Companies Act 2006. It appears that the concept of the "true and fair view" which is used in the

[131] The Commission in its Plan for Modernising Company Law considered these recommendations as a priority for the short term. See *Communication from the Commission to the Council and the European Parliament - Modernising Company Law and Enhancing Corporate Governance in the European Union - A Plan to move forward*, 21.5.2003, COM (2003) 284 final, p. 18.

[132] See for a comparative overview: P. van Ommeslaghe, 'La première directive du Conseil du 9 mars 1968 en matière de sociétés' [1969] CDE 619, 619–27; see also Edwards, *EC Company Law*, p. 34; S. Grundmann, *Europäisches Gesellschaftsrecht* (Heidelberg: C. F. Müller, 2003), para. 248.

[133] In Germany, a company is treated as acting through its organs: restrictions on their powers have no effect against third parties unless they are aware of that the representative in exceeding them are abusing their powers, or they collude with them in such abuse. The other original Member States adopt the mandate or agency theory, according to which the authority of an agent may be limited by his principal. They may be *ultra vires* in the absence of such authority. However, the effect of the *ultra vires* doctrine (which was also familiar in the United Kingdom) is ameliorated by a variety of legal devices in all the relevant legal systems.

[134] D. Wyatt, 'The First Directive and Company Law' [1978] 94 LQR 182, 184; W. Fikentscher and B. Großfeld, 'The proposed directive on company law' [1964] 2 CMLR 259; H. C. Ficker, 'The EEC Directives on Company Law Harmonisation', in: C. M. Schmitthoff (ed), *The Harmonization of European Company Law* (UK: National Committee of Comparative Law, 1973), pp. 66, 75.

[135] This provision was intended to implement Art. 9(2) of the First Directive, but it does not do so adequately, because it fails to apply to managing directors and chief executives and does not deal with limitations arising from board resolutions: note in this sense, Edwards, *EC Company Law*, 42–4. It seems that s. 40 of the Companies Act 2006 still suffers from the mentioned defects.

Fourth and Seventh Directives, is unfamiliar in most continental countries, and its implementation has given rise to difficulties in Germany.[136] The harmonisation of company law has also suffered from the fact that the Commission has limited resources, and cannot always take action against states which fail to implement it properly.

Another criticism of the harmonisation process is levelled against the failure of the Community to enact rules governing certain important matters, such as groups of companies and to make provision for a European private company, the creation of which has been proposed by J. Boucourechliev *et al.*[137] The 'salami' process of harmonisation, which involves the harmonisation of limited topics, leaving closely related ones unaffected has also been criticised.[138] Such an approach would seem however to be inevitable given the personnel and time constraints placed on the community institutions as well as the limitations of their powers.

The process of harmonisation may well become more difficult if the size of the Community expands very considerably in the near future. This process obviously often involves practical exercises in comparative company law, and would seem to have stimulated interest in this discipline among scholars and practitioners. The final section of this chapter will consider what problems arise in the study of this subject and indicate what use has been made of comparative law techniques at the Community level and in processes of national legal reform.

[136] M. Habersack, *Europäisches Gesellschaftsrecht* (Munich: Beck, 1999), para. 283 ff. See for the German law: § 264(2) HGB [German Commercial Code] and Case C-234/94 *Tomberger* [1996] ECR I-3145; 3153 para. 17 (true and fair view as overriding principle); Edwards, *EC Company Law*, pp. 128–30; See generally, P. Bird, 'What is "A True and Fair View"?' [1984] J Bus L 480; K. van Hulle, 'The EEC Accounting Directives in Perspective: Problems of Harmonization' [1981] 18 CMLR 121.

[137] J. Boucourechliev and P. Hommelhoff (eds), *Vorschläge für eine Europäische Privatgesellschaft – Strukturelemente einer kapitalmarktfernen europäischen Gesellschaftsform nebst Entwurf für eine EPG-Verordnung der Europäischen Gemeinschaft* (Cologne: O. Schmidt, 1999); P. Hommelhoff and D. Helms (eds), *Neue Wege in die Europäische Privatgesellschaft – Rechts- und Steuerfragen in der Heidelberger Diskussion* (Cologne: O. Schmidt, 2001); H-J. de Kluiver and W. van Gerven (eds), *The European Private Company?* (Antwerp: Maklu, 1995).

[138] Some regard the outcomes of European company law harmonisation as a fragmentary and compromise solution. See Schön, 'Das Bild des Gesellschafters im Europäischen Gesellschaftsrecht' [2000] 64 RabelsZ 1, 7; G. C. Schwarz, *Europäisches Gesellschaftsrecht* (Baden-Baden: Nomos, 2000), para. 3. See the present prevailing views in, e.g. Werlauff, *EU Company Law*, in the 'Introduction' at p. XV and S. Grundmann, 'The Structure of European Company Law: From Crisis to Boom' (2004) 5 *European Business Organisation Law Review* 601, where the title indicates the author's thesis.

II. Comparative company law

A. *Introductory remarks*

Comparative studies in the field of company law have become of more significance in recent years, but have been actively pursued by many scholars in different traditions for a considerable period of time.[139] Studies in comparative company law may entail identifying rules of different systems which have the same functions as each other. Comparisons have generally been made on a 'micro' basis, i.e. one particular topic such as directors' duties or minority protection is studied in more than one jurisdiction. The jurisdictions chosen may have similar systems of company law (e.g. those of Germany, Austria and Switzerland) or rather different ones, as in the case of the United Kingdom, France and Germany. It will often be necessary in particular jurisdictions to consider the relationship between company law and other system of law, e.g. commercial, civil or industrial law, and to take account of particular methods of reasoning in a given system, for example the German willingness to use provisions of Codes or statutes by way of analogy in the event that other applicable rules are not available.

Drury and Xuereb[140] advocate a counterfactual approach. It is only by an investigation which takes into account the underlying concepts, policy considerations and assumptions of each system that the real nature and relative importance of particular matters within each system can be more perceptively understood. The adequate performance of such a task would demand great scholarship. Furthermore there may be considerable difficulties and room for differences of opinion, in determining what these concepts, policy considerations and assumptions are, especially as they are likely to change with the passage of time.

139 Such studies were instituted by the Nordic Council as early as in 1925. The importance of comparative company law also received early recognition by German scholars, see, e.g. the 1929 Habilitation treatise by Walter Hallstein (the later first President of the EC Commission). See also Professor Gower's important article, 'Some Contrasts between British and American Company Law' [1956] 60 *Harvard Law Review*, 1360. In the 1960s, the Institute of Latin American Studies conducted a comparative study on corporations in the Latin American Free Trade Area. Professors Schmitthoff and Pennington, two leading British scholars, display an awareness of the importance of comparative studies in many of their extensive works in the field of company law.

140 See Drury and Xuereb (eds), *European Company Laws: A Comparative Approach* (Aldershot: Dartmouth, 1991), p. 87.

B. Comparative law and the harmonisation of company law

However scholarly they may be, persons engaged in the practical task of harmonising the company law of different states may have limited time for the above type of investigations. Their inclination will be to achieve workable compromises and prescribe possible alternatives, derived from certain national systems of law. They will thus frequently have to engage in comparative company law studies, if only to adopt a negotiating position which represents a compromise between different systems, which eventually has to be modified or abandoned. Certain proposals and Directives find their basis in the legal systems of only a few Member States: one may use as an example the Twelfth Directive on single-member companies,[141] which, at the time of the submission of the proposal for the Twelfth Directive in 1988, were only permitted in Belgium, France, Denmark, Germany and the Netherlands.[142]

Compromises which are made will depend on the perceived merits and demerits of each system as well as on practical and political considerations. Such compromises were made in the negotiation of the First Company Law Directive which, like most of the Directives mentioned below, contains elements ultimately derived from the laws of different Member States.

Two such compromises took place in the enactment of Articles 9(1) and (2) of the First Directive.[143] The first of these, relating to Article 9(1) will be mentioned below, since it is rather self-explanatory. This provision represents an accommodation between the German doctrine that the validity of a corporate transaction will not be influenced by whether it came within the scope of the Company's objects and is dependent only upon the ambit of the representative powers of the organs acting on the company's behalf, and the doctrine of *spécialité statutaire* or *ultra vires*

[141] See for more details: F. Wooldridge, 'The Draft Twelfth Directive on Single-Member Companies' [1989] EBLR 86; Edwards, *EC Company Law*, p. 219. The Twelfth Directive was part of the action programme for small and medium sized enterprises (SMEs). See Council Resolution of 3 November 1986, OJ 1986 C287/1.

[142] In Luxembourg already a draft legislation and in Portugal a form of sole-proprietor with limited liability existed. In the UK, Greece, Ireland, Italy and Spain the single-member limited company was not permitted. See Proposal for a Twelfth Council Directive on Company Law concerning single-member private limited companies, COM(88) 101 final, pp. 1–4; V. Ochs, *Die Einpersonengesellschaft in Europa – eine rechtsvergleichende Studie zum Recht der Einpersonen-GmbH in Deutschland, Frankreich, Italien und England* (Baden-Baden: Nomos, 1997), p. 29.

[143] See p. 22, above.

which was accepted subject to certain limitations relating to such matters as apparent authority and implied ratification in all the five other original Member States.[144] According to the latter doctrine, a transaction was invalid if it did not come within the objects of the company.

The nature of the compromise contained in Article 9(1) should be fairly obvious from the text of this provision, which stipulates that acts done by the organs of the company shall be binding on it even if these acts are not within the objects of the company, unless such acts exceed the powers which the law confers or allows to be conferred on such organs. As a result third parties are only protected if the organ acts within the limits of its powers. In its *Rabobank* decision,[145] the ECJ held that rules which provide for the invalidity of the agreement in case of a conflict of interest between the company and its organs, can be relied upon against third parties. The Directive was, however, not intended to coordinate the law applicable where there was a conflict of interest.[146]

Member States may provide that the company shall not be bound where such acts are outside the objects of the company, if it proves that the third party knew that the act was outside these objects, or could not in view of the circumstances have been unaware of it. But disclosure of the statutes shall not of itself be sufficient proof thereof.

The Second Directive has been said by Schmitthoff to combine the best features of national Company laws.[147] Certain of the provisions of this instrument, especially those relating to minimum subscribed capital, the distinction between public and private companies, distributions, the consequences of serious losses of capital, the valuation of non-cash consideration for shares and pre-emptive rights appear to derive from German and other civil law systems.[148] However, Articles 23–39, which

[144] See Edwards, *EC Company Law*, p. 36; H. J. Ault 'Harmonization of Company Law in the European Economic Community' [1968] 20 *Hastings Law Journal* 77, 103 f; E. Stein, *Harmonization of European Company Laws* (Bobb's Merrill, 1971), pp. 292–4; D. Wyatt, 'The First Directive and Company Law' [1978] 94 LQR 182.

[145] Case C-104/97 *Cooperative Rabobank* [1997] ECR I-7211.

[146] For that reason it was irrelevant if the third party knew about this conflict. See also Edwards, *EC Company Law*, p. 38; M. Habersack, *Europäisches Gesellschaftsrecht* (Munich: Beck, 1999), para. 105; and more critically Grundmann, *Europäisches Gesellschaftsrecht*, para. 261.

[147] Schmitthoff, 'The Second Directive on Company Law' [1976] 15 CMLRev 43, 53–4. The learned writer was considering the provisions relating to shareholders' rights of pre-emption.

[148] Grundmann, *Europäisches Gesellschaftsrecht* para. 349; Edwards, *EC Company Law*, p. 51 f; Schmitthoff, 'The Second Directive on Company Law' [1976] 15 CMLRev 43, 54.

are concerned with financial assistance given by a company for the purchase of its own shares and the redemption of shares, display the influence of English and Irish law and accountancy practice.[149] It may be said that certain English reactions to the Directive displayed an unfortunate suspicion of the civil law influences on the Directive,[150] which might perhaps have been less acute had an elementary knowledge of European company law been more widely disseminated. It appears that certain of the provisions the Second Directive was never especially well implemented in the United Kingdom. This appears particularly true of the complex provisions of section 108 of the Companies Act 1985 concerning the valuation of, and report on, non cash consideration.[151] It may well be the case that such legislation proved to be more complex in certain respects than the corresponding provisions of the company laws of other countries. The High Level Group of Company Experts suggested that with respect to contributions in kind, the requirement for an expert valuation should be eliminated in certain cases where clear and reliable points of reference for valuation already exist (market price, recent evaluation, recent audited accounts).[152] See above about the amendments in 2006.[153]

The disparate Anglo-Dutch and Franco-German influences on the Fourth and Seventh Directives have been mentioned above. Both Directives contain provisions concerning certain accounting techniques and related matters which will be unfamiliar to lawyers and accountants in certain Member States. One may mention as an example provisions concerning merger accounting (an alternative method of accounting for acquisitions according to which there is no requirement of establishing a share premium account) which were introduced at a late stage in Article 20(1) of the Seventh Directive as an option, at the request of the United Kingdom.[154] As already indicated, both the Fourth and Seventh Directive take account of the different requirements of the Member States by the use of options and alternatives, which

[149] Edwards, *EC Company Law*, p. 51; Grundmann, *Europäisches Gesellschaftsrecht*, para. 349.

[150] Note in particular the 24th Report of the Select Committee of the House of Lords on the European Communities (Session 1974–5, HL Paper, 239).

[151] See also G. Gansen, *Harmonisierung der Kapitalaufbringung im englischen und deutschen Kapitalgesellschaftsrecht – Vergleichende Studie zur Zweiten Gesellschaftsrechtlichen EG-Richtlinie* (Frankfurt: P. Lang, 1992).

[152] See Report of the High Level Group of Company Law Experts of 4 November 2002, 78–93, http://europa.eu.int/comm/internal_market/en/company/company/index.htm, p. 83.

[153] At p. 23, above.

[154] Merger accounting is now permitted under United Kingdom Law subject to the conditions set out in s. 131 of the Companies Act 1985: see also Schedule 48, paras. 10 and 11 to this Act.

makes individual company and consolidated accounts prepared in the various Member States markedly different from one another and sometimes not readily comprehensive to persons unfamiliar with the relevant accounting techniques, even though a certain level of harmonisation has been attained. However, as from 2005, the consolidated accounts of listed companies will have to be prepared in accordance with international accounting standards.

The use of options extended to the six definitions of a parent undertaking contained in Article 1 of the Seventh Directive for the purpose of the obligation to prepare consolidated accounts. Three of the relevant definitions are compulsory and must be adopted by Member States, whilst three are optional, and take account of the requirements of particular Member States: i.e. Germany, France and Italy, two of these three optional definitions were adopted by the United Kingdom in section 258(2)(c) and (4) of the Companies Act 1985.

It was possible to achieve a limited degree of harmonisation under the Fourth and Seventh Directives because account was taken of the different accounting techniques and practices of the Member States by the Community institutions, which did not encounter such significant political opposition to their proposals as was encountered to the proposal for the draft Fifth Directive. This Directive seems to have been abandoned. However, it has been suggested that the principle which it contained governing one share one vote might be adopted. The principle might be appropriate for quoted companies, but has met more resistance for other companies, for example those of a family character. In 2007, the European Commission published an impact assessment on the question of 'proportionality between capital and control in listed companies' that indicated that there was no link between voting systems and company profits. Previous Commission initiatives to legislate against restrictions on one share one vote was subsequently shelved. This is partly because of the persistent opposition of the United Kingdom to the introduction of a mandatory two-tier board system and compulsory employee participation. The first proposal was made in 1972.[155] The proposed mandatory two-tier board system was based upon the provisions of German and Dutch law, whilst the proposed compulsory employee participation was also based upon German and Dutch models.[156]

[155] Proposal for a Fifth Directive based on Art. 54 of the EEC Treaty concerning the structure of public limited companies and the powers and obligations of their organs, COM (72) 887 final.

[156] Edwards, *EC Company Law*, p. 387; H. C. Ficker, 'The EEC Directives on Company Law Harmonisation' in C. Schmitthoff (ed.), *The Harmonization of European Company Law*

Amendments made to the proposal in 1982[157] provided for greater flexibility in relation both to board structure and employee participation.[158] It was proposed that the single-board system might be maintained, provided that there was a distinction made between members of the board who were responsible for supervision, and those responsible for management.[159] Nevertheless, the Directive opts distinctively for the two-tier board system as the provisions regarding the unitary board have exactly the same wording except of using the words executive and non-executive instead of managing board and supervisory board.[160] Even though the functional separation of executive and non-executive members of the board can be found in many European company laws, certain varieties remain in particular in respect to their functions.[161] It was also proposed that the employee participation could take place in accordance with one of four models, which appear to have been influenced by German, Dutch and French law.[162]

The Directive contains a number of other provisions relating to the duties and liabilities of directors; the powers of the general meeting; the rights of shareholders; approval of the annual accounts and the functions and liabilities of auditors. Certain of these proposals appear to be based partly upon French[163] and German[164] models, and may be worthy of

(London: UK National Committee of Comparative Law, 1973), p. 66; J. Temple Lang, *The Fifth EEC Directive on the Harmonisation of Company Law; Some Comments from the Viewpoint of Irish and British Law on the EEC Draft for the Fifth Directive concerning Management Structure and Worker Participation* [1975] 12 CMLR 155, 345.

157 Amended Proposal for a Fifth Directive based on Art. 54(3)(g) of the EEC Treaty concerning the structure of public limited companies and the powers and obligations of their organs, COM (83) 185 final. See also the latest amended Proposal of 20 November 1991 for a Fifth Directive based on Art. 54 of the EEC Treaty concerning the structure of public limited companies and the powers and obligations of their organs, COM (91) 372 final.

158 See J. Welch, 'The Fifth Draft Directive – a False Dawn?' [1983] 8 EL Rev 83; A. J. Boyle, 'Draft Fifth Directive – Implications for Directors' Duties, Board Structure and Employee Participation' [1992] 13 *The Company Lawyer* 6.

159 See Art. 2(2) Fifth Directive.

160 See seventh consideration of the proposals 1982 and 1991. critical: C. Striebeck, *Reform des Aktienrechts durch die Strukturrichtlinie der Europäischen Gemeinschaften* (Frankfurt am Main: Lang, 1992), p. 33 f.

161 P. Davies, 'Board Structure in the UK and Germany: Convergence or Continuing Divergence?' [2001] 2 *International and Comparative Corporate Law Journal* 435.

162 See Fifth Directive, Art. 4.

163 The proposals for a minority shareholders' derived action contained in Arts. 42–4 of the Directive are paralleled to some extent by those of French law; see Art. L. 225–52 Code de commerce, and Art. 200 of the Decree of 23 March 1967.

164 The proposal suggests that directors should be jointly and severally liable for losses suffered by the company as the result of breaches of the law, the corporate constitution,

adoption. The High Level Group of Company Experts in its Report of 4 November 2002 made many proposals relating to the management responsibility, the introduction of a wrongful trading rule, the determination of sanctions for misleading statements and the disclosure of the remuneration policy for directors.[165]

Although the United Kingdom has now accepted the European Works Councils Directive,[166] which is applicable only to Community scale undertakings or groups of undertakings with more than a thousand employers across the twelve Member States, and at least two establishments in different Member States each employing at least 150 persons. Although the United Kingdom has recently accepted the framework Directive on informing and consulting employees,[167] it would still seem unwilling to accept the proposals for employee participation contained in the draft Fifth Directive, which now appears unlikely to be adopted, despite the evidently conscientious efforts of Commission officials to harmonise and develop the laws of the Member States such that Community wide rules could be enacted on employee participation and company structure.

As has been shown, the above proposal is much influenced by models provided by national law. The failure of the various draft proposals for a Ninth Directive on Groups of Undertakings for which Professors Van Ommerschlage and Würdinger as well as Dr K. Gleichmann were responsible, seems to have resulted in part from the fact that these proposals were biased to too great an extent on German rules on groups of companies: these rules were generally unfamiliar in the other Member States. Only Portugal, Brazil, Croatia and Slovenia have shown a willingness to incorporate provisions similar to those of German *Konzernrecht* into their national laws. Although this preponderant influence of German law on the Commission's draft proposals was probably unfortunate, it was perhaps somewhat inevitable as none of the other Member States attempted the

or other wrongful acts. However, an individual director could be exonerated if he could prove that no personal fault was attributable to him. Such joint and several liability is imposed on directors by Art. 93 of the German *Aktiengesetz* they may be exonerated of they can prove they are not personally at fault, Art. 93(1) 'diligence of a prudent businessman'. See Bundesgerichtshof in BGHZ 85, 293, 295 f; M. Roth, *Unternehmerisches Ermessen und Haftung des Vorstands* (Munich: Beck, 2001).

165 See Report of the High Level Group of Company Law Experts of 4 November 2002, 64–70, http://europa.eu.int/comm/internal_market/en/company/company/index.htm.

166 See above n. 85.

167 Directive 2002/14/EC of 11 March 2002 establishing a general framework for informing and consulting employees in the European Community – Joint declaration of the European Parliament, the Council and the Commission on employee representation, OJ 2002 L80/29.

systematic regulation of connected companies and groups of companies in the German fashion.

The successful negotiation of the draft Fourteenth Directive will evidently require the acceptance of a satisfactory compromise between the real seat and incorporation doctrines.[168] Such a compromise is attempted in draft Articles 2 and 3. However, the finalised Directive (and any ancilliary instruments) will also have to finalise satisfactory solutions to difficult problems concerning such matters as taxation (which is not dealt with in the proposal), employee participation, creditors' rights, the rights of minorities, and insolvency. The significance of these problems becomes apparent after a cursory examination has been made of the relevant laws and practices of the Member States, as well as such international instruments as the 1989 Rome Convention on the laws applicable to Contractual Obligations. Satisfactory solutions to the relevant problems will not only require a comparative law background, but will also necessitate a considerable degree of political skill as well as inventiveness on the part of the persons and bodies concerned.

There will need to be developments in tax law, which may involve the enactment of an appropriate directive, so as to endeavour to eliminate the present disadvantages suffered by companies in certain Member States in the shape of exit taxes on migration, or otherwise not much use would be made by the machinery provided for by the Directive, except in cases where the tax regime of the country of immigration was specially favourable.[169] The choice of the appropriate regime which would govern employee participation rights is obviously a difficult one. It is not clear whether, at present, such participation rights have to be regarded as company law rights or employment rights. If they are the latter kind of rights, it would seem to follow from Article 6(2) of the Rome Convention that (subject to the possibility of the enactment of a different rule) they would normally be subject to the law of the state of emigration, whilst if they are treated as company law rights, they would be subject to the newly applicable law.

The provisions of Article 7 concerning minority protection may be unsatisfactory, insofar as they provide for an optional procedure by

[168] Edwards, *EC Company Law*, p. 138.

[169] See especially, *Communication from the Commission to the Council, the European Parliament and the Economic and Social Committee – Towards an Internal Market without tax obstacles – A strategy for providing companies with a consolidated corporate tax base for their EU-wide activities*, 23 October 2001, COM (2001) 583 final.

which a Member State may introduce legislation to ensure 'appropriate protection for minority members who oppose the transfer'.[170] It is clear to anyone having a superficial knowledge of the company laws of more than one Member State that different rules may be applicable to such minority protection in different states, such that a different level of protection might be available in each such state. One may finally add that draft Article 13 of the proposal gives rise to difficulties.[171] It stipulates that migration with a change of applicable law may not take place if 'proceedings for winding up, liquidations, insolvency or suspension of payments or other similar proceedings' have been brought against the company. Although this provision appears to embrace many of the different kinds of insolvency procedures which are familiar within the Member States it does not appear to cover voluntary liquidations or receiverships begun in accordance with the provisions of a legal instrument. Both procedures are, of course, familiar in the United Kingdom and Ireland, but they do not involve legal proceedings.

III. Comparative company law and national legal reforms

A. Continental reforms

A knowledge of systems of company law other than that of the persons entrusted with reforms of national law coupled with a necessarily creative approach, may be of considerable assistance to such reforms. The German *Aktiengesetz* of 1965 appears to have been influenced by a number of studies in comparative company law which were published in the 1950s and early 1960s.[172] Aspects of Anglo-American company law were introduced into the debate by Professor Kronstein, who had been a refugee from the Nazis, and who also taught company law in the United States as well as in Germany. His contribution was particularly

[170] See also: Grundmann, *Europäisches Gesellschaftsrecht*, para. 911; J. Hoffmann, '*Neue Möglichkeiten zur identitätswahenden Sitzverlegung in Europa? – Der Richtlinienvorentwurf zur Verlegung des Gesellschaftssitzes innerhalb der EU* [2000] 164 *Zeitschrift für das gesamte Handels- und Wirtschaftsrecht*' 43, 64.

[171] See J. H. Priester, 'EU-Sitzverlegung – Verfahrensablauf' [1999] *Zeitschrift für Gesellschaftsrecht* 36, 49.

[172] Note, e.g. Wiethölter, *Interessen und Organisation der Aktiengesellschaft im deutschen und amerikanischan Recht* (Karlsruhe: C. F. Müller, 1961). According to E. Stein, *Harmonization of European Company Laws (1971)* (Bobbs Merrill, 1971), p. 100, n. 32, German law reformers considered Anglo-American law as early as 1926 at the 34th *Deutschen Juristentag* at Cologne.

concerned with American rules on company accounts, financial documents and disclosure requirements; it had some significant influence on German law. Mestmäcker, who spent some time in the United States, had a considerable influence on the provisions of the German law of 1965 governing connected companies and groups of companies. Belgian company law has also been significantly influenced in the past by comparative studies. The French Marin Report of 1998 makes certain favourable references to English law.

B. UK Company law reform and comparative law – DTI's strategic framework

The core document for the recently completed UK reform process was published in 1999. It contains two chapters which are of interest for the purposes of law reform. Chapter 3 deals briefly with the impact of the Community's company law harmonisation programme and the significant aspects of the European Convention on Human Rights. The restraints imposed by the Second Directive is discussed elsewhere in the Strategic Framework, which mentions the possibility of surmounting these abstracts by seeking derogations or general revision at Community level.[173]

Chapter 4 is entitled 'the Comparative Dimension'. It makes reference to the company laws of the Commonwealth, the European Union, and the United States. Perhaps rather unsurprisingly, the strategic framework takes the view that most inspiration is to be derived from recent reforms in Commonwealth countries, in particular in Canada, Australia and New Zealand. The Strategic Framework briefly examines the company laws of Germany, France and the Netherlands, but does not adopt a very positive approach to these systems of law. It finds nothing in the German system of employee participation or in the German regulation of groups of undertakings worthy of consideration by those responsible for the reform of United Kingdom company law.

Perhaps rather more surprisingly, the *Strategic Framework* treats certain recent developments in American company law rather dismissively. The approach taken in the *Strategic Framework* is probably to be explained by the selection of the company law review group;[174] although

[173] See the very useful note by Professor Boyle, 'The Use of Comparative law in the Strategic Framework' [2000] 21 Co Law 308–10.

[174] See Annex A to the *Strategic Framework* for relevant particulars.

this contained a number of representatives of the old Commonwealth it contained none from the EU countries or indeed from the United States.

The Law Commission's report on shareholder remedies[175] has also been criticised on the ground that it concentrates on relevant Commonwealth models, ignores the situation in the European Union, and almost completely ignores that in the United States. The Law Commission's consultation paper on *Company Directors: Regulating Conflicts of Interest*[176] does contain an account of the German law relating to directors duty of care.

It is surprising and disappointing that a more positive view was not taken in the *Strategic Framework* of the provisions of German law concerning employee participation, and indeed of developments in the law governing groups of companies in Germany, France and the United States. As Professor Boyle correctly points out,[177] in the future the corporate legal environment in the United Kingdom has come to be increasingly influenced by large enterprises taking European or American corporate forms (rather than those of Australia or Canada). The rather negative approach to European and American company law in the Strategic Framework is understandable from a traditional common law perspective, but still rather disappointing.

175 Law Commission No. 246, October 1997.
176 Law Commission Consultation Paper No. 153, 1998.
177 'The Use of Comparative Law' 21 Co Law (2000), 309.

3

Formation of companies

I. Introduction

The present chapter discusses the procedure for the formation of public and private limited liability companies in the United Kingdom, France, Germany, Italy, Spain, Belgium and the Netherlands. There are considerable differences between the process for the formation of public and private companies in France and Germany, and these processes will need to be more clearly differentiated from one another than in certain other cases. Because of the comparative rarity of such entities the process of formation of public companies with personally liable directors, such as the French *société en commandite par actions*, the German *Kommanditgellschaft auf Aktien* and the Italian *Società in accomandita per azioni* have not been considered in this chapter.

By reason of the impact of the First Company Law Directive, which applies to both public and private companies, there are similarities in the laws of the Member States concerning the disclosure of the basic documents on formation. There are however marked differences between these laws concerning other matters. The rules regarding the share and loan capital are considered in a subsequent chapter.

In all the countries considered in the present text, it is necessary to establish one or more documents which form the company's constitution. In all the relevant states the formation of the new company has to be registered in an official register. As already indicated, certain elements of the law relating to disclosure on formation of public and private companies have been harmonised by the First Company Law Directive. The minimum capital requirements relating to public companies have been harmonised by the Second Company Law Directive, which does not apply to private companies.[1] There would still seem to be some differences between the relevant rules in different Member States, both concerning the designation of documents and their content.

[1] This Directive has undergone recent amendment by Directive 2006/86 EC, OJ 2006 L264/32.

II. Formation of private and public companies in the United Kingdom

A. Process of formation

There is little difference between the process of formation of a public and a private company in the United Kingdom.[2] Most United Kingdom companies begin their existence as private companies, and some such companies are later converted to public ones. There is no optional or mandatory provision for a particular deed for the formation of an English or Scottish company, nor are there any special rules concerning the situation of a company prior to registration comparable to those which exist in German law relating to the *Vorgesellschaft*, which are explained briefly below in the section about the formation of German companies.

The formation and incorporation of an English or Scottish company takes place as the result of the registration. The issue of the certificate of incorporation by the registrar is conclusive evidence that all the requirements necessary for formation have been complied with.[3] There are no requirements concerning the minimum capital of an English private company which, like a public company, may do business and exercise borrowing powers immediately after its registration.

The rules regarding the documents required for registration are practically the same for public and private limited companies, and are set out in sections 9–13 of the Companies Act 2006 (formerly sections 10–12 of the Companies Act 1985). Certain documents must be presented to the registrar in order that registration may occur. These are a copy of the company's memorandum and proposed articles of association; a statement of the names and prescribed particulars of the first director(s) of the company and or the first company secretary (or joint secretaries); a statutory declaration of compliance signed by the solicitor concerned with the formation or by a person named as director of the company, and a statement of the company's capital and initial shareholders. In the case of a public company, the amount of the share capital stated to be that with which the company proposes to be registered must not be less than the authorised minimum (at present the minimum allotted share capital is £50,000 but the amount may be increased in the future). The statement as to the directors and secretary (or secretaries) must contain consents by

2 In this section we do not deal with unlimited companies or companies limited by guarantee.

3 Companies Act 2006, s. 15(4) (previously Companies Act 1985, s. 13).

these persons to act in the relevant capacity. The application for registration must also contain a statement of intended address of the company, registered office and the company's proposed name.

On the registration of the company, the registrar will grant a certificate that the company is incorporated which is conclusive evidence that the requirements concerning company registration have been complied with, and that the company is duly registered under the Act.

B. *Special rules applicable to public companies*

As is also the case with a private company, the statement of a public company's capital has to include the amount to be paid in and the amount unpaid on each share. If the applicable registered statement does not give particulars of these amounts, the company cannot be registered.[4] The amount consists of at least 25 per cent of the nominal value of the shares (authorised minimum capital is now £50,000) and any premium payable on them.[5]

Public companies are also subject to other detailed rules contained in the Second Directive concerning the method of payment for shares. These rules are reflected in certain of the provisions of the Companies Act 2006, especially by sections 91, 584–587 and 593–597.[6] Thus, such companies may not issue shares in return for a promise to perform services to transfer assets to the company in more than five years time. The allotment of shares wholly or partly for a non-cash consideration must, according to section 593, be preceded by a valuer's report as to the adequacy of the consideration. Section 584 of the Companies Act 2006 requires subscribers to the memorandum to pay for their shares in cash.[7] According to section 588,[8] any breach of the provisions contained in

[4] A public company was previously not permitted to do business or exercise any borrowing powers unless it had received a certificate from the registrar that it was entitled to do business. Such a certificate (which was different from the certificate of incorporation) would not be granted unless the company disclosed the amount of the share capital which has been allotted and paid up. The Company Law Review Steering Group's publication, *Modern Company Law for a Competitive Economy: Capital Formation and Capital Maintenance*, November 1999, p. 20, suggested that the two stage incorporation procedure for public companies should be abolished. This was done by the Companies Act 2006.

[5] Companies Act 2006, ss. 91, 585 and 586. The previous Companies Act 1985 provided for these matters in ss. 101 and 118.

[6] The new s. 593 corresponds with the former s. 103 of the Companies Act 1985.

[7] Previously s. 106 of the Companies Act 1985.

[8] Previously s. 112 of the Companies Act 1985.

Chapter V of Part 17 of the Companies Act 2006 regarding liability to payment for shares results in the holders' liability to pay the relevant amount under the provision contravened, jointly and severally with any other person liable, except where a shareholder is a bona fide purchaser without notice, liable to pay the full amount for them in cash. Private companies are not subject to these stringent rules, which may apply to public companies of the time of their formation or subsequently. The only rules applicable to the issue of shares for a non-cash consideration by private companies are rules prohibiting past (in England and Wales but not Scotland) and illusory consideration.

These rules like those applicable to non-cash consideration procured for shares in public companies do not specially relate to the formation process. The stricter rules applicable to non-cash consideration furnished at the time of the formation of continental private companies will be noted below.

C. *The memorandum and articles (constitution) of the company*

The most important documents for the formation of a company are its memorandum and articles. The Company Law Review Steering Group proposed that these two documents be replaced by one. This would roughly correspond with the articles.[9] The basic constitution of a company would thus be recorded in one document as opposed to two. This document would be delivered to the registrar together with a standard registration form, which would contain most of the matters currently required to be in the memorandum.

The memorandum was formerly the more important of the two documents. It was not abolished by the Companies Act 2006, but its importance has now been reduced. According to section 9, the memorandum shall state that the subscribers wish to form a company under the Act of 2006 and agree to become members of it, and in the case of a company that is to have a share capital, to take at least one share each.[10] It

[9] See the Company Law Review Steering Group's publication, *Modern Company Law for a Competitive Economy: Capital Formation and Capital Maintenance*, November 1999, p. 9.

[10] The Companies Act 1985 provided in s. 2 for the memorandum containing six clauses for private companies and seven clauses for public companies. The first clause contained the company's name; the second states the situation of the registered office and thus mentions whether this is to be in England and Wales or in Scotland. The third clause, which only applied to public companies, stated that the company is a public limited company. The fourth clause stated the object of the company, and often proved to be

also stipulates that the memorandum must be in the prescribed form and must be authenticated by each subscriber. Nothing further is mentioned about this prescribed form, but it would seem that the relevant form has to be prescribed by regulations made by the Secretary of State in accordance with section 1167 of the Companies Act 2006. The memorandum of a company was formerly required to state the company's name and registered office. It can change the location of its registered office within the United Kingdom but at present an international transfer of its registered office is impossible.[11] This will change if the draft EC Fourteenth Company Law Directive is adopted.[12]

The memorandum was formerly required to state the objects of the company. They were often set out in very prolix terms to avoid the possible effects of the *ultra vires* rule.[13] Public companies are required

very prolix so as to avoid the possible effect of the *ultra vires* rule, the impact of which had been much reduced by recent British legislation. The company's limited liability would be specified in the fifth clause of the memorandum. The next clause would set out the company's authorised capital, which had to be at least £50,000 in the case of a public company. The final clause was the subscription clause, according to which the founders subscribed their names to the memorandum, which had to determine the number of shares each subscriber took. A matter which might have been provided for in the articles of a company was instead often provided for in the memorandum. This was for instance often done in the case of the class rights attached to preferred shares, and served to entrench such rights.

[11] The possibility of legislation permitting such migration, and the jurisdiction migration of United Kingdom companies was envisaged by the Company Law Review Steering Group in its consultation document of November 2000, *Modern Company Law for a Competitive Economy: Completing the Structure.* However, in 2002, the Government rejected the proposal of the Company Law Review to allow an international transfer of the registered office of companies: it was feared that the proposal would cause a major tax loss for the UK, see the UK Government White Paper *Modernising Company Law* Cm 5553-I (July 2002), paras. 6.21–22.

[12] A proposal permitting the transfer of the registered office is likely to be made by the European Commission in the near future and would seem likely to be adopted. The European Court of Justice is in a case presently before the court, Case C-210/06 *Cartesio*, OJ C165, of 15 July 2006, p. 17, required to answer questions left open after Case 81/87 *R* v. *Treasury ex p Daily Mail* [1988] ECR 5483 which at that stage of the development of European company law allowed Member States to impose certain restrictions on companies leaving the jurisdiction since there was no mechanism in national or EU company law for relocating the registered seat and incorporation to another Member State. One question is now whether EU law requires that national law provides such a mechanism. If the Court of Justice does not reach such a conclusion, one will have to await the draft directive which will provide such a mechanism. See the discussion above in Chapter 2.

[13] According to this rule, anything outside the objects was regarded as *ultra vires*. The impact of the *ultra vires* rule have been much reduced by recent British legislation, see ss. 35, 35A, 35B, and 322A of the Companies Act 1985 as amended by the Companies Act 1989, now see ss. 29–41 of the Companies Act 2006.

by Article 2 of the Second Company Law Directive[14] to have an objects clause, setting out its object in its statutes or instrument of incorporation: no such requirement is imposed on private companies. According to section 3(1) of the Companies Act 2006, unless a company's articles specifically restrict the objects, the objects are unrestricted.[15] Certain commonwealth jurisdictions have dispensed with the need for an objects clause altogether, both for public and private companies.[16]

The memorandum was formerly required to state the company's authorised or nominal capital, but the Companies Act 2006 seems to have abandoned this concept.[17] According to section 7(1) of the Companies Act 2006, the minimum number of subscribers to the memorandum of a public or private company is now one.[18] The company is required by section 180 of the Companies Act 2006, to have articles prescribing regulations for it. The Secretary of State is empowered to make regulations prescribing model articles of association for companies, which may differ with the type of company.[19] If a company does not register articles on formation, or to the extent that it does not exclude or modify the relevant modalities where it registers articles, the relevant model articles remain applicable.[20] In the past, articles have usually defined class right, and provided for the calling of meetings and the voting rights of members. They could also provide for the appointment of a board of directors to manage the affairs of the company, and stipulate what power the board may exercise in the company's name. Furthermore, they would usually contain provisions governing the payment of dividends, the capitalisation of profits, the transfer and transmission of shares and the alteration of capital. Section 31(1) of the Companies Act 2006 may envisage that the objects are defined in the articles. The text provides that unless a company's articles specifically set out the objects of the company (which would seem to be a company of any type), the objects are unrestricted.

According to section 33(1) of the Companies Act 2006, the provisions of a company's constitution (which is defined in section 17 as its articles and certain types of resolutions set out in section 29) bind the company

[14] OJ 1977, L26/1.

[15] The Company Law Review Steering Group proposed to abolish the requirement of an objects clause for private companies, see its Consultation Document, *Company Formation and Capital Maintenance* (1999) p. 9.

[16] This is the law in Australia and New Zealand.

[17] A public company still has to have a minimum subscribed capital of £50,000.

[18] Companies Act 2006, s. 7(1). [19] *Ibid.*, s. 519(1). [20] *Ibid.*, s. 20(1).

and its members to observe these provisions to the same extent as if they were covenants on the part of the company and each member. Section 33(1) resembles the provisions of section 14(1) of the Companies Act 1985, which it repeals. Section 33(1) creates a contract which is binding on the members in their dealings with the company, [21] and binding on the company in its dealings with members as such.[22] A member may not evade the provision of the articles for his benefit where they relate to some capacity other than those of a member, the right to become the company's solicitor, secretary or director.[23] The effect of section 14(1) of the Companies Act 1985 was considered in the consultative documents from the Company Law Review Steering Group, *Modern Company Law for a Competitive Economy: Capital Formation and Capital Maintenance*,[24] and *Modern Company Law for a Competitive Economy: Developing the Framework*.[25] These consultative documents both questioned the concept of the deemed contract. The second consultative document suggests the redrafting of section 14(1) to make it clear to what extent it gives rise to rights and obligations binding on the company, and enforceable by members. However, neither document recommended significant changes in the existing legal position insofar as it concerned the unenforceability of outsider rights by members of the company. Its failure to do so is perhaps disappointing, because it has sometimes proved difficult to differentiate between outsider and member rights. The text of section 33 of the Companies Act 2006 does not appear to facilitate such differentiation.

D. *Constructive notice*

A company acquires legal personality when it is entered on the register, and it is then possible for members to inspect its file and the registry. A person who deals with a company is deemed to have notice of the contents of the company's articles and memorandum from the date when the company's incorporation was published in the *London*

[21] Note in particular, *Hickman* v. *Kent and Romney Marsh Sheep-Breeders Association* [1915] Ch 881.

[22] *Oakbank Oil Co.* v. *Crum* [1882] 8 App Cases 65.

[23] Note for example *Eley* v. *Positive Government Secretary Life Assurance Co* [1875] 1 Ex D 20, in which the court held that a person who was appointed as a solicitor for life by the company's articles was unable to enforce the contract because it did not relate to him as a member.

[24] (2000), see p. 7. [25] (2000), see pp. 109–19.

Gazette.[26] Such constructive notice would also appear to apply to the contents of other documents delivered to the Registrar of Companies which are open to inspection and their receipt has been notified in the *Gazette* where necessary. The doctrine of deemed or constructive notice has not been abolished, as appeared likely at one time. Section 711A(1) of the Companies Act 1985 as amended was intended to abolish this doctrine but was never brought into force.[27] A person was not deemed to have notice of a matter merely because it was disclosed on the companies register or made available at the Company's register. Section 711A(2) (which was also not brought into force) provided that 'this does not affect the question whether a person is affected by some or any matter by reason or a failure to make such inquiries as might reasonably be made'.

Today the doctrine may be of limited importance as it is only operative where complete or partial protection is not open to persons dealing with the company in good faith. Thus, section 40(1) of the Companies Act 2006 provides that in favour of a person dealing with a company in good faith, the power of the directors to bind the company or to authorise others to do so is deemed to be free of any limitation under the company's constitution. The requirements for good faith set out in section 40(2) are scarcely stringent. Thus a person is presumed to have acted in good faith unless the contrary is proved and is not to be regarded as acting in bad faith by reason of his knowing that an act is beyond the powers of the directors under the company's constitution.

E. Pre-incorporation contracts

It is frequently necessary for the founders of a company to enter into contract on the intended company's behalf prior to the incorporation. It was held in *Kelner* v. *Baxter*[28] the company would not become liable on such a contract under the law of agency, because the founders have been acting as agents for a non-existing principal. However, the founders will be liable on

[26] Note *Ernest* v. *Nicholls* (1853) 6 HL 401 and European Communities Act 1970, ss. 4(3) and 9(4), and also R. Pennington, *Company Law*, 8th edn (London: Butterworths, 1999), p. 129.

[27] The Company Law Review Steering Group proposed that the doctrine of constructive notice should be abolished as was intended by (the enacted but not brought into force) s. 711A(1), but that no provision corresponding to s. 711A(2) should be brought into effect, see *Modern Company Law for a Competitive Economy: Capital Formation and Capital Maintenance* (1999), p. 19.

[28] (1866) 2CP 174.

such a contract. The company may however enter into a new agreement specifically adopting the terms of the preliminary or earlier control; the existence of such a new contract may sometimes be inferred from the relevant circumstances and the behaviour of the parties. It may also be possible for the company to invoke such a preliminary contract in accordance with the Contracts (Rights of Third Parties) Act 1999. The decision in *Newborne* v. *Sensolid* (GB) Ltd[29] is one in which the court decided and came to a different conclusion concerning the liability of a person acting for a non-existent company than the Court of Common Pleas did in *Kelner* v. *Baxter.*[30] In this case, it was found that where a contractual document is signed by a company, the agent's signature being added only to authenticate that of the company, neither party was liable on the contract. The subtle distinctions between these two cases are no longer of significance.

According to section 51 of the Companies Act 2006 (replacing section 36C of the Companies Act 1985), which is intended to implement Article 7 of the First Company Law Directive, any person purporting to act for a company or as agent for a company which has not been formed is personally liable on the contract, unless there is an express agreement to the contrary. The former section 36C of the Companies Act 1985 was held to have altered the law such that *Newborne* would now be decided differently. This follows from *Phonogram* v. *Lane.*[31] In that case the court also held that section 36C was not confined to the case where the company was in process of formation. Although this is not entirely clear, it would seem that anyone made personally liable on the contract would have the right to enforce it. Like section 36C, section 51 of the Companies Act 2006 also applies to deeds executed on behalf of the company before its incorporation.

F. Transfer proposals in the consultation document 'Completing the structure'

It will be remembered that the proposed Fourteenth Company Law Directive contains detailed rules governing the transfer of the registered office and the real seat of a company from one Member State to another without any need for liquidation or reincorporation. The Consultation Document from the Company Law Steering Group entitled 'Completing the Structure' makes proposals for a possible regime for migration both

[29] (1954) 1 QB 45. [30] (1866) L.R. 2 C.P. 174 (Common Pleas). [31] (1982) QB 938.

between Great Britain and non-EU jurisdictions and between England and Wales and Scotland, which are based on the provision of Articles which resemble those of the 1997 version of the Fourteenth Directive. No such proposals have been adopted, but the draft Fourteenth Directive has not yet been enacted.

III. Formation of private and public companies in France

Although French and Italian law recognise the difference between companies and partnerships, they are all called by the same name in each country, in France *sociétés* and in Italy *società*. Partnerships generally have unlimited liability, whilst companies usually have limited liability. Partnerships are referred to as companies with unlimited liability, *sociétés à risque non limité* and *società a responsabilità illimitata.* Companies with limited liability are referred to as *sociétés à risque limité* and *società a responsabilità limitata*. The distinction largely corresponds to the one made between personal companies and capital companies, where the personal companies are characterised by the role of their members and the capital companies characterised by the capital.

Personal companies and capital companies, whether they have limited or unlimited liability have legal personality and have to be registered. There are certain exceptions relating to the civil partnership, *société civile*,[32] and de facto partnership, *société de fait*, which do not have legal personality and are not registered, and there are certain other exceptions relating to entities subject to special regimes and used for the exercise of the professions.

The division between commercial and civil law is an important feature of both the Italian and French legal systems. The civil partnership, *société civile*, belongs to civil law[33] whereas partnership created as a matter of fact can be created in both civil and commercial law.

[32] Civil partnerships have increased in importance in France in recent years, and are for instance often used in the building industry and in the professions.

[33] The distinctions between civil and commercial partnerships have become of less importance in recent years. According to Art. 1857 of the Civil Code, the members of civil partnerships do not incur joint and several liability for the obligations of the partnership, but only proportional liability for them. The rule is different for in the case of commercial partnerships in which the members are jointly and severally liable for the partnership obligations. They are so liable in the case of civil partnerships engaged in the professions. Furthermore, the French courts have held that the members of the civil partnership may incur joint and several liability by reason of the nature of the transaction, or of the underlying obligation.

A. *The* société à responsabilité limitée (*SARL*)

The formation of a *société à responsabilité limitée* (SARL) must comply with the general rules applicable to all French commercial companies. Thus the company contract must be a valid one; there must be an express or implied intention of all the members to act together in pursuit of a common purpose (*affectio societatis*), and an intention to make profits. They may be formed to pursue any activities apart from insurance, and investments,[34] and also those of banks, pharmacists, and public entertainment. Since 2003, there are no requirements concerning the minimum capital of a French private company.[35] An SARL may have a single member[36] In this case it will change its name to EURL, *entreprise unipersonnelle à responsabilité limitée.* Its membership must not exceed 100; if it does so, the company must be converted into an SA within one year, unless within that period of time the number of members is reduced to one hundred or less. If neither of these events occurs, the company is automatically dissolved.[37] All the company's shareholders are required to execute its statutes, either personally or through the medium of a specially authorised agent.[38] The statutes or articles (there is one governing document) of the company may take the form of a notarised deed or a contract signed by the parties.[39] The articles must contain similar information to that required in the case of an SA, where relevant. They must indicate the kind of company chosen, the duration (which must not exceed 99 years) and its name, location, the objects and the capital of the company.[40]

Before the signature of the articles, a statement must be given to the shareholders of all transactions entered into in the name of the company, together with an indication of the extent to which the company is intended to be liable for them.[41] This statement must be attached to

[34] French Commercial Code, Art. L223-1.

[35] *Ibid.*, Art. L223-2, amended by the law of 1 August 2003. Before, the minimum capital of a SARL needed to be at least €7,500. The new provision constitutes an exception to the general rule that for capitalistic companies (or with limited liability) the legislation imposes a minimum capital and the total value of the consideration must reach at least the minimum fixed by the law.

[36] French Commercial Code, Art. L223-1.

[37] *Ibid.*, Art. L223-3. [38] *Ibid.*, Art. L223-6.

[39] This is generally assumed to be the case. See Decree No. 67-236, Art. 20, which addresses the possibility of a private deed.

[40] See the French Commercial Code, Art. L 210-2 and Decree No. 67-236, Art. 2.

[41] Decree No. 67-236, Art. 26(1).

the articles, and the signature of the statutes by the shareholders will imply that the company will be liable upon registration.[42] Furthermore, if the articles or a separate instrument authorises one of the shareholders or a manager to enter into additional transactions, the company will be liable on them on registration: such liability includes obligations under executory contracts.[43] If the articles of the company take the form of a contract signed by the shareholders, enough copies must be made for one to be kept at the company's head office, three copies for fulfilling requisite procedural formalities and, in addition, one for each member of the company.

As in the United Kingdom and Germany, the company acquires legal personality on registration. Two copies of the statutes must be delivered to the registrar of the commercial court where the company will have its principal registered office, together with the instrument appointing the managers (if they are not appointed in the articles); where there are contributions in kind, a report of the special valuer is necessary. The valuer is appointed by the future members unanimously or, if they do not find an agreement, by the president of the commercial court. The report is attached to the articles. Members can, unanimously, decide not to appoint a special valuer if the value of any consideration in kind does not exceed €7,500 and in any case that the amount of the consideration does not exceed fifty percent of the capital.[44] Members will be held jointly and severally liable to third parties for five years for the value attributed to the shares if they decide not to appoint a valuer or if they give an overestimation of consideration in relation to the report of the valuer. Consideration in kind for shares must be given to the company before it is registered, and shares paid for in cash or kind must be fully subscribed. One fifth of the issue of shares issued for cash must also be paid up. In all cases a declaration of compliance with necessary procedural requirements must also be sent to the registrar.

When these requirements have been completed, the company will be registered on the Register of Commerce and Companies and the registrar will place a notice of such registration in the Official Bulletin of Commercial Announcements, which is annexed to the Official Gazette of the French Republic. It is not possible to withdraw capital from the company's bank

[42] *Ibid.*, Art. 26(2). [43] *Ibid.*, Art. 26(3).
[44] French Commercial Code, Art. L223-9.

account before the registrar of the commercial court issues a registration statement, which is called *Récépisse k bis* or *Extrait k bis.*

B. The société anonyme *(SA)*

A *société anonyme* (SA) has a separate existence as a legal entity when it is registered with the Registry of Commerce and Companies. Before that time it only exists as an agreement between its shareholders and is incapable of exercising or being the subject of any right. Two different procedures exist for incorporation: a public company may be formed as a publicly held company (*constitution avec appel public à l'épargne*), when there is a public call for subscriptions and investors are informed of the opportunity to participate in the formation of the company in newspapers and, after subscribing the capital, convene a meeting for the purpose of signing the articles. An SA may also be formed as a non-publicly held company, (*constitution sans appel publique public à l'épargne*). There is no public call for subscriptions. The founding members create the company after subscribing to the capital and do not publicly call for investors to participate in the creation of the company. Practically all French SAs are formed at first as non-publicly held companies, and only a few of them continue to be converted into publicly held companies. Admission to the stock exchange is conditional on having published a number of annual accounts. The minimum capital is €37,000 for a non-publicly held company and €225,000 for a publicly held company,[45] except in the case of certain specially regulated corporations, which must have a special provision in their articles.[46] The minimum capital of such corporations may be less than €37,000. If the capital falls below the minimum amount, the company must be converted into another type of company or otherwise may be dissolved.[47]

In case of a call for subscriptions, at least one founding member must sign the company's draft articles and deposit them at the Register of commerce and companies.[48] The whole of the share capital must be subscribed before the signature of the articles and deposited at the Register. Half of the par value of shares issued against cash consideration must be paid at the time of subscription. The draft articles of the

[45] French Commercial Code, Art. L224-2.

[46] These include companies carrying on such activities as legal advice and accounting.

[47] French Commercial Code, Art. L224-2 para. 2.

[48] *Ibid.*, Art. L225-2. Detailed rules governing the rare case in which there is a call for subscriptions are contained in Arts. 58-71 of Decree 67-236, but are not further considered above.

company are prepared by its founders, and must have certain minimum contents.[49] These include:

(a) the names of the persons signing the articles, or on whose behalf they are signed; a minimum number of seven shareholders is required;[50]
(b) the form of the company;
(c) the name of the company, which must be followed or preceded by the words *société anonyme* (if the company has a two-tier board the relevant words are *société anonyme à directoire et conseil de surveillance*);
(d) the place of the registered office (this determines the nationality of the company subject to the reservation that in certain situations, the court may decide that the company's real seat is where the principal decisions concerning its activities are made, and that the company is not governed by French law);
(e) the corporate purpose (some activities may not be carried out by public limited companies, for example the operation of a chemical laboratory) and are reserved to private limited companies (SARLs) or ordinary partnerships (*sociétés en nom collectif*));
(f) the amount of the share capital;
(g) the duration of the company, which may not exceed 99 years (subject to extension by a resolution of an extraordinary general meeting);
(h) for each class of shares the number of shares issued, together with their nominal value, or the amount of capital they represent;
(i) whether the shares are in registered or bearer form;
(j) the identity of persons making contributions in kind, the valuation of such contributions, and the number of shares issued against these contributions;
(k) the names of shareholders enjoying special advantages (and a description thereof);
(l) the rules governing the composition, powers and functions of the company's organs;
(m) the rules applicable to the allocation of profits and liquidation surplus, and the creation of a special reserve; and
(n) any restrictions on share transfer.

[49] Note in particular French Commercial Code, Art. L210-2 and Decree 67-236, Art. 55.
[50] French Commercial Code, Art. L225-1.

The articles must be in writing, and can be executed either under seal or in notarial form. As soon as they are so executed in their final form between the founding shareholders or their authorised representatives, there is a binding agreement between those shareholders. The articles must be accompanied by an act of formation, which must be attached to the articles, and which mentions the intention of the future shareholders to participate in a company. Further documentation must be attached to the articles giving the names of the directors and of the statutory auditors, and the report of the special valuer on non-cash contributions, and a list of the transactions carried out on the company's behalf by its founders. Transactions which are thus annexed to the articles in this way become the liability of the company upon its registration with the Register of Commercial Companies, provided particulars of such transactions are made available to the shareholders at least three days before they execute the articles.[51] Undertakings which are made after the execution of the articles but before registration become binding on the company when the latter is registered provided that they have been made under and in accordance with a special power of attorney given by all shareholders.[52]

Following the signing of the articles, the persons who have been nominated as directors hold their first meeting in order to elect the chairman of the board and the executive officer. After such signature, an announcement must be published in a legal newspaper giving prescribed particulars concerning the future corporation.[53] Application for registration of the company must be made at the Commercial Court, by depositing with the registrar two copies of the articles, a declaration that the necessary legal formalities have been completed with, the documents appointing the directors and executive officers, a certificate of deposit and a list of subscribers in the case of cash contributions, and the report of the special valuer in the case of contributions in kind. Registration takes place through the medium of the local *Centre de Formalités des Entreprises*, which contacts the Register of Commerce and Companies and a number of other bodies. A special administrative form has to be completed for the purpose of registration, to which a number of attachments have to be made, including the birth certificates of all members of the board of directors (or supervisory board and executive board). The law of 1 August 2003 'for the economic initiative' has simplified to a great extent the formalities which have to be complied with when establishing

[51] Decree No. 67-236, Arts. 73 and 74(2). [52] *Ibid.*, Art. 74(3). [53] *Ibid.*, Art. 285.

a new company in France. The registration of the company is published in a national official legal newspaper. The registrar must issue a statement known as *Extrait kbis*, which is a matter of public record. The company will then be given identification numbers, and exists as a legal person.

IV. Formation of private and public companies in Germany

A. *Formation of private companies*

A GmbH may be formed by one or more natural or legal persons for any lawful purpose. The statutes must be executed in notarised form by all its founders,[54] and must contain particulars of the name and registered office of the company, its objects, the amount of its share capital and the nominal value of the shares taken by each shareholder in the capital, as well as any additional obligations placed on the shareholders apart from making the capital contributions.[55] Since an alteration of the law in 1998 the firm's name does not have to derive from the objects of the company or the personal name of the shareholders.[56] Also invented or wholly made-up words or a combination of numbers and letters can be used. The name must also contain the additional designation *mit beschrankter Haftung*, 'with limited liability'. The common abbreviation, GmbH suffices for this purpose.[57] The registered office must be in German territory: otherwise the company will not be registered.[58] Normally, the seat of the company will be determined by the articles.[59] As a general rule the articles have to stipulate the place where the company has its premises or head office.[60] The relationship between this rule and the EU rules on the freedom of establishment is discussed elsewhere in this book and also much discussed in German scholarship.[61] The purpose of the company must be set out clearly.[62] The minimum

[54] German Private Limited Liability Companies Act (GmbHG), para. 2(1).

[55] *Ibid.*, para. 3. See F. Kübler and H. D. Assmann, *Gesellschaftsrecht – Die privatrechtlichen Ordnungsstrukturen und Regelungsprobleme von Verbänden und Unternehmen*, 6th edn. (Heidelberg: C. F. Müller, 2006), p. 275.

[56] T. Raiser and R. Veil, *Recht der Kapitalgesellschaften*, 4th edn. (Munich: Vahlen, 2006), § 25, para. 2.

[57] German Private Limited Liability Companies Act, para. 4.

[58] *Ibid.*, para. 7. [59] *Ibid.*, para. 4a(1). [60] *Ibid.*, para. 4a(1).

[61] Raiser and Veil (n. 56), § 25, para. 14.

[62] German Private Limited Liability Companies Act, para. 1 and 3 Nr. 2. See for more details: Raiser and Veil (n. 56), § 25, para. 17.

amount of the share capital (*Stammkapital*) is €25,000.[63] Contributions for the shares may be in cash or in kind. If provision is made for contributions in kind (*Sacheinlagen*), the amount of the contribution must be stated, and the amount of the original subscription covered by it. A report by the members on the valuation procedure must be attached to the articles. If the contribution consists of the transfer of an existing business, a statement of the profits and losses of the last two financial years must be attached.[64]

The amounts of the share capital contribution by different shareholders may be different.[65] The total nominal value of the shares must correspond to the capital of the company in formation.

The application for registration may not be made until one quarter of the nominal value of each share to be paid in cash has been paid to the company.[66] Contributions in kind must be fully performed[67] before such application may take place.[68] The total amount of the cash contributions and the contributions in kind made prior to registration must be at least €12,500. If a one-man GmbH is formed the shareholder must give the company in addition to the above-mentioned minimum contributions a security for that part of the cash contributions which he has not yet paid.[69] The application for entry in the Commercial Register, which is made to the commercial court of the place where the registered office is situated, must be signed in notarised form by all managers.[70] Such signature will usually take place at the time when the articles are notarised. A GmbH must have at least one manager who must be a natural person of full legal capacity.[71] The first managers must be appointed in the articles of a company, or by means of a members' resolution.[72]

[63] *Ibid.*, para. 5(1). A 2005 proposal to decrease the minimum capital to €10,000 failed to achieve parliamentary adoption, but a later one having the same effect appears likely to be adopted.

[64] German Private Limited Liability Companies Act, para. 5(4).

[65] However each shareholder may only acquire one share on formation: German Private Limited Liability Companies Act, para. 5(2).

[66] *Ibid.*, para. 7(2).

[67] The question when this requirement is met is subject to extensive case law.

[68] German Private Limited Liability Companies Act, para. 7(3).

[69] *Ibid.*, para. 7(2). This requirement is likely to be repealed by new legislation reforming the law governing the GmbH.

[70] *Ibid.*, paras. 8 and 78. See also Raiser and Veil (n. 56), § 26, para. 44.

[71] German Private Limited Liability Companies Act, para. 6. The manager of an English or French private company may, by way of contrast, be a legal person.

[72] German Private Limited Liability Companies Act, paras. 6 and 46, No. 5.

The following particulars must be included in an application for registration:-

(a) a copy of the articles;
(b) the full business address of the company;
(c) a list of shareholders signed by the managers giving the name, address and date of birth [and occupation] of each shareholder, and the nominal value of his contribution;
(d) where contributions in kind are made, copies of contracts on which their approval is based, or which were concluded for the purpose of their performance;
(e) an assurance by the managers that there are no legal impediments to their appointment;
(f) an assurance by the managers that all non-cash contributions and the minimum payments required in respect of cash contributions in addition to the security in respect of outstanding cash contributions required in the case of one-man companies have been made or given prior to the filing of the application and are at the free disposal of the managers;
(g) a statement giving particulars of the power of representation of the managers;
(h) documentary evidence that any required government licence has been granted;
(i) particulars regarding the optional supervisory board if there is one.[73]

If at the date when the company is registered the value of a contribution in kind has fallen below that attributed to it in the articles, the court should refuse to register the company.[74] If it fails to do so because of misinformation or some oversight, then the contributor must pay the shortfall to the company in cash.[75] Similarly, if the value of the cash contributions paid or outstanding has been reduced below the value of the stipulated cash contributions, either at the date of application for registration or the date when the company was to be registered, then the court should reject the application for registration. If it fails to do so, then all shareholders are required to pay the shortfall in cash, in proportion to the amount of their contributions.[76]

[73] *Ibid.*, paras. 8 and 52(2). [74] *Ibid.*, para. 9c. [75] *Ibid.*, para. 9(1).
[76] *Official Journal of the German Supreme Court* (BGHZ), 80, 129, 136 ff.

The company comes into existence on being entered in the Commercial Register maintained by the commercial court. Publicity must be given to the registration of the company in *Bundesanzeiger* (the Federal Gazette) and one other newspaper determined by the Commercial Court.[77]

B. *Special rules applicable to one-man companies*[78]

If a GmbH has only one member, it cannot be registered until such time as at least one fourth of the contribution required to be paid in cash has been paid, and any contribution in kind which was agreed upon has been placed at the disposal of the company. The total value of the cash contribution plus any contribution in kind must be at least €12,500. Security must be provided in respect of any remaining part of the cash contribution which is uncalled.[79]

A GmbH may become a one-man company by reason of the consolidation of all shares in the hands of one shareholder. If this takes place within three years of the registration of the company, the sole shareholder must within three months of such consolidation either pay all outstanding cash contributions, or provide the company with security in respect of the amounts so outstanding, or transfer his shares to a third party.[80] If the obligations contained in paragraph 19(4) GmbHG are not fulfilled, the court of the Commercial Register may declare that this failure has occurred and that if the position is not rectified within a given period of time the company will be dissolved.[81]

C. *Liabilities in respect of pre-registration activities*

The potential importance of liabilities in respect of pre-registration activities arises from the fact that it takes some time to get a company registered in Germany. Furthermore, if a contribution to a company in

[77] German Private Limited Liability Companies Act, para. 10 and German Commercial Code (HGB), paras. 10–11.

[78] See Kübler and Assmann (n. 55), 360 ff.

[79] German Private Limited Liability Companies Act, para. 7(2) sentence 3. See also Raiser and Veil (n. 55), § 26, para. 84 ff. The latter requirement is likely to be repealed.

[80] German Private Limited Liability Companies Act, para. 19(4). The provision is likely to be repealed.

[81] German Voluntary Jurisdiction Act (FGG), para. 144b.

process of formation is one to a trading company, the latter cannot be expected to suspend activities while registration is in progress.

The liabilities of managers and shareholders of a GmbH in respect of pre-registration activities have given rise to considerable controversies.[82] It is generally agreed that one must distinguish between the situation which occurs prior to the notarial authentication of the articles, and that which occurs between such notarisation and the registration of the company. [83] Prior to such notarisation, the intending company's shareholders are treated like members of a partnership. It is not yet settled whether the partnership is to be considered as a commercial law partnership (OHG) or a civil law partnership (GbR). The aim of the partnership is the formation of a GmbH. Whether this is a commercial purpose within the meaning of paragraph 105 HGB depends on the purpose of the GmbH. This distinction, however, plays a minor role since the imposed liability regime is almost identical, especially after the members start business.[84] It is generally agreed that they are jointly and severally liable in respect of any obligation arising out of the partnership's activities, whether or not they act within the scope of their authority.[85] Individuals who enter into transactions on behalf of the company before its articles are recorded by a notary will also be jointly and severally liable, unless the agreement with the third party provides otherwise.[86] Such liabilities remain in principle unaffected by the notarial recording of the articles, or the registration of the company.[87]

Once the articles have been duly executed, a pre-incorporation company (*Vorgesellschaft*) is deemed to come into existence, to which the provisions of the GmbHG and the articles will apply, so far as consistent with the fact that the company has not yet been registered.[88] In certain earlier Supreme Court[89] decisions, it has been held that the founders are

[82] See Raiser and Veil, *Recht der Kapitalgesellschaften*, § 26, paras. 94 ff.; K. Schmidt, *Gesellschaftsrecht* (Cologne: Heymanns, 2002), § 34 III.

[83] Generally on this issue in English: Volhard/Stengel, *German Limited Liability Company* (Chichester: Wiley & Sons, 1997), pp. 26 ff. and 31 ff.

[84] Schmidt, *Gesellschaftsrecht*, § 34, III, 2. [85] German Commercial Code, para. 128.

[86] This liability is based on the general principles of civil law. Individuals not acting within their authority of representing a partnership or in the name of a (non-existing) German private company can be liable according to German Civil Code, para. 179. See for more details and other examples: Schmidt, *Gesellschaftsrecht*, § 34, III 2 c.

[87] BGH NJW 1998, 1645; BGH NJW 2001, 1042.

[88] Schmidt, *Gesellschaftsrecht*, § 34, III 3.

[89] 'Supreme Court' denotes the *Bundesgerichtshof* (BGH) or German Federal High Court of Justice. Is should be noted that there is also a Federal Constitutional Court, the *Bundesverfassungsgericht* (BVerfG).

liable for obligations arising from activities between the time of execution of the articles and registration, but that such liability only extends to the amount of their contributions.[90] The Supreme Court in its decision of 1997 stated that founders must face an unlimited liability which is not directly to creditors of the company but primarily to the company (*Innenverhältnis*).[91] The Court held that limited liability during the pre-incorporation phase would not be consistent with the liability scheme arising upon incorporation. In addition to that, the founders use a company format with limited liability but in the pre-incorporation phase the pre-conditions for such a liability have not been verified by the commercial court.

Beside the liability of the founders, there is also a liability of the acting person. According to paragraph 11(2) of the GmbHG, persons acting in the name of the company prior to registration will be jointly and severally liable in respect of the relevant transaction. This liability, however, terminates when the company is duly registered unless the person acting on behalf of the company did so without authorisation. After incorporation the preincorporation company becomes a legal person. The personal liability of the founders terminates. Instead of the liability mentioned above the founders have to face a liability for shortfall (*Unterbilanzhaftung*),[92] where the assets of the company are insufficient to cover its capital.

D. Formation of an AG

The minimum number of members of an AG (*Aktiengesellschaft*) is now one.[93] The formation of an AG entails a complex process which must be accompanied by the subscription for all the company's shares which must not be issued until the company is entered in the commercial register.[94] Such an issue may be for cash, or be made in respect of contributions in kind, such as an existing business.[95]

[90] BGHZ 65.378, 382; BGHZ 72.45, 49 ff.; BGHZ 80.182, 183 ff.

[91] BGHZ 134, 333. See for more details: Schmidt, *Gesellschaftsrecht*, § 34 III 3 c.

[92] BGHZ 80, 129.

[93] German Public Limited Liability Companies Act, para. 2. Cf. F. Kübler and H. D. Assmann, *Gesellschaftsrecht – Die privatrechtlichen Ordnungsstrukturen und Regelungsprobleme von Verbänden und Unternehmen*, 6th edn (Heidelberg: CF Müller, 2006), p. 275.

[94] German Public Limited Liability Companies Act, paras. 41(4).

[95] *Ibid.*, para. 27.

The formation of a company commences with the preparation of the articles and minutes of formation in a notarial deed,[96] and finishes with its registration in the commercial register.[97] The articles (which are the single constitutional document) must be signed by the founder(s). The founder(s) do not have to appear personally before the attorney who prepares the statutes, but may do so through a representative who is authorised by means of a notarised power of attorney.[98] The minimum content of the articles is set out in paragraph 23(3) of the *Aktiengesetz* as follows:

(a) the name of the company. This must contain the designation *Aktiengesellschaft* or a generally comprehensible abbreviation thereof, such as AG.[99] The name does not have to be derived from the objects of the company or the personal name of the shareholders anymore;[100]
(b) the registered office of the company, which must be within Germany, and be a place where the company maintains an operation or where its management is situated, or its administration is carried on;[101]
(c) the company's purpose, if the company is engaged in trade or industry, the articles must explain what kinds of products or goods are to be produced and traded;
(d) the amount of share capital, which must be denominated in euros.[102] The minimum capital is €50,000.[103] Shares may be issued either as shares having a par value (*Nennbetragsaktien*) or as no par shares (*Stückaktien*);[104]
(e) the articles must give particulars of the subdivision of the share capital into par value or no par value shares. In the case of par value shares, they must specify their par value, and the number of shares of each par value. In the case of no par value shares they must specify their number, and in addition, if more than one class of shares exists, the classes of shares and the number of shares in each class;
(f) the registered or bearer nature of the shares;

[96] *Ibid.*, paras. 2 and 23(1).
[97] *Ibid.*, para. 41(1). See for more details: Raiser and Veil, *Recht der Kapitalgesellschaften*, § 11, para. 7; Kübler and Assmann *Gesellschaftsrecht – Die privatrechtlichen Ordnungsstrukktcuren* (above, n. 93), 187 ff.
[98] German Public Limited Liability Companies Act, para. 23(1) sentence 2.
[99] *Ibid.*, para. 4.
[100] German Commercial Code para. 18 f.; Raiser and Veil, *Recht der Kapitalgesellschaften* (above, n. 97), § 10, para. 2.
[101] *Ibid.*, para. 5(2). [102] *Ibid.*, para. 6. [103] *Ibid.*, para. 7. [104] *Ibid.*, para. 8(1).

(g) the number of members of the management board or the rules for determining such number;
(h) the journals in which company announcements are to be made. Such announcements must also be published in the electronic Federal Gazette (Bundesanzeiger). Additionally, the articles can provide for other journals or electronic media.[105]

The articles may contain additional provisions, except in relation to matters which are conclusively dealt with in the AktG.[106] Details of any obligation arising under agreements concerning special benefits granted to a particular shareholder or a third person, formation expenses, contributions in kind (*Sacheinlagen*) and existing or future assets to be acquired by the company (*Sachübernahmen*)[107] must be set out in the statutes.[108]

The appointment of the annual auditors of the future company for the first fiscal year and of the initial supervisory board (*Aufsichtsrat*) must take the form of a notarial deed.[109] Thus, the founders may make such an appointment at the same time as when the capital is subscribed and the statutes executed (which must be by a notarial document). There will be no employee representation in the first supervisory board,[110] but there will be such representation in the one which succeeds it at the first general meeting of the company, which decides on the release of the directors from liability (*Entlastung*) if an existing business employing more than 500 persons is being incorporated.[111] The first management board is appointed by the supervisory board.[112] At least 25 per cent of the lowest issue price must be paid on shares subscribed for by cash together with any premium before registration.[113] The management board is

105 *Ibid.*, para. 25.
106 *Ibid.*, para. 23(5). They may depart from or make different provisions from those of the Act only where the latter explicitly so permits. See for the so-called '*Satzungsstrenge*': M. Lutter, *Gestaltungsfreiheit im Gesellschaftsrecht: Deutschland, Europa und USA; 11. ZGR-Symposion "25 Jahre ZGR"* (Berlin: de Gruyter, 1998); H. Fleischer, 'Gesetz und Vertrag als alternative Problemlösungsmodelle im Gesellschaftsrecht' (2004) 168 ZHR 673. The difference between the situation in this regard in Germany and the UK, where the founders have significantly more freedom, should be emphasised.
107 The term *Sachübernahmen* is usually used to describe assets which the company acquires for valuable consideration from a shareholder or third party which do not give rise to rights in the company's shares, as do *Sacheinlagen* (contributions in kind). An asset which is acquired by a company or a contribution in kind to one, may be of an existing business or part thereof.
108 German Public Limited Liability Companies Act, paras. 26 and 27.
109 *Ibid.*, para. 30(1). 110 *Ibid.*, para. 30(2). 111 *Ibid.*, para. 30(3).
112 *Ibid.*, para. 30(4). 113 *Ibid.*, para. 36a(1).

responsible for obtaining this payment, which may not therefore take place until after the board has been appointed.

Paragraph 36a(2) AktG which deals with contributions in kind, is not clearly drafted.[114] The first sentence of this provision stipulates that contributions in kind must be made in full. The second sentence stipulates that where the contribution in kind consists, as it very frequently does, of the obligation to transfer assets to the company, this obligation must be fulfilled within five years of the registration of the company. The first sentence would seem to apply to such contributions as leases of assets. After such contributions in kind have been made or promised, the founders will have to prepare a written report (*Gründungsbericht*) on the formation of the company.[115] This report must cover the whole formation process, and contain certain details in respect of contributions in kind and acquisitions of assets.[116] If a business is being transferred to the company, accounts for the last two years are necessary.[117] The members of both boards of the future company are also required to make a formal examination of the foundation process. Furthermore, under certain special circumstances a special auditor (*Gründungsprüfer*) must be appointed by the court.[118] These are where there have been contributions in kind or acquisitions of assets (*Sachübernahmen*); where a founder is a member of either of the boards; where a member of either board subscribes for shares; and where a member of either board obtained a promise of preferential treatment or compensation or remuneration in connection with the formation of the company.

The examination by the members of the two boards and by any special formation auditor are essentially concerned with the accuracy of the formation report, and the adequacy of the value of assets acquired or contributed in kind.[119] A written report is made of each audit, which must describe each asset which has been contributed or acquired, and describe the valuation methods used in determining the value thereof.[120] One copy each of the report must be submitted to the court and the management board.[121] After the completion of the above steps, an

[114] Note in this sense U. Hüffer, *Aktiengesetz*, 7th edn (Munich: Beck, 2006), para. 36a, n. 4. See also Raiser and Veil, *Recht der Kapitalgesellschaften*, § 11, para. 22.

[115] German Public Limited Liability Companies Act, para. 32 ff. See for the details of the 'Gründungsprüfung': Raiser and Veil (above n. 114), § 11, para. 25; Kübler and Assmann, *Gesellschaftsrecht – Die privatrechtlichen Ordnungsstrukturen*, pp. 190 ff.

[116] German Public Limited Liability Companies Act, para. 34.

[117] *Ibid.*, para. 32(2). [118] *Ibid.*, para. 33(2). [119] *Ibid.*, para. 34(1).

[120] *Ibid.*, para. 34(2). [121] *Ibid.*, para. 34(3).

application for registration is made by the district registry of the appropriate commercial court. Except in the case of contributions in kind such application for registration may only be made after the amount called on each share has been paid up, and to the extent not already utilised for the payment of taxes and fees arising in connection with the formation, is at the free disposal of the management board.[122] If the company is a single-member one, the founder must in addition provide security for that part of the cash contribution which exceeds the amount called upon such shares.[123] The registrar of the commercial court will require evidence that these requirements have been complied with.

The application for registration should be accompanied by the following documents:[124]

(a) the articles and the deeds establishing the articles and relating to the subscription for the shares by the founder;
(b) as far as paragraphs 26 and 27 are concerned, the agreements on which the stipulations are based, or which were entered into in the execution of them, and particulars of the formation expenses to be met by the company; such particulars shall set out the kind and amount of remuneration and the recipients of such remuneration;
(c) the documents concerning the appointment of the management board and the supervisory board;
(d) the formation report and the audit reports of the members of the management and supervisory boards, together with underlying documentation;
(e) if the corporate purpose of the undertaking or any other provision of the statutes requires government approval, the documents providing for such approval; and
(f) according to paragraph 42 AktG, if the company has only one shareholder or if its shares are divided between such a shareholder and the company, particulars must be given to the registrar of the surname, first name, date of birth and domicile of such shareholder.

The registration of the company confers legal personality upon it.[125] Although this is difficult to reconcile with the rules relating to pre-incorporation transactions[126] which are discussed below and which include special rules for the assumption of pre-incorporation obligations by the company, the general view seems to be that in principle a company

[122] *Ibid.*, para. 36(2) sentence 1. [123] *Ibid.*, para. 36(2) sentence 2.
[124] *Ibid.*, para. 37(4). [125] *Ibid.*, paras. 1(1) and 41(1). [126] *Ibid.*, para. 41(2).

acquires all rights and liabilities agreed upon by the founders in the statutes.[127] However, in some circumstances because of the defective power of representation of the members of the management board, the company may not be bound by a particular pre-incorporation transaction and that in such a case paragraph 41(2) would remain useful.

E. Special rules relating to the one-man AG[128]

The special rules relating to outstanding cash contributions contained in paragraph 36(2) AktG correspond with those contained in paragraph 7(2) GmbHG, which have been considered above, as have the detailed particulars required by paragraph 42 AktG to be furnished for the register. Such particulars will also have to be furnished if a company initially formed as a multi-member company eventually comes to have only one shareholder, or if its shares are owned by such a shareholder and the company itself. There appears to be a good deal of academic discussion as to the nature of a single-member company before registration. Some writers take the view that it is an economic entity having partial legal capacity, whilst others adopt the view that it is a special property of the founder subject to the reservation that the pre-incorporation company is suitably organised.

F. Liability in respect of pre-incorporation transactions

Once the shares have been subscribed and the articles have been executed the company becomes a pre-incorporation one (*Vorgesellschaft*) capable of holding assets, to which certain of the provisions of the *Aktiengesetz* apply, although the entity has no legal personality. Persons acting in the name of an AG prior to registration are made jointly and severally liable.[129] However, paragraph 41(2) AktG provides that if the company shall assume obligations entered into in its name prior to its registration by agreement with the debtor (i.e. the person acting on behalf of the future company) by substituting itself for such debtor, the validity of such an assumption of obligations shall not require the consent of the

[127] Note in this respect, Hüffer, *Aktiengesetz*, § 41, para. 2, and see BGHZ, 70, 132 and BGHZ, 80, 129 and 137.

[128] See Schmidt, *Gesellschaftsrecht*, § 26, III, 2 c.

[129] German Public Limited Liability Companies Act, para. 41(1).

creditor (i.e. the other party to the transaction) provided that such assumption shall be agreed upon and communicated to the creditor by the company or the debtor within three months of the registration of the company.[130] As indicated above, paragraph 41(2) now appears of marginal importance. According to paragraph 41(3) AktG, the company may in no event assume obligations arising under agreements regarding special benefits, or contributions in kind or acquisitions of assets which have not been stipulated in the articles.[131]

V. Formation of public and private companies in Italy

A. Formation of public companies

The rules governing the formation of a public company (*Società per Azioni*, SpA) are very similar to those governing the formation of a private company (*Società a Responsabilità Limitata*, SRL). The latter type of entity was introduced much later than the SpA, and it appears convenient to consider the formation of an SpA first of all. The rules applicable to the formation of companies are stated by Article 2325 *bis* to apply also to companies which have recourse to the market for venture capital, insofar as the law does not provide otherwise. Such companies are defined as quoted companies and companies whose shares are sufficiently widely held by the public. Companies having more than 200 members are within this definition.

An Italian SpA and SRL may set out its constitution in two documents, the deed of incorporation (*atto costitutivo*) and articles. Even if the articles containing the rules governing the operation of the company are set out in a separate instrument, they are considered to be an integral part of the deed of incorporation and thus must be attached to it. In case of conflicting provisions between the rules of the deed of incorporation and those of the statutes, the deed prevails. They have to be deposited together with the Registrar of Enterprises for the place where the company's registered office is situated within twenty days of their execution. The steps in the formation of a SpA involve the preparation (stipulation) of the deed of incorporation, its deposit at the Register of Enterprises, and registration at the latter Registry.

The stipulation (preparation) of the deed of incorporation can take place in two different ways:

[130] *Ibid.*, para. 41(2). [131] *Ibid.*, para. 41(3).

(1) Simultaneous incorporation (*Stipulazione simultanea*);
(2) Incorporation by public subscription[132] (*Stipulazione per pubblica sottoscrizione*).

The first method involves the subscription of the company's initial capital in its entirety by its founders. This rather complicated serial method of formation of companies is rarely used. It consists of a presentation to the public of a prospectus of incorporation. Investors subscribe the shares through a public or a private deed authenticated by a notary and pay a quarter of the nominal value of each share before the deadline set by the promoters. The following steps are the attendance at a constitutive meeting at which at least half of the shareholders have to be present, and each of them has one vote irrespective of the number of shares subscribed. Then follows the agreement on the deed of incorporation.

The deed of incorporation of an SpA must be in the form of a public document executed by the founders (the company may have a single member), in the presence of a notary (Civil Code, Article 2328). It must indicate:

(1) the name and surname, the place and date of birth, the domicile (or seat) and citizenship of the members, and of the promoters if any, and the number of shares subscribed by each of them;
(2) the name of the company, which must include the words *società per azioni* or the abbreviation SpA and the address of its registered office, and if applicable, its branch office;
(3) the nature of the company's business (*l'oggetto sociale*);
(4) the amount of the subscribed capital and the amount actually paid up, the number of shares and their nominal value. The minimum capital of a SpA is €120,000. For some particular kinds of companies a higher minimum capital is required: for instance banks and financial companies[133];
(5) the number of shares subscribed by each shareholder, whether they are in registered or bearer form; and their method of issue or transfer;
(6) the value of assets contributed in kind for the allotment of shares;
(7) the rules according to which the profits will be apportioned, including provisions for the benefit of founders and promoters;

[132] Italian Civil Code, Arts. 2333–6.
[133] See Italian legislative decree 385/1993, Arts. 14 and 106, so-called *Tub, Testo unico delle leggi in materia bancaria e creditizia*.

(8) the system of management adopted, the number of directors and their powers, indicating those who have the power of representing the company;
(9) the number of members of the committee of auditors.
(10) The names of the first directors and auditors (or of the members of the supervisory board if the two tier board model is chosen) and of persons entrusted with the external audit of the accounts;
(11) The duration of the company; if this is for an indefinite period of time, the time limit, which may not be more than twelve months, after which a member may withdraw with six months' notice; and
(12) The amount of formation expenses.[134]

As already indicated, the method of simultaneous incorporation involves the founder in subscribing for the whole of the share capital,[135] and is in common use. The less common method of formation through public subscription is dealt with in Articles 2333–6 of the Civil Code. The method of formation involves the public subscription on the basis of a prospectus required by Article 2333(1). The subscription of shares must be evidenced by a public notarial act or an authorised private deed. Once the subscriptions have been made, time is given to the subscribers to make payments which must not exceed one month. Once the time limit has expired, a meeting of subscribers is called by the promoters (ie the founders who have signed the prospectus) within twenty days of the expiration of the time limit for payment.[136] The meeting of subscribers has the functions set out in Article 2335 which includes ascertaining the existence of the conditions necessary for the formation of the company, decision upon the contents of the deed of incorporation and the articles, and the appointment of directors, members of the committee of auditors or the supervisory board. Where provision is made for an external auditor, they are appointed by the meeting of subscribers. This meeting is validly constituted in the presence of half the subscribers. Each subscriber has one vote, irrespective of the number of shares he has subscribed for.

The consent of all subscribers is required to amend the conditions set out in the prospectus. According to Article 2336, once the requirements of Article 2335 have been complied with, those present at the meeting

[134] Italian Civil Code, Art. 2328(1). [135] *Ibid.*, Art. 2329(1) al 1.

[136] *Ibid.*, Art. 2334. The promoters may bring an action against the subscribers if the time limit expires without results or release them from their obligations. If such an action is taken, the company cannot be formed until disposal of the subscribed shares.

execute the articles which are deposited for registration at the Register of Enterprises in accordance with Article 2330.

Contributions for shares may be in cash or in kind. At the subscription of the deed of incorporation, at least 25 per cent of cash contributions must be deposited in a bank.[137] In case of a single shareholder company, the whole amount must be deposited.[138] If it is not, the single shareholder is personally liable for any obligation arising until the payment.

On each share the amount outstanding for payment is indicated.[139] Once the company is formed, the directors have the right to ask the shareholder to pay the residual cash contributions at any time, whatever the provisions of the articles. The original subscribers are still liable for the payment of the balance of the share value, even after transferring them to somebody else, for a period of three years from the registration of notice of the share transfer in the company's register book of members. The original subscribers' liability is residual, since he can be asked for the payment only when the actual holder of the share is unable to pay.[140]

As far as contributions in kind are concerned, the founders must obtain a report from an expert appointed by the President of the local civil court as to the value of any consideration in kind to be given for the company shares.[141] Since shares cannot be issued at a discount,[142] the report must demonstrate that the value of the consideration is at least equal to the nominal value of the shares to be allotted for it. The evaluations contained in the report must be verified or revised by the directors within 180 days of the incorporation of the company. If it results that the value of the contributions in kind was lower than the value for which contributions were made by more than one fifth, the company must reduce its capital in proportion by annulling the shares which are not covered. However, a contributing member may pay the balance of cash outstanding or resign from the company. If one essential element of those described above is missing, the notary can refuse to draft the deed of incorporation. After the incorporation procedure has been completed the notary must deposit the deed of incorporation within twenty days with the office of the Register of Enterprises – together with the documents showing payment of at least one quarter of the cash contributions, the experts report on contributions in kind and any authorisation required for the formation of the company – together with the application for the registration.[143] If the notary does not comply with

[137] Italian Civil Code, Art. 2342. [138] *Ibid.*, Art. 2342. [139] *Ibid.*, Art. 2354(2) no. 4.
[140] *Ibid.*, Art. 2356. [141] *Ibid.*, Art. 2343. [142] *Ibid.*, Art. 2346. [143] *Ibid.*, Art. 2330(1).

these rules, the directors or any single shareholder can deposit the deed of incorporation at the register and apply for registration. The officials of the Registry of Enterprises are required to ascertain whether the conditions required for the formation of the company have been complied with. If they find that this is the case, they will direct that the company shall be registered.[144] If the company has a branch, its deed of incorporation must also be deposited with the Register of Enterprises where the branch is situated.[145] Once the company is registered in the Register, it acquires legal personality.[146]

Persons who enter into transactions in the name of the company before it is registered are jointly and severally liable without limitation to the other contracting party in respect of such transactions. Such joint and several liability is also imposed upon a sole founding member and those of the members who, in accordance with the deed of incorporation or a separate instrument, have decided upon, authorised or consented to pre-incorporation transactions.[147] A company may become a party to a pre-incorporation transaction if it ratifies it after registration of the company, in which case it will become liable to the other party or parties to the transaction jointly with that (or those) previously liable to such party or parties.[148]

The issue and sale of shares prior to the formation of the company is prohibited and has no effect.[149] A call for subscriptions is also prohibited, except in the case of stipulations for public subscription.

B. *Formation of private companies in Italy*

One of the features of the recent legislation was that the private company was more clearly differentiated from the public company. However the rules governing the formation of SRLs are rather similar to those governing the formation of SpAs. In fact, Articles 2329–31 of the Italian Civil Code, concerning the conditions for the constitution, deposit of the deed of incorporation and registration of companies and effects of the registration are applicable to both kinds of companies. Both of them can be formed with only one member. The minimum capital is €10,000, as opposed to the €120,000 required for the SpA.[150] These shares may be of different amounts, in accordance with the contributions made by the

144 *Ibid.*, Art. 2330(2). 145 *Ibid.*, Arts. 2299 and 2330(3).
146 *Ibid.*, Art. 2331(1). 147 *Ibid.*, Art. 2331(2). 148 *Ibid.*, Art. 2331(3).
149 *Ibid.*, Art. 2331(5). 150 *Ibid.*, Art. 2463(2) sentence 4.

shareholders.[151] These shares will not be in registered or in bearer form, as the shares in an SRL cannot be represented by negotiable share certificates,[152] and cannot be transferred by endorsement and delivery. Only SRLs which so choose, or which for two consecutive financial years exceed two of the limits set out in Article 2435 *bis*, are required to have a board of auditors (i.e. internal auditors).

These limits are that the total amount of the assets does not exceed €3,125,000; the turnover does not exceed €250,000 and the average number of employees does not exceed fifty.

The requirements governing the contents of the deed of incorporation of an SRL are rather similar, although less detailed than those applicable to an SpA. The rules governing an SRL are contained in only one document, the deed of incorporation, while an SpA is organised on the basis of two document, the deed of incorporation and the articles. In order to obtain incorporation, an SRL, must be registered at the Registry of Enterprises.[153] If shares are allotted for a non-cash consideration, this has to be valued by an expert, as it is the case of the SpA. However, in contrast with the SpA, the expert does not need to be appointed by the court.[154] As is also the case with an SpA, the share capital must be fully subscribed, the detailed rules contained in Articles 2464 and 2465 of the Civil Code concerning contributions for shares complied with,[155] and any necessary authorisation obtained before the company can be registered.[156] The contributions in cash can be substituted, in an SRL, by drawing up a policy of insurance or a stand-by letter of credit.[157] In the latter cases the shareholder has the right at any time to pay the amount of cash corresponding to his subscription.

VI. Formation of private and public companies in Spain

A. Formation of private companies in Spain

The differences between the rules applicable to the formation of private and public companies in Spain are not so marked as those which are

[151] *Ibid.*, Art. 2468(2).
[152] *Ibid.*, Art. 2468(1). For this reason, shares in an SRL are sometimes translated into convertible bonds.
[153] Italian Civil Code, Art. 2463(2) which makes reference to Art. 2331.
[154] *Ibid.*, Art. 2343(1) (public companies) and Art. 2465(1) (private companies).
[155] These rules respectively govern cash contributions and contributions in kind.
[156] Italian Civil Code, Art. 2463(3), which makes reference to Art. 2329 (as well as to Arts. 2330–2 and 2341).
[157] *Ibid.*, Art. 2464(4).

applicable to the formation of these types of companies in France and Germany. Spanish private companies (*sociedades de responsabilidad limitada*) were introduced in Spain by the law of 17 July 1953, which underwent amendment by Act 19/1989 of 25 July 1989. Spanish law governing private companies (*sociedades de responsabilidad limitada*) was substantially reformed by Act 2/1995 of 23 March 1995, and was further reformed by Act 7 2003.[158] This type of company is considered separately below.

Like a public company, a private company is formed by a notarial deed of incorporation, which must be executed by the founders who are required to subscribe to the totality of the participations in the company. The notarial deed is required to include particulars of the members, or of the sole member (there is now no maximum number of members except in the case of the new type of a small private company introduced by Act 7/2003, the SLNE); a statement of intent to form a *sociedad de responsabilidad limitada* (SRL or SL); the contributions of each member and the shares assigned in payment; the articles (*estatutos*) of the company; a determination of the specific method of initial administrative organisation should the articles provide for particular alternatives; and the identity of the person or persons initially charged with the management and representation of the company.[159]

The notarial deed may, in addition include such provisions and conditions as the members deem appropriate, provided that they are not contrary to the law or the basic principles governing private limited liability companies. The articles must contain at least the following matters:

(a) the name of the company, which must be expressed either as a business name or a company name, to which must be added the words *sociedad de responsabilidad limitada* (SRL) or *sociedad limitada* (SL);
(b) the purpose and activities of the company;
(c) the closing date of its financial year;
(d) the company's registered office;
(e) the company's capital, the method of dividing the capital into shares (*participaciones*), their par value and relevant numbering;
(f) the method or methods of organising the management of the company, the appointment of administrators to represent the company

[158] On the differences between the rules applicable to the formation of private and public companies in Spain, see R. Uría and A. Menendez (dir.), *Curso de derecto mercantil* (2nd ed, Madrid 2006) pp. 827–845 and 1031–1162.

[159] Law governing SRL of 1995, Art. 12(2) as amended.

as well as the powers granted to them within the limits stipulated by law.[160]

After the execution of the notarial deed, this has to be recorded in the Commercial Register. The company acquires legal personality on being entered in the Register.[161]

The minimum capital of an SRL is €3,012. This must be fully paid up prior to incorporation.[162] Contributions to an SRL must either be in cash, or given a value in euros. Monetary contributions to an SRL have to be verified before the notary by obtaining a certificate from a bank or financial institution certifying that the money has been deposited in a bank account opened on behalf of the SRL.[163] Contributions in kind to an SRL do not require appraisal by an independent valuer appointed by the Commercial Registry, as is the case with public companies (*sociedades anónimas*, SA). However, the contributor is deemed to warrant that such contributions are free from any defects in title in accordance with the rules set out in the Civil Code. If the contribution consists of the assignment of a debt, the contributor is responsible for its existence and the solvency of the debtor.[164] If the contribution consists of a business, the provisions of the Civil Code are once again applicable concerning the statutory warranty that such contribution is free from any defects in title.[165] The statutory warranties described in this paragraph are also applicable to public companies.

Furthermore, by Article 21 of the law governing SRL of 1995, members who make contributions in kind shall be jointly and severally liable to the company and its creditors for the value of the contributions in kind set out in the notarial documents. Such liability shall expire five years after the date of the relevant contribution.[166]

B. Single member private companies

The law governing SRL of 1995 also contains certain provisions concerning single member limited liability companies, which are different from those

[160] *Ibid.*, Article 13. The name requires the consent of the Central Commercial Registry and if available, may be reserved for 15 months.

[161] *Ibid.*, Art. 11(1). [162] *Ibid.*, Art. 4. [163] *Ibid.*, Art. 19(2).

[164] Law governing SRL of 1993, Arts. 18(2) and 20(2) and Law governing SA of 1989, Art. 39(1) and (2).

[165] Law governing SRL of 1995, Art. 18(2).

[166] *Ibid.*, Art. 21. Art. 21(5) provides that persons relying on an expert valuation of non-monetary contributions in accordance with Art. 38 of the law of 1989 on the SA shall not be jointly and severally liable.

which are applicable to single member public limited companies. The formation of a sole member limited liability company must be evidenced in a notarial deed and recorded in the Commercial Registry. The entry in the register must expressly state the identity of the sole member.[167]

C. *Liabilities in respect of pre-incorporation transactions*

An SRL in the process of formation is subject to the provisions of Articles 15 and 16 of the law governing SA of 1989, as amended.[168] Persons carrying on any activity or entering into any contracts on behalf of a corporation before it is registered in the Commercial Registry are jointly and severally liable for them, unless the effectiveness of such acts was made conditional on the company's registration and where relevant, its later assumption of liability. A private company in the process of formation is liable for the acts and transactions necessary for the registration of the company and for the activities and agreements entered into by directors undertaken within the power granted to them in the notarial deed of incorporation in the period prior to registration. It is also liable for matters agreed to under any specific mandate given to persons designated for the purpose by all the shareholders. However, its liability is limited to paid-up capital, and the shareholders are liable for the amount they have agreed to contribute.[169]

The liability for the activities and contracts mentioned in the above paragraph begins with the company's registration. It can also be held bound in respect of other pre-incorporation transactions adopted during the three months period following registration. In both events, the joint and several liability of the shareholders, directors and representatives mentioned above ceases.

D. *Simplification of incorporation procedures*

Law No. 4/2003 is intended to simplify the incorporation procedure for private limited liability companies intended to operate small businesses. It may prove useful for certain such entities. Law No. 7/2003 modifies Law No. 2/1995 by incorporating a new chapter 12, consisting of fifteen sections. Articles 130–144 provide that companies known as new companies will be regulated as special categories of private limited liability

[167] *Ibid.*, Art. 126(1). [168] *Ibid.*, Art. 11(3).

[169] The liabilities mentioned in the present paragraph are set out in Art. 15(1) and (2) of the Law of 1989, on public companies, as amended.

companies. According to Article 131, the name of such a company is required to state the surname and first name of one of the founding members. The permissible objects are set out in Article 132: these include agriculture, fishing and the provision of professional services. Other activities will need to be approved by the registrar. Only natural persons may be shareholders, and the maximum number of members is five. A person who was a sole member of a private limited company could not become a sole member in such a company. The incorporation of the company is dealt with in Article 136 which stipulates that this shall take place by means of the execution of a deed before a notary public and due registration. According to Article 135, the maximum share capital is €3012 and the maximum €21,202. This may be paid in cash only. According to Article 139, the management of the company would be carried on by a sole director or board of directors.

An order was made on 4 June 2003 on the content of the articles for the new company. These are intended as guidelines and would for example permit the board and directors to assume powers to create or change the addresses of subsidiaries, branches or registered offices both in Spain and elsewhere[170] and permit meetings to be called by registered post or by email to the relevant electronic addresses.[171] Formation of the new private limited liability company may take place by means of the deed of incorporation and an electronic document only 48 hours from the execution of the deed.

E. *Formation of public companies in Spain*

The formation of an SA, like that of an SRL, takes place by means of a notarial deed which has to be registered in the Commercial Registry. Upon registration the company acquires legal personality for all purposes.[172]

The notarial deed (*escritura de constitución*) must contain detailed information concerning each founding member (an SA may be formed with only one member); a description of the cash, property or rights which each shareholder is providing or intends to provide (contributions in kind require appraisal by an independent expert); the number of shares which shareholder will receive in return for his contribution; an approximation of the expenses incurred in connection with the incorporation; the articles (*estatutos*) of the company; and particulars of the

[170] *Ibid.*, Art. 4. [171] *Ibid.*, Art. 5.
[172] Law governing SA of 1989, as amended, Art. 7(1).

natural and legal persons initially in charge of the management and administration of the company. The deed must also contain a statement of the intent of the incorporators to form a company. Founders of a public company are permitted by Article 11(1) of the Law of 1989, as amended, to give themselves special benefits not exceeding 10 per cent of the annual net profits and for a maximum period of ten years.

The minimum content of the article, which must be included in the notarial deed, is prescribed by Article 11 of the law governing SA of 1989. The statutes (the term is synonymous with articles or by-laws) must contain, inter alia, the following matters:

(i) the company's name, which must include the expression 'Sociedad Anónima' or 'SA'. The name must not be the same as that of another company, and must be derived either from the company's activities, or the name of one of the founders. It must not be misleading;[173]
(ii) the purpose and activities of the company;
(iii) the duration of the company, which may be indefinite;
(iv) the location of its registered office, which must be in the place where the company's business is situated, or at its centre of management and administration;
(v) the date when it is to commence business;
(vi) the authorised share capital, which must not be less than €60,101,21, and in addition, any amount not paid up;
(vii) the number, par values, classes and series of shares, and the rights attaching thereto; whether shares are represented by certificates or book entries and in the former event, whether they are in registered or bearer form;
(viii) the management structure of the company;
(ix) the procedure for general meetings;
(x) the closing date of the company's financial year;
(xi) any restrictions on the free transferability of the shares;
(xii) particulars of special rights reserved for the founders or promoters of the company. Such rights may be incorporated into registered certificates, separate from the shares.

As in France, Italy and Germany, there are two incorporation procedures; the first, which is the most common, is the simultaneous procedure (*fundación simultanea*) by which the deed is executed and the

[173] *Ibid.*, Art. 2.

capital subscribed by the founders.[174] The alternative or successive procedure is (*fundación sucesiva*) is applicable where prior to the execution of the notarial deed of incorporation, shares are offered to the public. It is governed by Articles 19–33 of the law of 1989, as amended.

When non-cash contributions are made during the course of the formation of the company, they have to be valued by one or more experts appointed by the Commercial Registrar.[175] Their report has to be attached to the notarial deed of incorporation and it must give particulars of each contribution, stipulate the valuation criteria and approve or disapprove of the number of shares issued in return. Contributions in kind must be rendered within five years from incorporation.

When a public company is formed by simultaneous incorporation, the founders are jointly and severally liable to the company, the shareholders and third parties for the authenticity of the share capital contribution, for the valuation of non-cash contributions and for the sufficient investment of funds to be utilised for payment of the incorporation expenses. Furthermore, they are also liable for the information required to be in the notarial deed of incorporation required by law, and for any inaccuracies in the statements required in such deed.[176] Furthermore, when the simultaneous incorporation procedure is used, the founders must present the notarial deed of incorporation to the Commercial Registry within two months of the date of its execution, and are jointly and severally liable for any damages arising to the company through the breach of this obligation.[177]

F. Liabilities in respect of pre-incorporation transactions

When an SA is formed by a single procedure/simultaneous incorporation, the rules contained in Article 15 of the law governing SA of 1989, as amended, which are applicable to SRL and which have been considered above, apply to transactions concluded on behalf of the company before incorporation. When the process of successive formation is used, the governing provisions are contained in Article 31.[178]

[174] *Ibid.*, Arts. 14–18. [175] *Ibid.*, Art. 38. [176] *Ibid.*, Art. 18. [177] *Ibid.*, Art. 17(2).

[178] Article 31 of the above law provides that the promoters shall be jointly and severally liable for any obligation incurred to third parties for the purpose of the formation of the corporation. Upon registration, the corporation shall assume any obligations lawfully assumed by the promoters, and shall reimburse them for any expenses they have incurred, provided that such actions were approved by the formation meeting or were necessary.

VII. Formation of private and public companies in Belgium

A. Formation

Belgian company law has recently undergone revision, a comprehensive *Code des Sociétés* being enacted on 7 May 1999, which was published in the *Moniteur Belge* of 6 August 1999. However, the rules relating to the formation of private companies (*sociétés de personnes à responsabilité limitée, SPRL*) and public companies (*sociétés anonymes, SA*) remain closely similar. An SPRL may, according to Article 211 of the *Codes des Sociétés* (Belgian Companies Act) be formed with only one member. In principle, an SA should have two members. According to Article 646 of the *Code des Sociétés*, if the membership drops below two for a period of more than 12 months, the remaining shareholder will be held jointly liable for the company's obligations which have been entered into by the company after the concentration of the shares in the hands of one shareholder, until the entry of a new shareholder, or the transformation of the SA into a closed held limited liability company, or its winding up. Such persons will have limited liability, but must pay in full the share capital they have promised to contribute. According to Article 214 of the Code, the minimum capital for a private company is €18,550, whilst Article 439 provides that it is €61,500 in the case of a public company. Companies must be incorporated by means of a notarial deed, which includes both the actual deed of incorporation and the articles (or statutes) of the company. In addition to submitting the articles of the company to a notary before incorporation, the founders must submit three other documents to him before that time. These include the financial report which has to be submitted to the notary in accordance with the provisions contained in Articles 215, 229(1) sentence 5, 440, and 456(1) sentence 4. This report should show that the company's share capital will be adequate to cover its normal projected activities during at least the first two years following incorporation. Should the company become insolvent within three years of its formation, the founders will be held jointly and severally liable to contribute to the company's debts if the competent judge finds that the share capital of the company was manifestly inadequate at the time of formation.

A further requirement consists of a certificate of an auditor (a certified public accountant) concerning the value of contributions in kind made to private and public companies. Such a certificate is required by Articles 219 and 395 of the Companies Code respectively in relation to the companies. The auditor is required to report on the description of the contribution in kind and on the methods of valuation used for it. The report must also indicate whether these methods of valuation lead to the conclusion that the value of the contribution in kind corresponds at least with that of the shares to be issued in consideration for it.

A private company may not be formed unless at least one fifth of its subscribed share capital, and at least €6,200, has been paid up.[179] A public company may not be formed unless over quarter of its share capital, and at least €6,200, has been paid up.[180] Contributions in kind to private and public companies must be capable of valuation by economic standards: they may not consist of promises to perform work or render services.[181] In addition to the certified accountant's certificate already mentioned, contributions in kind must be accompanied by a report by the founders explaining the significance of the contributions in kind for the company and, if appropriate, the reasons for which they disagree with the conclusions of the auditors. Both the accountant's certificate and the founders' report must also be deposited with the registry of the commercial court.[182]

Finally, the notary requires a receipt for money deposited with the Belgian Post Office (Postcheque) or with a Belgian bank in respect of cash contributions for shares. Such contributions have to be paid into a special blocked account in the company's name with the Belgian Post Office (Postcheque) or with a Belgian bank. The bank must not release the money until it receives a certificate from the officiating notary that the company has been incorporated. If the company is not formed within three months of the payment of the cash, the sums may be released on demand to the founders.[183] Cash contributions may be made by any legal means of payment.

The founders may either appear before the notary in person, or by means of agents whose power is derived either from a notarial deed or from a private document.[184] The company comes into being on the execution of the notarial deed.[185] Within fifteen days of the formation of the company, a copy of the deed and an extract thereof must be deposited with the registrar of the commercial court of the district in which the company has its registered office.[186] The required extract will be published in the *Moniteur Belge*[187] (*Official Gazette*). The Companies

[179] Companies Code, Art. 223. [180] *Ibid.*, Art. 397. [181] *Ibid.*, Arts. 218 and 394.
[182] *Ibid.*, Arts. 219 and 395. [183] *Ibid.*, Arts. 224 and 399.
[184] *Ibid.*, Art. 450, which applies only to public companies. [185] *Ibid.*, Arts. 66 and 450.
[186] *Ibid.*, Arts. 67 and 68. [187] *Ibid.*, Art. 73.

Act contains very detailed requirements concerning the contents of the required extract,[188] many of which will be contained in the company's articles. The extract must give particulars of such matters as the name of the company,[189] the situation of its registered office, particulars of the accounts period, the names of the auditors, and a precise definition of the company's objects and particulars concerning general meetings. The requirements differ somewhat for private and public companies, and relate to a number of other particulars as well as those mentioned. Although the Companies Code still contains provisions (Articles 451 and 452) governing the incorporation of an SA as a publicly held company, this rarely takes place in practice; the simultaneous method of incorporation is the one which is generally followed. Thus, all the capital is subscribed prior to formation.

B. Liability in respect of pre-incorporation transactions

The above matter is dealt with by Article 60 of the Companies Act. This provision stipulates that except where there is express contrary agreement on the part of the other contracting parties, the founders remain jointly and severally liable for the execution of pre-incorporation contracts, unless the company has deposited the extract from the notarial deed of incorporation required by Article 68 of the Code with the registrar within two years of the entry into the contract, and the contract has been ratified by the company within two months of such deposit. Creditors do not have to wait for the period of two months to expire, but may proceed against the founders immediately for the execution of the contracts.

VIII. Formation of private and public companies in the Netherlands

The formation procedures in respect of these kinds of companies are almost identical in the Netherlands. However, for a public company (*Naamloze Vennootschap*, N.V.), the minimum capital to be authorised and issued was DFL100,000, whilst for a private company (*Besloten Vennootschap*, B.V.), the required amount was DFL40,000. This requirement has changed to

[188] *Ibid.*, Arts. 69, 226 and 453.

[189] According to Art. 65(2) of the Code, if this is identified with that of another company, or if its resemblance is likely to induce error, interested parties may claim its modification and damages as well.

€45,000 in the case of the NV and €18,000 in the case of the B.V., but these figures are subject to subsequent alteration. However, companies formed before 1 January 2002 may continue to express their share capital in DFL.[190] Both types of companies may be formed by one or more persons, who must execute the deed of incorporation (*akte van oprichting*) before a notary. This deed contains the articles (*statuten*) which must be consistent with the law. The deed of incorporation cannot be executed prior to the receipt of a declaration of no objection from the Ministry of Justice, or more than three months thereafter. This requirement is a relic of the old concession system relating to the creation of companies. The certificate can only be refused upon certain statutory grounds.[191] These are principally that there is danger to the company that the company will be used for unlawful purposes, or that creditors will be prejudiced by its activities, or that the deed is contrary to public policy or law. It may take several weeks to obtain a certificate of no objection. The articles of association must contain provisions governing the name of the company, its official seat, the company's purposes or objects, its authorised capital,[192] and a provision governing the event that a member of the management board fails in or is prevented from exercising his duties.[193] The articles of an N.V. or B.V. usually provide for other matters as well.

The company's name must include the abbreviation 'N.V.' or 'B.V.'[194] The official seat is generally at the principal office of the company, and may be in any municipality in the Netherlands.[195] The articles must state the most important activities, but the purpose may otherwise be quite extensively formulated. According to B.W., Article 2.17, the company's articles may not contain any limitation on the duration of the company's existence. Unless there are bearer shares issued at the time of formation which have to be fully paid, at least 25 per cent of the nominal value of the shares of an N.V. or B.V. have to be paid up on formation. The minimum capital required must be in any event subscribed to and paid for at that time.[196] The latter requirement is likely to be relaxed in relation to the BV, where there will be some freedom to make agreements as to when the

[190] BW (*Burgerlijk Wetboek*, Civil Code) Arts. 2.67(2) and (5), 2.178(2) and (5). The requirement of a reduction of capital is likely to be abolished and be replaced by other safeguards in the case of a private company.

[191] BW, Arts. 2.68(2)/179(2).

[192] The issued capital must be stated in the deed of incorporation.

[193] BW, Arts. 2.66(1)/177(1); 2.67(1)/178(1); 2.134(4)/244(4).

[194] *Ibid.*, Arts. 2.66(2)/177(2). [195] *Ibid.*, Arts. 2.66(3)/177(3).

[196] *Ibid.*, Arts. 2.80(1)/191(1).

share capital is paid up. Cash contributions may be made in Dutch currency or in foreign currency. There are strict rules governing contributions in kind, which apply both when these are made at the time of formation and subsequently.[197] Contributions of property and other non-cash items to share capital are limited to assets which can be objectively assessed. Thus, as in Belgium, promises to perform work or render services cannot function as capital contributions.[198] Where a contribution in kind is made, the contributed assets must be described and particulars must be given of the value and valuation methods used. An auditor's statement must indicate that the value of the assets at least equals the total nominal value of the issued shares.[199] This certificate must be annexed to the deed of incorporation both of a public and private company. In the case of both types of company, a description of the assets contributed also has to be attached to the deed, and thus deposited with the Commercial Register for public inspection.[200]

The board of management or the notary acting on behalf of the company have to register it, and must deposit a certified copy of the deed of incorporation and the documents annexed thereto.[201] Until these requirements and the registration and deposit are complied with, the members of the management board of the company are jointly and severally liable for the obligations of the company in addition to the company itself.[202] An announcement is made by the chamber of commerce in the national gazette subsequent to registration and deposit.

A. *Liabilities in respect of pre-incorporation transactions*

Prior to its incorporation, legal transactions may be performed in the name of the company.[203] Such transactions are binding on the company only if after incorporation they are expressly or implicitly ratified.[204] Until such ratification takes place, the founders or other persons acting on behalf of the company in the process of formation are jointly and

[197] *Ibid.*, Arts. 2.94a/204a and 2.94b/204b.

[198] *Ibid.*, Arts. 2.80b(1)/191b(1).

[199] *Ibid.*, Arts. 2.94a(2)/204a(2) and B.W. Arts. 2.94b(2)/204b(2). The requirement of an auditor's statement to be submitted when a contribution in kind is made, is likely to be abolished in the case of private companies, but the founders of such companies will still be required to give a description of such a contribution.

[200] *Ibid.*, Arts. 2.94a(1), (2)/204a(1), (2) and B.W. Arts. 2.94b(2)/204b(2).

[201] *Ibid.*, Arts. 2.69(1)/180(1).

[202] *Ibid.*, Arts. 2.69(2)/180(2).

[203] *Ibid.*, Arts. 2.93(1)/203(1).

[204] *Ibid.*, Arts. 2.93(1)/203(1).

severally liable, unless otherwise stipulated.[205] The company is bound with retroactive effect on ratification. If the company is unable to fulfil its obligations and the founders or other persons acting on behalf of the company undergoing formation or their representative knows or could reasonably be expect to have known of the company's future inability to perform, they will be personally liable.

B. *Dutch legislation on pro-forma companies*

The fear has been expressed that the Court's decision in *Centros* may possibly herald a competition between jurisdictions and a resultant "race to the bottom" (the Delaware phenomenon), as has already happened in the United States.

It will thus be noted from the above account of the formation of companies in the Netherlands that the relevant rules are rather stringent and that a declaration of no objection will only be granted by the Dutch Ministry of Justice after the antecedents of the persons who will be responsible for the activities of a Dutch company have been investigated. Pro-forma foreign companies,[206] which can validly conduct business in the Netherlands, have sometimes been used to circumvent this requirement, as well as those regarding minimum capital. Both legitimate small businesses and less reputable ones have been formed as Danish and English private companies, and Delaware corporations, by Dutch persons living in the Netherlands.

The Pro-Forma Foreign Companies Act of 1998 endeavours to discourage the use of such companies.[207] The director or other persons charged with the day-to-day management of such a company are required to register it in the Commercial Register. This registration must be accompanied by a text of the deed of incorporation and the articles.[208] If the directors fail to comply with this requirement of

[205] *Ibid.*, Arts. 2.93(2)/203(2).

[206] Such companies are defined under s. 1 of the Dutch Pro-Forma Foreign Companies Act 1998 (*Wet op de puur formeel buitenlandse Venootschappen*) as follows: 'a pro-forma foreign company means a capital company with legal personality incorporated under a law other than Dutch law, which conducts its business entirely or almost entirely in the Netherlands, without having any further real tie with the state under whose law it was incorporated'.

[207] A detailed account of this Act may be found in Rammeloo, *Corporations in Private International Law* (Oxford: Oxford University Press, 2000), pp. 108–111.

[208] Pro-Forma Foreign Companies Act 1998, s. 2.

registration, they are jointly and severally liable for any legal act binding on the company performed during the course of their management.[209]

The pro-forma foreign company must give particulars of its full name, legal type, corporate seat and place of establishment in all the documents which it issues. Furthermore, it also has to state the register in which it appears and its identification number. It may not use any identification in its documents which contrary to the truth implies that the enterprise belongs to a Dutch legal person.

The paid up capital of a pro-forma foreign company is required to be to the amount of the minimum capital which is applicable to the Dutch Company Act, i.e. private and public companies. When it first falls within the definition of a pro-forma foreign company, its equity must amount to the minimum capital. In order to ensure that this requirement is satisfied, the directors are required to deposit a certificate by a registered accountant at the Commercial Register to this effect. If a pro-forma foreign company does not comply with the minimum capital and equity requirements, the directors shall once again be jointly and severally liable for any legal act binding on the company during their management.[210]

A pro-forma foreign company is required to prepare and publish annual accounts and an annual report which are in conformity with Dutch company law, unless it is a company subject to the law of any EU or EEA state, to which the Fourth and Seventh Company Law Directives apply.[211] Directors are liable for any misleading information arising out of accounts and auditing requirements.[212] For the purposes of sections 2–6, persons responsible for the day-to-day management of the company's enterprise are deemed to be directors of the company.[213]

The Dutch legislation represents an attempt to check abuse of the law by pro-forma foreign companies which may have been formed for example in Denmark, the United Kingdom or the Netherlands Antilles. The question arises whether the Dutch legislation is compatible with Community Law, and in particular with the Court's judgment in *Centros*, which the Court treated as involving questions of secondary establishment. Consideration (*considerant*) 34 of the Court's judgment refers to a general fourfold criterion according to which measures which hinder or render less attractive the exercise of fundamental Treaty freedoms may be justified. In consideration 38 of the judgment, the Court held that its

[209] *Ibid.*, s. 4(4). [210] *Ibid.*, s. 4. [211] *Ibid.*, s. 5. [212] *Ibid.*, s. 6. [213] *Ibid.*, s. 7.

interpretation[214] does not prevent the Member States concerned from adopting any appropriate measures for preventing or penalising fraud either in relation to the company itself, if need be in cooperation with the Member State in which it has been formed, or in relation to its members, where it has been established that they are in fact attempting, by means of the formation of a company, to evade their obligations towards public or private creditors established in the Member State concerned.

There are some reasons for thinking that the Dutch Act of 1998 may not be fully compatible with Community law. The Act appears to involve discrimination which may be contrary to Community law insofar as it involves pro-forma foreign companies formed in accordance with the law of a Member State: directors of such companies have more burdensome duties than directors of Dutch companies. It could be argued that it already followed from consideration 38 of the judgment of *Centros* that measures to protect creditors are only allowed in individual cases and on the basis of the existence of a concrete intention to defraud. The 1998 Act appeared to be motivated by the belief that pro-forma foreign companies necessarily harm creditors, and it does not operate on a case-by-case basis.[215] It is arguable however that the imposition of minimum capital requirements and of personal liability for non-compliance thereunto does not necessarily violate EC law.[216] The application to an English private company, which established a branch in the Netherlands, where all or nearly all its business activities took place, of the regime contained in paragraphs 2–5 of the Netherlands Pro-Forma Foreign Companies Act 1998, which governs such matters as capitalisation, publicity requirements, and the personal liability of directors in certain circumstances, was referred to the European Court of Justice. In *Kamer van Koophandel* v. *Inspire Art Ltd* [217] the European Court held these Netherlands rules to be contrary to the freedom of establishment contained in Articles 43 and 48 EC. These rules, which are stricter than those of English company law in some aspects, could not be justified by Article 46 EC; or by the need to combat fraud or abuse; or on the basis of the general interest.

[214] That the refusal of the Danish authorities to register the branch was contrary to Community law.

[215] This was pointed out by Prof Dr Timmermans at a symposium on *Centros* held at Kings College, London in 2000.

[216] Note in this sense Rammeloo, *Corporation in Private International Law*, p. 114.

[217] Case C-167/01 *Kamer van Koophandel* v. *Inspire Art Ltd* [2003] ECR I-10155.

The Advocate General and the Court placed considerable reliance on the Court's previous rulings in *Centros* and *Überseering* in reaching his conclusions. The application of the relevant Dutch legislation represented a failure to recognise the English private company, as was required by Community law. The 1998 Act will have little room for practical application in the future.

4

The types of business organisation

I. Introduction

The types of business organisation discussed in the present chapter are all governed by national law. However, the laws governing public limited liability companies and the more rarely encountered hybrid forms between a public company and a limited partnership, which are sometimes regarded as public companies with personally liable directors or limited partnerships with shares, perhaps more properly called *sociétés en commandite par actions* or *Kommanditgesellschaften auf Aktien*, as well as private limited liability companies, have been frequently influenced by provisions of Community directives, which have required implementation in the Member States. Partnerships have not generally been made subject to such directives and the same is true of the new French business entity, the *société par actions simplifiée* (SAS) as well as for the new German partnership form for use by the liberal professions, the *Partnerschaftsgesellschaft*.

The present chapter will not contain any detailed account of the European Economic Interest Grouping (EEIG), which is governed by a Community Regulation,[1] or the European Company,[2] or of the less well known proposals for a European Private Company.[3] These three matters are considered in a later chapter.

The substantive part of this chapter will begin with a discussion of public limited companies, which will be followed by one on the new French entity,

[1] Council Regulation (EEC) 2137/85 on the European Economic Interest Grouping, OJ 1985 L199/1.

[2] Council Regulation (EC) 2157/2001 of 8 October 2001 on the Statute for a European Company (SE) [2001] OJ L294/1 and Council Directive 2001/86/EC of 8 October 2001 supplementing the Statute for a European company with regard to the involvement of employees, OJ 2001 L294/22. The European Company is often referred to as 'Societas Europaea' = 'SE'. In more detail W. G. Ringe, *Die Sitzverlegung der Europäischen Aktiengesellschaft* (Tübingen: Mohr Siebeck, 2006).

[3] On which see R. Drury, 'A European Private Company?' (2001) 3 *International and Comparative Corporate Law Journal* 231–50 and C. Teichmann 'The European Private Company' [2004] ECL 162–5 .

the *société par actions simplifiée*, which is in essence a simpler form of the public (or share) company having a more flexible character than the French *Société anonyme* (SA). This discussion of the latter entity will be followed by a consideration of the limited partnership with shares, which is an amalgam of the public company and the limited partnership; despite the theoretical interest of this form, which exists in many Member States, it is no longer of much practical importance, although it was of considerable significance in the nineteenth century. Public companies are now often the chosen vehicle for large business entities.

The consideration of the limited partnership with shares will be followed by one of the private limited liability company, which is the business form frequently adopted by small and medium-sized enterprises. The proposals for a European private company will be briefly mentioned and considered in more detail in a later chapter. The main topic to be discussed is the various forms of partnership. Despite the obvious disadvantages of the partnership form, the most serious of which is the possibility of unlimited liability, the partnership is still used by many businesses in the EU. The present chapter will consider civil and commercial partnerships and limited as well as general partnerships. As is apparent from Article L210-1 of the French Commercial Code,[4] the latter two types of entities may be regarded as commercial by their nature. In France, as in Germany, this means that general and limited partnerships as well as public and private limited liability companies are subject to a special system of commercial courts.

Civil partnerships are partnerships which have no commercial objectives as this is defined by the parties. They may lack legal personality, as is the case in Germany. There is a useful alternative to the civil partnership in Germany called the *Partnerschaftsgesellschaft* which bears some resemblance to the commercial partnership, and which may be used by members of the professions. Spain also has a form of civil partnership: Spanish public and private limited liability companies are treated as being commercial by law.[5] The distinction between civil and commercial

[4] This provision stipulates that the commercial character of a company or a partnership is determined by its objects. However, general and commercial partnerships and public and private limited liability companies are commercial by reason of their form.

[5] See Art. 3 of the Spanish Law 19/1989 governing the public limited liability company at Art. 3 of the Spanish Law 2/1993 governing the private limited liability company. In Belgium (as in France) certain companies and partnerships are commercial by reason of their form; otherwise the civil or commercial nature of a company is partially determined by its objects: see Art. 3(2) of the Belgian Companies Act 1999.

activities has never existed in the United Kingdom or Ireland. It no longer exists in the Netherlands, although entities corresponding to civil and commercial partnerships (both general partnerships in which none of the members have limited liability, and limited ones, in which certain members do have such limited liability) exist in that country. They are called respectively the *maatschaap*, which is governed by Articles 1655–1688 of the Civil Code, and the *vennootschap onder firma*, and the *en commandite*, which are both governed by Articles 15–35 of the Commercial Code. In all the countries given consideration in this chapter the public and the private limited liability companies have legal personality and are thus distinct legal persons from their members. The same approach is not always taken to the partnership. Thus in England and Wales (as distinct from Scotland), general partnerships and limited partnerships have no distinct legal personality.

The law governing general partnerships (which are now considered an aggregate of persons) is likely to be changed in the future in the United Kingdom, where the law of partnership has been undergoing review by the Law Commission.[6] The twenty partner limits which formerly obtained have been repealed by the United Kingdom Regulatory Reform (Removal of 20 Member Limit in Partnerships) Order 2002. In Germany, the lack of legal personality applied to all German civil partnerships (*Gesellschaft bürgerlichen Rechts, GbR*) until 2001. In this year, the Federal Supreme Court (Bundesgerichtshof) delivered a landmark decision, according to which the civil partnership generally has both legal personality and the ability to be a party to legal proceedings.[7] However, in certain cases, the so-called Innen-GbR (which does not carry out any external activity) still lacks legal personality. The general (*offene Handelsgesellschaft*) partnership or the limited partnership (*Kommanditgesellschaft*), as well as the new entity called the *Partnerschaftsgesellschaft*, do not have legal personality but they can sue or be sued, enter into contracts and acquire rights and duties. Dutch commercial partnerships do not have legal personality. The situation is the same with the Dutch private partnership or *maatschap*. There have been proposals in the Netherlands that limited liability should be

[6] See *Partnership Law: A Joint Consultation Paper* LCCP159/SLCDP111 (Law Commission of England and Wales and Law Commission of Scotland, 2000) and *Limited Partnerships Act 1907: A Joint Consultation Paper* LCCP161/SLCDP118 (Law Commission of England and Wales and Law Commission of Scotland, 2002). A final report was produced in 2003, together with a draft Bill.

[7] BGH, judgment of 29 January 2001, II ZR 331/00, reported in BGHZ 146, 341.

conferred on certain partnerships by means of registration. Limited liability partnerships are registered in most states: they are popular in Germany, but rarely used in the United Kingdom, France or Italy. The traditional form of limited partnership familiar in many European countries (including the United Kingdom; see Limited Partnerships Act 1907, section 4(2)) is one of mixed liability, that is one in which some of the partners have unlimited liability while others have limited liability.

This entity should be distinguished from the new form of limited liability partnership recently introduced in the UK by the Limited Liability Partnerships Act 2000, where partnerships enjoy a qualified form of limited liability. The new entity has no other obvious parallel in continental European countries and bears some resemblance to the American limited liability partnerships which have now been introduced in practically all the states. Their introduction before the review of company law, which recently took place in the United Kingdom, has been completed, may be explained by the pressure exerted by professional organisations, which have been concerned with the increasing burden of liability claims. It is thus contended that in a large partnership, partners have no real ability to supervise and control the activities of other partners, and should not therefore be responsible for their misdeeds. However, it may also be argued that such monitoring may not be as difficult as contended, and that it may be unfair to reduce the opportunities for effective recourse available to an injured third party. It has also been contended that the new form of limited liability partnership may not effectively limit the liability of its members. This contention follows from the decision of the House of Lords in *Williams* v. *Natural Life Foods*.[8]

The United Kingdom limited liability partnership has legal personality and many of the characteristics of a corporation. Many of the provisions of the Companies Act 1985 and the Insolvency Act 1986 are applicable to it. Its members may be required to contribute to its assets if it is wound up. Furthermore, negligent members of such a partnership are liable to injured third parties to the full extent of their assets. The use of the new entity is not restricted to the professions.

In Germany (originally in order to avoid double taxation, i.e. the imposition of both corporation tax and income tax on the company's profits), considerable use has been made of an entity called the GmbH & Co. KG, which is considered below in the section on hybrid entities

[8] [1998] 1 WLR 830.

which follows that on limited partnerships. The permissibility of using this legal form was accepted by the *Reichsgericht* in 1922.[9] There are now few if any tax reasons for using this since the introduction of the imputation system of taxation on corporations in 1976, but there are other reasons for its use, and it remains popular in Germany. The usual form of this entity (which reserves recognition in a number of paragraphs of the German Commercial Code) is one in which the general (unlimited) partner in a limited partnership (*Kommanditgesellschaft*) is a private limited liability company.

In recent years, use has been made in Germany and France of new hybrid legal forms, the GmbH and Co. KGaA and the *société en commandite par actions à responsabilité limitée.* The legality of these entities has been questioned in France but upheld by some German courts. They consist of a limited partnership with shares, the shareholders of which have limited liability, and the corporate member of which, a private limited liability company, has unlimited liability. The directors of such an entity will usually also be directors of the private company which is a member thereof, and will often consist of members of the same family or personal friends. These persons enjoy the advantage of escaping unlimited liability, which they would incur in a KGaA or SCA (limited partnership with shares). These entities are useful for a number of purposes; in particular the SCA *à responsabilité limitée* has proved useful in France for the purpose of combating takeover bids. Some further brief reference will be made to them in the text which follows the discussion of the GmbH & Co. KG and *the société en commandite simple à responsabilité limitée.* These latter entities consist of limited partnerships in which the unlimited partner is a private company. The latter discussion is followed by a short account of the French GIE (*groupement d'intérêt économique*) which was introduced in 1967. It is used as a medium for cooperation and has some of the characteristics of a company, and some of those of a partnership.

II. Public limited liability companies

Companies similar to the UK's private limited liability company are familiar in all the relevant states. In France, the corresponding entity is called the *société anonyme* (SA); in Germany the *Aktiengesellschaft* (AG), in Italy; the *società per azioni* (SpA), in Spain; the *sociedad anónima*

[9] RGZ 105, 101.

(SA); in Belgium the *société anonyme* (SA) or *naamloze vennootschap* (NV); and in the Netherlands, the *naamloze vennootschap* (NV).

The public company is in not such frequent use as the private company in the Member States of the EU. It may be used for the purpose of gaining access to the capital markets, but is sometimes employed for the purpose of family businesses who may not seek such access. They may have a large number of shareholders but this is not necessarily the case. The *société anonyme* is quite frequently used by relatively small businesses in France. There is a general tendency to submit public limited liability companies to more detailed legal regulation than is the case with private limited liability companies.

The shares in public companies are commonly made freely transferable although national laws (note, e.g., the German *Aktiengesetz*, paragraph 68(2)) may provide for the imposition of restrictions on such transfer. There will usually be detailed rules governing minority shareholder protection, as well as rules governing the raising and maintenance of capital, and the composition and powers of the boards of the company, and the general meeting. Because of the enactment of the Community directives outlined in a previous chapter, there is some degree of similarity between the laws governing public companies in the various Member States of the EU. The similarity must not be exaggerated as in certain areas and in particular in relation to accounting, the relevant directives have given Member States options which have been exercised in different ways. The rules relating to share capital in the Member States have been approximated to a considerable extent by reason of the Second Company Law Directive.[10] There has, however, been an unfortunate failure to enact harmonising legislation in such areas as minority shareholder protection, groups of companies, employee participation and company structure.

[10] Second Council Directive 77/91/EEC of 13 December 1976 on coordination of safeguards which, for the protection of the interests of members and others, are required by Member States of companies within the meaning of the second paragraph of Art. 58 of the Treaty, in respect of the formation of public limited liability companies and the maintenance and alteration of their capital, with a view to making such safeguards equivalent [1977] OJ L26/1. This Directive was for some time under consideration with a view to reform; cf. the Commission's Proposal for a Directive of the European Parliament and of the Council amending Council Directive 77/91/EEC, as regards the formation of public limited liability companies and the maintenance and alteration of capital COM (2004) 730. It was recently amended by Directive 2006/68 of the European Parliament and Council, OJ 2006 L264/32.

A. The French SAS

The French *société par actions simplifiée* may serve as a model for legislation in other Member States. This simplified share company was introduced in France by Law 94-1 of 3 January 1994, which underwent amendment by Article 3 of Law 99-587 of 12 July 1999. The latter law was, interestingly, concerned with research and innovation.[11] It underwent further amendment by the Law on financial security of 1 August 2003.

In the new Commercial Code of 1999, the relevant provisions (Articles L227-1–L227-20) fall immediately below those which govern the *société en comandite par actions* (SCA), or limited partnership with shares which is a kind of corporation where a part of the members (namely those members called *commandités*) do not enjoy limited liability. The provisions governing the SCA come immediately after those governing the SA, or *société anonyme.*

According to the third paragraph of Article L227-1, insofar as they are compatible with the rules governing the SAS, the rules governing the SA, with the exception of those contained in Articles L225-17–L225-126 are applicable thereto. The Law of 15 May 2001 also excludes the provisions of Article L225-243 relating to the possibility of the conversion of public companies into companies of another kind after a duration of at least two years. The rules set out in Articles L225-17–225-56 govern the traditional management structures of SAs; those contained in Articles L225-57–L225-95 are provisions governing the alternative management system with an executive board (*directoire*) and a supervisory board (*conseil de surveillance*) Articles L225-96–L225-126 principally concern general meetings, voting rights and rights to documents and information. According to the third paragraph of Article L227-1; for the purpose of the applicability of the rules of the SA to the SAS, the functions of the board of directors or the president of an SA, are exercised by the president of an SAS, or those of the managers so designated in the company's articles.

The SAS may employ different forms of corporate governance from those provided for in the case of public companies. Certain mandatory rules are applicable to an SAS: thus such a company may not offer its shares (which may not take bearer form) to the public. Nevertheless, an SAS enjoys a considerable measure of constitutional freedom.

[11] For a fuller account of the SAS, see F. Wooldridge, 'The SAS Business Entity' (2000) *Amicus Curiae*, issue 26, 24.

As far as the management of the company is concerned, Article L227-5 states that the articles fix the conditions in which the company is directed. This freedom of organisation concerns the conditions for the appointment of the directors, their number and duration in the office, their remuneration and powers. The only requirement contemplated by the law is the presence of a chairman (*président*) who holds the most extended powers to represent the company in dealing with third parties.[12] The articles of the company may also stipulate the presence of one or more executive officers holding the same powers as the chairman. There is a scarcity of rules in the relevant legislation governing the SAS in relation to control over the management of the company and on the decisions of members, and the major part of the rules in these fields has to be included in the provisions of the articles.

The SAS is by nature more personalised than an SA. The contractual freedom granted may, however, be subject to certain abuses. Businessmen who do not benefit from proper legal advice may sometimes fail to provide, or provide fully, for certain important contingencies such as the calling of meetings and quorums, and the courts may sometimes be called upon to interpret their defective agreements. However, forms and precedents would seem likely to be available for the use of persons intending to form an SAS.

The new entity was devised to overcome certain rigidities in French law governing the SA and the SARL (*société à responsabilité limitée* – private limited liability company) which could not always be overcome by the use of special provisions in the company's articles, or by means of the provisions of shareholders agreements, which were sometimes of doubtful validity.

The SAS was at first made subject to limitations which resulted in the fact that it came to be used principally as a medium for cooperation between different companies, perhaps situated in different countries. Thus, until this requirement was repealed in 1999, such an entity had to be made up of members who were companies or partnerships having a capital of at least FF1,500,000. Certain public undertakings belonging to the state were also eligible for such membership. Now, both natural and legal persons may be members of an SAS. The SAS can still be used as a vehicle for co-operative ventures, and may prove useful as the holding company in a group of companies. It has advantages over the EEIG

[12] French Commercial Code, Art. L227-6. This function may be assumed by a legal person. See Art. L227-8.

(European Economic Interest Grouping) or its French counterpart the GIE (*groupement d'intérêt économique*) in that one of its objects may be the earning of profits, and that its members are only subject to limited liability and not (as in the EEIG or GIE) to joint and several unlimited liability for the debts of the entity. The one-person SAS (called SASU, *société par actions simplifiée unipersonnelle*) has been recognised by the amending law of 1999. The minimum capital requirement for an SAS is €37,000.

The SAS is not treated as a public company, but as a form of share company. It is probable therefore, that at least certain of the Community company law directives are applicable to it. However, it is taxed as a public company, although its creation seems to have been inspired by the Dutch *besloten vennootschap* (private or close company with limited liability). The new entity may prove very attractive to new and dynamic undertakings.

B. Limited partnerships with shares

The above entities are in restricted use in many of the Member States, including France, Germany, Italy and Spain, but are unknown in the United Kingdom and Ireland. They have allegedly been undergoing something of a revival in France, but their use has been discontinued in the Netherlands since the major company law reforms of 1971. The former popularity of this type of entity is explained by the fact that during the earlier part of the nineteenth century the formation of public limited liability companies used to require state permission. No such permission was required for the formation of a limited partnership with shares. Certain members of a limited partnership with shares have limited liability whilst others, most usually the directors or managers, have unlimited liability. The French SCA (*société en commandite par actions*), like its counterparts, the German KGaA (*Kommanditgesellschaft auf Aktien*), the Belgian *société en commandite par actions* and the Italian *società in accomandita per azioni* has legal personality. In the French SCA, the directors may be certain of the unlimited partners or outsiders, but may not be limited partners (*commanditaires*). The unlimited or general partners (*commandités*) cannot transfer their shares without the consent of all the other members. They are jointly and severally liable for the whole of the debts of the company without limitation. The limited partners hold transferable shares identical with those in an SA, and are only liable for the debts of the company to the extent of their contributions. An SCA may be quoted on a stock exchange.

The apparent revival of the French SCA in recent years may be explained, at least partly, by the fact that the use of such an entity permits a considerable amount of outside capital to be raised whilst the management of the company is kept in the hands of a comparatively small number of members, who hold only a small fraction of the company's capital. The management structure is also more flexible than that of the SA. In recent years, some limited use has been made of the *société en commandite par actions à responsabilité limitée*. The general partner in such an entity is an SARL (*société à responsabilité limitée*).

This form of the French SCA is similar to the German GmbH & Co KGaA. Both these hybrid legal forms are considered later on. Despite the apparent flexibility of the form, the German KGaA[13] appears to be in even less frequent use in Germany than is the SCA in France. According to paragraph 278(1) of the German Stock Corporations Act, *Aktiengesetz* (AktG), the limited partnership with shares is a partnership at least one of whose partners has unlimited liability towards the creditors (this general partner may be a GmbH or a GmbH & Co KG) and the other partners have shares in the entity's capital without incurring unlimited liability. Paragraph 278(2) AktG provides that the relationship between the personally liable partners, and the relationship of such general partners to the limited partners and towards third parties, is governed by the provisions of the Commercial Code governing limited partnerships.[14] The latter provisions also govern the powers of the general partners to manage and represent the limited partnership with shares. Furthermore, according to paragraph 278(3), the limited partnership with shares is also governed in other respects by the rules contained in paragraphs 1–277 of the AktG, insofar as the specific rules contained in paragraphs 279–290 AktG concerning this entity do not otherwise provide or insofar as an alternative conclusion must be reached by reason of the absence of a board of directors. The position of the corresponding entity in Spain (*sociedad en comandita por acciones*) is governed by Article 151–157 of the Commercial Code. Once again, as is apparent from the legal regime governing it, this entity is an amalgam between a public limited liability company and a limited partnership. The rules governing the relationship between the general partners and with third parties are in general those which would be applicable if the partnership were a

[13] K. Schmidt, *Gesellschaftsrecht*, 4th edn. (Cologne: Heymanns, 2002), § 32; F. Kübler and H. D. Assmann, *Gesellschaftsrecht*, 6th edn. (Heidelberg: CF Müller, 2006), p. 254 ff.

[14] German Commercial Code (HGB), paras. 161 ff.

sociedad comanditaria (limited liability partnership); the rules governing the public limited liability company (*sociedad anónima*) are otherwise applicable, except insofar as they contravene the provisions of the Commercial Code. In Belgium, the *société en commandite par actions* (*commanditaire vennootschap op aandelen*) is, as is apparent from Articles 654–660 of the new Companies Code of 1999, once again governed by a mixed legal regime.

III. Private companies

Private limited liability companies would appear to be in use in all the Member States. This type of entity is usually thought of as being suitable for small and medium-sized enterprises, which do not require access to public funding. However, the private limited liability company may be used for other purposes, especially for holding companies and subsidiaries. In Germany many large businesses take the form of a private company, and a special form of this company may be used for the purposes of attorneys (*Rechtsanwälte*).[15] Private companies are less subjected to the provisions of community directives than is the case with public ones. Severe restrictions may be placed upon the transferability of the shares in a private company, as is the case in Belgium, France and the Netherlands. No such mandatory restrictions are imposed by the law in the United Kingdom or Germany, but such restrictions are generally imposed by the statutes or articles of such companies. Private companies have proved to be a very popular business form, although they have often suffered from undercapitalisation and have sometimes been used as a vehicle for fraudulent practices. The number of such companies would seem to considerably outweigh that of public companies in most of the relevant states.

Some of the principal characteristics of private companies in the United Kingdom, France, Germany, Italy, Spain, Belgium and the Netherlands are briefly considered below. Particular points of interest in certain of these national laws receive some emphasis.

A. Private companies in the United Kingdom

Unlike a UK public company, which may only be limited by shares, a UK private company may be limited by shares or guarantee, or be unlimited.

[15] See F. Wooldridge, 'Germany: Legal Entities for Attorneys' (2000) *Amicus Curiae*, issue 26, 29.

By section 4(1) of the Companies Act 2006, all companies registered in the United Kingdom are treated as private companies, unless they are registered as public companies. Unlimited companies are not met frequently in practice; companies limited by guarantee are used for the purposes of non-profit making organisations such as educational establishments and professional bodies. Such a company's constitution will specify the amount which each member of the company must contribute to the debt in the case of a liquidation. There is no limit to the number of members of a private company, nor are there any minimum capital requirements as in certain other EU countries.

Private companies are no longer subject to statutory rules governing the giving of assistance for the acquisition of their shares, or the shares in their holding company. It was suggested that the requirements should be abolished insofar as they applied to private companies by the Company Law Review Steering Group.[16] A private company, whether limited by shares or by guarantee and having a share capital,[17] must not offer its shares to the public.[18]

The Companies Act 2006 grants private companies the facility – which is unavailable to public companies – of passing a written resolution (including passing a class resolution) with two exceptions.[19] A private company is not required to hold an annual general meeting, as is a public company under section 336 of the Companies Act 2006. It is thus not required to lay copies of its accounts and reports before such a meeting. The auditors' report on the annual accounts of the company must be sent out to the members in accordance with section 423 of the Companies Act 2006, but these are not required to be laid before a general meeting as is the case with a public company.[20]

Although English law no longer requires private companies to impose restrictions on the transfer of their shares, it remains true that such restrictions generally appear in the articles of private companies formed after the repeal of the former statutory requirements, as well as in private

16 The Company Law Review Steering Group's Consultative Document, *Modern Company Law for a Competitive Economy: Completing the Structure* (London: Department of Trade and Industry, 2000), ch. 2, p. 10. The former rules were contained in ss. 151–8 of the Companies Act 1985. Now see ss. 677–80 of the Companies Act 2006, which contains provisions applicable to public companies.

17 Such companies may no longer be formed.

18 Detailed rules concerning the matter are contained in ss. 288–300 of the Companies Act 2006. There is no longer any need for unanimity.

19 Section 755 of the Companies Act 2006. 'An offer to the public' is defined in s. 756.

20 Companies Act 2006, ss. 437 and 495.

companies formed at an earlier date, sometimes in combination and sometimes separately. The first type of restriction consists of a provision giving the directors power to refuse the transfer of shares, either for a particular reason, or for any reason whatsoever. The other common form of restriction is one granting other members of the company a right to pre-emption over shares. A pre-emption clause in a company's articles usually takes the form that a person wishing to sell or transfer his shares to a non-member must first of all offer them to the other members of the company at a price ascertained in accordance with a prescribed formula, or at a fair price to be determined by the company's directors or auditors. A pre-emption clause may be given a more extensive ambit and apply to transfers to fellow members as well. It may be possible to avoid a pre-emption clause by transferring or creating an equitable interest in shares. Because of the difficulties in finding a purchaser for shares in a private company which may arise from the fact that such shares may not be listed (and hence dealt in) on the London Stock Exchange (Listing Rule 3.2), as well as the possible impact of restrictions on their transfer, most of the cases concerning the statutory protection of the minority from unfair prejudice under what are now sections 994–996 of the Companies Act 2006[21] have concerned private companies. Special provisions sometimes occur in the articles of a private company or in a separate shareholders' agreement, which are intended to protect minority shareholders from being locked into an unfavourable situation. The use of alternative dispute resolution (including arbitration schemes) in cases involving shareholder disputes in private companies was recommended by the Company Law Review Steering Group in 2000.[22] According to section 270 of the Companies Act 2006, a private company is not required to have a secretary.

Single member private companies are in use in the United Kingdom as well as in the other Member States of the EU.

B. Private companies in France

The French private limited liability company (*société à responsabilité limitée*) like its English counterpart is the most popular type of company

[21] Previously ss. 459–461 of the Companies Act 1985.

[22] See, the Company Law Review Steering Group Consultative Document of November 2000, *Modern Company Law for a Competitive Economy: Completing the Structure*, pp. 14–15.

in the relevant country. It was introduced into France by a law passed in 1925, which displayed the influence of German law, and is currently regulated by Articles L223-1–L223-43 of the French Commercial Code. It is interesting to note that the enactment of the German law of 1892 introducing the GmbH (*Gesellschaft mit beschränkter Haftung*) into that country was itself much influenced by the English private company which was mentioned in the writings of Oechelhauser, a German jurist who championed the introduction of this new form of company in his country. The constitution of a single-member SARL (EURL or *Enterprise unipersonnelle à responsabilité limitée*) was permitted by the law of 11 July 1985. The rules applicable to this entity are generally speaking those applicable to SARLs, insofar as they are compatible with the existence of a single member. The single member can be a natural person or a legal entity. There is no minimum capital requirement[23] but the number of members of an SARL may not exceed 100.[24]

Shares in French private companies are called *parts sociales*, a different term from the one used for describing shares of public companies, *actions*. These terminological differences[25] reflect the more personalised approach to the shareholding in private companies than in public ones. Nevertheless, the difference with the shares of public companies is not only terminological and may be found in other characteristics of the *part sociale*, especially in relation to rules governing transfer.

In principle, the shares in an SARL carry equal rights. However, special classes of shares may be issued carrying different rights from other shares in respect of dividends and return of capital in the event of liquidation, in other words in respect of what French scholarship calls 'financial rights' (*droits financiers*). However, it follows from

[23] Before the law of 1 August 2003 the minimum capital required for the constitution of an SARL was €7,500, reduced to €500 in the case of newspaper companies as defined in Law No. 86-897 of 1 August 1986.

[24] French Commercial Code, Art. L223-3. It is the only kind of company in French company law for which the legislator fixes a maximum number of members.

[25] Which, to some extent, can be found also in the treatment of shares in Italian companies, with the differentiation between *quota* in the private company and *azione* in the public company. However, it is possible to note a fundamental difference between the shares of private companies in France and in Italy. In France, the company issues a fixed number of shares and every member has as many votes as the number of shares he holds. This regime does not differentiate very much between the *part sociale* and the *action* as far as the division of the capital in shares is concerned. However, with the Italian *quota* each member holds just one share which represents a determined percentage of the company's capital and at the general meeting every member (*socio*) hold just one vote, whose weight will be proportional to his stakeholding.

Article L223-28 of the Commercial Code that double or multiple voting rights may not be conferred on shares, nor may shares be deprived of voting rights. Any different provision in the articles is treated as unwritten.[26]

The main differentiation between shares in a private company and in a public company may be found in the rules governing transfer. In fact, private companies are considered to be capitalistic companies under French law, *sociétés de capitaux*, and the responsibility of the members is limited to what they contributed to the company's capital. However, it is generally recognised that they have some personal features. The regime governing the transfer of shares illustrates this personal character (*intuitus personae*) in the structure of private companies.

The shares in an SARL cannot be transferred in the same form as in an SA (public company). They may not be represented by registered or bearer share certificates.[27] The applicable rules governing the transfer of the *parts sociales* are those governing the transfer of credits contained in the Civil Code. Thus, the transfer of shares is in principle based upon consensus and is valid between the parties when it takes place orally but it is succeeded by a written instrument.[28] The company must be informed of the transfer in the prescribed manner,[29] and the transfer must be registered at the Commercial Register.[30] These two formalities make the transfer opposable to third parties. The transferor is charged a 4.8 per cent tax for the registration. For this reason, many SARLs are transformed into SAs before the transfer takes place.

A fundamental rule which governs the functioning of an SARL and that above all contributes to characterise this company as based on a

[26] French Commercial Code, Art. L223-28. Multiple voting rights may exist in an SAS, by contrast.

[27] French Commercial Code, Art. L223-12.

[28] French Commercial Code, Art. L223-17 which makes reference to Art. 221-14 which requires the transfer to be completed by a written instrument and take the form of required by Art. 1690 of the Civil Code. Questions concerning the transfer of a share in an SARL are as a matter of civil law within the competence of the civil courts, whilst those concerning that of the majority of the shareholding are dealt with by the commercial courts. See M. Cozian, A. Viandier, F. Deboissy, *Droit des sociétés*, 18th edn (Paris: Lexis Nexis Litec, 2005), p. 421.

[29] This can be done in two ways. The first and cheaper method is the deposit at the company's seat of the original act of transfer and the second and more expensive is to apply the procedure set out in Art. 1690 of the Civil Code, through the use of the official procedure carried out by a bailiff or notarised. The *Cour de Cassation* nevertheless treated a transfer as being valid when it was ratified by a resolution amending the statutes. Cass. Com., 3 May 2000, 811, note P. Le Cannu.

[30] French Commercial Code, Arts. L221-14 and L223-17.

personal or personalistic character or principle of the *intuitus personae*, is that the transfer of shares must be approved by the vote of the members. The approval is of two kinds. It is compulsory by law in the case of the transfer to third parties who are not members of the company. It is optional, and not required unless the statutes provide otherwise, for the transfer to other members or to relatives of the transferor.

The transfer of shares to persons who are not members of the company is dealt with by Article L223-14, which was amended in 2004, and provides that it must take place with the consent of the majority of the shareholders of the company (including the transferor), holding at least half the company's capital. Thus, there are two requirements:

(1) relating to number of the shareholders, which must consist of a majority, irrespective of the capital which they hold; and
(2) the other relating to the requirement of the vote of the holders of at least half the company's share capital, unless the articles provide for a larger majority.

If such consent is refused, other members of the company must acquire the shares or procure their acquisition by others, within a period of three months, which may be extended to six months on application to the court by a *gérant* (manager).[31] Alternatively, the company may reduce the capital by buying shares from the intending transferor. If neither of these actions is taken by the expiration of the relevant period, the intending transferor is allowed to make the transfer which was initially refused.

According to Article L223-16, shares are freely transferable between members. However, such free transferability may be restricted by the statutes, in which case Article L223-14, the provisions of which have been explained above, will apply, but the articles may provide for less stringent majorities or delays. In principle, shares are freely transferable also within the family of the transferor both on death and inter vivos, in the case of the division of matrimonial property held in co-ownership by spouses, between spouses and between persons related as ascendants and descendants. However, the articles may stipulate that these types of transfer as well as transmissions to heirs and legatees on death shall require the approval of the company. In this case, Article L223-14, explained above, will apply. The articles may in no case establish more

[31] But, according to Art. L223-14, 6th al., to benefit from this possibility the intending transferor must have hold the relevant shares for at least two years.

stringent majorities or shorter delays than those provided for in that article.[32]

The management of an SARL is carried out by one or more managers (*gérants*) under the direction and control of the shareholders. These managers have extensive powers, but these may be limited by the articles, and are restricted by certain rules of law. If the company fulfils certain requirements the members control over the management must be supplemented by the appointment of one or more statutory auditors (*commissaires aux comptes*). These requirements, which are contained in Article L223-35 of the Commercial Code and Articles 12 and 43 of Decree No. 67-236 of 23 March 1967 are that at the end of a financial year at least two of the three following conditions are satisfied: the balance sheet total is in excess of €1,550,000, the turnover excluding tax is in excess of €3,100,000 and the average number of employees in excess of fifty.

The function of the general meeting is to take the most important decisions which the company has to take. The requirements as to structure are perhaps rather more rigid than those applicable to an SAS. In the case of the latter kind of company, the rules governing the general meeting and management of an SA are inapplicable. It follows from Articles L227-1 and L227-5 of the Commercial Code that they may be replaced by special provisions in the articles.[33] Probably, an SAS has a greater degree of contractual freedom than an SARL, and it may well be that the numbers of the former type of business enterprise will eventually increase to the detriment of the SARL, and perhaps also that of the SA.

C. *Private companies in Germany*

The German private limited liability company (*Gesellschaft mit beschränkter Haftung*, GmbH) dates from 1892, and the German legislation, which has of course undergone considerable subsequent amendments, has had a

[32] French Commercial Code, Art. L223-13. Nevertheless, this latter article contemplates a number of exceptions to the rules normally governing the transmission of the shares by way of succession.

[33] French Commercial Code, Art. L227-9, paras. 1 and 2 provide that the articles determine the decisions which must be taken collectively by the members, in accordance with the forms and conditions which they prescribe. However, para. 2 of Art. L227-9 goes on to prescribe that certain decisions must be taken collectively in accordance with the articles. These include the increase, redemption and reduction of capital mergers, divisions, the dissolution of the company, the appointment of auditors, and the approval of the accounts documents.

considerable influence in many other states.[34] The GmbH was designed for small groups of shareholders with close personal links, who did not wish to transfer their shares easily but who desired considerable discretion to depart from the statutory model to suit their own requirements. The rules governing the public limited liability company (*Aktiengesellschaft*, AG) had shown themselves to be too complex or inflexible for this entity to be a convenient corporate vehicle for small and medium sized enterprises. Important amendments to the law governing the GmbH were expected to come into force by the end of 2008. These amendments would permit the GmbH to have an establishment in another Member State.

A GmbH may be formed for any lawful purpose.[35] However, the carrying out of certain types of insurance business as well as the carrying on of mortgage, ship mortgage and and building society business is not permitted.[36] GmbHs are sometimes used for the purpose of large business enterprises. They may constitute the controlling company in a group and provide a suitable legal from for charitable, research and artistic institutions. Many businesses take the hybrid form of a GmbH & Co. KG – which officially is not a GmbH; there are various types of such enterprise but the most common one is one in which the GmbH is the general partner, and the directors thereof are limited partners. The recognition of the one-man company (which may now be formed ab initio) has considerable advantages. A GmbH enjoys a separate legal personality and is deemed to be a commercial undertaking having limited liability, even if it does not pursue a commercial purpose.[37]

Apart from the *GmbH Gesetz* (as amended), the GmbH is regulated by a number of other statutes. Thus, for example, certain of the accounting rules contained in the Commercial Code are applicable to a GmbH fulfilling certain criteria. Lacunae in the rules of law governing the GmbH can be provided for by applying rules of law governing other bodies. Thus, in the event of such lacunae, certain of the rules of law relating to clubs (*Vereine*) which have a structure comparable to that of companies are applicable by way of analogy. Certain of the rules relating to civil and commercial partnerships, as well as to public companies have

[34] K. Schmidt, *Gesellschaftsrecht*, § 33.

[35] German Private Limited Liability Companies Act, para. 1.

[36] Insurance Control Act (*Versicherungsaufsichtsgesetz*, VAG), para. 7(1), Mortgage Bank Act (*Hypothekenbankgesetz*, HypBankG), para. 2(1), Ship Mortgage Bank Act. (*Schiffsbankgesetz*, SchBkG), para. 2(1), Building Society Act (*Bausparkassengesetz*), para. 2(1).

[37] German Private Limited Liability Companies Act, para. 13.

been applied in a similar fashion.[38] The Federal Supreme Court (formerly the *Reichsgericht*, now the *Bundesgerichtshof*) has applied the rules of law governing the nullity and annulment of resolutions of general meeting of AG by way of analogy to the nullity and annulment of resolutions of the general meeting of a GmbH in a number of cases.[39] Further, the rules governing the retirement and expulsion of partners in civil and commercial partnerships have been applied to private companies by the Supreme Court.[40] The minimum amount of the share capital of a private company is €25,000.[41] This amount may soon be reduced to €10,000.

The minimum value of each share is €100.[42] A member may have only one share.[43] Managers may be appointed by the articles or in a subsequent resolution.[44] The compulsory supervisory board appoints the managers in those few private companies having more than 2,000 employees, which are subject to the Codetermination Act 1976, and in any such private companies having more than 1,000 employees which are subject to the codetermination system applicable to iron, steel or coal companies, or iron, steel or coal holding companies (Codetermination Act 1951).[45] The principal duty of the managers is to manage the company with the skill and diligence of a lawful businessman.[46] A GmbH may set up a supervisory board voluntarily. The main function of such a board is to supervise the management. Large GmbHs employing between 500–2,000 employees are required to set up a supervisory board under the *Drittelbeteiligungsgesetz* of 2004[47] which replaced the Works Council Act (*Betriebsverfassungsgesetz*) of 1952. One-third of the members of such a board must consist of representatives of the employees. If a GmbH has more than 2,000 employees, it will be required to set up a supervisory board under paragraph 6 of the Codetermination Act (*Mitbestimmungsgesetz*) of 1976, one-half of which must consist of representatives of employees. The latter system of codetermination and

[38] Schmidt, *Gesellschaftsrecht*, (n. 34), § 33 I.

[39] *Official Journal of the former German Supreme Court* (RGZ) 166, 129; *Official Journal of the German Supreme Court* (BGHZ), 14, 25, 30; 14, 264, 268; 111, 224.

[40] RGZ 128, 1, 16; BGHZ 9, 157, 161 ff. See also T. Raiser and R. Veil, *Recht der Kapitalgesellschaften*, 4th edn (Munich: Vahlen, 2006), § 30 IV.

[41] German Private Limited Liability Companies Act, para. 5.

[42] *Ibid.*, para. 5(1). This may be reduced to €1 if a proposed reform of the law governing the GmbH comes into effect.

[43] *Ibid.*, para. 5(2). This limitation may be repealed in the near future.

[44] *Ibid.*, para. 6(3), 46 No. 5.

[45] Schmidt, *Gesellschaftsrecht*, § 36 IV 2.

[46] German Private Limited Liability Companies Act, para. 43(1).

[47] *Drittelbeteiligungsgesetz* or DrittelbG, BGBl. 2004 S. 974.

the special system of codetermination which applies to companies engaged in the coal, iron and steel industries, and to coal, iron and steel holding companies, have little or no significance for private companies. When such a company is required to set up a supervisory board by one of the Codetermination Acts the board's functions are prescribed by law and not subject to alteration by the articles.

The GmbHG does not require the company articles to place any restrictions on the transfer of shares; it resembles the United Kingdom Companies Act 2006[48] in this respect. However, such transfers are required to take place by a notarial deed.[49] Such a deed is required as well if a shareholder assumes a contractual obligation to transfer his share.[50] These requirements entail that stock exchange dealings in shares are impossible. The shareholders may however place restrictions on the transfer (transferability) of shares. Common examples of such restrictions are the requirement that the general meeting, the supervisory board or other persons shall approve the transfer. Sometimes the restriction on transfer takes the form that a person desirous of transferring his shares shall transfer them to certain named persons, for example the other members of the company. It has been held that a new restriction cannot be imposed by the articles on the transfer of shares without the unanimous consent of all the shareholders affected.[51] As far as the company is concerned, a person may only be treated as a shareholder if he has given it notice that he has acquired the relevant share and provides proof for this.[52] German law relating to the recently established concept of unlimited shareholder liability for causing the insolvency of a private company ('*Existenzvernichtungshaftung*') underwent some revision as the result of an important judgment of the Federal Supreme Court (BGH) of 16 July 2007 (II ZR 3/04, *Trihotel*). Such shareholder liability would in principle only be towards the company itself, and not towards its creditors. It will be based upon Artical 826 of the German Civil Code (BGB), which imposes delictual liability for damage caused intentionally, and in violation of good moral behaviour. It will constitute 'eine besondere Fallgruppe der sittenwidrigen vorsätzlichen Schädigung'.

[48] And the previous UK legislation.

[49] German Private Limited Liability Companies Act, para. 15(3). See also Raiser and Veil, *Recht der Kapitalgesellschaften*, § 30 I.

[50] German Private Limited Liability Companies Act, para. 15(4).

[51] *Ibid.*, para. 53(1) in combination with para. 53(3). This somewhat controversial view has been taken in certain of the decided cases, where such a restriction has been held to involve an increase in the obligations on the shareholders (a '*Vermehrung der den Gesellschaftern obliegenden Leistungen*').

[52] German Private Limited Liability Companies Act, para. 16. This provision is likely to undergo revision when the proposed amending legislation is adopted.

The requirement mentioned in certain earlier cases that unlimited shareholder liability is only incurred if the loss cannot be fully recovered under Article 31 and 30 GmbHG will no longer be applicable. ('§826 BGB sind gegenüber Erstattungsansprüchen aus §§31,30 GmbHG nicht subsidiär Schadensersatzanspruche aus Existenzvernichtungshaftung gemäß §826 BGB sind gegenüber Erstattungsansprüchen aus §§31,30 HmbHG nicht subsidiär.')

D. Private companies in Italy

The SRL (*società a responsabilità limitata*) was until recently considerably similar to the SpA (*società par azioni*). The rules governing the former entity were largely based on those governing the SpA, and many of the latter rules were incorporated by reference into the Civil Code. The 1882 Commercial Code contemplated a *società anonima*, the original model of limited company, which was of two kinds, *anonima per quote* (private limited company) or *anonima per azioni* (public limited company) depending on the different kinds of participation of the members. In the 1942 Civil Code the Spa replaced the *società anonima per azioni* and the newly introduced SRL was not very different from the previous *società anonima per quote*, sharing the main part of the discipline with the public company. The reforming Decree No. 6 of 17 January 2003 now provides a separate system of rules for SRLs which is substantially different from that relating to SpAs. It is hoped that this reform will encourage the more widespread use of the private company, which has both certain capital and personalsied features. There is no need for two separate documents to form an Italian private company. Two such documents may be necessary to form an Italian public company.

As in the German GmbH, there is substantial scope for private agreement. Many of the rules are default rules, and certain others resemble those applicable to partnerships. The minimum capital of an SRL is €10,000.[53] This capital is divided into shares (*quotas*) and in principle, the rights of the shareholders are in proportion to their contribution and consequently to their shareholding.[54] In principle because, given the only imperative rule is that shares cannot be issued at a discount and the value of all the contributions must be at least equal to the total nominal value of the capital, the deed of incorporation (*atto costitutivo* or articles of association) can determine the amount of a member's participation in a way which is not proportional to his contribution. Individual shares will be measured on

[53] Italian Civil Code, Art. 2463(1) al 4. [54] *Ibid.*, Art. 2468(2).

the basis of the total amount of the share capital but a member who has contributed for instance with X% can be allotted according to the rules contained in the deed, a participation of X + Y% or of X – Y%.[55]

Financial and other rights will be accorded to the members in proportion to their participation. Nevertheless, the articles could state that single members shall be accorded particular rights regarding the management of the company and the distribution of dividends.[56]

The shares in a private company may not be represented by negotiable instruments, nor may they be offered for public subscription.[57] These rules help in particular to differentiate the private company from public companies (SpA). In the SRL every shareholder has only one share (*quota*) in proportion to his participation to the capital and each shareholder can be allotted a different sized share, whilst in the public company every shareholder has a certain number of shares, all of the same amount.

Shares may be transferred inter vivos by a notarised deed and they are also transmissible on death: however the deed of incorporation may exclude or limit their transfer.[58] The freedom of transfer of the shares, unless otherwise stated in the deed, is a feature of SRLs which differentiate them from those 'personalised' companies (*società semplice, s.s., società in accomandita semplice, s.a.s.*, and *società in nome collettivo, s.n.c.*, not having legal personality) in which the transfer of the participation requires a modification of the partnership agreement or deed (contratto sociale). If the deed of incorporation provides that shares in a private company cannot be transferred, or is subject to the consent of organs of the company, the members or third parties, no conditions or limits being placed on the discretion of such persons or bodies; or if the deed imposes limitations or conditions which, impede the transmission of shares on death, Article 2469(2) provides that the shareholder or his heirs may withdraw from the company. This is a consequence of the principle that a shareholder should not be unconditionally bound to the company. However, the deed of incorporation may prescribe a period of time, not more than two years, from the formation of the company or the acquisition of the shares, before which the right of withdrawal can be exercised.[59]

The transfer takes effect with the company from the time when it is entered in the company's register of members[60] and with third parties from the time when the notary, responsible for authenticating the instrument of transfer, has deposited it at the office of the Register of

[55] B. Libonati, *Diritto Commerciale, Impresa e Società* (Milan: Giuffrè, 2005), p. 449.
[56] Italian Civil Code, Art. 2468(2). [57] *Ibid.*, Art. 2468(1).
[58] *Ibid.*, Art. 2469(1). [59] *Ibid.*, Art. 2469(2). [60] *Ibid.*, Art. 2470(2).

Enterprises in the district where the company's seat is situated. The entry into the register of members may be made at the request of the transferor or transferee. In the case of transmission on death the request is made by the deceased's heirs or legatees, providing a copy of the certificate of death and a copy of the will, if it exists, or of a judicial or notarial certificate of the standing of heirs or legatees.

If a share is transferred which is not fully paid up, it follows from Article 2472 of the Civil Code that the transferor is jointly and severally liable together with the transferee for a period of three years from the date of transfer for the sum unpaid on the shares unless a request for payment made to the defaulting member has been unsuccessful.

The single member SRL has been recognized in Italy since 1995.[61] When the entire shareholding belongs to a single member, the directors have to deposit a declaration containing particulars of that person with the appropriate office of the Register of Enterprises for entry therein.[62] If they fail to comply with that rule, and neither the transferor or transferee does comply, within thirty days from the constitution of the company or of the time when the shareholding comes to belong to the one member, or the transfer of the single member's shareholding, that shareholder will be held personally liable for the obligations incurred during the period when the shareholding belonged to him or the company becomes insolvent.[63]

Article 2473 of the Civil Code contains detailed provisions concerning the withdrawal of a member.[64] According to Article 2473(1) of the Civil Code, the deed of incorporation determines when a member may withdraw from the company, and the modalities of such withdrawal. In any event, the right to withdraw is available to any member of the company who has not assented to the alteration of the objects; or the type of the company; or to the merger with another company; or its division; or to the revocation of a state of liquidation of the company; or to the transfer of the company's seat abroad; or the removal of one of the causes of withdrawal set out in the statutes or modification of its rights granted to shareholders under Article 2468(2). It follows from Article 2443(2) that if a private company is formed for an indefinite period of time, a member may withdraw from it at any time on giving six months' notice, which may be increased to twelve months in the deed of incorporation.

[61] This is now apparent from Art. 2470(4) of the Italian Civil Code.

[62] *Ibid.*, Art. 2470(4). [63] *Ibid.*, Art. 2462(2).

[64] See F. Wooldridge, 'The New Provisions Governing Italian Private Companies' (2003) EBLR 99, 104–5 for a detailed account.

An Italian private company may issue debt securities in accordance with the provisions of Article 2483 of the Civil Code.

According to Article 2475, unless the deed of incorporation provides otherwise, the management of the company is entrusted to one or more members, appointed in accordance with a decision taken by the members. If there is more than one director, the directors may be treated as forming a board, or power may instead be conferred on each of them, or on all the directors acting unanimously.[65] Each director has the general power of representing the company.[66] The deed of incorporation may provide for the establishment of a committee of auditors.[67] It must do so if the capital of the company is at least €120,000,[68] or if for two successive financial years, two of the three limits set out in Article 2435 *bis* which is concerned with the presentation of the annual balance sheet, have been exceeded.[69] The limit for the balance sheet total is now €3,125,000; for the annual turnover, €6,250,000, and for the average number of employees fifty. If there is a committee of auditors, the rules governing it are the same as those governing the same body in the SpA.[70]

E. Private companies in Spain

The laws governing private companies (*sociedades de responsabilidad limitada*, SL) in Spain are completely revised by Law 2/1995 of 23 March 1995 regarding limited liability companies. The capital of such a company may not be less than €3,012.[71] Single member private companies are recognised in Spain, and there is no limit on the number of members of such companies. Company participations are not treated as having the characteristics of shares in a public company, nor may they be represented by negotiable securities; they may not be referred to as shares.[72] Transfers of participations must take place by means of a public document executed before a notary and must be recorded in the company's registry of members.[73] The company is in essence a type of closed company: this is demonstrated by the detailed and substantial restrictions which may be imposed on the transfer of participations to non-members.[74] According to Article 29(1), except for provision in the *estatutos* to the contrary, certain

[65] Italian Civil Code, Arts. 2257 and 2258 and D. Santosuosso, *Il nuovo diritto societario* (D&G *diritto e guistizia, supp al fasc.* 6/2003) 103–4.

[66] *Ibid.*, Art. 2475 *bis* (1). [67] *Ibid.*, Art. 2477(1).

[68] *Ibid.*, Art. 2477(2). [69] *Ibid.*, Art. 2477(3).

[70] *Ibid.*, Art. 2477(4). These rules are discussed in relation to the SpA in Chapter 5.

[71] Article 4 of Law 2/1995. [72] *Ibid.*, Art. 5(2). [73] *Ibid.*, Arts. 26 and 27.

[74] Restrictions of transfer are dealt with by Arts. 29–34 of Law 2/1995.

voluntary transfers *inter vivos* of company participations are free from restrictions. These include a members' transfer to a spouse, a fellow member's ascendant or descendant, or to companies within the same group. In all other cases such transfers are subject to the rules and limitations contained in the articles or, in the absence thereof, the provisions of the 1995 Law. Article 29(2) provides that in the absence of such rules, detailed pre-emption provisions shall apply. Furthermore, Article 30(1) provides that provisions in a company's *estatutos* (these correspond to the articles of a UK company) which would practically allow the free and voluntary transfer of company participation, inter vivos shall be null and void. Article 30(3) provides that provisions prohibiting the inter vivos transfer of participation in the company shall only be valid if the articles recognise the right of the member to withdraw from the company at any time. The incorporation of such provisions in the statutes requires the consent of all the members. Transfer of company participations not conforming to requirements of the law or the articles have no effect, and are not binding on the company.[75] An SL is not permitted to issue bonds. The new law is characterised by a greater degree of flexibility than was formerly the case. A considerable measure of freedom is given to structure the company in accordance with the wishes of its members. Thus, for example, the articles may provide for enhanced majorities at company meetings.[76] The articles may also make provision for restrictions upon transfer which depart from the model provided for by the Law of 1995. They may also provide for different rules from those contained in Article 46(1) for giving notice of a general meeting.[77] According to Article 57(1) the management of the company may be entrusted to a single administrator, or to several administrators who may act separately, or must act jointly, or to a board of directors (*consejo de administración*). The articles are required by the third sentence of Article 57(1) to set out the rules of organisation and operation of the board of directors. However, according to Article 57(2) the articles may provide for different methods of organising the management body (i.e. the administrator(s) or board of directors) and may give power to the general meeting to select which method.

The 1995 Law also places considerable emphasis on the protection of minorities in private companies, which is a matter of fundamental importance given their closed character. Thus members of a company

[75] *Ibid.*, Art. 34. [76] *Ibid.*, Art. 43.

[77] *Ibid.*, Art. 46(2). According to Art. 46(1) such notice must be given in the *Official Gazette of the Commercial Registry* and in one of the major daily newspapers of the municipality in which the company has its registered office.

who do not vote in favour of certain types of resolution are given the right to withdraw from the company by Article 95(1). The articles of the company may, according to Article 96, make provision for other causes of withdrawal. Article 98 provides that members of a private company may be removed in certain circumstances.

The provision of Article 52 excluding the right of a member to vote in certain cases where that member is subject to a conflict of interest appear to be directed towards the protection of the other members of the company.

A new simplified type of private limited liability company has been introduced in Spain, the SLNE, which is especially designed to operate small businesses. The new Law 1/2003 of 2 April 2003 introducing such companies contains 15 sections, and was followed by an Order of 4 June 2003 providing for draft statutes for such companies which contains the principal characteristics of such an entity mentioned in connection with its formation. Article 14 of the Law governing private limited liability companies of 1995, as amended by the new law, provides for the rules applicable to the amendment of the articles, and Article 141 for a simplified form of articles for such companies. Such a company may be registered by means of a public deed of incorporation and an electronic document within 48 hours of execution of the deed. Only individuals may be members of the company and they may not exceed five at the time of incorporation. The corporate purpose should be one of those provided for in Law 1/2003, but different activities may be included. It appears that not much use has been made of this new corporate form, although it does enjoy certain tax concessions.

F. Private companies in Belgium

The Belgian private company, *société privée à responsabilité limitée* (SPRL) or *besloten vennootschap met beperkte aansprakelijkheid* (BVPA) is dealt with in detail in Articles 210–349 of the new Belgian Companies Code of May 1999. It may be formed with only one member, but, as in Spain, there is no upper limit to its membership. According to Article 212, when an SPRL has only one member who is a natural person, such member is treated as guaranteeing the obligations of any other single member private company which he sets up by himself, or of which he eventually becomes the single member, except if the shares were transmitted to him by reason of death. Furthermore, notwithstanding any stipulation to the contrary, if the member of an SPRL is a legal person who set it up, the latter is jointly and severally liable for the obligations which the SPRL enters into whilst it has only one member. When an SPRL becomes a single-member company subsequent to the formation and this single member is a legal person, and no additional person becomes a member of the company within a period of one year, and the company is not dissolved within that period, the single member is treated as guaranteeing all the obligations of the single member company which come into existence between the time when the legal person acquired all the shares in the company and the time when the company acquires a new member or consent is given to its dissolution.[78]

The minimum capital of a SARL is €18,550, at least €6,200 of which must be paid up on formation.[79] In addition, if the shares are subscribed for cash, they must be paid up to the extent of one-fifth; the consideration for the shares allotted other than for a cash consideration must be fully paid up.[80] The capital of the company must be subscribed for in full.[81] If shares are issued for a non-cash consideration, such consideration must be valued by an expert (*réviseur des entreprises*). The founders must prepare a report on contributions in kind, in which they may explain any reasons they may have for departing from the expert's conclusions.[82]

Before the formation of the company, the founders are required to send the officiating notary a financial plan in which they justify the amount of the share capital of the company in formation. This plan is not made public but is retained by the notary. If the company becomes insolvent within a period of three years from its incorporation, and it appears that at the time of such incorporation this amount was manifestly insufficient to pursue the proposed activities of the company for a period of at least two years, the founders are jointly and severally liable for the commitments of the company to the extent determined by the court.[83] The capital of the company is divided into shares (*parts*) of equal amounts, which may or may not have a nominal value.[84] Without prejudice to what is provided for in the case of non-voting shares, each share carries equal rights in the distribution of profits and of surplus assets in the liquidation.[85]

An SRL may issue bonds (*obligations*) as well as shares. These must be in registered form,[86] and the company is required to keep separate registers of shares and bonds at its registered office.[87] The new Code

[78] Belgian Companies Code, Art. 213. [79] *Ibid.*, Arts. 214 and 223.
[80] *Ibid.*, Art. 223. [81] *Ibid.*, Art. 216. [82] *Ibid.*, Art. 219.
[83] *Ibid.*, Arts. 215 and 229, sentence 5. [84] *Ibid.*, Art. 238. [85] *Ibid.*, Art. 239.
[86] *Ibid.*, Arts. 232 and 243. [87] *Ibid.*, Art. 233.

contains a number of detailed rules concerning the issue of bonds and related matters.

The transfer of shares and bonds is dealt with by Articles 249–254 of the Companies Code. According to Article 249, a member (*associé*) of an SRL cannot transfer his shares, nor can the transmission of shares on death take place without the consent of at least half of the other members of the company, who must possess at least three-quarters of the remaining shares. Whilst the company may impose more stringent conditions than this requirement, it cannot impose less stringent ones. However, such consent is not necessary for the transfer or transmission of shares to another member, or to the transferor, or the testator's spouse, or to any of his or her lineal ascendants or descendants, or to other persons to whom the articles permit shares to be transferred or transmitted. Transfers and transmissions of shares have no effect against the company or against third parties until they are entered in the share register.[88] By virtue of Article 251, except where the articles provide otherwise, where the transfer of shares is refused, the intending transferor(s) is able to challenge such refusal before a court which is competent to give summary relief in urgent cases. If the court decides that such refusal is arbitrary, the opponents of the transfer will be given three months from the date of the order to find purchasers at the price and conditions laid down in the articles. In the absence of such a provision in the articles and agreement between the interested parties the price and terms of payment are fixed by the competent court. In any event, the court may not stipulate a period of more than five years from the date of the above mentioned order for the complete performance of the condition contained in it (e.g. as to payment). Shares which are purchased may not be transferred until the full payment of the purchase price. If the purchase of the shares is not agreed upon within the three month period, the transferor may request the dissolution of the company, but he must do so within the forty days which follow the expiry of that period.[89] Heirs and legatees who have been refused membership are given similar rights to those granted by Article 251 of the Companies Code to intending transferors by Article 252 of that Code.

According to Article 253, the transfer of bonds does not take effect as with the company or third parties until such time as the declaration of transfer dated and signed by the transferor and the transferee, or by their authorised agents, is entered on the bonds register: It may however take

[88] *Ibid.*, Art. 250. [89] *Ibid.*, Art. 251.

place in accordance with the special rules governing the assignment of obligations contained in Art 1690 of the Civil Code.[90]

The affairs of a private company are managed by one or more managers (*gérants*) who do not need to be members of the company.[91] They may be appointed for a limited time, or for an unlimited time, in which case they are reputedly appointed for the duration of the company. The latter type of managers may only have their powers wholly or partially removed for serious reasons.[92] Each manager may perform all the acts which are necessary or useful for the achievement of the company's objects, except those which are reserved by the Code to the general meeting.[93] The articles may impose restrictions on the powers of the managers, but these are not opposable to third parties even if they are published.[94] Each manager represents the company with regard to third parties and in court. However, the articles may provide that such powers of representation be conferred on one or more specially chosen managers, or by several managers acting jointly. This clause is only opposable to third parties if it concerns the general power of representation and it is duly published.[95] The company is bound by acts done by the managers which fall outside its objects, unless the company proves that the third party know or must have known that this was so. Mere publication of the statutes is not sufficient proof of such knowledge.[96]

The managers are jointly and severally liable towards the company and third parties for all damages arising from infractions of the Code or of the company's articles. However, they may be discharged from liability for breaches in which they have not participated, provided that no fault is imputable to them, and they have condemned the infractions at the general meeting following their acquisition of knowledge of them.[97] If a private company becomes bankrupt and has insufficient assets, and it is established that a grave fault in which they have participated has contributed to such bankruptcy, each manager or former manager, as well as any other person who has effectively possessed managerial powers may be declared personally liable, with or without joint and several liability, for the whole or part of the debts up to the account of the insufficiency of assets. This provision, contained in Article 265(1), is not however applicable when the bankrupt company has, during the three financial years

[90] This provision stipulates that the transferee is entitled with regard to third parties only where notice of the transfer is given to the debtor. However, he may also be so entitled through an acceptance of the transfer made to the debtor by means of a certified instrument.

[91] Civil Code, Art. 255. [92] *Ibid.*, Art. 256. [93] *Ibid.*, Art. 257(1).

[94] *Ibid.*, Art. 257(2). [95] *Ibid.*, Art. 257(3). [96] *Ibid.*, Art. 258. [97] *Ibid.*, Art. 263.

preceding the bankruptcy, an average turnover of less than €620,000, excluding value added tax, and when the balance sheet total for the financial year preceding the bankruptcy has not exceeded €370,000.

G. *Private companies in the Netherlands*

The *besloten vennootschap met beperkte aansprakelijkheid* (BV) was introduced into the Netherlands in 1971, and has proved popular in that country. The legal provisions governing this type of entity are largely the same as those applicable to the *naamloze vennootschap* (NV or public company), but the implementation of certain recent proposals could result in some significant differences. However, its formation appears to be less onerous than is the case with the NV. This applies to some extent to the required content of the *statuten* (statutes or articles). No founders report has to be made on contributions in kind made on formation or subsequently and such contributions do not have to be valued by a registered and qualified accountant. However, a founders statement has to be made about such contributions. The law governing private companies is likely to be amended in the near future; it will retain the requirement of such a statement, but will not require the independent audit of contributions in kind by a valuer.

The shares of a BV must be in registered form and the articles of a BV must impose one of the restrictions on transfer required by Article 2-1295 of the Civil Code, except for certain complex exemptions made in favour of a relative. The clause restricting transfer is called the blocking clause (*blokkeringsclausule*). Article 2-195 provides for two forms of restrictions, the requirement that transfers shall be approved by an organ of the BV, and the imposition of pre-emption rights in favour of the other shareholders. It is possible to combine the two restrictions by means of a suitable provision in the articles. One of the restrictions contained in Article 2-195 of the Civil Code must be included in the statutes in any event. According to Article 2-195(8), a restriction on transfer must not be such as to render transfer impossible or exceedingly burdensome. An NV may impose restrictions on the transfer of its shares but is not required to do so. It is likely that the present rules governing restrictions on transfer of shares in a BV will be amended in the near future. Such restrictions will be made optional, and may involve the requirement that the directors or the general meeting consent to a particular transfer. If a company imposes restrictions on share transfers in its articles it will be able to make detailed agreements as to how the price of its shares is determined.

The issue of *certificaten* (shares in Dutch companies are often represented by such certificates)[98] which are issued by an *administratiekantoor* (which is usually a subsidiary of a bank, or a subsidiary of an associated company of the NV in which the shares are held) to the bearer in respect of shares in a BV, with or without the consent of the BV, is prohibited by Article 2-202 of the Civil Code. As long as *certificaten* to bearer are outstanding in respect of a BV, no rights can be exercised in respect of the shares in question.

At present the minimum capital requirements for a BV[99] is €18,000 as opposed to the €45,000 required for an NV.[100] It is likely that the requirement of a minimum capital will be abolished.

There are certain other significant differences between a BV and an NV. Thus a BV may give loans for the purpose of the subscription or purchase by third parties of its shares or depository receipts (*certificaten*) issued up to an amount which does not exceed the distributable reserves provided that the articles so permit.[101] An NV can only give loans for the purchase of its shares by employees or depository receipts by employees.[102] A BV may acquire up to 50 per cent of its issued shares,[103] whilst an NV may only acquire 10 per cent.[104]

A BV and an NV can both be 'large' corporations. The same criteria are applicable for large BVs[105] as well as large NVs.[106] The rules concerning the appointment, composition and functions of the supervisory boards of both types of company are the same.[107]

H. Proposals for the European Private Company

The impact of the harmonising directives has not been as great on private limited liability companies as on public ones. In addition to the recently introduced European company it has been suggested that the establishment of a European private company might be beneficial, especially for countries which have yet to join the EU, and exporters from the EU. The proposed model articles of association on which Drury, Hicks and Hommelhoff have been collaborating would be annexed to proposed

[98] Netherlands Civil Code, Art. 2.202 [99] *Ibid.*, Art. 2.178(2). [100] *Ibid.*, Art. 2.67(2).
[101] *Ibid.*, Art. 2.207(c). This provision is likely to be repealed. [102] *Ibid.*, Art. 2.98c(1).
[103] *Ibid.*, Art. 2.207(2)(b). It is proposed that this limitation should be replaced. However, the company will not be able to purchase its own shares if this will involve the distribution of reserves which it is required to maintain by the law or articles, or such a purchase would result in the company being unable to pay its debts as they fall due.
[104] *Ibid.*, Art. 2.98(2)(b). [105] *Ibid.*, Art. 2.263(2). [106] *Ibid.*, Art. 2.153.
[107] For the BV see Netherlands Civil Code, Arts. 2.268–274, *ibid.*

regulations, which had already been drafted. The European type of private company is further discussed in a later chapter dealing with business enterprises governed by European law.[108]

A recent report by K. H. Lohne, a member of the European Parliament, on the European Private Company, was adopted by the Legal Affairs Committee of the European Parliament on 21 November 2006. The report stipulated that the European Commission should bring forth a proposal for an EPC Statute in 2007. It recommended that the minimum capital should be €10,000 and suggests that model articles of association should be annexed to any proposed regulation.

IV. Partnerships

The partnership remains an enterprise of considerable economic importance both in the United Kingdom and in other EU countries. In the United Kingdom, the partnership is of considerable significance in the retail and construction industries, as well as in manufacturing, agriculture and tourism. These partnerships may be informal associations between two persons engaged in a short-term profit making enterprise without any formal agreement, or small family businesses; or major business enterprises with a large number of members, an elaborate partnership agreement and a sophisticated management structure.

The fiscal transparency of partnerships sometimes leads to tax advantages. At one time (especially in Germany), partnerships were used to avoid the mandatory disclosure of annual accounts. This is no longer possible because Council Directive 90/605/EEC extended the scope of the Fourth Directive to partnerships where members having unlimited liability were public or private companies or limited partnerships with shares. Germany has only in 2000 complied with the requirements of this Directive.[109] The personal element is of considerable importance in partnerships. Thus, the shares in a partnership are usually not transferable without the consent of the other members, and the death or bankruptcy of a member of a partnership may lead to its dissolution. The partners generally have a

[108] For an account of the proposed European Private Company, see R. Drury, 'A European Private Company?' (2001) 3 ICCLJ 231 and C. Teichmann, 'The European Private Company' [2004] ECL 162.

[109] See Act of 24 February 2000 transposing, inter alia, Directive 90/605 into German Law [2000] *Federal Gazette* I 154. See in more detail D. Eisolt and W. Verdenhalven, 'Erläuterung des Kapitalgesellschaften und Co-Richtlinie-Gesetzes (KapCoRiLiG)' [2000] NZG 130; D. Zimmer and T. Eckhold, 'Das Kapitalgesellschaften & Co. – Richtlinie-Gesetz – Neue Rechnungslegungsvorschriften für eine große Zahl von Unternehmen' [2000] NJW 1361.

considerable measure of freedom to decide on the internal construction of a partnership. The personal element is once again manifest in the fact that in general partnerships, which do not grant limited liability to certain of their members, all the latter members are jointly and severally liable for the whole of the debts and obligations of the partnership.

Despite the unlimited liability of at least certain members of a partnership, certain partnerships are granted legal personality in certain Member States, including France, Belgium and Spain. Where they do not have such personality, their members are treated as being co-owners of the partnership's property.

A. *Civil partnerships*

This type of entity consist of partnerships which do not have a commercial objective, as defined by national legislation, generally contained in the Commercial Code, and which are not stated to be commercial by reason of their form. The civil partnership has no longer been in use in Italy since 1942, when the system of separate codification of civil and commercial law was abolished. However, they remain of some significance in France and Germany; in both countries, they are a matter for agreement by the partners.

Many forms of civil partnerships exist in France; civil partnerships are of considerable importance in the liberal professions. Special forms of civil companies or partnerships have also been detailed for the purpose of the building industry, and for the purposes of agriculture. Indeed, such entities have undergone something of a renaissance in recent years. Civil partnerships have been granted personality by Article 1842 of the Civil Code. The *Gesellschaft bürgerlichen Rechts* (GbR) remains of considerable importance in Germany. It is used for the purposes of the liberal professions and has other uses as well, in particular for consortium operations. Under German law, every group of persons associating together to pursue a common purpose without making use of the general or limited partnership of one of the three forms of company available under company law is treated as being such a partnership. As is the case with an English partnership, such a partnership may come into being through an unwritten agreement. The partnership is covered by Articles 705–740 of the Civil Code, and there are few mandatory provisions other than those governing duration and liquidation. The partnership has a number of defects insofar as members of the liberal professions are concerned, and it may be that it will be gradually replaced by the

Partnerschaftsgesellschaft, which was introduced in 1994. Until 2001, the opinion prevailed that a GbR lacked legal capacity, and that it could not enter into transactions, acquire obligations or sue or be sued in its own name. However, in 2001, the Federal Supreme Court (*Bundesgerichtshof*) delivered a landmark decision, according to which the civil partnership generally has both legal personality and standing in court.[110] However, in certain cases, the so-called Innen-GbR (which does not carry out any external activity) still lacks legal personality. Furthermore, difficulties have sometimes occurred in determining whether and to what extent the individual partners are liable to third parties.[111] However, the Civil Code partnership form is still used by some of the largest law firms in Germany.

Civil partnerships are also in use in Belgium and Spain. In Italy, they have been replaced by the simple partnership (*società semplice*).

B. Silent partnerships and other forms of partnership without legal personality

In addition to the civil partnerships mentioned above, entities which are sometimes referred to as silent partnerships because they do not have to be registered and the relationship does not have to be disclosed to third parties, exist in France, Germany and Belgium. The French silent partnership (*société en participation*) is governed by Articles 1871-3 of the Civil Code. It is recognised by Article 1871-1 of the Civil Code that a silent partnership may have a civil or a commercial character. The French silent partnership is not subject to the publicity formalities required of other companies and partnerships. However, the partners may decide that the partnership shall be disclosed to third parties. If they do so, then according to Article 1872-1 of the French Civil Code, each one of the partners is held bound by obligations arising from acts done as a partner by one of the others. The liability is joint and several if the enterprise is commercial. There is no such joint and several liability if the object is civil. The same rule as is applicable to disclosed partnerships is applicable where a partner with whom a third party has not dealt with personally has acted in such a way as to lead the third party to believe he intended to bind himself to the latter, and where that partner received a profit from the transaction in which he participated. The normal rule in relation to silent partnerships, to which the two above

[110] BGH, judgment of 29 January 2001, II ZR 331/00, reported in BGHZ 146, 341. See the discussion article by K. Schmidt, 'Die BGB-Außengesellschaft: rechts- und parteifähig – Besprechung des Grundlagenurteils II ZR 331/00 vom 29. 1. 2001' [2001] NJW 993.

[111] On this aspect, see BGH, judgment of 7 April 2003, II ZR 56/02, reported in BGHZ 154, 370.

rules are exceptions, is that each partner contracts in his personal name and is alone bound to third parties.

A silent partnership does not have legal personality according to Article 1871 of the Civil Code, and thus has no assets of its own. Consequently each partner retains the ownership and control of whatever he contributes to the partnership. The silent partnership has proved itself to be a very flexible form, and especially suitable for consortium operations or research activities. If, as is frequently the case it pursues a commercial objective, then subject to agreement to the contrary the rules governing the general partnership (*société en nom collectif*) apply. If on the other hand, the silent partnership pursues a civil objective then, subject to contrary agreement, the rules applicable to civil partnerships apply.[112]

The German form of silent partnership (*Stille Gesellschaft*) differs somewhat from the French *société en participation.* A silent partnership exists where a person participates in a commercial undertaking carried on by another, by means of a capital contribution, and all the assets remain in that other person's possession.[113] The owner alone has rights and obligations in relation to transactions concluded by the business with third parties. The partnership is correctly called silent because it is not registered in the Commercial Register and the relationship is not apparent to third parties. Silent partnerships between individuals and private limited liability companies have been used in the past for tax reasons. Silent partnerships are governed by the rules applicable to civil partnerships, as modified by the special rules contained in paragraphs 230–7 of the Commercial Code. A silent partner participates in the profits of the partnership and shares in its losses up to the amount of his contribution. The partnership agreement may provide that a partner shall not participate in the losses at all, or provide that he shall participate in them beyond the amount of his contribution, but cannot exclude him from participation in the profits.[114]

The owner of the commercial undertaking is bound by the general duties of loyalty and good faith toward the silent partner. The latter has a right to information and is entitled to a copy of the annual balance sheet and to determine its correctness by inspecting the books and records of the business undertaking. The court may, if there are serious reasons, order the provision of a balance sheet and the production of books and records to the silent partner, on being requested by him.[115] The silent partner does not participate in the management or representation of the commercial

112 Civil Code, Art. 1871-1. 113 See Kübler and Assmann, *Gesellschaftsrecht*, pp. 110 ff.
114 Commercial Code, Art. 232. 115 *Ibid.*, Art. 233.

undertaking, unless otherwise agreed. However, the partnership agreement may require the consent of the silent partner if the owner of the commercial undertaking wants to enter into certain types of transactions.

Articles 46–54 of the Belgian Companies Code recognises three forms of partnership which are different from the general partnership (*vennootschap onder firma, société en nom collectif*) and the limited partnership (*société en commandite simple*). None of these forms of partnership have legal personality. The first of these is the partnership according to the ordinary law (*droit commun*), which may have a civil or a commercial subject. It is not entirely clear what entities come within the above category. The second is the *société momentanée*, which is formed for the purpose of carrying out one or more commercial operations. This is often used as a vehicle for a joint venture. The third type of partnership, which would seem to correspond to the silent partnership, is the so called internal partnership, which is one in which one or more members involve themselves in operations which one or more other persons manage in their own name.

Article 50 of the Companies Code provides that the stipulation that an obligation is entered into on behalf of a partnership only binds the contracting partner and not the other partners, unless the latter have empowered him to act, or the transaction entered into has transpired to be for the benefit of the partnership. This provision is apparently intended to apply to all the three types of partnership lacking legal personality that have been mentioned above.

According to Article 51, one of the members of a partnership according to the ordinary law cannot bind the other members unless they confer such power on him. Furthermore, Article 52 provides that the members of such a partnership are liable to third parties to the extent of their share in the partnership if it has a civil object, and are jointly and severally liable to such persons if it has a commercial one.

By Article 53, the members of a *société momentanée* are jointly and severally liable to third parties with whom they deal. They may be sued individually and directly. However, it follows from Article 54 that no such direct action is possible by third parties against the members of an 'internal' partnership who supply funds thereto.

The type of Dutch partnership called the *maatschap* may function as a silent partnership. If it does so, it can be used for commercial purposes. However, if the object is commercial, the use of a firm name will convert it into a general partnership (*vennootschap onder firma*) in accordance with Article 16 of the Dutch Commercial Code (*Wetbook voor Koophandel*).

C. General partnerships

1. General partnerships in the United Kingdom

Somewhat controversially, a partnership is defined as a relationship by section 1(1) of the United Kingdom Partnership Act of 1890, according to which it is the relation which subsists between persons who carry on a business for profit. Thus, a partnership is treated as an aggregate of persons rather than a separate legal entity; an English partnership lacks legal personality. This lack of personality, which is not parallel in Scotland, leads to certain legal difficulties relating for example to such matters as the ownership of property and the execution of deeds. In certain European countries, such as France, Belgium, Norway, Greece and Sweden, a general partnership acquires personality by the registration of the deeds. A partnership may arise under English law from a course of dealings between the partners.

It follows from section 2 of the Partnership Act 1890 that the mere sharing of the profits of a business does not necessarily lead to the conclusion that a partnership exists, nor does the mere co-ownership of land. As is generally the case with corresponding forms in other EU countries, an English partnership is largely a matter of agreement. Thus, for example, section 24 of the Partnership Act 1890 contains rules concerning the rights and duties of partners subject to special agreement. There are however certain mandatory provisions of the 1890 Act, for example those of section 28, which impose on partners the duty to render the accounts, and those of section 29, which concern the accountability of partners for private profits.

According to section 26 of the Partnership Act 1890, a partner in a partnership at will may determine the partnership by giving notice of his intention to do so. It has been suggested in the English and Scottish Law Commission's Joint Consultation Paper on partnership law that this rule should be replaced by a right to withdraw from the partnership.[116]

There are some exceptions to the aggregate approach to partnerships taken by English law, principally for administrative reasons. A firm name is recognised for the purpose of court proceedings.[117] Furthermore, the firm name may be recognised for VAT purposes and, where it is, account is not taken of changes in the membership of the firm.[118] A Scottish

[116] Law Commission's Consultation Paper, No. 159 (2000), p. 23.

[117] CPR, Sched. 1, RSC 081, R1; CPR, Sched. 2, CCR, 05, R9(1).

[118] Value Added Tax Act 1994, s. 45.

partnership is regarded as having separate personality, but this doctrine is subject to certain limitations. Thus it is doubtful whether the legal personality of such a partnership can survive changes in its composition.

Every partner in a firm is liable jointly with the other partners, and in Scotland generally also for all the debts and obligations of the firm incurred when his is a partner.[119] Because an English partnership lacks legal personality and cannot own property, it is necessary to distinguish between the property owned by the partnership and the property owned by the partners. Section 20(1) of the Partnership Act 1890 does this though the employment of the concept of partnership property. Such property which is property brought into the partnership or acquired on its behalf, must be applied by the partners exclusively for the purposes of the partnership and in accordance with the partnership agreement. The concept of partnership property is of fundamental importance in determining what assets are available to meet the claims of creditors, of individual partners and the creditors of the firm. Considerable difficulties sometimes arise in determining what is partnership property.

Each partner is deemed to be an agent for his co-partners in respect of transactions carried out in the ordinary course of the partnership business.[120] Under Scottish law, partners are agents of the firm which has the primary liability for the debts and obligations it incurs through such agency. The liability of the partners is subsidiary in a Scottish partnership. The position differs in an English partnership, where each partner has unlimited liabilities for the acts of the other partners. Partners place mutual trust and confidence in one another, and thus stand in a fiduciary relationship. A partner cannot make a profit at the expense of his co-partners without their full knowledge. A partner who makes such a profit is under a duty to account for it to the other partners, which requirement may be avoided if the partner makes full disclosure of his interest in a transaction (e.g. a sale to or purchase from his firm)[121] to his co-partners. Under Scottish law, it would seem that the duty to account may be to the firm rather than to the fellow partners. However, in both jurisdictions, the duty to render the accounts and full information on all things affecting the partnership is a duty owed to co-partners rather than the firm.[122]

The Joint Consultation Paper of the Law Commissions of 2000 made a number of proposals for the reform of the law of partnership.[123] The

[119] Partnership Act 1890, s. 9. [120] Partnership Act 1890, s. 5.
[121] *Gordon* v. *Holland* (1913) 108 LT 385. [122] Partnership Act 1890, s. 28.
[123] See para. 3.11 of the Joint Consultation Paper.

most important of these would seem to be that English and Welsh partnerships should be entitled to have legal personality, and that this may, or may not be, dependent on registration, as is the case in some continental countries. This proposal has proved somewhat controversial. The Joint Consultation Paper also proposes that an outgoing partner should not have the right to force a winding up, unless this is provided for in the agreement. It also suggests that the liability of partners for the debts and obligations of the partnership should be joint and several in both England and Wales, and in Scotland, where the partnership has legal personality, it should be made clear that the partnership has liability, with the partners' liability being subsidiary. The two Law Commissions published a report on partnership law reform in November 2003.[124] It included recommendations in respect of general partnership law and limited partnership law, together with a draft Bill designed to replace both the Partnership Act 1890 and the Limited Partnerships Act 1907. After a consultation by the DTI in 2004, the government in 2006 announced its decision to implement the limited partnership law reforms recommended by the Law Commissions in their joint report. However, the recommendations in respect of general partnership law reform were not taken forward at this time. There is a considerable literature concerning the proposals for the reform of partnership law.[125]

D. General partnerships in some other European countries

1. General Partnership in France

The French *société en nom collectif* (SNC) has a long history and is subject to rather detailed legal provisions, some of which resemble those applicable to capital companies. Like the general partnership in the United Kingdom, this entity is in widespread use. An SNC is defined in Article L221-1 of the Commercial Code as a partnership the members of which are all merchants (*commerçants*)[126] who are jointly and severally

[124] Law Commission No. 283; Scot Law Commission No. 192.

[125] Note, for example, E. Deards, 'The Partnership Bill under starter's orders' (2004) 25 Co Law 41; J. Henning, 'The review of Partnership Law: the entity approach prevail' (2004) 25 Co Law 143; M. Baron, 'Partnership law reform: a review of the new changes to the partnerships law of England proposed by the Law Commission and the Scottish Law Commission' (2004) 25 Co Law 293; and J. Henning, 'Partnership law reform and the first RIA' (2005) 26 Co Law 831.

[126] Those persons who do not comply with the legislative requirements for the acquisition of the status of merchant cannot become members of an SNC.

liable for the debts and obligations of the partnership.[127] However, the creditors of an SNC can sue an individual partner for a partnership debt only if previous action has been undertaken against the company's assets and these did not entirely satisfy the creditor. An SNC is designated by a business name which may include the names of one or more members, and must be preceded or followed by the words '*société en nom collectif*.'[128]

A contract which is negotiated and signed privately is sufficient for the formation of an SNC. It must be in writing for the purposes of evidence and for the registration of the company at the Register of Commerce and Companies. However, if land is to be transferred to the partnership, a private deed is necessary. Several copies of a private contract are required, such that one may be deposited at the registered office, whilst the others are necessary to comply with the necessary formalities. A declaration of compliance with the necessary procedural requirements has to be signed by all the partners. The partnership acquires legal personality on being entered in the Register of Commerce and Companies.[129] The shares in an SNC (*parts d'intérêt*) may not, according to Article L221-13 of the Commercial Code, be transferred without the consent of all the partners, but pre-emption clauses are permissible. Furthermore, such shares may not be represented by negotiable securities. According to Article L221-3, all the partners have the right to participate in the management, except where the articles or a subsequent act provides otherwise. The members, according to the articles or a procedure stipulated therein, may appoint one or more managers who may or may not be partners. In the absence of such a provision in the articles, each member is a manager. A legal person may be appointed as a manager and, if such an appointment is made, the legal representatives of the latter body are subject to the same requirements and to the same duties and liabilities, civil and penal, as if they were individually managers of the partnership.

The court has the power to remove a manager for good reasons (which include dishonesty or incompetence) at the request of one or more partners. In addition to this power, the partners are empowered to remove the managers in accordance with rules which vary in accordance with the manner of their appointment, and whether they are partners. According to Article L221-12 of the Commercial Code, a partner or partners who are appointed manager(s) by the articles or by a modification thereof can only be dismissed by the unanimous vote of the other partners. Such dismissal

[127] See in more detail M. Cozian *et al.*, *Droit des sociétés*, 18th edn (Paris: Litec, 2005), pp. 453 ff.

[128] *Ibid.*, Art. L221-2. [129] *Ibid.*, Art. L210-6.

entails the dissolution of the partnership unless the articles provide otherwise, or the partners unanimously decide to continue it.

If one or more partners are managers and who are not designated as such in the articles, they may be dismissed in the circumstances provided for in the articles and in default of such provision, by a unanimous decision of the other partners. A manager who is not a partner may be dismissed under the conditions provided for in the statutes (if any), and otherwise by a unanimous decision of the partners.

If a manager (however appointed) is dismissed without good cause he is entitled to damages. It may be the case that the articles can derogate from this obligation: they may do so in the case of a civil company, and a similar rule may apply to a partnership. As far as third parties are concerned, the manager can bind the partnership by entering into transactions which fall within its objects. Any act of the manager which is not within the company's purposes as indicated in the articles is not binding on the company in dealing with third parties. On the other hand, provisions in the articles which limit the powers of the managers cannot be invoked against third parties.[130]

Such limitations are however, effective as between partners and managers. Article 221-4 covers the situation in which the powers of the managers are not stipulated in the articles. In such an event, the manager may bind the partnership by any act of management in its interests.

The articles may confer on the partners the power to authorise or overrule acts which fall within the province of the managers. When this step is taken the partners can be regarded as having a sovereign power of decision. Furthermore, the partners are empowered to decide unanimously on certain matters which fall outside the powers of the managers such as the appointment, supervision, and removal of managers, and the alteration of the articles.[131] An annual general meeting of the partners must be held six months after the end of the financial year for the purpose of approving the accounts and the manager's report and deciding on the division of profits.[132] The general meeting cannot be replaced by a written consultation.

The above type of decisions, which are beyond the powers of the managers are taken by the partners at a general meeting, or by a written

[130] French Commercial Code, Art. L221-5. If there are several managers, each one binds the company by acts falling within its objects. The opposition by one manager to the acts of another has no effect against third parties unless they are aware of such opposition.

[131] *Ibid.*, Art. L221-6. The statutes may also provide that decisions may be taken by written consultation if the calling of a meeting is not requested by one of the partners.

[132] *Ibid.*, Art. L221-7.

consultation if a general meeting is not made necessary by the terms of the articles and one of the partners does not demand it. Decisions must be taken unanimously, unless the articles provide otherwise.

The distribution of profits or losses takes place in accordance with the provisions of the articles and the members are entitled to vote on a distribution of profits at the annual general meeting. A contribution which takes the form of a promise to perform work is treated for the purposes of profits distribution as equivalent to the smallest contribution made by any other partner in cash or in kind unless the articles otherwise provide.[133]

The partners who are not managers have the right to examine the accounts and records of the partnership twice a year and to ask the managers written questions about the management to which they must reply in writing[134].

An SNC may appoint one or more auditors. It is bound to do so when at the end of a financial year two of the following three conditions are satisfied. These are that the balance sheet total exceeds €1,550,000, the turnover (less VAT) exceeds €3,100,000 and the average number of employees exceeds fifty.[135]

Certain grounds of dissolution are common to all companies and partnerships (for example dissolution by the court in accordance with Article 1844-7 of the Civil Code where there is just cause), and are thus applicable to the SNC. Furthermore, special grounds for dissolution exist relating to the capacity and competence of members. A SNC is dissolved if a partner becomes bankrupt or the subject of a decision ordering a complete transfer of his assets (*plan de cession total*), or becomes disqualified from exercising a commercial activity, or is pronounced subject to an incapacity, unless the continuation of the partnership is provided for by the articles, or the other members unanimously decide on such continuation. In the event of such continuation, the continuing partner must pay the person who may no longer continue to be a partner the value of his shares, to be determined by agreement or in accordance with an order of the court.[136]

Article L221-15 of the Commercial Code contains somewhat complex rules governing the effect of the death of a partner. In principle, such death results in the dissolution of the partnership. However, it is possible

[133] *Ibid.*, Art. 1844-1. [134] *Ibid.*, Art. L221-8.
[135] *Ibid.*, Art. L221-9 and Decree 67-236 of 23 March 1967, Art. 12.
[136] *Ibid.*, Art. L221-16.

for the articles to provide that in the event of the death of a partner, the partnership shall continue with his heirs taking his place or simply between the surviving partners. If it is stipulated in the articles that the partnership will continue with the heirs of the deceased partner, the other members must agree unanimously to their entrance into the partnership. If the articles expressly stipulate that the partnership shall continue either with the surviving spouse, or one or more heirs of the deceased, or any person mentioned in the articles or in the will of the deceased, the rule mentioned in the last sentence remains applicable. If the partnership is to be continued by the surviving partners there must be at least two in number and the value of the deceased partner's share must be paid to his heirs. The value of the shares is also paid to them if the other partners do not agree upon their entry into the partnership. If the statutes provide that a partnership shall continue with the heirs of the deceased partner, and any of these are unemancipated minors (that is, minors who do not possess legal capacity), they will be responsible for the company's debts within the limits of what they received by way of succession and furthermore the partnership must be transformed into a limited partnership (SCS) in which the minors are limited partners within one year of the death of the deceased partner, or otherwise to be dissolved by the end of one year.

2. General partnership in Germany

An *offene Handelsgesellschaft* (OHG) comes into being where the partners agree to carry on a commercial undertaking (for profit) (the intention to make profit is actually not necessary, albeit probably inherent in the term 'commercial undertaking'), in a common firm name (*Firma*) and no partner has limited liability for the debts of the partnership.[137] A commercial undertaking is defined in paragraph 1(2) of the Commercial Code. This provision (designed as a rebuttable presumption) states that every undertaking is a commercial undertaking unless it does not require to be managed like a commercial undertaking. Thus if a commercial (general) partnership declines in size as not to require the latter, it becomes a civil partnership. In addition to that, an undertaking has to be considered as a commercial undertaking if it is registered in the commercial register irrespective of the fact that it does not require to

[137] German Commercial Code, para. 105. See in detail Kübler and Assmann, *Gesellschaftsrecht*, pp. 68 ff.

be managed as a commercial undertaking.[138] Furthermore, to the extent that no special provisions may be found in the Commercial Code, the provisions of paragraphs 705–40 of the Civil Code are applicable to a general partnership.[139]

The formation of a general partnership requires an agreement, which may be oral. The partnership will be entered in the Commercial Register which will contain particulars of the firm's name and the names and particulars of the partners and the address of the registered office.[140] A general partnership must use its firm's name in transactions with third parties. Although a general partnership does not have full legal personality, it may acquire rights and liabilities, may be granted title to corporeal or incorporeal property (all the partners form a community of owners or a *Gesamthandsgemeinschaft*), be registered as the owner of property, and sue or be sued in the firm's name.[141]

Without prejudice to differing stipulations in the partnership agreement, each of the partners is authorised to manage the business of a general partnership and enter into transactions for the purpose thereof without the consent of the other partners. The authority of a partner to manage the business of the partnership is restricted by paragraph 116(1) of the Commercial Code to transactions within the normal scope thereof and by paragraph 115 giving other managing partners the right to object to particular measures (*Widerspruch*). The partnership agreement may contain what different provisions are thought desirable concerning the management of the partnership. It may thus, for example, require majority decisions for certain acts, and exclude individual partners from management altogether. The breach of these rules by the management may give rise to a claim against a manager for breach of his duties, but it normally does not affect his ability to enter into transactions on behalf of the company and has, therefore, no impact on the validity of the contract.[142]

A general partnership enters into transactions with third parties in the name of the firm. In principle, each partner has authority to bind the partnership in all judicial and extra judicial business and legal transactions.[143] This authority can only be restricted if an entry in the commercial register provides that a partner is excluded from representation, or

[138] German Commercial Code, para. 2. [139] *Ibid.*, para. 105(3).
[140] *Ibid.*, para. 106. [141] *Ibid.*, para. 124.
[142] *Ibid.*, para. 126. See Kübler and Assmann, *Gesellschaftsrecht* (n. 137), 83.
[143] *Ibid.*, para. 125(1).

that the partnership is represented by two or more partners, or that unless several partners act together, individual partners are empowered to represent the partnership only jointly with an authorised signatory (*Prokurist*).[144] Other limitations on the authority of the partners have no effect on third parties, unless they know or ought to know of them.[145] A partner is not permitted to undertake business of the same nature as that of the partnership on his own account, in the absence of the consent of the other partners. He is also not allowed to become a partner in another partnership engaged in the same kind of business as the original partnership.[146] The partners have the same rights in the partnership unless it is agreed that their rights shall be proportional to their original contributions.[147] They owe a duty of good faith to the partnership and the other partners, and must exercise the same degree of care as exercised in their own affairs.[148]

Partners are jointly and severally liable without limitation to satisfy the debts and obligations of the partnership out of their own personal property.[149] In practice, creditors often bring an action against the partnership and all the partners together.

By paragraph 717 of the Civil Code, a partner may not transfer his rights in a general partnership, unless the partnership agreement so permits, or all the other partners agree. The entry of a new partner requires the consent of all the other partners.[150] A person who joins an existing partnership is responsible for all the debts and obligations of the partnership existing at the date of his entry, whether or not he is aware of them.[151] Any agreement to the contrary has no effect. Where the partnership agreement provides that if one of the partners dies, or gives notice of termination of the partnership, or bankruptcy proceedings are instituted against his property, the partnership agreement shall continue between the other partners, the relevant partner is deemed by paragraph 736 of the Civil Code to retire on the occurrence of such an event. A partner who retires from the partnership is entitled to the payment for his shares out of the partnership assets.[152]

If a partner retires, he continues to be liable for the debts and obligations of the partnership incurred before retirement.[153] However, he is entitled to

[144] *Ibid.*, para. 125. [145] *Ibid.*, para. 126(2). [146] *Ibid.*, para. 112.
[147] *Ibid.*, para. 125(1). [148] Schmidt, *Gesellschaftsrecht*, § 47 II.
[149] German Commercial Code, para. 128. [150] BGHZ 13, 179, 185; BGHZ 71, 296, 299.
[151] German Commercial Code, para. 130.
[152] German Civil Code paras. 737–740 – applicable via German Commercial Code para. 105(3).
[153] German Commercial Code, para. 160(1).

an indemnity against such liabilities by the remaining partners if when his share of the assets of the partnership on retirement was calculated, account was taken of the firm's existing debts and obligations.[154]

The expulsion of a partner is permitted by paragraph 140 of the HGB in circumstances in which the other partners would be justified in applying to the court for an order dissolving the partnership because of the partner's conduct. The court is empowered to make such an order at the request of another partner when there are substantial grounds for such dissolution. General partnerships may be dissolved on certain other grounds set out in paragraphs 131–5 of the HGB.

3. The German *Partnerschaftsgesellschaft*

The regulations governing certain professions in Germany used to not permit them to make use of limited companies.[155] The commercial partnership and the limited partnership (KG) have not been open to persons carrying on liberal professions because their activities are not classified as 'commercial' in the sense of § 105 German Commercial Code. It proved politically impossible for Germany to adopt the same approach as had been taken in Austria, which was to make the general and limited partnership available to members of the liberal professions and persons carrying out activities which were not regarded as fully commercial.[156] The new *Partnerschaft*, which was introduced in Germany by the Law of 25 June 1994,[157] had certain apparent defects and underwent amendment in 1998.[158]

Membership of the new type of partnership is open to natural (but not to legal) persons engaged in the liberal professions. These professions are defined widely. The rules of particular professions may exclude their members from partnership in a *Partnerschaft*, or make such partnership subject to additional requirements. The new entity is governed by the rules contained in the Civil Code governing civil partnerships except where the law provides otherwise.[159] Several provisions of the Commercial Code are also of importance. The articles must be in a prescribed form, in writing and contain certain details.[160] The formation of a *Partnerschaft* must be entered in a separate *Partnerschaft* register which is open to public inspection.[161]

[154] Schmidt, *Gesellschaftsrecht*, § 51 II.
[155] Schmidt, *Gesellschaftsrecht* (n. 154), § 33 I 1. Now, § 59c of the Federal Lawyers Act. (*Bundesrechtsanwaltsordnung*, BRAO) permits a so-called *Rechtsanwalts-GmbH*.
[156] Schmidt, *Gesellschaftsrecht* (n. 154), § 64 I 2. [157] [1994] BGBl. I 1744.
[158] [1998] BGBl. I 1878. [159] *Partnerschaftsgesellschaftsgesetz* (PartGG), para. 1.
[160] PartGG, para. 6. [161] Commercial Code, para. 15.

The *Partnerschaftsgesellschaft* has to be given a name, which is taken from that of one of the partners, and contains an indication of their professional activities, and which adds the words '*und Partner*' or '*in Partnerschaft*'. The entry in the registry will contain the name and place of the partnership, the names and addresses of each partner, and the objects of the partnership. It follows from paragraph 7(1) of the Law of 1994 (as amended) that the new entity does not have legal personality, but is rather a community of persons. However, it may acquire rights as the owner of property. The rules concerning the representation of the *Partnerschaftsgesellschaft* are contained in paragraph 7(3) which makes reference to paragraphs 125–127 of the Commercial Code.[162] Paragraph 125 provides that each partner is entitled to represent the partnership, if he is not excluded from doing so by the partnership agreement. The latter (like the articles of a private company) may provide that the partnership shall be represented by all the partners or several of them jointly.

Paragraph 8 of the PartGG, which concerns liability for the obligations of the *Partnerschaftsgesellschaft*, appears to be the most important provision of that law.[163] Paragraph 8(1) provides that the creditors of the partnership do not only have access to the assets of the *Partnerschaft* in satisfaction of their obligations but in addition the partners thereof are jointly and severally liable to them in respect of such obligations. Paragraph 8(1) also provides that paragraphs 129 and 130 of the Commercial Code (HGB) are applicable by way of analogy. Paragraph 129 contains rules governing the defence of a partner against a claim, and paragraph 130 provides that a person who joins an existing partnership has the same liability as the other partner for the obligations of the partnership incurred before its entry. Paragraph 8(2) PartGG provides that where only certain partners are concerned with the execution of a task, they alone among the partners are jointly and severally liable to the creditors for professional fault. The latter also have recourse to the partnership's assets. The former rule is inapplicable to work of secondary importance. The stipulations of paragraph 8(2) say nothing about contractual liability and are not as detailed as is generally the case with the relevant provisions of American Limited Liability Partnership Statutes. Paragraph 8(3) provides that statutes (laws) may make provision for the limitation of liability in certain professions up to a certain specified amount in respect of a professional default, on condition that

[162] Schmidt, *Gesellschaftsrecht*, § 64 IV 1.
[163] Kübler and Assmann, *Gesellschaftsrecht*, p. 67.

they also provide for the imposition of an obligation to insure on the individual partners of the *Partnerschaft*. Such a limitation of liability is available to *Rechtsänwalte*.[164]

According to paragraph 9(1) PartGG, the provisions of paragraphs 131–144 of the Commercial Code (HGB) applicable to the dissolution of and withdrawal from a commercial partnership shall apply by way of analogy to the *Partnerschaft*, except where the law governing that entity otherwise provides. It is thus clear that any member may request the dissolution of the partnership without notice if there is an important ground therefore. The expulsion of a partner is apparently only possible if the court so orders on the petition of the other partners. Shares in a *Partnerschaft* are stated by paragraph 9(4) No. 1 PartGG not to be inheritable. However, the statute does not say anything about the situation where a share is left to a legatee who is qualified for partnership.

The new entity may eventually prove more useful than the civil law partnership to the professions. However, it does involve a greater element of disclosure consequent on registration. Furthermore, certain civil law partnerships benefit from limitations of liability. These include partnerships between attorneys and tax consultants. Such bodies may suffer however from their lack of legal personality and the absence of a clear legal structure.[165]

4. General partnership in Italy

Italian partnerships having non-commercial objects,[166] like those having commercial ones, may make use of the general partnership (*società in nome collettivo*), and the limited partnership (*società in accomandita semplice*). The first mentioned entity is in widespread use. The civil law partnership has been replaced by the *società semplice* or simple (non-commercial) partnership. The latter entity is of significance insofar as the rules applicable to such partnerships also apply to commercial (i.e. general) partnerships where no special rule is applicable to the latter. They are also applicable to a considerable extent to limited partnerships. A general partnership is required to register at the local office of the Register of Enterprises and in this case all the rules provided for this kind

[164] See paragraph 51(a)(1) No. 2 of the *Bundesrechtsanwaltsordung*, as amended. Cf. Schmidt, *Gesellschaftsrecht*, § 64 IV 1 and H. J. Hellwig, 'Die Rechtsanwalts-GmbH' (1997) 161 ZHR 337.

[165] Schmidt, *Gesellschaftsrecht*, § 64 V.

[166] The distinction between commercial and non-commercial objects follows from the Italian Civil Code.

of partnership will apply.[167] On the contrary, an unregistered general partnership (*società irregolare*) is treated, as far as dealings with third parties are concerned,[168] as a simple partnership until it is registered. General partnerships and limited partnerships do not have legal personality under Italian law.

The partnership agreement must contain the details mentioned in Article 2295 of the Civil Code governing the particulars of the partners, the business name, the partners who have powers of management and representation, the legal address and objects of the partnership, the contribution of each partner, the services to be provided from members whose contribution consists of work, rules for the distribution of profits and for each shareholder his participation in profits and losses and the duration of the partnership.

Unless the partnership agreement otherwise provides, each partner acting individually and separately from the others, is entitled to participate in transactions involving the management of the partnership.[169] If there is no express provision to the contrary in the agreement, the power of representation belongs to each managing partner, and extends to all acts done within the partnership's objects.[170] A stipulation which grants representation to some of the partners only, or which limits the power of representation of a partner, may be enforced against a third party if it appears in the Register of Enterprises, or if it can be proved that the third party had actual notice of it.[171] Should a general partnership not be registered, the limitation may be enforced against a third party only if the partnership can prove that the third party had notice of it.[172]

In a general partnership, whether registered or unregistered, the partners are all jointly and severally liable without limit for the obligations of the partnership.[173] Any agreement between the partners having a contrary effect is inoperative against third parties, irrespective of whether they are aware of it.[174] However, it is valid between the partners themselves.[175]

167 Italian Civil Code, Art. 2296(1).

168 This means both in respect of the liability and power of representation. The partners are all, jointly and severally liable for all the debts of the partnership, while in simple partnerships the contract may exclude the liability of one or more members under Art. 2267(2) of the Italian Civil Code. See F. Di Sabato, *Diritto delle società* (Milan: Giuffrè, 2005), pp. 162–3.

169 Italian Civil Code, Art. 2257(1). 170 *Ibid.*, Art. 2266(2). 171 *Ibid.*, Art. 2298(1).

172 *Ibid.*, Art. 2297(2). 173 *Ibid.*, Art. 2291(1). 174 *Ibid.*, Art. 2291(2).

175 In a simple partnership such an agreement is valid also against third parties if brought to their knowledge in suitable ways under Art. 2267(2) of the Civil Code.

The creditors of a registered general partnership must have recourse to and exhaust the assets of the partnership before they can avail themselves of the individual liability of the partners.[176] In all types of partnership a personal creditor of a partner can attach the profits accruing to that partner by way of execution, and is entitled to apply to the court for protective measure against the share of assets to which the defendant partner is entitled in the liquidation of the partnership.[177] In the case of a registered commercial partnership, the creditor cannot have the partner's share realised whilst the partnership continues.[178] The only exceptions to this rule are: (1) in case of a declaration of insolvency of the member who will become unable to partake in the collective management of the undertaking and is automatically excluded; and (2) when the duration of a partnership is extended by a court judgment, and the personal creditors of the partner opposes the judgment providing for the extension and has the partner's share realised.[179] However, in the case of an unregistered commercial partnership a creditor may attach profits belonging to the debtor and require the firm to realise the debtor's share in the partnership if the debtor's assets are insufficient to meet the claims of the creditor.[180]

The death, expulsion or withdrawal of a partner is not a reason for the dissolution of any type of Italian partnership, unless the partnership agreement stipulates otherwise.[181] Nevertheless, the partnership is required to realise and pay the value of the share of a partner who dies or is expelled, or withdraws from the firm within six months from the date when he ceased to be a partner.[182]

5. General partnership in Spain

The *sociedad colectiva* (general partnership) is one of the four types of commercial companies mentioned in Article 122 of the Spanish Commercial Code (*Código de Comercio*). The general partnership is in in frequently use in Spain. The incorporation or partnership agreement must be converted into a public deed (*escritura de constitución*) by a notary, and must contain certain prescribed particulars mentioned in Article 125 of the Commercial Code. These include, inter alia, the names

[176] Italian Civil Code, Art. 2304. [177] *Ibid.*, Art. 2270(1). [178] *Ibid.*, Art. 2305.

[179] *Ibid.*, Art. 2307. See B. Libonati, *Diritto Commerciale, Impresa e Società* (Milan: Giuffrè, 2005), p. 162.

[180] Italian Civil Code, Art. 2270(2).

[181] This follows from the Italian Civil Code, Art. 2272 which does not include such contingencies in the reasons for dissolution of a partnership.

[182] Italian Civil Code, Art. 2289.

and addresses of the partners, the objects of the partnership; the name and address of the partners who will manage the partnership, the partnership capital, stating each member's share and the bases on which its value has been arrived at, and the duration of the partnership.

A *sociedad colectiva* (SC) acquires legal personality as the result of registration.[183] Unless it is specifically provided otherwise, all partners are equally entitled to participate in partnership management. The partners are, according to Article 127 of the Commercial Code, jointly and severally liable to the full extent of their individual assets for the partnership's debts. Partnerships have a personalised character, and a partner in an SC may not transfer his interests in the partnership without the unanimous consent of the other partners.[184] General partnerships conduct business and contract obligations under the collective or partnership name which distinguishes them from other companies. This name must include that of all the partners, except where it contains the words '*y compañía*' (and company),[185] when it may include only some of them.

In addition to their right to participate in management enjoyed by all partners except those who only contribute their work, in the absence of other provisions in the partnership agreement, partners have a right to information, which enables them to examine the partnership's management and accounts.[186] They also have a right to share in profits and in the division of partnership assets, or in surplus assets on a liquidation, in the manner stipulated by the partnership agreement or, if this contains no relevant provision, in proportion to their shares in the partnership. If a partner only contributes his work, he is considered to have the same share as the 'capitalistic' partner with the lowest partnership share.[187] It may be recalled that a similar rule applies to the French general partnership (*société en nom collectif*). In addition to their obligation to contribute capital, work or both, partners are obliged by Article 144 of the Commercial Code to compensate the partnership for damages caused as the result of malicious conduct, abuse of powers or gross negligence. They are required to contribute to the losses in accordance with the provisions of the partnership agreement, or in proportion to their shares in the partnership. A partner may not compete with the partnership in the same field of activity.[188] Furthermore, he must not abstract amounts

[183] Spanish Commercial Code, Art. 119. [184] *Ibid.*, Art. 143. [185] *Ibid.*, Art. 126.
[186] *Ibid.*, Art. 133. [187] *Ibid.*, Art. 140. See also Civil Code, Arts. 1689–1691.
[188] Spanish Commercial Code, Art. 139. See also Arts. 170, 171, and 218(4), *ibid.*

from partnership funds in excess of what is granted to him in respect of expenses.[189]

There are various forms of management of general partnerships. Thus, for example, instead of management by agreement between all the partners, except those who contribute their work, the partnership agreement may delegate the task of management jointly and severally (or simply jointly) to two or more partners. In the former case, any management act done by any of the managers will bind the partnership, even if the other managers have expressed their objection to it. In the latter case, the agreement of all the managers is normally required for the performance of any management act.

The power of management may be granted to one partner only. In this case it follows from the Commercial Code that the other partners may not obstruct or impede him in the exercise of his activities. If a partner is appointed as the manager in the partnership agreement, he may not be removed from office according to Article 132 of the Commercial Code. However, if a sole manager abuses his powers or acts in a way which is manifestly prejudicial to the partnership, the other partners may appoint an administrator who will participate in all transactions or may seek rescission of the agreement before the competent court.

Managers are usually entrusted with powers of representation as well as powers of management. Only persons who are expressly authorised to use the partnership's name may exercise powers of representation.[190] It follows from Article 128 of the Commercial Code that persons not so authorised do not bind the partnership by the contracts they enter into, even if these are on its behalf.

6. General partnership in Belgium

The new Belgian Companies Code has surprisingly little to say about such partnerships. Article 201 of the Code provides that the *société en nom collectif* (SNC) or *vennootschap onder firma* (VOF) is a partnership

[189] Special rules are contained in Art. 136 of the Commercial Code to cover the case where the partnership has no special category of activities. In such partnerships, partners may not operate on their own without the agreement of the other partners, which agreement may be refused if there is actual manifest prejudice to the partnership. Partners who act on their own behalf without the agreement of the other partners are required to give any resulting profit to the partnership funds and will be required to bear any resulting losses. Furthermore, the partnership agreement may be rescinded in relation to such a partner.

[190] Commercial Code, Art. 128.

in which the responsible partners enter into contracts, and are jointly and severally liable without limits, and which may have a civil commercial object. According to Article 2 of the Code, such partnerships have legal personality. Article 203 provides that any judgment involving the personal liability of partners pronounced on account of the obligations of a general or limited partnership may not be pronounced until such time as there is a judgment against the partnership. By Article 204, the partners are jointly and severally liable for all the obligations (*engagements*) of the partnership, provided that one partner has given his signature and so long as the firm name is mentioned.

The partnership must be incorporated by a deed drawn up by a notary or one under private signature.[191] The partnership acquires legal personality on execution of the deed. It appears that even if no deed is executed, lasting and public collaboration of persons may still be regarded as a SNC: this takes place in accordance with the idea that a de facto entity (*société de fait*) has been created. It appears from Article 69, sentence 9 of the Companies Code that all the partners do not have to be entrusted with the task of administering and representing the partnership.

7. General partnership in the Netherlands

There have been recent suggestions that a new form of legal entity will be created in the Netherlands called the public partnership, which will have legal personality. The *vennootschap onder firma* (VOF), or partnership, and the *vennootschap bij wijze van geldschieting* (*en commandite*) or limited partnership would be forms of public partnership, and would (contrary to the present position) have legal personality.

Special rules concerning the general (or commercial) partnership are contained in Articles 15–34 of the Commercial Code, but certain of the provisions of the Civil Code are relevant to it as well. Furthermore some matters are left to the discretion of the partners. According to Article 16 of the Commercial Code, a general partnership has the object of conducting business under a firm name. This name may contain the names of some or all of the partners. The use of the phrase (*en compagne*) is not mandatory, but is reserved to the general and limited partnership. The partnership agreement must be contained in a notarised deed, or a deed under private signature.[192] A VOF must be registered at the commercial register kept by the chambers of commerce, but such registration is not essential to the validity of the partnership.

[191] Companies Code, Art. 66. [192] Commercial Code, Art. 23.

The general partnership may be represented by each partner unless the partnership agreement provides otherwise.[193] Limitations on the authority to enter into transactions on behalf of the general partnership only have effect as against third parties if they are entered in the commercial register.[194] Each partner is jointly and severally liable for the obligations of the partnership which arise out of contract or statutes.[195] The partnership is in principle only liable for the acts of a partner who is authorised to act on its behalf.[196] Partners may not compete with the partnership in the absence of agreement between the partners to the contrary effect.

New legislation governing Dutch partnership law is expected to come into force early in 2009. A partnership acting under a common name will be empowered to acquire legal personality and to give up such personality; and to convert itself into a BV (limited company). Irrespective of whether such a partnership has legal personality, all its partners will be jointly and severally liable to the company creditors, except for the limited partners in a limited partnership who will, generally speaking, be exempt from such liability.

E. Limited partnerships

1. United Kingdom limited partnership

The UK limited liability partnership has been discussed in the introductory part of this chapter, where it was indicated that it does not correspond to the types of limited partnership familiar in continental countries.[197] The limited partnership form introduced by the Limited Partnerships Act 1907 does so correspond, but probably because of the lateness of its introduction, little use has been made of it in this country, although it has sometimes been used in the film industry, for the purposes of North Sea oil operations, and also in the venture capital and private equity industries. The private limited liability company came into use in the United Kingdom in the late nineteenth century, and is usually preferred to the limited partnership.

As is the case with the general partnership, the law governing the limited partnership has recently undergone review by the Law Commission.[198]

[193] *Ibid.*, Art. 23. [194] *Ibid.*, Art. 31. [195] *Ibid.*, Art. 18. [196] Civil Code, Art. 1679.

[197] Limited partnerships were familiar in many other European countries well before the introduction of private limited liability companies.

[198] On 6 November 2001, the Law Commission and the Scottish Law Commission published a Joint Consultation Paper on the Limited Partnerships Act 1907. In November 2003, they produced a joint report on the consultation proposing, inter alia, to amend

At present the United Kingdom limited partnership governed by the 1907 Act, lacks personality. It has been recommended in the Law Commission and Scottish Law Commission's Joint Report on Partnership Law Reform that (for tax reasons) English limited partnerships, which should normally have legal personality, may belong to a category of special limited partnerships which do not possess it. It was proposed that this exception should not apply to Scottish limited partnerships. The limited partnership must be registered with the Registrar of Companies, and the registration details must contain certain prescribed particulars mentioned in Section 8 of the Act. These include the general nature of the partnership's business, the principal place of the business, a statement that it is a limited partnership, the names of the limited partners, the sum contributed by each limited partner and the method of contribution.

A limited partner may lose his limited liability if he takes part in the management of the firm.[199] This is not the case in Germany, where limited partners may be given rights of management without losing their limited liability. It is not clear what actions involve taking part in the management for the purposes for Section 6 of the United Kingdom statute.

The ordinary rules of United Kingdom partnership law are modified to some extent in relation to limited partnerships. Thus, a limited partner has no implied authority to represent the firm. He may fully assign his share with the consent of the other partners, but he has no right to dissolve the partnership on giving notice.

2. French limited partnership

The French *société en commandite simple* (SCS) (limited partnership) is not made much use of in practice, although there has apparently been some revival in the use of the *société en commandite par actions* (limited partnership with shares) in recent years.[200] According to Article L222-2 of the Commercial Code, the rules applicable to general partnerships are applicable to limited ones, apart from those rules contained in the chapter applicable to the SCS.

The *commandités* or general partners are jointly and severally liable for the whole of the debts and obligations of the partnership, and are

the law to create separate personality for all general partnerships. The DTI followed this with a consultation document on the economic impact of reform of partnership law. The government intends to bring forward proposals for the reform of limited partnership law based on the Law Commissions' recommendations.

199 Limited Partnership Act, s. 6.

200 The principal difference between these two entities is the fact that the limited partnership with shares is a public company while in a limited partnership shares may not be represented by negotiable securities.

subject to most of the rules applicable to an SNC.[201] The *commanditaires* or limited partners are liable up to the amount of their contributions. They need not be qualified as merchants, and cannot make a contribution consisting of services.[202] An SCS must have at least one general partner, but there can be as many limited partners as it thought desirable.

According to Article 222-6 of the Commercial Code, a limited partner may not enter into any transaction with a third party as part of the management of the partnership's affairs. He cannot do this by acting as an agent appointed by the general partners or the managers. If this rule is broken, the limited partners together with the general partners are jointly and severally liable without limit for the debts and obligations of the partnership which result from the prohibited acts. Furthermore, depending on the number and significance of such acts, he may be declared jointly and severally liable in respect of all the obligations of the partnership, or only certain of them. There is nothing in the law to prevent a limited partner participating in management decisions provided he does not enter into transactions with third parties. However, such participation is usually excluded by the statutes of the partnership, which generally reserve all management powers to the general partners or managers.

The contributions of both general and limited partners are represented by shares or participations (*parts sociales*). In the absence of different provisions in the statutes, such shares may be transferred only with the consent of all the general and limited partners. The articles may provide that the shares belonging to the limited partners are freely transferable as between the partners. They may also provide that the limited partners' shares may be transferred to a person who is not a partner with the consent of all the general partners, and of a majority in number of the limited partners who hold more than one half of the capital attributed to all the limited partners.[203]

3. Limited partnership in Germany

A partnership whose purpose is the operation of a commercial enterprise under a firm name is a limited partnership (*Kommanditgesellschaft*, KG), if the liability of one or more member partners is limited to the amount their contributions[204] and the other partners are liable without limitation

[201] Commercial Code, Art. L222-1, para. 1.

[202] Commercial Code, Art, L221-1(2). This is because that such a contribution might entail participation in management.

[203] *Ibid.*, Art. L222-8.

[204] German Commercial Code, paras. 161 and 171.

for the debts and obligations of the partnership.[205] As is the case with the French SCS, the rules governing general partnerships are applicable to the KG, except where the law provides otherwise.[206] The special rules contained in paragraphs 162–177a of the Commercial Code are generally applicable to limited partners only. Both natural and legal persons may be members of a limited partnership. Since the 1998 reform the name of a limited partnership does not have to contain the name of at least one general partner anymore.[207] The application for registration must, inter alia, mention this name, the names of the partners, and the contribution due from each limited partner.[208] Limited partners are liable without limit with regard to transactions entered into by the partnership before the registration of the fact that their liability is limited unless they did not give their consent to the transaction or the creditor was aware of their limited liability.[209]

Limited partners are in principle excluded from the management of the partnership.[210] They may not oppose a transaction by the ordinary partners unless it goes beyond the scope of the ordinary business of the partnership.[211] A limited partner may request a copy of the annual balance sheet and determine its accuracy in the light of the books and records.[212] A limited partner is not authorised to represent the partnership.[213]

The above rules only apply if the partnership agreement fails to contain different provisions. In practice it always contains special provisions. Limited partners are sometimes given rights of management. If a limited partnership has a large number of partners, the partnership agreement often provide for a committee of limited partners exercising control over the managing partner, or taking part in the management of the partnership. The partnership agreement may provide that the share of a limited partner shall be transferable, in which case such transfer only takes effect in favour of an outsider when registered.

The commonest form of limited partnership met with in practice in Germany is the GmbH & Co. KG.[214] This entity together with certain

[205] *Ibid.*, para. 161(1). Cf. Kübler and Assmann, *Gesellschaftsrecht*, p. 100 f.
[206] German Commercial Code, Art. 161.
[207] Schmidt, *Gesellschaftsrecht*, § 53 II 3; Kübler and Assmann, *Gesellschaftsrecht*, p. 101.
[208] German Commercial Code, para. 162. [209] *Ibid.*, para. 176. [210] *Ibid.*, para. 164.
[211] *Ibid.*, para. 164. [212] *Ibid.*, para. 166.
[213] *Ibid.*, para. 170 states that limited partners are generally excluded from representing the partnership. Nevertheless, they can be individually given power to represent the partnership.
[214] Schmidt, *Gesellschaftsrecht*, § 56 I; Kübler and Assmann, *Gesellschaftsrecht*, p. 103.

other similar entities of a hybrid character of much less importance, the GmbH & Co. KGaA and the *société en commandite par actions à responsabilité limitée*, will be considered briefly, after limited partnerships have been fully discussed. The hybrid form of entity which has been described as the limited partnership with shares has already been considered above.

4. Limited partnerships in Italy

According to Article 2315 of the Italian Civil Code, the provisions relating to general partnerships apply to the limited partnerships (*società in accomandita semplice*) except where they are incompatible with the special rules contained in Articles 2316–2324 governing such limited partnerships. As follows from Articles 2293 and 2315, the rules concerning the limited partnership are to a considerable extent based on those governing the general partnership.

By Article 2314 of the Civil Code the business name (*ragione sociale*) must consist of the name of at least one of the general partners; with an indication of the limited partnership status. Once again, a distinction is made between the position of the general unlimited partners (*soci accomandatari*[215]) who are jointly and severally liable without limit for all the debts of the partnership, and the limited partners (*soci accomandanti*), who are liable to the extent of their contributions.[216] Limited partners who permit their name to be included in the business name, or who perform acts of management, lose their limited liability.[217] However, it follows from Article 2320(1) of the Civil Code that limited partners can perform managerial acts or negotiate or conclude business in the name of the partnership if they are fully authorised in respect of a particular such act or transaction by the general partners. The prohibition on assuming the powers of the managers does not prevent them from exercising certain powers and rights. Thus, by Article 2320(3) of the Civil Code, the limited partners are in all cases entitled to receive the annual accounts, and profit and loss statement, and to check their accuracy by consulting the books and other partnership documents. As is generally the case in other jurisdictions, the unlimited partners have the same rights and duties as partners in general partnerships. As already

[215] Because of linguistic similarities, one might well think that the *soci accomandatari* corresponds to the *commanditaires* in a French limited partnership (*société en commandite simple*). However, this is not the case: they actually have the same role as the *commandités* (limited partners) in such a partnership.

[216] Italian Civil Code, Art. 2313. [217] *Ibid.*, Arts. 2314(2), 2320(1).

indicated, the management of the partnership may only be conferred on an unlimited partner.[218]

It follows from Article 2317(1) of the Civil Code that an unregistered limited partnership is treated in the same way as an unregistered general partnership. Nevertheless, the liability of limited partners remains limited unless they have participated in partnership transactions.

5. Limited partnership in Spain

The limited partnership in Spain is governed by Articles 145–150 of the Spanish Commercial Code. The limited partners (*socios comanditarios*) do not involve themselves in the business transactions, and have a liability limited to their contribution: the unlimited partners (*socios colectivos*) have joint and several liability for debts and obligations of the partnership. At least one partner's name must be used in the partnership name, which may not include names of limited partners. The transfer of the participations (or shares) of a limited or unlimited partner is only permissible with the consent of all the other partners. According to Article 148(4), limited partners have no rights to participate in the management of the partnership, and may not represent or bind it by their acts. By Article 150(2) of the Commercial Code, limited partners are entitled to examine the accounts at the end of the year, unless the partnership agreement provides otherwise. However, limited partners have the same rights as general partners to participate in the partnership profits, and they participate on a pro rata basis in the liquidation surplus.

A limited partnership, like a general partnership, has to be formed by means of a public notarial deed, which must contain certain similar particulars to those required in the case of a general partnership.

Limited partnership with shares (*sociedades en comandita por acciones*) are rarely encountered in Spain, and are governed by the provisions of Articles 151–157 of the Commercial Code. They are thought of as a special category of limited partnerships, but they function in such a way so that they could also be regarded as a special type of public company with personally liable directors.

6. Limited partnership in Belgium

The Belgium limited partnership is called the *gewone commanditaire vennootschap* (GCV) or *société en commandite simple* (SCS). The names of the unlimited partners must be published in the Annexes to the

[218] *Ibid.*, Art. 2318(1).

Moniteur Belge together with the amount of the contributions and anticipated contributions of the limited partners.[219] Similar publicity must also be given to the name, registered office, and duration of the partnership, if this is not unlimited.

A judgment cannot be given against the partners by imposing personal liability on them until such time as judgment has been given against the partnership.[220] The general partners are jointly and severally liable without limitation for the partnership's obligations. The limited partners are only liable to contribute to the debts and losses of the partnership up to the amount of their promised contribution. However, according to Article 206(2) of the Belgian Companies Code, they may be required by third parties to pay them interest and dividends which they have received if these have not been paid out of real profits of the partnership. In such an event, if there is fraud, bad faith, or gross negligence, on the part of a manager or managing partner, the limited partner may bring an action against him for the restitution of the amounts he has had to pay to the third party. According to Article 207(1), limited partners may not, even when granted authorisation by the other partners, participate in any act of management. However, this prohibition does not apply to the giving of advice, the exercise of supervisory functions, and the authorisation of managers to do acts which are outside their powers. Nevertheless, they are jointly and severally liable without limitation to third parties for all the partnership's obligations in which they have participated despite the prohibition on their performance in managerial acts. They are jointly and severally liable without limitation to third parties even if they have not so participated if they have habitually managed the partnership, or if their name appears in that of the partnership.[221]

If the manager dies, or becomes subject to a legal incapacity or impediment, and it has been stipulated that the partnership shall continue, the president of the commercial court may, unless the partnership agreement provides otherwise, order the appointment of a limited partner as administrator entrusted with the task of carrying urgently necessary acts and simple administration for a period of no more than one month. The administrator may only carry out the tasks assigned to him. The commercial court's order may be opposed by any interested party. Such oppositional proceedings will be dealt with by the court entrusted with hearing urgent cases.[222]

[219] Belgian Companies Code, Arts. 69, 72 and 73.
[220] *Ibid.*, Art. 203. [221] *Ibid.*, Art. 207. [222] *Ibid.*, Art. 208.

7. Limited partnership in the Netherlands

When the Dutch *commanditaire vennootschap* (CV)[223] is formed, it is necessary to register the number, nationality and domicile of the limited partners, and also the amount of their contributions.[224] At present, unlike its Belgian counterpart, a Dutch limited partnership lacks legal personality. Once again, the limited partners are only liable to the extent of their contributions to the partnership, but they may not perform act of management on its behalf.[225]

F. *Special type of limited partnership in Germany and France*

1. GmbH & Co. KG and *société en commandite à responsabilité limitée*

The most common type of limited partnership in Germany is the GmbH & Co. KG. In recent years, a similar form, the *société en commandite simple à responsabilité limitée* has been in use in France, where it is much less commonly employed than its German counterpart. There appears to be considerably more literature on the German GmbH & Co. KG than on its French counterpart.[226] Many German jurists have expressed their disapproval of the hybrid form of business entity in the past, and there is a great deal of jurisprudential writing on this entity. It now must be regarded as a generally accepted business form. In 1933 the highest fiscal court, the *Reichsfinanzhof*, gave full recognition to the GmbH & Co KG.[227] This entity was often looked at with disapproval by the German tax authorities, as it appeared to constitute a means of tax avoidance. It is possible that the French courts might treat an *SCS à responsabilité limitée* as an entity the sole purpose of whose formation was to avoid mandatory

[223] The Dutch limited partnership is also called *vennootschap bij wijze van geldschieting*.

[224] Article 7 of the *Handelsregisterwet* (Dutch law on the Commercial Registry).

[225] Dutch Commercial Code, Art. 19.

[226] See, e.g. M. K. Binz and M. H. Sorg, *Die GmbH & Co. KG*, 10th edn (Munich: CH Beck, 2005); M. Hesselmann *et al.*, *Handbuch der GmbH & Co. KG*, 19th edn (Cologne: Otto Schmidt, 2005); H. Klauss and J. P. Birle, *Die GmbH & Co. KG. Gesellschaftsrecht, Steuerrecht*, 7th edn (Ludwigshafen: Kiehl Friedrich Verlag, 1988); K. Schmidt and W. Uhlenbruck, *Die GmbH in Krise, Sanierung und Insolvenz*, 3rd edn (Cologne: Otto Schmidt, 2003); H. Sudhoff, *GmbH & Co. KG*, 5th edn (Munich: CH Beck, 2000); H. Wagner and H. J. Rux, *Die GmbH & Co. KG*, 10th edn (Freiburg: Haufe, 2004); T. Raiser and R. Veil, *Recht der Kapitalgesellschaften*, 4th edn (Munich: Vahlen, 2006), § 42.

[227] Decision of 18 February 1933, RStBl 375. The Federal Supreme Court *Bundesgerichtshof* has continued to adopt the same approach.

rules of law.[228] Both the French and German entities consist of one or more limited partners and a general (or unlimited) partner or partners which is a private limited liability company.[229]

2. Uses and forms of the GmbH & Co KG

A GmbH & Co KG in which the limited partners are also the shareholders in the GmbH has been frequently used in Germany for the purpose of family businesses in the early stages of their development.[230] Many other types of GmbH & Co are met with in practice. This entity has been used to provide for the situation in which a general partner dies or departs from a family business taking the form of a KG by means of transferring his share to a GmbH which continues the business with the limited partners.[231] Certain large types of GmbH & Co. are quoted on a stock exchange. In such partnerships, a GmbH is usually the general partner and the investors are the limited partners.[232] Since such companies have lost the tax advantages which they enjoyed before 1976, when the new imputation system of corporation tax was introduced, they have tended to be used less frequently in recent years.[233] Although these undertakings have proved to have a successful role as finance companies, they have fallen into a certain amount of disrepute in Germany, owing to the frequency of insolvencies which have occurred.[234] The courts have been developing rules to protect investors in such companies.

One-man GmbH & Co. KGs are also recognised in which the sole shareholder of the GmbH, who is the general partner, is the same individual as the limited partner.[235] The sole shareholder may instead be the limited partnership itself. The formation of such entities has sometimes proved useful to sole traders. However, it has been suggested

[228] Note in this sense, A. Guineret-Brobbel Dorsman, *La GmbH & Co. KG allemande et la commandite à responsabilité limitée française* (Paris: LGDJ, 1998), p. 115.

[229] At least in Germany, it is possible to replace the GmbH by any other limited liability company. Therefore, it is equally permissible to form an 'AG & Co. KG' or a 'KGaA & Co. KG'. It is even allowed to use a foreign limited liability company, for instance the English private limited liability company (which would give the 'Ltd. & Co. KG'). See on the latter, M. K. Binz and G. Mayer, 'Die ausländische Kapitalgesellschaft & Co. KG im Aufwind? – Konsequenzen aus dem "Überseering" – Urteil des EuGH vom 5.11.2002' [2003] GmbHR 249. In more detail Raiser and Veil, *Recht der Kapitalgesellschaften*, pp. 625 ff.

[230] Schmidt, *Gesellschaftsrecht*, § 56 I; Kübler and Assmann, *Gesellschaftsrecht*, p. 350 f.

[231] The conversion of this capital is now permitted by para. 226 of the new Umwandlungsgesetz (UmwG, Conversion Act) of 1994, *Federal Law Gazette* (BGBl) 1994 I-3210.

[232] Schmidt, *Gesellschaftsrecht* (n. 230), § 56 II 1 a. [233] *Ibid.*, § 56 I. [234] *Ibid.*, § 56 I 3.

[235] *Ibid.*, § 56 II 3 c; Kübler and Assmann, *Gesellschaftsrecht* (n. 230) p. 351.

that French jurists would be likely to oppose the use of a similar entity in France on the grounds that what is in reality an entity composed of a single person cannot be treated as a *société des personnes.*[236]

The type of entity in which the sole shareholder of the GmbH is the same person as the limited partner, must be distinguished from the unitary type of GmbH & Co. KG (*Einheits-GmbH & Co KG*) in which the sole shareholder of the GmbH is the limited partnership itself.[237] The use of such an entity, which is acknowledged by paragraph 172(6) of the HGB, has the advantage of coordinating the activities of the GmbH and the limited partnership. Such coordination is sometimes difficult to achieve because of the differences between the law applicable to the private limited liability company and the limited partnership.[238] The employment of the unitary type of entity does however give rise to certain problems in relation to the use of voting rights by the manager(s) of the GmbH as representatives of the partnership in the general meeting of the GmbH.[239] Such managers are prevented by paragraph 47(4) GmbHG from voting on certain resolutions affecting them. Furthermore, the members of a GmbH are required to decide on the dismissal of its managers(s) by paragraph 46(5) GmbHG. This appears to entail that, because the GmbH has no natural persons as its members, the manager(s) must vote upon their own dismissal.

These difficulties are circumvented by permitting the limited partners to exercise voting rights in such circumstances. This pragmatic solution may well have an inadequate legal basis.[240]

A final rather curious variant of the GmbH & Co. KG which has been employed in Germany in the past consists of the three tier GmbH & Co. KG in which the general partner in the GmbH & Co. KG is itself a GmbH & Co. KG.[241] The use of this complex form of undertaking (which apparently is now only rarely employed) was explained by efforts to circumvent the rules which used to be contained in the former *Umwandlungsgesetz* (UmwG) (Conversion Law) concerning the change of form of a company as well as the rules governing employee codetermination.

[236] Note in this context, Guineret-Brobbel Dorsman, *La GmbH & Co. KG allemande*, (n. 228), 164.

[237] Kübler and Assmann, *Gesellschaftsrecht* (n. 230) p. 351; Raiser and Veil, *Recht der Kapitalgesellschaften*, p. 628.

[238] A. Guineret-Brobbel Dorsman, *La GmbH & Co. KG allemande et la "commandite à responsabilité limitée française"*, pp. 156–7.

[239] Schmidt, *Gesellschaftsrecht*, § 56 II 3 e.

[240] Schmidt, *Gesellschaftsrecht*, § 56 II 3 e.

[241] *Ibid.*, § 56 II 3 f.

3. Advantages of the GmbH & Co KG and the corresponding French entity

Although the GmbH & Co. KG no longer has the advantage over capital companies of avoiding the double taxation of company profits since the imputation system of taxation was introduced in 1976, it may have other tax advantages. The tax position of its French counterpart, the *société en commandite à responsabilité limitée*, is rather complex, and may not offer any particular advantage which is not available to capital companies.

A GmbH & Co. KG and its French counterpart appear to have a number of advantages over an ordinary limited partnership and a private limited liability company.[242] As compared with an ordinary limited partnership, both entities have the advantage that all their members have limited liability.[243] As compared with a German KG, there is a greater freedom to choose a manager. This is because in principle, in the GmbH & Co. KG, a member having unlimited liability should be chosen as a representative of the partnership. Thus, the representative of a GmbH & Co. KG must be the unlimited partner, i.e. the GmbH. However, because the latter is a legal person, it has to exercise its task of management and representation through the medium of its manager(s), who may be any natural person (including a limited partner) of full legal capacity. Such managers do not have joint and several liability. The formation of a GmbH & Co. KG rather than a KG may thus be contemplated if none of the founders wish to incur unlimited liability, or if none of them feel capable of assuming managerial tasks.

The advantage consisting of a greater freedom of choice of the managers which applies to the German GmbH & Co. KG as compared with the German KG is inapplicable to the French *société en commandite simple à responsabilité limitée* as compared with the French SCS. In the latter entity, an outsider may be a manager if the articles so permit.[244] However, the use of the GmbH & Co. KG will permit a limited partner to act as manager of the constituent GmbH. Such a person cannot act as a manager of a SCS, even if he is given specific authorisation[245] by the general partners or managers. Both the GmbH & Co. KG and the corresponding French entity can be used to circumvent difficulties which sometimes occur on the death of general or unlimited partners. In France, unless the partnership agreement provides otherwise, the

[242] Note in this context, Guineret-Brobbel Dorsman, *La GMBH & Co. KG allemande*, 136–148.
[243] Schmidt, *Gesellschaftsrecht*, § 56 II 4 a.
[244] French Commercial Code, Arts. L221-3, L222-2. [245] *Ibid.*, Art. L222-6.

death of such a partner entails the dissolution of the partnership.[246] In Germany, the contrary is true: unless otherwise laid down in the agreement, the death of a partner entails his retirement from the partnership.[247] A private limited liability company is not subject to mortality.

The use of the German GmbH & Co KG and the French *société en commandite simple à responsabilité limitée* appears to make possible the use of more flexible structures to meet the needs of particular businesses, than appears to be the case with the GmbH or SARL.[248] Furthermore, in both entities, those who provide capital may well be limited partners whose influence on the management of the partnership may not be significant. A person who holds the necessary majority of shares or capital in a GmbH[249] or SARL[250] which is the unlimited partner in one of the two special types of limited partnership mentioned above should be able to become manager of the GmbH or SARL and indirectly of the limited partnership. This might not be possible if the entity took a different form. This possibility of separating the managerial and capital providing functions explains the success of the large GmbH & Co. KGs which offer their shares to the public.

The *Drittelbeteiligungsgesetz* of 2004[251] which replaced the Works Council Act (*Betriebsverfassungsgesetz*) of 1952, is not directly applicable to GmbH & Co. KG, and thus this type of undertaking can be used to avoid employee codetermination when the number of relevant employees does not exceed 2,000. The limited partnership employees are attributed to the GmbH if a majority of the limited partners holds a majority of the shares or votes in the GmbH.[252] It follows from Articles L225-23 and L225-71 of the French Commercial Code that there is only limited scope for compulsory codetermination at board level in French public companies. Furthermore, the rules contained in Article L432-6, paragraph 1 of the Labour Code (*Code du Travail*) provide for a merely consultative role for the members of the works committee at the meetings of the executive

246 *Ibid*., Art. L222-10.

247 This follows from para. 131 (3) no. 1 Commercial Code for the OHG and from paras. 161, 177 Commercial Code for the KG. See K. J. Hopt in A. Baumbach and K. J. Hopt, *Handelsgesetzbuch*, 32nd edn (Munich: CH Beck, 2006), § 139, para. 1. Instead of the retirement, the articles of association can provide for a continuation clause with the partner's heirs.

248 Schmidt, *Gesellschaftsrecht*, § 56 III 4.

249 German Private Limited Liability Companies Act, para. 6 al 5.

250 French Commercial Code, Arts. L223-18, L223-29(1).

251 *Drittelbeteiligungsgesetz* or DrittelbG, BGBl. 2004 S.974.

252 Codetermination Act (*Mitbestimmungsgesetz*, MitBestG) 1976, para. 4(1).

board or supervisory board of a company. Thus the use of the French *SCS à responsabilité limitée* provides no great advantage from the viewpoint of codetermination at board level.

As already pointed out above, Council Directive 90/605/EEC, which amends Directive 78/660 on Annual Accounts and Directive 83/349 on consolidated accounts as regard the scope of the Directive has recently been implemented in Germany by the *Kapitalgesellschaften- und Co. Richtliniengesetz* (KapCoRiLiG) of 14 February 2000.[253] The former exemption of German GmbH & Co KGs from the accounting requirements of the Fourth and Seventh Directives have now ceased.[254]

4. Disadvantages

The French *SCS à responsabilité limitée* and the German GmbH & Co. KG have substantially the same disadvantages. This type of entity suffers from a certain lack of transparency insofar as it may be difficult to determine what or who lies behind the entity which is the unlimited partner. Furthermore, these entities have a complex structure and are governed by a complex legal regime and partnership contract. Although they have the apparent advantage of imposing limitations on the liability of members, such persons may often in practice be asked to give guarantees to banks or other creditors.[255]

5. Protection of creditors and the limited partners

The German GmbH & Co KG has acquired a somewhat dubious reputation which it does not entirely deserve, on the grounds that it is sometimes used as a vehicle for fraudulent practices.[256] However, many family undertakings which are run with scrupulous honesty take this form. Rules have been developed by the courts and the legislature which are intended to protect the creditors of and the limited partners in such an undertaking.[257] Similar rules to those governing the preservation of the capital of a GmbH have been applied to the GmbH & Co. KG. Thus, in a number of decisions, the Supreme Court has held that if a limited partner

[253] Act of 24 February 2000 transposing, inter alia, Directive 90/605 into German Law [2000] Federal Gazette I 154. See on this D. Eisolt and W. Verdenhalven, 'Erläuterung des Kapitalgesellschaften und Co-Richtlinie-Gesetzes (KapCoRiLiG)' [2000] NZG 130; D. Zimmer and T. Eckhold, 'Das Kapitalgesellschaften & Co. – Richtlinie-Gesetz – Neue Rechnungslegungsvorschriften für eine große Zahl von Unternehmen' [2000] NJW 1361.

[254] Schmidt, *Gesellschaftsrecht*, § 56 IV 6; Kübler and Assmann, *Gesellschaftsrecht*, 353.

[255] A. Guineret-Brobbel Dorsman, *La GMBH & Co. KG allemande*, 149.

[256] Schmidt, *Gesellschaftsrecht*, § 56 I 3. [257] Kübler and Assmann, *Gesellschaftsrecht*, 357.

receives a payment out of the funds of a GmbH & Co. KG, he may be liable to refund it if such payment has the effect of making the liabilities of the GmbH exceed its assets.[258] It is noteworthy that the laws governing the preservation of the capital of a GmbH have been applied directly to the GmbH & Co. KG by way of analogy. Furthermore, paragraph 172a of the Commercial Code (HGB) makes the rules contained in paragraphs 32a and 32b GmbH, which are concerned with loans from shareholders of a GmbH applicable by way of analogy to loans from partners or shareholders in a GmbH & Co. KG in which no natural persons are unlimited partners. Under these rules, certain loans may be treated as if they were capital, and are not repayable in insolvency proceedings. It seems likely however that these rules may be repealed in the near future. The partnership agreements of publicly held GmbH & Co. KGs are frequently orientated in favour of the GmbH. They may be reviewed by the courts to protect the limited partners therein.

6. GmbH & Co KGaA and *société en commandite par actions à responsabilité limitée*

The above two entities which correspond with one another to a considerable extent are limited partnerships with shares, in which the unlimited partner is a private limited liability company.[259] Such a company is often managed by a person or persons who wish to expand their business and to obtain finance whilst maintaining control, such that they are not in danger of being outvoted or removed from their office. Under French law, the first managers of a *société en commandite par actions* are, according to Article L226-2 of the Commercial Code, appointed by the articles. Subsequent managers must be appointed by the general meeting with the consent of all the unlimited partners, unless the statutes otherwise provide. Furthermore, Article L226-2 provides that the removal of the managers is governed by the articles, which may provide that the unanimous consent of the partners is necessary for such removal. In the entity under consideration, the private limited liability company will be appointed as the managing partner; there may be no other unlimited partners. It will obviously be very difficult to remove it from office. For this reason, the French *SCA à responsabilité limitée* has been treated as providing a useful means of combating contested take-over bids in France. Such bids are still not very common in Germany, but it appears

[258] BGHZ 60, 324; BGHZ110, 342; Schmidt, *Gesellschaftsrecht*, § 56 V 1. b.
[259] Schmidt, *Gesellschaftsrecht*, § 32 I.

that the GmbH & Co. KGaA could be used for a similar purpose. Nevertheless, the use of the French entity has not shown itself to be an infallible protection against corporate 'raiders' in France. It also seems to involve the danger of entrenching an ageing and inefficient management.

French literature has generally welcomed the introduction of the *SCA à responsabilité limitée*: in one case, the Supreme Court (*Cour de Cassation*) condemned the formation of such an entity for the sole purpose of enabling the majority shareholder to appropriate power and dividends to himself.[260] The Stock Exchange showed itself reluctant to allow the admission of the shares of the *SCA à responsabilité limitée* (which are freely transferable) to quotation, on the official market, but permitted this step in 1988. An attempt to enact legislation introduced by Senator Dailly having the intention of drastically limiting the use of the *SCA à responsabilité limitée* failed.

A large number of German academics showed themselves opposed to the use of the GmbH & Co KGaA because of the circumventions of the law which it permitted. However, the German Supreme Court (*Bundesgerichtshof*), after having failed to pronounce on the matter in its judgment in *Holzmüller*[261] in 1982, held in a decision of 24 February 1997 that German law did not prevent a KGaA from having a private limited liability company as an unlimited partner, even if the company was the only unlimited partner.[262] In 1998, the German legislator followed this decision by amending paragraph 279(2) AktG.

7. French *groupement d'intérêt économique*

Unlike the French *SCA à responsabilité limitée* which is a hybrid form of business entity which owes its existence to the inventiveness of entrepreneurs, the French *groupement d'intérêt économique* (GIE), which is in more general use than the former type of entity, owes its existence to the French legislature. It was introduced by the Ordonnance of 23 September 1967, which was amended by the Law of 13 June 1989. The French GIE is a new type of business association which may be formed for a stipulated period of time, and which has fiscal transparency, and legal personality. It has some of the characteristics of a partnership and certain of those of a company and enjoys a considerable measure of flexibility. Thus, it can be set up without any capital, need not be designed to make profits, and may have commercial or civil objects. Its members may be individuals,

[260] Cass 24 January 1995 *Revue des Sociétés* 1995 46 (note by Jeantin).
[261] BGHZ 83, 122, 133. [262] BGHZ 134, 392; BGH [1997] NJW 1923.

partnerships or companies, whether civil or commercial, and may be of French or any other nationality. However, the objects of a GIE are subject to certain limits. These must be to facilitate or develop the economic activities of its members or to improve or increase the profits or benefits of such activities. The grouping is often used for the purpose of research activities and ancillary services.

One of the reasons for the invention of this new legal form in France was that at the relevant time, a company could not be set up for the purpose of providing economic benefits for its members. The only entity which could then be set up for this purpose was an *association* coming within the law of 1901. Law 78-9 of 4 January 1978 changed the definition of a company contained in Article 1832 of the Civil Code so as to include within this provision all contracts by which one or more persons combine their assets or activities in order to participate in the profits or to benefit from the economies which may result. This amendment of Article 1832 now allows companies to be formed for the purpose of providing economic benefits for their members. The *association* can be used for this purpose as well, provided that its object is not to obtain pecuniary gains or material gains which add to the assets of its members. However, the use of the *association* has certain disadvantages when compared with that of the company.

The French GIE formed the inspiration for the setting up of the European Economic Interest Grouping, which owes its existence to a Community regulation.[263] This entity, which was the first supranational business form to be set up within the Community, is governed by a rather complex legal regime, and does not appear to have enjoyed outstanding success, although it has been used by firms in the professions and in other activities situated in different countries as a means of cooperation. The EEIG is dealt with in a separate chapter, which also considers the European Company and the European private company.

[263] Council Regulation (EEC) No. 2137/85 of 25 July 1985 on the European Economic Interest Grouping (EEIG) OJ 1985 L199/1.

5

Share (or equity) capital and loan capital

A wide variety of shares,[1] other equity securities and debt securities[2] may be issued under the laws of the Member States. There are considerable differences in the nature of the rights appertaining to, the methods of transfer, and the forms of such securities. The variety of such instruments appears especially extensive in France. The public issue of shares and other securities may be rendered impossible by law in the case of private companies and often proves to be difficult for small and medium sized enterprises. Such companies may have to rely at least temporarily on their retained earnings and borrowings from banks as sources of finance.

In the present chapter a brief account will be given of the types of equity securities issued in the relevant Member States. This will be followed by an account of the increase and reduction of shares, and certain other matters relating to share capital. The phrase 'equity security' is generally (but not always) used in the present chapter to denote a security which may usually be regarded as the counterpart to the shareholder's contribution to the company's capital, and which generally confers both patrimonial (proprietary) and personal rights. Some securities are difficult to classify. The phrase 'equity security' is used in a restrictive sense in section 560 of the UK Companies Act 2006, which excludes shares which with respect to dividends and capital carry a right to participate only up to a specified amount in a distribution from the definition of such a security.[3]

[1] In some countries, such as Spain, France and Germany, shares in a private company are given a different name from those in a public company. However, the difference is of minor importance for the purpose of this chapter.

[2] The fixed dividend is characteristic of bonds which may, however, be given further rights of participation. The analogy with bonds is specially relevant when, as in the case of French *actions de priorité*, a preference shareholder has no voting rights, or has them only if his dividend is in arrears, as is often the case in the United Kingdom.

[3] Note the similar provisions of s. 94(2) of the Companies Act 1985.

The distinction between debt and equity securities has become rather blurred as the result of recent developments in several Member States. Thus, for example, in both United Kingdom and France preference shares often entitle their holders to a fixed cumulative or non-cumulative preferential dividend, but to no further rights of participation. In many countries, bonds may be issued which are convertible into shares. In both the United Kingdom and France warrants to subscribe for shares may be issued by companies either as a supplement to other securities, or as autonomous securities.

Ordinary shares and various types of preference shares are issued by companies in all Member States considered in this work. Other types of equity securities, such as the above-mentioned subscription warrants, are also recognised in of these states.[4] A detailed account of the various equity securities (using the phrase in a broad sense) recognised as such, is beyond the scope of the present work and only a brief and illustrative account is attempted below.

The formation and maintenance of share capital of public companies forms the subject matter of the Second Company Law Directive.[5] Articles 25–37 of the Second Directive deal with the increase and reduction of the capital of public limited companies. There are considerable differences in the law governing these matters in the members states. The relevant provisions of German law regarding these matters are especially complex. There have been a number of decisions of the European Court of Justice concerning the effect of Article 25 of this Directive, which enshrines the basic principle that a decision to increase capital must ultimately remain with the shareholders.[6] In most jurisdictions, an increase of share capital appears to require an alteration of the articles.

The acquisition by a company of its own shares is dealt with in some detail in this chapter. It forms the subject matter of Article 1(4) of

[4] For the position in the United Kingdom, see ss. 548 and 560 of the Companies Act 2006. According to s. 548, equity share capital means the issued share capital of a company exceeding any part of that capital which neither as respects dividends or as respects capital carries any right to participate beyond a specified amount on a distribution. In the Companies Act 2006, s. 560, an equity security is defined so as to include rights to subscribe for or convert securities into ordinary shares of a company. Relevant shares were defined somewhat restrictively so as to exclude shares such as ordinary preference shares but not preferred ordinary or participating preference shares which have only limited rights of participation.

[5] OJ 1977 L26/, amended by Directive 2006/68/EC, OJ 2006 L264/32.

[6] See the discussion of certain of these decisions in V. Edwards, *EC Company Law* (Oxford: Clarendon Press, 1999) pp. 77–82.

Directive 2006/68/EC. The final part of the present chapter will consider the rules governing loan capital in the relevant Member States. There has been no harmonisation of these rules at EU level.

I. Equity securities issued by United Kingdom companies

As already indicated, the phrase 'equity security' is used in a broad sense in this chapter. The capital structure of UK companies has apparently undergone some simplification in recent years, and it seems that less use is being made of non-voting ordinary shares by public companies than was formerly the case. However, for various reasons, more than one class of shares is frequently issued by UK companies. There may thus be several classes of preference shares,[7] one of which will be given priority as regards dividend and capital over the other classes of preference shareholders in addition to priority in respect of dividends and capital over the ordinary shareholders.

Preference dividends are generally expressed as being cumulative by the terms of issue of the shares. This means that if the profits of one financial year available for dividend are insufficient to pay the preference dividend in full, the unpaid balance is carried forward and is payable out of the profits of later financial years. A preference dividend is presumed to be cumulative, unless the terms of issue make it clear that it is not intended to be cumulative.[8] There is no such presumption that shareholders are entitled to repayment of capital in respect of their shares on a winding up in priority to the repayment of the ordinary shareholders.[9] Preference shareholders are not entitled to priority for the repayment of their capital share in the net assets rateably with the other shareholders on a winding up. Even if they are entitled to priority for the repayment of their capital, they only receive repayment of the nominal value of their shares, plus any premium to which they are entitled, before the ordinary shareholders receive any capital

[7] The distinguishing feature of a preference share is that the holder thereof is entitled to a fixed dividend based usually upon the nominal or paid up value of the share before any dividend is paid on the company's ordinary shares in a financial year, or such shorter period as may be prescribed by the company's memorandum and articles. Preference shares are frequently also given priority for repayment of capital in a winding up, and may have further rights of participation in profits.

[8] *Henry* v. *Great Northern Ry Co* (1957) 1 De G & J 606 at 638; see R. Pennington, *Company Law*, 8th edn (London: Butterworths, 2001), p. 244.

[9] *Birch* v. *Cropper* (1889) 14 App Cor 525.

repayment.[10] Convertible preference shares have sometimes been issued by UK companies in recent years. The terms of issue of such shares will contain an option for the holders to convert their share into ordinary shares at or after a certain fixed date or during certain future periods.[11]

United Kingdom companies sometimes issue debentures or other debt securities which are convertible into ordinary shares, or which carry the right to subscribe for them, as well as subscription options for ordinary shares. It should be noted that these securities are classified as equity securities in section 560 of the Companies Act 2006,[12] but it is also possible to consider them as more akin to debt securities.

The facility given by sections 684–9 of the Companies Act 2006 to companies to issue redeemable shares, which may be ordinary or preference shares, as well as that given by section 690 of the Act[13] to companies to purchase their own shares, may be useful to small and medium-sized companies, including private companies, which have no ready market for their shares. The redemption and purchase of shares is considered in the text below in the section dealing with the reduction of capital.

II. Equity securities issued by French companies

The main distinction in the regime of securities in French company law lies between capital securities (*titres de capital*) and loan securities (*titres d'emprunte*).[14] The distinction is based on the fact that the owners of the former category enjoy also the position of members of the company and capital securities. Their shares represent a division of the company's capital into many parts of the same size. The members accept the risk of losing the value invested in their participation. The owners of loan securities are only creditors of the company, expecting to gain from their investment, and not undergo the risk of limited liability securities that shareholders do. Both kinds of securities may be in registered or in bearer form. The law relating to equity securities in France underwent a considerable reform as a result of the Administrative Order of 24 June 2004. This Order introduced the category of preference shares (*actions de*

[10] *Scottish Insurance Capital Corp* v. *Wilson and Clyde Coal Company* L1949 JAC 462; see also Pennington, *Company Law*, pp. 249–252.

[11] For further details, see Pennington, *Company Law*, pp. 252–3.

[12] Replacing s. 94(2) of the Companies Act 1985.

[13] These provisions are replacing ss. 159 and 162 of the Companies Act 1985.

[14] See M. Cozian, A. Viandier and F. Deboissy, *Droit des sociétés*, 18th edn (Paris: Lexis Nexis Litec, 2005), pp. 375–8.

préférence) and no longer permitted the issue of some of the previous types of shares and securities.[15] The rules related to equity securities in France are characterised by their strictness, due to the fact that French law has traditionally limited the possibility for companies to issue shares entitling the holders to specific rights which are not given to other shareholders.

The above brief discussion has touched on securities issued by public companies (*sociétés anonymes*). However, there is nothing preventing a private company (*société à responsabilité limitée*) from issuing special classes of shares having different rights as to dividends or the repayment of capital out of profits. Furthermore, where the articles so provide, the shares in a private company may be reimbursed out of profits. Such *actions de jouissance* (reimbursed shares) will continue in existence, and have the same rights as before, except in relation to the repayment of capital. *Actions de jouissance* may also be issued by public companies. Multiple voting rights are not allowed in respect of shares in an SARL, nor may a shareholder be deprived of his vote, while double voting shares are admitted for SAs and multiple voting shares may be issued for an SAS. By Article L223-11 of the French Commercial Code, an SARL may not issue investment securities (*valeurs mobilières*). Its shares may thus not be transferred by the same commercial means of transfer as it is the case for shares of an SA.[16] According to Article L223-12 of the

[15] The Administrative Order of 24 June 2004 in particular removed the non-voting preference shares (*actions à dividende prioritaire sans droit de vote*) and investment certificates (*certificats d'investissement*). Companies can no more create this kind of share and those shares and certificates already issued will circulate until their conversion into ordinary or preference shares. Investment certificates are securities constituted of two separate certificates, voting certificates (*certificats de droit de vote*) and investment certificates (*certificats d'investissement*). The latter type of certificates represents the pecuniary rights attached to shares, and gives the holder limited information rights. The former one represents the voting and other rights attached to shares. This type of division was intended to make it possible for a company to increase its equity without modifying its control and was first permitted in 1983. Investment certificates are negotiable instruments and enjoy all the pecuniary rights attached to the shares, and the right to receive company documents. These pecuniary rights concern such matters as the right to receive dividends and liquidation surplus, to be reimbursed the par value of the securities on winding up the company, to exercise preferential subscription rights on capital increases and to claim redemption of their securities on a reduction of capital. Voting certificates are not negotiable, and must be in registered form. They cannot be transferred to anyone who does not hold an investment certificate.

[16] In fact in the French terminology for the share of a private company has a different name (*part social* or simply *part*) than the share of an SA (*action*). The terminological difference reflects the substantial divergence of the regimes governing the transfer of such shares.

Commercial Code, such shares cannot be represented by the usual registered or bearer share certificates. As is the case with the shares of a German GmbH, such shares cannot be dealt in on the stock exchange. The transfer of the participation in a French private company follows the general regime of the transfer of credits and in principle it needs to be approved by the other members.[17]

Currently, it is possible for French companies to issue only two kinds of shares and one type of related security. These are:

(1) ordinary shares (*actions ordinaires*);
(2) preference shares (*actions de préférence*); and
(3) securities giving eventual access to the capital (*titres donnant accès à terme au capital*).[18]

An account is given below of certain types of securities which have been treated as classifiable as equity securities.

A. *Preference shares* (actions de préférence)

Preference shares have been introduced in French legislation by the Law of 24 June 2004 and are now governed by Article L228-11 of the Commercial Code. They may be created when a public company is formed, or subsequently on the increase of its capital. They may receive a preference dividend which may be cumulative or non-cumulative. This preferential right is frequently combined with a preferential right to repayment on the reduction of the capital of the company or its liquidation. They may be with or without vote and enjoy any kind of particular treatment. An increased power in certain matters may also be accorded by the statutes to the holders of such shares. There is a limit to their issue: a maximum of half of the capital may be issued as preference shares, the limit being even lower for quoted companies, that is only one quarter of the company's capital.

The terms of the preference shares may be set out in the articles or by the decision of an extraordinary general meeting. Such meetings are subject to stricter rules as to quorum and majority than ordinary ones. At least one-quarter of the capital carrying voting rights must, according to Article L225-96 of the Commercial Code, be represented at the meeting by shareholders or their proxies. If such a quorum is not present,

[17] See Civil Code, Art. 1690. [18] See Cozian *et al.*, *Droits des sociétés*, p. 378.

Article L225-96(2) of the Commercial Code requires the meeting to be held a second time. The quorum is then relaxed to one-fifth of the issued capital carrying voting rights. Resolutions are passed at an extraordinary general meeting by a two-thirds majority of the shareholders present or represented thereat.

When the preference shares are allotted to one or more specific shareholders it is necessary to follow the procedure for the allotment of particular advantages (*procédure des avantages particuliers*), involving the nomination of a special appraiser (*commissaire aux avantages particuliers*) who reports on the value of the advantages to be given to the intended preference shareholders.[19]

B. *Securities giving rights of conversion into shares* (titres donnant accès à terme au capital)

In 2004, the French legislator introduced securities giving the right of conversion of the security into a share at a certain date.[20] The final decision whether or not to convert the security into a share is always left to the holder of the security. The manner of the conversion will follow the rules established in the contract of issue. This kind of securities may be independent or attached to other securities. When the security are independent, they will give the holders access to the capital at a certain time. On the other hand, the securities may be related to other securities, which can be either loan securities or capital securities. For instance, in the first case a bond will be convertible into an ordinary share and in the second an ordinary share will be convertible into a preference share (*action de préférence*). A resolution of an extraordinary general meeting of the shareholders is necessary for the issue of such securities. Every shareholder has a right of preferential subscription of such securities, and any contrary provision of the statutes is treated as null and void by Article L229-95 of the Commercial Code. After the date of the issue of such securities the company cannot change the company's purposes contained in the articles, nor is entitled to be transformed into another kind of company,[21] unless authorised by the contract of

[19] French Commercial Code, Arts. L225.8, L225-14, L225-147 and L. 225-148. See Cozian *et al.*, *Droit des sociétés*, p. 380.

[20] Which, together with the ordinary shares and the preference shares, constitute the third category of shares (*titres de capital*) that may be issued by French companies. French Commercial Code, Art. L 228–91. See Cozian *et al.*, *Droit des sociétés*, p. 380.

[21] French Commercial Code, Art. L228-98.

issue of the securities or if in accordance with special rules governing the construction of such a contract covered in Article L228-103 of the Commercial Code.

III. Equity securities issued by German companies

The provisions of German law concerning the kinds of securities that German public companies may issue do not appear to be as complex as those considered above in relation to France. According to paragraph 11 of the German *Aktiengesetz* (AktG) of 1965 (as amended), shares may confer different rights, in particular with regard to the distribution of profits and assets. Shares conferring identical rights are deemed to constitute a class; paragraph 12(1) AktG provides that every share shall confer voting rights. However, preferred shares, which confer no voting rights, may be issued in accordance with the provisions of the Act. These provisions are paragraphs 139–141 AktG, and are of a rather complex nature.[22] They receive separate consideration below. It is now clear from paragraph 12(2) AktG that multiple voting rights are prohibited under all circumstances in German public companies. Various kinds of preference shares are issued by such companies, which sometimes have different classes of such shares, with differing priorities as to dividend and capital.

A. Private companies

The transfer of shares in a private company and an agreement creating an obligation to make such a transfer has to be in a notarial form.[23] This requirement prevents such shares from being dealt in on a stock exchange, but there have been suggestions that the law should be changed.[24] Shares in a GmbH can be given enhanced voting rights (sometimes on particular occasions), or may have no voting rights. According to paragraph 3(2) of the *GmbH Gesetz* (GmbHG), shareholders in a GmbH may have additional duties in addition to that of providing capital.

22 T. Raiser and R. Veil, *Recht der Kapitalgesellschaften*, 4th edn (Munich: Vahlen, 2006), p. 282.

23 German Private Limited Liability Companies Act, para. 15(3) and (4).

24 German private limited liability companies are permitted to, and sometimes do issue *Genußscheine*, which embody rights rather similar to those of bondholders. This type of security is discussed briefly below.

Shares in a GmbH can also be given a preference as to dividend, repayment of capital on liquidation, or liquidation surplus.

B. *Public companies: the provisions of Articles 139–141 of the German* Aktiengesetz (*AktG*)

According to paragraph 139(1) AktG, shares which have a cumulative preference dividend (*nachzuzahlenden Vorzug*) may be issued without voting rights.[25] It remains possible to issue such shares with voting rights,[26] but considerable use has been made of the present facility which arguably contravenes the principle of shareholder democracy. Paragraph 139(2) AktG, which provides for a limitation on the issue of cumulative preference shares without voting rights, stipulates that the total par value of such shares may not exceed half the issuing company's capital.[27]

Cumulative preference shares without voting rights have been increasingly issued by German public companies since the 1980s. They have sometimes been issued when a family company makes its first public offer of shares on a stock exchange. Such shares have sometimes been issued to employees, and use has also been made of them as a defence mechanism against takeover bids.[28] The issue of voteless cumulative preference shares has the effect of concentrating power into the hands of ordinary shareholders.

Voteless cumulative preference shares may be entitled to a fixed dividend only. However, as is the case with participating preference shares in the United Kingdom, they may be given the right to participate in surplus profits available for dividend. The right to payment of unpaid preference dividends (or amounts thereof) has priority over the payment of current preference dividends. Earlier arrears of such dividends have priority over later ones. In principle, the right to repayment subsists until all the arrears of dividends are repaid.[29] However, it seems that this right can be limited to a specific period of years in the future, provided that the shareholders affected acquire voting rights after the termination of this right. The same principle may apply where the right to payment of

[25] Kübler and Assmann, *Gesellschaftsrecht*, p. 197 have criticised this denomination, preferring the denomination '*Vorzugsaktien, die Anspruch auf eine aus dem Jahresgewinn vorab zu entrichtende Vorzugsdividende gewähren*'.

[26] On the absence of the right to vote, see U. Hüffer, *Aktiengesetz*, 5th edn (Munich: CH Beck, 2002), § 139, paras. 13 ff.

[27] Raiser and Veil, *Recht der Kapitalgesellschaften*, p. 283.

[28] *Ibid.*, p. 283. [29] *Ibid.*, p. 282 f.

unpaid dividends is subject to a condition, for example, that it shall end after a number of years without profits, the affected shareholders then acquiring voting rights.

The original articles of a public company may provide for the issue of voteless cumulative preference shares; these may be created instead as the result of an alteration of the articles, which may be accompanied by an increase of capital. Their creation may also take place by an amendment of the articles withdrawing the vote from existing cumulative preference shareholders, or by means of the conversion of ordinary shares into voteless cumulative preference shares. Both the latter two types of operation would require the consent of all the shareholders affected. Such consent would not be required where the new shares were issued on an increase of capital.[30]

The provisions of paragraph 140 of the *Aktiengesetz*, like those of paragraph 141, are somewhat complex and perhaps require setting out in full for purposes of clarity. The former text provides as follows:

Paragraph 140 AktG. Rights of preference shareholders:

(1) Apart from the right to vote, non-voting preference shares confer the same rights as those enjoyed by the other shareholders.
(2) If the preferential dividend is wholly or partly unpaid in any particular year, and if the amounts in arrears are not paid in the next succeeding year, together with the total preference dividend for that year, the preference shareholders shall have voting rights until the amounts in arrears have been paid. In such an event, the preference shares shall be taken account of in calculating any capital majority required by law or by the articles.
(3) Unless the articles provide otherwise, the fact that a preference dividend is not paid or not fully paid in any given year does not give rise to any claim for any arrears of preference dividend, which is contingent on later resolutions governing the distribution of profits.

The provisions of the above sub-paragraphs, although sometimes rather complex, are fortunately somewhat self-explanatory. Paragraph 140(1) leads to the conclusion that, apart from the right to vote, cumulative preference shareholders enjoy the same rights as those enjoyed by the other shareholders such as that of participating in a general meeting, and rights of pre-emption in relation to the issue of new shares or an

[30] Note in this context, Hüffer, *Aktiengesetz*, § 139, para. 11.

increase of capital.[31] They also enjoy the extensive minority rights granted to shareholders by the *Aktiengesetz*. It follows from paragraph 140(2) AktG that voting rights revive under two conditions, i.e. the non-payment of the full preferential dividend in one year, and the failure to pay the arrears of such dividend, or the full preferential dividend in the succeeding year. The voting right arguably revives when the deficit becomes apparent on the approval of the relevant annual financial statements by the supervisory board or by the general meeting.[32]

Paragraph 141 AktG provides as follows: it has not been thought necessary to include those provisions of paragraph 141(3) AktG which concern pre-emptive rights.[33]

Paragraph 141 AktG. Withdrawal or limitation of preferential rights:

(1) Any resolution which withdraws or limits preferential rights requires the consent of the holders of the preference shares in order to be effective.
(2) Any resolution requiring the issue of preference shares having priority over or the same rights as non-voting preference shareholders in respect of the distribution of profits or assets needs the consent of the holders of the preference shares. Such consent is unnecessary if a reservation was expressly made for such an issue when the preferential right was granted or, if the voting rights were later withdrawn, when such withdrawal took place, provided that the pre-emptive rights of the holders of the preference shares are not excluded.
(3) The holders of preference shares shall decide at a special meeting whether to pass a resolution granting such consent. Such a resolution must be passed by a majority of three quarters of the votes cast. The statutes may not provide for any other majority nor may they stipulate any additional requirements (the second sentence concerning pre-emptive rights is omitted).
(4) The shares carry voting rights if the preference is withdrawn.

The type of resolution mentioned in paragraph 141(1) AktG must be one amending the articles, which requires a majority consisting of at least three quarters of the capital represented when the resolution is passed (unless the articles provide otherwise).[34]

[31] Raiser and Veil, *Recht der Kapitalgesellschaften*, p. 283.
[32] For a good discussion of this matter, see Hüffer, *Aktiengesetz*, § 140, para. 4 f.
[33] Kübler and Assmann, *Gesellschaftsrecht*, p. 197.
[34] See para. 179(2) German Public Limited Liability Companies Act.

The preferential right (*Vorzug*) referred to in paragraph 141(1) AktG appertains to the preferential right to a dividend, or the right to receive fully or partly unpaid dividends due from previous years. It is generally thought that for an action to come within paragraph 141(1) AktG, it must directly withdraw or restrict a preferential right.

Paragraph 141(1) AktG does not apply to alterations of the company's articles which restrict the distribution of profits to the shareholders, or to resolutions governing the distribution of profits according to which the balance sheet profit is wholly or partly allocated to purposes other than the distribution of a dividend. According to the predominant opinion, it is inapplicable to reductions of capital because, like the contingencies mentioned in the last sentence, such reductions have no effect on preferential rights, but influence their enjoyment.[35] Paragraph 141(1) AktG is inapplicable to situations in which the preferential right has become extinguished through the effluxion of time or the operation of a condition.[36]

Paragraph 141(2) AktG is concerned with the issue of new preference shares having priority over or the same rights as non-voting preference shareholders in respect of the distribution of profits or assets. This normally requires the consent of the non-voting preference shareholders. The new shares may be voting or voteless preferential shares, and there is no need for them to be cumulative preference shares, provided they are given other preferential rights. The requirement of consent contained in the first sentence of paragraph 141(2) AktG is applicable where the relevant new shares are issued on an increase of capital, and where ordinary shares are converted into preference shares, provided that the new shares have priority over, or the same rights as the existing non-voting preference shares in respect of the distribution of profits and assets. The protective provisions contained in paragraph 141(1) and (2) AktG are not always paralleled by corresponding ones in other jurisdictions. Thus in the United Kingdom, an issue of new shares ranking equally or in priority to an existing class of shares has been held not to fall within the scope of a variation of rights clause unless, in the latter case, there is a contractual promise that such an issue would not take place.[37]

[35] Raiser and Veil, *Recht der Kapitalgesellschaften*, p. 283.

[36] Hüffer, *Aktiengesetz*, § 141, para. 11; also Werner, *AG 1971*, pp. 69–70.

[37] See A. Boyle and J. Birds, *Boyle and Birds' Company Law*, 4th edn (Bristol: Jordans, 2000), p. 242. Note also *Allen* v. *Gold Reefs of West Africa* (1900) Ch 656.

IV. Equity securities issued by Italian companies

The discipline concerning shares in private companies in Italy differs sharply from that provided for public companies. Even the denomination used to indicate the stake in the two different kinds of companies differ, together with their meaning.[38] As already pointed out before, in a private company the division of the capital among shareholders is governed in a more personal or personalistic way than in public companies. The capital is divided in as many shares as the number of shareholders, and each member receives only one share whose size corresponds to the amount of capital subscribed. Consequently, every share in a private company may have, and this is usually the case, a different size. A shareholder who buys a share from another will remain holder of only one share, which consequently by reason of the purchase will increase in value. The difference from public companies is quite important: in those latter companies the capital, at the time of the subscription, is divided in a number of shares all of the same size and every shareholder holds a number of them.

It is generally accepted that an Italian private company may issue shares carrying preferential rights as to the payment of dividends and the repayment of capital. According to Article 2468(3) of the Italian Civil Code, the deed of incorporation of an Italian private company may attribute particular rights governing the administration of the company or the distribution of profits to individual shareholders[39]. On the contrary, all shares in public companies confer equal rights, different rights being attributed only if special classes of shares are issued. One quarter of the cash contributions on shares must be paid upon subscription to the deed of incorporation: in the case of single-member companies, the full amount must be paid. Such payment may be replaced by the provision of a bank guarantee or policy of insurance covering the full amount. The latter may itself be replaced by the payment of the relevant amount in cash, in accordance with the provisions of Article 2464(4) of the Civil Code. Article 2466(6) of the Civil Code makes similar rules applicable to obligations assumed by members of private companies to contribute

[38] The stake in a private company, '*quota*', as well as the stake in a public company, '*azione*', are both translated in English with the same word, namely 'share'. This may somewhat obscure the difference in the methods of transfer and rights and other characteristics of such shares.

[39] This privilege, unless the articles provide otherwise, may be modified or removed only with the consent of all the shareholders, Art. 2469(3) and (4).

work or services to the company. Such contributions may be made by stipulating a policy of insurance or bank guarantee covering the full value attributed to such contributions. In such an event, if the deed of incorporation so provides, the policy of insurance or bank guarantee may be replaced by the payment of the full amount attributed to the work or services by the member, as a security. Any share in private companies may be divided into two or more parts, while shares in public companies are indivisible. Shares of private companies may not be offered through a call for investments.[40] It has also already been pointed out how the shares in private companies can be allotted to shareholders in a manner which is not proportional to their contribution[41] and may not be represented by negotiable instruments, nor may they be offered for public subscription.[42]

Shares in public companies are very different. They represent standardised fractions of the amount of the share capital, all of the same size and value, conferring identical rights, indivisible, distinct from each other even when they belong to the same member. When two or more persons own the same share they must elect a common representative for the exercise of the rights in dealing with the company.[43] They are usually represented by certificates which determine the rules applicable to their transfer (*Titoli di credito*).

By Article 2346(2) and (3) of the Italian Civil Code, the shares in an Italian public company may be given a nominal value or have no par value.[44] Furthermore, Article 2346(6) provides that such a company may issue financial instruments conferring financial (patrimonial) rights or rights in respect of the administration of the company in return for contributions made by a member or by a third party, which may also consist of work or services. In such an event, the articles must contain stipulations governing the terms of issue, the rights conferred, the sanctions imposed in the event of failure to make the necessary contributions, and the rules governing the transfer of the financial instruments.[45]

[40] Italian Civil Code, Art. 2468 (1). [41] This does not appear possible in France.

[42] Italian Civil Code, Art. 2468(1). [43] Italian Civil Code, Art. 2347.

[44] Article 2346 states also that the choice between shares with a nominal value or no par value, must be applied without exceptions, to all the shares issued.

[45] Such financial instruments were introduced in Italian law by the reform of 2003 permitting contributions of work or services which are not allowed in return for shares and also creating an alternative to the distribution of shares to company's employees.

Article 2348(1) of the Italian Civil Code provides that all the shares must be of the same value and confer the same rights.[46] This principle is tempered by the second paragraph of the same article, which provides that the articles of a public company may create classes of shares having different rights even in relation to participation in losses.[47] Within the limits provided for by law, the company may freely determine the incidents attached to the different classes of shares. Shares having multiple voting rights are prohibited by Article 2351(4) of the Civil Code: In principle, each share carries one vote. Article 2351(2) stipulates that, subject to rules contained in special laws, the articles may provide for the issue of shares carrying no voting rights, or voting rights on particular matters, or in the event that certain conditions are fulfilled. It is stipulated by Article 2351(3) that the articles of a public company which does not have access to the market for venture capital may provide that individual shareholders shall have a maximum number of votes, or that their voting power shall be grouped in echelons (that is, in accordance with a sliding scale) according to the number of shares that they hold. The holders of financial instruments may be permitted to vote on particular matters. They may also be permitted to appoint an independent member of the management board (*consiglio d'amministrazione*), or of the supervisory board (*consiglio di sorveglianza*), or of the committee of auditors (*sindaci*).

An Italian company may issue preference shares, but such issues do not appear very frequently. Savings shares (*azioni di risparmio*) may be issued by companies which are quoted on an Italian regulated market, or on a regulated market in another Member State. The present legal provisions governing such shares are Articles 145–147 of Decree Law No. 58 of 24 February 1998 as amended by Legislative Decree No. 37 of 6 February 2004. The holders of such shares have no right to attend and vote at general meetings, but may attend and vote at class meetings, and a common representative of the holders of savings shares appointed by a class meeting is responsible for the implementation of resolutions of such

[46] This rule can usefully be compared with the corresponding rules of French law, which prevent the issue of two types of shares as well as securities giving contractual access to the capital by public companies.

[47] The creation of classes of shares implies a modification in the internal organisation of the company, entailing the consequent holding of class meetings of shareholders. In the chapter concerning the management of the public company, the role of class meetings will be considered in relation to the general meeting.

a meeting, and may also attend general meetings.[48] The total nominal values of savings shares and shares carrying limited voting rights in accordance with Article 2351 of Italian Civil Code[49] may not exceed half the company's capital.[50] If they come to exceed this amount, the balance must be restored by means of the issue of ordinary shares, to offer an option to ordinary shareholders, within two years. If the amount of the capital represented by the ordinary shares is reduced below one quarter of the company's capital, the amount must be increased to at least one-quarter within six months. The company is treated as being dissolved if the relationship between the amount of the capital represented by the ordinary shares and that represented by savings shares and shares having limited voting rights is not restored within the required period of time.[51]

The deed of incorporation (*atto costitutivo*) determines the nature of the patrimonial (pecuniary) privileges granted to the holders of savings shares, the conditions and limitations attaching to them, and the method and time within which they may be exercised.[52] The shares may be in bearer form, if they are fully paid.[53] However, if such shares belong to administrators, auditors or directors, they must be in registered form.[54] Savings shares my be issued on an increase of capital, or by means of the conversion of ordinary or other shares into such shares.[55]

Italian law also provides for the reimbursement of the shares of the company out of profits and their replacement with a new type of share called enjoyment shares (*azioni di godimento*).[56] Such shares do not have one of the usual characteristics of equity shares, because they are no longer a counterpart of the shareholders' contribution to the public company's capital, since the capital on the original shares which the

[48] Decree Law No. 58 of 1998 Arts. 145(1), 146 and 147(3). It is thought that savings shareholders are also entitled to the exercise of all the other rights not related to the right to vote at the general meeting, such as the right to ask for the convocation of the general meeting and to activate judicial control on the management as provided for in Art. 2409 of the Civil Code. Their position should also be considered equivalent to that of normal shareholders insofar as this is not expressly excluded from the law. See G. F. Campobasso and M. Campobasso (eds.), *La riforma delle società di capitali e delle cooperative* (Turin: UTET, 2004).

[49] Such shares will be granted special financial privileges, for example in relation to the distribution of dividends and the repayment of capital.

[50] Decree Law No. 58 of 1998, Art. 145(5) and Civil Code, Art. 2351(2).

[51] *Ibid.*, Art. 145(5). [52] *Ibid.*, Art. 145(2). [53] *Ibid.*, Art. 145(3).

[54] *Ibid.*, Art. 145(3). [55] *Ibid.*, Art. 145(7).

[56] Which may be compared with French and Belgian *actions de jouissance*.

new enjoyment shares replace has been repaid. However, like other equity shares, they confer certain personal and pecuniary rights on their holders. According to Article 2353 of the Italian Civil Code, unless the articles provide otherwise, enjoyment shares allotted to the holders of redeemed shares do not carry the right to vote at the shareholders' meeting. They participate in the profits which remain after the payment to the non-redeemed shares of a dividend equal to the legal rate of interest and, in the event of liquidation they participate in the distribution of the residual assets of the company after the capital in respect of the other shares has been repaid.[57]

Shares may be allotted to the employees of the company on an increase of capital by the reservation to them of a preferential right of subscription over not more than one quarter of the capital comprised in the increase.[58] Such shares may be considered as constituting another category of shares, which also includes shares allotted to employees of a company, or one controlled by it, on a capitalisation of profits,[59] and such shares are governed by very specific rules contained in the articles of the company concerning their form, the manner of their transfer, and the rights possessed by the holders thereof.[60] It is possible to give such employees financial instruments (as described above) instead of shares. Article 2350 of the Civil Code permits the issue of tracking shares, which have financial rights corresponding to the results of the company's activities in a particular field. Such shares are familiar in the US.[61]

A resolution passed by a general meeting which prejudicially affects the rights of one class of shareholders or financial instruments is invalid unless it is ratified or approved in advance by a resolution of a class meeting (Civil Code, Article 2376). It appears that indirect as well as

[57] It is uncertain whether such securities, despite their name, shall be classified as shares or, more properly as financial instruments. See B. Libonati, *Diritto Commerciale, Impresa e Società* (Milan: Giuffrè, 2005), p. 249.

[58] Italian Civil Code, Art. 2441(8). If members holding more than one-half of the company's capital agree this amount may be increased.

[59] *Ibid.*, Art. 2349. See D. U. Santosuosso, *Il nuovo diritto societario* (D&G Diritto e Guistizia, 2003), p. 26 for a useful discussion of employees' shares.

[60] Italian Civil Code, Art. 2349(1).

[61] The articles determine the criteria for identifying the costs and receipts attributable to the relevant sector, the rights attributable to such shares, the method of accounting, and the conditions and modalities for conversion into shares of another class. Tracking shares are not entitled to a dividend insofar as it exceeds the distributable profits shown in the balance sheet. It is thought that the use of such shares may well give rise to accountancy problems: see Santosuosso, *Il nuovo diritto*, pp. 26–27.

direct prejudice is covered by Article 2376, at least in some situations. The rules relating to extraordinary general meetings apply to class meetings if the company is unquoted. In quoted companies, the rules governing savings shareholders' meetings applies instead.

V. Equity securities issued by Spanish companies

Article 5(1) of the law of 1995 provides that shares (*participaciones*) in a private company (SRL) shall grant to members the same rights, with the exceptions provided for in this law. There does not seem to be any exception specifically permitting the issue of shares with a preferential right to dividend. However, the possibility of granting such a preference may follow from Article 85 of the Law of 1995 which stipulates that unless the statutes provide otherwise, the distribution of dividends to the members shall be made in proportion to their participations in the company's capital.

According to Article 50(1) of the Law of 1989, as amended, which governs public companies, shares which confer more privileges than ordinary shares may be issued, provided that the requirements for the amendment of the statutes are complied with. However, Article 50(2) provides that shareholders shall not be entitled to receive interest (*interés*) in any form, and that it is also impermissible to create shares which directly or indirectly alter the ratio between the par value and the right to vote, or the pre-emptive rights. Articles 90 and 91 contain detailed requirements governing the issue of non-voting shares. The share capital represented by such shares may not be more than 50 per cent of the total share capital including that represented by non-voting shares.

The holders of non-voting shares are entitled to be paid dividends before any distribution is made to ordinary shareholders. They are no longer entitled to a minimum dividend which used to be fixed at 5 per cent of the paid up share capital for each non-voting share. However, in some circumstances, failure to distribute the minimum dividend as set out in the articles, may result in the non-voting shares being treated as ordinary shares, and as such entitled to vote. According to Article 91(2), non-voting shares are not affected by a reduction of capital due to losses, unless the reduction is for an amount greater than the par value of the remaining shares. If after reduction, the par value of the non-voting shares is greater than half the par value of the paid up share capital, this proportion must be adjusted to achieve equality within two years;

otherwise the company is dissolved. Holders of non-voting shares have a preferential right to obtain repayment of their paid up contributions should the company be in liquidation, prior to any distributions to other shareholders.

According to Article 92(1), the owners of non-voting shares have all the other rights of ordinary shareholders except the right to vote. Article 92(3) provides that any amendment to the articles directly or indirectly prejudicing the rights of the non-voting shares requires the approval of the majority of shareholders.

VI. Equity securities issued by Belgian companies

In addition to ordinary shares, preference shares may be issued by Belgian public and private companies. Such shares may also carry voting rights, or have no such rights. Public companies may issue founders' shares (*parts bénéficiares*), which lack one of the features usually attributed to equity shares, insofar as they do not represent the capital of the company.[62] The statutes determine what rights are attached to them. If founders' shares are issued by a company which makes a public offering of its securities, and they are to be subscribed for by cash contributions, they must be paid in full at the time of such subscription.[63] Founders' shares are only transferable by a notarial act or by a written instrument notified to the company, until ten days have expired following the publication of the second set of annual accounts following the issue of the shares.[64] However, according to Article 509 of the Companies Code, so far as companies making or having made a public offer of their securities are concerned, founders' shares which are subscribed in cash are immediately negotiable.

As is the case with shares in Dutch companies, ordinary shares, founders' shares and convertible bonds issued by Belgian public companies may be represented by certificates issued by a legal person which retains or acquires the property in such securities. The certificates may be in bearer, registered, or dematerialised form. The issuer of the certificates exercises all the rights attached thereto, including the right to vote. The issuer pays dividends and other products received in respect of shares or founders' shares (e.g. shares in surplus assets on liquidation) as well as sums resulting from the reduction or cancellation (*amortissement*) of

[62] Companies Code, Art. 483. [63] *Ibid.*, Art. 484. [64] *Ibid.*, Art. 508.

capital to the certificate holder. Except where it is otherwise provided, the certificate holder may exchange his certificate for a share, founder's share, bond or subscription rights to which the certificate relates.[65]

A. *Belgian provisions concerning preference shares*

Belgian law contains detailed provisions concerning the issue of voteless preference shares by private and public companies. These appear to be the only type of voteless share that a company may issue. The relevant provisions concerning private companies are contained in Articles 240 and 241 of the Companies Code, whilst those concerning public companies are contained in Articles 480–2 of that Code. Like the relevant provisions of German law, these provisions are rather complex.

B. *Private companies*

Article 238 of the Companies Code provides that the capital of a private company is divided into equal shares, which are indivisible, and which may or may not have a nominal value. According to Article 239, apart from what is provided for in the case of voteless shares, each share has an equal right of participation in the profits and in the surplus assets on liquidation.

Article 240(1) stipulates that if voteless shares are issued, they may not represent more than one-third of the capital of the private company. Provided that there is a distributable profit, a preferential dividend must be paid on such shares and, except where the articles provide otherwise, one which is cumulative, and the terms of which are fixed at the time of issue, as well as a right to participate in surplus profits which is at least equal to that given to the voting shares. They also confer a preferential right to reimbursement of the capital contributed, as well as one to participate in surplus assets on liquidation. Furthermore, Article 240(2) stipulates that such shares have the right to vote in certain situations. These include where one of the conditions set out in Article 240(1) is not fulfilled. When the requirement as to the amount of share capital represented by voteless shares is breached, the existence of the right to vote excludes the enjoyment of all the preferential and other rights mentioned above. The right to vote may also be exercised where class rights are modified, or where one class of shares is replaced by another. It is also

[65] *Ibid.*, Art. 503(1).

given where the general meeting decides on the reduction of capital, the alteration of the objects of the company, on the conversion of the company into a company of another type, or its merger with another company, or its division. Finally, voting rights may be exercised where, for whatever reason, preference dividends which are due are not fully paid for three successive financial years, and continue in being until such dividends are fully recovered. The Belgian provisions concerning voting rights appear more detailed and explicit than the corresponding French and German ones.

Article 241 is concerned with the creation of non-voting preference shares by means of the conversion of voting shares already issued into such shares. The general meeting has to decide on the maximum number of shares which may be converted and the conditions of such conversion. However, the articles may authorise the managers to take these decisions. If they are left to the general meeting, they may be taken by the same procedure as is required for the alteration of the articles. According to Article 286 of the Companies Code, the object of the proposed modification has to be set out in the notice convening the meeting at which at least half the capital of the company must be represented. If the latter requirement is not fulfilled, a new meeting has to be called without any requirement of a quorum so that it can make decisions, whatever the percentage of capital represented. The required modification of the statutes has to be approved by a majority consisting of at least three-quarters of the votes cast.

The conversion offer has to be made at the same time to all the members in proportion to their shareholdings; it must mention the period within which the conversion rights may be exercised, which may not be less than one month. The rules concerning the conversion of voting into non-voting preference shares are similar to those contained in Article L228-35-3, paragraph 1 of the French Commercial Code, but unlike Article L228-35-3, paragraphs 1 and 4 of that Code they do not also cover the conversion of non-voting preference shares into voting shares.

C. Public companies

The rules contained in Articles 480–82 of the Companies Code concerning non-voting preference shares are similar to those contained in Articles 240–41. A minor difference between Article 480 and Article 240(1) is that the former article gives the preference shareholders the right to share in surplus assets on a liquidation which must be at least equal to that attributed to the ordinary shareholders having the right to vote. There is also a slight difference between Article 240(2) and Article 481 insofar as the latter provision stipulates that non-voting preference shareholders shall have the right to vote in one further circumstance, i.e. when authorisation is given to the board of directors to exclude or limit preferential rights of subscription. This provision may be compared with Article 228-35-7 of the French Commercial Code which provides, inter alia, that in case of the increase of capital by cash contributions, non-voting preference shareholders benefit from a preferential right of subscription under the same conditions as the ordinary shareholders. After seeking the opinion of a class meeting of the voteless shareholders an extraordinary general meeting of the company may also decide that those shareholders shall have a preferential right to subscribe for new voteless shares under the same conditions as the shareholders having votes. The French provision may have a more protective effect than the Belgian one.

There are also some slight differences between Article 241 and Article 482. In addition to imposing the requirements already mentioned in relation to Article 241, Article 482 also requires notice to be given of a conversion offer to be given in the *Moniteur Belge*, as well as in national and regional newspapers. When all the shares are in registered form, the shareholders may be informed of the offer by registered letter.

VII. Equity securities issued by Dutch companies

Except where a different provision is contained in the articles, shareholders in Dutch public and private companies have equal rights in proportion to the nominal value of their shares.[66] Provisions in the articles concerning such matters as voting rights, participation in profits and in surplus assets on liquidation may limit, but cannot completely exclude, these rights. Non-voting shares do not exist in the Netherlands, but the position will be different if Article 228(5) of Part 2 of the Dutch Civil Code enters into force. Although, at the current time, non-voting shares do not exist in the Netherlands, it is possible in that country, as in Belgium, for shares to be vested in a trust company (*administratiekantoor*) which is the legal owner of the shares, which issues depository receipts representing the shares, which take the form of registered depository receipts and bearer depository receipts. Usually, the trust company (*administratiekantoor*) exercises the voting rights in the shares. It is often a foundation (*stichting*) formed by the issuing company, but

[66] Civil Code, Art. 2.118/228, 2.92(1)/201(1).

may be an independent bank. The rights possessed by the receipt holders are set out in the conditions (*administratievoorwaarden*) according to which the receipts are issued.

Although voteless shares may not be issued, at the current time, both public and private companies which have an appropriate provision in their articles are empowered to grant profit participation rights to persons who are not shareholders.[67] Such rights can be issued in a negotiable form as a profit participation certificate (*winstbewijs*). The holders of such securities can never vote at shareholders' meetings, but other rights may be granted to them in addition to sharing in the profits of the company. It appears difficult to classify such profit participation certificates; they do confer certain personal and proprietary rights and to that extent at least, they are similar to equity securities.

A. *Preference shares*

Ordinary shares and the various types of preference shares which may be created by Dutch companies do not give rise to such problems of classification. Preference shares have a preference over ordinary shares as regards the payment of dividends up to a certain percentage of their nominal value. That preference may also extend to the liquidation surplus. Preference shares may be given the same voting rights as ordinary shares or more limited ones. As in Germany and in other countries, preference shares are sometimes issued to a friendly person to enable the managing directors to maintain control. The shareholders in a public company normally have the right to decide on the issue of new shares, but this power may be delegated to the management board or supervisory board for a period not exceeding five years in the case of a public company and for an unlimited period in the case of a private one.[68] If there are different kinds of shares, for example preference shares as well as ordinary shares, the shareholders' power to issue shares of a particular type, and to delegate that power to the board is conditional on the prior approval of the holders of that type of share.[69] The rules are similar in the case of private companies except that the issue of shares may be delegated to the management board for an unlimited period in such companies.[70]

Cumulative preference shares are sometimes issued by Dutch companies. Such companies sometimes issue cumulative profit sharing preference shares. These are cumulative preference shares which, after their

[67] *Ibid.*, Art. 2.105(1)/216(1). [68] *Ibid.*, Art. 2.96(1)/206(1).
[69] *Ibid.*, Art. 2.96(2). [70] *Ibid.*, Art. 2.206(1).

right to a preferential dividend has been satisfied, confer on their holders the right to dividends out of the remaining profits on an equal or proportional basis with the ordinary shareholders.

B. Priority shares

Preference shares must be distinguished from priority shares (*prioriteitsaandeelen*) which are used by their holders, who are usually members of the management or supervisory board of public or private companies to acquire control over certain actions of the general meeting or the management board. The priority shares are often vested in a foundation (*Stichting*), the board of which is made up of founders and members of the supervisory board or management board of the company. Priority shares are often used as a means by which minority shareholders can maintain control of the company. Their powers include making 'binding' proposals for the appointment, supervision and dismissal of members of the management and supervisory boards. However, such proposals may always be overruled by a two-thirds vote of the shareholders' meeting, representing more than one-half of the issued share capital.[71] These powers of making binding proposals are excluded in large companies,[72] which are fully exempt.[73] Priority shareholders may also be given the right to veto the issue of new shares, and propose amendments to the articles. They may also have the power to create reserves out of profits.

C. Warrants

Warrants are securities issued by Dutch public companies which create an option to acquire shares at a specific price during a specific period of time. This type of security is familiar in other jurisdictions, including the United Kingdom and the United States.

[71] *Ibid.*, Arts. 2.133(2)/243(2), 2.134(2)/244(2).

[72] Large companies (*Structuurvennootschappen*) are characterised by the extended power of their supervisory boards. They are defined in Arts. 2.153(2) and 2.263(2) of the Dutch Civil Code as companies which satisfy three requirements. These are that according to its balance sheet, the issued share capital of the company and its reserves amount to €16,000,000 or any subsequently adjusted amount; the company, or any other company in which it holds at least half the issued share capital directly or indirectly for its own benefit, or any partnership in which the corporation or a dependent company is a fully liable partner has been required to establish a works council; and the company together with its dependent companies normally employ one hundred or more persons in the Netherlands.

[73] Such companies are defined in Arts. 2.155 and 265 of the Dutch Civil Code.

VIII. Increase and reduction of capital

The company laws of all the relevant states contain provisions concerning the increase and reduction of capital which are similar in many respects, especially in relation to creditor protection. The reduction of capital may take place (as in the Netherlands) through the redemption and purchase of shares. French and Belgian law provide for procedures analogous to a reduction of capital by means of redemption without reduction. The acquisition, redemption and purchase by a company of its own shares are considered after the section dealing with the increase and reduction of capital. The provision of financial security for the purchase of shares has been dealt with in a further short section, which will not attempt a comprehensive survey of the relevant laws of the Member States. This matter has given rise to considerable difficulties in the United Kingdom, and apparently also in the Netherlands, but perhaps not so much elsewhere. Thus, only the position in the United Kingdom and the Netherlands will be discussed in any detail. It should be noted, however, that all the Member States discussed in this work have legislation prohibiting such assistance in the case of public companies, subject to certain exceptions. It was necessary for such legislation to be enacted in order to conform with Article 23 of the Second Company Law Directive.

A. Applicable legal rules in the United Kingdom

1. Increase of capital

The rules relating to the increase of capital have undergone some simplification with the abolition of the concept of authorised share capital,[74] in the sense that no companies must determine in their constitution a ceiling on the number of shares with its directors may issue.[75] The

[74] UK public and private companies were previously allowed to increase their share capital up to the amount authorised by the memorandum by issuing more shares. Where an increase beyond the authorised amount was required, that increase could take place by an ordinary resolution of the company's general meeting, if the articles so permitted, Companies Act 1985 s. 121. The power to issue shares remained with the general meeting unless the articles or a resolution of the company gave the power to issue shares to directors either generally or for a particular issue, Companies Act 1985, ss. 80 and 80A. In the case of a public company, the maximum period for the grant of such authority to the directors was five years; in the case of a private company, an authority of indefinite duration could be given to the directors by means of a unanimous elective resolution.

[75] Such abolition was recommended at para. 7.7. of the Consultative Document, *Modern Company Law for a Competitive Economy: Completing the Structure*. It remains the case that public companies are required to have a minimum capital equivalent to £50,000.

allotment of shares in a private company with only one class of shares is now governed by section 550 of the Companies Act 2006, which stipulates that where a private company only has one class of shares, its directors may exercise any power to allot shares of that class, or to grant rights to subscribe for or convert any security into shares, except to the extent that they are prohibited from doing so by the company's articles. The company's articles may require a resolution of the general meeting for an increase of share capital.[76] The provisions of section 551 of the Companies Act 206 concerning the powers of directors to allot shares in the company are complex. In order to exercise such powers, the directors need to be authorised by the articles or by a company resolution. Such an authorisation may be given for a particular exercise of the power, or for exercise generally, and may be conditional or subject to conditions. The authorisation must stipulate the maximum amount of shares which may be allotted under it, and the date of expiry. Section 551 is not only applicable to public companies, but may be relevant to certain private ones. If the latter companies have only one class of shares, the special rules contained in section 550 apply to them.

According to section 561 of the Companies Act 2006,[77] which applies to shareholders in both public and private companies, shareholders have pre-emption rights when the company makes a new issue of equity securities.[78] Such pre-emption rights may be excluded by the articles of a private company.[79] The Companies Act 2006 contains a number of other detailed rules concerning exceptions, exclusions and disapplications of rights of pre-emption.[80]

[76] This or some other restrictions on the directors' powers may be required when the private company issues classes of shares.

[77] See previously, s. 89 of the Companies Act 1985 on pre-emption rights and the definition of equity securities in s. 94(2) and 94(5) of the Companies Act 1985. Equity securities were defined as relevant shares in the company. Such shares did not include non-participating preference shares, and shares held by a person who acquired them in pursuance of an employees' share scheme. Such pre-emption rights might be excluded by the memorandum or articles of a private company, s. 91 of the Companies Act 1985. For public companies, s. 95(1) of the Companies Act 1985 provided that where the directors of a company are generally authorised for the purposes of section 80, they may be given power by the articles or by a special resolution to allot equity securities pursuant to their s. 80 authority as if s. 89(1) was not applicable to the allotment.

[78] Equity shares are defined in s. 548 of the Companies Act 2006, and do not include non-participating preference shares for the purposes of the Act.

[79] See Companies Act 2006, s. 567.

[80] See *Ibid.*, ss. 564–566, 568 and 569–573.

2. Reduction of capital

The rules concerning the reduction of capital[81] are set out in sections 641–657 of the Companies Act 2006.[82] According to sections 642–44 of this Act, a private company may reduce its capital by means of a special resolution supported by a solvency statement made by its directors. The consent of the court is not necessary in the case of a private company. Any company is permitted by section 641 to reduce its capital by a special resolution confirmed by the court. A company is allowed by this section to reduce its capital in certain ways. In particular, it may extinguish or reduce its liability on any of its shares in respect of share capital not fully paid up; or either with or without extinguishing or reducing such liability, cancel any paid-up share capital which is lost or unrepresented by available assets; or repay any share capital in excess of the company's needs. Where a company (either public or private) has passed a resolution for reducing the share capital, it is permitted to apply to a court for an order confirming it, if the proposed resolution involves the diminution of liability in respect of unpaid share capital or the payment to a shareholder of any paid-up share capital, and unless the court orders otherwise, creditors are entitled to object to the reduction. Such an objection may be made by every creditor who at the date fixed by the court, is entitled to any debt or claim that, if that date were the commencement of the winding up of the company, would be admissible as proof against it.[83]

[81] The previous English rules concerning the reduction of capital were considered to be complex and time consuming. Their simplification in the Companies Act 2006 was based on the proposals of the Company Law Review Steering Group, see the Consultation Document, *Modern Company Law for a Competitive Economy, Company Formation and Capital Maintenance*, October 1999 and *Modern Company Law for a Competitive Economy, Developing the Framework*, March 2000, paras. 7–26.

[82] This was previously governed by ss. 135–141 of the Companies Act 1985. According to s. 135, a company limited by shares or one limited by guarantee and having a share capital could, if authorised by its articles, reduce its capital in any way by passing a special resolution and obtaining the consent of the court. Section 135(2) stated expressly that such a company could reduce its capital in certain ways, which include the extinction or reduction of liability on any of its shares in respect of share capital not fully paid up, the cancellation of any paid-up share capital which is lost or unrepresented by available assets, and the repayment of any paid-up share capital which is in excess of the needs of the company. The rule about the need for consent of the creditors if the proposed reduction involved the return of assets to the shareholders or any diminution in their liability, was found in s. 136 of the Companies Act 1985.

[83] This rule is rendered necessary by Art. 32 of the Second Company Law Directive, which provides that any creditor has the right to object to the court in relation to any reduction of capital other than one designed to write off losses or which would create an undistributable reserve of less than 10 per cent of the reduced capital to be used only to offset losses or increase the subscribed capital.

The court will ascertain whether the reduction is fair between different classes of shareholders, and that the reduction has been properly explained to them. Where different classes of shareholders have different rights to return of capital in a winding up, there is a general rule that a reduction of capital should take place in accordance with these rights. Several decided cases deal with preference shareholders who have priority in respect of the return of capital, but no further right of participation in surplus assets. When capital is returned in excess of the company's needs, the preference shareholders should be paid off first before any ordinary shareholders. This rule may sometimes have an unfortunate impact on preference shareholders, who find that the prior repayment of their capital defeats expectations of future participation in profits.[84]

Certain types of reduction of capital have a similar effect to the redemption and purchase of shares. These latter types of operation are not deemed to be reductions of capital within the meaning of the Companies Act 2006,[85] and they are treated separately, together with similar operations in other countries considered in the present work. The rules governing such operations in certain such countries are sometimes complex, and it appears better to consider them separately from those which concern the increase and reduction of capital.

B. *Applicable legal rules in France*

1. Increase of capital

The capital of a private company may be increased by means of cash contributions or contributions in kind. As such a capital increase involves an alteration of the company articles. It must be passed by the votes of members who together hold at least three-quarters of the share capital if the company was formed before 2 August 2005. If the company was formed after that date, the required majority is two-thirds of the shareholders present or represented at the relevant meeting.[86] Law No. 2005-882 of 2 August 2005 also contains especially permissive rules

[84] Note, e.g. *Scottish Insurance Corp Ltd* v. *Wilson and Clyde Coal Co Ltd* [1949] AC 462 and *House of Fraser plc* v. *ACGE Investments* [1987] AC 387.

[85] These operations are dealt with separately in ss. 684–9 (redemption of shares) and in ss. 690–708 (purchase of own shares) of the Companies Act 2006. See previously, ss. 160(4) and 162(2) of the Companies Act 1985.

[86] French Commercial Code, Art. L223-30, as amended. Article L223-30 does not apply to single-member companies, see Art. L223-31.

governing quorums at meetings. The required quorum at the first such meeting consists of the holders of one quarter of the share capital, present or represented at the meeting. If such a quorum cannot be achieved, the required number is reduced to one-fifth of the share capital present or represented at the second meeting. Private companies that were formed before 2 August 2005 may submit themselves to the new rules if their members unanimously so decide.[87] It still remains the case that a decision to increase the share capital by means of the capitalisation of profits or reserves, has to be taken by the votes of shareholders holding at least one-half of the company's capital.[88] It appears that an increase for cash contributions may be undertaken only if the shares already issued have been fully paid up. It would seem that new shares for cash contributions in an increase of capital must be fully paid up too.[89] Cash contributions have to be lodged with a bank, notary or the *Caisse des Dépôts et Consignations* within eight days of their receipt.[90] When contributions in kind are made when the company is formed, a special appraiser is appointed by the court on the application of the managers, and the appraiser must prepare a report on the value of the assets.[91] The managers of the company and the allottees of the shares are jointly and severally liable for five years to third parties (i.e. creditors of the company) for any shortfall when no appraiser is appointed or the actual value of the contributions differs from that proposed by the appraiser.[92]

The Decree of 24 June of 2004 simplified to some extent the rules governing the increase of capital of public companies, but this remains characterised by a rather strict formalism, with the purpose of protecting the shareholders. A French public company may increase its capital in return for cash contributions, contributions of assets, the set-off of

[87] *Ibid.*, Art. L223-30, as amended, para. 4. [88] *Ibid.*, Art. L223-30, as amended, para. 6.

[89] At the time of the formation of the company, at least one-fifth of the subscribed share capital must be paid up. See French Commercial Code, Art. L223-7.

[90] *Ibid.*, Art. L223-32.

[91] At the time of the formation of the company a unanimous decision of the shareholders may decide that an appraiser will not be appointed if any contribution in kind does not exceed €7,500 in value, and the total amount of contributions in kind does not exceed half of the company's capital. See French Commercial Code, Art. L223-9. This rule is inapplicable in case of increase of capital contributions in kind.

[92] French Commercial Code, Arts. L223-9.

liquidated debts owed by the company,[93] and by the conversion of securities into capital.[94] In addition, it may increase its capital by the capitalisation of reserves, profits or premiums.[95] As is the case for private companies, new shares for cash contributions may only be issued if the entire amount for the already issued shares have been fully paid up.[96] The power to make such an increase rests with an extraordinary general meeting, acting upon a report of the board of directors or the executive board.[97] This is due to the fact that the increase of capital entails a modification of the articles, as capital is one of the matters which must be indicated there. Resolutions are passed at extraordinary general meetings by a two-thirds majority of the votes held by the shareholders present or represented.[98] An ordinary general meeting is sufficient where the capital increase takes place by the capitalisation of reserves, profits or premiums.[99]

The increase in capital may be made either by an increase in the number of the shares, ordinary shares or preference shares, or an increase in their nominal values.[100] All the shareholders must consent unanimously to an increase in the nominal value of the shares unless this takes place as the result of the capitalisation of reserves, premiums or profits.[101] A law was passed on 8 August 1996 which limited the power of the general meeting to delegate the power to increase capital to the board of directors or the executive board. However, this law still permitted the general meeting to confer power on the board of directors or the executive board to issue all investment securities which might be converted into the capital of the company, within certain limits for a period of twenty-six months. The decree of 24 June 2004 extended consistently the power of delegation of the extraordinary meeting to the board or the

[93] Such a contribution can be considered in French law both as a contribution in kind or in cash. In the first case the procedure provided for contributions in kind will be applied, with consequent appointment of a special appraiser.

[94] French Commercial Code, Art. L225-127. [95] *Ibid.*, Art. L225-128.

[96] *Ibid.*, Art. L225-131. [97] *Ibid.*, Art. L225-129.

[98] *Ibid.*, Art. L225-96. Such meetings are also subject to stricter quorum requirements than ordinary meetings.

[99] *Ibid.*, Art. L225-130. The ordinary general meeting is regulated in Art. L225-98 of the Commercial Code, referred to in Art. L225-130. When the general meeting is first called, it cannot validly deliberate unless the shareholders who are present or represented there together hold one-fifth of the share capital having voting rights. No such quorum requirement exists if the meeting is called a second time. The meeting takes decisions by a simple majority of the votes cast.

[100] *Ibid.*, Art. L225-127. [101] *Ibid.*, Art. L225-130.

executive board, which now includes also the decision on whether or not to undertake the increase of capital.[102] Therefore, when the delegation concerns only the modalities of the increase it must be undertaken within five years[103] from the date when the general meeting authorising it took place. On the other hand, when the delegation from the meeting to the administrative organ involves also the decision on whether or not to undertake the increase, the requirements are a little more complex.[104] The meeting must fix a maximum period of time (not more than twenty-six months), during which the delegation may be used, and the maximum amount of share capital that can be issued.[105] The board of directors or the executive board must also prepare, after having used the power delegated by the meeting, a complementary report on the increase to be presented at the following ordinary general meeting and also attach to the annual management report a list of all the delegations of power given to them and the extent to which each of them has been used.[106] Whatever the limits of the delegated powers given by the general meeting, the board of directors or the executive board is empowered to fix the terms of issue, certify the realisation of the increase of capital which has resulted, and proceed to the necessary modifications of the articles.[107]

In quoted companies the board may even sub-delegate the power received from the meeting to decide whether or not to increase the company's capital. This sub-delegation in the case where the company has a board of directors, will be to the to the *directeur général* or, with his consent, to one or more of the assistant general directors, *directeurs généraux délégués*, Where the company has an executive board, it would be to the chairman of the executive board or to one of its members. The delegates must give a detailed account on how the power has been used to the board of directors or the executive board.[108]

Shareholders in a public company have preferential rights to subscribe for the new shares issued for cash consideration,[109] but these may be excluded or limited by the general meeting which must consider two

[102] See Cozian *et al.*, *Droit des sociétés*, p. 339.

[103] French Commercial Code, Art. L225-129-1 and Art. L225-129.

[104] More strict rules are provided in the interest of the shareholders. See Cozian *et al.*, *Droit des sociétés*, p. 339.

[105] French Commercial Code, Art. L225-129-2.

[106] *Ibid.*, Art. L225-100, para. 7.

[107] *Ibid.*, Art. L225-129-2, para. 4.

[108] *Ibid.*, Art. L225-129-4.

[109] The preferential right is excluded in case of issue of new shares for consideration in kind.

reports, one from the executive board or board of directors, and another from the auditors.[110] Individual shareholders are also permitted to renounce their preferential rights.[111] In case some of the shareholders renounce the preferential rights of subscription, the other shareholders may be able to subscribe the remaining shares in proportion to their preferential rights (*Souscription à titre réductible*).[112] If, after the share having been offered to the other shareholders, the entire amount of capital established for the increase still has not yet been subscribed, the board of directors or the executive board may use one of the following options:[113]

(1) limit the amount of the increase to the capital already subscribed, unless the general meeting decides otherwise; the amount may not be less than three-quarters of that decided on;
(2) decide freely how to distribute the remaining shares; or
(3) offer the remaining shares totally or partially to the public, if there was a previous authorisation by the general meeting to do so.

If, after the use of one or more of these options the increase has still not been subscribed for entirely or at least to the extent of three-quarters of the increase decided on, the operation is not valid. Nevertheless the board, irrespective of any contrary instruction from the meeting, can realise a valid increase if the amount of capital remained unsubscribed is less that 3 per cent of the planned increase.

Where shares are issued for a non-cash consideration, no preferential rights are provided for the other shareholders. The rules governing consideration in kind on an increase of capital are rather similar to those governing the formation of the company. Therefore, a report must be prepared by an expert or experts appointed by the court. An extraordinary general meeting decides in the valuation of the contributions in kind, after receiving a report from an expert appraiser. If the contributor is a member he is not entitled to vote at the meeting deciding on his contribution in kind. The shareholders may reduce the value of the contributions in kind if they have the contributors' approval, and that of the beneficiaries or their agents.[114]

[110] French Commercial Code, Art. L225-135. [111] *Ibid.*, Art. L225-132.
[112] *Ibid.*, Art. L225-133. This depends on the express decision of the board of directors or the executive board.
[113] *Ibid.*, Art. L225-134. See Cozian *et al.*, *Droit des sociétés*, p. 341.
[114] French Commercial Code, Art. L225-147.

2. Reduction of capital

The principal rules governing the reduction of the capital of an SARL are set out in Article L223-34 of the French Commercial Code. A private company may reduce the number or nominal value of the shares issued by it by means of an extraordinary resolution. Provision must be made for the equal treatment of all shareholders. If the company has auditors, the proposed reduction must be referred to them, such that they may report on it at the meeting. If the meeting approves a reduction which is not occasioned by losses, the creditors whose claims predate the deposit of the minutes of the resolution with the registrar of the commercial court may oppose the reduction by applying to the court within one month of such deposit. The court may reject their opposition, or order that their debts are paid, or satisfactorily secured. The reduction may not take place until the time period for objections has expired.

An SARL is forbidden to purchase its own shares. However, a general meeting which decides upon a reduction of capital which is not motivated by losses may authorise the managers to acquire a given number of such shares for the purpose of cancelling them.[115]

Where consent is refused to the transfer of shares in a private company, they may be acquired by other members of the company or other persons, or the company may reduce its capital by purchasing the shares from the intending transferor.[116]

If owing to losses evidenced in its accounting documents, the value of the assets of a private limited company become less that half of the capital indicated by the articles the manager (*gérant*) must convoke the members to decide whether to wind up the company. If no such decision is made, the company must reduce its capital by the amount of the losses which cannot be written off against reserves, or increase its assets and thus reconstruct its capital to an amount at least equal to half the nominal amount.[117]

In French public companies, a reduction of the capital must take place by a resolution of an extraordinary general meeting, involving a modification of the articles. A reduction of the capital of an SA may be made to write off losses (*réduction motivée par des pertes*), or to repay part of the capital which is thought to be in excess of the company's needs. When the reduction is motivated by losses, an extraordinary general meeting decides after receiving reports from the board and from the auditor. Shareholders must be

[115] *Ibid.*, Art. L223-34. [116] *Ibid.*, Art. L223-14, paragraphs 3 and 4.
[117] *Ibid.*, Art. L225-48.

treated equally.[118] Shareholders will experience the reduction in proportion to their shareholding. Creditors cannot oppose such a reduction because it does not entail a reduction in the assets (*capitaux propres*) of the company. Stricter rules are provided if the assets of the company fall below half the amount of the company's share capital.

A reduction not motivated by losses may take place in two different ways, but it will always be through the medium of a purchase of shares. First, it can consist of an offer of purchase by the company to any shareholders or, secondly, it can be reserved to one or more specific shareholders.[119] In the first case the company may purchase its own shares and cancel them, except where warrants attached to bonds, convertible bonds or exchangeable bonds which have been issued by the company remain outstanding.[120] Such purchase will take place by means of a tender offer made to all shareholders.

Special rules are applicable to the protection of creditors of an SA where a reduction in its capital is not motivated by losses.[121] These rules resemble those governing the protection of the creditors of an SARL in certain respects.[122] Shares can be purchased after a minimum delay of twenty days from the deposit of the text of the general meeting's deliberation concerning the reduction with the registrar of the court. During this period, creditors of the company can object to the reduction and until the court has decided on such objections, such reduction cannot take place. The shares must be cancelled within one month of the expiry of the offer of purchase.[123]

Further detailed protective rules are contained in Article 181–183 of Decree No. 67-236 but are inapplicable where the general meeting has authorised the executive board or board of directors to purchase a small number of shares in order to cancel them to facilitate an increase of capital, an issue of convertible bonds, or a merger or division. The latter exception is

[118] *Ibid.*, Art. L225-204.

[119] This kind or reduction allows the withdrawal of a member wishing to leave the company. It is used also when, given a provision of the articles which requires the consent of the other shareholders for the transfer of shares, such consent is not given and the company decides to purchase and cancel the member's shares. For further details, see Cozian *et al.*, *Droit des sociétés*, p. 347.

[120] This latter restriction applies also when the reduction concerns only one or more specific members.

[121] French Commercial Code, Art. L225-205; Decree No. 67-236 of 23 March 1967, Art. 180. Cf. J. Simon, 'A Comparative Approach to Capital Maintenance: France' (2004) 15 EBLR 1037, 1041.

[122] French Commercial Code, Art. L223-34.

[123] Decree No. 67-236 of 23 March 1967, Art. 185(3).

only applicable where during the same financial year the number of shares purchased is no more than 0.25 per cent of the company's capital.[124] Special rules are applicable to the market purchase of shares by listed companies, which are explained below in the section relating to the acquisition, purchase and redemption by a company of its own shares. If it is not instead dissolved, a public company's capital must be reduced if the assets of the company fall below half the amount of the company's share capital. Such reduction may take place either through the cancellation of shares or a reduction in their par value. Thus, Article L225-248 of the French Commercial Code provides that if at the time of the annual general meeting, accounts show that the value of the company's assets have fallen below the half of the nominal value of the capital, the board of directors or the executive board must call an extraordinary general meeting within four months which decides whether to continue the company or dissolve it. If they decide to continue the company, they must either reduce the capital by the amount of losses which cannot be set off against reserves within the two financial years following that in which the losses were established, unless within this period of time, the capital assets of the company have come to amount to half the nominal capital. Information for third parties is provided through the medium of a newspaper carrying legal notices, and through the Commercial Registry. If the board does not call such an extraordinary general meeting, any third party may request the court to dissolve the company. If the shareholders decide to reconstruct the assets they can do so through a reduction of the capital which takes account of the current assets owned by the company.[125]

C. *Applicable rules of law in Germany*

1. Increase of capital

The rules governing issues of shares on the increase of capital of a GmbH are rather strict. Such an increase will require an alteration of the company's articles, by means of a notarised resolution of the members passed by a three-quarters majority of the votes cast.[126] It also requires a notarised filing of the amendment with the commercial registry[127] and notarised subscriptions.[128] The resolution must contain particulars of the increase and the consideration involved. If contributions in kind are

[124] Decree No. 67-236 of 23 March 1967, Art. 184.
[125] See Cozian *et al.*, *Droit des sociétés*, pp. 348–9.
[126] German Private Limited Liability Companies Act, paras. 53(2) and 55.
[127] *Ibid.*, para. 54. [128] *Ibid.*, para. 55.

made, the resolution must give particulars of their nature, and of the amount of the share capital covered by such contributions.[129] Special rules govern the capitalisation of reserves.[130]

There is no rule that a GmbH should have a capital commensurate with its requirements or range of activities. In fact, as in certain other countries, under-capitalisation has been a perennial problem with the GmbH. Capitalisation through loans rather than the issue of new shares has been very common, and has often proved prejudicial to the rights of creditors in the insolvency of the company. The Supreme Court has made a number of decisions concerning loans from and securities for loans given by shareholders to the company, many of which relate to transactions which took place before the provisions of paragraphs 32a and 32b GmbHG concerning loans and securities came into force on 1 January 1981. The majority view in the relevant literature, which has received support from the Supreme Court, is that the principles, enshrined in the earlier decisions, remain good law:[131] they have sometimes been applied in conjunction with paragraphs 32a and 32b GmbHG. Most of these decisions applied paragraphs 30 and 31 GmbHG by way of analogy to loans from shareholders, in cases in which private companies had suffered capital losses.[132] According to certain of these decisions, loans and similar payments which a shareholder makes to a private company which cannot pay its debts as they fall due, or whose liabilities exceed the assets, or to a company which would not have obtained credit under normal market conditions, are to be treated as capital. Paragraph 32a(1) GmbHG[133] has a narrower ambit than the principles enshrined in the former cases, but had been frequently applied in conjunction with these principles.[134] The scope of paragraph 32a(1) GmbHG compared with the analogical application of

129 *Ibid.*, para. 56. 130 *Ibid.*, para. 57c–57o.

131 Note, e.g. BGHZ 75, 334 and 76, 335 for some important earlier decisions. The earlier decisions of the Supreme Court were held to remain good law in BGHZ 90, 378.

132 Schmidt, *Gesellschaftsrecht*, § 37 IV 3.

133 Paragraph 32a(1) sentence 1 of the German Private Limited Liability Companies Act provides that a shareholder who grants a loan to a private company at a time when the shareholder, if he had acted as competent businessman would have provided it with capital, cannot claim the loan back in bankruptcy proceedings or in judicial composition proceedings to avoid bankruptcy. It is now proposed that paragraph 32a(1) will be repealed but that the repayment of such loans will be postponed to the claims of other creditors in insolvency proceedings in accordance with paragraph 39 of the Insolvency Act 1998 (*Insolvenzordnung*).

134 Schmidt, *Gesellschaftsrecht*, § 37 IV 3.

paragraphs 30 and 31 is both narrower and wider. It is narrower in a temporal sense, since its application requires the commencement of insolvency proceedings (whereas paragraphs 30, and 31 which forbid the return of capital to the shareholders and require the restoration of sums paid in breach of the former requirement, are applicable as soon as the company is undercapitalised). The scope is wider in the sense of liability. Paragraphs 30 and 31 only provides for the re-characterisation of loans to a more limited extent than does paragraph 32a(1). This has been of much importance when arguing for a parallel application of both systems, it has been argued that since only the interplay of both sets of rules ensures sufficient creditor protection. It seems doubtful whether the principles so stated in its earlier decisions will continue to be invoked if the proposed amendments to the existing law as outlined below are made.

It appears to follow from the rules contained in paragraphs 30[135] and 32a GmbHG that a shareholder may not be able effectively to make a payment for shares consisting of a loan outstanding to him, or set off such a debt due against a cash payment for shares, unless the company is in financial difficulties and he acquires the shares for the purpose of overcoming the crisis (*Sanierungsprivileg*, privilege of recapitalisation).[136] However, it is likely that if the proposal of the Federal Ministry of Justice for the amendment of the law governing the GmbH is adopted, paragraph 30(1) of the GmbHG and paragraph 57 of the *Aktiengesetz* will be amended, and paragraphs 32a and 32b GmbHG would be repealed. The proposed amendments would come into force by the end of 2008.

The GmbHG does not expressly grant existing shareholders any preferential rights of subscription for new shares. Such rights may, however,

[135] This provision forbids the return of capital to shareholders. The German Federal Ministry of Justice proposed (2007) that new sentences be added to paragraph 30(1), which would then read as follows:

> The assets required to maintain the company's capital may not be returned to the shareholder. This rule is inapplicable to performances which take place on the basis of a control or profit transfer contract, or which are covered by a fully effective claim against or counter-performance by the relevant shareholder. It is also applicable to the return of a loan from a shareholder made at a term according to the judgment of a competent business man, the company required capital, and to performances which take place on the basis of transactions similar to such a loan.

[136] Raiser and Veil, *Recht der Kapitalgesellschaften*, § 38 para. 39 f; Schmidt, *Gesellschaftsrecht*, § 37 IV 4. Cf. Kübler and Assmann, *Gesellschaftsrecht* p. 294.

be granted by the articles or be derived from the principle of equality.[137] If a shareholder in a private company agrees to pay for his share in cash, but subsequently sells assets belonging to him to the company, he cannot set the price of these assets against the cash payment he is required to make except where the nature of the assets and the value of the share is stated in the company's articles, or in the resolution providing for the increase of capital.[138] It is not sufficient to state the nature of the assets in the statutes or the resolution, but additionally to prepare a written report (*Sachgründungsbericht*) to ensure the value of the assets, see above.

An increase in the capital of a public company involves two essential stages,[139] as does that of a private company.[140] These are a shareholders' resolution amending the articles and subscription for the shares. Both steps have to be notified to the commercial registry.[141] Unless the articles provide otherwise, the necessary resolution to increase the capital against contributions requires a three quarters majority of the votes cast.[142] If the shares to be issued are preference shares without voting rights the articles may only require a larger majority.[143] If there are more than one class of shares, class voting is necessary.[144] Where shares are to be issued at a premium the relevant resolution(s) must specify the lowest issue price.[145] Share capital should not be increased when significant amounts of capital contributions are outstanding and collectible.[146] Contributions in kind made on an increase of capital are subject to strict requirements, which are set out in paragraph 183 AktG. These include an examination of their value by one or more auditors, as happens when contributions in kind are made on formation.

Shareholders in an AG have a pre-emptive right to subscribe for new shares in proportion to their holdings in the existing share capital. A period of not less than two weeks must be provided for in which to exercise such rights.[147] They may, however, be limited or excluded by the resolution on the increase of share capital, which limitation or exclusion must be approved by at least three-quarters of the share capital represented at the meeting, or by any larger majority required in the articles.[148] The management must

[137] Schmidt, *Gesellschaftsrecht*, § 37 V 5. 1. a) ee).
[138] German Private Limited Liability Companies Act, para. 19(5) and para. 5(4).
[139] Raiser and Veil, *Recht der Kapitalgesellschaften*, § 20.
[140] See in more detail, *ibid.*, § 39.
[141] German Public Limited Liability Companies Act, paras. 184 and 188.
[142] *Ibid.*, para. 182(1) sentence 1. [143] *Ibid.*, para. 182(1) sentence 2.
[144] *Ibid.*, para. 182(2). [145] *Ibid.*, para. 182(3). [146] *Ibid.*, para. 182(4).
[147] *Ibid.*, para. 186(1). [148] *Ibid.*, para. 186(3).

report to the general meeting in writing on the reason for the partial or total exclusion of the rights of pre-emption.[149]

The increase in capital cannot be entered in the commercial register unless the amount called on the shares, which must not be less than one quarter of the lowest issue price has been paid. As is also the case on the formation of a company, contributions in kind must be made in full. The report for registration made by the management board must contain evidence that the amount paid in is at the free disposal of the management board.[150] Once the increase in capital is entered in the commercial register it becomes effective.[151]

In addition to the above type of capital increase, special rules apply to certain other kinds of capital increase, they include conditional capital increases, authorisations to the management board to increase the capital up to a specified amount, and the conversion of capital and profits reserves into share capital. These operations are described briefly below.

Conditional capital increases (*Bedingte Kapitalerhöhung*) may take place in connection with the issue of convertible bonds or bonds with warrants, mergers and stock option plans.[152] The conditional capital may not exceed one-half of the share capital and, in the case of stock option plans for employees, one-tenth of the share capital.[153] Detailed rules concerning such matters as contributions in kind and the registration and publication of the resolution on the increase are contained in paragraphs 194–200 AktG.

If the original or amended articles of the company so provide, the general meeting is also permitted to authorise the management board for a period not exceeding five years to increase the share capital up to a specified amount, not exceeding one half the share capital at the date of the authorisation (*Genehmigtes Kapital*).[154] The issue of such share capital also requires the consent of the supervisory board.[155]

The articles may provide that the new shares shall be issued to the employees of the company.[156] Insofar as the authorisation does not contain relevant provisions, the management board may stipulate the rights and conditions of issue of the new shares.[157] The issue of such new shares is otherwise dealt with by paragraphs 203–6 AktG, which make reference to other relevant provisions of the German *Aktiengesetz.*

The increase in capital from the company's reserves (*Kapitalerhöhung aus Gesellschaftsmitteln*) is dealt with by paragraphs 207–220 AktG.

[149] *Ibid.*, para. 186(4). [150] *Ibid.*, para. 188(1) and (2). [151] *Ibid.*, para. 189.
[152] *Ibid.*, para. 192(1) and (2). [153] *Ibid.*, para. 192(3). [154] *Ibid.*, para. 202(1) and (2).
[155] *Ibid.*, para. 202(3) sentence 2. [156] *Ibid.*, para. 202(4). [157] *Ibid.*, para. 204(1).

According to paragraph 207 AktG, the shareholders' meeting may resolve an increase of the share capital by means of the conversion of the capital reserve or profits reserve into capital. Paragraph 212 AktG provides that new shares shall be allotted to the shareholders in proportion to their holdings in the existing share capital. New shares not claimed by the shareholder within one year of notice of the resolution capital increase may be sold on behalf of the person entitled thereto on the stock exchange, if the company is listed, or otherwise by public auction.[158]

2. Reduction of capital

The rules governing the reduction of capital of a GmbH which are contained in paragraph 58 GmbHG are somewhat complex, and serve a number of purposes, for example the return of capital in excess of requirements to shareholders, the payment of compensation to withdrawing shareholders, and the writing off of losses.[159] The reduction of capital involves an alteration of the company's articles, and thus requires the passing of a resolution, which must be notarially recorded, by a majority of at least three quarters of the votes cast.[160] Notice of the passing of such a resolution must be given three times in official newspapers such that creditors of the company may inform it of their existence.[161] Creditors who do so and do not express their consent to the reduction must have their claims satisfied or secured.[162] Application may not be made for the entry of the resolution on the reduction in capital in the commercial register until a year has expired since the third request was made to creditors.[163] The entry of the resolution in the commercial register gives it legal effect, and thus enables the reduction to take place.[164]

As is also the case with the AG, there is a simplified form for the reduction of capital of a GmbH.[165] This appears to be rather similar to that applicable to the AG, and to enable the restructuring of the company's losses without any significant distribution of assets to shareholders and without providing security to creditors. The rules governing simplified reductions of capital include other means of protecting creditors, limiting the possibility of distributions to shareholders; for example funds obtained from the release of capital and profits reserves may only be

[158] *Ibid.*, para. 214. [159] Schmidt, *Gesellschaftsrecht*, § 37 V 3.

[160] German Private Limited Liability Companies Act, para. 53. Cf. Raiser and Veil, *Recht der Kapitalgesellschaften*, § 40, para. 3.

[161] German Private Limited Liability Companies Act, para. 58(1) No. 1.

[162] *Ibid.*, para. 58(1) No. 2. [163] *Ibid.*, para. 58(1) No. 3. [164] *Ibid.*, para. 54(3).

[165] *Ibid.*, para. 58a. See Raiser and Veil, *Kapitalgesellschaften*, § 40, para. 2.

used for the purpose of compensating for the decline in the value of assets or to offset other losses.[166] A simplified reduction of capital may only take place for the latter purposes. The necessary resolution must be passed by at least three quarters of the votes cast at the general meeting; the company's articles may provide for an enhanced majority.[167] Simplified reductions of capital are governed by the detailed provisions of paragraphs 58a–f GmbHG.[168]

A private company is not permitted to make payments to its members if the net worth of its assets is no longer equal to the amount of its issued capital.[169] If any payment is made to the shareholders in violation of this obligation, it must be refunded by the recipient to the company.[170] However, if such a recipient can demonstrate that he is in good faith, he is only required to refund the amount necessary to satisfy the creditors.[171] It is noteworthy that this is a debt owed to the company by one of its shareholders and since a creditor cannot sue the shareholder for the amount, one may raise the question as to how the money will be recouped if the shareholders of the company have to file an action on behalf of the company against themselves. Although this mechanism appears to be inefficient to ensure a sufficient equity capital, it harmonises with the underlying notion of limited liability and separate personality of the company.

Both the rules developed by the courts before 1980 on the basis of the interpretation of paragraphs 30 and 31 GmbHG by way of analogy, and the new rules contained in paragraphs 32a and 32b GmbH impose limitations on capitalisation by means of loans, which has frequently taken place in the context of the GmbH. Paragraph 32a and 32b are complex, but their most important features appear to be contained in the first sentence of each provision.[172] Paragraph 32a(1) s 1 GmbHG provides that if a shareholder has granted a private company a loan at a time when, if he had acted as a competent businessman, he ought to have provided it with capital,[173] he is treated as a creditor ranking behind all

[166] Furthermore, para. 58d(2) of the German Private Limited Liability Companies Act provides that distributions to shareholders are limited to four per cent of the share capital until the financial year which begins more than two years after the reduction unless the creditors claims are satisfied or secured. A similar rule is contained in para. 233(2) of the German Public Companies Act, which restricts the relevant period to two years.

[167] German Private Limited Liability Companies Act, paras. 53 and 54.

[168] Schmidt, *Gesellschaftsrecht*, § 37 V 3. b).

[169] German Private Limited Liability Companies Act, para. 30. As already indicated above, this provision is likely to undergo amendment in the near future.

[170] *Ibid.*, para. 31(1). [171] *Ibid.*, para. 31(2). [172] Schmidt, *Gesellschaftsrecht*, § 37 IV 2.

[173] What is referred to as 'crisis' in the case law.

other creditors (*nachrangiger Gläubiger*).[174] In employing this mechanism the law recharacterises the loan into de facto equity capital, hence the name 'capital-replacing-loan' (*kapitalersetzendes Darlehen*). Paragraph 32a(2) GmbHG applies to loans given by third parties at a time when the company should have been provided with capital, which have been guaranteed or secured by a shareholder. It stipulates that in such cases, the third party may, in insolvency proceedings, only claim the balance of the loan after recourse has been made to the guarantee or security. Paragraph 32a(3) GmbHG provides that the foregoing provisions apply by way of analogy to other legal transactions by a shareholder or by a third party which economically correspond to the granting of a loan in accordance with paragraph 32a(1) or (2) GmbHG.

Paragraph 32b GmbHG provides that if in situations governed by paragraphs 32a(2) and (3) GmbHG the loan has been repaid within one year of the opening of insolvency proceedings, the shareholder who has provided security or given a guarantee must restore the amount repaid to the company.

These rules place important restrictions upon the repayment of loans which can be regarded as substitutes for the capital of a private company, and they place restraints on what may substantially be a reduction of the company's capital. As already indicated, paragraphs 32a and 32b may be repealed in the near future. The view has been taken that there is no need for a distinction between loans which replace capital and other loans to a company.

The forms of capital reduction which are open to German public companies are ordinary capital reduction, simplified capital reduction, and capital reduction through the mandatory redemption or purchase of shares. An ordinary capital reduction is governed by paragraphs 222–8 AktG. If the shares in an AG have a par value, the capital reduction requires a reduction of this value. Should the reduced share capital of each share not reach the minimum amount of €1, the reduction has to be made through the consolidation of shares.[175] Reductions of capital have to be approved by a resolution adopted by holders of at least three quarters of the share capital represented at the meeting.[176] Class voting is necessary if there is more than one class of shares.[177] An amendment of

[174] See also para. 39, (1) No. 5 and 174 (3) of the German Insolvency Act, 1998 (*Insolvenzordnung*).

[175] German Public Limited Liability Companies Act, para. 222(4).

[176] *Ibid*., para. 222(1). The statutes may provide for a higher capital majority and additional requirements.

[177] *Ibid*., para. 222(2).

the articles is also necessary.[178] The reduction of capital takes effect once the resolution on reduction of share capital is registered.[179]

The rules governing the protection of creditors are simpler than those applicable to the ordinary reduction of the capital of a GmbH. According to paragraph 225 AktG, creditors whose claims arise before the date of registration of the resolution have the right to demand security within six months of the publication of the reduction, if they cannot obtain satisfaction of their claims. Any distribution to shareholders must be delayed until the six month period has elapsed, and the claims of creditors have been satisfied or secured.

The rules governing the simplified reduction of capital of an AG are somewhat similar to those applicable to a GmbH. The simplified procedure may be used for a capital reduction for the purpose of compensating for a decline in the value of assets, offsetting other losses or transferring amounts to the capital reserve.[180] The company's losses are restructured with only limited distributions of assets, and no security is given to creditors. Before the reduction take place, all free (i.e. profits) reserves must be employed to cover losses.[181] The transfer to the legal (or statutory) reserve (*gesetzliche Rücklage*) of amounts obtained from the use of profits reserves (*Gewinnrücklagen*) and to the capital reserves of amounts obtained from the capital reduction may take place only to the extent that the sum of the legal reserve and the profits reserves after the transfer does not exceed ten per cent of the share capital. As in the case with simplified reduction of the capital of a private company[182] after the reduction has taken place distributions are limited to four per cent of the share capital until the financial year which commences at least two years after the reduction, unless the outstanding creditors are paid or secured.[183] As is also the case with the GmbH reductions can be made retroactively with the financial statements.[184] They may also be made at the same time as a retroactive capital increase if the new shares have been fully subscribed for, no contributions in kind have been stipulated and one-quarter of the part value plus the whole premium is paid on each share.[185] Such a combined increase and reduction of capital enables a

[178] *Ibid.*, para. 23(3). [179] *Ibid.*, para. 224.
[180] *Ibid.*, para. 229(1). [181] *Ibid.*, para. 229(2).
[182] German Private Limited Liability Companies Act, para. 58d(1).
[183] German Public Limited Liability Companies Act, para. 233(2).
[184] German Public Limited Liability Companies Act, para. 234: cf. the German Private Limited Companies Act, para. 58e.
[185] German Public Limited Liability Companies Act, para. 235: cf. the closely similar para. 85f of the German Private Limited Liability Companies Act.

company, which has suffered capital losses to raise new equity share capital. If an increase took place without a reduction, this would have the effect of depriving new shareholders of a return on their shares until the lost capital had been restored through earnings.

The rules contained in Articles 237–239 AktG permit the reduction of capital by means of the compulsory redemption or purchase of shares by the company. Such operations, unlike other reductions of capital, will not affect all shareholders equally. They may take place in accordance with an ordinary or a simplified capital reduction procedure (which is applicable under the conditions set out in paragraph 237(3) and must not be confused with the simplified procedure described above) but are only permissible if prescribed or allowed by the company's statutes or an amendment thereof which became effective prior to the issue of the shares. The mandatory redemption or purchase of shares can be carried out by the directors, without any need for a resolution of the general meeting.

D. Applicable legal rules in Italy

1. General remarks

In Italian company law scholarship, the distinction between real and nominal modification of the capital (that is for both, increase or reduction) is generally accepted. A *real* modification is spoken of when the numerical change in the value of the capital contained in the statutes or deed corresponds to a concrete loss or increase in the company's assets. This happens for instance when the reduction is undertaken by means of returning capital to the shareholder or the increase takes place by means of the new provision of new consideration. A *nominal* modification instead is represented by situations in which the numerical modification of the value of the capital in the statutes or deed is not accompanied by an increase or loss in the assets of the company, for example in the case of capitalisation of the reserves or reduction of the capital for losses, where the change is only a matter of formalising an alteration of the assets already incurred.

An increase or a reduction of the share capital of an Italian public company will usually require the passing of a resolution at a general meeting. Because such a resolution involves an amendment of the statutes, the rules governing extraordinary general meetings apply.

In private companies, where there is no difference between ordinary and extraordinary meetings, the law provides that resolutions involving a modification of the deed of incorporation, like those of increase and reduction of capital are, must be adopted at a general meeting of shareholders by an affirmative vote of the holders of more than one-half of the share capital.[186]

In certain cases the competence in respect of an increase or reduction may be given to the directors both in public and private companies. The control on the regularity of the relevant resolutions is as a general rule entrusted to the notary who is responsible for drafting the minutes of the shareholders or board meetings (Article 2436 of the Civil Code). Under certain circumstances the court may be invested with the competence to decide on the increase or reduction.

2. Increase of capital

If a private company has a suitable provision in its deed of incorporation, (*atto costitutivo*) it is permitted by Article 2481 to empower its directors to increase its capital up to a certain amount. Otherwise, such an increase is a matter for the general meeting; the holders of a majority representing at least half of the company's capital will be required to vote in favour of it.[187] Articles 2444 and 2481 *bis* (6) require the directors of a public or private company, within thirty days of the full subscription for the new shares, to deliver a declaration to the Register of Enterprises that the increase of capital has been carried out.

In both public and private companies an increase in capital may take place through the medium of contributions in cash or in kind (*aumento reale*), or by means of the capitalisation of reserves (*aumento nominale*). The rules governing the first two types of operations are somewhat different for both public and private companies.[188] Articles 2438 and 2481(2) of the Civil Code prohibit the issue of new shares unless the company's existing shares are fully paid. Subscribers of new shares in cash must pay at least 25 per cent of the issue price to the company when the shares are issued.[189] Where there are contributions in kind, they have to be valued by an expert both in the case of public and private companies. If the value of the assets contributed is less than four-fifths of that attributed to the assets by the expert, a public company must reduce its capital proportionately, annulling the shares which are not covered.[190]

[186] Italian Civil Code, Art. 2479 *bis* (3). [187] *Ibid.*, Art. 2479 *bis* (3).

[188] Italian Civil Code, Arts. 2439–40 and Art. 2442 (public companies) and Arts. 2481–81 *ter* (private companies).

[189] *Ibid.*, Art. 2439(1) Note the similar provisions of Art. 2481 *bis* (4), which apply to private companies. They require any premium agreed upon to be fully paid, as does Art. 2439(1).

[190] Italian Civil Code, Arts. 2343 and 2440 (public companies); the applicable provision for private companies is Art. 2465.

Shareholders in a public company have extensive preferential rights of subscription in accordance with Article 2441(1) of the Civil Code. These extend to all new issues of shares, and to issues of convertible bonds (which issues cannot be made in an SRL), and are available to all existing shareholders, who hold ordinary shares and to the holders of convertible bonds.[191] Furthermore, in a public company, shareholders and convertible bondholders who so request when they exercise their original right of subscription have preferential rights of subscription for bonds and shares which are not originally taken up. If such shares are quoted on a regulated market, the preferential rights of subscription not taken up must be offered on the stock exchange by the directors on behalf of the company in at least five successive sessions.[192]

Preferential rights of subscription for shares in public companies do not exist where shares are issued for contributions in kind and they may be excluded or restricted in certain other cases.[193] Where the exclusion or limitation is on the grounds of the issue of shares for contributions in kind or of the interests of the company, it has to be justified by the directors in a special report. Where the exclusion or limitation is in the interests of the company, it must be provided for in the decision to increase the capital and approved by members representing more than one-half of the share capital, even if on second or third call.

The preferential right may also be excluded in case new shares are offered to employees of the company or of a controlled or a controlling company. If the right is excluded with regard to more than 25 per cent of the shares to be issued the resolution deciding on the increase must be taken with votes of more than half of the share capital even in second or subsequent convocations.

Article 2442 of the Civil Code contains provisions governing the capitalisation of the reserves of a public company (*Aumento nominale*). This article stipulates that the shareholders' extraordinary meeting of a public company may increase its capital by attributing the reserves or other disposable funds appearing in the balance sheet to capital. If it does so, the increase may take place by an increase in the nominal values of the existing shares, or by an allotment to members of bonus shares. The

[191] *Ibid.*, Art. 2441(1). [192] *Ibid.*, Art. 2441(2).

[193] *Ibid.*, Art. 2441(4)–(8) They may thus be excluded within the limit of 10 per cent of the pre-existing share capital where a company has its shares quoted on a regulated market, provided that the issue price of the shares corresponds to their market value, and this is confirmed by the report of the auditors of the issuing company's accounts.

newly issued shares must be of the same class as those already held by the members, and distributed freely to members in proportion to their shareholding. Article 2481 *ter* makes provision for the capitalisation of the disposable reserves of a private company.

The minutes of the resolution to increase the capital of a public or private company must be deposited at the office of the Registry of Enterprises by the responsible notary, such that the modifications of the articles may be registered within thirty days from the meeting in accordance with Articles 2436 and 2480 of the Civil Code if the documents are in order. If the notary believes that conditions required by the law are not fulfilled, he communicates this fact to the directors who can call a meeting or submit the relevant resolution to the court of first instance. The latter may, after a verification of fulfilment of the condition provided by the law for the passing of the resolution, order the registration thereof at the register of companies.[194] The further requirements of Articles 2444 and 2481 bis(6) concerning the registration of the fact that the resolution has been implemented have already been explained above. Such registration must take place within thirty days of the subscription for the shares.

3. Reduction of capital

Both in relation to public and private companies, the Civil Code contains general provisions governing the reduction of capital of companies, as well as other more specific provisions which are applicable when the capital has been diminished by more than one-third owing to losses, and when the capital has by reason of the loss of more than one-third thereof, been reduced below the legal minimum. The relevant provisions relating to public companies may be found in Articles 2445–7, and those relating to private companies are in Articles 2482–2482 *quater*.

The capital must not be reduced below the minimum amount required.[195]

[194] The verification of compliance with the conditions established by law for the purpose of the registration of alterations of the statutes is undertaken by the notary after the conclusion of the relevant meeting. The *Corte di cassazione* has made a number of decisions concerning the exercise of the notary's functions when drafting the minutes. He cannot fail to do so unless he considers that an unlawful resolution may have been passed. However, he may refuse to submit the minutes for registration and inform the directors of this refusal. See R. Rosapepe, 'Modificazioni statutarie e recesso' [2005] *Diritto delle Società di Capitali* 382.

[195] Italian Civil Code, Art. 2445(1) and Art. 2482 *ter*.

The capital of a public or private company may be reduced in a number of circumstances. A reduction may take place where a company's assets exceed what is required for it to achieve its objects. The extraordinary general meeting of a public company which decides on this matter must indicate the method of reduction and the reason for it. The reductions may take place by means of the return of capital, or release from the obligation to make contributions in both public and private companies. The resolution for the reduction may be implemented three months after the date of the registration of the resolution in the Companies Register; unless within that period a creditor whose claims arose before the registration of the resolution has filed an objection to it with the court.[196] A reduction of capital may be carried out notwithstanding such opposition if it has been sanctioned by the court which believes that there is no risk of prejudice for the creditor by reason of the reduction and after the company has given suitable security for the objecting creditor's claims.[197]

A reduction of capital by repayment must not result in the remaining capital falling below the minimum amount prescribed by Article 2327 in the case of a public company, and by Article 2463(1) sentence 4 in the case of a private company. Furthermore, Article 2413 of the Civil Code imposes certain limitations on the reduction of the capital of a public company which has bondholders. Such a company may not voluntarily reduce its capital if to do so would mean that the total amount outstanding on the bonds becomes more than twice the value of the share capital, the legal reserves and the disposable reserves appearing in the latest balance sheet. However, there are a number of exceptions to this principle. If the reduction is compulsory, or if the reserves are diminished by reason of losses, profits may not be distributed if the amount of the share capital and legal reserves is less than that of the bonds in circulation.

A reduction of capital in excess of a company's needs may be carried out in a number of different ways. Thus shareholders may be released from their obligation to contribute capital in respect of their shares; or the nominal value of the company's shares may be reduced, the resulting capital being repaid to shareholders either rateably or by drawings. In the latter case, shareholders whose capital is repaid may be allotted enjoyment or profit sharing shares (*azioni di godimento*). Sometimes it is possible for a company to write off losses against reserves or by the

[196] *Ibid.*, Art. 2445(3), and Art. 2482(2); the latter provision mentions a period of ninety days.

[197] *Ibid.*, Art. 2445(4) and Art. 2482(3).

revaluation of assets. If a private or public company incurs losses which cannot be written off in such a manner, the company may not pay dividends until its capital has been restored or reduced.[198] Thus companies sometimes reduce their capital in order to be able to make distributions. As frequently happens in Germany and in other countries, reductions of capital are sometimes made in order to permit the company to make a subsequent increase of capital, which would otherwise have only an insignificant chance of being taken up.

A reduction of capital must take place if a company suffers losses whose total exceeds one-third of its issued capital. The rules differ in the present instance according to whether the company's capital, as diminished by the losses, is not less than the required minimum capital, or has fallen below that amount.[199]

If the losses mentioned above do not cause the capital of a public company to fall below the statutory minimum, a reduction of capital is not immediately necessary. However, the directors or the executive board and, in the event of their inaction, the board of auditors or the supervisory board must without delay convene an extraordinary general meeting to take the necessary actions after receiving a report as to the state of the company's assets with the observations thereon of the committee of auditors, or the internal control committee (*comitato per il controllo sulla gestione*) where the new single board structure is used. Copies of the report and the observations on it must be deposited at the registered office of the company eight days before the meeting such that they may be examined by the members.[200] Should the total loss suffered by a company have not been reduced to less than one-third of the company's capital before the end of the following financial year, then the ordinary general meeting or the supervisory board which approves the company's balance sheet for that year must resolve on a reduction of capital in proportion to the remaining loss. The rules are similar in relation to private companies.

Should the above mentioned bodies fail to resolve on the necessary reduction of the company's capital, the directors, committee of auditors

[198] *Ibid.*, Art. 2433(3) and Art. 2478 *bis* (5).

[199] *Ibid.*, Arts. 2446 and 2447(public companies) and Art. 2482 *bis* and *ter* (private companies).

[200] *Ibid.*, Art. 2446(1) (public companies). The rules are somewhat similar in relation to private companies: see *ibid.*, Art. 2482 *bis* (1) and (2).

or supervisory board must request the court to order the necessary reduction of capital.[201]

Where the company's capital, after being diminished by losses, falls below the statutory minimum, the directors of a public or private company and, in the event of their inaction, the board of auditors or the supervisory board,[202] must convene an extraordinary general meeting without delay either to resolve on an appropriate reduction of capital accompanied by a simultaneous increase thereof to an amount equal at least to the statutory minimum, or to resolve on the conversion of the company into a company of another kind.[203]

Reductions of the capital of public and private companies may take place by reason of the withdrawal of shareholders, which may for example take place when they dissent from resolutions involving the changing of the objects or type of the company, or the transfer of its registered office abroad.[204] The shares of a shareholder who withdraws may be cancelled in certain circumstances and the capital then reduced. However, the law aims to preserve the integrity of the company providing rules on the purchase of these shares by remaining members or third parties and reimbursement for the shares by recourse to the reserves if any. The reduction of the share capital or winding up are the extreme alternatives.

If a shareholder in a public company has made contributions in kind for shares and directors discover that the real value of the assets was less than four-fifths of the nominal value of the shares issued for them, the shareholder may withdraw from the company, or instead pay the difference in cash.[205] Should the allottee withdraw, the shares are cancelled and the company's capital is reduced.

If a shareholder in a public company omits to pay calls or instalments in respect of shares, and the company cannot find a purchaser for them by exercising its power of sale under Article 2344 of the Civil Code, the directors may declare the expulsion of the member. If it proves impossible to put the unsold shares back into circulation within the accounting

201 *Ibid.*, Art. 2446(3) (public companies); Art. 2482 *bis* (4) and (5) (private companies). Article 2446 (5), applicable to public companies, and as far as compatible also to private ones, provides that in companies whose shares have no nominal value the articles or a modification thereof or a resolution passed at an extraordinary general meeting may entrust the reduction to the board of directors.

202 The recourse to the latter organs is expressly provided for in the case of public companies only.

203 Italian Civil Code, Art. 2447 (public companies) and Art. 2482 *ter* (private companies).

204 *Ibid.*, Arts. 2437 and 2473.

205 *Ibid.*, Art. 2343(4). The same rule is not applicable to private companies.

year during which the expulsion is declared, the shares must be cancelled and the capital correspondingly reduced.[206]

E. Applicable legal rules in Spain

1. Increase of capital

A Spanish SRL (*sociedad de responsabilidad limitada*) may increase its capital by issuing new shares if shareholders holding more than half the votes in respect of the shares in the company vote in favour of such an increase at a general meeting.[207] As is the case with a public company (*sociedad anónima*), the increase of the capital of an SRL (private company) may take place either by issuing new shares, or increasing the nominal values of the existing shares.[208] Where the latter operation is contemplated, the consent of all the members in writing is required, except where the increase is to take place by the capitalisation of profits or reserves.[209] Where the increase of capital is to take place through the set-off of debts owing by the company, the debts must be fully liquidated and payable.[210] When contributions in kind are to be made, the members must be provided with a report by the directors giving particulars of them when the meeting is convoked.[211] The capitalisation of reserves in a private company must take place on the basis of a balance sheet approved by the general meeting which must relate to a date less than six months before the meeting. A similar rule is applicable to the capitalisation of the reserves of a public company, where the balance sheet has in addition to be verified by an auditor. In the case of a private company, the balance sheet has to be included in the notarial deed which reflects the increase of capital.[212]

[206] *Ibid.*, Arts. 2344 and 2466(3) which contains a similar provision applicable to private companies.

[207] Law of 1995 concerning private companies (*sociedades de responsabilidad limitada*), Art. 53(2). The required majority may be increased by the articles which may not, however require unanimity: see Art. 53(3), *ibid.*

[208] Law of 1989 concerning public companies as amended. Art. 151(1); Law of 1995 concerning private companies, Art. 73(1).

[209] Law of 1995 concerning private companies, Art. 74(1); cf. Law of 1989 concerning public companies (*sociedades anónimas*), as amended, Art. 152(2).

[210] Law concerning private companies of 1995, Art. 74(2); cf. Law of 1989, as amended, Art. 156(1), which requires such debt to be payable within five years.

[211] Law concerning private companies of 1995, Art. 74(3). Similar rules apply to an SA: see Law concerning public companies of 1989, as amended, Art. 155(1).

[212] See Law of 1995 concerning private companies, Art. 74(4) and Law of 1989 concerning public companies, as amended, Article 157(2).

Pre-emptive rights are enjoyed by shareholders in an SRL when the capital increase has resulted in the issue of new shares, which shareholders are then entitled to subscribe for a number of shares proportionate to the par values of their shareholdings. The pre-emptive rights must be exercised within the period set out in the resolution for the capital increase. Unless the articles provide otherwise, the directors may offer the shares not subscribed in accordance with the pre-emptive rights, to members who have acquired such rights for subscription and payment within not more than fifteen days from the end of the period prescribed to the exercise of pre-emptive rights. If more than one person is interested in acquiring the relevant shares, they must do so in proportion to their shareholdings. These supplementary pre-emption rights do not have any parallel in the rules governing pre-emption rights in public companies, which are not only available to existing shareholders but also to the holders of convertible bonds issued by such companies.[213] In both types of companies, pre-emption rights can be wholly or partially excluded under certain prescribed (and to a considerable extent similar) conditions. The resolution excluding or limiting such rights must be preceded by a report from the directors explaining the reasons for such proposed action.[214]

The resolution for an increase or reduction of capital of a public or private company will involve an amendment of the articles which must be recorded in a notarial deed which must be filed with the Commercial Register and published in the *Official Gazette*.[215] The notarial deed recording the increase of the capital of a private company must contain the details prescribed by Article 78(1) of the Law of 1995, which include particulars of property or rights contributed. A resolution evidencing the execution of the increase must be recorded simultaneously with that on the increase at the Companies Register. If the necessary documents have not been filed at the Companies Register within six months of the beginning of the period for such increases the subscribers may demand the return of the capital contributed.[216]

[213] Law concerning private companies of 1995, Art. 75; Law concerning public companies of 1989, as amended, Art. 158.

[214] Law concerning private companies of 1995, Art. 76; Law concerning public companies of 1989, as amended, Art. 159, as amended by Law 37/1998, Law 50/1998, and Law 44/2002, providing special rules for public listed companies.

[215] Law concerning private companies 1995, Art. 79(2); Law concerning public companies of 1989, as amended, Art. 162(1).

[216] Law concerning private companies of 1995, Art. 78(3); Law concerning public companies of 1989 as amended, Art. 162(2).

As already indicated, the rules governing capital increases in public companies are generally similar to those applicable to private companies, but there are a few significant differences. Thus, a resolution for the increase of the capital of a public company has to be adopted in accordance with Articles 151 and 152 of the Law of 1989, as amended. A resolution for the increase of capital can only be validly adopted when the meeting is first convoked if shareholders representing at least 50 per cent of the voting capital are present in person or represented by proxy. On a second call, this requirement is reduced to 25 per cent of the voting share capital. However, if the shareholders present in person or by proxy represent less than 50 per cent of the voting share capital, the resolution must be passed by a vote of two thirds of the share capital present or represented at the meeting. These rules are the same as those applicable to the amendment of the company's articles, and are contained in Article 103 of the Law of 1989, as amended.

When debts owed to the public company are converted into shares, at least 25 per cent of the debt must be due and payable.[217] The articles (*statutos*) or a resolution passed by the general meeting may authorise the directors to carry out increases of capital. Such authorisations must either involve a specific amount, and be carried out within one year, or be up to a specified maximum amount, which must not be greater than one half the company's capital. In the latter event, the increase must take place by way of cash contributions made within five years.[218] If a public company's shares are the subject of a public offer for subscriptions, the offer is subject to the regulations governing the securities market.[219]

2. Reduction of capital

The rules governing the reduction of capital of a public company are more complex than those governing the reduction of capital of a private company, and there are considerable differences between certain of the relevant provisions. Thus, Article 79, of the Law of 1995 concerning private companies, which sets out the purpose of the reduction of capital of such companies, is simpler than the corresponding provisions of Article 163 of the Law of 1989, as amended. Article 79(1) provides that a reduction of capital may be carried out for the purpose of reimbursing contributions, or the restoration of the balance between capital and the

[217] Law of 1989, as amended, Art. 156.
[218] Law concerning public companies of 1989, as amended, Arts. 153 and 155(2).
[219] *Ibid.*, Art. 160.

net assets of the company caused by losses. Article 163(1) paragraph 1, which applies to public companies, provides for the same contingencies as are provided for in Article 79(1), but is somewhat more detailed. According to Article 163(1), paragraph 2, a company must reduce its capital where as the result of losses, the value of its net assets has been reduced below two thirds of the total capital, and a financial year has passed without the restoration of the value of the assets.

Article 81 of the Law of 1995 concerning private companies (SRL or SL) unlike Article 166 of the Law of 1989 concerning public companies (which provides that creditors whose claims are not secured may object to the reduction until they receive a guarantee)[220] does not contain any mandatory provisions for the protection of creditors. Its dispositions are of a dispositive nature; the first paragraph of Article 81 stipulates that the articles may provide that no resolution for the reduction of capital involving the repayment of contributions made by members may be carried out until after three months notice given to creditors has expired. Creditors may object to the reduction within this period.

According to Article 82(1), the capital may not be reduced to restore the balance between capital and net assets to the extent that the private company has any kind of free reserves. A rather similar rule is contained in Article 168(1) of the Law of 1989 concerning public companies as amended. By Article 82(2) of the Law of 1995, the balance sheet that will serve as the basis for the reduction must have been prepared within six months of the date of such reduction, and must be approved by a general meeting after having been verified by auditors. The rules contained in Article 168(2) of the Law of 1989 (as amended) are similar except insofar as they do not mention any time period within which the balance sheet should be prepared.

The reduction of capital of an SRL or SA (public company) will require an alteration of the articles which must be reflected in a notarial deed registered in the commercial Registry and published in the *Official Gazette*. In the case of an SA, the resolution to reduce capital has to be published not only in the *Official Gazette* but also in two major newspapers which circulate in the province in which the company's registered office is situated.[221] The resolution of the general meeting on the reduction of capital of an SA is required to state the reason for the resolution,

[220] They may not raise such an objection in the cases mentioned in Art. 167, e.g. where the sole aim of the reduction is to re-establish the balance between the capital and the net assets of the company that has been reduced by losses.

[221] Law of 1989, as amended, Art. 165.

the form it will take, and any amount to be repaid to shareholders.[222] No such detailed requirements appear in the Law of 1995 concerning private companies.

Article 83 of the Law of 1995 concerning private companies covers the situation in which a simultaneous reduction and increase of capital is necessary, which is where a resolution is to be passed reducing the capital below the legal minimum. This may only take place if a resolution is passed to convert the company into a company of another type, or to increase its capital. Article 169 of the Law of 1989 governs this situation as far as public companies are concerned, and is similar in content.

F. Applicable legal rules in Belgium

1. Increase of capital

The rules contained in the new Companies Code concerning the increase and reduction of capital (like those concerning bonds) are rather detailed and complex, and the account below will generally concentrate on the position in the public company (NV or SA) as far as the increase of capital is concerned. It will also contain some indication of the ways in which this position resembled and differs from that in the private company (BVBA or SPRL). A detailed account of all the provisions will not be attempted.

The increase of the capital of a public or private company requires the passing of a resolution by the same procedure as is required for the modification of the articles.[223] If a public company has authorised capital, an increase of capital within the limits of such authorised capital may be decided on by the directors. If a proposal is to be discussed at a general meeting to issue shares without mention of their nominal value at a price lower than the accounting par value of shares already issued of the same kind, this fact must be mentioned specifically in the notice

[222] Law of 1989, as amended, Art. 164(2). A reduction of the capital of a public company may take place by lowering the par values of the shares, by their redemption, or by grouping them together and exchanging them; the latter would presumably apply to fractional shares: see Law of 1989 as amended, Art. 163(2).

[223] Companies Code, Arts. 286, 288 and 302 (private companies); Arts. 558, 560 and 581 (public companies). The power to make an increase within the limits of authorised capital may be granted to the directors of a public company for a period of five years by the articles, either in their original form or as amended by the general meeting. There are a number of situations in which such authorised capital cannot be utilised: see Arts. 605–6 of the Companies Code. The rules governing authorised capital do not apply to private companies. According to Article 603, if the company has appealed to the public for subscription, its authorised capital may not exceed its existing capital.

calling the meeting. Reports are also required from the directors, and from a qualified accountant on such an operation. If no such report is provided, the decision of the general meeting has no effect.[224] If convertible bonds or subscription rights are to be issued, the directors are required to make a special report explaining the object of the operation and justifying it in detail. Once again, the absence of the relevant report entails the nullity of the decision of the general meeting.[225]

In both public and private companies, if the increase of capital is not fully subscribed this does not entail that the capital is increased to the extent of the subscriptions recovered, unless such a contingency is provided for in the terms of issue.[226]

Shares issued for cash or for non-cash contributions on an increase of capital have to be paid up, or the contribution has to be made to the extent of one quarter of its value in a public company. A contribution in kind has to be fully performed within five years of the date of the resolution on the increase of capital.[227] In both private and public companies, any premium on the shares has to be paid on subscription.[228]

A single notarial act may set out both the fact of the proposed increase and its execution: however in the past it has usually been found that a second deed is necessary for this purpose. The rules are similar both in the case of private and public companies.[229]

When new shares are issued for cash, or convertible bonds or subscription warrants are issued, they must be offered to the existing shareholders in a public company in proportion to the amount of capital represented by their shares. The same is true of the issue of shares for cash in a private company.[230] In both types of company, the holders of non-voting shares have a right of pre-emption in the case of the issue of new shares, whether or not they carry voting rights except where the increase in capital takes place by means of the issue of two proportionate blocks of shares, one carrying voting rights and another carrying no such rights, and existing voting shareholders are given a preferential right to

[224] Companies Code, Art. 582. There is no parallel provision relating to the SPRL (private companies).

[225] Companies Code, Art. 583. No corresponding provision exists in the case of the SPRL.

[226] Companies Code, Art. 303 (private companies); Art. 584 (public companies).

[227] Companies Code, Art. 586. The position is somewhat different in a private company, in which one-fifth the amount of any cash contribution has to be paid up, and any contribution in kind performed in full on subscription: *ibid.*, Art. 305.

[228] *Ibid.*, Art. 306 (private companies); Art. 587 (public companies).

[229] *Ibid.*, Art. 307 and 308 (private companies); Arts. 588 and 589 (public companies).

[230] *Ibid.*, Art. 309(1) (private companies); *ibid.*, Art. 592(1) (public companies).

subscribe for the new voting shares and existing non-voting shareholders a corresponding right in respect of the new non-voting shares.[231]

Pre-emption rights cannot be excluded or limited by the articles of a public company.[232] According to Article 596, a general meeting of a public company which is called upon to deliberate and decide upon an increase of capital, the issue of convertible bonds, or subscription rights, may exclude or limit rights of pre-emption in the interests of the company by the same conditions as to quorum and majority as is required for the amendment of the articles.[233] The directors must justify their action on the basis of a detailed report made by an auditor (*commissaire*) or another expert (*reviseur d'entreprise*) if the company does not have an auditor.

By Article 311, cash contributions paid on an increase of the capital or a private company must be paid into a special account with the post office or a bank, and this account must be at the sole disposal of the company. No similar rule is made applicable to cash contributions on an increase of capital of a public company. In both private and public companies, contributions in kind made for shares on an increase of capital must take the form of assets whose value is capable of economic evaluation, and may not take that of work to be done or services to be performed.[234] In both cases, contributions in kind to be made for shares on an increase of capital have to be reported on by the company's auditor (*commissaire*) or, if it has not got one, by an expert (*reviseur d'entreprise*). The report is deposited with the registrar of the local commercial court, and it must be included in the agenda of the meeting which decides on the increase of capital.[235]

[231] *Ibid.*, Art. 309(2) (private companies); *ibid.*, Art. 592(2) (public companies).

[232] *Ibid.*, Art. 595. There is nothing in the Code permitting the exclusion or limitation of the pre-emption rights of shareholders of private companies. If pre-emption rights are not exercised by the shareholders of such companies, it follows from Art. 310(3) that third parties may only take shares if they are approved by at least half of the existing members holding at least three-quarters of the share capital. An exception to this rule is made for spouses, ascendants and descendants in the direct line of the shareholder, persons specifically mentioned in the articles and other shareholders by Art. 249(2).

[233] The alteration of the articles of a public company is dealt with by Art. 558 of the Companies Code, Art. 286 of which applies to the alteration of the articles of private companies, is in similar terms. The proposed alteration must be set out in the notice calling the meeting. The meeting must be attended by persons representing at least half of the company's capital. If this condition is not fulfilled a further meeting must be called which deliberates validly, whatever fraction of capital is represented at such meeting. However, the relevant resolution must be passed by at least three-quarters of the votes cast.

[234] Companies Code, Art. 312 (private companies) and Art. 601 (public companies).

[235] *Ibid.*, Art. 313 (private companies) and Art. 602 (public companies).

2. Reduction of capital

The provisions governing the reduction of capital of Belgian private and public companies are virtually identical. They are mercifully considerably less detailed than those which relate to increase of capital.

A reduction of the nominal capital of a public or a private company is required to take place in accordance with the procedure necessary for the alteration of the articles, and must treat shareholders in the same situation equally. The notice calling the meeting must explain the manner in which the proposed reduction will be carried out, and the objective of such reduction.[236] If the proposed reduction involves the return of assets to the members, or their total or partial dispensation from liability in respect of unpaid capital, creditors may request security for their debts within two months of the announcement of the reduction resolution in the Annexes to the *Moniteur Belge*. If the company does not provide such security, or it does not pay a creditor, the matter can be referred to the local commercial court, which makes use of a summary procedure (*procédure en référé*). Without prejudice to the merits of the case, the president of the local commercial court shall determine the security to be furnished by the company and the period within which it is to be provided, taking into account the guarantees or privileges which the creditor has, and the solvency of the company.[237]

If the creditors who have requested security within the two months period already mentioned have not obtained security or had their debts paid, no return of capital can be made to shareholders, and such shareholders may not benefit from any cancellation of liability in respect of unpaid capital. This is subject to the reservation that their claim to receive security has not been rejected by an enforceable decision of the competent court.

Creditors have no right to demand security, or apply to the court, in accordance with Articles 317 and 613 of the Companies Code where the reduction of capital takes place because of losses suffered by the private or public company,[238] or because of the company's need to create a reserve to cover foreseeable losses. The latter type of reserve may not exceed 10 per cent of the subscribed capital after account has been taken of its reduction. This reserve may not be distributed to the shareholders, except in the case of a later reduction of capital. It may only be utilised for

[236] *Ibid.*, Art. 316 (private companies) and Art. 612 (public companies).
[237] *Ibid.*, Art. 317 (private companies) and Art. 613 (public companies).
[238] *Ibid.*, Art. 318 (private companies) and Art. 614 (public companies).

the purpose of compensating for losses suffered or for that of increasing capital through the incorporation of reserves.[239] In the situations envisaged by Articles 318 and 614, the company's capital may be reduced below the minimum amount required. Such a reduction has no effect until the capital is increased to at least the minimum amount.[240]

G. *Applicable legal rules in the Netherlands*

1. Increase of capital

The issued capital of an NV or BV is increased by the issue of new shares. The increase of capital requires the amendment of the articles of both private and public companies. The certificate of no objection of the Minister of Justice will not be given if when the notarial deed which is required for the amendment of the articles is executed, subscription has not been made for one fifth of the newly authorised capital.[241] Shares in both private and public companies are sometimes issued at a premium.[242] In the case of an NV, this must be paid at the time of issue:[243] no such restrictive rule applies in the case of a BV.

The issue of new shares in a private or public company needs a resolution of the general meeting. However this task may be delegated to another organ by the general meeting of a public or private company,[244] or the articles of either kind of company.[245] In the case of a public company, the period of delegation to the directors or supervisory board may not exceed five years, and may be renewed from time to time. Once the delegation has been granted in a public company, it may not be withdrawn unless it provides otherwise.[246] If there are different classes of shares, the power of the NV's shareholders to issue shares of a particular class and to delegate this power to the board may not be exercised without the prior or simultaneous approval of the holders of the class of shares whose rights are prejudiced by the issue.[247] Information concerning the number and type of new shares issued must be filed with the commercial register within eight days of such issue.[248] The rules are less detailed and restrictive in the case of a BV. In such a private company, the

[239] *Ibid.*, Art. 318 (private companies) and Art. 614 (public companies).
[240] *Ibid.*, Arts. 318 and 614.
[241] *Ibid.*, Arts. 2.68(2)/179(2) and 2.67(4)/178(4). This requirement is likely to be repealed as far as BVs are concerned.
[242] *Ibid.*, Art. 2.80(1). [243] *Ibid.*, Art. 2.80(1).
[244] *Ibid.*, Arts. 2.96(1) and 2.206(1). [245] *Ibid.*, Arts. 2.96(1) and 2.206(1).
[246] *Ibid.*, Art. 2.96(1). [247] *Ibid.*, Art. 2.96(2). [248] *Ibid.*, Art. 2.96(3).

shareholders can delegate their power to issue shares to the management board or the supervisory board. Furthermore, the power to issue new shares may be conferred on one of these boards by the articles.

The power to issue new shares and to determine the consideration given them (which power usually accompanies the former one) is often of significance in the context of a hostile takeover bid.[249] This power is, however, subject to the stock exchange regulations in the case of a public offer.

In public and private companies, existing shareholders have a statutory pre-emptive right to purchase shares of the class they own, in proportion to their existing shareholdings.[250] The shareholders in a public company are entitled to limit or exclude this pre-emptive right. This may also be done under the company's articles. They may also delegate their power to exclude or limit the shareholders' pre-emptive rights to the company organ (that is, the management or supervisory board) which was initially permitted to issue new shares.[251] This power of delegation is limited to a period of five years and can be renewed from time to time.[252] The public company must file the complete text of the resolution limiting or excluding pre-emptive rights with the commercial register within eight days of its being passed.[253]

According to Article 2.96a(1) of the Civil Code, pre-emptive rights are not available when new shares are issued by a public company for a non-cash consideration unless the articles otherwise provide. They are also unavailable in respect of shares held by employees of a public company or its group companies. Except where there are different provisions in the articles, the holders of preference shares in a public company[254] have no pre-emptive rights and the holders of ordinary shares have no pre-emptive rights with respect to preference shares.[255]

[249] Note in that sense, S. R. Schuit, *Corporate Law and Practice of the Netherlands* (The Hague, London: Kluwer Law International, 2002), p. 57. The writer points out that the management board or the holders of priority shares may be able to place preference shares so as to repel a hostile bidder.

[250] BW, Arts. 2.96a(1) (public companies) and 2.206a(1) (private companies). The new proposals will exclude such a right for shareholders in a private company who have only a limited right to participate in the profits; or who have no right or limited right to participate in the liquidation surplus; or who have no voting rights.

[251] This power of delegation or designation is sometimes used by Dutch listed companies as a protection against hostile takeovers.

[252] BW, Art. 2.96(a)(6). [253] *Ibid.*, Art. 2.96(a)(7).

[254] Their position is usefully (if briefly) considered in A. Dorresteijn, *European Corporate Law* (Deventer and Boston: Kluwer Law and Taxation, 1994), p. 92. See BW, Arts. 2.96a(2) and 2.206a(2).

[255] *Ibid.*, Art. 2.96a(2) and (3).

Furthermore, no pre-emptive rights are available in respect of shares issued to the employees of a private company or one of its group companies.[256] In such a company, the shareholders are permitted to restrict or exclude the pre-emptive rights of existing shareholders, unless the articles provide otherwise. However, they may only do this each time in respect of single issues of shares, unless there is a different provision in the articles.[257] In addition unless the articles provide otherwise (as is also the case with the public company), holders of preference shares have no pre-emptive rights, and the holders of ordinary shares have no pre-emptive right with respect to preference shares.

When new shares are issued, this may be for a cash consideration. Similar rules apply to non-cash consideration furnished at the time of a new issue as on foundation.

2. Reduction of capital

A reduction of the issued capital of a private or public company may take place by means of a resolution of the general meeting either to cancel shares (*intrekking*) or to reduce their nominal amount by amending the articles. A resolution to cancel shares may only concern shares held by the company itself[258] or all shares belonging to the class in respect of which the articles permit the cancellation of shares by means of redemption, perhaps by drawing lots, before their issue.[259] Otherwise, such cancellations can only take place if all the shareholders of the relevant class agree. Any reduction in the nominal value of shares without redemption and without release from the obligation to pay up must be pro rata in respect of all the shares of the same class, except where all the shareholders involved otherwise agree.[260] The partial repayment or release from the obligation to contribute may only take place on the implementation of a resolution to reduce the nominal value of shares.[261] The resolution for the reduction of capital must be filed with the commercial register. A notice of such filing must also be published in a

[256] *Ibid.*, Art. 2.206a(1). [257] *Ibid.*, Art. 2.206a(1).

[258] An NV together with its subsidiaries can own 10 per cent of its own shares whilst a BV and its subsidiaries may own 50 per cent; see BW, Art.2.98(2)(b) (public companies) and BW, Art.207(2)(b) private companies. The lower limitation for private companies is likely to be abolished.

[259] BW Arts.2.99(2) and 2.208(2) (public and private companies respectively). It is proposed that Article 2.208(2) shall be amended slightly.

[260] *Ibid.*, Arts.2.99(3) and 2.208(3).

[261] *Ibid.*, Arts.2.99(4) (public companies) and 2.208(4) (private companies).

nationally circulating daily newspaper.[262] Creditors may oppose the intended action within two months of such publication by filing a petition with the competent district court (*rechtbank*).[263] The creditor must make it clear what security he wants. The company must provide such security or otherwise guarantee the payment of the claim, unless the latter is sufficiently secured, or the company's financial situation prevents the giving of security.[264]

A resolution for the reduction of the issued share capital may not have effect until such time as the opposition of any creditor has been withdrawn, or has been set aside by the district court.[265] In no circumstances may the reduction of capital bring the issued capital below the minimum amount.

It follows from Article 2.100(6) of the Civil Code that public and private companies which have suffered losses do not need to provide security when purchasing their shares. However, this type of operation may only take place provided that the acquisition price for the purchased shares does not bring the amount of shareholders equity (net worth) below the issued and called up part of the share capital together with any statutory reserves and reserves required by the articles.[266] Thus, the price for the purchased shares has to be paid out of the company's distributable reserves. The reduction of capital takes place upon the subsequent redemption of the shares. As already indicated, if the company is a public one, it may, together with its subsidiaries, hold only 10 per cent of its own shares, but if it is a private one, this amount is increased to 50 per cent. A cancellation of treasury shares facilitates future repurchases. The present law relating to the acquisition of its own shares by a private company is likely to undergo change with the enactment of recent government proposals. The existing 50 per cent limitation is likely to be abolished.

The articles of a public company must permit the acquisition of the company's shares, but no such permission is required when the acquisition

[262] *Ibid.*, Art.2.100(1) (public companies) and Art.2.209(1) (private companies). Article 209 will be repealed if the new government proposals for the reform of the law relating to the BV are adopted.

[263] *Ibid.*, Art.2.100(3) (public companies).

[264] *Ibid.*, Art.2.100(2) (public companies).

[265] *Ibid.*, Art.2.100(5) (public companies).

[266] *Ibid.*, Art.2.100(2)(a) (public companies) and Art.2.209(2)(a) (private companies). See also Schuit, *Corporate Law and Practice*, pp. 66–7. It is proposed that the law should be changed governing this matter; the new Article 207(2) would impose a balance sheet test and a liquidity test for such acquisitions.

is for no consideration. A similar rule applies to a private company.[267] In a public company, repurchase has to be authorised by the general meeting. In a private company, the power of authorisation may in addition be conferred on another corporate body appointed to do so by the articles or the general meeting.[268] It is likely that this power will be given to the directors of a private company if the new government proposals are enacted.

IX. Acquisition, purchase, and redemption by a company of its own shares

A. Applicable legal rules in the United Kingdom

The UK rules governing the purchase and redemption of its own shares by a company are rather complex, as are the rules governing the acquisition of its own shares by a German public company.[269] Some changes have been made in the rules which were formerly applicable by the Companies Act 2006. Until recently,[270] UK public and private companies were not allowed to hold their own shares, unlike their counterparts in certain other countries.[271] This is now possible where a limited company purchases its own shares in accordance with Chapter 4 of Part 18 of the Companies Act 2006, provided such shares are qualifying shares within the meaning of section 724(2) of the Act. The aggregate value of shares so held must not at any time exceed 10 per cent of the nominal value of the issued share capital of the company or of any class of shares held as treasury shares. Redeemable shares may be issued by a public or private company, provided that, if it is a public company, it is

[267] BW Art.98(4) (public companies) and Article 2.207(2)(c) (private companies). It is now proposed that the articles may specifically exclude or limit a company's power to purchase its own shares.

[268] *Ibid.*, Art.2.98(4) and Art.2.207(2)(d). [269] See paras. 71–71d, AktG.

[270] Shares which were redeemed or purchased, had to be cancelled immediately. Redeemable shares could be issued by a public or private company in the United Kingdom if authorised by the articles; the shares had to be fully paid up, Companies Act 1985, section 159. Public and private companies were also allowed to purchase their own shares in accordance with the rules set out in ss. 162–170 of the Companies Act 1985. A distinction was made between market and off market purchases. Section 163(3) of the Companies Act 1985 defined a market purchase as a purchase made on a recognised investment exchange other than a purchase on a recognised stock exchange of shares not subject to a marketing arrangement. The majority of purchases of shares in companies whose shares were listed on a stock market were market purchases.

[271] German public companies may hold their own shares with certain limitations. Treasury shares are common in the United States.

authorised to do so by its articles. The articles of a private company may exclude or limit the issue of redeemable shares.[272] Such shares are required to be fully paid up,[273] and they are annulled on redemption.[274] Public and private companies are permitted to purchase their own shares in accordance with the detailed rules set out in sections 690–708 of the Companies Act 2006, which continues to make a distinction between market and off-market purchases.

A market purchase is defined in section 693(4) of the Companies Act 2006 (making reference to section 693(2)(b)) as a purchase made on a recognised investment exchange other than a off-market purchase by reason of the fact that the shares are not subject to a marketing arrangement on the exchange.[275] Public listed companies occasionally transact off-market purchases but most of them are made by private companies and unlisted public ones.

An off-market purchase is defined in section 693(2) as a purchase in which either the shares are purchased otherwise than on a recognised investment exchange; or they are purchased on such an exchange but are not subject to a marketing arrangement on that exchange. According to section 694(2) the terms of the contract for an off-market purchase must be authorised by a special resolution before the contract is entered into, or the contract must provide that no shares may be purchased in pursuance of the contract until its terms have been authorised by a special resolution of the company. If the vendor exercises voting rights on the relevant shares, and the resolution would not have been passed if he had not done so, it is ineffective.[276] In the case of the public limited company, the resolution must specify a date by which the transaction must take place, which is limited to eighteen months after the passing of the resolution in the case of public companies.[277] Any contingent purchase option by which a public or private limited company may become entitled or obliged to purchase its own shares (contingent purchase option) is subject to the same procedural requirements.[278]

In accordance with the provisions of Article 19(1) of the Second Company Law Directive (as amended), market purchases require the prior authority of an ordinary resolution. Thus, according to section 701(1) of

[272] Companies Act 2006, s. 686(1). [273] *Ibid.*, s. 684(2) and (3).
[274] *Ibid.*, Companies Act 2006, s. 688.
[275] See previously, Companies Act 1985, s. 163(3). [276] Companies Act 2006, s. 695(3).
[277] *Ibid.*, s. 694(5). The same requirements were previously in the Companies Act 1985, ss. 163 and 164.
[278] Companies Act 2006, s. 694(3).

the Companies Act 2006, a company may only make a market purchase of its own shares if it has been authorised by a resolution of the company. The authorising resolution must, according to section 701(3) specify the maximum number of shares to be acquired, the maximum and minimum prices which are to be paid for them, and a date within eighteen months on which the authority will expire. These provisions are in accordance with the former provisions of Article 19(1) of the Directive, which has been replaced by Article 1(4) of Directive 2006/68/EC.[279]

The purchase or redemption of shares is not intended to lead to a reduction of capital. Thus, apart from the special rules relating to the redemption or purchase of shares in private companies set out below, shares may only be redeemed or purchased out of distributable profits, or out of the proceeds of a new issue of shares.[280] Where shares are redeemed or purchased wholly out of the company's profits, the amount by which the company's issued share capital is diminished on cancellation of the shares redeemed or purchased is transferred to a reserve called the 'capital redemption reserve'.[281]

However, if they are so authorised by the articles, private companies may redeem or purchase their shares out of capital if other available funds are inadequate for this purpose.[282] The present provisions[283] remain rather complex.[284] The permissible capital payment which may be made in respect of the redemption or purchase of a company's own shares which together with other permissible funds[285] is equal to the price of redemption or purchase has to be determined by reference to accounts which are dated not more than three months before the required statutory declaration by the directors.[286] This statutory declaration is in essence one of existing and future solvency after the making of the payment, which must be supported by a report from the company's auditors.[287] The payment out of capital must be approved by a special resolution within one week of the directors' statement.[288] The payment out of capital may be made only between five and seven weeks after the

[279] See previously Companies Act 1985, s. 166(1) and (3).
[280] Companies Act 2006, ss. 687(2)(a) and 692(2)(a).
[281] *Ibid.*, s. 733. [282] *Ibid.*, ss. 709–12.
[283] See the previous rules in Companies Act 1985, s. 171: note in particular s. 171(3). See the good account of the previous provisions in A. J. Boyle and J. Birds, *Company Law*, 5th edn (Bristol: Jordans, 2004), p. 214.
[284] The criticism made by the above authors of the complexity of the rules still remains valid.
[285] These consist of available profits plus the proceeds of any fresh issue of shares required to meet the price of redemption or purchase.
[286] Companies Act 2006, s. 712(2) and (7). [287] *Ibid.*, s. 714. [288] *Ibid.*, s. 716(1).

date of the resolution.[289] Within one week from the date of the resolution, the company must publish notice in the Gazette and also notice in a national newspaper. The further notice is not necessary if the company gives notice in writing to each of its creditors.[290]

Within five weeks of the date of the resolution, any creditor or dissenting shareholder may apply to the court to have it set aside.[291] The court has extensive powers to confirm, amend or cancel the resolution.[292] It is not clear under what conditions the court might accede to an application to set aside the resolution.[293] It may alter or extend any date or time in the resolution, or in any provision in chapter 5 of part 18 concerning the redemption or purchase of shares by private companies out of capital.[294]

B. *Applicable legal rules in France*

An SARL is not given the power to subscribe for or redeem its own shares, and it may only purchase (and annul) its own shares on a reduction of capital not motivated by losses. In the latter circumstances, the general meeting which decides on the reduction may authorise the managers to purchase a certain number of shares for the purpose of cancelling them.[295]

An SA is specifically prohibited from subscribing for its own shares[296] but there are some exceptions which will be explained below. It may also redeem them if permitted to do so by the articles or by a decision of an extraordinary general meeting. The latter operation takes place by the equal reimbursement of the par values of the shares belonging to the same class out of profits or distributable reserves.[297] As indicated above, shares which have been reimbursed are called *actions de jouissance* (enjoyment shares or profit participation shares). Their holders lose the right to a first dividend and to be reimbursed the par value of the shares on a winding up, but retain all other rights appertaining to them, first of all the vote.

An SA is permitted to purchase its own shares in a number of circumstances.

Reduction of capital not motivated by losses has already been explained above. This usually takes place through a tender offer directed

[289] *Ibid.*, s. 723. [290] *Ibid.*, s. 719.
[291] *Ibid.*, s. 721(1) and (2). [292] *Ibid.*, s. 721(3)–(7).
[293] See the discussion of this matter A. J. Boyle and J. Birds, *Company Law*, p. 216.
[294] Companies Act 2006, s. 721(5). [295] French Commercial Code, Art. L223-34, para. 4.
[296] *Ibid.*, Art. L225-206, para. 1. [297] *Ibid.*, Art. L225-198.

to all the shareholders. It is sufficient to add that when the company is quoted the offer must be previously authorised by the French Stock Exchange Authority, the AMF (*Autorité des marchés financiers*).

Article L225-210 of the Commercial Code provides that a public company cannot in any circumstances hold more than 10 per cent of its own shares, either directly or through a nominee. Furthermore, it cannot hold more than 10 per cent of any class of shares. The shares must be in registered form and fully paid up. The purchase of its own shares by the company may not have the effect of reducing its equity (*capital propre*) below the amount of its share capital together with any non-distributable reserves. In addition, the company's reserves other than the legal reserve must be at least equal to the value of the shares which the company holds. Such shares do not confer any right to dividends, votes or preferential subscription rights.[298]

Public companies which encourage the participation of their employees in their profits by allowing employees to purchase their shares in conformity with the provisions of Article L225-208 of the Commercial Code may purchase their own shares for this purpose. The shares must be distributed or the options to purchase them granted within one year from the acquisition of the shares by the company.[299]

A special regime applies to the purchase of own shares by SAs whose shares are admitted to trading on a regulated market in Article L225-209 and the following articles. The general meeting of such a company may authorise its board of directors (*conseil d'administration*) or its executive board (*directoire*) to purchase not more than ten per cent of its own shares. The general meeting decides upon the conditions under which the shares are to be purchased and sold. The authorisation given by the general meeting may be granted for not more than eighteen months.[300] Shares purchased by the company may be annulled on a reduction of capital up to the amount of ten per cent of the share capital of the company during periods of twenty-four months.

Public companies whose shares are admitted to trading on a regulated market and which encourage the participation of employees in the benefits of expansion by granting them shares as well as public companies which grant share options or free shares to their employees may

[298] *Ibid.*, Art. L225-210. [299] *Ibid.*, Art. L225-208.

[300] *Ibid.*, Art. L225-209. The works council must be informed of the passing of the relevant resolution. Compliance must be made with the requirements of the Stock Exchange Authority, AMF (*Autorité des marchés financiers*), concerning a notice for information.

make use of all or part of the shares which are acquired in accordance with the provisions of Article L225-209 for these purposes. If shares which are purchased are cancelled, the reduction of capital has to be permitted by an extraordinary general meeting, which may delegate power to the board of directors or the executive board to carry it out.[301]

C. *Applicable legal rules in Germany*

A GmbH may redeem its own shares in accordance with the provisions of paragraph 34 GmbHG. According to paragraph 34(1), the redemption of a share may only take place if this is permitted in the articles. Article 34(2) provides that such redemption may only take place without the consent of the shareholder concerned, if the provisions governing such redemption were included in the articles before he or she acquired the share. Such redemption may be accompanied by a reduction of capital, which might free funds necessary to indemnify the shareholder whose share(s) is cancelled.[302] The cancellation of a share through such redemption does not of itself reduce the share capital of the company, but has the effect of increasing the contributions required from the remaining shareholders. The cancellation of a share requires the passing of a resolution by the general meeting or other competent organ, and the making of a declaration to the departing shareholders. Shares are sometimes cancelled as a means of ending disputes in private companies: there are other methods of remedying such situations, such as the compulsory transfer of shares in accordance with the provisions of the articles, or the exclusion of a member in accordance with the law or the articles.

There is nothing in the GmbH *Gesetz* of 1892 (as amended) concerning the company's power to subscribe for or purchase its own shares, and it would seem that such a company cannot engage in such transactions.

Paragraph 56(1) and (3) of the German *Aktiengesetz* make it clear that a public company may not subscribe for its own shares, and if it issues shares to a person who holds them on its behalf, or on behalf of a company controlled by it, or by a company in which it holds a majority of the issued shares or voting rights, the subscriber is personally liable to

[301] French Commercial Code, Art. L225-209.

[302] The shareholder whose shares are cancelled (amortised) may not receive compensation out of assets necessary to maintain the share capital: paras. 30(1) GmbHG and 34(3) GmbHG.

pay the issue price, but cannot exercise any rights in respect of the shares until he acquires the shares on his own behalf.

The German rules concerning the acquisition by a company of its own shares are rather complex. Such acquisition is limited to eight precisely defined situations which are set out in paragraph 71(1)AktG. The provisions of paragraph 71 are reinforced by those of paragraphs 71a–71e. It follows from these stipulations that the acquisition by a company of its own shares is generally forbidden.[303]

According to paragraph 71(1) Nos. 1–7 AktG, a public company may acquire its own shares:

(1) to avoid severe and imminent damage to itself;
(2) in order to be offered to employees; in order to compensate minority shareholders in connection with the conclusion of a control agreement or carrying out integration;
(3) when the acquisition takes place without consideration, or is by a bank in executing a purchase order;
(4) when the acquisition is one by a successor in title by operation of law;
(5) when the shares are redeemed by the company under a resolution for a reduction of capital governed by paragraph 237 AktG; and
(6) when the company is a credit or financial institution, and its general meeting has passed the necessary resolution, for the purposes of dealing in securities.

Furthermore, by paragraph 71(1) No. 8 AktG, the general meeting may authorise the company to purchase its own shares under particular conditions for a period not exceeding eighteen months.[304]

Many of the enabling clauses mentioned above are made subject to specific thresholds and other requirements by Article 71(2). Article 71a forbids a company from granting credit for the purchase of its own shares. According to Article 71b, a company has no rights in its own shares. The company is required by Article 71c(2) to sell shares in excess of ten per cent of the share capital not later than three years from the date of their acquisition. If shares have not been sold within this stipulated period, they must be redeemed. Article 71e (which corresponds to Article L225-215 of the French Commercial Code) forbids a public company from accepting a pledge of its shares.

[303] See in more detail, Raiser and Veil, *Recht der Kapitalgesellschaften*, § 19, paras. 13 ff.; Kübler and Assmann, *Gesellschaftsrecht*, p. 158 f.

[304] Cf. Raiser and Veil, *Recht der Kapitalgesellschaften*, § 19, para. 23.

D. Applicable legal rules in Italy

According to Article 2474 of the Italian Civil Code, an SRL can in no circumstances (*in nessun caso*) acquire or accept as security its own shares or grant loans or guarantees for their subscription or purchase. There does not seem to be any exception to this provision. A public company is not permitted to subscribe for its own shares. If it does so, the promoters, founders or directors will be required to pay for them unless they can show that they are without fault.[305]

A public company may reimburse the amount of capital paid up out of profits. Such reimbursed shares (*azioni di godimento*) carry no voting rights unless the articles otherwise provide. They also carry the right to an equal dividend with the non-reimbursed shares only after interest at the legal rate has been paid on the latter, and they only participate on surplus assets in a liquidation after capital on non-reimbursed shares has been paid.[306]

According to Article 2357 of the Italian Civil Code a public company cannot acquire its own shares except out of profits available for distribution and distributable reserves shown in the last regularly approved balance sheet. Only fully paid shares may be purchased. The acquisition must be authorised by the general meeting, which must indicate the minimum amount to be acquired, the duration of the authorisation, which must not exceed eighteen months. In no event must the nominal value of the shares acquired exceed one-tenth of the share capital. Shares acquired in violation of the latter rules must be sold within one year, and if the shareholders' meeting fails to provide for such sale, it must instead provide for their annulment and a corresponding reduction of capital. Should the shareholders' meeting take neither action, in directors and auditors must apply to the court to order the reduction.

A number of special cases in which the limitations set out in Article 2357 are inapplicable where the acquisition of a company's own shares by the company takes place are provided for in Article 2357 *bis* of the Civil Code. These comprise:

(1) the implementation of a resolution to reduce the company's capital to take place through the redemption (*riscatto*) and cancellation of shares;
(2) the acquisition of fully paid shares free of charge;

[305] See Civil Code, Art. 2357 *quater*. [306] *Ibid.*, Art. 2353.

(3) the acquisition of shares in consequence of universal succession or a merger or division; and
(4) their acquisition on the occasion of a forced execution in satisfaction of a debt owing to the company, provided the shares are fully paid.

If in consequence of purchases made pursuant to clauses (2)–(4), the nominal value of the company's shares which are owned by it exceeds 10 per cent, the excess shares must be sold within a period of three years, as opposed to one year, or cancelled.

A public company whose shares are listed and which acquires its own shares under Article 2357, or under Article 2357 *bis* for the purpose of implementing a reduction of capital, must do so through the medium of a public offer for the purchase or exchange of such shares,[307] under which the equal treatment of all relevant shareholders must be ensured.

As long as the shares are owned by the company the dividends and rights of pre-emption in respect of them are transferred proportionately to the other shareholders. Voting rights in respect of such shares are suspended.[308]

According to Article 2358 of the Civil Code, a public company cannot grant a loan or provide security for the acquisition or subscription of its own shares. Such a company is not permitted to accept its own shares as a security. Article 2359 *bis*(1) provides that a controlled company may acquire or subscribe shares in the controlling company only out of distributable profits and free reserves shown in the last regularly approved balance sheet. The par value of the shares so acquired may not exceed one-tenth of the controlling company's capital. A controlled company may not exercise the voting rights attached to shares held by it in its controlling company.[309] Shares of a controlling company which are acquired, purchased or held in violation of the prohibitions contained in Article 2359 *bis* must be sold within the prescribed time limit of one year or cancelled with a consequent reduction of capital or otherwise the court may order the reduction of capital on application being made by the directors

[307] See Art. 132(1) of Decree Law No. 58 of 24 February 1998. According to Art. 132(2) of this Law, a similar rule is made applicable to the acquisition of the listed shares of a controlling company by a controlled company. The concept of controlled companies and associated companies is explained in Art. 2359 of the Civil Code. Art. 132(3) of the Law of 24 February 1998 provides for certain exceptions from Art. 132(1) and (2) thereof in relation to employees shares.

[308] Civil Code, Art. 2357 *ter*(2). [309] *Ibid*., Art. 2359 *bis* (5).

and auditors.[310] Article 132(2) of Decree Law No. 58 of 24 February 1998 provides that the acquisition of the listed shares of a controlling company by a controlled company must take place through the medium of a public offer.

A company, whether an SpA or SRL is regarded as being controlled by another company in three situations, namely:

(1) when the other company holds enough of its shares to be able to cast a majority of the votes which may be cast at an ordinary general meeting;
(2) when the company is subject to the dominant influence of the other company in consequence either of the number of shares the latter holds, or of particular contractual commitments entered into with the other company;
(3) when the other company holds a controlling shareholding in a third company which itself controls the company in question under (1) or (2).

E. *Applicable legal rules in Spain*

The rules of Spanish law governing the acquisition and purchase of the shares of an SA or SRL by the company itself appear much influenced by Italian law, for example in the use of the concept of a controlling company. As is true in France, Germany and Italy and in other EU States, the rules governing the acquisition by an SA of its own shares have been much influenced by Article 19(1) of the Second Company Law Directive. The possibility of the redemption of shares on a reduction of capital is recognised by Article 163 of the Law of 1989 governing public companies, as amended.

Public companies are not allowed to subscribe for their own shares or shares in the controlling company (which is defined in Article 87 of the Law of 1989, as amended) by Article 74(1) of the Law of 1989, as amended. A somewhat similar prohibition is contained in Article 39(1) of the Law of 1995 governing private companies, which stipulates that in no case may an SRL subscribe to its own shares, or those of its controlling company. If such a subscription is made through a nominee the founders and directors are jointly and severally liable for payment of the subscribed or acquired shares.[311] Article 75 of the Law of 1989, as amended,

[310] *Ibid.*, Art. 2359 *ter* (2). Such application may be made if the necessary meeting does not take place.

[311] Law of 1989, as amended, Art. 74(1); Law of 1995, Art. 39(2).

and Article 40 of the Law of 1995 prescribe circumstances under which a public or private company may acquire its own shares or those issued by its controlling company. In the case of a public company such acquisition must be authorised by a resolution of the general meeting which stipulates the method of purchase, the maximum number of shares to be purchased, the minimum and the maximum purchase price and the period of authorisation which may not exceed eighteen months. The total par value of the shares held by the acquiring company and its subsidiaries and the controlling company and its subsidiaries must not exceed 10 per cent of the acquiring company's capital. The acquisition must allow the acquiring company and, if applicable, the controlling one to maintain the mandatory reserve required by Article 79(3),[312] as well as other mandatory reserves required by the law or the articles. Only fully paid shares may be acquired.

Article 40(1) of the Law of 1995, which enumerates cases in which a private company may acquire its own shares, for example to satisfy a judgment in favour of the company against the holder of the shares, is rather less complex than Article 75 of the Law of 1989, as amended. According to Article 40(2), the own shares or participations acquired in a private company by the company itself, must be redeemed or sold during a maximum period of three years, and according to Article 40(3) the participations or shares acquired from the controlling company must be sold in one year. Shares in a private company acquired by the company itself must be fully paid up. Furthermore, Article 40(4) provides that a private company cannot accept a pledge or other form of security based on its shares, or on those of another company in the same group. The sanction for the breach of any prohibition placed on a private company in respect of the acquisition of its shares consists of a fine on the directors of that company.[313]

The rules governing transactions by a public company involving its own shares are rather more demanding and complex then those governing the corresponding transactions by private companies. Shares acquired in violation of Article 75 of the Law of 1989 as amended (except in breach of the requirement that the relevant shares should be fully paid) must be disposed of

[312] Article 79(3) of the Law of 1989, as amended, provides as follows: a mandatory reserve shall be created on the liabilities side of the balance sheet of the acquiring company equal to the value of the shares held by it in itself, or shares of the controlling company that are included in the assets. The reserve must be maintained until the shares are sold or redeemed.

[313] Law of 1995, Art. 42.

within one year of the date of first acquisition. If no such disposal takes place, the company must immediately proceed to redeem its shares and reduce its capital accordingly. If the company fails to carry out such measures, any interested party may petition the court to order their performance.[314]

According to Article 77 of the Law of 1989, as amended (which corresponds to some extent to Article 40(1) of the Law of 1995 governing private companies), a public company may acquire its own shares without being subject to Articles 74–6 in certain situations. These are where a company acquires its own shares pursuant to a resolution of the general meeting to reduce the company's capital, where the shares form part of an estate acquired in its entirety; where fully paid shares are acquired gratuitously; and where fully paid shares are acquired as the result of a court order for the payment of a debt owed by the shareholder to the company. It follows from Article 78 of the Law of 1989, as amended, that where shares are acquired under normal conditions (*regularamente adquiridas*), they should be disposed of within three years of such acquisition except where they are redeemed on a reduction of capital or where when added to the shares already possessed by the acquiring company and its subsidiaries or by the controlling company and its subsidiaries do not exceed 10 per cent of the company's capital.

According to Article 79(1) of the Law of 1989, as amended, the right to vote and all other non-economic rights attached to the company's own shares or attached to the shares held by the company in the controlling company shall be suspended. Dividend rights attaching to a company's own shares except the right to free subscription for new shares[315] are distributed proportionately among the remaining shares.

F. Applicable legal rules in Belgium

The Belgian legal rules concerning the acquisition, redemption and purchase by private or public companies of their own shares are rather complex and extend to founders' shares (*parts bénéficiaires*)[316] and certificates representing shares (*certificats*)[317] as well as to share in the

[314] Law of 1989, as amended, Art. 76(1).
[315] This presumably refers to bonus issues: the Spanish text uses the words: '*a la asignación gratuita de nuevas acciones*'.
[316] Such shares are sometimes issued by public companies. They do not form part of the capital of the company, and their rights are governed by the articles.
[317] Such *certificats* resemble Dutch *certificaaten* and may be issued by a legal person with respect to the shares of a private or public company: see Companies Code, Arts. 242 and

company's capital. There are considerable similarities in the relevant rules governing private and public companies. However, Belgian public companies may redeem their shares without a reduction of capital: this facility is not open to private companies.

The articles of a Belgian public company may thus stipulate that a determinate part of the profits shall be devoted to the repayment of share capital at par on shares chosen by the drawing of lots without the capital being reduced thereby. Such redemption must take place out of distributable assets and results in the replacement of the relevant shares by *actions de jouissance* which retain all their rights in the company other than that to a first dividend.[318] Both Belgian private and public companies may require the purchase of voteless shares, or classes of such shares from their holder if the articles so provide before the issue of such shares, and the general meeting so decides by the majority required for the alteration of the articles, on condition that all shareholders in the same position are equally treated. Furthermore, the preferential dividends payable on the shares in respect of earlier financial years and for the current financial year must have been fully paid. The decision of the general meeting will be carried out by a reduction of capital, and thus security may be demanded by creditors in respect of their debts within two months of the publication of the decision in Annex to the *Moniteur Belge* (*Official Gazette*). The shares purchased will be annulled.[319]

Both Belgian private and public companies may purchase or exchange their shares or certificates without a reduction of capital. Any such transaction must (in the case of a private company) be approved by the general meeting, which must reach its decision by a majority comprising at least half the members, possessing three-quarters of the share capital, no account being taken of those members the acquisition of whose shares is proposed.[320] In public companies, the general meeting fixes the maximum number of shares or certificates to be acquired,[321] the minimum and maximum price at which they may be acquired, and the duration of

503. The issuer must divulge its existence to the company which issued the shares. It exercises all the rights attached to the shares to which it relates, including the right to vote, but reserves all the products and income arising from the shares for the holders of the certificates.

318 Companies Code, Art. 615. Such shares obviously carry no right to reimbursement.

319 Companies Code, Arts. 331 and 626.

320 *Ibid.*, Art. 321. For the position in a public company, see Arts. 559 and 620(1).

321 The decision may relate to founders' shares in a public company. The quorum at the meeting consists of at least half the members and the requisite majority consists of at least four-fifths of the votes cast.

its authorisation which may not exceed eighteen months.[322] The acquisition may only be of fully paid shares, and a capital reserve must be created out of other distributable assets, whose value is equal to that at which the shares acquired appear in the inventory.[323] Shares so acquired together with shares already acquired, must be limited to 10 per cent of the total share capital.[324] In the case of a public company, Article 620(1) no. 5 of the Companies Code provides that the offer of acquisition must be made under the same conditions to all the shareholders, and if relevant, to all the holders of founders' shares or certificates. In the case of a private company, shares and certificates must be disposed of or cancelled within two years, in accordance with a resolution of the general meeting.[325] The rules in relation to public companies are more complex, but the general one is that set out in Article 622(2) of the Companies Code, according to which the relevant shares, founders' shares or certificates acquired by the company can only be alienated as the result of a decision of a general meeting, which will determine the conditions under which such disposals may take place. Article 622(2) prescribes different periods within which the securities must be alienated, depending on the nature of the securities, and the process for, or method of, their acquisition.

In the case of a private company, the rights attaching to the shares acquired by it are suspended until the shares are disposed of or cancelled.[326] In a public company, the voting rights in respect of shares or founders' shares remain in suspense, and the board of directors may suspend the dividend rights on such securities as well.[327]

No resolution of the general meeting is required when a public company acquires its shares, founders' shares or certificates relating to its shares for distribution to its employees.[328] Furthermore, a public company's statutes may provide that a decision of a general meeting is not necessary where the acquisition of the shares is necessary to avoid serious and imminent harm.[329] The latter rules are inapplicable to private companies. Article 627 of the Companies Code provides that the

[322] Companies Code, Art. 620(1) (public companies). Note the similar rules contained in Arts. 321(1) and 322 concerning private companies.

[323] *Ibid.*, Art. 325 (private companies) and Art. 623 (public companies).

[324] *Ibid.*, Art. 322(1) (private companies) and Art. 620(1) (public companies).

[325] *Ibid.*, Art. 326. [326] *Ibid.*, Art. 325(2).

[327] *Ibid.*, Art. 622(1). [328] *Ibid.*, Art. 622(2) no. 3.

[329] *Ibid.*, Art. 620(1). This facility is not available until three years after the publication of the deed of incorporation (*act constitutif*) or any relevant amendment of the articles (*statuts*).

subsidiaries of a public company which are subject to direct control in accordance with certain of the provisions of Article 5 of the Companies Code[330] as well as persons acting as a nominee for a subsidiary, may not possess, together with the parent company, shares or founders' shares of that company, or certificates relating to such securities except, subject to certain exceptions, in accordance with the provisions of Articles 620–623 thereof. Thus, the 10 per cent limit and the requirement of the full payment of the relevant shares or certificates described above are applicable to such holdings, as also are many of the other important rules already described. However, if the parent company is a private company, no rules exist corresponding to those in Article 627.

G. Applicable legal rules in the Netherlands

A Dutch company, whether private or public, may not subscribe for its own shares, whether on formation of thereafter.[331] The same rule applies to certificates or depositary receipts issued in respect of shares.[332] Shares in the company held by a Dutch public company must be fully paid.[333] A company may acquire fully paid-up shares in its own capital for no value, but otherwise only if the shareholders' equity (net worth) less the acquisition price is not less than the aggregate of the paid and called up capital, statutory reserves and reserves required by the articles.[334] The amount of shares which a BV may hold in its capital, or hold through subsidiaries, or as a pledge must not be more than 10 per cent of its issued capital.[335] This amount is increased to 50 per cent in the case of a BV,[336] which cannot hold its shares in pledge. This limitation is likely to be abolished.

[330] The relevant provisions make it clear that there is an irrebuttable presumption of control where a company holds the majority of all the voting rights attached to the shares or otherwise existing in another company; where a company has the right to appoint or dismiss the majority of the directors or managers of another company; and where, by reason of agreement concluded with the other members of the company, another company holds the majority of all the voting rights attached to the shares or otherwise existing in a company.

[331] BW, Art. 2.95(1) (public companies) and Art. 2.205 (private companies).

[332] *Ibid.*, Art. 2.98(9) (public companies) and Art. 2.207(5) (private companies).

[333] *Ibid.*, Art. 2.98(1) (public companies).

[334] *Ibid.*, Art. 2.98(2)(a) (public companies) and Art. 2.207(2)(a) (private companies). The latter rule is likely to be changed to permit the private company to acquire its own shares if this will not result in a depletion of the reserves it has to maintain by the law or the articles, or in the company becoming unable to pay its debts as they fall due.

[335] *Ibid.*, Art. 2.98(2)(b) (public companies) and Art. 2.207(2)(b) (private companies).

[336] *Ibid.*, Art. 2.207(2)(b), which is likely to be repealed.

An acquisition of shares in a public company by the company itself other than one for no consideration must be permitted by the articles, and the shareholders' meeting must have authorised the management board to make such acquisition. Such authorisation is not necessary for an acquisition for the purpose of transferring shares purchased by the company to employees of a public company, or a company in the same group,[337] provided that the shares are listed on a stock exchange.[338] The authorisation is valid for not more than eighteen months. The shareholders' meeting must stipulate in the authorisation the number of shares which may be required, the manner by which they may be acquired, and the limits within which the price must be fixed.[339] The relevant rules governing private companies are in general similar to those governing public companies considered above. In such companies, the articles or the shareholders' meeting may designate a corporate body other than the management board to authorise the purchase of the shares such as the supervisory board, or the holders of a specific class of shares.[340] The period of authorisation in a private company is not limited to eighteen months.

A repurchase of the shares of a private or public company may not take place in the final six months of the company's financial year if the annual accounts for the previous year were not adopted, and approved, where relevant, during the first six months of the current financial year.[341] The rules governing the repurchase of shares in a private company will undergo fundamental change if draft Article 2-207 becomes law. The directors will be required to decide on the acquisition of its own shares by the private company. Such acquisitions will be subject to a balance sheet and liquidity test.

Certain rules of Dutch law restrict the circular ownership of shares.[342] The provisions contained in Article 2.98d of the Civil Code, which relates to public companies, and Article 2.207d thereof, which relates to private

[337] For the definition of a group of companies in Dutch law, see BW, Art. 2.24b and Schuit, *Corporate Law*, p. 31.

[338] BW, Art. 2.98(5). No such rule applies to private companies whose shares cannot be so listed.

[339] *Ibid.*, Art. 2.98(4).

[340] *Ibid.*, Art. 2.207(2)(d). Such purchase must be permitted by the BV's articles, *ibid.*, Art. 2.207(2)(c).

[341] *Ibid.*, Art. 2.98(3) (public companies) and Art. 2.207(3) (private companies).

[342] See Schuit, *Corporate Law*, p. 59.

companies, are almost identical. A subsidiary of an NV or a BV is not permitted to subscribe for shares issued by the parent company. It may purchase shares of a parent company and purchase its own shares held by such a company only to the extent that the parent company is permitted to.[343] In the event of breach of this requirement, the managing directors of the parent company are jointly and severally liable to compensate the subsidiary for the acquisition price and for statutory interest.

Shares purchased by the company are treated as remaining part of the issued capital until they are redeemed. Such redemption has the effect of reducing the company's issued capital. No votes may be cast in respect of such shares.

X. Financial assistance for the acquisition of shares

Article 23 of the Second Directive requires Member States to maintain a prohibition on the giving of financial assistance by public companies for the acquisition of their shares, subject to certain limited exceptions. This matter receives detailed regulation in the United Kingdom by section 678(1) of the Companies Act 2006, which imposes a general prohibition on the granting of financial assistance by public companies and subsidiaries of such companies for the acquisition of shares in these companies. The present rules are very complex, and there are certain exceptions to them.

Rules of law prohibiting the giving of such financial assistance (with certain limited exceptions) exist in all the other Member States considered in this work[344] but sometimes, as in Germany,[345] they are only applicable to public companies. The relevant provisions in Belgium apply both to private[346] and public companies,[347] with certain minor exceptions. There are some differences in the exceptions applicable to private and public companies in Belgium. There are also some differences between the relevant rules governing private[348] and public companies[349] in the Netherlands. For both types of companies, the financial assistance

[343] BW, Art. 2.98d(1) (public companies) and Art. 2.207(d)(1) (private companies). Article 207d will undergo considerable modifications if the government proposals for the reform of the law governing private companies are accepted. A subsidiary will not in principle be able to acquire shares in its parent company, but there will be an exception to this rule where such acquisition is based on a special title (*bijzondere titel*) provided the directors of the parent company agreed to such acquisition.

[344] Such rules are required by Art. 23 of the Second Company Law Directive.

[345] AktG, para. 71a. [346] Companies Code, Art. 329. [347] *Ibid.*, Art. 629.

[348] BW, Art. 2.207c. [349] *Ibid.*, Art. 2.98c.

rules prohibit the company from providing security, guaranteeing payment of the acquisition price, or otherwise binding itself to or for third parties for the purpose of the subscription or acquisition by third parties of its shares or *certificaten* (certificates or depositary receipts). Public companies may not grant loans for this purpose.[350] The relevant prohibitions applicable to both types of companies also extend to subsidiaries.[351]

It was suggested in the UK Company Law Review Steering Group's Consultative Document, *Company Formation and Capital Maintenance*, that it might be desirable to make the provisions of UK Companies Act 1985 concerning financial assistance by a company for the acquisition of its own shares applicable to public companies only.[352] The Government White Paper of March 2005 accepted this proposal.[353] A conditional exception was made for the giving of financial assistance by private limited companies in section 682(1) of the Companies Act 2006 in respect of certain transactions' carried out by such companies. The wording of section 153(1)(a) of the Companies Act 1985 gave rise to difficulties but it has been used again in section 678(2) of the Companies Act 2006. This provision contains an exception to the prohibition of giving financial assistance for the acquisition of shares where the principal purpose of such assistance is not the acquisition of shares. This wording received a narrow interpretation by the House of Lords in its controversial judgement in *Brady* v. *Brady*,[354] and it has been suggested that the exception should be reformulated in terms of the company's predominant reason. As pointed out by the Steering Group in its Consultative Document, *Company Formation and Capital Maintenance*, the latter wording may give rise to some difficulties, as well as did that of section 153(1)(a) of the Companies Act 1985. Section 682(1) of the Companies Act 2006 also contains a conditional exception for the giving of assistance by a public company where the company has net assets which are not reduced by the

[350] *Ibid.*, Art. 2.98c(1).

[351] *Ibid.*, Art. 2.98c(1) and Art. 2.207c(1). However, the new proposals for the reform of Dutch law governing private companies provide for the repeal of Article 2.207c of the Dutch Civil Code.

[352] See *Company Formation and Capital Maintenance* (October 1999), 39–40. Cf. Company Law Review, *Modern Company Law for a Competitive Economy: Completing the Structure*, URN 00/1335 (November 2000), ch. 2, p. 10.

[353] DTI, *Company Law Reform White Paper* (March 2005), pp. 41, 48.

[354] [1989] AC 755.

giving of assistance, or to the extent that these assets are reduced, the assistance is provided out of distributable profits.

The existing Dutch legislation gives rise to problems: contested take-over bids take place occasionally in the Netherlands, as they of course do frequently in the United Kingdom. The provisions of Dutch law have a wide ambit.[355] They discourage various forms of leveraged acquisition which are common in the United States. A leveraged buy-out in the form of an asset acquisition is often easier to finance in the Netherlands than one which takes the form of a share acquisition: this is because the financial assistance provisions are inapplicable to the former type of acquisition.

A. *Loan capital*

Companies may borrow money either by raising a loan from a particular lender, such as a bank or finance house, or by means of an issue of bonds, which are debt securities. Bonds may be issued in the same way as shares. However, they differ from the latter securities in many ways. The holders of debt securities rank in priority to shareholders, and are remunerated through interest. Frequently, bond issues are secured by the issuer. Debt securities are usually issued for a defined term, and are reimbursed to their holders. The distinction between debt and equity securities has become blurred in recent years by reason of the introduction of new forms of securities in several Member States. Thus, the perpetual subordinated bonds (*titres subordonnés à durée indéterminée*) which may be issued by French public companies cannot be redeemed until all the other creditors are paid off.[356] They are regarded from an accounting point of view as a kind of equity. The same is true of participation certificates (*titres participatifs*), which may be issued by public companies belonging to the public sector and by cooperatives with the form of an SA or a SARL.[357] Such certificates are only repaid in the event of the company's liquidation or if the issuer so decides, within at least seven

[355] Note in this context, S. R. Schuit, *Corporate Law*, p. 60. Dutch law generally prohibits companies from giving financial assistance to third parties, whether shareholders or not, if such assistance is for the purpose of the subscription or acquisition by third parties of their shares or depository receipts issued on their shares. See BW, Art. 2.98c (public companies) and Art. 207c(1) (private companies). The relevant provisions extend to subsidiaries. The rules contained in Article 2.207c governing private companies will be repealed if the proposed legislation comes into force in its draft form.

[356] French Commercial Code, Art. L228-97. [357] *Ibid.*, Art. L228-36.

years, and carry no voting rights. The interest which they receive is in part variable and in part fixed, being dependent partially on the results and activity of the issuer.

Only a brief outline of the laws of the Member States concerning debt securities can be attempted here. The emphasis will be on bonds, rather than on other special types of debt securities, and it will be impossible to give more than a superficial account of the laws of the Member States governing the issue of such securities, and the rights attaching to their holders. Various different kinds of bonds are issued in the relevant Member States, and the position in France is specially complex. Some emphasis is placed on the account below on convertible bonds, and other types of bonds will be referred to in outline only.

B. The position in the United Kingdom

According to United Kingdom Law, loan capital may be raised by public or private companies by means of the issue of debentures or debenture stock. A debenture has been defined as a document which creates a debt or acknowledges it.[358] It is, perhaps somewhat unhelpfully, defined in section 738 of the Companies Act 2006 as including debenture stock, bonds and any other securities of the Company, whether constituting a charge on the assets of the company or not.

Where a collective loan is to be made by a number of persons, this company will issue debentures or debenture stock under the terms of a trust deed. In a modern trust deed, the company agrees with the trustees to repay the total amount of the loans secured by an issue of debentures, together with interest until the principal is paid, such payments to be made either to the trustees on behalf of the debenture holders or to the debenture holders themselves, in proportion to their individual subscriptions. The individual subscribers are issued with debenture stock certificates, which evidence their individual rights, but there is no promise by the company to repay them. However, the company covenants with the trustees to pay the principal sum of the loan plus interest directly to the holders of the debenture stock.[359] The security vested in the trustees may

[358] By Chitty J in *Levy* v. *Abercorris Slate and Slab Co* (1887) 37 Ch D 260 at 264. This definition may be too wide, and there is probably no entirely satisfactory legal definition of a debenture. This was recognised by Mummery J in *Re SH & Co (Realisations) 1990 Ltd* [1993] BCC 60; [1993] BCLC 1309.

[359] See R. Pennington, *Company Law*, pp. 530–1.

consist of a legal mortgage over the land and fixed assets of the company, and/or a floating charge over the generality of its assets and undertaking. It is now apparently rare to find a legal mortgage, over land or fixed assets when large-scale issues of loan securities are made by leading public companies.[360] Sometimes no floating charge exists over the generality of the company's assets and undertaking. The relevant debentures or debenture stock are then commonly known as unsecured loan stock, or if the loan is for a period of up to ten years, unsecured loan notes. Debentures quoted on the stock exchange are subject to the rules of that exchange. The power to issue them is usually granted to the directors of the company.

Debentures may be in registered on in bearer form. There is no obligation to maintain a register of debenture holders, but if this is done, sections 743–746 of the Companies Act 2006 impose certain obligations concerning the inspection and the provision of copies thereof. Debentures secured by a floating charge cannot be created by ordinary or limited partnerships, but they may be by the new type of limited liability partnership. The difference between fixed and floating charges has become somewhat blurred in recent years, as the result of a number of decisions concerning charges on book debts, or other debts and receivables.[361]

Debentures, unlike shares may be issued at a discount. However, convertible debentures may not be issued at a discount so as to evade the rule that shares may not be issued at a discount.[362] Thus where, as in *Mosely* v. *Koffyfontein Mines*, the debentures are immediately convertible, their issue at a discount is an obvious method of issuing shares at a discount. It is possible however, that an option to convert is valid if it may not be exercised until some time in the future.[363]

C. *The position in France*

Since 2004,[364] a French private company (SARL) has been empowered to issue registered bonds. The relevant legal rules are now contained

[360] Pennington, *Company Law*, pp. 530–1.

[361] See E. Ferran, *Company Law and Corporate Finance* (Oxford: Oxford University Press: 1999), pp. 517–29 and G. McCormack, 'The nature of security over receivables' (2002) 23 Co Law 84.

[362] *Mosely* v. *Koffyfontein Mines* [1904] 2 Ch 108.

[363] See the judgment of Cozens-Hardy LJ in *Moseley* v. *Koffyfontein Mines*, at 120. The learned judge left the question open.

[364] See Ordinance 274 of 2004, Art. 12.

in Article L223-11 of the Commercial code. This possibility is reserved to SARLs which comply with the requirements indicated in Article L223-11:

(1) the company must appoint an auditor in accordance with Article L223-35 of the Commercial Code;
(2) the company's accounts of the last three financial years must have been approved.

Debt securities issued by a private company must be in registered form and cannot be offered to the public. The competence to provide for such an issue is vested in an ordinary general meeting in compliance with the rules governing general meetings of public companies. The rules concerning debt securities issued by public companies apply to those issued by private companies, but Articles L228-39 – L228-43 and L228-51, concerning the offer to the public of debt securities, are specifically excluded from such applicability.

French SAs issue a wide variety of bonds: they may do so provided that the company has prepared two approved balance sheets and has no unpaid share capital.[365]

As we have seen above, the issue of capital securities, shares and securities giving access to the capital, in French company law, entails a modification of the articles and therefore requires the approval of an extraordinary general meeting.[366] Such approval is not required for the issue of bonds. An issue of bonds may be decided upon by the board of directors or by the executive board, unless the articles reserve this matter to the general meeting, or the latter decides to exercise it. Furthermore the board of directors may delegate the power to make such an issue within one year, also of deciding the modalities of the issue, to one or more of its members or to the managing directors (*directeurs généraux*) or, with the agreement of the latter, to one or more assistant managing directors (*directeurs généraux délégués*). Similarly, in a company with the dual board system, its executive board of may delegate such power to its chairman or to one or more of its members. In financial

365 French Commercial Code, Art. L228-39. The requirement that the company must have prepared two approved balance sheets need not be complied with if the value of its assets and liabilities has been examined by a special appraiser: see Art. L225-8 and Art. L225-10 of the Commercial Code.

366 This is also due to the fact that the capital and the participations in it entail that shareholders should have a significant influence on the decisions concerning the company.

institutions (*établissements de crédit*), the same power may be delegated to any person chosen.[367] If the bonds are convertible into shares, an extraordinary general meeting is needed.[368] Listed companies may also issue bearer bonds.[369] Usually, the existing shareholders in a company do not enjoy any pre-emptive rights in an issue of bonds, as such an issue do not affect the composition of the capital and, therefore, the decision making power of the shareholders. Nevertheless when the bonds are convertible, pre-emptive rights are given to the shareholders by Article L228-91 of the French Commercial Code.[370]

Ordinary bonds may take a number of different forms. They may thus be payable in instalments, or give special premiums to persons selected by lottery, or have warrants attached to them which entitle the holder to take up more bonds or shares. The principal debt or the interest due may be indexed against inflation, or be dependent on the company's profits or some other factor, such as its turnover. Zero coupon bonds are bonds which pay no interest until redemption and in which all interest payments are capitalised and paid on the redemption of the bond.[371]

The holders of a series of bonds form a class or entity (*masse*), which has legal personality, and which may hold meetings which are convened either by the bondholders' representative, or the company or on the request of the holders of one-thirtieth of the outstanding bonds. The convocation of such meetings is governed by the same rules as to time and form as ordinary general meetings of shareholders.[372] A meeting of a class of bondholders must appoint up to three representatives (*mandataires*) to protect their interests.[373] The issuing company and the other companies which hold one-tenth or more of the issuing company's

[367] French Commercial Code, Art. L228-40. Before 2004, the general competence to decide on an issue of bonds was given to an ordinary general meeting, which could delegate this power to the directors. Ordinance no. 604 of 2004 introduced a more flexible regulation of this matter, and responded to criticism made of the past regime by placing more reliance on the managing directors executive and finance officers, who could more readily determine the appropriate time for such an issue.

[368] French Commercial Code, Art. L228-92.

[369] Law of 30 December 1981, governing the dematerialisation of securities, applies both shares and to bonds in registered or in bearer form, see Cozian and others, *Droit des sociétés*, pp. 337 and 385.

[370] For further details of the pre-emptive rights of shareholders, see French Commercial Code, Art. L225-135.

[371] The issue of such securities is based on tax considerations.

[372] French Commercial Code, Arts. L228-46, L228-58 and L228-59.

[373] *Ibid.*, Art. L228-47. If the company makes a public offer for subscriptions, the representatives may be appointed in the terms of issue.

capital, or in which the issuing company holds one-tenth or more of their capital, any company giving security on the bonds, together with all the officers of the issuing company or of the company giving a security on the bonds are prohibited from being appointed bondholders' representatives.[374] The representatives may perform any acts in the interests of the bondholders, unless restrictions are imposed by the general meeting thereof. They require, on the other hand, authorisation by a meeting of bondholders to bring actions having the object of defending the common interests of the bondholders.[375]

An ordinary general meeting of bondholders is required to give its consent to important decisions which have to be taken by the company and which have consequences on the rights of the bondholders. For instance, it has to approve an alteration of the company's objects or claims, and a modification of any security they may have, or a deferment of the payment of interest or the repayment of capital, but no resolution may treat different bondholders in an unequal way.[376]

D. The position in Germany

Private companies (GmbHs) may enter into loan transactions with third parties. They may grant such persons interest linked to the profits of the company on loans granted to them (*partiarische Darlehen*). Furthermore, they may also grant participation rights (*Genussrechte*) which are evidenced by negotiable certificates (*Genusscheine*)[377] which do not carry any voting rights or any rights in the management or control of the company, but which give rise to a share in the profits, and often a right to participate in surplus assets on the liquidation of the company. The use of this type of security would seem to make capital markets, such as the stock exchanges, open to the company. The issue of participation rights requires the passing of a resolution of a general meeting by a three-quarters majority of the votes cast.[378] Finally, private companies may be

[374] *Ibid.*, Art. L228-49. [375] *Ibid.*, Arts. L228-53 and L228-54.

[376] French Commercial Code, Arts. L228-65 and L228-68. Nevertheless if the approval is not granted by the general meeting of the bondholders, the board of directors or the executive board may undertake certain measures affecting the rights of the bondholders, notwithstanding their opposition, and is empowered to offer payment for their bonds, see Arts. L228-72 and L228-73 of the Commercial Code and P. Le Cannu, *Droit des sociétés*, 2nd edn (Paris: Montchrestien, 2003), p. 688.

[377] See M. Lutter and H. Hummelhoff, *GmbH Gesetz*, 15th edn (Cologne: Verlag Dr Otto Schmidt, 2000), paras. 44–46 of the commentary to para. 55, GmbH.

[378] See for more details, Schmidt, *Gesellschaftsrecht*, § 18 II 2b(aa).

financed by silent partnership (*stille Gesellschaft*) arrangements. In such an event, the silent partner who makes finance available to the company will often be one of its directors.[379]

As pointed out above, debt can be reclassified as share capital under certain circumstances, set out in paragraphs 32a and 32b GmbHG (which are likely to be repealed). This is true of participation rights if they are placed at the company's disposal on a permanent basis, and rank after the company's creditors, such that they may not be withdrawn, or withdrawn arbitrarily without any compensation. Furthermore, a participation in a silent partnership may be classified as share capital if the silent partner is placed on an equal basis with a full shareholder insofar as proprietary interests are concerned, as is the case where he participates fully in the profits and losses of the company.[380]

Public companies may issue bonds (*Schuldverschreibungen*) which may be in registered or (as is most usually the case) bearer form. It follows from paragraph 793 of the Civil Code that such bonds are negotiable instruments. German public companies may also issue bonds which enable their holders to convert them into shares or to subscribe for further shares, often in accordance with warrants attached to the bonds (*Wandelschuldverschreibungen*).[381] In addition, public companies in Germany may issue bonds which entitle their holders to a payment proportionate to the dividends paid to the shareholders in addition to or instead of interest (*Gewinnschuldverschreibungen*).[382] Furthermore, Germany public companies frequently issue participation rights (*Genussrechte*) which may be evidenced by certificates (*Genusscheine*).[383] Participation rights are not properly defined in German law. Such rights usually involve the right to share in the company's profits, and often involve contributions to losses on the liquidation.[384] Sometimes the holders of participation rights are entitled to fixed interest payment. The exact rights which these securities convey depend on their terms of issue, which may be determined by the provisions of the articles of the

[379] For more details, Schmidt, *Gesellschaftsrecht*, § 62 II 1.

[380] For further details concerning the so called atypical silent partnership ('*atypisch stille Gesellschaft*') and the participation in a GmbH ('GmbH & Still'), see Schmidt, *Gesellschaftsrecht*, § 62 II 2.

[381] These types of financial instrument are in common use in Germany. See Raiser and Veil, *Recht der Kapitalgesellschaften*, § 17 para. 14 for details.

[382] *Ibid.*, § 17 para. 12.

[383] Such certificates may be in order, registered or bearer form.

[384] See Schmidt, *Gesellschaftsrecht*, § 29 I 1c.

company.[385] The holder of participation rights has no voting rights, and no right to challenge the validity of company resolutions.[386]

The issue of bonds and of participation rights requires the approval of a general meeting of shareholders by a three-quarters majority of the share capital represented at the meeting.[387] The articles may provide for a different capital majority, and additional requirements.[388] Furthermore, the management board may be authorised by the general meeting to issue convertible bonds or bonds granting an option to subscribe for other shares for a period of up to five years.[389] Unless a shareholders resolution waives this requirement, the latter kinds of bonds may first be offered to the shareholders in proportion to their existing holdings.[390] Bonds may be secured on the property of the company, or a third person, or by means of a guarantee given by a bank or another company, but they are (as in France), frequently unsecured. Secured bonds are protected by mortgages of land (*Hypothek*) and of fixed assets, such as equipment, intellectual property rights and investments (*Sicherungsübereignung*). Floating charges are not met with in practice in Germany or France.

Where convertible bonds, or bonds granting an option to subscribe for more shares are to be issued,[391] the right to convert such bonds must be secured through the medium of an increase of capital, which may consist of an ordinary capital increase in accordance with paragraph 182 AktG, or through the medium of an increase of conditional capital (*bedingtes Kapital*) or through the use of authorised capital (*genehmigtes Kapital*). Conditional capital increases (*bedingte Kapitalerhöhungen*) are permissible in connection with the issue of convertible bonds, or bonds granting an option to subscribe for new shares, employees' share schemes and mergers.[392] The conditional capital may not exceed one-half of the existing capital, except in the case of employees' share schemes, where it may not exceed one-tenth.[393] The conversion rights may be exercised

[385] Raiser and Veil, *Recht der Kapitalgesellschaften*, § 17 para. 19.

[386] Schmidt, *Gesellschaftsrecht*, § 18 II 2b(dd).

[387] Raiser and Veil, *Recht der Kapitalgesellschaften*, § 17 para. 15.

[388] German Public Limited Liability Companies Act, para. 221(1) and (3).

[389] *Ibid.*, para. 221(2). The same seems to be true of bonds in which the rights of the holders are related to the dividends paid to the shareholders.

[390] *Ibid.*, paras. 186 and 221(4).

[391] These are sometimes called warrant bonds because the option to subscribe for the new shares are often contained in a warrant attached to the bond.

[392] German Public Limited Liability Companies Act, para. 192(1) and (2).

[393] *Ibid.*, para. 192(3).

through the subscription for new shares created as the result of the capital increase.

The general meeting may, in accordance with paragraph 202 AktG, authorise the management board for up to five years to increase the share capital up to a specified amount not exceeding one-half of the share capital as of the date of authorisation. The issue of such authorised capital requires the consent of the supervisory board.[394] Such authorisation may include the authority to issue convertible bonds, or bonds granting an option to subscribe for new shares.

E. The position in Italy

The amendments made to the Civil Code in 2003 involve a number of changes in the law relating to bonds. An SRL is permitted by Article 2483 of the Civil Code to issue debt securities provided that its deed of incorporation so allows. If the deed so provides, then it must grant the competence to issue such securities to the members or the directors and determine the limits and method of such issues, and the majorities necessary for the decision.[395] Such securities may only be subscribed for by professional investors who are subject to prudential supervision the rules governing which are contained in special legislation.[396] If the securities are subsequently transferred, the transferor is answerable if the company defaults, to a transferee who is not a professional investor or a member of such company.[397] According to Article 2483(3), the decision to issue debt securities must make provisions for the conditions of the loan and the method of reimbursement. This decision must be entered in the Registry of Enterprises: the directors are responsible for taking the necessary steps. It may also provide that, on condition that the majority of the shareholders so consent, the company may modify the relevant conditions and modalities. Debt securities issued by Italian private companies must be considered financial instruments and are subject to the Legislative Decree no. 58 of 1998.[398]

[394] *Ibid.*, para. 202(3) sentence 2. [395] Italian Civil Code, Art. 2483(1).

[396] These professional investors are subject to the control of CONSOB (*Commissione Nazionale per le Società e la Borsa*).

[397] If securities are transferred to third parties which are not professional investors or members of the company the transfer will be subject to rules in Legislative Decree no. 58 of 1998.

[398] See B. Libonati, *Diritto Commerciale, Impresa e Società* (Milan: Giuffrè, 2005), p. 462.

The issue of bonds by public companies is a task for the directors unless the law or the articles provide otherwise. Bonds may be in registered or bearer form. The minutes of the resolution permitting such issue must be notarised in accordance with Article 2410(2) of the Civil Code, and communicated to the Registry of Enterprises for entry therein.[399] According to Article 2411 of the Civil Code, the bondholders' rights to repayment of capital and interest may be subordinated to the rights of other creditors. Such subordinated bonds are familiar in other jurisdictions, particularly in the United States. The time and extent of the payment of interest may, in accordance with Article 2411(2), vary in accordance with objective criteria even based on the financial position of the company.

Article 2412(4) of the Civil Code removes quantitative restrictions on the issue of listed bonds by listed companies.[400] The restrictions on the issue of bonds have also been relaxed for unlisted companies, which are now permitted by Article 2412(1) to issue bonds up to twice the amount of the company's equity (i.e. its capital, disposable reserves and the legal reserves in accordance with the last approved balance sheet).[401] So that if the capital is 100, the legal reserve 20 and the other optional reserves 30, the issue of bonds may not exceed 300.[402] According to Article 2413, a company which has issued bonds may not reduce its capital voluntarily or distribute reserves if the limit provided in Article 2412 will be exceeded. In case of compulsory reduction of the capital for losses the company is not allowed to distribute dividends until the above-mentioned proportion is restored. The members of the committee of auditors are entrusted with the control on the compliance with the restrictions. The limit of Article 2412 (1) may be exceeded if the excess consists of bonds placed with professional investors who are subject to professional regulation and supervision and who, if they transfer them to non-professional bondholders, are liable to them if the issuer defaults. There is a further exception for the issue of bonds secured by a first-grade mortgage on the immovable property of the company, covering up to two-thirds of its

399 Also in this case, Art. 2410 refers to Art. 2436 which regulates the registration of the modifications of the articles and the intervention of the notary in the procedure.

400 Separate rules are also provided for in special laws for other categories of companies.

401 In the original provisions of the Code of 1942, the issue of bonds was restricted to a maximum corresponding to the amount of capital paid up mentioned in the last balance sheet. The new rule has been introduced by the reform of 2003.

402 See G. F. Campobasso (ed), *La riforma delle società di capitali e delle cooperative* (Turin: UTET, 2004), p. 175.

value. The latter type of transaction does not come within the limit set by Article 2412(1). The limits imposed by Article 2412 may be exceeded if there are particular reasons in the public interest for so doing, and the relevant public authority gives its permission.

Although bonds may be secured by a mortgage of the company's movable or immovable property, it is not possible for a floating charge over the whole of the company's undertaking to be created, as in the United Kingdom and Ireland and most Commonwealth countries. However, there is now a new way in which public companies may raise funds, which is to set aside part of their assets (which must not exceed more than one-tenth of their net assets) as exclusive security for the providers of finance for a particular project (*patrimonio destinato ad uno specifico affare*). A further new method of financing is also provided for by Legislative Decree No. 6 of 2003, according to which public companies are permitted to give providers of finance exclusive or non-exclusive security, based upon future revenues arising from the project financed (*finanziamento destinato ad uno specifico affare*). These methods of finance are mentioned in Article 2447 *bis* of the Civil Code, and are regulated in detail by the provisions of Article 2447 *ter* – Article 2447 *decies*.[403]

Bondholders may hold meetings which resolve on the appointment or dismissal of a bondholders' representative (*rappresentante comune*); on the amendment of the conditions of the loan; on proposals for supervised or controlled administration (*amministrazione controllata*) and settlement with creditors; and other matters of common interest.[404] The directors or the bondholders' representative may call a bondholders' meeting when they consider it necessary, and such a meeting must be called on the requisition of the holders of one-twentieth of the outstanding bonds.[405] The bondholders' representative may even be a non-bondholder or chosen from among their number for a period of not more than three years by a meeting of the bondholders. If they fail to agree on such a representative, the appointment is made by the court at the request of one or more bondholders or the directors. The representative may not be a director, auditor or employee of the company, or

[403] It remains to be seen whether such methods have any advantages over floating charges.

[404] Italian Civil Code, Art. 2415(1). However the latter may have lost some advantages in the United Kingdom since the enactment of the Enterprise Act 2002.

[405] *Ibid.*, Art. 2415(2). The bondholders' meeting is made subject to the provisions governing extraordinary general meetings by Art. 2415(3).

person disqualified for appointment to the committee of auditors under Article 2399 of the Civil Code. According to Article 2418 of the Civil Code, the representative must provide for the implementation of the resolutions of the bondholders' meeting and protect their interests generally. The appointment of a common representative does not prevent the individual bondholders from bringing an action against the company on their bonds, except where such an action is incompatible with a resolution passed by the bondholders meeting.[406]

A public company may issue various kinds of bonds, for example ordinary bonds, granting a fixed rate of interest and payment of the nominal value of the bond on maturity, bonds which give a right to a share in the profits or the payment of additional sums contingent on the profits; indexed bonds; and convertible bonds, which are of considerable importance. Such bonds are regulated by Article 2420 *bis* of the Italian Civil Code. An issue of convertible bonds must be approved by an extraordinary general meeting of the company. Convertible bonds must be offered to the shareholders and previous holders of convertible bonds, in order to maintain their proportions in the shareholding. This rule aims to prevent the dilution of the members' participation. Other rules are provided similar to those concerning the issue of new shares. The resolution cannot be passed if the capital of the company has not been fully paid up. The company must also resolve to increase its capital by an amount equal to the aggregate nominal values of the shares which would be issued if the bondholders' conversion rights were fully exercised.[407] Until the end of the term fixed for their conversion, the company is not permitted by Article 2420 *bis*(4) to decide on the voluntary reduction of capital, or the amendment of the provisions of the articles regarding the distribution of profits, unless the holders of the convertible bonds have been given the power, by means of a notice published at the office of the Registry of Companies at least three months before the convening of the shareholders' meeting, to exercise the right of conversion within the period of one month from the publication.

F. The position in Spain

According to Article 9 of the law governing limited liability companies of 1995, a limited liability company (SRL) may not issue or guarantee an issue of bonds or negotiable securities grouped in a series (*agrupado en*

[406] *Ibid.*, Art. 2419. [407] *Ibid.*, Art. 2420 *bis*(2).

emisiones). Although the issue of such bonds is not open to them, such companies are able to finance themselves through bank loans and by other methods.

Spanish public companies may issue bonds in registered or bearer form, or represented by accounting entries through the medium of direct computerised annotation. Representation by accounting entries is now compulsory for bonds which are to be traded on organised markets.[408] Various terms and conditions as to repayment may be attached to bonds, including a redemption premium. The power to issue bonds is given to the general meeting, at which the quorum at first call is the holders of shares representing 50 per cent of the subscribed voting capital.[409] The relevant resolution must be registered at the Companies Registry. The board of directors may have the power to issue bonds delegated to it by the general meeting, subject to what limitations the general meeting wishes to impose, but such delegation is not possible where the issue is of convertible bonds. The issue takes the form of a contract between the company and the representative of the future bondholders (*concisario*).[410] The amount of the bond issue may not exceed the amount of the paid up share capital and reserves of the company as shown in the most recent approved balance sheet, except where the bonds are secured by mortgages on real estate or chattels, or are issued with a state or other governmental guarantee, or a bank guarantee.[411]

The issue of bonds requires the consent of the Ministry of Economy and Finance,[412] and must always be recorded in a notarial deed, which may itself be registered, and notified in the *Official Gazette* of the Commercial Registry.[413] Bond certificates for a particular issue must be identical, and must contain certain prescribed particulars, including particulars of the issuing company, the place of payment of the bonds, and of any security, and the total value of the issue.[414]

Convertible bonds are in frequent use in Spain; their issue requires the consent of the general meeting, which must receive reports from the directors and the company's auditors.[415] Such bonds may not be issued for less than their par value. In addition, bonds may not be converted

[408] See Royal Decree, 116/1992 of 14 February 1992.
[409] Law of 1989, as amended, Art. 103. [410] *Ibid.*, as amended, Art. 283(2).
[411] *Ibid.*, as amended, Arts. 282(1) and 284(1) and (2).
[412] A prospectus would have to be published and other formalities complied with if the bonds were issued by listed companies.
[413] Law of 1989, as amended, Arts. 285 and 286(1). [414] *Ibid.*, as amended, Art. 291.
[415] *Ibid.*, as amended, Art. 292(1).

into shares when the par value of the bond is less than that of the shares.[416] Where convertible bonds exist, the company may not reduce its capital except if prior to the reduction and with adequate security, the bondholders are offered the chance of effecting the conversion.[417]

Unless the general meeting decides on a different procedure, bonds may be converted at any time, in which case the directors issue the new shares during the first month of each prescribed six-month period. To those shareholders who have required a conversion in the previous six months period. At other times, a resolution providing for the relevant increase of capital would be required.[418]

G. *The position in Belgium*

Both public and private companies may issue bonds, but in the case of the latter type of company these must be in registered form.[419] A private company may grant a mortgage to secure a loan which takes the form, or is to take the form of a bond issue.[420] Furthermore, like public companies, private companies may issue lottery bonds, subject to certain conditions, ie that the rate of interest on the bonds is at least 3 per cent; that all such bonds receive the same sum on repayment; and that the amount of the annuity received comprising interest payments and repayments of capital remains the same during the existence of the loan. The total value of such bonds may not be more than the paid up share capital.[421] The transfer of bonds in private companies is subject to the special rules contained in Article 253 of the Companies Code, and like the transfer of shares, does not take effect against the company until it is entered in the appropriate register. The rules governing the transfer of bonds in a public company are the same as those applicable to the transfer of other securities, including shares.

The articles (*statuts*) of a public or private company determine the formalities which have to be complied with for admission to the bondholders' general meeting.[422] Articles 292–301 of the Companies

[416] *Ibid.*, Art. 292(2). [417] *Ibid.*, Art. 294(3). [418] *Ibid.*, Art. 294(1).

[419] Belgian Companies Code Art. 243. [420] *Ibid.*, Arts. 246 and 248.

[421] *Ibid.*, Art. 245; for the similar rule applicable to public companies, see *ibid.*, Art. 488. In public companies such bonds may not be issued in a dematerialised form.

[422] *Ibid.*, Art. 295 (private companies) and Art. 571 (public companies). Both provisions state that the statutes determine the formalities which have to be accomplished to be admitted to the general meeting. Article 571 contains further provisions imposing special requirements where the relevant public company has made, or is to make an appeal to the public for funds.

Code provides for bondholders' meeting in private companies, and Articles 568–580 thereof for such meetings in public companies. The relevant provisions frequently resemble one another closely. A general meeting of the bondholders may be called by the directors and auditors, and must be held on the requisition of one-fifth of the holders of the outstanding bonds.[423]

Provided that all the company's capital has been called up, the general meeting of bondholders may decide to delay the payment of one or more instalments of interest, to consent to a reduction in the rate of interest, or a modification in the conditions of payment. It may also prolong the period of repayment, suspend repayment or agree to modifications that are appropriate in the circumstances. It may also accept that shares should be substituted for the bonds, but unless the shareholders have already given their consent to such substitution, they will have to agree to it within a period of three months in accordance with the procedure required for the modification of the articles. The meeting may also decide on the release or modification of the bondholders' security, on acts of conservation in the bondholders' interests, and also on the appointment of one or more representatives to carry out decisions taken at the meeting and to act on behalf of bondholders in procedures relating to the alteration or removal of particulars concerning any charge created by the company securing the bonds which have to be published in the Annexes to the *Official Journal* (*Moniteur Belge*).[424]

A bondholders' meeting cannot validly deliberate and make decisions on first call unless the holders of at least half of the outstanding bonds are present. No such quorum requirement exists when the meeting is called on a second occasion. Votes are cast at bondholders' meetings in proportion to the nominal value of the bonds, and resolutions are passed by a three-quarters majority of the votes cast. However, unless the resolution is supported by the holders of at least one-third of the outstanding bonds, it has effect only if approved by the Court of Appeal for the district in which the company is domiciled. Nevertheless, the quorum requirements are inapplicable, and only a simple majority vote is required to decide on measures of conservation, and on the appointment of representatives for the purpose specified at the end of the above paragraph.[425]

423 *Ibid.*, Art. 293 (private companies); Art. 569 (public companies).
424 *Ibid.*, Art. 292 (private companies); Art. 568 (public companies).
425 *Ibid.*, Art. 297 (private companies); Art. 574 (public companies).

If there are more than one class of bonds and if the deliberations of the bondholders' meeting is of such a nature as to modify their respective rights, the conditions relating to quorum and three-quarters majority which have been explained above must be satisfied in relation to each class of bondholders. Separate meetings of each class of bondholders, or a single meeting of all the relevant classes may be held.[426]

A Belgian public company (SA) may issue fully paid convertible bonds or bonds carrying the right to subscribe for shares in the company, but the conversion or subscription options must be exercisable not later than ten years after the bonds are issued.[427] The issue must be approved in advance by a general meeting of the company by a three-quarters majority vote, unless the directors were authorised to issue them by reason of provisions in the articles, delegating such powers to them.[428]

When convertible bonds or rights to subscribe for bonds are to be issued, the purpose and the justification for such an issue must be explained in a special report to be circulated to the shareholders before any meeting takes place. If this report is inadequate, the Belgian Finance and Banking Commission may postpone the meeting or delay the proposed issue for a maximum period of three months.[429]

The existing shareholders have a preferential right to subscribe for convertible bonds or bonds (usually accompanied by warrants) carrying the right to subscribe for shares in the company, but such right may be excluded or limited by the resolution which authorises the issue.[430] Whilst convertible bonds or bonds carrying subscription rights are outstanding, the company may not do any act which reduces the advantages attributed to the bonds by the terms of issue or the law.[431] According to Article 491 of the Companies Code, if the capital of a company is increased by cash contributions, the holders of convertible bonds may, notwithstanding any provision of the articles or the terms of issue, obtain the conversion of their bonds, and participate in the new issue as shareholders to the extent that this preferential right belonged to the old shareholders.[432]

426 *Ibid.*, Art. 298 (private companies) and Art. 575 (public companies).
427 *Ibid.*, Art. 489 (convertible bonds) and Art. 499 (rights to subscribe for shares).
428 *Ibid.*, Art. 603. 429 *Ibid.*, Art. 583. 430 *Ibid.*, Arts. 592 and 596.
431 *Ibid.*, Arts. 490 and 501. 432 *Ibid.*, Art. 491.

H. *The position in the Netherlands*

The question of loan capital and bonds (*obligaties*) is covered by Dutch private law rather than company legislation. Unless the articles otherwise provide, the board is empowered to raise loan capital on behalf of the company. If bonds are to be listed they have to comply with the requirements of the Amsterdam Stock Exchange. Bonds may be secured by a mortgage. The mortgage deed will usually appoint a trustee to exercise all the rights belonging to the bondholders collectively. The legal relationship between the trustee, the company and the bondholders will be regulated by a trust deed. It should be emphasised that a Dutch trustee does not have the same position as one appointed under English law.

Convertible bonds are frequently met with in the Netherlands and it would seem that, because the issue of such bonds eventually involves an increase of capital, a resolution of the general meeting is necessary for their issue. Furthermore, when such bonds are issued, the existing shareholders have pre-emptive rights, which may be excluded by the articles or by a resolution of the general meeting.[433]

[433] BW, Art. 96a (public companies) and Art. 206a (private companies). However, if the shares come within the special categories mentioned in Article 96a(2) and Article 206a(2), they have no such pre-emptive rights.

6

Management and control of companies

I. Introduction

In only a limited number of small companies is it possible for all the members to participate in management. This task has to be delegated to directors and managers, who have the power of taking binding decisions on behalf of the company. The national laws of the EU Member States under consideration provide for suitable management bodies for their companies. They also provide for controlling mechanisms which endeavour to ensure that the directors and managers do not make improper use of their extensive powers. Thus, rights may be vested in such bodies as the general meeting, the supervisory board or the works council to require information, be consulted about certain matters, and to give their consent to certain important proposals, for example the alteration of the company articles (statute), its merger with another company, or its conversion into a company of a different type.

In all the Member States under consideration, there are significant legal controls on the activities of the directors and managers, which are intended to ensure that such officers act within their powers, and conduct their business efficiently. Such controls vary in their detail and in the sanctions provided for in case of their breach. Furthermore, in all the relevant states, requirements exist as to financial disclosure, and the accounts of most companies have to be audited by a qualified auditor who has to report on them. The latter requirements should, but do not inevitably, succeed in guarding against financial irregularities. The provisions governing financial disclosure are supplemented by certain requirements set by stock exchanges and other relevant bodies in the Member States.

In the United Kingdom, listed companies have to comply with the Combined Code, which emphasises certain structural issues concerning membership of the board of directors, the appointment of directors, directors' remuneration and the relationship between board and shareholders. The Combined Code also deals with certain accountancy matters, such as financial reporting and internal control. However, the criticism has been made of this Code, and earlier codes concerning corporate governance that it focuses too much on the internal structure of the company, and takes inadequate account of the needs of creditors and suppliers. The recent proposals contained in the Higgs Review which provides retailed guidance on the role of non-executive directors, and are designed to strengthen existing corporate governance provisions within the Combined Code, have also given rise to criticism, and have undergone certain modifications before being adopted.

The so-called market for corporate control, which subjects inefficient managers and directors to the threat of loss of office through the medium of a takeover bid, may well operate as a further control mechanism in jurisdictions in which hostile bids are common place.

There are considerable differences in the rules concerning management and control in the Member States under consideration. These differences depend to some extent on historical accidents as well as on differences between political and social ideologies which have proved surprisingly difficult to transcend, as is shown by the prolonged and unrelated debate on employee participation, which has so far helped to prevent the adoption of the Fifth Directive. However, in all the Member States under consideration the general meeting has, in theory, certain powers of control, especially in private companies. The possibility that the majority (who may be the same persons as or closely associated with the managers) may abuse their position receives recognition in the rights given to minority shareholders in many states. However, the double-board system only exists in three of the states considered in this book, Germany, the Netherlands and France, and in France on a facultative basis.

The role of non-executive directors has been emphasised in the United Kingdom by the Cadbury, Hampel and Higgs Reports on Corporate Governance, and is recognised in the Combined Code.[1] It will obviously be impossible to consider all the detailed rules in the seven relevant

[1] *The Combined Code on Corporate Governance* (2003). This Code superseded and replaced the Combined Code issued by the Hampel Committee on Corporate Governance in 1998. It derived from a review of the role and effectiveness of non-executive directors by Derek Higgs, *Review of the Role and Effectiveness of Non-executive Directors* (London: Department of Trade and Industry, 2003), and a review of audit committees by a group led by Sir Robert Smith, *Audit Committees Combined Code Guidance* (London: Financial Reporting Council, 2003). The Financial Services Authority responded that it would replace the 1998 Code that is annexed to the Listing Rules with the revised Code and would make the consequential rule changes. There was a consultation on the necessary rule changes but not further consultation on the Code provisions themselves.

countries concerning management and control, but an attempt will be made to cover the salient features of the legal rules in these fields. No attempt will be made to cover the detailed requirements set by stock exchanges and regulatory bodies, and there will be no detailed consideration of the rules relating to financial disclosure and auditing. Detailed attention has not been given to the codes of corporate governance which have effect in certain Member States, such as the United Kingdom, Germany and Italy. The recent Commission proposal on the modernisation of Company Law of 9 April 2003 suggests that a framework directive should be enacted containing the principles applicable to an annual corporate governance statement.

II. The position in the United Kingdom

A. General considerations

The Companies Act 2006[2] requires every company to have a director or directors; but fails to define the term 'director'. The Act attributes certain powers to directors, and imposes certain general duties on them.[3] There is no difference between the management and control structures relating to public and private companies. The need for minority protection is generally considered to be greater in private companies. As far as listed companies are concerned, the Act is supplemented by the provisions of the Combined Code.[4]

Many of the existing rules governing the duties of directors of companies are derived from decisions of the courts, in which principles of common law and equity have been applied. The actual management of a company is left to its articles which will frequently adopt, subject to modifications, the relevant provisions of Table A. Certain matters remain

[2] Companies Act 2006, s. 151 (previously Companies Act 1985, s. 282). Every private company must have at least one director and every public company at least two. Companies must have one director who is a natural person. Under the previous Companies Act, corporations could be directors.

[3] This situation should be compared with the position in Germany: see German Public Companies Act, para. 93 and German Limited Companies Act, para. 43, which contain general rules governing the duty of care and liabilities of members and managers.

[4] The duty of a director to act in good faith, has been replaced by s. 172 of the Companies Act 2006, which requires directors to act in the way which they consider, in good faith, would be most likely to promote the success of the company for the benefit of the company as a whole. In doing so, they must have regard to the matters set out in s. 172(1)(a)–(f). It may be doubted whether the relevant provision will have much effect on the various actions of directors.

within the scope of the general meeting, for example the alteration of the company articles, the reduction of its capital, or its winding up.

In addition to the Combined Code, which is concerned with corporate governance, and which most recently underwent amendments as the result of the Higgs Report, on the role and effectiveness of non-executive directors, the Financial Services Authority, which is responsible for the listing of securities, the Stock Exchange which is concerned with their admission to trading, and the City Code on Takeovers and Mergers, provide for the use of regulatory functions which concern or may concern directors and their conduct, and which operate independently of the framework of the Companies Act.

B. *The appointment, vacation of office and removal of directors*

The first directors may be named in the articles. Subsequent directors are usually appointed in accordance with the provisions of the articles. There are no binding rules concerning the mode of appointment, or the period of such appointment. Directors of private companies are sometimes appointed for life. The articles often provide that vacancies occurring other than through retirement by rotation shall be filled or further directors appointed by the board and that a certain proportion of directors, usually one-third shall retire at each general meeting, and their place shall be filled by the company at the meeting. In addition it is often provided that a director retiring by rotation shall be deemed to be reappointed if his place is not filled, unless it is expressly resolved not to appoint him.[5]

Directors are not required to have a share qualification, but the articles may provide for one; if they do section 291 of the 1985 Act requires directors to acquire it within two months of appointment, or such shorter time as may be prescribed. It also stipulates that any director not acquiring his qualification within the prescribed time, or ceasing to hold it after such time, shall vacate office. No corresponding provision exists in the Companies Act 2006.

Directors are not entitled as of right to any remuneration. However, the articles may provide for directors' fees,[6] and a director may be

[5] See Art. 75 of Table A of the Companies Act 1985.

[6] Thus, Art. 82 of Table A of the Companies Act 1985 provides that a director is entitled to such remuneration as the company may by ordinary resolution determine. It should be noted that s. 19 of the Companies Act 2006 enables the Secretary of State to prescribe such articles in the future. Meanwhile many companies will continue to be governed by Table A, perhaps with modifications.

entitled to a salary or other remuneration under the terms of a service contract between himself and the company. Furthermore, if he performs services which are not contemplated under the terms of a service contract, he may be entitled to a *quantum meruit*. No such entitlement to payment for services as a *quantum meruit* or an equitable allowance exists where the articles provide that remuneration is only payable if granted by the board or the general meeting.[7]

Directors may be required by the provisions of articles similar to Table A Article 73, to retire by rotation. Such provisions are rarely found in the articles of private companies. A director may become disqualified by law, or by the memorandum and articles of the company from continuing as director: if this occurs he automatically vacates office. An undischarged bankrupt may be subject to criminal sanctions if he acts as director of a company without leave of the court which adjudged him bankrupt.[8] A person may be disqualified from acting as a director by order of the court in accordance with the provisions of a number of other sections of the Company Director Disqualification Act 1986.[9]

The articles often provide that a director shall vacate office if he does or suffers particular things.[10] These may include becoming bankrupt or insolvent, failing to acquire or hold the necessary share qualifications, prolonged absence from meetings, or becoming subject to a mental illness with consequent hospitalisation, or the making of a court order.

According to section 168(1) of the Companies Act 2006,[11] a director may be dismissed at any time despite anything to the contrary in the articles. It is surprising, and perhaps unacceptable, except possibly in private companies, that it is possible to circumvent this provision by giving every director multiple votes on any such resolution so that, in fact, he cannot be dismissed. It is noteworthy that if a director has a service contract with the company, dismissal may be expensive for it.

C. Powers of directors

The division of powers between the general meeting and the board is in principle a matter for the articles. The position may be contrasted with

7 *Guinness plc* v. *Saunders* [1990] 2 AC 663.

8 Company Directors' Disqualification Act 1986, ss. 1 and 2.

9 For a full account of these provisions see R. Pennington, *Company Law*, 8th edn (London: Butterworths, 2001), pp. 652–660.

10 Companies Act 1985 Table A, Art. 81.

11 Replacing s. 303 of the Companies Act 1985.

that in the United States and many other European countries, where certain functions are treated as managerial ones, which must be entrusted to the board. However, the tendency of modern articles is to follow the pattern of Article 70 of Table A to the 1985 Companies Act, and confer on the board all the powers of the company except those which the Companies Act 1985 and the memorandum and articles require to be exercised by the general meeting. The directors are not bound by any ordinary resolution of the general meeting when the articles are in the form of Article 70 of Table A, but under this article, directions can be given to them by special resolution.

Unless the articles confer power on the board to delegate its functions, directors must exercise their managerial powers collectively as a board.[12]

The quorum is usually fixed by the articles, and it may be fixed as one.[13] In practice, the articles of a company cover wide powers of delegation by the board both to individual directors[14] (such as managing directors)[15] and other agents.[16] Acts which are within the actual, implied (or usual) or apparent authority of directors and other agents will be binding on the company as against third parties who act in good faith. The latter may also receive protection from section 40(1) of the Companies Act 2006[17] quite independently of the agency principles already mentioned, or the rule in *Royal British Bank* v. *Turquand*.[18]

[12] However, by virtue of s. 35A of the Companies Act 1985, an act done by a single director might perhaps have been binding on the company, even where the single director has no actual implied or apparent authority.

[13] It is questionable whether the statutory provision protects a person dealing with an inquorate board. The Companies Act 2006, s. 40 (power of directors to bind the company), (1) provides 'In favour of a person dealing with a company in good faith, the power of the directors to bind the company, or authorise others to do so, is deemed to be free of any limitation under the company's constitution'. This replaces s. 35A of the Companies Act 1985 which is in identical terms.

[14] Companies Act 1985, Table A, Art. 72.

[15] *Ibid.*, Table A, Art. 84.

[16] *Ibid.*, Table A, Art. 71.

[17] Section 35A(1) of the Companies Act 1985 provided that in favour of a person dealing with the company in good faith, the power of the board of directors to bind the company, or to authorise others to do so, would be deemed to be free of any limitation in the company's constitution.

[18] (1855) 5 E and B 248. This rule enables persons dealing with a company to assume that its internal procedures at meetings of directors and shareholders have been conducted correctly, when they do not have notice to the contrary.

D. Duties of directors

The general duties of directors of British companies are set out in sections 171–177 of the Companies Act 2006.[19] The directors of British companies owe fiduciary duties to their companies which are not closely paralleled in other European jurisdictions, apart from the Republic of Ireland. These fiduciary duties were originally owed by trustees, and the analogy of trusteeship (*Treuhandschaft*) is sometimes used by German authors when mentioning the duties of directors under paragraph 93 of the German *Aktiengesetz*. Although section 172 of the Companies Act 2006 places the general obligation on directors to consider the interests of other stakeholders, such as employees, suppliers, customers and the community, it still appears to remain the case that the fiduciary duties of directors are primarily owed to the company and its shareholders. Furthermore, directors of British companies are subject to detailed statutory rules of various kinds. In addition, they owe a statutory duty under section 174 of the Companies Act 2006 to exercise reasonable care, skill and diligence.[20] This means the care, skill and diligence which could be exercised by a reasonably diligent person with the general knowledge, skill and experience which might reasonably be expected of a person carrying out the functions of a director in relation to the company, and to the general knowledge, skill and experience that the director has.[21] A number of duties are imposed by the complex provisions of Part X of the Companies Act 1985: the Law Commissions suggested various amendments to Part X, the deletion of various of its provisions, and the establishment of a single code of remedies applying to the provisions of Part X.[22] It has been held that directors are bound to exercise the powers conferred on them bona fide in what they consider, as opposed to what a court may consider, is in the interests of the company.[23] It is accepted

[19] It is impossible to treat these complex duties in detail here. Some of the directors' duties were previously uncodified, other such duties were imposed by the complex provisions of Part X of the Companies Act 1985.

[20] This previous common law duty was codified by the Companies Act 2006.

[21] There have been a number of important recent developments in the case law concerning directors' duties of care and skill in recent years. Note in particular *Norman* v. *Theodore Goddard* [1991] BCLC 1028 and *Re D'Jan of London* [1993] BCC 646.

[22] Law Commission, *Company Directors: Regulating Conflicts of Interest and Formulating a Statement of Duties* (Law Com No. 153, 1998). Although certain of the Part X provisions appear in the Companies Act 2006, there is no part of that Act that corresponds exactly to Part X.

[23] See the dictum of Greene MR in *Re Smith and Fawcett Ltd* (1942) Ch 304 (CA) at 306 in this sense.

that the interests of the company include those of present and future shareholders and when the company is insolvent or on the brink of insolvency, the interests of the creditors.[24] It has been accepted in the past that the interests of the company do not only include those of its present and future shareholders, but may include those of its employees in accordance with section 309 of the Companies Act 1985, and when the company is insolvent or on the brink of insolvency, the interests of its creditors.[25] The question whether directors should be allowed to further the interests of other entities, such as the state, the local community, the general public and the company's customers has received much consideration in recent years,[26] and will continue to be debated. The effect of the relevant provisions of section 172(a)–(f) of the Companies Act 2006, is as yet unclear.

If directors use the power conferred by the articles for a purpose other than that for which it was conferred, their conduct may be impugned, and they may not avail themselves of the defence that they honestly believed that what they did was in the interests of the company.[27] The present rule is applicable even when the directors derive no profit from the transaction, and believe themselves to be acting bona fide in the interests of the company.[28]

It has been held in a number of decided cases that directors must make no unauthorised profit by or as a result of exercising their functions as such. Because this is a fiduciary duty, it is independent of fault or loss to the company. Thus, the company may recover the profit, even if there is no loss, and it could not have made the profit itself.[29] A director who makes such an unauthorised profit must account to the company for it. The duty embraces the use of corporate information and opportunities, but not that of information of a general nature.[30] It appears that where an opportunity to enter into a transaction from which a profit arises has been offered to and

[24] Note in this context, *Brady* v. *Brady* [1989] AC 755 (HL) and see Companies Act 2006, s. 172(2).

[25] Note in this context, *Brady* v. *Brady* [1989] AC 755(HL).

[26] Company Review Steering Groups' Consultative Document, *Modern Company Law for a Competitive Economy: Developing the Framework* (March 2000), paras. 3.20–3.36, in which the Steering Group expressed its opposition to any pluralist duty of loyalty.

[27] Note in particular *Howard Smith* v. *Ampol Petroleum Co Ltd* [1974] AC 821 (PC).

[28] Section 171(b) of the Companies Act 2006 requires directors to use their powers only for the purpose for which they were conferred.

[29] Note especially, *Regal (Hastings) Ltd* v. *Gulliver* [1967] 2 AC 134.

[30] Note e.g., *Canadian Safeway* v. *Thompson* [1951] 3 DLR 295 (information) and *Cook* v. *Deeks* [1916] 1 AC 554 (corporate opportunities).

rejected by the company, and is then offered to the individual directors after a significant period of time has passed, the court may conclude that the profit was not derived from the directors' office as such.[31]

Directors are also under a fiduciary duty under section 175 of the Companies Act 2006 not to place themselves in a position in which there might be a conflict between personal interest and their duty to the company. This rule is said to apply to any exploitation of any property, information or opportunity. It is immaterial whether the company could take advantage of the property, information or opportunity. This requirement is not infringed if authorisation is given by the directors. Such authorisation is provided for by section 175(5) and (6).

Section 177 of the Companies Act 2006[32] requires a director to disclose the nature and content of any direct or indirect interest in a transaction or arrangement or proposed transaction or arrangement with a company of which he is a director, to the other directors. Such disclosure may be made at a meeting of the directors or by means of a general notice to the directors of the existence of the interest. Section 177 is applicable to shadow directors. A 'shadow director' is defined in section 251(1) as a person in accordance with whose directions or instructions the directors of the company are accustomed to act.[33]

It was held that non-disclosure of an interest in accordance with section 317, which was rather similar to section 177 of the Companies Act 2006, did not make the contract voidable at the instance of the company.[34] The Law Commissions recommended that breach of the disclosure requirement under section 317 should make the arrangement or transaction in which the director or a person connected with him had an interest, voidable at the instance of the company unless certain conditions were fulfilled.[35] There is no explicit provision in the Companies Act

[31] See the Canadian case, *Peso Silver Mines Ltd* v. *Cropper* (1966) 58 DLR (2d) 1 and the Australian case, *Queensland Mines Ltd* v. *Hudson* (1978) 52 AJLR 399 (PC).

[32] This provision has some resemblance to Companies Act 1985, s. 317 which is no longer in force. It required disclosure to the shareholders' meeting but the company articles almost always contained provisions releasing directors from the duty of disclosure to the general meeting. What remained was the duty to disclose their interest to a meeting of directors or by way of a general notice to the other directors.

[33] A shadow director was previously defined in s. 74(2) of the 1985 Companies Act. Section 317 of the 1985 Act, like a number of other controls on directors imposed by Part X of the 1985 Act, was applicable to shadow directors.

[34] Note *Hely-Hutchinson* v. *Brayhead Ltd* [1968] 1 QB 549 to this effect.

[35] See part 8 of the Law Commission's report, *Company Directors: Regulating Conflict of Interests and Formulating a Statement of Duties* (Law Com No. 153, 1998).

2006 covering this matter. However, section 178 of the 2006 Act stipulates that the consequences of a breach of sections 171–7 are the same as the corresponding common law or equitable principles applied.

Other important controls are placed on directors and shadow directors by Chapter 4 of Part 10 of the Companies Act 2006.[36] These include provisions governing substantial property transactions with directors,[37] loans to directors,[38] and payment for loss of office to directors and past directors.[39] The provisions are rather complex and detailed. They are made applicable to shadow directors by section 223 of the Companies Act 2006.

Directors or shadow directors may be liable for fraudulent or wrongful trading under section 213 or 214 of the Insolvency Act 1986. The need to prove fraud in order to make any person knowingly a party to the carrying on of business liable to make a contribution to the assets of an insolvent company undergoing liquidation is an obstacle to the successful invocation of section 213.

The liability for wrongful trading under section 214 is only applicable to directors and shadow directors. It makes such persons personally liable to contribute to the assets of a company which has gone into indirect liquidation if at some time before the commencement of the liquidation, they knew or ought to have concluded that there was no reasonable prospect that the company would avoid going into insolvent liquidation. In deciding whether this condition is fulfilled, the court takes account of whether a director or shadow director has failed to show the general knowledge, skill and care which might be expected from a reasonably diligent person in their position, and also of someone with the general knowledge, experience and skill that director or shadow director has. The latter requirement obviously imposes an additional burden on persons who have attained higher standards than may usually be expected.

Directors also incur liability if they are responsible for negligently managing the company's affairs. The earlier decisions on the required standard of care and skill tended to impose a subjective criterion based upon the degree of care and skill which might be expected of a person of

36 Replacing provisions in Part X of the Companies Act 1985. Amendments were proposed by the Law Commission in parts 10–11 of their report, see n. 35 above.

37 Companies Act 2006, ss. 190–196.

38 *Ibid.*, ss. 197–214 (loans, quasi-loans and credit transactions).

39 *Ibid.*, ss. 215–222.

the director's knowledge and experience.[40] However, an objective standard of care and skill is now required of directors employed under a service contract.[41] The same is true of non-executive directors, who do not have such a contract. In two fairly recent cases, the court held that the standard of care and skill which is made applicable to directors under section 214 of the Insolvency Act, which has been considered above, constitutes a correct statement of the directors' standard of care and skill.[42] The Law Commissions adopted an approach depending on a similar dual objective/subjective test to that which is contained in section 214(4) of the Insolvency Act 1986.[43] This approach has now been adopted in the Companies Act 2006.[44]

E. The general meeting

The formal rules about holding general meetings often prove to be ignored in the case of private companies,[45] and the stipulations of section 336 of the Act which provide that public companies are required to hold an annual general meeting, do not apply to private companies.[46] In the

[40] *Re City Equitable Fire Insurance* [1925] Ch 407. In this case the court also held that a director was not bound to attend board meetings and that a director might escape liability when he entrusted functions to subordinates.

[41] Note in this sense, Pennington, *Company Law*, p. 734.

[42] *Norman* v. *Theodore Goddard* [1991] BCLC 1028 and *Re D'Jan of London Ltd* [1993] BCC 646 at 648 (Hoffmann LJ).

[43] This test has been criticised by Riley, *The Company Director's Duty of Care and Skill: the Case for an Onerous but Subjective Standard* (1999) 62 MLR 697.

[44] Section 174(2).

[45] Written resolutions of the members of a private company now have effect as if they were passed at a general meeting or class meeting, according to s. 288(1) of the Companies Act 2006. There are exceptions to this rule, which are set out in s. 288(2) of the Act.

[46] There were special rules concerning the passing of resolutions by private companies and annual meetings also before the 2006 Act. Thus s. 381A of the Companies Act 1985 permitted such companies to avoid the need for a general meeting, and pass resolutions by means of a resolution in writing signed by or on behalf of all the members. The auditors could in accordance with s. 381B, object to the use of this procedure. It is not clear whether the written procedure provided for in s. 381A intended to supersede the provisions frequently found in the articles of private companies permit ting the passing of such resolutions without any need to refer them to auditors.

Private companies were also permitted by section 379A of the Companies Act 1985 to pass unanimous elective resolutions dispensing with the need to comply with certain requirements of the Companies Act 1985, e.g. the need to hold an annual general meeting or appoint auditors annually.

It was suggested by the Company Law Review Steering Group that the elective regime might operate automatically unless the company decides otherwise. Company Review Steering Groups' Consultative Document, *Modern Company Law*, pp. 254–6. The 2002

case of public companies, such meetings are often poorly attended but pressure which may be exerted by institutional investors which often takes place outside the general meeting, may entail that the board is unable to exercise de facto control on all occasions in large public companies.

It follows from the overview above that the general meeting normally has fairly limited powers, as the articles normally vest managerial powers in the board. It has of course to approve the annual accounts, and is empowered to dismiss directors. The directors will usually be able to get their way on contested issues by reason of their control of the proxy voting system.

In principle, if the directors are responsible for a breach of duty, the general meeting has to decide whether to take action against them, and a minority shareholder cannot normally bring an action on the company's behalf if the members in general meeting choose not to do so.[47] The directors have sometimes been treated as entitled to vote as shareholders against the bringing of such an action.[48] The present view appears to be that the decision not to sue must be taken by an independent majority of disinterested shareholders.[49] However, a minority shareholder may bring an action on behalf of the company, a so-called derivative action, where the general meeting fails to take action against directors in certain circumstances.[50]

A public company must hold a general meeting at least once a year.[51] By section 303 of the Companies Act 2006, the directors are required to hold a general meeting upon a members' requisition, which may be made

White Paper proposed that the norm should be that private companies will not have an AGM unless they decide to do so by ordinary resolution.

[47] *Foss* v. *Harbottle* (1843) 2 Hare 461.

[48] See *North West Transportation Co* v. *Beatty* [1887] 12 AC 589 (PC). This case concerned ratification rather than a decision not to sue, but its effect on the minority of such a decision is the same as ratification.

[49] *Smith* v. *Croft* (No. 2) [1988] Ch 144.

[50] See the detailed provisions of Chapters 1 and 2 of Part 11 of the Companies Act 2006 which deal respectively with derivative claims in England and Wales, Northern Ireland and Scotland. Derivative actions are further considered in the section dealing with minority protection. The concept of fraud on the minority, which has been regarded as providing an exception to the *Foss* v. *Harbottle* rule in the past is learnedly discussed in Pennington, *Company Law*, pp. 804–806. This concept is not entirely clearly defined but fraud on the minority appears to mean dishonest conduct or an abuse of power which has benefited the directors.]

[51] Companies Act 2006, s. 336(1). The meeting must be held in each period of six months beginning with the day following its accounting reference date. See previously, Companies Act 1985, s. 366.

by the holders of at least 10 per cent of the paid-up share capital carrying voting rights. Section 303(3) contains certain exceptions to this requirement. Directors who receive a requisition under section 303, are required to call a general meeting within forty-nine days of such receipt.[52]

Such a meeting may be replaced by written resolution except in the two cases set out in section 288(2) of the Companies Act 2006. Private companies are not required to hold an annual general meeting: see Companies Act 2006, section 336. They may include such requirements in their articles.

Business may not be transacted at a company meeting unless a quorum is present. According to section 318(2) of the Companies Act 2006, subject to certain exceptions for representatives and proxies of the same person, two members personally present are a quorum, unless the articles otherwise provide.

Furthermore, section 357 of the Companies Act 2006 provides for the recording of decisions by one-person companies.[53] Where a member of such a company limited by share or guarantee takes any decision which may be taken by the company in general meeting, and which has effect as if agreed on by the company in general meeting, he must (unless that decision is taken by written resolution) supply the company with details of that decision.

Chapter 3 of Part 13 contains special requirements governing the results of, and independent reports on, polls taken at such meetings.

According to section 307(1) and (2), general meetings of both public and private companies require 14 days' notice, except in the case of the annual general meeting, which requires twenty-one days' notice. The company's articles may prescribe a longer period of notice,[54] or a shorter one, under rather stringent conditions.[55] An ordinary resolution is one passed by a simple majority of the votes cast by shareholders and their proxies,[56] whilst a special resolution is one passed by at least three quarters of the votes cast by such persons.[57]

The Companies Act 2006 requires special notice to be given of certain resolutions. Section 312(1) provides that such a resolution is ineffective

[52] Companies Act 2006, s. 304(1).

[53] Regulations promulgated in 1992 provided that in the case of single member private companies, one member present in person or by proxy constitutes a quorum. See the Companies (Single Member Private Limited Companies) Regulations 1992, SI 1992, No. 1699 which inserted a new s. 370A into the Companies Act 1985.

[54] Companies Act 2006, s. 307(3). [55] *Ibid.*, s. 307(4)–(7).

[56] *Ibid.*, s. 282. [57] *Ibid.*, s. 283.

unless notice of the intention to move it is given to the company at least twenty-eight days before the meeting at which it is moved.

Voteless shares may be less common than they formerly were in the United Kingdom: shares may however have different voting rights attached to them, and shareholders' voting and other agreements are commonplace in private and joint venture companies. In private companies, the directors often hold the majority of the shares, and the general meeting, assuming that it takes place,[58] may prove to be an ineffective control over their activities, this may be the case in certain public companies as well.

The Company Law Steering Committee reviewed the introduction of electronic voting[59] which has not been provided for in specific terms in the 2006 Act.

F. *Minority protection*

The shareholders' derivative action is not much used by minority shareholders but was generally regarded as one of the principal remedies available to them. The former weakness used to be the need to show fraud on the minority and, according to many authorities, that the wrongdoers controlled the company. The concept of a fraud on the minority was somewhat vague but it has been held not to include negligence unless the wrongdoers benefit themselves at the expense of the company.[60]

The Law Commission suggested that the existing principles underlying the derivative action should be replaced by a new statutory derivative action in cases where there was an alleged breach of directors'

[58] Such a meeting may be replaced by written resolution except in the two cases set out in s. 288(2) of the Companies Act 2006. Private companies are not required to hold an annual general meeting: see Companies Act 2006, ss. 336. They may include such requirements in their articles.

[59] Company Review Steering Groups' Consultative Document, *Modern Company Law* suggested a number of possibilities for the reform of the law relating to shareholders' meetings, e.g. allowing electronic voting. A useful summary of its suggestions appears in A. J. Boyle and J. Birds, *Boyle and Birds' Company Law*, 4th edn (Bristol: Jordans, 2000), pp. 419–420.

[60] See *Pavlides* v. *Jensen* [1956] Ch 565 and *Daniels* v. *Daniels* [1978] Ch 406, 414. In the latter case, Templeman J held that a minority shareholder who has no other remedy may sue where directors use their powers intentionally or unintentionally, fraudulently or negligently, in a manner which benefits themselves at the expense of the company.

duties.[61] The leave of the court to maintain a derivative action would have to be sought at an early stage in the proceedings, and the court would have to have regard to all relevant circumstances. The Law Commission failed to consider what changes should be made in the substantive law regarding ratification. However, its positive suggestions have obviously influenced the new statutory rules governing derivative actions contained in Chapters 1 and 2 of Part 11 of the Companies Act 2006.

According to section 260(1) and (2), a derivative action may be brought by a member of a company in proceedings in England and Wales and Northern Ireland in respect of a cause of action vested in the company and seeking relief on its behalf. Such a claim may only be brought under Chapter 1 or in pursuance of an order of the court in proceedings under section 994 (proceedings for protection of members against unfair conduct). The scope of the derivative action is wide: section 260(3) states that it may be brought only in respect of a cause of action arising from an actual or proposed act or omission involving negligence, default, breach of duty or breach of trust by a director of the company. The cause of action may be against the director or another person.

Applications must, according to section 261, be made to the court to continue the claim. Section 262 contains provisions governing an application for permission to continue a company's claim as a derivative action. Section 263 contains provisions governing whether permission should be given to a member of a company to bring a derivative claim under section 261 or 262. Thus, for example, Article 263(2) provides that where the cause of action arises from an act or omission that has already occurred, such permission should be refused if the act or omission was authorised by the company before it occurred or has been ratified since it occurred. The ratification of acts of directors is governed by the detailed provisions of section 239; a resolution of members of the company is necessary for such ratification, and neither the director (if a member of the company) nor a person connected with him may take part in a written resolution. The votes of such persons in favour of such a resolution must be disregarded in determining whether the necessary majority has been obtained for ratification. Furthermore, according to section 239(7), section 239 does not affect any other enactment or rule of law imposing additional requirements for valid ratification or any rule of law as to acts which are incapable of being ratified by the company. The existence

[61] Law Commission, *Shareholder Remedies* (Law Com No. 246, 1997) [Cm 3769].

of such unratifiable wrongs has been much discussed in the relevant literature.[62] In some circumstances a minority shareholder who brings a derivative action may be entitled to an indemnity against his costs.[63]

It remains to be seen whether the provisions governing the derivative actions will succeed in making resort to this remedy more common in the future. The improper or vexatious use of the new procedure should be prevented or contained as the result of the exercise of the discretion of the court. In some, but not all cases, the remedy under section 994 might be a viable alternative.[64] It does not seem that the latter remedy can always be used instead of a derivative action. Thus, for example, it is of little utility in the case of public companies.[65] The wrongdoers are not specifically required to control the company in order that permission should be given for a derivative action to be brought; however, similar considerations would have to be taken into account by the court in accordance with the provisions of sections 262(3)(c) and (d) of the 2006 Act.[66] The court may also take into consideration whether the relevant act or omission in respect of which the claim is brought gives rise to a cause of action which the member could pursue in his own right rather than on behalf on the company, and whether the bringing of an action under section 994 is a more appropriate remedy.

In some circumstances a minority shareholder who brings a derivative action may be entitled to an indemnity against his costs.[67]

[62] For example, the discussion of ratification in E. Ferran, *Company Law and Corporate Finance* (Oxford: Oxford University Press: 1999), pp. 144–53.

[63] See *Wallensteiner* v. *Moir* (No. 2) [1975] QB 373; note, however the more conservative approach of Walton J in *Smith* v. *Croft* [1986] 1 WLR 580.

[64] See in this connection, s. 263(3)(f) which requires the court when considering whether to give permission or leave, to consider whether an act or omission in respect of which the claim is brought, gives rise to a cause of action which a member could pursue in his own right rather than on behalf of the company.

[65] On the relationship between these two remedies, see A. Reisberg 'Shareholders' Remedies in Search of Consistency of Principle in English Law' [2005] 15 EBLR 1065 Certain petitions under the former s. 459 of the Companies Act 1985, now replaced by s. 994 of the Companies Act 2006, have alleged wrongs which are both personal (to the petitioner himself) and derivative. This may have been the case in *Clark* v. *Cutland* [2003] EWCA 810 in which a s. 459 petitioner was given an indemnity order against costs. Note also the decision of the Privy Council in *Gamlestaden Fastigheter AB v Baltic Partners Ltd & Ors (Jersey)* [2007] UKPC 26, [2007] 4 All ER 164, [2007] BCC 272, [2008] 1 BCLC 468.

[66] The provisions of s. 268(2)(c) and (d), which apply to Scotland, are in similar terms to those applicable to England and Wales and Northern Ireland. This appears to be governing the case with the other provisions of ss. 265–269 that apply to England and Wales and Northern Scotland.

[67] See *Wallensteiner* v. *Moir* (No. 2) [1975] QB 373; note, however the more conservative approach of Walton J in *Smith* v. *Croft* [1986] 1 WLR 580.

Sometimes, a shareholder does not wish to enforce a right belonging to the company but instead to bring an action in respect of wrongs done to his personal rights, for example where the company proposes to do an illegal or *ultra vires* act, or to refuse to record the shareholders' vote. The possibility of bringing such personal actions does not constitute a true exception to the rule in *Foss* v. *Harbottle*. The plaintiff may sue in his own name, or instead, where the rights of other shareholders as well as himself are affected, bring an action in a representative form.

A further kind of minority protection is available to a shareholder under section 122(1) of the Insolvency Act 1986, under which he may petition for the winding up of the company on the ground that it would be just and equitable to grant this remedy. The court will not grant this remedy when a alternative remedy is available, and the petitioner is acting unreasonably in not pursuing it. The principal modern case on the just and equitable jurisdiction is the decision of the House of Lords in *Ebrahimi* v. *Westbourne Galleries Ltd.*[68] The court upheld Ebrahimi's petition. It found that although two of the three directors had acted within their legal rights in removing Ebrahimi from the board, such legal rights would be treated as being subject to equitable considerations. It held that the petition would be successful, in a case in which the company was a quasi-partnership which was formed on a basis of mutual confidence, or on that of conducting equal management rights. The advantage of a petition under section 122(1)(g) is that it results in the valuation of the petitioner's interest on an assets basis: such a remedy has the obvious disadvantage of putting an end to the life of the company. The reasoning of the House of Lords in *Ebrahimi* has had a considerable influence on the decisions of the courts under section 459 of the Companies Act 1985 (now replaced by section 994 of the Act of 2006).

A perhaps more useful form of minority protection is available under section 994 of the Companies Act 2006[69] which permits any member to petition the court on the ground that the company's affairs are being conducted in a way which is unfairly prejudicial to him or some or all of the members. The concept of unfair prejudice under the forerunner of this section has received considerable attention in the abundant case law, and has recently been considered by Lord Hoffmann in his judgment in *O'Neill* v. *Phillips.*[70] His Lordship took the view that a member of a company will not ordinarily be entitled to complain of unfairness unless

[68] *Ebrahimi* v. *Westbourne Galleries Ltd* [1973] AC 360.

[69] Previously, s. 459 of the Companies Act 1985.

[70] *O'Neill* v. *Phillips* [1999] 2 BCLC 1.

there is some breach of the terms on which he agreed that the affairs of the company should be conducted has occurred. These terms were enshrined in the articles of association, and might also be found in collateral agreements between shareholders. Lord Hoffmann added that equitable principles might be invoked by the court for the purpose of determining that these terms were used in a way that could be regarded as a breach of good faith. Lord Hoffmann's judgment has been criticised because it cast doubt on the significance of the concept of legitimate expectations which had previously been invoked in section 459 cases involving small partnership-like companies.

The Law Commission made a number of recommendations for the reform of the remedy based on unfairly prejudicial conduct in its Report on Shareholder Remedies of 1997.[71] It placed emphasis on the need for active case management, and suggested that there should be a presumption of unfair prejudice where a director who held at least 10 per cent of the voting rights was excluded from participation in a private company limited by shares, all or substantially all of whose members were directors. It was doubtful whether the latter presumption can easily be reconciled with *O'Neill* v. *Phillips*, because such dismissal does not necessarily involve a breach of an agreement or of equitable principles.[72] The new provisions of sections 994–996 of the Companies Act 2006 do not depart greatly from those of sections 459–461 of the Companies Act 1985. A new provision is contained in section 996(2)(d) which enables the court to require the company not to make any, or any specified alterations in its articles without the court's leave.

The courts are empowered to make what order they think fit if they uphold a petition under section 996. The commonest type of order which has been made in practice is an order for the purchase of the petitioner's shares. The court have used different methods of valuation, but where a petitioner is excluded from participation in a partnership like company, the courts have generally treated such exclusion as unfairly prejudicial, and have ordered that the respondent must purchase his shares on a pro rata basis. An offer to purchase the petitioner's shares is not necessarily a bar to proceedings under section 994, but it may well be if the offer can be

71 Law Commission, *Shareholder Remedies*. See H. Farrar, *Company Law*, 4th edn (London: Butterworths, 1998), pp. 460–2 for a useful concise account of its proposals.

72 Note in this context, Company Review Steering Groups' Consultative Document *Modern Company Law*, p. 123.

regarded as a reasonable one within the criteria set out by Lord Hoffmann in *O'Neill* v. *Phillips*.[73]

III. The position in France

A. *Managers of an SARL; their powers and duties*

The rules of law governing the management and control of public and private companies differ from one another to a greater extent in France and Germany than they do in the other countries under consideration in the present work. A French SARL is managed by one or more managers (*gérants*), who are placed under the direction and control of the shareholders. The managers must be natural persons, but need not be members of the company or French citizens. The first managers are appointed by the articles (*statuts*), and all subsequent appointments are made by resolutions passed by the members in general meeting.[74] The holders of more than half the capital of the company must vote for such a resolution, but if this majority is not obtained and the articles do not provide otherwise, a second meeting must be called or the members be consulted a second time, when appointment may take place by a simple majority of the votes cast.[75] Unless the articles provide otherwise, the managers are appointed for the period of the company's existence.[76] Managers frequently have service contracts with the company, subject to the consent of the members.

Managers may be removed by a resolution passed by the votes of members holding more than half the company's capital; unless the articles require a larger majority. If a second meeting has to be called, removal may take place by a simple majority of the votes cast unless the articles provide otherwise. The resolution is not required to specify any reason for dismissal, but if this takes place in the absence of just cause (incompetence or mismanagement), the manager may bring an action against the company for damages. Furthermore, a manager may be removed by the court for just cause on the application of any member.[77] It appears that a manager may resign at any time, but the company may claim damages from him if he resigns without just cause, and this has a prejudicial effect on the company.

The managers may act on behalf of the company in all circumstances, but must not do acts which the law reserves to the members, or which are

[73] *O'Neill* v. *Phillips* [1999] 3 BCLC 15. See also A. J. Boyle and J. Birds, *Boyle and Birds' Company Law*, p. 581.

[74] French Commercial Code, Art. L223-18. [75] *Ibid.*, Art. L223-29.

[76] *Ibid.*, Art. L223-18. [77] *Ibid.*, Art. L223-25.

contrary to the company's articles or outside the scope of managing the business which it carries on. The latter two categories of restrictions unlike the first one have an internal effect only. These two types of restriction are not binding on third parties who are unaware that the relevant transaction was outside the scope of the articles, or unrelated to the company's activities and who act in good faith.[78]

Certain statutory restrictions are imposed on the powers of managers of an SARL by Articles L223-19 and L223-21 of the Commercial Code. The latter provision forbids managers and shareholders of an SARL from borrowing from the company or having it guarantee or secure their personal debts. This prohibition also extends to the spouses, issue and ascendants of managers and shareholders. Article L223-19 provides that contracts between an SARL and any of its managers or members must be ratified by a general meeting after considering a report by the managers or the company's auditor, if any. If there is no auditor, contracts concluded between a manager who is not a member of the company require the prior approval of the general meeting. If the company is a single-member company, and the contract is concluded with the sole member, it is only necessary to mention it in the company's register of decisions. If the contract is not ratified, it remains valid, but the relevant manager or member is liable for any losses which occur as the result of the contract being concluded.

B. *Control over the managers of an SARL*

The members' power to dismiss the managers has already been mentioned above. The members in general meeting have to approve the company's accounts, which consist of the managers' reports, inventories of assets, trading accounts, profit and loss accounts and balance sheets no more than six months after the end of the financial year.[79] These documents together with (if relevant) consolidated accounts and a report on the management of the group, have to be placed at the disposal of the statutory auditors (if any) at least one month before the relevant general meeting takes place.[80] The managers are also required to send to every shareholder at

[78] *Ibid.*, Art. L223-18(6). [79] *Ibid.*, Art. L223-26.

[80] Decree No. 67-236 as amended, Art. 44. A company has to appoint at least one statutory auditor if at the end of a financial year at least two of the three following requirements are fulfilled. These are that it has a balance sheet total in excess of €1,550,000, a turnover excluding tax in excess of €3,100,000, and a workforce averaging more than fifty people, Decree No. 67-236 as amended, Art. 12.

least fifteen days before the annual general meeting a copy of the company's trading account, profit and loss account, balance sheet and managers' report (and also any group report) for the preceding financial year, together with the report of the auditor (if any) on the accounts and any group accounts, as well as the text of the resolutions to be proposed at the meeting.[81]

The enforcement of the managers' duties is dealt with in detail by Article L223-22. According to this provision, the managers are individually or jointly liable for damages according to the circumstances, both towards the company, its members and third parties, for infringements of the provisions of law relating to the SARL, or for violation of the articles of their company, or for negligent acts of mismanagement. If the company does not take action against the directors, one or more of the members of the company may bring a derivative action against them. The damages will be paid to the company.

C. Position of the members of an SARL

The members exercise controlling powers in respect of the managers as has already been indicated. They take the major decisions which the company has to take, for example the alteration of the company's articles,[82] or the conversion of the SARL into a company of another type.[83] They have important rights to be kept informed about the company's affairs,[84] and to inspect and copy its principal records and documents at its registered office.[85] Members have the right to be consulted on particular matters either by the holding of general meetings or by means of individual written consultation. As already indicated, a general meeting must be held within six months of the end of the financial year to approve the company's annual accounts and the managers' report.[86] It is also necessary to call a general meeting when requested by shareholders who together hold half of the company capital, or if they represent at least one fourth of its shareholders, by shareholders amounting to at least one-quarter of the company's capital.[87]

[81] Decree No. 67-236, Art. 36(1). [82] French Commercial Code, Art. L223-30.
[83] *Ibid.*, Art. L223-43.
[84] The requirements governing information which must be given to members consisting of the communication of accounts and other documents before the annual meeting have already been considered above.
[85] Decree No. 67-236 as amended, Art. 33. [86] French Commercial Code, Art. L223-26.
[87] *Ibid.*, Art. L223-27.

Apart from decisions approving the annual accounts, the articles may provide that a decision shall be taken by a written consultation of the members. If the articles so provide, it is then up to the managers (who are entrusted with the task of calling general meetings) to choose between calling a general meeting or conducting a written consultation. A written consultation takes the form of a registered letter giving particulars of the proposed resolutions and necessary decisions despatched to each member, in which he is given fifteen days to reply by casting his vote.[88]

Each shareholder has the right to participate in decisions, and has a number of votes at a general meeting equal to the number of shares which he holds.[89] Multiple voting rights may not be given to particular shares, nor may any shares be deprived of voting rights.

Whether a matter has to be decided by an ordinary or an extraordinary resolution depends on the law. Ordinary resolutions take place where the relevant matter does not involve the alteration of company's articles. They are passed on the first poll by the holders of a majority of the company's shares, and unless the articles otherwise provide (e.g. by excluding a second poll) on a second poll by a majority of the votes cast.[90] Extraordinary resolutions involve changes in the company's articles, and must be passed by the votes of members who together hold at least three-quarters of the company's shares.[91] In certain cases, the alteration of the nationality of the company,[92] unanimity is required for the relevant resolution. Act No. 2005-882 of 2 August 2005 contains provisions regarding quorums at meetings for the purpose of making alterations to articles.[93]

D. *Different management structures in an SA*

Two different management structures are open to French public companies. As is the situation in the majority of cases, they may have a single board of directors, but companies may adopt the dual board system either originally, or by a subsequent amendment of their articles.[94] There is a distinction between management and controlling functions under both systems. The management of a single-board company is sometimes carried out by the chairman of the board (*président directeur général*, PDG) and a number of delegated executive officers (*directeurs généraux délégués*). The latter persons may, but do not have to, be

[88] Decree No. 67-236 as amended, Art. 40. [89] French Commercial Code, Art. L223-28.
[90] *Ibid.*, Art. L223-29. [91] *Ibid.*, Art. L223-30(3). [92] *Ibid.*, Art. L223-30(1).
[93] *Ibid.*, Art. L223-30(3). [94] *Ibid.*, Art. L225-57.

directors. The other members of the board (*conseil d'administration*) exercise a controlling function, and have only the theoretical right to manage. Sometimes however, the two offices of chairman of the board and managing director are held by different persons, and the managing director may be assisted by *directeurs généraux délégués*. In the dual board system, (*directeur général*) are held by different persons. In the two-board system, the supervisory board has a controlling function, whilst the executive board is responsible for management. Under both systems, the general meeting retains certain controlling rights: it is thus responsible for the approval of the annual accounts and consolidated accounts and the management report,[95] and for the allocation of the profits.[96]

The distinction between managing and controlling functions is more clearly defined under the two board system than it is under the single board system. However, although the duties and the liabilities of the members of the supervisory board are less burdensome than those of the members of the boards of directors, all such persons are subject to similar rules in particular areas, for example in relation to agreements with the company, and the age limits for holding office. The rules governing the necessary management structures in an SA or an SARL are not applicable to the new simplified share company, which is governed by a flexible regime which may prove useful for many kinds of enterprise.[97]

E. The single board system

Both natural and legal persons may be directors of a public company. Directors and the permanent representatives of legal persons who are approved directors must hold qualification shares in the company. However, a person who is not a shareholder may be elected as a director, but he is deemed to have resigned unless he becomes a shareholder within three months.[98] The first directors are designated in the articles, except in the rare case in which the company is formed as a publicly held one.[99] All other directors are appointed by the general meeting.

The total number of directors of a public company must not be less than three and no more than eighteen.[100] In addition to these directors,

[95] *Ibid.*, Art. L225-100. [96] *Ibid.*, Art. L232-12.
[97] See F. Wooldridge, 'The French SAS business entity' (2000) *Amicus Curiae*, June issue, 44.
[98] French Commercial Code, Art. L225-25.
[99] *Ibid.*, Arts. L225-16 and L225-18. If the company (rather unusually) is formed as a publicly held one, the first directors are appointed by the members thereof.
[100] French Commercial Code, Art. L225-17.

who are appointed in the manner already explained, not more than four employees' representatives may be appointed to the board of directors if the articles so permit. Such appointment will take place by the personnel of the company, and of its French subsidiaries. This membership may be increased to five in companies whose shares are admitted to dealings on a regulated market, but it may in no case exceed one-third of the total number of directors.[101] The articles of the company may authorise the appointment of censors (*censeurs*), who are able to attend board meetings, but cannot vote at them. They have sometimes been held to have the same duties as directors of a public company and to be subject to the same requirements and obligations and under the same civil and criminal liabilities as though they were directors in their own right.[102] Directors who are appointed by the articles cannot hold office for more than three years; if they are appointed by the general meeting, this period is increased to six years. They may, however, be re-elected unless the articles provide otherwise.[103] The number of directors who are more than seventy years old may not exceed one third the number of all the directors holding offices unless the articles provide otherwise. Furthermore, unless the articles stipulate otherwise, when this proportion is not maintained, the older directors are treated as having resigned.[104]

A director's office may terminate by resignation or dismissal. Although this situation may be open to criticism, the courts have decided that by reason of certain principles of the law of agency contained in the Civil Code, dismissals may take place at any time by a resolution of the shareholders' ordinary or extraordinary general meeting. This right cannot be restricted by the articles or otherwise, and damages are only available if the dismissal occurred in prejudicial circumstances. The general meeting may grant the directors a global sum for attendance fees (*jetons de presence*), and they may pay themselves reasonable remuneration for special tasks.[105] An employee of the company can become a director and keep the benefit of his employment contract if the contract relates to effective categories. He or she does not lose the benefit of their contract of employment.[106] A natural person cannot serve on the board of directors of more than five public companies having their

[101] *Ibid.*, Art. L225-27. Not much use has been made of this facility.

[102] *Censeurs* are often persons of considerable distinction and have mostly been used by banks, insurance and investment companies but are not mentioned in the Commercial Code. Their function appears to have been to exercise control over the management.

[103] French Commercial Code, Art. L225-18. [104] *Ibid.*, Art. L225-19.

[105] *Ibid.*, Arts. L225-45 and L225-46. [106] *Ibid.*, Art. L225-22.

registered office in France. Legal persons may hold any number of directors' offices.[107]

According to Article L225-35 of the Commercial Code, the board of directors determines the scope of the activities to be carried on by the company, and supervises their execution, subject to the limitations imposed by a company's objects and the powers which are expressly granted by law to the general meeting (e.g. the approval of accounts); it has the power to deal with all questions concerning the proper running of the company, and deliberates on matters which concern it. However, the board limits itself in practice to defining the policies to be followed by the company. It takes, or assents to strategic decisions, and exercises supervision over the managing director. The business of the company is, as has already been pointed out, conducted by the managing director (who may also be the chairman) and by assistant managing directors, or executive officers. As far as third parties are concerned, limitations on business transactions imposed on the board by the articles or otherwise have no effect (even where such transactions fall outside the ambit of the company's objects), unless it can be proved by the company that the third party knew that the transaction was outside the company's objects, or that such person should have known of this in the circumstances. The board of directors carries out such checks as it deems necessary. Each director must be given all the information necessary to carry out his tasks, and receive all the documents that he deems useful.

The board of directors are granted certain specific powers and duties for example preparing the annual accounts and drawing up an inventory of the company's assets;[108] calling general meetings;[109] and authorising all agreements entered into between the company and its chairman, one of its directors or executive officers, or with a shareholder possessing more than 10 per cent of the voting rights.[110] It is also responsible for appointing and dismissing the chairman of the board and the executive officers and determining their remuneration;[111]and authorising the chairman to give guarantees on behalf of the company.[112]

The chairman (*président du conseil d'administration*) must be a natural person, and is appointed by the board of directors, which fixes his

[107] *Ibid.*, Art. L225-21. However, where the person holds posts as the director of companies whose shares are not admitted to listing on a regulated market and which are controlled in the sense of Art. L233-16 by a company of the same kind, such posts only count as one, with the reservation that such mandates may not exceed five.

[108] *Ibid.*, Art. L232-1. [109] *Ibid.*, Art. L225-103. [110] *Ibid.*, Art. L225-38.

[111] *Ibid.*, Art. L225-47 and Art. L225-53. [112] *Ibid.*, Art. L225-35(4).

remuneration. The period of his appointment must end with his directorship, and he may be reappointed. His appointment may be terminated at any time.[113] The age limit is sixty-five years, unless the articles otherwise stipulate.[114]

According to Article L225-56, the managing director has, subject to certain limitations, the widest powers to act on behalf of the company in all circumstances. The managing director may not encroach on the powers given to the general meeting and the board of directors by law, and is only permitted to exercise his powers within the limits of the company's objects. However, acts of the managing director bind the company in relation to third parties in the same way as acts of the board of directors do.[115]

The maximum number of executive officers or assistant managing directors (*directeurs généraux délegués*) who can be appointed to help the managing director or *directeur général* is five.[116] They are appointed by the board on the proposal of the managing director,[117] and their powers in relation to third parties are the same as those of the managing directors.[118] Their remuneration is determined by the board of directors. The executive officers may be dismissed by the board on the proposal of the managing director. Unless the board determines otherwise, if the managing director resigns or is dismissed from office, or is prevented from exercising his powers, the executive officers retain office until a new managing director is appointed.[119] When a director is an executive officer, the latter office terminates with his directorship.

F. The dual board system

The double board system is only applicable if provided for in the company's articles.[120] The rules applicable to traditional companies are applicable to companies having a dual board system, with the exception of Articles L225-17–L225-56, which has been considered immediately above.[121] The executive board (*directoire*) is collectively responsible for

[113] *Ibid.*, Art. L225-47. Such termination would be by the board. [114] *Ibid.*, Art. L225-48.
[115] *Ibid.*, Art. L225-56(2), cf. Art. L225-35 which applies to the board of directors.
[116] *Ibid.*, Art. L225-53.
[117] *Ibid.*, French Commercial Code Art. L225-53. As indicated above, the managing director may also be the chairman.
[118] *Ibid.*, Art. L225-56.
[119] *Ibid.*, Art. L225-55. This is subject to the proviso that the board does not decide otherwise.
[120] *Ibid.*, Art. L225-57.
[121] These provisions are of course applicable to the single board system.

the management of the company's affairs, and is the equivalent of the managing director of an SA having a single board. The maximum number of members of the executive board is five, which is increased to seven for companies whose shares are admitted to dealings on a regulated market.[122] The number of members is fixed in the articles or if they contain no relevant provision, by the supervisory board. If a company's capital is less than €150,000, the executive board may consist of one person.[123] The chairman is referred to as the *président du directoire* (chairman of the executive board).

The members of the executive board must be natural persons, but need not be members of the company. They may be employees of the company at the time of their appointment, or become such subsequently, but they may not be members of the supervisory board of the same company. Subject to exceptions for groups of companies and unlisted companies it is only permissible natural persons to serve on the executive board of one company.[124]

The members of the executive board are appointed by the supervisory board for a period of between two and six years.[125] They may be removed by the general meeting, or if the articles so provide, by the supervisory board. Should such removal take place without just cause, it will give rise to a claim in damages.[126]

The members of the executive board may act collectively, and bind the company in relation to third parties, in the same way as the board of directors of a traditional company.[127] However, by way of exception, certain transactions require the approval of the supervisory board to be valid, such as the giving of guarantees, the sale of real property, or the creation of mortgages or charges over the company's assets.[128] Furthermore, the articles may provide that the conclusion of certain other transactions requires the prior consent of the supervisory board.[129]

Restrictions imposed on the powers of the chairman of the executive board or on the sole executive director[130] cannot be invoked by the company against third parties.[131] The articles may empower the supervisory board to confer the same power of representation enjoyed by the latter persons

122 French Commercial Code, Art. L225-58. 123 *Ibid.*, Art. L225-58.
124 *Ibid.*, Art. L225-67.
125 *Ibid.*, Art. L225-62. If the articles fail to mention the period of the appointment, it is treated as being four years.
126 *Ibid.*, Art. L225-61. 127 *Ibid.*, Art. L225-64. 128 *Ibid.*, Art. L225-68.
129 *Ibid.*, Art. L225-68. 130 *Directeur général unique.*
131 French Commercial Code, Art. L225-66.

with respect to third parties on one or more members of the executive board, who are then called executive officers (*directeurs généraux*), although there are differences between their position, and that of similar officers of a traditionally managed company.[132]

The executive board has to submit a quarterly report on its management to the supervisory board. It must also prepare the company's annual accounts and report for submission to the annual general meeting.[133]

The principal function of the supervisory board is to exercise control over the executive board. It has a minimum of three and a maximum of eighteen members.[134] Provided that the articles so stipulate, representatives of the company's employees may be elected to the supervisory board, and they do not count towards this maximum and minimum.[135] The first members of the supervisory board are designated in the articles, when the company is formed as a non-publicly held company (which is usually the case) and hold office for three years. Subsequent members of the supervisory board, who are appointed by the general meeting (from among the shareholders) or the existing employees (from among their number) hold office for a period stipulated in the articles, which may not exceed six years.[136] As is the case with the directors of a traditional company, the members of the supervisory board may be dismissed at any time by the general meeting. A natural person cannot (subject to certain exceptions) belong at the same time to more than five supervisory boards of companies having their registered office in France.[137]

The board elects a chairman and vice-chairman from among its members,[138] who have the task of calling and presiding over board meetings. Resolutions may only be passed if half the members are present.[139] The supervisory board is permitted by Article L225-68(3) to carry out such inspections and inquires into the management of the

[132] *Ibid.*, Art. L225-66. [133] *Ibid.*, Art. L225-68 and Art. L225-100.

[134] *Ibid.*, Art. L225-69. Legal as well as natural persons may be members of the supervisory board, and must appoint a person to be a permanent representative at board meetings.

[135] *Ibid.*, Art. L225-79(3). The number of such directors may not exceed four nor one-third of the other directors in office: see Art. L225-79(2).

[136] *Ibid.*, Arts. L225-75 and L225-79.

[137] *Ibid.*, Art. L225-77. An exception is made for membership of the supervisory board of a company which is controlled by the company of which the relevant person is a member of the supervisory board.

[138] *Ibid.*, Art. L225-81.

[139] *Ibid.*, Art. L225-82. However, the internal rules of the company may provide that persons who participate by means of audio-visual links or other forms of telecommunication shall count for the purpose of determining quorums and majorities.

company as it thinks appropriate, and it may require access to any document which it thinks necessary. It also is responsible for the appointment of the members of the executive board and their chairman, and plays an important role in their dismissal. The supervisory board is also required to provide the annual general meeting with comments on the report of the executive board and the company's accounts.[140]

G. *Directors' liability*

Directors, managing directors, and the executive officers (*directeurs généraux*) of public companies adopting the traditional single board system as well as members of the executive supervisory boards of such companies employing the double board system are subject to a number of statutory controls which have features in common. The purpose of the strict rules governing agreements between such persons and their company is to avoid a conflict between the personal interests of the persons concerned and their duty to the company. According to Articles L225-43 and L225-91, the making of loans and the giving of guarantees by companies to their managing director, directors and executive officers (*directeurs généraux délégués*), or to members of their executive and supervisory boards, where the alternative double board system is employed, is prohibited and void. This rule also applies to the personal representatives of legal persons who are members of the board of directors or the supervisory board, and to the spouses and close relatives of directors or executive officers or members of the executive and supervisory boards. The relevant prohibition does not apply to current transactions entered into on the usual terms where the company is a bank or finance house, nor is it applicable where the director is a legal person, as may be the case in a group of companies.

The provisions of Articles L225-38 and L225-86 are concerned with agreements between a company and its managing director, one of its directors, or executive officers, and agreements between a company and a person holding more than ten per cent of the voting rights; and where the dual board system is employed, between a company and a member of its executive or supervisory board, or between the company and a shareholder possessing more than 10 per cent of the voting rights. These two provisions are in similar terms. They are applicable where there

[140] *Ibid.*, Art. L225-68(6). However, the supervisory board is not entrusted with the approval of the accounts as is generally the case under the Italian dualistic system.

is an agreement entered into directly or indirectly between the company and one of the persons already mentioned; or between the company and another undertaking which is owned by a director, an executive officer, or member of one of the two boards, or in which such a person; is a general partner, manager, director, executive officer, or a member of the supervisory board.

In the case where the company has a traditional structure, and the agreement is with the managing director, one of the directors or, executive officers, or the holder of shares carrying more than ten per cent of the voting rights, it must receive the prior approval of the board of directors before execution. If it is directly between a member of the supervisory or executive board, and the company, or between a person possessing more than 10 per cent of the voting rights and the company, it must be approved by the general meeting before execution. The same rule applies where such persons are indirectly interested in a contract with the company and also where there is a contract between it and another undertaking in which they have one of the positions mentioned in the above paragraph. Furthermore, agreements which have been so authorised must be notified to the auditor, reported on by him and considered and approved by the general meeting.[141] The interested party cannot vote on the agreement either at the meeting of the board of directors or the supervisory board.[142] If the agreement is not approved by the general meeting, the company may claim damages from the relevant parties (which may include other directors etc) for any loss suffered, even in the absence of fraud. However, the agreement will remain binding on third parties, unless it is annulled for fraud.[143] The rules relating to approval are inapplicable to current transactions entered into under normal conditions. However, such transactions must be disclosed to the president of the board of directors or of the supervisory board, who must provide a list of such transactions to the other directors and the auditors, unless they are insignificant for any of the parties by reason of their objects or financial implications.

The managing director and the executive officers in traditionally managed public companies and the members of the executive board and supervisory boards of companies adopting the dual board system are also required to comply with a number of other more general rules. They must take account of the limitations on their powers provided for

[141] *Ibid.*, Arts. L225-40 and L225-88. [142] *Ibid.*, Arts. L225-40(4) and L225-88(4).
[143] *Ibid.*, Arts. L225-41(1) and L225-89(1).

by law, in the articles or otherwise and abstain from acting outside the corporate purpose, as well as from taking any action which is not within the best interests of the company. An action for damages may be brought against directors if specific fault or negligence can be proved against them. Many types of self interested or dishonest behaviour by directors are classified as criminal offences.

Minority shareholders may bring a derivative action against the directors (*administrateurs*), the managing director or the members of the executive and supervisory boards in the company's name if the company does not wish to bring such an action.[144] The articles may not subordinate the bringing of such an action to the preliminary consultation or the consent of the general meeting.[145] A common representative may bring such an action in the minority shareholders name, if such shareholders represent at least 5 per cent of the capital.[146] If the personal rights of members have been infringed, they may also bring an action on this account.

H. The position of the shareholders

The shareholders in general meeting are treated as being the supreme body of the company. However, a shareholders' meeting may not usurp the powers belonging to the chairman or executive board. The law of 1966 attempted to increase the involvement of shareholders, and improve the provision of information to them. However, the results of this legislation, which has been incorporated in the Commercial Code, have been somewhat unsatisfactory, partly owing to the apathy of shareholders. The general meeting must assent to certain transactions, for example the conversion of the company into an undertaking of a different type, or a reduction of capital. The general meeting has the power to appoint and dismiss directors as well as members of the executive and supervisory boards of companies having dual boards. It is also responsible for the approval of the accounts[147] and the apportionment of profits.[148]

Meetings may be ordinary or extraordinary ones. The annual general meeting falls within the former category, as does a meeting called to pass an ordinary resolution. Ordinary meetings may only be held if the

[144] *Ibid.*, Art. L225-252. [145] *Ibid.*, Art. L225-253.

[146] Decree No. 67-236 as amended, Arts. 200 and 201. This amount is reduced proportionally when the capital exceeds €750,000.

[147] French Commercial Code, Art. L225-100. [148] *Ibid.*, Art. L232-12.

shareholders present or represented hold at least one-fifth of the shares issued by the company which carry voting rights. Should the latter quorum requirement not be satisfied, the meeting must be called again, when no quorum is required. Resolutions are passed at ordinary meetings by a simple majority of the votes[149] held by the shareholders present or represented. Extraordinary meetings are necessary for the purpose of altering the company's articles. The extraordinary general meeting may not increase the financial obligations of shareholders. At least one-quarter of the shares carrying voting rights must be represented at the meeting by their holders or their proxies when it is first called. If such a quorum is unavailable the meeting has to be called a second time, when the quorum is reduced to one-fifth of the shares carrying voting rights. If there is no such quorum then, the meeting can be adjourned for a date no later than two months hence. Resolutions are passed at a general meeting by a two thirds majority of the votes held by shareholders present or represented at the meeting.[150]

A general meeting is convoked either by the board of directors or the executive board. In default of such convocation, it may also be called by the supervisory board (if any) or the auditors, or an agent appointed by the court at the request of the holders of 10 per cent of the share capital, or the liquidators.[151] The holders of a minimum of 5 per cent of the share capital, which is reduced in the case of large companies in which there are shareholders' associations, may require resolutions proposed by them to be placed on the agenda of any meeting.[152]

In principle, shares carry one vote, but there are some exceptions to this general rule. Thus, double voting rights may be conferred on fully paid shares which have been in registered form for at least two years in the name of the same shareholder.[153] If the shares are converted into bearer form, they no longer enjoy this double voting right.[154]

Shareholders are required to employ their voting rights in the interests of all the members of the company, and not in order to promote their own personal interests. Resolutions of the general meeting or of the board of directors which violate this principle may be annulled, whether they are detrimental to the interests of the minority or the majority shareholders. Detriment to the minority may be established where there

[149] *Ibid.*, Art. L225-98. A higher quorum may be provided for the case of unlisted companies.

[150] *Ibid.*, Art. L225-96. [151] *Ibid.*, Art. L225-103. [152] *Ibid.*, Art. L225-105.

[153] *Ibid.*, Art. L225-123. [154] *Ibid.*, Art. L225-124.

are decisions refusing to distribute profits over a period of years, and the profits retained are not reinvested.

Minority shareholders have been held to have acted abusively when they have failed to vote for necessary amendments to the company's articles.

Shareholders acting either individually or collectively may exercise particular rights. Individual shareholders have an extensive right to obtain access to certain documents.[155] Shareholders holding individually or collectively 5 per cent or more of the company's capital and shareholders' associations also have a number of rights, for example to submit questions to the chairman of the board of directors or of the executive board about one or more management transactions.[156] Copies of the answers to these questions must be sent to the company's auditors. If there is no reply within one month, or if the question receives an unsatisfactory answer, the shareholder can ask the court dealing with urgent matters to appoint experts to report on one or more such transactions. Furthermore, the Public Prosecutor, the works committee and, in companies which offer their shares to the public, the Financial Markets Authority (*L'Autorité des marches financières*, AMF) are empowered to act in the same way.[157]

IV. The position in Germany

A. The management and control of a GmbH

The powers of management in a German private company are divided between the manager(s) and the general meeting, in accordance with the provisions of the *GmbH Gesetz*, as amended, and the articles of the company. When a private company has few members, who are also managers, the shareholders may be able to take decisions falling within the powers of the managers and the general meeting whenever they meet. The controlling functions of the general meeting may, to a considerable extent, be exercised by the supervisory board, which may be provided for in the company's articles. Such a board has to be set up in accordance

[155] *Ibid.*, Arts. L225-115–L225-118.

[156] *Ibid.*, Art. L225-231(1). In companies whose shares are admitted to dealings on a regulated market, shareholders whose shares have been in a registered form for at least two years and which have at least 5 per cent of the voting rights may form associations which represent their interests, and which may also submit such questions: see also Art. L225-120.

[157] *Ibid.*, Art. L225-231(2). Previously, these powers lay with the Stock Exchange Commission (*Commission des opérations de bourse*, COB).

with the *Drittelbeteiligungsgesetz* (One-Third Participation Act) of 2004[158] when the company employs more than 500 workers. The employees of companies integrated with a controlling company (which may be a GmbH) or which are subject of a control contract with that company, are added to those of the controlling company for the purpose of determining the relevant number of employees, according to paragraph 2(1) of article 1 of the 2004 Act.[159] Coal, iron and steel companies which employ more than 1,000 workers, as well as certain coal, iron and steel holding companies, also have to establish a supervisory board, in accordance respectively with the Coal, Iron and Steel Codetermination Act (*Montan-Mitbestimmungsgesetz, Montan-MitBestG*) 1956. Furthermore, companies employing more than 2,000 workers have to set up a supervisory board in accordance with the Codetermination Act (*Mitbestimmungsgesetz, MitBestG*) of 1976. The two-tier system of management has received considerable criticism in Germany in recent years; supervisory boards have been said to be insufficiently independent, and the members thereof have not always been found to observe the requirements of confidentiality.[160] The problems may be especially acute in relation to the large supervisory board of big public companies[161] which have to comply with the Codetermination Act 1976.

The requirements set out above concerning the establishment of a supervisory board apply both to public and private companies, but there are certain differences in the composition and powers of the respective supervisory boards under the four principal Codetermination Acts mentioned above. Under the *Drittelbeteiligungsgesetz* of 2004, one third of the board must consist of representatives of employees:[162] the remaining two-thirds are representatives of the shareholders. Under the Coal, Iron

[158] *Drittelbeteiligungsgesetz* or DrittelbG, BGBl. 2004 p. 974. The DrittelbG replaced the Works Council Act (*Betriebsverfassungsgesetz*, BetrVG) of 1952. The issues discussed here were provided for in paragraph 77 BetrVG.

[159] The Act is also applicable to public companies registered before 1 August 1994 which employ less than 500 workers unless they are family companies. However, paragraph 1 of the Act excludes companies which in a direct and preponderant sense have political, confessional, educational, scientific or artistic objectives or which have the purpose of reporting.

[160] See K. J. Hopt, *'The German Two-Tier Board: Experience, Theories, Reforms'*, in K. J. Hopt *et al.* (eds), *Comparative Corporate Governance – The State of the Art and Emerging Research* (Oxford: Clarendon Press, 1998), p. 227.

[161] The new German Corporate Governance Code of 2002, which is applicable to listed companies, and is of a voluntary character, contains a number of recommendations concerning the supervisory boards of such companies.

[162] Previously, the BetrVG 1952, para. 76(1).

and Steel Codetermination Acts, the board consists of an equal number of shareholder and employees' representatives, together with a 'neutral' number who are elected by a special procedure.

Supervisory boards established in accordance with the Codetermination Act 1976 have an equal number of representatives of employees and shareholders, but the chairman, who is always a representative of the shareholders, has a casting vote.[163] The employees' representatives consist of representatives of trade unions as well as employees of the company.[164] Under this Act, and under the Coal, Iron and Steel Codetermination Acts, the supervisory board is responsible for the appointment and dismissal of the managers or directors.[165] The latter two Acts have very little significance for private, as opposed to public, companies.[166]

Private companies which are not required to set up a supervisory board under one of the codetermination acts may set up one voluntarily, the composition and functions of which may be stipulated in the articles: where these are silent, the relevant matters are governed by paragraph 52 (1) of the *GmbH Gesetz*, which refers to parallel articles of the German *Aktiengesetz*.

1. Managers

Managers may be appointed in the articles of a private company, or by a subsequent resolution of the company.[167] A shareholder may vote on such a resolution, even if he is nominated for appointment. As already indicated, the compulsory supervisory board appoints the managers of companies having more than 2,000 employees and of companies in the coal, iron and steel industries. Such companies must have one labour director, who is responsible for work and social matters. The number of such companies has declined in recent years and few, if any of them, are private companies.

Every natural person with the legal capacity to enter inter into contracts may be appointed as a manager.[168] However, persons who are not permitted to dispose of property without the consent of a guardian cannot be

[163] MitBestG 1976, paras. 7(1) and 29(2). [164] MitBestG 1976, 7(2).

[165] MontanMitBestG 1956, para. 12; MitBestG 1976, para. 31.

[166] The most important Codetermination Act for such companies seems to be the *Drittelbeteiligungsgesetz* (One-Third Participation Act) of 2004 (here replacing the Works Councils Act 1952), the relevant provisions governing such companies are contained in Art. 1, paras. 1–15.

[167] German Private Limited Liability Companies Act, paras. 6(3) and 46(5).

[168] German Public Limited Liability Companies Act para. 76(3). The position is basically the same as in a private company: see German Private Limited Liability Companies Act, para. 6(2).

appointed manager of a private company. The same is applicable to persons who have been convicted of an offence relating to insolvency under paragraphs 283–283d of the Penal Code, who may not become managers for five years after the date of the final conviction. Furthermore, the same is true for the duration of the prohibition of persons who have been prohibited from carrying out any profession or trade, by a court judgment or a decision of administrative authority where the relevant company's purpose consists wholly or partly of the prohibited activity.[169] It is likely that additional grounds for exclusion from office will be enacted in new legislation.

Managers may be dismissed at any time without prejudice to claims arising from the employment contract.[170] The articles may however limit this power of dismissal to situations when there is good cause for such dismissal, such as gross breaches of the managers' duties or inability to carry out their duties.[171] A manager of a private company can only be dismissed for good cause if he is appointed for life, by the articles, or whilst he remains a shareholder, or for the duration of the company's existence.[172] Dismissal for good cause will not affect any service contract that the manager may have; thus, in some circumstances, such dismissal may prove to be a costly affair.

In principle the organ which appoints the managers may dismiss them.[173] If a company is subject to codermination under the Coal and Steel Codetermination Act 1951, the Supplementary Coal and Steel Codetermination Act 1956, or the Codetermination Act 1976, only the supervisory board may dismiss the managers, and such dismissal must be for good cause. [174] In the absence of special provisions in the articles or a codetermination law, a manager of a private company may be dismissed from office by a resolution of the shareholders in general meeting passed by a simple majority vote.[175] It is possible for the articles to require a qualified majority for such dismissal.

[169] For more details, K. Schmidt, *Gesellschaftsrecht* (Cologne: Heymanns, 2002), § 28 II 2b.

[170] German Private Limited Liability Companies Act, para. 38(1). For more details, Schmidt, *Gesellschaftsrecht*, § 14 III 2b.

[171] German Private Limited Liability Companies Act, para. 38(2).

[172] In certain such situations, the manager might be treated as having a special right to manage the company, in which case he could also only be dismissed for good cause. See also T. Raiser, *Recht der Kapitalgesellschaften* (Munich: Vahlen, 2001), § 32, paras. 54, 59.

[173] Schmidt, *Gesellschaftsrecht*, § 14 III 2b; BGH, [1995] NJW 1359; [2000] NJW 2983.

[174] Raiser, *Recht der Kapitalgesellschaften*, § 32, para. 56 referring to German Public Limited Liability Companies Act, para. 84(3) 1, 2.

[175] German Private Limited Liability Companies Act, paras. 38(2), 46 No. 5, 47(1) and for more details, Raiser, *Recht der Kapitalgesellschaften*, § 32, para. 60.

According to the dispositive provisions of paragraph 35(2) GmbHG, the managers are collectively entrusted with the management of the company and its representation in transactions with third parties. The articles often provide that each manager, or two or more managers acting together, or a manager acting together with a duly authorised officer called a *Prokurist*, may enter into binding transactions on behalf of the company. The managers may not represent the company in transactions with themselves, but the articles may free them from this prohibition.[176] The sole manager of a one-man private company is subject to the same rules.[177] The exact extent of the powers of the managers is a matter for the articles, but limitations contained in them are not binding on third parties unless the third party knew or had reason to believe that the director was acting outside his authority.[178] However, as far as the company is concerned, the managers are bound to abide by restrictions imposed on them by the articles or by resolutions of the general meeting.[179] If they do not respect such restrictions, they are liable to the company in damages, and also to be instantly dismissed.

The principal duty of the managers is to manage the company with the degree of care and skill of a conscientious businessman.[180] Certain duties of the managers may be stipulated in the articles, the service agreements, or in resolutions of the general meeting. The managers are jointly and severally liable to the company in damages for any violation of the former duties, and in particular for making payments out of the assets required to preserve the company's capital, and for acquiring the company's shares where these have not been fully paid.[181] A company may not grant loans to managers, authorised signatories (*Prokuristen*) or managing agents (*Handlungsbevollmächtigten*), out of the assets of the company required to maintain its share capital, as stated in the articles.[182] A resolution may be passed formally releasing a manager from liability to the company, or waiving a company claim against him, but he may not vote on the resolution.[183] It has been held that a manager has no actionable claim that the company should pass a resolution formally releasing him from liability towards the company.[184]

176 German Commercial Code, para. 181.

177 German Private Limited Liability Companies Act, para. 35(4). For more details, Schmidt, *Gesellschaftsrecht*, § 40 III 2b.

178 German Private Limited Liability Companies Act, para. 37(2).

179 *Ibid.*, para. 37(1); Raiser, *Recht der Kapitalgesellschaften*, § 32 para. 82.

180 German Private Limited Liability Companies Act, para. 43(1).

181 *Ibid.*, para. 43(2) and (3). 182 *Ibid.*, para. 43a.

183 *Ibid.*, para. 47(4). 184 BGHZ 94, 324.

Apart from those mentioned above, other specific duties are placed upon managers, the violations of which may lead to criminal sanctions. If a private company becomes insolvent and the mangers fail to file a bankruptcy petition or one for the institution of judicial composition proceedings without undue delay, and at the latest within three weeks of the date on which the insolvency occurred, they may be liable to a fine or imprisonment of up to three years.[185] However, no culpable delay will be deemed to have occurred if the managers pursue the institution of judicial composition proceedings with the diligence of competent businessmen.[186] Furthermore managers who disclose trade or business secrets which become known to them as members of the management board are liable to criminal sanctions.[187]

Managers may incur personal liability under certain circumstances, for example where they act on behalf of their company, but fail to mention or indicate that it is a GmbH.[188] Furthermore, the managers will also incur liability if they wrongfully infringe a statutory provision intended for the protection of others. (*Schutzgesetz*).[189] If managers neglect to file a bankruptcy petition or one for the institution of judicial composition proceedings within the appropriate time period, (and do not exercise proper care in relation to the opening of such judicial composition proceedings)[190] they may incur liability to creditors whose claims came into being before the date when insolvency proceedings should have been instituted, for the depletion in assets caused by their failure to institute such proceedings at the appropriate time.[191] They are also liable to creditors whose claims come into being after that time, but before the actual opening of insolvency proceedings, for the damages arising from transactions which took place when insolvency proceedings should have been instituted.[192] These liabilities arise because paragraph 64 has been treated as a provision designed for the protection of creditors, and is intended to prevent insolvent companies from engaging in commercial transactions.[193]

185 German Private Limited Liability Companies Act, para. 84.
186 See Raiser, *Recht der Kapitalgesellschaften*, § 32, para. 90.
187 German Private Liability Limited Liability Companies Act, para. 85
188 BGHZ 64, 11. For more details, Schmidt, *Gesellschaftsrecht*, § 36 II 5a.
189 Schmidt, *Gesellschaftsrecht*, § 36 II 5b.
190 German Private Limited Liability Companies Act, para. 64.
191 *Ibid.*, para. 64(2).
192 [1994] ZIP 1103. According to the more recent jurisprudence, these new creditors can make a claim for the full sum, not only for the quota claim (BGHZ 126, 181, [1995] NJW 398). The *Quotenschaden* or quota damages claim is a claim to a dividend in insolvency.
193 K. Schmidt, *Gesellschaftsrecht*, § 36 II 5b.

If a third party enters into contractual negotiations with a private company and it is apparent because of the trust that the third party had in one or more of the managers, the latter should have informed him that the company was heavily indebted, the manager or managers may incur liability in damages to the third party if the contract is concluded, and the company is unable to carry out its obligations. Such liability is said to arise out of *culpa in contrahendo* (fault in contracting). Much will depend on the particular circumstances of the case: a duty to warn a third party of a company's parlous condition may be more readily implied if the three-week period from the time when insolvency (*Zahlungunfähigkeit*) or excessive indebtedness occurred (when assets were insufficient to cover liabilities), had already begun.[194] The view has been taken that liability on the ground of fault in contracting may be more readily implied when the manager(s) has a strong economic interest in the outcome of the transaction, which goes beyond that of his company. Liability for fault in contracting is not confined to situations where a company is insolvent or on the brink of insolvency. There have been a number of rather inconsistent Supreme Court decisions concerning the basis of such liability: sometimes emphasis has been placed on the reliance on the part of the third party on the conduct of the manager rather than on the manager's economic interest in the transaction.[195]

Managers have been held personally liable in tort, even where such tort has not resulted in any depletion of the assets of the company. They may also incur very significant liabilities to third parties as the result of recent developments in the law relating to product liability and the environment.[196] Furthermore, managers may incur personal liabilities if they fail to make tax returns, or make them on time.[197]

2. Supervisory board

If a supervisory board is set up by a GmbH on a voluntary basis, the articles cannot provide that it shall not exercise its basic function of

[194] See German Public Limited Liability Companies Act, para. 64(1) for this period.

[195] See the decisions in Lutter and Hommelhof, *GmbH Gesetz*, 15th edn (Cologne: Dr Otto Schmidt, 1995) pp. 800–802. The authors emphasise the existence of reliance by the third party but also mention that the manager's economic interest in the result of the transaction may be conducive to such reliance only in a limited number of exceptional cases.

[196] See *Official Journal of the German Supreme Court in Criminal Proceedings* (BGHSt) 37, 106 *Erdal* (1990).

[197] AO (*Abgabenordnung*, General Tax Code), para. 69.

supervising the managers. The statutory requirement contained in paragraph 42a(1) sentence 3 of the GmbHG that if a company is required to have auditors, their report must be laid before the supervisory board, is also applicable in cases where such a board has been set up voluntarily. Such a board may be granted powers in addition to its supervisory functions, for example, the approval of the board may be necessary before the company enters into certain transactions.[198] Managerial functions may not, however, be transferred to the supervisory board.[199]

When a GmbH is required to establish a supervisory board by one of the codetermination laws, the board's functions are prescribed by law and are not subject to alteration by the articles[200] The powers and duties of a supervisory board of a GmbH set up in accordance with one of the principal codetermination laws correspond largely with those of the supervisory board of an AG. Such a supervisory board supervises the managers and may require a report from them at any time on any matter.[201] It may enquire into the conduct of the managers and call general meetings.[202] Furthermore, it is also entitled to inspect and examine the books, records and assets of the company, and to commission the auditor to audit the annual financial statements.[203] The articles or the supervisory board may require the consent of the supervisory board for any types of transaction entered into by the managers.[204] If such consent is refused, the managers may refer the matter to a general meeting, which may give its consent by a resolution passed by at least three-quarters of the votes cast.[205] A supervisory board set up in accordance with the codetermination laws mentioned below represents the company in transactions with its managers and in actions against them.[206] Members of such a board must preserve silence about company secrets which become known to them, and exercise the standard of care

[198] German Private Limited Liability Companies Act. para. 52(1) refers to the German Public Companies Act, para. 111(4) sentence 2.

[199] German Private Limited Liability Companies Act, para. 52(1) refers to the German Public Companies Act, para. 111(4) sentence 1.

[200] See MontanMitBestG 1951, para. 3(2); *Drittelbeteiligungsgesetz* 2004, para. 1 and MitBestG 1976, para. 25(1) sentences 2 and 3; very few GmbH carry on business in the coal, iron or steel industries. The relevant provisions make reference to certain (or all) of those of the *Aktiengesetz* concerning the supervisory board.

[201] German Public Limited Liability Companies Act, para. 90(3) and (4).

[202] *Ibid.*, para. 111(1) and (3). [203] *Ibid.*, para. 111(2).

[204] *Ibid.*, para. 111(4) sentence 2. [205] *Ibid.*, para. 111(4). [206] *Ibid.*, para. 112.

of a conscientious and prudent businessman.[207] The burden of proving that they have exercised the necessary care is on them.[208]

The articles of a GmbH sometimes provide that it shall have an advisory board (*Beirat*) as distinct from a supervisory board. The tasks of such a board will be stipulated in the articles, and may involve participation in certain decisions and perhaps the exercise of arbitral functions.[209] Such a board may sometimes exercise many of the competences of the managers and the general meeting.[210]

3. The general meeting

The shareholders take decisions by passing resolutions in a general meeting, or by means of written resolutions which may require unanimity. It is generally thought that the general meeting is the supreme organ of the company which has competence in all company matters, except where the law (including the GmbH) or the articles otherwise provide.[211] It has the power of giving instructions to the manager or managers.[212] However, as the real status as the superior organ may be less clear in companies which have to establish a supervisory board under the Codetermination Act 1976 or the *Drittelbeteiligungsgesetz* of 2004, and where this supervisory board has the power of appointing and dismissing the manager or managers. Unless the articles provide otherwise, the shareholders are competent to decide all the eight matters listed in paragraph 46 of the GmbHG.[213] These are the approval of the annual accounts and the application of the profits, the calling up of contributions on shares, the repayment of additional contributions, the division and cancellation of shares, the appointment, dismissal and release from liability of managers, the appointment of *Prokuristen* and *Handlungsbevollmächtigten* (these are special agents authorised to represent the company having a wide authority deriving from the Commercial Code) and the assertion of claims for damages against the managers or the members.

[207] *Ibid.*, para. 116 sentence 1 refers to German Public Limited Liability Companies Act, para. 93(1).

[208] *Ibid.*, paras. 93 and 116. [209] Raiser, *Recht der Kapitalgesellschaften*, § 34, para. 3.

[210] Luther and Hummelhof, *GmbH Gesetz*, 811 ff.

[211] German Private Limited Liability Companies Act, paras. 45 (1), 48.

[212] For Schmidt, *Gesellschaftsrecht*, § 36 I 2a this is one of the main reasons for the popularity of a GmbH as a subsidiary company.

[213] German Private Limited Liability Companies Act, para. 45(2).

The articles may extend the powers of the members in general meeting.[214] On the other hand, they may delegate many of the powers of the shareholders as a group to the supervisory board, the managers or the *Beirat*, a shareholders committee or individual shareholders. However, no such delegation may take the place of the shareholders' power to alter the articles (and thus to increase or reduce the company's capital),[215] to call for additional contributions in accordance with the articles,[216] to pass a resolution for the dissolution of the company,[217] or for the appointment and dismissal of liquidators.[218]

Resolutions of the shareholders normally take place in a meeting.[219] However a vote in writing may take place if all the shareholders agree with the proposed resolution, or if all of them agree to a written consultation prior to the casting of the votes, which need not then be unanimous.[220] Apart from certain special resolutions, resolutions are passed by a simple majority of the votes cast.[221] Unless the articles provide otherwise, each share carries one vote for €50 of its nominal value.[222] By paragraph 47(4) of the GmbHG, a shareholder may not vote on a resolution dealing with his formal release from liabilities to the company, or a waiver by the company of claims against him, or the approval of a business transaction entered into by the company with him, or the institution or settlement of an action against him. Many legal authors, supported by court decisions, take the view that shareholders are prohibited from voting in other cases where a conflict of interest arises.[223] However, voting agreements between shareholders and (within certain limitations) between shareholders and non-shareholders are permitted, and will be enforced by the courts.[224]

It is not necessary to take minutes of resolutions of general meetings.[225] However, in the case of a one-man company, the shareholder must prepare and sign a record without delay after the passing of the

[214] *Ibid.*, para. 45(1). [215] *Ibid.*, para. 53(1). [216] *Ibid.*, para. 27.
[217] *Ibid.*, para. 60(1) No. 2. [218] *Ibid.*, para. 66. [219] *Ibid.*, para. 48(1).
[220] *Ibid.*, para. 48(2). [221] *Ibid.*, para. 47(1).
[222] *Ibid.*, para. 47(2). The latter provision is likely to be altered so as to provide that every euro of the nominal value carries one vote.
[223] Schmidt, *Gesellschaftsrecht*, § 21 II 4a referring to further decisions and documents.
[224] See Schmidt, *Gesellschaftsrecht*, § 21 II 1e.
[225] However, a notarial record is sometimes necessary: note, e.g. German Private Limited Liability Companies Act, paras. 53(2) and 55(1) (alteration of articles and increase of capital).

relevant resolution.[226] Resolutions of a general meeting may be avoided or declared a nullity for similar reasons as those which apply to resolutions of an AG. A resolution passed by the general meeting of a GmbH may, for example, be annulled where the meeting has not been properly convoked, or where the content of the resolution violates some compulsory provision of the GmbH G or some other statute. A resolution may be avoided, as opposed to being declared a nullity, because of some breach of the law or the articles, which is of a less serious character.[227]

B. *The management and control of an AG*

1. Dual board system

The double board system has long been an essential feature of German law relating to the public company. The management board is entrusted with the task of managing the company, whilst the supervisory board has a controlling function. The general meeting plays a less significant role than is the case in the GmbH, but it still has important functions. As already indicated, employee participation is compulsory in many German public and private companies.[228] It is not however required in the case of small AG employing less than 500 employees.[229] The dual board system has been subjected to some criticism in recent years. [230]

2. The management board

The above board is entrusted with responsibility for managing the company.[231] Its members are appointed by the supervisory board for renewable periods not exceeding five years.[232] The board can consist of one or more persons.[233] But, if the articles do not provide otherwise, companies whose share capital exceeds €3 million must have at least two persons on the management board.[234] Members of the management

226 *Ibid.*, para. 48(3). 227 See Schmidt, *Gesellschaftsrecht*, § 36 III 4a.

228 German Public Limited Liability Companies Act, para. 96(1); MitBestG 1976 para. 1(1) al 1 Montan-MitBestG 1951, para. 4(1), BetrVG 1952, para. 76(1).

229 A liberalisation was introduced by the Law of 10 August 1994, BGBl 1994 1, 1961. However, public companies formed before that date may be subject to the codetermination regime unless they are family companies which have only one member who is a natural person or whose members are related by consanguinity or marriage.

230 See K. J. Hopt, 'The German Two-Tier Board: Experience, Theories, Reforms', in K. J. Hopt *et al.* (eds), *Comparative Corporate Governance – The State of the Art and Emerging Research* (Oxford: Clarendon Press, 1998) for details.

231 German Public Limited Liability Companies Act, para. 76(1). 232 *Ibid.*, para. 84(1).

233 *Ibid.*, para. 76(2) sentence 1. 234 *Ibid.*, para. 76(2) sentence 2.

board (directors) must be natural persons of full legal capacity, who have not been convicted of an offence relating to insolvency; and not prohibited from practising a trade or profession or branch thereof by court judgment, or a decision of an administrative authority, where the company's purpose consists wholly or partly of the prohibited activity.[235] In principle a member of the supervisory board may not be a member of the management board.[236] However, the supervisory board may fill vacancies on the management board with its own members for up to one year, during which time they may not serve on the supervisory board.[237]

Appointments to the management board may only be revoked for good cause during the term of such appointment.[238] 'Good cause' in paragraph 84(3) sentence 2 AktG includes gross breaches of duties, inability to manage the company, or a vote of no confidence by the general meeting, unless the vote took place for clearly unsatisfactory reasons. A person who is dismissed may obtain damages from the court if the dismissal is a breach of his employment contract.[239] According to paragraph 85 AktG, the court may fill vacancies in the management board in urgent cases.

Except where the articles provide otherwise, all the members of the management board have a joint power of managing and representing the company.[240] It is frequently the case that the articles provide that any two members, or any member of the management board together with a duly authorised officer called a *Prokurist*, may represent the company.[241] Unless this power is reserved for the supervisory board, the management board may make by-laws providing for committees and prescribing what matters require the consent of the management board.[242] The articles or the by-laws for the management board may not provide that a member or members of the management board may overrule a majority.[243] However, the chairman is frequently given a casting vote.[244] Business letters must

[235] *Ibid.*, para. 76(3). The scope of the disqualification from membership is likely to be increased when new legislation, reforming GmbH law and combating improper conduct (*Missbrauch*), comes into force.

[236] *Ibid.*, para. 105(1). [237] *Ibid.*, para. 105(2). [238] *Ibid.*, para. 84(3) sentence 1.

[239] Clarified by German Public Companies Act, para. 84(3) sentence 5, which refers to the general labour law provisions.

[240] German Public Limited Liability Companies Act, paras. 77(1) and 78(2).

[241] *Ibid.*, para. 78(3). A *Prokurist* has an authority to represent the company which is prescribed by HGB, paras. 49 and 50 and is registered as such in the appropriate commercial register.

[242] German Public Limited Liability Companies Act, para. 77(2).

[243] *Ibid.*, para. 77(1) sentence 2.

[244] U. Hüffer, *Aktiengesetz*, 5th edn (Munich: C. H. Beck, 2002), § 77, para. 11.

contain the first names and the surnames of each member of the management board.[245]

Paragraph 87 AktG is concerned with the principles governing the remuneration of the directors. The aggregate remuneration of each member is required by paragraph 87(1) first sentence AktG to bear a reasonable relationship to the duties of the relevant director, and the condition of the company but may be reduced by the supervisory board if there is a deterioration in the situation of the company.

Members of the management board may not engage in any trade or enter into any transaction in the same branch of activity as their company without the consent of the supervisory board. Similar consent is required to their acting as a director, manager, or general partner of another commercial undertaking.[246] Members of the board of management, and their spouses and minor children may only have credit extended to them with the consent of the supervisory board. The same rule is applicable to *Prokuristen*, *Handlungsbevollmächtigten* having a general power of management[247] and their spouses and minor children.[248]

The management board's power to manage the company may not be delegated to the supervisory board.[249] However the managing board, which normally acts on its own responsibility, is subject to the directions of the controlling enterprise when a control contract is concluded,[250] or where the AG is integrated with another (principal) company.[251] If a controlling shareholder causes an AG to enter into a detrimental transaction in the absence of a control contract, it is made liable by paragraph 311 AktG to compensate it for any disadvantages that follows.

The management board is required by paragraph 90 AktG to report to the supervisory board at stipulated times on intended business policy and other fundamental matters relating to the future strategy of the company, in particular on finance, investment and personnel plans. The principal responsibility for calling a shareholders' meeting is vested in the management board.[252] It must call such a meeting if it appears that the company has lost one half of the share capital,[253] and must apply to the court within three weeks of the company becoming unable to make payments

[245] German Public Limited Liability Companies Act, para. 80(1) sentences 1 and 2.

[246] *Ibid.*, para. 88(1).

[247] *Handlungsbevollmächtigten* are senior officials who are empowered to represent the company in its whole field of business; German Commercial Code, para. 54(1).

[248] German Public Limited Liability Companies Act, para. 89.

[249] *Ibid.*, para. 111(4) sentence 1. [250] *Ibid.*, para. 308. [251] *Ibid.*, para. 323.

[252] *Ibid.*, para. 121(2). [253] *Ibid.*, para. 92(1).

as they fall due, or becoming over-indebted.[254] Where the interests of the company so require, the general meeting may be called by the supervisory board, as well as by the holders of at least 5 per cent of the share capital, or who hold share capital equal to €500,000.[255] If such a demand by the shareholders is not complied with by the company, the court may authorise them to call the meeting and also determine who shall be the chairman.[256] Furthermore, the articles may provide that the right to call a meeting shall be exercised in another form, and by the holders of a lesser amount of the company's share capital.[257]

Members of the management board of a German public company must exercise the care of a careful and conscientious businessman.[258] This general clause is thought to be applicable to all the duties of directors, for example in relation to their managerial responsibilities, their fiduciary duties[259] and their duties arising out of specific provisions of the AktG.[260] The standard is not that of an ordinary businessman, but that of a person in a leading and responsible position in a specific enterprise. The test is generally thought to be an objective one. Individual abilities are not being taken into account.[261] When an action is brought against them, it appears that directors have to show compliance with this strict rule.[262] The view is often taken that the due care requirement is an absolute one, irrespective of subjective fault including some degree of blameworthiness (*Vorwerfbarkeit*) and that any failure, however slight, may result in a requirement to pay damages. However, the German courts and academic commentators have not always adopted this view. Members of the management board who violate their duties are jointly and severally liable to the company for any resulting damage.[263] If a public company is a listed one, the management and the supervisory boards are required by paragraph 161 AktG to state annually whether they have complied with the recommendations of the Corporate Governance Code, and if not, what recommendations were not applied.[264]

[254] *Ibid.*, para. 92(2). [255] *Ibid.*, para. 122(1). [256] *Ibid.*, para. 122(3).
[257] *Ibid.*, para. 122(1) sentence 2. [258] *Ibid.*, para. 93(1) sentence 1.
[259] These have come to be recognised by academic commentators and in the decisions of the courts. See also Raiser, *Recht der Kapitalgesellschaften*, § 14, para. 80.
[260] For example, German Public Limited Liability Companies Act, paras. 80, 81, 83, 88, 91(2) and 92.
[261] See Raiser, *Recht der Kapitalgesellschaften*, § 14, para. 76.
[262] German Public Limited Liability Companies Act, para. 93(2) sentence 2.
[263] German Public Limited Liability Companies Act, para. 93(2) sentence 1.
[264] Such recommendations do not have a binding effect.

Directors are not liable to the company for damages if they acted pursuant to a lawful resolution of the general meeting.[265] But liability for damages is not excluded by the fact that the supervisory board has consented to the act.[266] Provided the requirements of paragraph 93(4) No. 3 AktG are complied with, a compromise of a claim for damages against a director under paragraph 93(2) AktG is possible. The period of three years which is required before such a compromise may take place is intended to give sufficient time for the quantification of damages. Such a compromise will not extinguish a director's liability towards the creditors if he or she has been guilty of a gross violation of the duty of care of a diligent and conscientious manager.[267]

Directors have a statutory duty of confidentiality, certain breaches of which may result in criminal liability.[268] Other breaches of statutory provisions concerning the duties of the management board may also result in criminal liabilities.[269]

3. The supervisory board

If any of the codetermination articles apply, the members of the supervisory board are chosen by the general meeting and by the employees.[270] The number of members of the supervisory board depends on the articles and the amount of the company's capital, where the Codetermination Act 1976 or one of the two coal, iron and steel codetermination Acts is inapplicable.[271] The *Aktiengesetz* contains very detailed rules designed to ensure that the composition of the supervisory board is in accordance with any relevant codetermination statute.[272] However, the efficacy of the double board system, especially where the supervisory board has to be set up in accordance with the Codetermination Act of 1976 requiring quasi-paritative codetermination, has been doubted by some commentators.[273]

Members of the supervisory board must be natural persons having full legal capacity.[274] Their term of office may not exceed approximately five years, and may be less if the articles or resolution on appointment so

265 German Public Limited Liability Companies Act, paras. 93(4) and 119(1).

266 *Ibid.*, para. 93(4) sentence 2. 267 *Ibid.*, para. 93(5) sentence 3.

268 *Ibid.*, para. 404. 269 *Ibid.*, paras. 399–403.

270 *Ibid.*, para. 101(1). Note, however, AktG, para. 101(2), which permits one third of the shareholders' representatives to be designated by shareholders mentioned in the articles, or by the holders of specified shares which must be in registered form, and which according to the articles, may only be transferred with the consent of the company.

271 German Public Limited Liability Companies Act, para. 95 sentence 5.

272 *Ibid.*, paras. 96–99. 273 See Hopt 'The German Two-Tier Board: Experience'.

274 German Public Limited Liability Companies Act, para. 100(1).

stipulate.[275] A person may not serve on the supervisory board if he already is a member of the supervisory boards of ten enterprises required by law to form a board (the position of chairman counts double); or if he is the legal representative of another enterprise controlled by the company; or if he is the legal representative of another company whose supervisory board includes a member of the management board of the company.[276] The removal of members of the supervisory board is dealt with by paragraph 103 AktG. If a member is elected by the shareholders, without being bound by nominations they may remove him without cause by a vote cast by three quarters of the shareholders actually voting on a general meeting.[277] Persons who appoint members to the supervisory board pursuant to the articles may replace them at any time, and they may be removed by a simple majority vote in the general meeting if they no longer satisfy the requirements specified in the articles in relation to the right to appoint.[278] Furthermore, the court may remove a member of the supervisory board for cause on the motion of the supervisory board, or on that of a specified majority of the shareholders if he has been appointed to the board pursuant to the articles.[279] If the company is subject to one of the Codetermination Acts the provisions of the relevant act must be obeyed in relation to the removal of members who were not elected by the shareholders' meeting without being bound by nominations, nor appointed to the supervisory board pursuant to the articles.[280]

The supervisory board appoints members of the management board, and may dismiss them for good cause.[281] It represents the company in its dealings with the management board; this includes entry into employment agreements with its members.[282] As already pointed out above, the management board is required by paragraph 90 AktG to report to the supervisory board about various matters. The supervisory board is also empowered by paragraph 111(2) to inspect the company's books, records and properties.

The articles or the rules of the supervisory board must set out a list of transactions of fundamental importance, for example decisions that alter

[275] *Ibid.*, para. 102. [276] *Ibid.*, para. 100(2).

[277] *Ibid.*, para. 103(1). [278] *Ibid.*, para. 103(2).

[279] *Ibid.*, para. 103(3). The shareholders are required to have an aggregate holding of one-tenth of the share capital, or have share capital the normal value of which amounts to €1 million.

[280] *Ibid.*, para. 103(4). Such persons will include the representatives of employees on the supervisory board.

[281] *Ibid.*, para. 84(3). [282] *Ibid.*, para. 112.

assets, financial or earnings situation of the company which require the consent of the supervisory board.[283] However, the supervisory board must not restrict the ability of the management board to manage the company by means of burdensome consent requirements. If the supervisory board refuses its consent, the management board can nevertheless act if it has the support of a three-quarters majority of the votes cast at a general meeting.[284]

The supervisory board has an important role to play in the preparation of the annual financial statements. These, which consist of a balance sheet, profit and loss account and an annual report, together with an auditor's report if necessary, and a proposal for the allocation of distributable profits, must be submitted by the management board to the supervisory board.[285] The supervisory board examines all these documents and reports on its conclusions to the general meeting within one month of their receipt.[286] The annual financial statements must be approved by the supervisory board[287] or, exceptionally by the shareholders' meeting, if the management and supervisory boards resolve that the statements should be so approved, or if the supervisory board has refused to approve them.[288] The general meeting resolves on the appropriation of distributable profits, based upon the annual financial statements.[289]

According to paragraph 116AktG, paragraph 93 AktG regarding the duty of care and responsibility of the members of the Management board is applicable analogously to the duty of care and skill of the members of the supervisory board. Similar criminal provisions apply to members of the supervisory board as are applicable to those of the management board.[290] It has been held in *Holzmüller*,[291] and in subsequent cases that the management board should exercise the discretion granted to it to refer matters to the general meeting positively in certain circumstances.[292]

[283] *Ibid.*, para. 111(4), as amended by the Transparency and Disclosure Act, which came into force on 1 August 2002.

[284] *Ibid.*, para. 111(4) sentences 3 and 4. [285] *Ibid.*, para. 170(1) and (2).

[286] *Ibid.*, para. 171. [287] *Ibid.*, para. 172. [288] *Ibid.*, para. 173(1).

[289] *Ibid.*, para. 174(1). [290] *Ibid.*, paras. 399, 400, 404 and 405.

[291] BGHZ 83, 122. In *Holzmüller*, the company transferred most of its assets to a subsidiary which was set up for this purpose. The decision in *Holzmüller* has given rise to considerable controversy, but would seem worthy of support. See also German Court of Appeal, Munich (*Oberlandesgericht* (OLG), Munich), [1995] Die AG 232, 233 (*EKATIT/Riedinger*).

[292] See for more details, Schmidt, *Gesellschaftsrecht*, § 28 V 2b.

4. The general meeting

Management and supervisory board members should attend general meetings.[293] The auditors if any, should be present at the deliberations on the approval of the annual financial statements.[294] The directors generally call general meetings, but as has been pointed out above, such a meeting may be called by the supervisory board, or by the holders of at least five per cent of the share capital. Shareholders holding not less than five per cent of the share capital or shares having a nominal value equivalent to €500,000 may request the inclusion of a particular item on the agenda of any general meeting.[295] If the management refuses to comply with such requests, the court may authorise the shareholders who made the demand to call a shareholders' meeting, or to include the items on the agenda.[296]

The functions of the general meeting are set out to a large extent in paragraph 119(1) AktG. They consist principally of passing resolutions governing the company's legal and financial structure,[297] electing certain members of the supervisory board, ratifying acts of members of the management board and the supervisory board, or instituting proceedings against such members, and appointing auditors. The general meeting has to give its consent to measures to increase or reduce the share capital and to the allocation of profits. [298]

An annual general meeting must be called within the first eight months of the company's financial year to receive the report of the board of management and the supervisory board, to approve the conduct of the directors, and to declare dividends out of the previous year's profits.[299]

The functions of the supervisory board and the general meeting with respect to the accounts have been discussed above. Whether or not the annual general meeting approves the accounts, the profits shown by them are at its disposal, and it must determine what part of the profits shall be paid out as dividend and what part carried forward and transferred to reserve.[300] However, the latter power is subject to the limitation

[293] German Public Limited Liability Companies Act, para. 118(2).
[294] *Ibid.*, para. 176(2). [295] *Ibid.*, para. 122(2). [296] *Ibid.*, para. 122(3) sentence 1.
[297] *Ibid.*, paras. 170(2) and (3) and 175(1). [298] *Ibid.*, para. 119(1) sentences 2 and 6.
[299] *Ibid.*, para. 175(1) sentences 1 and 2. The approval of the general meeting is required for amendments to the articles, the conclusion of enterprise agreements, conversion of the company into a company of another type, or the transfer of all the company's assets or a substantial part of them: see BGHZ 83, 122 (*Holzmüller*).
[300] German Public Limited Liability Companies Act, para. 174(1).

that one-twentieth of the annual profits must be transferred to the statutory reserve (after deducting any loss carried forward) until this, together with capital reserves,[301] amounts to one-tenth of the share capital, or any higher amount prescribed by the articles.[302] The relevant power is also subject to the limitation that the directors and the supervisory board may transfer up to half the year's profits (or a greater or lesser amount if the articles so prescribe) to the free or revenue reserves until they amount to one-half of the company capital.[303] In addition, the articles may provide in respect of those cases where the shareholders meeting has to approve the accounts, that amounts not exceeding one half of the year's profits be transferred to free reserves.[304]

According to paragraphs 21 and 23(1) AktG, notices concerning general meetings must be published in the journals mentioned in the articles at least thirty days before they are held. However, the articles are permitted to make participation in the general meeting or the exercise of voting rights dependent on notification by the shareholder of his intention to participate. In such an event, the date by which shareholders are to give notice of their intention to attend, is substituted for the date of the meeting for the purpose of determining the period of notice. The notification must be received by the company at the appropriate address at least seven days before the meeting for the purpose of determining the period of notice, unless the articles provide for a shorter time period.[305] In the case of bearer shares, the articles may provide how the entitlement to take part in a meeting or to exercise voting rights shall be evidenced. Where the shares are listed on the stock exchange, a notice in a textual form provided by the depository institution shall be sufficient evidence of a relevant entitlement. In the case of such listed companies, evidence of ownership of the shares twenty-one days before the date of the meeting must be given by the depository banks and must reach the company at the appropriate address at least seven days before the meeting, unless the articles provides for a shorter time period. The notice of the meeting given by the company consists of the publication of the date, time and place of the meeting, the agenda, and the conditions for the participation

[301] German Commercial Code, para. 272(2) 1–3.

[302] German Public Limited Liability Companies Act, para. 150(2).

[303] *Ibid.*, para. 58(2). If the company is a listed one, only a greater amount may be so transferred.

[304] *Ibid.*, para. 58(1).

[305] *Ibid.*, para. 123(2), as amended by UMAG, BGBl (2006) 1. 2002. See also para. 123(3) as amended.

of shareholders, and the exercise of voting rights. The notice must be accompanied by the agenda.[306] If an annual general meeting is called, the annual accounts, the director's report and the report of the supervisory board to be placed before it must be available for inspection by any shareholder, and upon his request, he must be provided with a copy of these documents.[307]

Shareholders have the right to the information necessary to evaluate an item on the agenda. The management board may refuse to provide information in certain circumstances, for example where providing such information would be likely to cause harm to the company or an affiliated company, or if the information relates to the acceptability of certain balance sheet items for tax purposes or the calculation of special taxes, or if the information is available on the company's internet site at least seven days before the meeting, and is generally available there.[308]

Every fully paid share entitles its holder to vote at general meetings, and votes are cast according to the nominal value of shares: in the case of no-par value shares, they are cast in proportion to their number.[309] Voting rights may be granted to partly paid up shares, in which case they are determined in accordance with the amounts paid up on the fully and partly paid up shares.[310] Shares may not carry multiple voting rights, but in unlisted companies voting rights may be limited with respect to shareholders having more than one share providing for a maximum par value or a sliding scale.[311] Shares may not be issued without voting rights, apart from cumulative preference shares (*Vorzugsaktien*) which may have no voting rights if the preference dividend is not more than one year in arrears. Such shares may not exceed one-half of the share capital of the company. They carry voting rights on any resolution to reduce or extinguish the preference dividend granted to them, and their consent is required to a resolution to issue more preference shares with prior or equal ranking rights.[312]

A shareholder may vote by proxy, which should be in writing.[313] But proxies given to banks and shareholders' associations, which often act a depositaries of share certificates and vote thereon as permanent proxies, are only valid to the extent that the shareholder has given specific

[306] German Public Limited Liability Companies Act, paras. 121 and 124.
[307] *Ibid.*, para. 175(2) and (3). [308] *Ibid.*, para. 131. [309] *Ibid.*, para. 134(1).
[310] *Ibid.*, para. 134(2), sentence 2. The minimum contribution must be paid up on the shares for such voting rights to arise.
[311] *Ibid.*, para. 134(1), sentence 2. [312] *Ibid.*, paras. 139–141. [313] *Ibid.*, para. 134(3).

instructions regarding the items on the agenda.[314] The proxy given to a credit institution lasts for a period of fifteen months, but the bank has to point out and clearly emphasise in writing the possibility of a revocation at any time.[315] Depositary banks and shareholders' associations which are notified by the company of a general meeting are required to pass the information given to them regarding the meeting to the shareholders whom they represent. If they intend to exercise votes on behalf of a shareholder they must inform him of their proposals of how to vote on each item on the agenda, and give a statement of the manner in which the bank or association will vote if it does not obtain instructions from the shareholder to the contrary.[316]

Resolutions of the general meeting require a simple majority of the votes cast, unless the law or the articles provide for a larger majority or additional requirements.[317] Certain resolutions must be passed by a majority consisting of three quarters of the capital represented at the meeting. These include resolutions amending the articles[318] and resolutions increasing and reducing the company's capital.[319] In certain cases, class voting may be required, as in the case of alterations to the relationship between classes to the detriment of any class.[320] Such class voting may take place either by a separate resolution of the shareholders adversely affected at the same meeting as that at which the resolution adversely affecting them is to be passed, or at a separate meeting. The required majority for the resolution passed by the disadvantaged class of shareholders is three quarters of the share capital represented at the passing of such resolution. The votes of shareholders who abstain from voting are not counted.[321] In addition, to casting such a majority vote, the disadvantaged shareholders must also hold the majority of the votes cast.[322]

Each resolution of the general meeting must be recorded in minutes of the meeting taking the form of a notarial deed, except where the company is an unlisted one.[323] A certified copy of the minutes and the

314 *Ibid.*, para. 135(1), (8) and (9). 315 *Ibid.*, para. 135(2) sentence 2.

316 *Ibid.*, para. 128(1)–(4). 317 *Ibid.*, para. 133(1).

318 *Ibid.*, para. 179. The articles may provide for a different majority but if the alteration involves a change in the company's purpose, this may only be an enhanced majority.

319 *Ibid.*, paras. 182(1) and 222(1). 320 *Ibid.*, para. 179(3).

321 *Ibid.*, para. 179(3) sentence 2; para. 179(3) sentence 3 refers to para. 179(2).

322 Official Journal of the former German Supreme Court (RGZ) 125, 356, 359; BGH [1975] NJW 212, 213.

323 German Public Limited Liability Companies Act, para. 130(1). In this case, a minute signed by the chairman of the supervisory board is sufficient, insofar as no resolution is made which requires a majority of three quarters or more by law.

appendices thereto must be submitted to the Commercial Register promptly after the closure of the meeting.[324]

5. Minority protection

In addition to the rights already mentioned to request the calling of a general meeting,[325] to place certain items on the agenda,[326] to receive such information as is necessary to properly evaluate an agenda item,[327] and to put a motion to the court for the dismissal of a supervisory board member appointed by the articles,[328] minority shareholders (who are usually required to hold a minimum percentage or fixed amount of the shares) have certain other rights specified in the *Aktiengesetz* or the articles. Thus the holders of at least 10 per cent of the company's share capital are empowered to prevent a waiver or compromise of certain claims that the company may have against members of the management or supervisory boards or others,[329] or against controlling enterprises.[330]

The provisions of paragraph 147 AktGG concerning derivative actions have been found to be unsatisfactory, and have recently been amended. In addition, a new provision has been introduced in paragraph 148 AktGG, involving a preliminary procedure. Paragraph 147(1) now provides that the claims of the company against persons concerned with the formation of the company or members of the two boards in connection with its management, or arising from paragraph 117 AktGG, shall be brought if the general meeting so resolves by a simple majority.[331] Furthermore, paragraph 147(2) sentence 1 provides that the general meeting may appoint special representatives to assert the claim for damages. The court may, upon the motion of shareholders whose

[324] *Ibid.*, para. 130(5). [325] *Ibid.*, para. 122(1).
[326] *Ibid.*, para. 122(2). [327] *Ibid.*, para. 131.
[328] German Public Limited Liability Companies Act, para. 103(3). If a member has been appointed to the supervisory board by the articles, a motion for his or her removal by the court may be made by the holders of one-tenth of the share capital, or of an amount equivalent to €1,000,000.
[329] German Public Limited Liability Companies Act, paras. 50, 53, 93(4), 116 and 117(4) and Schneider and Heidenhain, *The German Stock Corporation Act* (Munich: Beck and Devenber: Kluwer, 2000), p. 13.
[330] German Public Limited Liability Companies Act, paras. 309(3), 310(4), 317(4), 318(4) and 323(1).
[331] Paragraph 117 AktGG provides that a person who intentionally uses influence on a company and so induces a director or a member of the supervisory board to act in a manner detrimental to the company or its shareholders, is liable (together with directors or members of the supervisory board who collaborated with him) in damages to the company and the shareholders who suffered loss.

aggregate shareholdings exceed one tenth of the share capital or the holders of shares having a nominal value of at least €1 million, appoint persons other than those authorised to represent the company pursuant to paragraphs 78 and 112, if sentence 1 above as the company's representatives to assert the claim for damages. The court shall make such appointment if in the opinion of the court, this is appropriate for the proper assertion of the claim. Thus it may be asserted by persons other than the directors or members of the supervisory board.

This procedure has been found unsatisfactory in the past.[332] The holders of one tenth of the shares are often represented in the supervisory board, and have frequently been satisfied with a settlement between directors and supervisory board, which represents the company in actions against them. Employees' representatives on the supervisory board have also sometimes shown themselves satisfied with such a compromise.

The procedure under paragraph 148 has a preliminary stage. A minority consisting of the holders of 1 per cent of all the shares or a nominal capital of at least €100,000 may invoke this procedure before the local *Landgericht*, which may result in permissions being given for a direct action by them against the company. Such permission will be granted if certain requirements are satisfied. Shareholders desirous of suing or their predecessors in title must have acquired the shares before they become aware of the alleged breach of duty or damage. In addition, they must have endeavoured to induce the company to sue the defaulting officers before they make an application to the court. Furthermore, the relevant facts must give rise to the suspicion that there has been dishonest conduct or a serious breach of the law or the articles which has caused damage to the company. There must be no overriding grounds based upon the welfare of the company for abstaining from bringing an action against the relevant officers of the company. The new provisions governing costs contained in paragraph 148(6) AktGG may be more favourable to plaintiffs than were those of former paragraph 147(4) AktGG which have been repealed.[333]

A general meeting is empowered to appoint special examiners to inquire into matters relating to the formation and management of the

[332] It has been criticised in German academic writing.

[333] The rules contained in para. 147(4) concerning costs were not favourable to minority shareholders, requiring them to reimburse costs to the company where it has been wholly or partly unsuccessful in the litigation, insofar as such costs exceed what has been gained by the other party to the action.

company.[334] If it fails to do so, the holders of at least one-tenth of the share capital or an amount equivalent to one million euros may apply to the court to appoint special examiners (*Sonderprüfer*). It will do so if it has reason to suspect that improprieties or gross violations of the law or the articles have taken place in relation to any matter concerned with the formation or management of the company during the past five years.[335]

V. The position in Italy

A. Public companies

The rules applicable to the public company (SpA) are to some extent made applicable to the private company (SRL),[336] and we here deal with the public company first. There is scope for the use of the dual board system in Italian public companies. The committee of auditors (*collegio sindicale*) which has to be established by Italian public companies has special significance in those Italian companies which make use of the traditional board model. It then has a role not entirely dissimilar from that of the German supervisory board. Its function is not generally one of auditing the accounts but rather one of exercising internal controls. Italian public companies are able to make use of two alternative board models, the dualistic and monistic ones, instead of the traditional model of a single board. Those companies which are quoted on an Italian regulated market, or on a regulated market belonging to another Member State, are subject to special rules concerning their committee of auditors, as well as rules governing minority protection, and the granting of proxies to vote, at general meetings.[337] Italian public companies which are listed on the Italian Stock Exchange have to comply with the guidelines contained in the Code of Corporate Governance, or explain why they do not do so. This Code emphasises the need for the presence of an adequate number of independent non-executive directors on the board of directors. Furthermore, they are required by the Code to set up an Internal Code Committee and a Remuneration Committee consisting mainly of independent directors. The recent extensive amendments to the Civil Code often contain provisions which are applicable to

[334] German Public Limited Liability Companies Act, para. 142(1).

[335] *Ibid.*, para. 142(2).

[336] And continues to be so also after the major reform of Italian company law by Decree Law No. 6 of 17 January 2003.

[337] The latter rules are contained in Decree Law No. 58 of 24 February 1998.

companies quoted on a regulated market, or which have more than 200 shareholders.

A public company may accept the traditional system of management and control which is outlined below. It may however adopt either the new dualistic or monistic systems for this purpose. According to Article 2380 of the Civil Code, except when provided otherwise, the rules which are applicable to directors apply both to the executive committee (*consiglio di amministrazione*) under the single board system and to the executive board (*consiglio di gestione*) under the dual board system.

1. Management in accordance with the traditional model

The directors of a public company who manage the company's affairs (*amministratori*) may number one or more persons, whose term of appointment may not exceed three years.[338] They need not be members of the company. The first directors are appointed by the deed of incorporation (*atto costitutivo*), whilst the later ones are appointed by the general meeting.[339] Persons who are disqualified, or who are mentally ill, or who are bankrupt or who have been made subject to a penalty which results, even temporarily, in their disqualification from public office are not eligible to be directors of a public company and if they are appointed, they forfeit office.[340] The shareholders may reappoint a retiring director unless the articles provide otherwise, and they may remove a director from office by a resolution of the general meeting, without prejudice to an action for damages if the dismissal has no just cause.[341] The directors are required to appoint one of their number to be the chairman (*presidente*), unless such an appointment has been made by the shareholders in general meeting.[342] The chairman's role is simply to preside over board meetings.

The board of directors (*consiglio di amministrazione*) cannot deliberate validly unless the majority of its members are present, unless the articles provide otherwise. Subject to a different provision in the articles, the board exercises its powers by a majority vote at board meetings. Provided the articles so stipulate or a general meeting so resolves the board may delegate its powers to one or more of its members (*direttore generale or comitato esecutivo*), except in relation to the preparation of the annual accounts, the directors' report, the increase of the company capital, the reduction of its capital because of losses, and the requirement

[338] Italian Civil Code, Arts. 2380 *bis* and 2383(2). [339] *Ibid.*, Art. 2383(1).
[340] *Ibid.*, Art. 2382. [341] *Ibid.*, Art. 2383(3). [342] *Ibid.*, Art. 2380 *bis* (5).

of calling of a general meeting if the capital has fallen below the minimum by reason of the loss of more than one third thereof.[343] The managing director of an Italian public company (*direttore generale*) or one of them is frequently the same person as the chairman.

The directors who represent the company may perform any act which falls within the company's purpose, except for the limitations which result from the articles or decisions of the competent bodies. Such limitations on the power of representation are not opposable to third parties, even if they are published, unless it is proved that such third parties, acted knowingly to the detriment of the company.[344]

The remuneration (which may take the form of a salary or a share in the profits) of members of the board of directors or the executive committee is determined in their terms of appointment or by the general meeting. Those of the directors who are entrusted with particular tasks in accordance with the articles is fixed by the board of directors in consultation with the committee of auditors.[345]Particulars of the remuneration received by the directors and the auditors must appear in the notes on the accounts (*nota integrativa*) and be given on a cumulative basis for each category.[346] Directors and auditors of companies whose shares are listed on the Stock Exchange must declare annually to the National Commission for Companies and the Stock Exchange (*Commissione Nazionale per la Società e la Borsa*, – CONSOB) the total amount of remuneration of any kind whatsoever obtained from the company or its subsidiaries.[347]

Directors must fulfil the duties imposed on them by law and the articles with the diligence required by reason of their office and that of their specific competence, and they are jointly and severally liable to the company for damages resulting from their failure to observe this requirement, unless the relevant tasks come within the competence of the executive committee or one or more specific directors. The directors are also jointly and severally liable where they become aware of prejudicial acts and do not do all within their power to prevent them and eliminate or diminish their harmful consequences. However a director who is himself without fault, may avoid liability for an improper

[343] *Ibid.*, Arts. 2381, 2428 *ter*, 2443, 2446 and 2447. The same is true in relation to the directors' powers in relation to the preparation of a merger proposal (Art. 2501 *ter*) and in relation to a proposal for a division (Art. 2506 *bis*).

[344] *Ibid.*, Art. 2384. [345] *Ibid.*, Art. 2389.

[346] *Ibid.*, Art. 2427, clause 16. [347] Law No. 216 of 7 June 1974, Art. 17.

transaction resolved on by the board by recording his dissent in the minutes and giving written notice to the chairman of the board (committee) of auditors.[348]

A director may not take any part in the management of a business which competes with that of the company, nor be a general partner in a competing firm, except where he is authorised to do so by the general meeting. If he fails to observe these prohibitions, he may be dismissed from his directorship and also be liable for damages.[349] If a director is personally interested on his own account or on that of a third party in a transaction concerning the company, he must disclose details of that interest to his fellow directors and the committee of auditors, and if the director is empowered to conclude the transaction, he must abstain from so doing, and refer the matter to the board of directors. If the board or the executive committee's decision is adopted by reason of the vote of the interested director, and is liable to cause harm to the company, it may be challenged by the absent or dissenting directors or the board of auditors within ninety days of the relevant decision but the rights acquired by third parties acting in good faith are preserved.[350] If the relevant directors failed to disclose their interests the decision may also be challenged. In the latter event, directors who voted in favour of the decision may also take such proceedings. The directors are liable to the company for damages suffered by it by reason of the utilisation for their own advantage, or that of third parties, of facts, information or opportunities about which they have become acquainted in the course of their duties. This principle reminds one of the corporate opportunity rule familiar in Germany, the United Kingdom and the United States.

An action for breach of director's duties may be brought by the company, even if it is in liquidation if the shareholders in general meeting so resolve, and the resolution is passed by the favourable votes of the holders of at least one-fifth of the company's capital. The passing of such a resolution means that the relevant director is automatically dismissed. The company may waive the bringing of the action, or compromise it if such action is not opposed by shareholders holding at least one-fifth of

[348] Italian Civil Code, Art. 2392. This rule is also applicable where the dualistic or monistic board systems are adopted. The same is true in the case of Art. 2391, which is considered below.

[349] Italian Civil Code, Art. 2390.

[350] *Ibid.*, Art. 2391. The rules contained in this article are inspired by a concern for transparency, and are applicable even when there is no conflict of interest. See Santosuosso, *Il nuovo diritto societario* (D&G Diritto e Guistizia 2003), pp. 63–66.

the share capital.[351] Individual shareholders holding at least one-fifth of the share capital may bring a derivative action against the company.[352] Furthermore, individual shareholders and creditors may sue the directors for the diminution in value of their shares,[353] or the loss caused to them by the directors' fraud or negligence.[354]

A derivative action is available to shareholders in both quoted and non-quoted companies in accordance with Article 2393 *bis* of the Italian Civil Code. Certain detailed particulars regarding this action are set out under the heading 'the rights of minority shareholders' which appears below.

2. Committee (or board) of auditors

Position in unquoted companies The rules governing the functions of the committee (or board) of auditors differ according to whether or not the company is a quoted one, and as explained below, whether the traditional rules governing management are adopted, or whether the new dualistic or monistic system is used instead. The rules governing the committee of auditors of unquoted companies, certain of which remain applicable to quoted ones, will be considered first of all. These rules are principally contained in Articles 2397–2409 of the Civil Code, although certain subsidiary rules relating to the committee of auditors are contained in other provisions thereof. These provisions underwent some revision under Decree Law No. 88 of 21 January 1992; the amendments came into force on 27 April 1995, and provided for a more stringent regime. Persons lacking professional qualifications may no longer be members of the committee of auditors of an unquoted company.

The committee of auditors of an unquoted company consists of three to five persons who may or may not be members of the company. In

351 Italian Civil Code, Art. 2393(5). The fraction is reduced to one-twentieth, or the lesser amount permitted by the articles, where the company is admitted to the market for venture capital, because it is a listed company or has more than 200 members.

352 Italian Civil Code, Art. 2393 *bis* (1) and (2). This required fraction is reduced to one-twentieth in the case of companies which have recourse to the market for venture capital. These are quoted companies and companies having more than 200 members.

353 This remedy would be useful to creditors who wished to complain that they had suffered a loss because the directors had wrongfully paid dividends out of capital.

354 Italian Civil Code, Art. 2395: for the special position of creditors, see Art. 2394(1) which provides that the directors are answerable to the company's creditors for non-compliance with the obligations regarding the preservation of the company's assets. The rules continued in Articles 2394 and 2395 remain applicable to the executive board where the new monistic or dualistic system is employed by the company.

addition, two alternate auditors must be appointed. A least one auditor and one deputy must be chosen from the register of auditors (*registro del revisore contabile*) kept by the Ministry of Justice.[355] The other auditors must be entered on a professional register specified by decree of the Minister of Justice, or be tenured university teachers in the field of economics or law. The auditors are appointed for a period of three years by the shareholders in general meeting and, in the case of the first auditors, by the deed of incorporation.[356] According to Article 2399 of the Civil Code, certain persons are ineligible for appointment to the committee of auditors of an unquoted company, or are required to vacate office if they are so appointed. These are the spouses and parents (including parents-in-law) of, and persons within the fourth degree of relationship to, the directors, and persons who are connected with the company, or companies controlled by it or which controls it, by a continuous remunerated consultancy or an employment relationship.[357] The removal of, or the suspension of an auditor from the official register of company auditors, results in his loss of membership of the committee of auditors.

The annual accounts of a company which does not have recourse to the market for venture capital (typically unquoted and with less than 200 members) and which is not required to prepare consolidated accounts, may be audited by the committee of auditors, which is entitled to proceed with acts of inspection for these and other purposes.[358] The accounts of a company which has recourse to the market for venture capital are subject to external controls. They must be audited by a properly qualified auditing firm (*società di revisione*) approved by CONSOB (*Commissione nazionale per le societa e la borsa*), whose members are independent of the company audited and professionally qualified.[359] In the case of

[355] *Ibid.*, Art. 2397. [356] *Ibid.*, Art. 2400(1).

[357] Similar disqualifications are applied to quoted companies under the provision of Art. 148(3) of Decree Law No. 58 of 1998.

[358] Italian Civil Code, Art. 2409 *bis* (3), and 2403(1) and (2). The rule contained in Art. 2409 *bis* (3) is an exception to the general rule contained in Art. 2409 *bis* (1) which is that the accounts of a company are externally audited by a company auditor or an auditing company entered on a register maintained by the Ministry of Justice. Art. 2409 *bis* (3) requires the committee of auditors to be made up of auditors registered in the register maintained by the Ministry of Justice.

[359] Italian Civil Code, Art. 2409 *bis* (2). The position is similar in quoted companies, see Art. 159(1) of Decree Law No. 58 of 24 February 1998, it has undertaken and blameworthy acts revealed.

unquoted companies, the committee of auditors is required to report to the general meeting.[360]

The members of the committee of auditors must attend board and general meetings, and may also attend meetings of the executive committee of the board of directors.[361] They are required to check the adequacy of the accounting arrangements adopted by the company and their actual functioning. Their mandate includes the compliance with the law and the articles, the principles of correct administration and the organisational, administrative and accounting arrangements.[362] They may make use of their own employees for this purpose, unless these are disqualified under Article 2399 of the Civil Code.[363] The auditors are empowered to proceed to acts of inspection and control at any time on an individual or collective basis.[364] They must carry out an investigation without delay if required to do so by the holders of one-twentieth of the company's share capital.[365]

The holders of one-tenth of the capital of the company (the amount is reduced to one-twentieth in companies having recourse to the market for venture capital) may take a report to the competent court if there is justified suspicion of grave irregularities in the fulfilment of the duties of the directors or the auditors which cause damage to the company or to one or more companies controlled by it. The court may order an investigation into the management of the company. It will not do so and will suspend the proceedings for a determinate period if the general meeting of the company replaces the directors and auditors with persons of adequate professional competence, who must determine without delay whether irregularities have taken place and, if they find that they have, make reference to the court on the results of such determination and the activities carried out. If such action proves insufficient to eliminate

[360] *Ibid.*, Art. 2429(2). The position is similar in quoted companies: Art. 153(1) of Decree Law No. 58 of 24 February 1998 provides that the committee of auditors reports to the general meeting convened for the purpose of approving the accounts on the supervisory activities it has undertaken and blameworthy acts revealed. A similar obligation is imposed on the supervisory board and on the internal control committee (when the monistic system is used).

[361] Italian Civil Code, Art. 2405(1).

[362] *Ibid.*, Art. 2403(1). [363] *Ibid.*, Art. 2403 *bis* (4). [364] *Ibid.*, Art. 2403 *bis* (1).

[365] *Ibid.*, Art. 2408(2) the same rule applies to companies which have recourse to the market for venture capital: note the similar rule contained in Decree Law No. 58 of 1998, Art. 128 which applies to quoted companies. The required percentage for an investigation in the latter two cases is the holders of at least two per cent of the company's share capital.

the irregularities, the court may order provisional measures, and call a general meeting for the purpose of passing the necessary resolutions. In the most serious cases it may remove the company's directors and auditors from office and order the appointment of a judicial administrator, who will be charged with the temporary management of the business. The relevant provisions governing the matters discussed in the present paragraph are contained in Article 2409 of the Civil Code, and may be usefully compared with those of Article 152 of Decree Law No. 58 of 1998, which are only applicable to quoted companies. Article 152 of Decree Law of No. 58 of 1998, which like certain other provisions of the Decree Law, was amended in 2006, provides that the committee of auditors, the supervisory board or the internal control committee may, if they have reason to suspect that grave irregularities have occurred in the management of the company which may cause harm to it or to companies controlled by it, report the matter to the competent court, which is empowered to dismiss the directors.

Position of quoted companies We will deal with the position of quoted companies here, although the duties of the auditors of such companies will be lessened where they do not adopt the traditional system of management, but instead adopt the dualistic system now permitted. The rules applicable to the committee of auditors of a quoted company are contained principally in Articles 148–154 of Decree Law No. 58 of 24 February 1998. Certain of these rules were amended, and made applicable to the corresponding organs of control, the audit committee and the supervisory board, under the monistic and dualistic systems of administration, by Legislative Decree No. 37 of 2004. The rules governing the committee of auditors of unquoted companies became stricter as the result of reforms made in 1992, the corresponding rules governing quoted companies are stricter. Article 154 of Decree Law No. 58 of 24 February 1998 absolves a member from provisions of the Civil Code applicable to unquoted companies, but not all such provisions.[366]

[366] The inapplicable provisions are Arts. 2397–2399, 2403, 2403, *bis*, 2405(1) 2426, sentences 5 and 6, 2429(2), and 2441(6). Thus the rules governing the appointment of auditors contained in Art. 2400, those governing their remuneration contained in Art. 2402; those governing their meetings and resolutions contained in Art. 2404; those concerning the giving of notice of general meetings by auditors if directors fail to do so contained in Art. 2406; those governing the liabilities of auditors contained in Art. 2407; and those governing reports to auditors and the courts contained in Arts. 2408 and 2409 are applicable to the auditors of quoted companies.

The detailed provisions applicable to quoted companies must state the number of regular members of the committee of auditors which must not be less than three, and the number of alternate members, which must not be less than two. They must also stipulate the method of and requirements for, nomination as president of the committee, and the limitations on the number of offices that may be held by the members. The articles must contain provisions ensuring that the minority shareholders may elect at least one regular member of the committee. If the committee has more than three members, this number is increased to two.[367] Certain persons are made ineligible for appointment as auditors, including spouses, parents and parents-in-law of, and persons within the fourth degree of relationship to, directors of the company, or of the directors of any company which controls it, or of any subsidiaries; and senior and other employees of the company, or any company which controls it, or any subsidiaries.[368] Certain of the rules contained in Article 48 were made applicable to the supervisory board and internal control committee when the dualistic and monistic board structures are used by Article 9.77 of Legislative Decree No. 37 of 2004.

The duties of the committee of auditors of a quoted company are set out in Article 149(1) of Decree Law No. 58 of 1998. It is required to examine whether the law and the articles of the company are observed, and whether the principles of correct administration are adhered to. It must also examine the adequacy of the organisation of the company particularly from the viewpoint of the allocation of competences, the system of internal control, and that of management accounting as well as the appropriateness of that accounting system for the purpose of representing management transactions (*fatti di gestione*). The committee of auditors is also required to examine the adequacy of the provisions made by a controlling company for the purpose of ensuring that a subsidiary has given the notices to it which are required by law.

Article 149(2) of Decree Law No. 58 of 1998 requires the members of the committee of auditors to assist at general meetings and at meetings of the board of directors, and the executive board. If such a person fails to give assistance at general meetings, or two meetings of the board, without good reason, he vacates office.

According to Article 149(3) of this law, the committee of auditors is required to communicate to CONSOB without delay any irregularity it

[367] Decree Law No. 58 of 1998, Art. 148(1) and (2).
[368] Decree Law No. 38 of 1998, Art. 148(3).

finds in exercising its supervisory tasks, and to send it the relevant minutes of the particular meeting and of the investigations undertaken together with any other useful documentation. Paragraph 3 is inapplicable to companies which are only quoted in a regulated market in another EC State.

The directors are required by Article 150(1) of Decree Law No. 58 of 1998 to report to the committee of auditors in good time and in accordance with the requirements of the articles. Reporting should take place at least on a three monthly basis. The reporting should cover activities which have been carried on and on operations of major economic, financial or patrimonial importance effected by the company, or by a company controlled by it. The reporting should in particular deal with operations in which the directors or third parties have an interest, or which have been influenced by the entities which exercise direction and control over the company.

The powers of the committee of auditors are set out in Article 151 of Decree Law No. 58 of 24 February 1998. Paragraph 1 of this provision stipulates that the auditors have the power, acting individually or otherwise, to ask the directors to notify them of the progress of company operations or of a determinate matter, as well as to proceed at any time to measures of inspection and control. According to paragraph 151(2), the committee of auditors may exchange information with the corresponding organs of controlled companies, as to the merits of the system of administrative control. The committee of auditors may on giving notice to the chairman of the company, call a general meeting, a meeting of the board of directors or of the executive board, and may call upon employees of the company to explain their exact functions. No less than two members of the committee of auditors may call meetings of the above bodies, and may also require the collaboration of employees of the company.

Article 151(3) stipulates that, for the purpose of determining the adequacy and appropriateness of the company's system of management accounting, the committee of auditors may make use of its own employees at its own responsibility on an individual or other basis, and at its own expense, provided that such employees are not disqualified under Article 148(3) of Decree Law No. 58 of 1998. Furthermore, Article 151(4) provides that the auditors are responsible for recording the investigations made by them in the register of meetings and deliberations of the committee kept at the company's head office. Article 151 *bis* is concerned with the powers of the supervisory board under the dualistic system: it is given certain of the powers of the committee of auditors of quoted companies by this provision. Article 151 *ter* is concerned with the powers given to the internal control committee (*comitato per il controllo sulla gestione*) under the monistic system and is similar in content to Article 151 *bis*.

According to Article 152(1) and (2) of Decree Law No. 58 of 24 February 1998, if they have justified suspicion of grave irregularities in the fulfilment of the duties of the directors that can cause damage to the company or one or more companies controlled by it, the committee of auditors, the supervisory board or the internal control committee may report the matter to the competent court. In such an event, the costs of the investigation may be borne by the company, and Accordingly directors may be dismissed by the court. When it has serious reasons to suspect that the committee of auditors, or the supervisory board or the internal control committee have manifestly failed to exercise their supervisory tasks, CONSOB may make a report to the competent court (the court that deals with urgent matters). The costs of the investigation must be borne by the company.

Finally, Article 153(1) of Decree Law No. 58 of 1998 provides that the committee of auditors (or where the monistic or dualistic system is used, the internal audit committee or the supervisory board) reports to the general meeting convened for the purpose of approving the accounts, on the supervisory activities it has undertaken, and blameworthy acts revealed. Furthermore, Article 153(2) provides that the committee of auditors may make proposals to the general meeting concerning the accounts and their approval as well as on other matters within its competence.

The application of certain of the provisions of the Civil Code to the committee of auditors of traditionally structured listed companies, is dealt with in Article 154 of Decree Law No. 58 of 1988, as amended, which also excludes certain of the provisions of the Civil Code form applying to the supervisory boards and internal control committees under the new dualistic and monistic board structures.

3. The dualistic system

The dual board system, the use of which is optional, bears some relationship to that employed in German public companies, and that available under the European Company Regulation. The rules governing the executive board (*consiglio di gestione*) as in general the same as those applicable to the directors under the traditional system. However, the supervisory board has some of the powers which, under the latter system, are entrusted to the general meeting, for example the appointment and dismissal of the members of the executive board, and many of those which are entrusted to the committee of auditors when the traditional system described immediately above is used. These include the supervision of the conduct of executive board members referred to in Article 2403(1). The supervisory board is also empowered by Article 2409 *terdecies* (1)(e) to make a report to the competent court in accordance with Article 2409.

The powers of the supervisory board are set out in Article 2409 *terdecies* of the Civil Code. Under the dual board system, this board is responsible for the approval of the annual accounts, in accordance with the provisions of Article 2409 *terdecies* (1)(b). Under all three different systems of management, the accounts have also to be approved by external auditors. The only exception to this rule applies to public companies which do not have recourse to the market for venture capital and which do not have to produce a consolidated balance sheet. By Article 2409 *bis* (3), the articles of such companies may entrust the committee of auditors with auditing functions provided that they are suitably qualified.

The supervisory board must consist of at least three members; the original members must according to Article 2409 *duodecies* (1) be appointed in the deed of incorporation, whilst later appointments, which like the original ones are for a maximum period of three years, are made by the general meeting. According to Article 2409 *nonies* sentence 4, the members of the first executive board are appointed by the deed of incorporation; subsequent appointments are made by the supervisory board: the maximum period for appointments is three years. Article 2409 *nonies* sentence 5 provides that members of the executive board may not be appointed to the supervisory board.

4. The unitary board system

This model involves a board of directors, one third the members of which must, in accordance with Article 2409 *septiesdecies* (2) be persons who fulfil the requirements of independence contained in Article 2399(1), which relates to the committee of auditors. The company is also required to establish an internal audit committee (*comitato per il controllo sulla gestione*) which is appointed by the directors unless the articles otherwise provide. If the company has recourse to the market for venture capital, this committee must consist of at least three persons. The members of the committee must not exercise management functions in the company or one which controls it, or one which it controls, and also fulfil the requirements of independence contained in Article 2399(1). At least one of the members of this committee must be entered on the register of auditors (*revisori contabili*). The functions of this committee are set out in Article 2409 *octiesdecies* (10). It examines the adequacy of the organisational structure of the company and the system of internal control, administration and accounting. Furthermore, it examines the performance of other duties entrusted to the directors, and in particular their relationship with those entrusted with the audit of the accounts.

Certain of the rules made applicable to the committee of auditors under the traditional system are made applicable to the internal audit, committee under the unitary board system. Article 2409 *noviesdecises* (1) of the Civil Code applies most of the rules applicable to the board of directors under the traditional system to a board of directors constituted under the new unitary system. The two new models may well appeal to companies having different needs.

5. General meetings

Types General meetings of shareholders are either ordinary meetings (*assemblea ordinaria*) or extraordinary meetings (*assemblea straordinaria*). When a company does not have a supervisory board, ordinary meetings are held annually once a year within a period not exceeding 120 days of the end of the financial year. The period of 120 days may be extended to a period of 180 days by the articles when the company has to prepare a consolidated balance sheet and when so required by particular exigencies relating to the structure and objects of the company.[369] The general meeting shall approve the accounts, appoint and dismiss directors (or the members of the supervisory board where a company has a supervisory board), appoint the chairman and members of the committee of auditors, appoint an external auditor (if necessary), determine the remuneration of directors and auditors unless this is set out in the articles, and deliberate on the responsibilities of directors and auditors.[370] When a company has a supervisory board, the general meeting is responsible for appointing and dismissing the members and determining their remuneration when this is not provided for by the articles. General meetings may also resolve on other matters (apart from those on which an extraordinary meeting is required) which are placed within the competence of the shareholders by the law or the articles.[371] A general

[369] Italian Civil Code, Article 2364(1).
[370] *Ibid.*, Art. 2364. [371] *Ibid.*, Art. 2364.

meeting cannot validly pass a resolution on a management matter unless this is placed before it by the board; this is because, by Article 2384 of the Civil Code, management questions are reserved for the directors of the company.

Extraordinary meetings are called to resolve on the alteration of the articles, including the increase and reduction of capital, the issue of bonds, the appointment, replacement and powers of the liquidators,[372] and other matters expressly placed within their competence by the law or the articles.

Convocation of and participation in meetings Meetings are normally called by the directors or by the executive board. The holders of at least one-tenth of the company's capital (or any lesser percentage required by the articles) may require the directors to call a meeting, and specify the items to be put on the agenda.[373] If the directors or the executive board fail to do so, the meetings may be called by the committee of auditors or the supervisory board or the internal audit committee (*comitato per il controllo sulla gestione*). If these bodies fail to call such a meeting, the president of the local civil court may do so: if he thinks such action justified he must designate who shall preside over the meeting.[374]

If the company is a quoted one, Article 125(1) of Decree Law No. 58 of 24 February 1998 provides that the directors shall call a meeting within thirty days of being requested to do so by the holders of at least 10 per cent of the company's capital, who must specify the items to be placed on the agenda. However, by Article 125(2) the directors may decide not to hold a meeting within that time period if, having regard to the proposed agenda, this is not in the interests of the company.[375] The president of the

[372] *Ibid.*, Art. 2365. Certain of the powers of an extraordinary general meeting may be delegated to the directors or on the supervisory board by the articles. When there is a supervisory board, the general meeting's competences are lessened. It appoints and dismisses members of the supervisory board and determines their remuneration, decides on distribution of profits and appoints the external auditor, see Art. 2364 *bis* of the Civil Code.

[373] The power of the members to request the calling of a meeting is excluded in the circumstances set out in Art. 2367(3), which include matters which, in accordance with the law, the meeting would decide on proposals of the directors or on the basis of projects or reports drawn up by them.

[374] Italian Civil Code, Art. 2367(2).

[375] The provisions of Art. 125 of the Decree Law No. 58 of 1998 resemble those of Art. 2367 of the Civil Code, which have been dealt with in the present paragraph. If the deed of incorporation so provides, a meeting may be called by the holders of a lesser percentage of the capital.

local civil tribunal may, according to Article 125(3) on being requested to do so by the shareholders, order the holding of a meeting after having heard the directors and auditors, and designate who is to preside over it. If requested by the holders of one-fifth of the share capital of a quoted company, Article 2367 of the Civil Code remains applicable, such that the directors have no discretion to refuse to call the meeting.[376] According to Article 151(2) of the Decree Law No. 58 of 1998 at least two members of the committee of auditors may call a general meeting.

The latter provisions apply only to quoted companies. However, Article 2406 of the Civil Code, like Article 2408, applies both to quoted and unquoted companies. Article 2406 provides that the committee of auditors may call a meeting where the directors have been guilty of omission or unjustifiable delay in doing so. The committee of auditors may also call a meeting if, in carrying out its tasks, it discovers seriously wrongful acts, and there is an urgent need to take measures.[377]

If a complaint is made to the committee of auditors by a shareholder concerning facts which he considers worthy of censure, it must take account of such a complaint in its report to the general meeting.[378] Should the complaint be made by shareholders holding 5 per cent of the share capital or two per cent in a company having recourse to the market for venture capital, the committee of auditors is required to investigate the complaint without delay and present its conclusions and proposals, if any, to the general meeting. In cases provided for in Article 2406(2), it must also call a general meeting.

When the dual board system is used, the supervisory board, or two members thereof, may call a meeting in accordance with Article 151 *bis* (3) of Decree No. 58 of 1998. It may also call a meeting of the directors.

Meetings are called by giving at least 15 days' notice in the Official Gazette (*Gazetta*) or in a daily newspaper indicated in the articles. According to Article 2366(3) of the Civil Code, in companies which do not have recourse to the market for venture capital, the articles may provide that notice may be given by means which ensure its receipt at least eight days before the meeting. Failure to give such notice does not render a meeting invalid if all the shareholders attend or are represented, together with the majority of directors and members of the controlling organs (the supervisory board or the committee of auditors).[379] Members who hold at least one-third of the company's capital represented at a meeting may

[376] Decree Law No. 58 of 24 February 1998, Art. 125(4).
[377] Italian Civil Code, Art. 2406(2). [378] *Ibid.*, Art. 2408(1). [379] *Ibid.*, Art. 2366(4).

declare that they are insufficiently informed of a matter on the agenda, and require the postponement of the meeting for not more than three days. This right cannot be exercised more than once with regard to the same matter.[380] The articles may require the deposit of the shares or share certificates at the seat of the company or with a particular bank within a specified period before the meeting at which the vote is to be cast. If a company which has recourse to the market for venture capital, this period may not be more than two days. The reduction of this period to two days was intended to encourage the increased participation of institutional investors in meetings.

Proxies The holders of shares in a public company may vote by correspondence or electronically.[381] Proxies are governed by the rules contained in Article 2372 of the Civil Code. In quoted companies, the somewhat complex rules contained in Articles 136–144 of the Decree Law No. 58 of 24 February 1998 apply to the solicitation and accumulation of proxies,[382] in derogation from Article 2372 of the Civil Code. Article 2372(1) stipulates that unless the articles provide otherwise, members may appoint proxies to represent them. Such appointments must be in writing. In companies which have recourse to the market for venture capital such an appointment is only valid for the particular meeting for which the appointment is made, unless it is a general proxy (*procura generale*), or a proxy conferred by a company, association, foundation or other collective entity or institution on one of its employees.[383] The proxy remains effective for meetings called subsequent to an adjournment.[384] The full name of the proxy must appear on the proxy form: proxies may not be granted with the representative's name blank.[385] A proxy cannot be granted to members of the management or supervisory bodies, members of the committee of auditors, or to employees of the company.[386] A proxy may not represent more than twenty members at the same meeting. If the company has recourse to the market for venture capital the proxy may not represent more than 50 shareholders if the capital of the company is not in excess of €5 million; or more than 100 shareholders if it does not exceed €25 million; or more than 200 shareholders if it exceeds the latter amount.

380 *Ibid.*, Art. 2374(2). 381 *Ibid.*, Art. 2370(4)

382 Article 137(1) of the Decree Law No. 58 of 1988 provides that the solicitation and accumulation of proxies is governed by the relevant part of the Decree Law.

383 Italian Civil Code, Art. 2372(2). 384 *Ibid.*, Art. 2372(2).

385 *Ibid.*, Art. Italian Civil Code, Article 2372(3).

386 *Ibid.*, Art. Italian Civil Code, Article 2372(4).

Special provisions apply to the solicitation of proxies and their accumulation in the case of quoted companies.[387] The solicitation of proxies is defined in Article 136(1)(b) of Decree Law No. 58 of 1998 as a request for the grant of proxies (*deleghe di voto*) made to the general body of shareholders. The phrase 'accumulation of proxies' is defined in Article 136(1)(e) as meaning the request for the grant of proxies made by a shareholders' association exclusively to its members.

According to Article 138(1) of Decree Law No. 58 of 1998, the solicitation of proxies must be effected by an intermediary at the request of the *committente* (agent)[388] by means of the dissemination of a prospectus and proxy forms. The votes in respect of the shares in respect of which proxies have been granted are exercised by the *committente* (agent) or, the intermediary which has made the solicitation, if the *committente* has given it the task.[389] The *committente* is required by Article 139(1) of the Decree Law No. 58 of 1998 to possess at least one per cent of the shares carrying the right to vote at the meeting at which proxies are sought, and must have held these shares for at least six months. CONSOB may prescribe a lesser percentage requirement if the capital of the company is particularly large, or the shareholding widely diffused. Article 140 of the Decree Law of 1998 reserves the solicitation of proxies to particular bodies, comprising investment undertakings, banks, companies which manage investments, investment companies having a variable capital, and capital companies having the exclusive object of carrying on the activity of soliciting proxies and representing shareholders in meetings.

Associations of shareholders which are permitted to collect proxies are defined in Article 141 of Decree Law No. 58 of 1998. They must be established by a private deed, and not exercise any activity as an undertaking except one which is directly instrumental in achieving the purpose of the association. Their membership must consist of at least fifty natural persons, each of which must own at least 0.1 per cent of the share capital having voting rights. Their task of collecting proxies is exercised in accordance with the provisions of Article 142. The first paragraph of

[387] Article 137(1) of Decree Law No. 58 of 1998 provides that solicitation and accumulation of proxies (*raccolta delle deleghe di voto*) is governed by the relevant part of the Decree Law in derogation from Art. 2372 of the Civil Code.

[388] The *committente* is defined in Art. 136(1)(c) of Decree Law No. 58 of 24 February 1998 as the person or persons that jointly promote the solicitation, requesting the adhesion to a specific voting proposal.

[389] Decree Law No. 58 of 24 February 1998, Art. 138(2).

the latter article provides that the person granting the proxy, must sign it, and the proxy must be revocable and be granted in respect of one meeting which has already been convoked, with effect for adjourned meetings. The proxy may not be granted with the proxy's name blank; it must state the date, the name of the proxy, and instructions as to voting. According to Article 142(2), the proxy may be conferred as well in respect of certain of the voting proposals indicated on the proxy form. Whether the grant is on a full or partial basis, all the shares in respect of which proxies are granted must be counted after the end of the regular holding of the meeting.

Article 143 of Decree Law No. 58 of 24 February 1998 contains rules governing the information which must be given when proxies are solicited, and makes the intermediary, i.e. the person or body which carries out the solicitation on behalf of the *committente*, responsible for the completeness of the information circulated during the solicitation. By Article 143(3), if an action for damages is brought against the *committente*, a shareholders' association or an intermediary for breach of the requirements of Articles 136–144 or of the related regulations, they bear the burden of proving that they have exercised the necessary degree of care. The solicitation of proxies and their accumulation by shareholders' associations, is further regulated by regulations made by the Ministry of Justice and CONSOB.[390]

Quorums and majorities A distinction is made by Italian company law doctrine between the quorum needed to start a meeting (*quorum costitivo*) and the quorum needed to adopt a resolution (*quorum deliberativo*). The rules governing ordinary general meetings are the same for quoted and non-quoted companies. The constitutive quorum for a general meeting of a public company consists of the holders of at least half the company's share capital represented in person or by proxy. Shares which (like saving shares) have no voting rights are not taken account of for the purposes determining the quorum.[391] The meeting reaches its decisions by an absolute majority, unless the articles provide for a higher one. An extraordinary general meeting reaches decisions by a majority consisting of the holders of more than one-half of the

[390] Decree Law No. 58 of February 1998, Art. 144.

[391] Italian Civil Code, Art. 2368(1) and (3). The meeting reaches decisions by an absolute majority, unless the articles require a larger one.

company's share capital unless the articles provide for a higher majority.[392] In companies which have recourse to the market for venture capital, the extraordinary general meeting is properly constituted, in accordance with Article 2368(3), in the presence of the holders of at least half of the share capital, or the larger quorum required by the articles, and passes resolutions by the affirmative votes of the holders of at least two-thirds of the share capital represented in the meeting.[393] Shares in respect of which votes cannot be exercised, are taken into account for the purpose of determining whether the meeting is regularly constituted. Such shares, and other shares in respect of which voting rights cannot be exercised by reason of a conflict of interests, are not taken account of for the purpose of determining requisite majorities and the capital necessary for the passing of resolutions.[394]

If a quorum is not present at an ordinary or extraordinary general meeting of a public company, the meeting must be called again. The meeting cannot take place on the same day as that set for the first meeting. If the date for the second meeting is not included in the notice at the first meeting, the meeting must be called again within thirty days of the first meeting. This is done by publishing a notice in the Official Gazette at least eight days before the date of the second meeting.[395] In the case of an unquoted company, the original notice of the meeting may set out the date of the second meeting.[396]

There is no quorum requirement for an adjourned ordinary general meeting, and it may deliberate on matters which should have been dealt with at the first meeting whatever the percentage of capital represented.[397] An adjourned second extraordinary general meeting cannot deliberate unless shareholders representing more than one-third of the share capital are present.[398] The affirmative votes of shareholders representing two-thirds of the company's share capital present or represented are also necessary for the passing of a resolution at an adjourned extraordinary general meeting.[399] The articles may require a higher majority except for

392 *Ibid.*, Art. 2368(3) and Decree Law No. 58 of 1998, Art. 126(1).
393 Note in the same sense Art. 126(4) of the Decree Law of 1998.
394 Italian Civil Code, Art. 2368(4).
395 *Ibid.*, Art. 2369(1) and (2) and Decree Law No. 58 of 24 February 1998, Art. 126(2) which applies to adjourned extraordinary general meetings of quoted companies.
396 Note the different rule contained in Art. 126(2) of Decree Law No. 58 of 1998.
397 Italian Civil Code, Art. 2369(3)
398 *Ibid.*, Art. 2369(3) and Decree Law No. 58 of 24 February 1998, Art. 126(1).
399 Italian Civil Code, Art. 2369(3) and Decree Law No. 58 of 24 February 1998, Art. 126(4). The latter rule also applies when a meeting is convened by the board.

the approval of the annual accounts and the appointment and dismissal of corporate officers.

According to Article 2369(5) of the Civil Code, in the case of companies not having recourse to the market for venture capital,[400] the favourable votes of shareholders representing more than one-third of the share capital are necessary at the second meeting for certain important resolutions. Such resolutions involve matters such as the alteration of the objects of the company, the conversion of the company into a company of another type, the dissolution of a company before the end of the period fixed for its existence, the transfer of the registered office abroad, and the issue of preference shares.[401]

According to Article 2369(6) of the Civil Code, where the articles so provide, meetings may take place subsequently to the second one.[402] Where companies have recourse to the market for venture capital, an extraordinary general meeting is properly constituted on a third or subsequent call given the presence of shareholders representing at least one fifth of the share capital, unless the articles require a higher quorum.[403] However, the deliberative quorum remains the same: resolutions have to be passed by the affirmative votes of the holders of two-thirds of the capital represented.

Voting rights Each share usually confers the right to one vote on its holders. Shares of the same class shall be of equal value and confer the same rights. However, the articles may confer different rights on different classes of shareholders.[404] The articles may provide that the holders of shares which have preferential rights to the distribution of profits, and the reimbursement of capital in winding up, only have voting rights at extraordinary general meetings. Shares without voting rights and limited voting rights may not exceed one-half of the company's capital. A company cannot issue shares conferring multiple voting rights.[405] Savings shares (*azioni di risparmio*) may be issued not carrying the right to vote, or the

[400] These include unquoted companies and companies having less than 200 members.

[401] Italian Civil Code, Art. 2369(5).

[402] *Ibid.*, Art. 2369(6). The provisions of Art. 2369(3)–(5) are applicable to such meetings.

[403] *Ibid.*, Art. 2369(7): compare Decree Law No. 58 of 1998, Art. 126(3) which contains similar rules.

[404] Italian Civil Code, Art. 2348. See the discussion of the types of shares in Santosuosso, *Il nuovo diritto societario*, pp. 24–29.

[405] Italian Civil Code, Art. 2351.

right to attend meetings.[406] 'Tracking' shares may also be issued (as in the case of France and the United States). As is clear from Article 2350(2) of the Civil Code, the patrimonial rights attaching to such shares are connected with the results of the company's activities in a particular sector of business. Shares held by the issuing company itself carry no voting rights.[407] Companies without recourse to the market for venture capital (this market includes some large unquoted companies) are permitted by Article 2351(2) of the Civil Code to include provisions in their articles providing for the limitation of the voting rights to a certain amount of the capital held by the shareholders, or, as in France, to provide for voting by echelons, or by gradual decreasing amounts depending on the amount of capital held.

Resolutions adopted by the votes of a shareholder who has a direct interest which conflicts with that of the company, can be challenged in accordance with Article 2377 of the Civil Code when they are likely to harm the company. Should a shareholder vote despite the prohibition, and the necessary majority to pass the resolution would not have been obtained without his vote, the local civil court is empowered to set the resolution aside upon the application of a member having one-thousandth of the company's capital if the company has recourse to the market for venture capital, and on that of the holders of 5 per cent of the share capital in other companies. The articles may reduce or exclude these requirements. Such reductions may also be challenged by the directors, the supervisory board and the committee of auditors.[408]

Voting and other agreements (*patti parasociali*) According to Article 122(1) of Decree Law No. 58 of 24 February 1998, agreements in whatever form stipulated, which govern the exercise of the vote in quoted companies, and companies which control them must be notified to CONSOB within five days of their conclusion, published within ten days, and deposited within fifteen days within the Registrar of Enterprises. Such agreements are void if the notification obligations are not respected.[409] The votes in respect of all quoted shares affected by such a void agreement may not be exercised in a quoted company or one

406 Decree Law No. 58 of 24 February 1998, Art. 145(1) and (2).

407 Italian Civil Code, Art. 2357 *ter* 2.

408 *Ibid.*, Art. 2373 and 2377. The latter article contains detailed rules governing the annulment of resolutions: their nullity is governed by Art. 2379: see Santosuosso, *Il nuovo diritto societario*, pp. 48–56.

409 Decree Law No. 58 of 1998, Art. 122(3).

that controls it. The present article applies to certain other types of agreement.[410] Agreements governed by Article 122 have a maximum duration of three years if made for a determinate period. If they are made for an indeterminate period, there is a right of withdrawal from them on giving six months notice.[411]

Shareholders' voting and other agreements are now also regulated by the provisions of Articles 2341 *bis* and 2341 *ter* of the Civil Code. These provisions resemble those contained in Legislative Decree Law No. 58 of 1998 in some respects but there may be certain conflicts between the two sets of provisions.[412]

Article 2341 *ter* provides that a shareholders' agreement in a company having recourse to the market for venture capital must be communicated to the company, and declared at the beginning of every meeting. The minutes of such a declaration must be deposited at the Register of Enterprises. Failure to make such a declaration means that shareholders who are parties to the agreement may not exercise their right to vote, and decisions adopted by meetings as the result of their vote may be challenged in accordance with Article 2377. The directors, the members of any supervisory board or committee of auditors, shareholders who voted for or against such a resolution or who abstained from voting may challenge it within ninety days of its being passed. If registration of the

410 *Ibid.*, Art. 122(5).

411 *Ibid.*, Art. 123(1) and (2). Six months notice of withdrawal is required. A fuller account of shareholder agreements is given by F. Wooldridge and L. Davies (2006) 27 Co Law 190–92.

412 Article 2341 *bis* stipulates that agreements which are intended to safeguard the proprietary arrangements or the governance of the company and which have as their subject matter the exercise of the vote in a public company, or a company which controls it; or which impose limitations on the transfer of particular shares or participations in the company or in the controlling company; or which have as their object or effect the exercise of a joint dominant influence over the company may not remain in force for more than five years, and are renewable. Clauses which are ancillary to joint venture agreements concerning the production or exchange of goods and services and which relate to a company entirely owned by the parties to the agreement are excluded from the provisions of Art. 2341 *bis*. This provision, unlike Art. 122 of Decree Law No. 58 of 1998, also does not apply to agreements to consult before exercising a vote in a company, or to agreements governing the acquisition of shares or financial instruments. See the account of shareholders' agreements (*patti parasocialii*) in Santosuosso, *Il nuovo diritto societario*, pp. 56–58. The relevant period for Art. 2341 *bis* agreements clearly differs from that in Art. 123(1) of the Decree Law No. 58 of 1998, which arguably prevails over the provisions of Art. 2341 *bis* as far as quoted companies are concerned. This may, however not have been the intention of the legislature.

resolution is necessary, the relevant period is three months after such registration at the Register of Enterprises.[413]

Annulment of resolutions Resolutions which are not passed in accordance with the law or the articles are invalid, and may be annulled upon application being made to the competent court of the place where the company is registered (the local civil tribunal). The directors, the supervisory board and shareholders who voted for or against it, or who abstained, may challenge the resolution within ninety days of the date of its passing, or where registration with, or deposited with the office of the Registrar of Enterprises, within three months of it being so registered or filed.[414]

Right of withdrawal The Italian rules governing the withdrawal of shareholders are quite complex.[415] Certain imperative causes for withdrawal are included in Article 2437 of the Civil Code. Shareholders have a right of withdrawal who dissent from or abstain from voting for resolutions which alter the company's objects in such a way as to make a substantial change in the activities of the company, or transform it into another a company of another kind, or transfer its registered office outside Italy, or which modify the articles with regard to voting rights or rights of participation; which amend the criteria for determining the value of the shares in the event of withdrawal. Rights of withdrawal from a company subject to an activity of direction and coordination by another entity are also provided for by Article 2497 *quater*. Any agreement which excludes the right of withdrawal or which makes it more burdensome is without effect.

According to Article 2437(2), unless the articles provide otherwise, dissenting or abstaining shareholders have the right to withdraw if a resolution is passed extending the period of existence of the company, or introducing or removing a restriction on the transfer of shares. Companies which do not have recourse to the market for venture capital may provide for additional grounds for withdrawal in their articles.

413 Italian Civil Code, Art. 2377. The challenge may be made by the holder of 0.1 per of the share capital if the company has recourse to the market for venture capital, and otherwise it may be made by the holder of 5 per cent.

414 *Ibid.*, Art. 2377, as discussed above in the context of the procedure relating to shareholders' agreements.

415 *Ibid.*, Arts. 2437, 2437 *bis* and 2437 *ter*.

A shareholder may withdraw from an unlisted company which has an indefinite duration on giving 180 days' notice, which may be extended to one year.

If the shares are quoted on a regulated market, the shareholders may obtain reimbursement for their shares on the basis of the average price for the last six months. If the shares are not quoted on a regulated market, other methods of valuation indicated in Article 2437 *ter* are available. Written notice of the shareholders' intention to withdraw must be sent by registered letter to the company within fifteen days of the registration at the Register of Enterprises of the resolution which permits it. If the withdrawal is not legitimated by a meeting, it must be exercised within thirty days of the time when the shareholder had notice of the legitimating event.

Article 131 of Decree Law No. 58 of 24 February 1998, unlike the relevant provisions of the Civil Code, is only applicable to quoted companies. It provides that shareholders who dissent from deliberations concerning mergers or divisions which involve the allocation to them of non-quoted shares have a right of withdrawal pursuant to Article 2437 of the Civil Code.

The shares of withdrawing shareholders are offered to the existing shareholders in proportion to their shareholdings. Any shares which remain may be sold to third parties. If the shares are not sold, the company must buy them. If there are no distributable profits or adequate reserves, the company must either reduce its capital or be wound up.

Where a resolution prejudicially affects the rights of a special class of shareholders they do not have a right of withdrawal without approval by an extraordinary general meeting of that class in order to be valid.[416] However, this rule applies only where the rights of the special class of shareholders are affected without similar rights of all other shareholders being modified or abrogated.

6. Accounts

A public company's accounts consists of a balance sheet, profit and loss account and explanatory notes (*nota integrativa*).[417] These must be forwarded by the directors together with their report on the situation of the company and on the conduct of the management, to the committee of auditors at least thirty days before the date of the meeting which

[416] *Ibid.*, Art. 2376(1) and (2). [417] *Ibid.*, Art. 2423(1).

has to approve them.[418] If the company is an unquoted one, the committee of auditors is required to make a report to the general meeting on the results of the financial year, and on the state of the accounts, and their approval, with particular reference to certain derogations allowed by Article 2423(4) of the Civil Code,[419] If the company is a quoted one, the above mentioned provisions of Article 153 of Decree Law No. 58 of 24 February 1998, are applicable rather than those of Article 2429(2) of the Civil Code. The committee of auditors may thus make proposals to the general meeting, correcting the accounts and their approval.

In both quoted and unquoted companies the balance sheet, profit and loss accounts, explanatory notes on the accounts, the directors and auditors' reports, together with a copy of the last accounts of controlled companies[420] and a summary of the essential parts of those of associated companies,[421] and the reports of the directors and the committee of auditors, and the persons responsible for external control must be kept available for inspection at the company's head office for fifteen days before the annual general meeting, and remain there until the accounts are approved.[422]

Under all the three models governing board structure, subject to a minor exception contained in Article 2409 *bis* (3), which has already been mentioned above, it follows from Article 2409 *bis* (1) that the accounts of companies are externally audited by a company auditor or an auditing company, on a register maintained by the Ministry of Justice. Companies which have recourse to the market for venture capital are required to have their accounts audited externally by an auditing company which is subject to special safeguards, being subject to the special rules governing auditing which are applicable to companies issuing shares quoted on a

[418] *Ibid.*, Art. 2429(1). In companies which make use of the new dualistic system the approval of the accounts is a matter for the supervisory board: see Italian Civil Code, Art. 2409 *terdecies* (b).

[419] *Ibid.*, Art. 2429(2).

[420] Controlled companies are defined in Art. 2359 of the Italian Civil Code as companies in which another company holds the majority of votes which can be exercised at a general meeting, or has sufficient votes to exercise a dominant influence at such a meeting, as well as companies which are under the dominant influence of another company by reason of a contractual relationship with it.

[421] Associated companies are defined in Art. 2359 of the Italian Civil Code as companies in which another company may exercise a dominant influence. This is presumed when such a company can exercise 20 per cent of the votes at a general meeting, or 10 per cent of the votes that can be exercised if the company is quoted on the stock exchange.

[422] Italian Civil Code, Art. 2429(3).

regulated market and to the control exercised by CONSOB.[423] An auditor or auditing company may have their appointment revoked by the general meeting after consultation with the committee of auditors, if there is good cause.[424] The holders of at least one-twentieth of the share capital of a quoted company may, subject to an exception contained in Article 156(4) of Decree Law No. 58 of 1998, challenge the deliberations of the annual general meeting which approved the accounts for the relevant financial year, on the ground that the accounts do not properly conform with the rules governing their compilation.[425]

After the accounts have been approved, the general meeting may declare a dividend out of the net profits shown. It may instead resolve to transfer the whole or part of the profits to reserves or carry them forward. However, dividends may not be paid to shareholders unless they are in reality available, and result from properly proposed accounts. The capitalisation of undistributed profits or reserves may be the subject of a resolution of an extraordinary general meeting, which will issue new fully paid bonus shares, or increase the nominal value of the existing shares, by means of capitalisation.[426]

7. The rights of minority shareholders

Many of the rights of minority shareholders have been mentioned above, for example those of a stipulated minority of shareholders in public companies to bring derivative actions,[427] the power of a specific minority of shareholders to report auditors or directors suspected of grave irregularities to the local civil tribunal,[428] and the powers of a particular minority of shareholders of a quoted or unquoted company to request the calling of a meeting,[429] and the power of a stipulated minority of shareholders in a quoted company to challenge the deliberations of the annual general meeting which approves the accounts.[430] The derivative action available to shareholders in quoted companies against directors, auditors and members of the executive committee under Article 129 of

[423] *Ibid.*, Art. 2409 *bis* (1) and Decree Law No. 58 of 24 February 1998, Art. 159(1). Subject to minor exceptions contained in Art. 2409 *bis* (3), the accounts of all public companies are externally audited.

[424] Italian Civil Code, Art. 2409 *quater* (3) and Decree Law No. 58, Art. 159 sentence 2.

[425] Decree Law No. 58, Art. 157(1). [426] Italian Civil Code, Art. 2442.

[427] Decree Law of 24 February 1998, Art. 129; and Italian Civil Code, Arts. 2393 and 2393 *bis*.

[428] Italian Civil Code, Art. 2409.

[429] Decree Law of 24 February 1998, Art. 125 and Italian Civil Code, Art. 2367.

[430] Decree Law of 24 February 1998, Art. 157(1).

Decree No. 58 of 1998 will be considered futher below. In a quoted company, it is available to the holders of at least 5 per cent of the company's share capital, or of such lesser percentage as is stipulated in the articles. In an unquoted company, the percentage is raised to at least 20 per cent. In either kind of company, if the action is brought against the directors or members of the executive committee, the initiation of process against the company is notified to the president of the committee of auditors. The shareholders responsible for bringing the action against the company must nominate one or more common representatives for the purpose of such litigation and for consequential acts. The company may waive the bringing of the action or it may settle it provided that there is no contrary vote of a minority of members representing one-fifth of the company's capital if the company is unquoted, and one-twentieth if it is quoted, at the general meeting which decides on the waiver or settlement. If the shareholders' claim is successful, the company has to pay the plaintiffs costs in respect of the judgment, insofar as the defendants have not been required to pay them, or it proves impossible to recover them following the judgement. The derivative action is also regulated by the rather similar provisions of Article 2393 *bis* of the Civil Code, which are applicable to companies which have recourse to the market for venture capital. Article 2393 *bis* also applies to other companies which do not have such recourse. The action must be brought by persons representing at least one-fifth (which may be increased by the articles to one-third) of the share capital, where the company does not have venture capital. Otherwise it is made available under the same conditions as in Article 129 of Decree Law No. 58 of 1998.

B. *Private companies*

The rules governing private companies (SRL) are in essence based to a considerable extent upon those governing public companies (SpA). There are more opportunities for departing from these rules by specific provisions in the deed of incorporation than there is in the case with the SpA. The rules governing the general meeting are of a flexible character as is made clear by Article 2479(4) and (5) of the Civil Code. Like the French and German rules governing private companies, those governing Italian private companies have some features of a personal or personalistic character.[431]

[431] See F. Wooldridge, 'The New Legal Provisions Governing Italian Private Companies' [2005] EBLR 99.

1. Directors

Articles 2475–2476 of the Civil Code contain rules governing the directors of private companies which often resemble the corresponding rules for the SpA, although there are some differences between them. Unless the deed of incorporation (*atto costitutivo*) provides otherwise, the directors (*amministratori*) of a private company must be members of the company. No period of office is prescribed for directors: if the deed of incorporation is silent about these matters, it may appear they may be appointed for whatever period is thought appropriate. Such appointment is by resolution of the general meeting, unless the deed of incorporation provides otherwise. According to Article 2475(3), when the administration of a private company is entrusted to more than one person, they form the board of directors. The deed of incorporation may provide that the directors shall act individually or jointly, in which case the special rules contained in Articles 2257 and 2258 which are applicable to partnerships, apply to the decision making process. However, they cannot act individually in relation to the preparation of the balance sheet and proposals for merger or division, as well as the increase of capital, (when this task is delegated to the directors).[432] They must act together in these matters. According to Article 2475(4), when a board of directors is established, the deed of incorporation may provide that decisions shall be adopted by means of a written consultation or on the basis of a written consensus. The documents signed by the directors must clearly state the matters decided on and the consensus reached. It would seem that if the directors wish to reduce the importance of meetings and place emphasis on such methods of communication as the telephone, fax or internet, the results of such deliberations must be transcribed into a written document.

The directors have, in accordance with Article 2475 *bis* (1), the power of general representation of the company. As is the case with public companies, the limitations on the powers of the directors are not opposable to third parties even if published, except where it can be shown that the latter have knowingly acted to the detriment of the company. The provisions of Article 2475 *ter*, which govern transactions concluded by directors who have a personal interest therein are somewhat different from those of Article 2391, which apply to directors of public companies. According to the former provision, contracts concluded by directors who

[432] The exceptions to the general principle contained in the Italian Civil Code, Art. 2475(3) appear in Art. 2475(5).

have a personal interest therein, either on their own account or on that of a third party, may be annulled on the initiative of the company if the interest was known to or recognisable by the third party. Furthermore, decisions adopted by the board of directors by the determining vote of a director who is personally interested, either on his own account or on that of a third party, and which cause damage to the company's assets, may be challenged within three months by the directors or by the committee of auditors, or by an external auditor, should such persons exist. Rights acquired by third parties acting in good faith on the basis of acts carried out in implementation of the decision are unaffected.

Article 2476 of the Civil Code governs the liabilities of directors. Paragraph 4 somewhat controversially provides for a derivative action against them by individual members when they have been guilty of grave faults. Furthermore, Article 2476(6) provides that unless the deed of incorporation stipulates otherwise, actions against the directors may be settled or renounced by the company if such a procedure is supported by the holders of two-thirds of the share capital, and is not opposed by shareholders holding one-tenth of the share capital.

2. The committee of auditors

An Italian SRL must appoint a committee of auditors if the deed of incorporation so stipulates. It is required to do so by law if for two successive financial years, two out of the three following limits are exceeded. The first limit is that the company's balance sheet total is the equivalent to €3,125,000; the second that its receipt from sales and services is €6,250,000; and the third that its average number of employees is fifty. The obligation to appoint a committee of auditors terminates if, for two successive years, two of the three limits are not exceeded.[433] The rules relating to the committee of auditors of an unquoted SpA apply to the committee of auditors of an SRL which has to be set up by law.[434]

In such an SRL, members representing one-tenth of the share capital may report a well funded suspicion of serious breaches of duties of the directors or internal auditors to the appropriate court, in accordance with Article 2409 of the Civil Code.[435] Members who do not participate in the management of a private company are entitled to obtain

[433] Italian Civil Code, Art. 2477(3). [434] *Ibid.*, Art. 2477(2).

[435] Article 2409 provides for the procedure of judicial investigation of the management of the company. In serious cases, the court can dismiss the directors and appoint a judicial manager and determine his powers and duration of office.

information from the directors concerning the progress of the company's affairs and to inspect its books and documents.

3. Decisions of the members

The provisions of Article 2479 of the Italian Civil Code display the influence of the concept of private autonomy according to which the members are free to make the rules they find appropriate. Article 2479(1) provides that members decide on matters reserved for their competence by the deed of incorporation, and also on matters referred to them by one or more directors or members holding at least one third of the company's share capital. Certain matters are exclusively within the competence of the members. By Article 2479(2), these include:

(1) the approval of the accounts and the distribution of dividends;
(2) the appointment, if provided for in the deed of incorporation, of the directors;
(3) the appointment of the committee of auditors and the external auditor;
(4) the amendment of the deed of incorporation; and
(5) decisions to carry out activities which would involve substantial changes in the objects of the company set out in the deed of incorporation, or substantial changes in the rights of shareholders.

As already mentioned, the deed of incorporation may provide that the decisions of the shareholders shall be adopted on the basis of a written consultation or consents expressed in writing.[436] According to Article 2479(4) of the Civil Code, if the deed of incorporation does not contain any provisions governed by paragraph (3) of Article 2479 concerning written consultation, and in any event with regard to the matters dealt with by clauses (4) and (5) of Article 2479(2), or if such action within clauses (4) or (5) of Article 2479(2) is requested by one or more directors or shareholders representing at least one-third of the company's share capital, the members' decisions shall be adopted by a resolution of the general meeting.

[436] Italian Civil Code, Art. 2479(3). These requirements do not prevent the articles from providing that meetings shall be called by telephone, email or fax. However, a meeting is required when the deed of incorporation does not make provision for the appointment of a committee of auditors or an external auditor, and is always required in relation to alterations in the deed of incorporation or substantial modifications in the objects of the company. A meeting is also required where one or more directors, or shareholders holding at least one third of the share capital so request.

The key paragraph of Article 2479 *bis* of the Civil Code stipulates that the deed of incorporation determines the mode of calling the general meeting, which must be such as to provide for the timely provision of information on the matters to be dealt with. It seems that the meeting may be called by means of fax and email. In the absence any provisions any provisions governing the method of calling the general meeting, this is done by sending a registered letter to the members at least eight days before the meeting is to take place, to their place of residence as stated in the company's register of members. It follows from Article 2479 *bis* (2) that, unless the deed of incorporation provides otherwise, members may be represented by another person at the meeting. Article 2479 *bis* (3) provides that, unless the deed of incorporation provides otherwise, the meeting takes place at the seat of the company and in the presence of the holders of at least half the company's capital. Each member has the right to participate in the meeting and has a number of votes in proportion to his share in the capital. Decisions are taken by an absolute majority.[437]

The annulment of members' decisions is governed by Article 2479 *ter*.[438] Decisions of the company which has not been taken in conformity with the law or the deed of incorporation may be challenged by members who have not consented to them, and by any director and by the committee of auditors within six months of their entry into the company's register of the decision. The court may, if it deems it opportune fix a period of not more than six months for the adoption of a new decision aimed at removing the ground of invalidity of the earlier decision. The request for such adoption should be made by the company or the person who has requested the annulment of the original decision.[439]

According to Article 2479 *ter* (2), where there is a possibility of their harming the company, decisions taken by the determining vote of a person having an interest of his own or on behalf of another party, which conflicts with that of the company, may be annulled in accordance with the rules set out in Article 2479 *ter* (1). Decisions having objects which are illegal or impossible and decisions taken in the absolute absence of information, may be challenged by an interested party within three years of being entered in the company's register of decisions. A decision which

[437] Decisions taken on matters within clauses (4) and (5) of Art. 2474(2), (alterations of the deed of incorporation or substantial alterations in the objects of the company), require the favourable vote of shareholders representing at least one-half of the company's capital.

[438] Which apparently cover informal decisions and deliberations of the general meeting.

[439] Italian Civil Code, Art. 2479 *ter* (1).

changes the company's objects so as to provide for the carrying out of illegal or impossible activity, may be challenged a any time.[440]

4. Accounts and the distribution of profits

The accounts must be prepared in accordance with the detailed provision of Articles 2423–2431 of the Civil Code, which apply also to public companies. They must be presented to the shareholders within a period not exceeding 120 days from the end of the financial year but according to Article 2478 *bis* (1), an extension of time may be granted in certain circumstances. The decision of the members approving the accounts also deals with the distribution of the profits of the company. Such profits may not be distributed except when they were really earned, and are based upon a balance sheet which has been regularly approved.

5. Minority rights

As already indicated above it follows from Article 2476(4) that each shareholder may bring a derivative action against the directors. However, according to Article 2476(6) if a majority of shareholders representing at least two-thirds of the share capital so resolve, such an action may be abandoned or compromised, unless the holders of at least 10 per cent of the share capital object to such an event. Article 2476(3) entitles shareholders who do not participate in the management to be informed by the directors of the development of the business of the company. Every shareholder has the right to participate in the decision-making process, and his voting rights are proportional to his shareholding.

As is the case in the public company, the shareholders of an Italian private company have an extensive right to withdraw from the company. Such withdrawal is governed by the provisions of Article 2473(1), which provides that the deed of incorporation determines when a shareholder may withdraw and the modalities of the exercise of such withdrawal. The provision also stipulates that a member may always withdraw if he has not consented to the alteration of the objects of a the company, or to the conversion of the company into a company of another kind; or to its merger with another company or to its division; or to the carrying out of activities which involve a substantial modification of the company's objects. Furthermore, rights of withdrawal exist when a private company is subjected to direction or coordination by another company. In addition to these rather extensive rights of withdrawal, Article 2473 *bis* provides that shareholders in an

[440] *Ibid.*, Art. 2479 *ter* (3).

Italian private company may be excluded for good reasons in accordance with the provisions of the deed of incorporation.

VI. The position in Spain

A. Private companies (SRLs)

1. Management

Spanish law does not make provision for a double board system in public or private companies, although provision has recently been made for audit committees in quoted companies.

The enactment of the Spanish Limited Liability Companies Act 1995 (LSRL), governing private companies, has resulted in the rules governing the management of such companies sometimes being identical with, and sometimes reflecting the corresponding rules relating to public companies (LSA), to which reference is sometimes made. However, there are some differences between the two sets of rules.

The management organ of a Spanish private company, like that of a German GmbH, is not conceived as being the supreme organ of that company; this role is given to the general meeting, which according to Article 44(2) of the LSRL, may issue instructions to the company's management or require it to obtain authorisation to adopt resolutions regarding certain areas of the company's business, unless the articles (*estatutos*) provide otherwise.

A private company (*sociedad de responsabilidad limitada*) may have one or more directors (*administradores*) who may act separately or jointly, or a board of directors, which must comply with requirements concerning the maximum (twelve) and minimum (three) number of members.[441] The company's articles must set forth the rules governing the organisation and operation of the board, including the rules concerning meetings thereof.

The articles may contain different methods of organising the administration, and give the management board the facility of choosing between them.[442] The general meeting has the exclusive power to appoint directors, and is also empowered to remove them, even if such removal is not on the agenda of the meeting. Unless the articles otherwise provide, there is no need to be a member of the company to be appointed

[441] Spanish Private Limited Liability Companies Act 1995, Art. 57(1).
[442] *Ibid.*, Art. 57(2).

director thereof.[443] Certain persons including minors, persons without legal capacity and bankrupts may not act as directors.[444] Unless the articles provide for a specific term of office, the directors serve for an indeterminate period of time.[445] They are required to discharge their duties with the degree of care of a conscientious business man and a faithful representative. They must maintain secrecy about confidential information, even when they have vacated office.[446] The directors are responsible for the preparation of the annual financial statements, the directors' report and any necessary consolidated accounts, within a maximum period of three months from the end of the financial year.[447]

The powers of representation of the directors are set out in Article 62 of the LSRL. Thus, if there are several directors acting jointly, the power of representation is exercised jointly by at least two of them, in accordance with the provisions of the articles. If there is a board of directors, this acts as a single body. However, the articles may grant individual or joint powers of representation to one or more members of the board. The latter may (as is the case with an Italian public or private company) appoint an executive committee (*Comisión ejecutiva*) or one or more executive directors. If it does so, the board determines the rules governing its or their actions.[448]

The scope of representation extends to all activities included in the objects of the company, as set out in the articles. Any limitation on such powers of the directors has no effect as against third parties, even if it is entered in the Commercial Registry. The company is bound in relation to third parties who have acted in good faith and without serious fault even when it is clear from the limitations registered at the Commercial Registry that the activity is not within the company's objects.[449] The directors are prohibited from competing with their company in accordance with the provisions of Article 65 of the LSRL. Directors of a private company are not entitled to any remuneration, unless the articles provide otherwise, and determine the manner of remuneration.[450] When this is not based upon participation in profits, it is determined annually by the general meeting.[451]

[443] *Ibid.*, Art. 58(1) and (2). [444] *Ibid.*, Art. 58(3).
[445] *Ibid.*, Art. 60(1). [446] *Ibid.*, Art. 61.
[447] *Ibid.*, Art. 84; and Spanish Public Companies Act 1989, Art. 171 ff.
[448] Spanish Private Limited Liability Companies Act 1995, Art. 62(2)(d).
[449] *Ibid.*, Art. 63. [450] *Ibid.*, Art. 66(1). [451] *Ibid.*, Art. 66(3).

According to Article 69(1) of the LSRL, concerning private companies, the liability of the directors of such a company is governed by the provisions of Articles 133–135 of the LSA, concerning public companies. Article 133(1) provides that directors shall be liable to the company, its shareholders and auditors for damages caused as the result of unlawful acts and for failure to exercise due care. Articles 134 and 135 provide for derivative and personal actions against the directors. It is noteworthy that Article 134(5) provides that creditors of the company may bring derivative suits against the directors when the company or its shareholders fail to do so, and the company's net worth is insufficient to satisfy its debts. According to Article 69(2) of the LSRL a resolution to bring an action against the directors must be approved by a majority of the shareholders who exercise their votes and are entitled to do so, provided that such votes represent at least one-third of those belonging to the outstanding shareholders.

Directors may challenge void and voidable resolutions of the board in accordance with the provisions of Article 70 of the Law of 23 March 1995, as also may members holding at least 5 per cent of the share capital. Directors may attack such resolutions within thirty days of their approval. Members may challenge them within thirty days of becoming aware of them.[452] Such resolutions may not be challenged if more than one year has elapsed since their adoption.

The new type of private company (*sociedad limitada de nueva empresa*), introduced by Law 7/2003, which can be registered within forty-eight hours of the execution of the deed of incorporation, has on formation, no more than five members and it is restricted in its fields of activity.

2. General meetings

The general meeting is competent to pass resolutions on a wide variety of matters, which include the supervision of the company management; the approval of the annual accounts; the distribution of dividends; the appointment and removal of directors; the alteration of the articles; increase and reduction of the company's capital; its conversion into a company of another type, merger with another company, or its division; and its dissolution[453] As already indicated, it may issue instructions to the company's directors.[454]

[452] *Ibid.*, Art. 70. [453] *Ibid.*, Art. 44(1). [454] *Ibid.*, Art. 44(2).

The directors have the task of convening the general meeting.[455] They must do so within the first six months of each financial year for the purpose of reviewing the company's management, approving its accounts, and on the application of the distributable profits.[456] A general meeting must be called by the directors at any time when they deem necessary, or when requested to do so by the holders of at least 5 per cent of the company's capital. If the directors do not properly respond to the request it may be called by the Court of First Instance of the place where the company has its registered office.[457] Unless the articles otherwise provide, notice of the general meeting must be published in the Official Gazette and in any one of the daily newspapers of the municipality in which the company has its registered office.[458] At least fifteen days must pass between the calling of the meeting and the date thereof.[459] The meeting must be held in the municipality where the registered office is situated, unless the articles provide otherwise.[460] If all the members or their proxies are present at a meeting which has not been duly called, and the persons present unanimously agree upon the holding of the meeting and its agenda, the meeting (*junta universal*) is treated by Article 48 of the LSRL as being validly called. Such a universal meeting may take place within Spain or outside that country.

All members have the right to attend general meetings, and they may be represented there by proxies.[461] Members may request in writing before the meeting or verbally at the meeting such information or clarification as they deem necessary concerning matters on the agenda. The directors must provide such information unless they deem the disclosure requested would be harmful to the company's interests.[462] This exception is not applicable if the request is supported by members holding at least 25 per cent of the company's capital. A member may not vote in certain conflict of interest situations enumerated in Article 52. Thus, when the resolution proposed would authorise a member to transfer his shares or would remove him from the company, he may not vote on it. If a member is a director, he cannot vote on a resolution concerning the waiver of non-competition provisions.[463]

[455] *Ibid.*, Art. 45(1). [456] *Ibid.*, Art. 45(2). [457] *Ibid.*, Art. 45(3).
[458] *Ibid.*, Art. 46(1). [459] *Ibid.*, Art. 46(3). [460] *Ibid.*, Art. 47. [461] *Ibid.*, Art. 49.
[462] *Ibid.*, Art. 51. This exception does not apply if the request is supported by members representing at least 25 per cent of the company's capital.
[463] *Ibid.*, Art. 52(1).

Resolutions are normally required to be passed by a majority of the votes cast which must consist at least one third of the votes on the outstanding shares in the company.[464] Larger majorities are required for resolutions concerning the increase or reduction of the share capital, as well as resolutions involving conversions, mergers, and the exclusion of preferential rights on an increase of capital. The former two types of resolution require a favourable vote of the holders of more than half the votes in respect of the outstanding shares of the company. This amount is increased to two-thirds the votes in respect of the outstanding shares in the case of the latter types of resolutions for reorganisations, mergers, divisions, and waiver of pre-emptive rights in a capital increase.[465] The articles may require higher majorities in all or certain matters, but not unanimity.[466] Each share carries one vote, unless the articles provide otherwise.[467] All resolutions of the company must be evidenced in its minutes, which may, if the directors so require, be prepared by a notary. The latter requirement is compulsory if members representing at least 5 per cent of the company's shares so request at least five days before the scheduled meeting. In the latter case, resolutions are only valid if they appear in the minutes prepared by the notary.[468]

Resolutions passed by a general meeting of a private company which are contrary to law, or the articles or which prejudice the interests of the company for the benefit of one or more shareholders or third parties may be challenged in the courts. Resolutions which are contrary to law are void, whilst the other categories mentioned above are voidable. Void resolutions may be challenged by shareholders, directors and third parties who can demonstrate a legitimate interest. Voidable resolutions may be challenged by shareholders attending the meeting whose opposition thereto is recorded in the minutes, by absent shareholders, and by shareholders illegally prevented from voting, as well as by directors. The detailed rules governing the impugning of company resolutions are the same as those which apply to public companies.[469]

[464] *Ibid.*, Art. 53(1). Abstentions are not counted. [465] *Ibid.*, Art. 53(2).
[466] *Ibid.*, Art. 53(3). [467] *Ibid.*, Art. 53(4). [468] *Ibid.*, Arts. 54 and 55.
[469] See Spanish Private Limited Liability Companies Act 1995, Art. 56, which makes reference to the relevant provisions of the Spanish Public Limited Liability Companies Act 1989.

B. Public companies (SAs)

1. Management

The directors of a public company (*sociedad anónima*) are appointed in the deed of incorporation or elected by the shareholders within the number stipulated therein. They are entrusted with the tasks of managing the company and representing it in relation to third parties.[470] They may be natural or legal persons, do not have to be members of the company, and must not be undischarged bankrupts, minors or other persons prohibited from acting as directors.[471] When the company's management is entrusted jointly to more than two persons, they form a board (*Consejo de administración*). By Article 137, board members may be appointed by a form of proportional representation, according to which shareholders pool their votes and elect a proportional number of directors, provided that their total votes exceed the total number of votes cast divided by the number of directors. When this right is exercised, the shares so pooled do not carry any votes in respect of the election of the other directors.

The appointment of a director takes effect from the time when it is accepted. The resolution making the appointment must be registered in the Commercial Registry within ten days of being made.[472] The directors hold office for the period specified in the articles, which may not exceed five years.[473] They may be re-elected, and their remuneration is fixed in the articles.[474] As is the case in private companies, directors may be dismissed at any time by a resolution of the general meeting.[475] Directors who are also directors of a competitor, and any person who has interests in any way conflicting with those of the company may be dismissed from office by such a resolution, on the request of any shareholder.[476]

The board must have a chairman and a secretary. As in Italy, it may delegate, certain of its managerial tasks to one or more managing directors or to an executive committee. However, it may not delegate the

[470] Spanish Public Limited Liability Companies Act 1989, Arts. 128 and 129. Further duties have been imposed on the directors of quoted and other companies by Law 26/2003 of 17 July 2003, which amends the law on the Securities Markets Act of 1988 and the Spanish Public Companies Act 1989 in certain respects. The Law of 2003 amends the Spanish Securities Markets Act of 1988 to require a detailed annual corporate governance statement from quoted companies.

[471] Spanish Public Limited Liability Companies Act 1989, Arts. 123(2) and 124.

[472] *Ibid.*, Art. 125. [473] *Ibid.*, Art. 126. [474] *Ibid.*, Arts. 126 and 130.

[475] *Ibid.*, Art. 131. [476] *Ibid.*, Art. 132.

tasks of presentation of the accounts and the annual balance sheet to the general meeting, unless the members consent to such delegation.[477]

As is the case with a private company, the directors are empowered to represent the company in respect of all activities which comes within the company's objects. The company is liable to third parties who have acted in good faith, and without serious fault, even when it is clear from the articles registered in the Commercial Registry that the activity does not come within the company's objects.[478]

The rules governing the liability of directors of public companies were until recently similar to those which apply to directors of private companies. According to Article 133(1) and (2) of the Spanish Public Limited Liability Companies Act 1989 (LSA), the directors (including de facto directors) are liable to the company, the shareholders and the creditors for any damage they cause by infringement of the law or the articles, and for failure to exercise the degree of care necessary to fulfil their duties. This degree of care in that of a competent business man and a loyal representative.[479] The liabilities of the directors are further regulated by Article 133(3) and 133(4). Article 134 contains detailed rules governing derivative actions by the company and its creditors. Personal actions for damages by shareholders and third parties are also possible.[480]

2. General meetings

A number of matters are placed within the competence of the general meeting, which include the appointment and dismissal of the directors,[481] the alteration of the articles[482] and the approval of the accounts.[483] A meeting to review the company's management, to approve the accounts for the previous financial year and to declare a dividend must be held within the first six months of every financial year.[484] This meeting is treated as an ordinary general meeting; all other meetings count as extraordinary general meetings.[485] The latter type of meetings may be called by the directors when they deem necessary, and also upon the

[477] *Ibid.*, Art. 141. [478] *Ibid.*, Art. 129.

[479] *Ibid.*, Art. 127(1). According to Art. 127(2), each one of the directors must inform himself conscientiously about the business of the company. Further duties are imposed on the directors by Arts. 127 *bis*, 127 *ter* and 127 *quater* of the Spanish Public Companies Act 1989. These comprise a duty of good faith, loyalty, and one of safeguarding business secrets.

[480] Spanish Public Limited Liability Companies Act 1989, Art. 135.

[481] *Ibid.*, Arts. 123 and 131. [482] *Ibid.*, Art. 144. [483] *Ibid.*, Art. 95.

[484] *Ibid.*, Art. 95. [485] *Ibid.*, Art. 96.

requisition of the holders of at least 5 per cent of the capital, who must state in their request, the matters to be discussed at the meeting.[486] Such a meeting must be called within thirty days of the request.[487] An ordinary meeting requires fifteen days' notice which may be given by the insertion of an advertisement in the official journal of the Commercial Registry and in a provincial daily newspaper. The notice of the meeting shall state the date of the first call of the meeting, and the matters to be discussed.[488] It may also state the date when the meeting is to be held on second call. There must be at least a twenty-four hour period between the first and second calls.[489] If a duly called general meeting was not held on the date scheduled, and the notice did not state the date for a second meeting, the meeting must be called again, within fifteen days of the date when the original meeting was to have been held, and eight days' notice of it must be given prior to the date of the new meeting.[490]

The minimum quorum requirement is set out in Article 102 of the Law of 1989, as amended, and in the case of a first call, the shareholders present or represented at the meeting must hold 25 per cent of the subscribed shares; however any amount is sufficient on a second call.[491] The quorum requirement on first call is increased for specific resolutions, and it is thus the holders of 50 per cent of the subscribed shares for resolutions to issue bonds or for the increase or reduction of capital.[492] In the case of such resolutions, it is reduced to 25 per cent on second call. In principle resolutions are passed by a majority of those present and voting. This is subject to the qualification that, in the case of those resolutions requiring a higher quorum on first call, if the shareholders present on second call represent less than 50 per cent of the subscribed voting capital, the relevant resolution can only be validly passed by a vote of two thirds of the capital present or represented at the meeting.[493]

The company's articles may limit the number of votes that any shareholder may exercise, and can also require a minimum shareholding in order to attend the general meeting. By Article 105(1) this amount cannot be greater than one-thousandth of the total share capital. As in the case of the private company, universal meetings are provided for, and may be useful to companies having few shareholders. Despite failure to

[486] *Ibid.*, Art. 100.
[487] *Ibid.*, Art. 100. For the judicial call of an ordinary general meeting, see Art. 101.
[488] *Ibid.*, Art. 97. [489] *Ibid.*, Art. 98(1), (2). [490] *Ibid.*, Art. 98(3).
[491] *Ibid.*, Art. 102. [492] *Ibid.*, Art. 103(1) and (2). [493] *Ibid.*, Art. 103(3).

comply with notice requirements, such members can attend and pass valid resolutions when all the shareholders are present in person or by proxy, and agree to hold the universal meeting.[494]

Articles 115–122 of the LSA contains detailed provisions governing the challenging of resolutions of the general meeting of a public company which are also applicable to resolutions of general meetings of private companies. These provisions have been referred to in the section above relating to such companies.

3. Special rules applicable to quoted companies

Public companies which issue shares or bonds which are admitted to negotiation on the securities market are required by Law 44/2002 to establish a committee of auditors. According to Law 26/2003 of 17 July 2003, which amends title X (Articles 111–117) of the Securities Markets Act 1988, companies whose shares are admitted to quotation on an official market must publicise certain types of shareholders' agreements in accordance with Article 112 of the former Act. Article 113 requires the general meeting of quoted companies to approve a regulation governing all matters concerning the general meeting, whilst Article 115 requires the board of directors of such companies, in consultation with the general meeting, to formulate rules governing the internal regime and functioning of the board, in conformity with the law and the articles. Proper publicity must be given to the regulations governing the general meeting and the board of directors. Article 114 imposes certain duties with regard to their abstention from voting on certain matters on directors who are granted proxies.

Article 116 of the Securities Markets Act requires the making of a detailed corporate governance statement, which has to be communicated to the National Commission for Securities Markets (*Comisión Nacional del Mercado de Valores*). The latter body is charged with securing the observation of the rules governing such a statement: administrative penalties are imposed in the event of failure to provide the required documents or information in such a statement, and for omissions or misleading or erroneous particulars therein. Particulars concerning the methods of providing information required from quoted companies are contained in Article 117 of the Securities Markets Act.

[494] *Ibid.*, Art. 99.

VII. The position in Belgium

A. *Patterns of management and control*

There are only a few significant differences between the rules governing management and control applicable to Belgian private and public companies. For this reason, it appears convenient to deal with the public company (*société anonyme*) first of all, and then to consider the private company (*société privée par responsabilité limitée*).

B. *Public companies*

1. Management

Belgian law recognises a unitary board system. The management of a public company is entrusted to its board of directors, but the members in general meeting exercise certain controlling and other functions. A public company must have at least three directors, who are not required to be natural persons. However, if such a company is established with only two members, or it is found at a general meeting to have only two members, the number of directors may be limited to two until it is ensured that by taking appropriate steps that the company has more than two members at the subsequent general meeting.[495] The first directors must be appointed by the deed of incorporation whilst subsequent ones are appointed by the general meeting.[496] The term of appointment, which is renewable unless the articles provide otherwise, may not exceed six years.[497] Directors may always be dismissed by the general meeting.[498] Unless the articles provide otherwise, if the position of a director falls vacant, the remaining directors have the right to officiate until the next general meeting, which must then proceed to a definitive appointment.[499]

According to Article 522(1) of the Civil Code, the directors have the power to perform all the activities necessary or useful for the fulfilment of the objects of the company, with the exception of those which the law reserves for the general meeting. Restrictions imposed by the articles on the power of the directors, as well as provisions allocating particular tasks to individual directors cannot be invoked against third parties, even if they are published.[500] The board of directors represents the company in relation to third parties, and in court, whether as plaintiff or defendant.

[495] Belgian Companies Code, Art. 518(1). [496] *Ibid.*, Art. 518(2).
[497] *Ibid.*, Art. 518(3). [498] *Ibid.*, Art. 518(3). [499] *Ibid.*, Art. 519(1).
[500] *Ibid.*, Art. 522(1) sentence 2.

The articles may confer this task of representation on one or more directors, acting individually or jointly. Such a provision may be invoked against third parties.[501]

The day-to-day management of the affairs of a public company, as well as the representation of the company in matters concerning such management may be delegated to one or more persons acting individually or jointly. Any restrictions on such powers of delegation for the purpose of daily management have no effect against third parties. Particulars of the appointment of such delegates must be entered in the annexes to the Official Journal, if such appointment is to have effect against third parties.[502]

The board of directors is treated as forming a collegiate body: it acts by majority decision, but the minority are bound by the majority. It normally acts by meeting together, but in exceptional cases duly justified by their urgency and the interests of the company, its decisions may be taken, if the articles so provide, by the unanimous consent of its members, given in writing. This procedure may not be used for decisions taken in relation to the accounts, and on the employment of authorised capital, or in any other cases excepted by the articles.[503]

According to Article 526 of the Companies Code, the company is bound by acts done by the board of directors and by directors having the power of representation conferred on them in accordance with Article 522(2) as well as by persons having delegated powers of day-to-day management, even if such acts go beyond the scope of the company's objects, unless it can be shown that the third party was aware of the latter fact, or could not ignore it in the relevant circumstances. However, publication of the articles does not constitute evidence for the latter purposes.

2. Directors' liability

Provisions exist designed to prevent the misuse of the directors' powers as the result of conflicts between their personal interests and their duties to the company. Article 523 of the Companies Code provides that any director who has a direct or indirect interest of his own of an economic nature which conflicts with those of the company in a decision or operation envisaged by the board must inform the other members thereof before the decision or operation is considered by the board. This statement must appear in the minutes of the board which will decide

[501] *Ibid.*, Art. 522(2). [502] *Ibid.*, Art. 525. [503] *Ibid.*, Art. 521.

on the proposed transaction. The auditors, if any, must be informed of the directors' interest.

In contemplation of the publication of the relevant particulars in the directors' report or in a document which has to be deposited at the same time as the annual accounts, the board of directors must describe the nature of the decision or operation in the board's minutes, and must justify the approach which has been taken in respect of it, and state its economic consequences for the company. The auditors must also make a separate report. In the case of companies which have made, or are making, an appeal to the public for investments, the interested director cannot take any part in any discussion of the proposed transaction or vote on it.

Furthermore, the company may seek a declaration of the nullity of decisions or operations which have been taken in violation of the above rules, provided that the other party was aware, or ought to have been aware of such violation. In addition, according to Article 529 of the Civil Code, directors are jointly and severally liable to the company and third parties for damages suffered by them as a result of decisions or operations carried out in accordance with Article 523, if such transactions have procured for them, or one of them an improper financial advantage to the detriment of the company. However, a director may escape such liability if he has not participated in the wrongdoing, is not guilty of fault and has denounced the relevant infringements at the general meeting which took place immediately after he had knowledge of them.[504] Article 523(1) is inapplicable in certain situations set out in paragraph (3) of this provision.

A separate procedure set out in Article 524 has to be complied with in relation to decisions or operations made or undertaken in execution of a decision taken by a quoted company which concerns relationships between that company or a subsidiary thereof and another company in the same group. The procedure does not apply to dealings with subsidiaries of the quoted company, or subsidiaries of subsidiaries. It is also inapplicable to dealings at arm's length, and to dealings representing less than one per cent of the net assets of the company.

All relevant items on the agenda governing inter group dealings, must be presented to a committee of three independent directors fulfilling the four criteria set out in Article 524(4). The committee is assisted by one or more independent experts. It describes the transaction, assesses its

[504] *Ibid.*, Art. 528(2).

financial impact, and gives advice on its possible unlawful or detrimental nature. After having received the non-binding advice of the committee, the board of directors decides whether to follow it. The members of the board should indicate whether the relevant procedure was followed, and if relevant, the reasons why the committee's advice was not followed. The auditors draft a separate report on the reliability of the figures and information contained in the advice and in the minutes of the board of directors.

Dealings between an unlisted Belgian subsidiary of a Belgian listed company with other entities in the group require, in accordance with Article 524(5), the authorisation of the parent company, and compliance with the procedure outlined above. According to Article 529(2) the directors are jointly and severally liable for the damage suffered by a company or a third party as the result of decisions or operations approved by the board, even when Article 524 has been complied with, where such decisions have resulted in an improper financial loss to the company for the benefit of another company in the group.

In addition to the specific liabilities outlined above, the directors also may incur other ones. The directors and those charged with the day-to-day management of the company are responsible for carrying out the mandate (authority) granted to them, and for faults committed during the course of their management.[505] This latter requirement imposes the duty on them to act honestly and conscientiously, and to exercise proper care and skill. Directors are also jointly and severally liable to the company for breaches of the legislation relating to companies, and the provisions of the company's articles.[506] If they are aware of breaches of the law or the articles by other directors, but did not participate in them personally and are not themselves at fault, they may escape liability by reporting the breaches to a general meeting or directors' meeting as soon as they become aware of them.[507] If a director is guilty of a breach of his duty of care or does not conform to the terms of the legislation or the articles, he may be sued by individual shareholders who have suffered from personal damage which is distinct from that suffered by the company.[508]

The general meeting can give the directors a discharge from liability, provided the correct state of affairs has been disclosed to it. It may on the other hand decide to sue the directors, and appoint representatives for this purpose.[509] Minority shareholders who possess shares carrying at

[505] *Ibid.*, Art. 527. [506] *Ibid.*, Art. 528(1). [507] *Ibid.*, Art. 528(2).
[508] *Pasicrise* [1994] Trib comm. Ghent 348. [509] Belgian Companies Code, Art. 561.

least 1 per cent of the votes attached to the issued share capital or shares whose total value is at least €1,250,000, at the date when the resolution exonerating the directors from liability is considered are entitled to sue the company's directors.[510] If the minority shareholders succeed in their action, the costs of the litigation, which the plaintiffs have paid in advance, and which are not charged to the defendants, must be met by the company. If the action fails, the plaintiffs may be made liable for costs and in an appropriate case, may have to pay damages to the defendants.[511]

If a company is insolvent,[512] and has insufficient assets to meet its debts and it is established that such involuntary liquidation or bankruptcy has been contributed to by serious faults on the part of the directors, the directors and former directors, together with any de facto directors who have effectively had the power of managing the company, may be held personally liable to contribute to the whole or part of the company's debts, insofar as these are not covered by the company's assets. Such liability may be joint and several.

3. General meetings

It follows from Articles 522(1) of the Companies Code that the directors can perform acts which are necessary or useful for the realisation of the company's objects, except when the law reserves competence to the general meeting. According to Article 531, the general meeting has the most extensive powers to do or ratify acts which affect the company. It is not clear whether these provisions must be read subject to an implied limitation similar to that contained in Article 522(1). The general meeting has special powers granted on it by Articles 556 and 557 of the Companies Code when public offers to acquire the shares of public companies take place.

Meetings may be called by the directors, and by the auditors, if any, as well as by the holders of at least one-fifth, of the share capital.[513] Notices of all general meetings together with the agenda must appear in the *Moniteur Belge* at least fifteen days before they are held. Such particulars must also be advertised in a national and a regional newspaper at least fifteen and eight days before the holding of the meeting.

An ordinary general meeting must be held once a year for the purpose of approving the annual accounts and the directors and auditors report.

[510] *Ibid.*, Art. 562. [511] *Ibid.*, Art. 567.
[512] That is in involuntary liquidation or bankruptcy, see the Belgian Companies Code, Art. 530.
[513] *Ibid.*, Art. 532.

After the accounts have been approved, the general meeting votes on the discharge of the directors and auditors from responsibility. Such discharge is only effective if the accounts do not contain any omission, or any false statement concealing the true situation of the company, and that any acts done that were not permitted by the articles, or which were in contravention of the Companies Code, have been specially indicated in the notice convening the meeting.[514] Other general meetings may be held during the course of the year if called by the directors or the holders of one-fifth of the company's share capital.

Resolutions are passed at ordinary general meetings by a simple majority of those present and voting. However, extraordinary general meetings, to which special quorum and majority requirements are applicable, are necessary for certain transactions. These include the alteration of the articles,[515] the increase[516] and reduction[517] of capital, and the prolongation of the life of the company.[518] In all relevant cases, a quorum of the holders of 50 per cent of the share capital is required on first call. If an alteration of the articles,[519] involves a change in the objects of the company, the required quorum must include members representing at least 50 per cent of the share capital and 50 per cent of the holders of founders' shares (*parts bénéficiares*). If the former conditions are not fulfilled, a second meeting may be held to which no quorum requirements are applicable. No alteration of the articles[520] can take place unless at least three-quarters of the votes cast are in its favour. This number is increased to four-fifths if the alteration involves a change in the company's objects. If there are different classes of shares or different classes of founders' shares have been issued, the general meeting may, despite any contrary provisions in the articles, modify their respective rights, or replace shares or founders' shares of one class with shares or founders' share of another class. A report has to be made by the directors justifying the proposed modification. In the absence of such a report, the decision of the general meeting is a

[514] *Ibid.*, Art. 554.

[515] *Ibid.*, Art. 558. Where such an alteration affects the objects of the company, the special rules contained in Art. 559 are applicable. These require the directors to give a reasoned justification for the proposed alteration and gives rights to the holders of founders' shares. Special quorum and majority requirements for the alteration of the articles are also applicable: see Art. 559(4) and (5).

[516] Belgian Companies Code, Art. 581. [517] *Ibid.*, Art. 612. [518] *Ibid.*, Art. 645.

[519] The increase and reduction of capital and the extension of the life of the company will normally require such an alteration.

[520] The increase and reduction of capital and the extension of the life of the company will normally require such an alteration.

nullity. The holders of founders' shares possess voting rights in respect of the proposal, irrespective of any contrary provisions in the articles. The quorum and majority requirements explained above must be satisfied in relation to each class of shares.[521]

The articles may restrict the number of votes which each shareholder has in general meetings, provided that such limitation is imposed on each shareholder, irrespective of the shares in respect of which he participates in the vote.[522] Founders' shares enjoy voting rights if the articles so provide:[523] they are sometimes granted such rights by the Companies Code, irrespective of the provisions of the articles. Proxy voting is recognised by Belgian law, and special rules apply to the solicitation of proxies by companies which make appeals to the public for investments.[524]

C. *Private companies*

There is a considerable similarity between the Belgian rules governing the management and control of private and public companies. A private company (*société privée par responsabilité limitée*) is only required to have one director or two directors acting jointly.[525] Directors of a private company may be appointed for an unlimited period of time. Directors who are so appointed are deemed to hold office for the lifetime of the company and cannot be dismissed except for serious reasons, unless the articles or unanimous agreement of the shareholders otherwise provides.[526] Each director may carry out any act which is necessary or appropriate for the realisation of the company's objects, except such acts as are reserved for the general meeting. Individual directors also have the power of binding the company in relation to third parties.[527] It is possible for the articles to confer the power of representation on more than one director. Such a limitation is binding on third parties if it relates to the general power of representation, and not to specific instances thereof, and if it is duly published.[528]

The complex rules relating to directors who have a direct or indirect interest in decisions or operations contemplated by a public company, which are considered by its board, contained in Article 523 of the Companies Code are largely reflected by those of Article 259, which deals with the parallel situation in relation to private companies. Minority

[521] Belgian Companies Code, Art. 560. [522] *Ibid.*, Art. 544. [523] *Ibid.*, Art. 542.
[524] *Ibid.*, Arts. 547–549. [525] *Ibid.*, Art. 255. [526] *Ibid.*, Art. 256. [527] *Ibid.*, Art. 257.
[528] *Ibid.*, Art. 257(3); cf. Art. 522(2), which relates to public companies.

shareholders representing 10 per cent of the company's share capital as of the date when the resolution exonerating the directors from liability is considered may bring a derivative action against the directors.[529] According to Article 265 directors of a private company who commit a serious breach of their duties which contributes to the insolvency of the company, may incur liability to creditors if during the three financial years preceding the insolvency, the insolvent company had an average turnover of at least €620,000 (after the deduction of VAT), and the balance sheet total for the last financial year was more than €370,000. No such limitation is contained in Article 530, which is the corresponding provision relating to public companies, and which is considered above.

VIII. The position in the Netherlands

A. Management structures

The rules relating to the private company (*besloten vennootschap*, BV) and the public company (*naamloze vennootschap*) are practically identical. This is true in relation to management structure, the powers of the management and supervisory board, (if any), and the powers of the shareholders. A company may have a single board, or adopt a double board system on a voluntary basis which is not subject to the special rules applicable to 'large' companies, or be required to adopt the compulsory two board system applicable to such companies, which can be applied to other companies on a voluntary basis, provided that the company, or a company controlled by it, has a works council (*ondernemingsraad*)[530] The management board is in essence the executive board, and it may be made up of one or more individuals or companies who, if the company is not a 'large' one, are appointed and dismissed by the shareholders in general meeting.[531] If the management board has more than one member, each member may have different powers or duties. As in most jurisdictions,

[529] *Ibid.*, Art. 290; cf. Art. 562, which is the corresponding provision in relation to public companies, where the holders of only 1 per cent of the share capital may bring a derivative action against the directors. In both cases, successful plaintiffs can recover their costs from the company: see Belgian Companies Code, Arts. 291 and 562. Shareholders who voted for the discharge cannot usually bring a derivative action under either provisions.

[530] Dutch Civil Code Book 2, Arts. 157(1) and 267(1).

[531] Dutch Civil Code Book 2, Arts. 132 and 242; and Arts. 134(1) and 245(1). In a 'large' company which is not wholly or partly exempt, the members of the management board are appointed, suspended and removed by the mandatory supervisory board: See the Dutch Civil Code Book 2, Arts. 162/272 and 134(1)/244(1).

the management board is responsible for the management and representation of the company.[532] As far as the appointment of executive directors and supervisory directors of a company which is not a 'large' one are concerned, the shareholders may find it necessary to accept nominations made to these boards by a particular class of shareholders, who are frequently the holders of priority shares, or other persons stipulated in the articles. However, such nominations may always be overridden by a qualified majority consisting of two-thirds of the votes cast, representing more than one half of the issued shares.[533]

The functions of the supervisory board are more extensive when the company is subject to the legal regime applicable to large companies (*structuur vennootschappen*), which is explained below. The legal regime for large companies involves a particular method of constituting the supervisory board. Where the company is not subject to this legal regime the powers of the supervisory board are less extensive than when it is so subject. In the former event, it has primary supervisory and advisory functions, but may be granted more extensive power by the articles,[534] but it cannot, whatever its basis, be given the power to manage the business. However, the supervisory board of a 'large' company has the task of approving certain important decisions of the management board.

There are also important Dutch proposals which would permit Dutch public and private companies to adopt either a dualistic or a monistic board model. As in Germany, the dualistic model would involve the use of a supervisory and a management board. The option would not be available where the company was required by law to have a supervisory board. Furthermore, there are also proposals in the Netherlands for the introduction of a new type of business entity, the socially oriented company which should prove useful for schools, universities, hospitals, care institutions and housing corporations. The new type of company would have a management and a supervisory board and a representative body of interested parties.

B. The regime applicable to 'large' companies

'Large' companies are defined as companies which comply with three conditions.[535] The company's issued capital plus reserves and retained

[532] Dutch Civil Code Book 2, Arts. 129/239 and 130/240.
[533] *Ibid.*, Arts. 133(2)/243(2) and 142(1)/252(1). [534] *Ibid.*, Arts. 140(2) and 250(2).
[535] *Ibid.*, Arts. 153(2) and 263(2).

earnings must be at least €16,000,000. The company, or a dependent[536] company, must have established a works council. It must, together with its dependent companies, usually employ one hundred or more persons in the Netherlands. In practice, the regime covers medium sized companies, and is only applicable when the majority of employees are in the Netherlands.

A private or public company which meets the above requirements for a period of three financial years, and which is not fully exempt, is required to have a supervisory board with fairly extensive powers. Special rules (which were amended in 2004) apply to the appointment and removal of its members.[537] When the 'large' company rules become applicable, the members of the works council have the right to suggest candidates up to a maximum of one-third for membership of the supervisory board. The supervisory board is in principle required to accept these nominations, but it has a right of objection, and may apply to the Enterprise Chamber of the Amsterdam Court to declare the objections well founded. This enhanced right of the works council persists until the maximum of one third of the members of the supervisory board are filled with employees' representatives. The general meeting is empowered to dismiss the entire supervisory board, including the members nominated by the works council, subject to an enhanced majority and quorum requirement. Subject to similar requirements, the general meeting may also refuse to appoint a person nominated by the supervisory board.[538]

Unless a 'large' company is partially or wholly exempt from the special regime applicable to such companies, the supervisory board is, in addition to its normal supervisory and advisory functions, responsible for the

[536] A dependent company is defined in Dutch Civil Code Book 2, Arts. 152/262 as (a) a legal person in which the company or any of its dependent companies, solely or jointly and for its or their own account contributes at least half the issued capital, and (b) a partnership, a business enterprise of which is entered on the commercial register and for which a company limited by shares or a dependent company has unlimited liability towards third parties.

[537] Dutch Civil Code Book 2, Arts. 158 and 268.

[538] According to Arts. 161(2) and 271(2) of Book 2 of the Dutch Civil Code, an individual member of the supervisory board cannot be dismissed without the consent of the Enterprise Chamber of the Court of Appeals of Amsterdam. Such removal may take place because of breach of duties, other important reasons or significant changes in circumstances which could not be anticipated by the company and which make it unreasonable for the relevant member of the board to continue in office. A request to the Enterprise Chamber for the dismissal of a member of the board may be made by the company itself, or by the general meeting, the shareholders' committee or the works council. The supervisory board may suspend one of its members: see Arts. 271(3) and 161(3).

appointment and dismissal of the directors of the company and for the approval of certain important resolutions of the company, for example proposals to amend the articles or to dissolve the company.[539] If a company is partially exempt from the regime applicable to large companies, the supervisory board is not entrusted with the tasks of appointing and dismissing the members of the management board. A 'large' company is partially exempt where it is controlled from outside the Netherlands, and where it belongs to an international group with a Dutch based holding company.[540] A company which would otherwise be a large company is fully exempt from the special regime under the four circumstances set out in Articles 153(3) and 263(3) of Book 2 of the Civil Code. An application to the Enterprise Chamber for the dismissal of a member of the board may be made by the company itself, or by the general meeting, the shareholders' committee or the works' council.

C. Powers and duties of the management board

The powers of the management board differ according to whether or not the company is a 'large' one. As already indicated, the management board is made responsible for the management and representation of the company by Articles 129 and 130 and 239 and 240 of Book 2 of the Dutch Civil Code: however, in large companies, its managerial powers are subject to special rules which require the approval of the supervisory board if certain transactions (for example the commencement or termination of a significant long lasting cooperation between the company or a dependent company with another company or partnership) are to be undertaken.[541] The articles of the company may supplement the relevant requirements. Furthermore, the Works Councils Act 1971 (*wet op de ondernemingsraad*) requires the management board to seek the approval of the works council for certain important decisions.

The company's business policies are determined by the management board in accordance with the company's objects. The board is responsible for the preparation of the annual accounts and the annual report; the accounts must be submitted to the shareholders' meeting within five

[539] Dutch Civil Code Book 2, Arts. 162 and 164; Arts. 172 and 274.

[540] *Ibid.*, Arts. 155(1) and 265(1). Few partially exempt Dutch companies exist.

[541] *Ibid.*, Arts. 164 and 274. However, the supervisory board cannot require the management board to take action on any of the relevant matters.

months of the end of the financial year. This period may be extended by one month.[542]

The articles of a company which is not subject to the special rules governing large companies may require the management board to comply with guidelines issued by the supervisory board or the shareholders concerning policy matters, especially where the company belongs to a group of companies.

As is the case in common law jurisdictions, directors are treated as having duties of good faith and care and skill. These duties are applicable both to members of the management and the supervisory boards.[543]

If a company is declared bankrupt (i.e. placed in involuntary liquidation) the members of the management board and others (including members of the supervisory board) who have been responsible for the de facto management of the company are personally liable for any deficit if the bankruptcy is caused to an appreciable extent, by the apparent negligence of the management board during the period of three years prior to the date of the bankruptcy. The company is required to maintain financial records and to file the accounts with the Commercial Register within thirteen months of the end of the financial year.[544] In the event of failure to discharge one of these duties, Articles 138(2) and 248(2) of Book 2 provide for two irrebuttable presumptions, which are that there has been apparent negligence, and that the negligence is a significant cause of the bankruptcy. New liabilities are to be placed on the directors of a private company which becomes insolvent within one year of making a distribution if draft Article 216(3) of Book 2 of the Dutch Civil Code is adopted.

If there is a conflict of interests between the management board and certain of its members and the company, the supervisory board or a special representative (or representatives) designated by the general meeting must act on its behalf, unless the articles of the company provide otherwise.[545] The rules contained in the latter provisions are somewhat permissive, but they have been rendered more stringent in the relevant decisions.

[542] The supervisory board no longer has any role in the adoption of the accounts as was formerly the case. The accounts are adopted by the general shareholders' meeting, see the Dutch Civil Code Book 2, Arts. 101(3) and 210(3).

[543] This is made clear in respect of duties of care by Arts. 9, 138/248, 149/259 of Dutch Civil Code Book 2, which require that members of such boards must properly perform management and supervisory duties.

[544] Dutch Civil Code Book 2, Arts. 10 and 394.

[545] *Ibid.*, Arts. 146 and 256.

D. The general meeting

The powers of the general meeting vary in accordance with the nature of the company and the provisions of its articles. The latter may give powers normally exercised by the general meeting to other organs of the company, e.g. power to the management board to issue shares, or give the right to the holders of priority shares to propose or approve certain categories of resolution. The powers of the general meeting vary according to whether the company is a large company, and if it is, whether it is fully or partly exempt. The general meeting does not play such an important role in the Netherlands as in certain other jurisdictions. However, it always has the right to approve major changes in the structure of the company, such as amendments to the articles, mergers, divisions, the conversion of the company into an entity of another type,[546] and its dissolution.

As already indicated, the general meeting of a company, has the power to adopt the annual accounts. The general meeting is responsible for the allocation of the profits, subject to any provisions contained in the articles governing the establishment of reserves.[547] In cases in which the accounts are required to be audited by law or the articles, the shareholders are empowered to appoint the auditors.[548] However the auditors' report is not submitted to the general meeting, but instead to the management board[549] and, in appropriate cases, to the supervisory board.

General meetings must be held in the Netherlands. They must take place at least once a year.[550] All other meetings are called special or extraordinary meetings. Unless the articles provide for a shorter period, the general meeting must be held within six months of the end of the financial year.[551] Subject to different provisions in the articles, a general

[546] Note, e.g., Dutch Civil Code Book 2, Arts. 18, 72 and 183.

[547] *Ibid.*, Arts. 105(1) and 216(1). It is proposed that the latter provisions, which apply to private companies, shall be amended so as to provide that no distribution can be made on its authority of the general meeting if the directors have expressed their opposition to it. No such distribution should be made according to the proposal, if this would result in a depletion of the reserves.

[548] *Ibid.*, Art. 393(2).

[549] *Ibid.*, Art. 393(4). The auditors' report is called the management report. An auditors' opinion must be submitted to the shareholders by the management board: See Dutch Civil Code Book 2, Art. 393(5).

[550] *Ibid.*, Arts. 108(1) and 218(1).

[551] *Ibid.*, Arts. 108(2) and 218(2).

meeting is convened by the board of directors or the supervisory board by giving notice in a national newspaper at least fifteen days prior to the date of the meeting.[552] Should the board refuse to call a meeting, shareholders representing at least 10 per cent of the issued capital may call one by obtaining an order from the president of the competent District Court.[553] The persons calling the meeting usually set out the agenda. The law does not set out any quorum requirements, but the articles frequently contain quorum provisions.

E. Rights of minority shareholders

Minority shareholders may secure the nullification or avoidance of decisions taken by any company organ on the ground that such decision may be annulled if it violates principles of reasonableness or fairness.[554] There is no derivative action under Dutch law. Furthermore, shareholders are not entitled to inspect the books and records which must be kept by the company with the exception of the share register.

However, shareholders (or the holders of depository receipts) representing ten per cent of the issued shares, or who are entitled to shares or depository receipts with a nominal value of €225,000, or any lower percentage or amount prescribed by the articles, have the right to ask the Enterprise Chamber of the Amsterdam Court of Appeal for an inquiry to be made by experts into the policy and the conduct of the business of the company.[555] Such court appointed experts are entitled to access to the company's books and records. The court has statutory powers to make any order which it thinks fit in the interests of the inquiry or those of the company.[556] However, the order has to be of a temporary character. The existence of the remedy has made the inquiry procedure popular.

In addition to their right to ask the Amsterdam Court for the appointment of an expert, the holders of depository receipts or *certificaten* have

[552] *Ibid.*, Arts. 109 and 219. [553] *Ibid.*, Arts. 110–112 and 220–222.
[554] This does not mean that shareholders must promote the company's interests, or have any obligations towards other shareholders.
[555] Dutch Civil Code Book 2, Art. 344 and subsequent. The owners of depository receipts (*certificaaten*) representing ten per cent of the issued shares also have the right to petition for an inquiry: see Dutch Civil Code Book 2, Art. 346(b).
[556] *Ibid.*, Art. 349a

certain other rights to information on an equal basis with shareholders. They are thus entitled to receive the agenda of a general meeting,[557] and to attend such a meeting and participate in discussions,[558] without exercising any right to vote. In addition, they are entitled to obtain the annual accounts[559] and the auditors' opinion, as well as to request a meeting.

Furthermore, Articles 335–343 of Book 2 of the Civil Code provides for the remedy of compulsory purchase or compulsory sale of shares in private companies and in closely held public companies which limit the transfer of shares in the same way as in a public company. Such companies must only have registered shares and issue no bearer depository certificates. This remedy has not been much used in practice, because of many procedural difficulties, enabling reluctant parties to delay the proceedings for years by initiating appeal procedures. Many of these provisions will be revised if the proposed amendments to Part 2 of the Civil Code come into effect.

The above amendments will permit the company and its shareholders to adopt dispute settlement procedures in the articles or by agreement. It follows from proposed new Article 2.337 that the company must be able to make its own arrangements for dispute settlement and depart from all, or certain of the statutory provisions, unless that arrangement would render the transfer of shares impossible or extremely difficult. It will be possible to have disputes settled by the Enterprise Chamber of the Court of Appeal of Amsterdam or by arbitration. According to proposed new Article 2.339(3), the court will not be required to appoint experts to determine the price of the shares of an oppressed shareholder who wishes to leave the company, if it can determine it itself, which would be the case if the parties agree upon the prices or the agreement between the company and its shareholders establish clear criteria for establishing their value. A shareholder whose rights or interests have been prejudiced through the actions of other shareholders will, according to Article 2.343(1) of the Dutch Civil Code, be able to demand to be bought out by such shareholders or by the company. Article 343(4) of Book 2 of the Dutch Civil Code will enable a shareholder who wishes to be brought out to request

[557] *Ibid.*, Arts. 113(1)/223(1) and 114(1)/224(1).
[558] *Ibid.*, Arts. 117(2)/227(2). [559] *Ibid.*, Arts. 102(1)/212.

the court to take account of a depreciation in the value of its shares caused by the activities of the other shareholders or the company itself. The provisions governing the settlement of disputes will also make it clear that a shareholder who prejudices the interests of the company can also be bought out.

7

Business entities governed by Community law

The present chapter will consider the EEIG (European Economic Interest Grouping) and the SE (European Company).[1] The EEIG is partly governed by Community law, i.e. Council Regulation (EEC) No. 2137/85; and this will also be true of the SE.[2] After these two entities have been considered, the European Cooperative Society is dealt with in outline. The consideration of this proposal will be followed by a brief treatment of the proposal for a European private company, which does not emanate from the Commission, but which may from the basis of or influence further Community legislation.

I. European Economic Interest Grouping

A. History and scope

The Regulation on the European Economic Interest Grouping (EEIG) was inspired by a French entity called the *groupement d'intérêt économique*, which was introduced in France in 1967, and which is regarded as an intermediate form between the *société* (company or partnership) and the *association* (club). The Regulation provides a somewhat original framework for natural persons, companies and firms within the meaning of Article 48(2) EC and other entities governed by public or private law to enable them to cooperate effectively when carrying on business activities across national frontiers. An EEIG must have at least two members from different Member States. The registered office of a corporate member must be in a Member State. Furthermore,

[1] This was adopted on 31 July 1985, see OJ 1985 L199/1.

[2] Council Regulation (EC) No. 2157/2001 of 8 October 2001 on the Statute for a European Company SE, OJ L294/1, 10 November 2001, did not come into force until 8 October 2004. This Regulation is accompanied by Council Directive 2001/86/EC of 8 October 2001 supplementing the Statute for a European Company with regard to the involvement of employees.

either the central administration or the principal activity, of at least two of the members must be within such a state. Individuals must demonstrate a link with the Community by carrying on any industrial, commercial or agricultural craft or agricultural activity or providing professional or other services within the Community.[3] The official address of an EEIG must be either where it has its central administration, or one of its members has its central administration, or in the case of a natural person, his principal activity, provided that the grouping carries on an activity there.[4] This rule, which reminds one of the *siège réel doctrine*, may be unduly restrictive, and possibly at variance with the decision of the European Court in *Űberseering*[5] or the future development of the law concerning freedom of establishment.

As an EEIG has its either central administration or principal activities within the Community, there is no need for a third member who is a natural person to comply with this requirement. Thus even though a person's principal activity is outside the Community, they may nevertheless become a member of an EEIG, if they carry on an economic activity there.

An EEIG is governed by a mixed legal regime consisting not only of supranational provisions of the Regulation, but also, in certain circumstances, of provisions of the contract of formation; as well as of the national or internal law of the Member State where the grouping has its official address. Reference to internal law, as opposed to that to national law, excludes the provisions of private international law of the relevant state.

According to Article 3(1) of the Regulation, the purpose of a grouping shall be to facilitate or develop the economic activities of its members and to improve or increase the results of those activities. This provision also states that a grouping's purpose is not to make profits for itself, and that its activities shall be related to those of its members and no more than ancillary to such activities. It is questionable whether acts which violate Article 3(1); and which would seem to be *ultra vires* and void, are saved by Article 20 of the Regulation, or by relevant provisions of national law governing the effect of *ultra vires* contracts on third parties. The answer

[3] Council Regulation (EEC) 2137/85 of 25 July 1985 on the European Economic Interest Grouping (EEIG), OJ L199/1, Art. 4.

[4] *Ibid.*, Art. 12. The official address may be transferred, provided that the new official address conforms with the above provisions.

[5] Case C-208/00 *Überseering BV* v. *Nordic Construction Company Baumanagement GmbH* [2002] ECR I-9919.

to this question is probably in the negative, at least as far as Article 20 is concerned.[6]

In order to obviate difficulties arising from the German system of codetermination at board level, a grouping may not have more than 500 employees.[7] It has legal personality in all the Member States other than Germany and Italy. This is because Article 40 of the Regulation stipulates that the profits and losses of a grouping shall be taxable only in the hands of its members. In order to allow this fiscal transparency in Germany and Italy, the grouping had to be denied legal personality in those countries.

Groupings have been envisaged as a useful means of collaboration between small and medium-sized firms, and to be useful for such purposes as research and development, buying and selling, the packaging of finished products, the processing of goods, and the provision of services for their members. In certain cases, where they involve the pooling of research, development or manufacturing activities, an exemption or negative clearance under EC competition law may be necessary. Groupings have been used for a number of different kinds of economic activity, for example cooperation between lawyers, the promotion of audio-visual communications, and the provision of services of various types.

A grouping has some of the characteristics of a contractual arrangement, and some of those of a business association. The Regulation required the passing of implementing legislation, which in the United Kingdom took the form of two statutory instruments, one of which (SI 1989 No. 638) extended to Great Britain, and another, which was in almost identical terms, extended to Northern Ireland. These instruments tend to assimilate the grouping to an unregistered company rather than a partnership. It should be noted that many of the provisions of the Companies Act 1985 concerning the investigation of companies and their affairs, books and papers have been made applicable to an EEIG with an official address in the United Kingdom.

[6] Regulation 2137/85, Art. 20 provides that each of the managers shall bind the grouping as regards third parties when he acts on behalf of the grouping, unless the grouping proves that the third party knew or could not under the circumstances, have been unaware that this act fell outside the object of the grouping. Particulars of the publication referred to in Art. 5(c), shall not of itself be proof thereof.

[7] The requirement is retained in the *Drittelbeteiligungsgesetz* of 2004 (*Zweites Gesetz zur Veireinfachung der Wahl der Arbeitnehmervertreter*, 'the One-Third Participation Statute') BGBl (2004) 1.974.

B. Profits of the grouping

It appears clear both from Articles 21 and 40 of the Regulation that, although the purpose of a grouping may not, according to Article 3(1), be to make profits for its members, it may make such profits. Article 21 stipulates that the profits of a grouping shall be deemed to be the profits of its members, and shall be apportioned among them in the proportions laid down in the contract for the formation of the grouping or, in the absence of any such provision, in equal shares. It follows from the fourteenth recital to the Regulation that Member States were required to enact legislation stating what profits made by a grouping shall be subject to taxation, and upon what basis they shall be apportioned among members for the purposes of Article 40. The Regulation does not make it clear in which country the profits should be taxed in the hands of the members. This would seem to be that of the permanent or usual address of the members, but in some circumstances at least, the profits may be taxable in the country of registration of the grouping.

C. Prohibitions

A number of prohibitions are contained in Article 3(2) which have rather disparate objects. The reason behind those contained in Article 3(2)(a) and (b) is to prevent the formation of an integrated enterprise to the detriment of the independence of the participating ones. Article 3(2)(a) provides that a grouping may not exercise, directly or indirectly, a power of management or supervision over its members' own activities, or over the activities of another undertaking, in particular in the fields of personnel, finance and investment. Article 3(2)(b) stipulates that a grouping may not directly or indirectly, on any basis whatsoever, hold shares of any kind in a member undertaking. The holding of such shares is, according to Article 3(2)(b) only possible insofar as it is necessary for the achievement of the grouping's objects, and it is done on its members' behalf. Article 3(2)(c) forbids the grouping from employing more than 500 persons. Article 3(2)(d) contains certain detailed prohibitions on the uses of an EEIG by a company to make loans to its directors, or for the transfer of property between a company and a director in circumvention of national rules of company law. This provision was inserted at the request of the United Kingdom, and was reflected by certain provisions of the Companies Act 1985, which are now replaced in chapter 4 of Part X of the Companies Act of 2006. According to the sixteenth recital to the preamble, a Member State may impose appropriate sanctions in the event of the abuse or circumvention of national laws by a grouping.

Article 3(2)(e) provides that an EEIG may not be a member of another EEIG. This provision is intended to prevent the creation of a chain of liabilities which might diminish the liability of individual members.

Article 4(4) provides that any Member State may, on the grounds of public interest, prohibit or restrict participation in groupings by certain classes of natural persons, companies, firms or other legal bodies. It is understood that the inclusion of this provision in the Regulation resulted, at least partly, from anxiety felt about the possibility that British savings banks would become members of groupings and that, in consequence, losses might be suffered by investors.

D. Limitation on membership

It is not clear from Article 4 of Regulation 2137/85 whether partnerships which do not have legal personality but which have legal capacities, as is the case with English, Dutch and German partnerships may be members of a EEIG, but the view has been taken that such entities may be.[8]

There is no limit to the number of members of an EEIG. However, Article 4(3) provides that a Member State may stipulate that groupings registered in its registries in accordance with Article 10 may have no more than twenty members. In addition, a Member State may provide that for this purpose in accordance with its laws, each member of a legal entity formed under its laws, other than a registered company, shall be treated as a separate member of a grouping.

E. Formation and publicity

The formation of an EEIG requires the conclusion of a contract, and its registration in a registry designated by the Member State in which the official address is situated.[9] The contract must include the name of the grouping preceded or followed by the words 'European Economic Interest Grouping' or their equivalents in the other Community languages, and at least the official address, the objects of the grouping, the

[8] See Van Gerven and Aalders (eds), *The European Economic Interest Grouping* (Deventer: Kluwer, 1990), pp. 7–8 in this context.

[9] Regulation 2137/85, Arts. 6 and 39(1). If the official address is in Great Britain, the registry would be the Registrar within the meaning of the Companies Act 1985.

name of each member thereof, and other information relating to the members and the duration of the grouping, except where this is indefinite.[10] If the contract contains no provision governing the duration, it is presumed to be indefinite.

If a state has different territorial units, each having its own system of law relating to the states of capacity of natural persons and the capacity of legal persons, each one is considered as a state.[11] The United Kingdom consists of three territorial units, England and Wales, Scotland and Northern Ireland. One statutory instrument (SI 1989 No. 638) implements the Regulation in the first two units, whilst another very similar one implements it in Northern Ireland.

The contract for the formation of a grouping must be filed at the commercial registry, together with certain other particulars and documents.[12] The most important of these would seem to be notice of the appointment of the manager or managers, their names and any other identification particulars required by the law of the Member State in which the register is kept, and notification that they may act alone or must act jointly. If a grouping has an establishment or establishments in a Member State other than that of its official address, such an establishment is required to be registered in the Member State in which it is situated.[13] Such secondary registration takes place by means of copies of the documents which have to be filed for the purposes of initial or primary registration, together with, where necessary, a translation which conforms with the practice of the registry in the state in which the secondary establishment is situated.

Once an EEIG undergoes primary registration, it has the capacity, in its own name, to have rights and obligations of all kinds, to make contracts and accomplish other legal acts, and to sue and be sued. As from registration, the grouping may assume liability for activities carried out on its behalf prior to registration. If it fails to do so, the persons who carried out such activities have unlimited joint and several liability for them.[14]

After registration takes place, it is necessary to publish certain documents and particulars in the national official gazette. These include the mandatory minimum content of the contract, the number, date and place of registration, and practically all the documents and particulars which must be filed at the registry.[15] Such publicity has no effect on the existence of the grouping, but according to Article 9 of the Regulation,

[10] *Ibid.*, Art. 5. [11] *Ibid.*, Art. 2(2). [12] *Ibid.*, Arts. 7 and 8. [13] *Ibid.*, Art. 10.
[14] *Ibid.*, Art. 9(2). [15] *Ibid.*, Art. 8.

has the effect that the relevant documents and particulars may be relied on by the grouping as against third parties in accordance with the applicable national law.[16] After publication takes place, in the national gazette, notice that it has been formed must be published in the Official Journal of the European Communities.[17] Because of the wording of Article 11, it is arguable that such publication cannot be relied upon by the grouping against third parties.

F. Transfer of the official address

The rules governing the place where the official address of a grouping may be situated contained in Article 12 have been considered above. The transfer of the official address is covered by Article 13 when there is no change in the applicable law,[18] and by Article 14 when there is such a change. These provisions also state the consequences of such a transfer. The official address may be transferred within the EC provided that the new official address complies with the requirements contained in Article 12. If the transfer will give rise to a change in the applicable law, a transfer proposal must be drawn up, filed and published in the same way as is necessary when a grouping is formed. The decision to transfer may only be taken two months after such publication and must be unanimous. A Member State may provide (the UK and Spain have done so) that as regards a grouping registered in that state, the transfer of the official address which would result in a change of the applicable law has no effect if, within the two-month period after the publication of the proposal, a competent authority in that Member State opposes it on grounds of public interest. Review by a judicial authority must be possible.[19] It seems that Member States which have not expressly exercised the relevant option may intervene as well, for example to ensure that the tax obligations of the grouping are complied with.[20]

The new official address has immediate effect following publication,[21] but third parties can rely upon the old address as long as the termination of the groupings registration is at this address, unless they can be shown to have actual knowledge of the new address.

[16] *Ibid.*, Art. 9. [17] *Ibid.*, Art. 11.

[18] In such an event, the change is treated as being governed by the formation contract.

[19] Regulation 2137/85, Art. 14(1), sentence 4.

[20] See A. Dorrenstein *et al.*, *European Corporate Law* (Deventer and Boston: Kluwer Law and Taxation, 1994), para. 6.08 and the work cited there.

[21] Regulation 2137/85, Art. 14(3).

G. Structure and functioning of the grouping

1. Organs

Although the Regulation makes provision for certain binding rules and rules which apply in the absence of an express agreement to the contrary, the grouping is intended to be a flexible instrument which may, generally speaking, be adapted to the needs of the participants. It is required to have two organs, consisting of the members acting collectively, and the manager or managers.[22] It may have other organs, such as a supervisory body corresponding to the German *Aufsichtsrat*. The members acting collectively constitute the decision making body of the EEIG, and they may take any decision for the purpose of achieving the objects of the grouping. Article 17(1) provides that each member may have one vote, but that the contract may give more than one vote to certain members, provided that no member shall have a majority of the votes. A unanimous decision is always required for particular matters,[23] for example to alter the objects of the grouping, and to extend the period fixed for its duration. It is necessary for certain other matters, except where the contract otherwise provides.[24]

It follows, from Article 17(3) that in all other cases, the contract must prescribe the conditions for a quorum, and the majority by which decisions, or certain of them may be taken. If it fails to do so, unanimity is necessary. Decisions maybe taken by means of a postal vote or by teleconference.

A grouping must be managed by one or more natural persons. The appointment, powers and removal of such persons are determined in the contract, or by means of a unanimous decision of the members.[25] A person may not be appointed a manager if he is not permitted to belong to the administrative or management board of a company by virtue of the law which applies to him, or by virtue of the internal law of the state where the grouping has its official address, or following an administrative or judicial decision made or recognised in a Member State.[26] Legal persons may be appointed as managers, but such legal persons must appoint a natural person to represent them.[27] A manager who exceeds

[22] *Ibid.*, Art. 16. [23] *Ibid.*, Art. 17(2)(a)–(e).
[24] *Ibid.*, Art. 17(2)(f) and (g). [25] *Ibid.*, Art. 19(3).
[26] *Ibid.*, Art. 19(1). See also Art. 20 of the UK European Economic Interest Grouping Regulations, SI 1989 No. 638.
[27] See Regulation 2137/85, Art. 19(2) and UK European Economic Interest Grouping Regulations, SI 1989 No. 638, Art. 5.

his powers will incur liability towards the grouping. Article 20(1) contains the same rule as is to be found in Article 9(1) of the First Company Law Directive. It provides that each of the managers binds the grouping when he acts on its behalf, even where his act does not fall within the objects of the grouping, unless the grouping proves that the third party knew, or could not have been unaware, that the act fell outside its objects. The mere publication of these objects does not constitute proof of this matter. It should be observed that the contract may validly provide that the grouping shall be validly bound only by two or more members acting jointly. Such a restriction may be invoked against third parties if it is properly published.[28]

The liability of managers towards members is governed, by the internal law of the state where the official address is situated, whilst their liability towards third parties is governed by national law.[29]

2. Contributions

The contract or a decision of the members, may provide for contributions to be made to the grouping in cash, or in kind, and by way of services. Article 21(2), which deals with the situation when no such provision is made for contributions, provides that the amount by which the expenditure of the grouping exceeds its income shall be met in accordance with the contract and, in the absence of any such contractual provision, in equal shares.

3. Assignment or charging of participations

The above matter is dealt with by Article 22, which makes it apparent that the grouping has some of the characteristics of an association of individuals. Article 22(1) stipulates that any member of a grouping may assign his participation in the grouping, or a proportion thereof, either to another member or a third party, and that the assignment shall not take effect without the unanimous authorisation of the other members. This text does not state how an assignment is to take place, nor does the Regulation state how a member's rights in a grouping shall be represented. It may follow from Article 22(1) that the validity and effect of an assignment against the grouping is determined by the internal law of the Member State where the grouping has its official address. This matter depends on whether (as seems to be the case) the matter can be regarded as one concerning the internal organisation of the grouping.

[28] Regulation 2137/85, Art. 20(2). [29] *Ibid.*, Art. 2(1).

Article 22(2) stipulates that a member of a grouping may use his participation as security only after the other members have given their unanimous consent, unless otherwise provided in the contract for formation of the grouping, The holder of the security may not at any time become a member of the grouping by virtue of that security. This would appear to indicate that a security which has a similar effect to a charge by way of legal mortgage may not be created in respect of a member's participation.

4. Rules concerning liability

The rules governing liability are similar to those which apply to a partnership. Article 24(1) provides that the members of a grouping shall have unlimited joint and several liability for its debts and liabilities of whatever nature. Although members cannot limit their liability towards third parties, they may, according to Article 21(2), contract among themselves to limit contributions to losses. According to the tenth recital to the Regulation, tax and social security debts must be treated as debts of the grouping. Creditors may only proceed against a grouping if they first of all request payment from it, and such payment does not take place within an appropriate period.[30]

The consequences of joint and several liability are determined by national law which includes conflict of laws rules. The United Kingdom European Economic Interest Grouping Regulations (SI 1998 No. 638) do not contain any provisions concerning this matter, but it would seem that British courts would apply partnership rules to determine the relevant consequences.

The liability of a new member of a grouping is provided for in Article 26. This provision allows a new member to be exempted from the payment of debts and other liabilities arising out of the group's activities before he became a member, provided that such exemption is provided for in the contract for the formation of the grouping, or the instrument of admission thereto,[31] such a clause can be relied upon against third persons in accordance with the applicable national law provided that the relevant provisions have been published in accordance with Article 8. The rules contained in Articles 34 and 37(1), which govern the position of members who cease to belong to a grouping, are more severe. It follows from these provisions that any member who ceases to belong to a grouping

[30] Regulation 2137/85, Art. 24(2).

[31] This rule may be compared with that contained in s. 17(1) of the UK Partnership Act 1890.

remains liable for a period of five years from the publication of notice of the cessation of this membership for debts and other liabilities arising out of the grouping's activities before he ceased to be a member. Member States appear free to continue to impose a shorter period for such liability if they already do so.

5. Termination of membership

The personalistic character of a grouping is also reflected in the provisions governing withdrawal therefrom. Article 27(1) provides that a member of the grouping may withdraw under the conditions provided for in the contract and, in the absence of such conditions, with the unanimous agreement of the other members. It also provides that any member of a grouping may withdraw on just and proper grounds. The provisions concerning withdrawal are rather sketchy, and need amplification by contractual provisions.

Furthermore, any member of a grouping may be expelled for reasons set out in the company's contract or if he seriously fails in his obligations or if he causes or threatens to cause serious disruption to the operation of the grouping. These provisions are clearly modelled on those of German law relating to the ordinary commercial partnership. Article 27(2) requires that expulsion shall take place as the result of the decision of a court unless otherwise provided in the contract of formation.

Article 28(1) provides that a member of a grouping shall cease to belong to it on death, or when he ceases to comply with the requirements of Article 4(1) concerning membership. Article 28(1) also permits a Member State to provide, for the purpose of its liquidation, winding up, insolvency or cessation of payments laws, that a member shall cease to be a member of any grouping at the moment determined by those laws. The legal consequences of cessation of membership are dealt with by Articles 29, 30, 33 and 37 of the Regulation.

H. Winding up and dissolution

Articles 31, 32 and 35 govern the winding up of groupings on grounds other than insolvency or cessation of members. Article 31(1) stipulates that a grouping may be wound up by a decision of its members which must be unanimous unless the contract otherwise provides. Winding up must take place

(a) if the fixed term provided for in the contract has expired;
(b) on any of the grounds set out in the formation contract;

(c) where the purpose for which the grouping has been formed is accomplished or it is impossible to fulfil it; or
(d) where the grouping ceases to comply with the requirement in Article 4(2) that it shall have two members from different states.[32]

If no decision regarding winding up is taken within three months of one of the events mentioned in (a)–(c) above, any member may petition the court to order a winding up of the grouping. An application may be made to the court to wind up a grouping by any person concerned or by a competent authority[33] in the event of an infringement of Article 3 (purposes of and prohibitions imposed on a grouping), Article 12 (situation of the registered office) or Article 31(3) (winding up must take place by a decision of the members where the requirements of Article 4(2) as to membership are no longer fulfilled). The court must order a winding up, unless the grouping's affairs can be and are put in order before the court makes a substantive ruling.[34] According to Article 32(2), on application by a member, a court may order a winding up on just and proper grounds. Furthermore, by Article 32(3), the court may on the application of a competent authority order the winding up of a grouping which acts in contravention of the public interest of the state where its official address is situated, if the relevant state provides for such a possibility in relation to its registered companies or other legal bodies.

Article 35(1) provides that the winding up of a grouping shall entail its liquidation and that the liquidation of the grouping and the conclusion of such liquidation are governed by national law. This is so even though the grounds for winding up are prescribed by Community law, i.e. in Articles 31 and 32 of the Regulation. Groupings are made subject to national law by Article 36 sentence one in relation to insolvency and the cessation of payments. This solution which is somewhat unsatisfactory results from the fact that the EC Bankruptcy Regulation had not been concluded or come into force when Regulation (EEC) 2137/85 was enacted.

It is of interest to note how the winding up and insolvency of the EEIG is treated under the UK European Economic Interest Grouping Regulations (SI 1985 No. 638). Regulation 8 of these Regulations provides that

[32] Regulation 2137/85, Art. 31(2) (3).
[33] This is the Secretary of State for Trade and Industry in the United Kingdom: see SI 1989 No. 638, reg. 1.
[34] Regulation (EC) 2137/85, Art. 32(1).

groupings will be wound up as unregistered companies under Part V of the Insolvency Act 1996. It appears to follow from section 221(4) of the Insolvency Act 1986 that no company can be wound up voluntarily under it. However, this seems contrary to Article 31, which provides for the voluntary winding up of a grouping by a decision of its members: this provision appears directly effective, and thus to prevail over section 221(4) in the British legal order.

Section 221(5) of the Insolvency Act states the circumstances under which an unregistered company (and hence a grouping) having an official address or principal place of business in England and Wales may be wound up. These are:

(a) if it has ceased to carry on business or is carrying on business only for the purpose of winding up its affairs;
(b) if the company is unable to pay its debts; or
(c) if the court is of the opinion that it is just and equitable that the company should be wound up.[35]

The first of these grounds is not reflected precisely by any of those of the Regulation. The second may not be entirely appropriate considering the unlimited joint and several liability of the members of the grouping to creditors. It is noteworthy that managers of a grouping may, in appropriate circumstances, be liable for fraudulent or wrongful trading under sections 213 and 214 of the Insolvency Act 1986. In addition (although such an action may sometimes be inappropriate), it follows from regulation 19 of the European Economic Interest Regulations (SI 1985 No. 638) that it would be possible for an administrative receiver to be appointed by a debenture holder where the grouping had been financed by a debenture. However, the appointment of an administrator is not made possible under the Insolvency Act 1986 or elsewhere.

I. Legal regime applicable to the grouping

This matter has already been dealt with in outline above. The Regulation contains provisions governing the structure and functioning of groupings from formation to winding up. The governing hierarchy of rules applicable to groupings concerning these matters is as follows:

[35] Note the additional ground for winding up applicable to Scottish unregistered companies, contained in s. 221(7) of the Insolvency Act 1986.

(a) the mandatory provisions of the Regulation itself;
(b) the contract for the formation of the grouping in many situations where the Regulation is silent, as well as where the Regulation makes specific reference thereto;
(c) the provisions of the Regulation about what the contract shall or may provide certain rules about; and
(d) the national or internal law of the Member State where the grouping has its official address.

The structure and functioning of the grouping are, to a marked extent, governed by the provisions of the Regulation. This is especially true as far as the protection of members and third parties at different stages in the existence of the grouping.[36] Sometimes, instead of trying to provide for a particular matter itself, the Regulation grants options to Member States to legislate concerning certain matters. Furthermore, national law governs the liquidation of a grouping and the whole winding-up process (including the making of the winding up order) in the event of insolvency or cessation of payments. As has already stated the Regulation sometimes fails to contain mandatory provisions, and leaves specific matters to be regulated by the contract, or by a decision of the members. In such an event, the Regulation will contain default provisions which will apply in the absence of a provision in the contract, or a decision of the members.[37]

As far as problems concerning the contract for the formation of the grouping and its internal organisation cannot be resolved by applying the rules already mentioned, they must be resolved by applying the internal law of the Member State where the grouping has its official address.[38] An exception to this is made as regards the status and capacity of persons, which is governed by national law.[39]

It follows from the eleventh, fourteenth, fifteenth, sixteenth and seventeenth recitals that a grouping will be subject to the laws of Member States in certain areas other than those mentioned above, for example labour law, competition law and intellectual property law, where Community law is also of importance.[40]

[36] Note, however, Art. 9 of the Regulation, which stipulates that the documents and particulars which must be published pursuant to the Regulation, may be relied on by a grouping against third parties under the conditions laid down by the national law applicable under Arts. 3(5) and 3(7) of the First Directive.
[37] Note, e.g. Regulation 2137/85, Arts. 17(3), 21(2) and 27(1).
[38] Regulation 2137/85, Art. 2.
[39] See the eleventh recital in the Preamble to Regulation 2137/85.
[40] Note the see the fifteenth recital in this sense.

J. Implementation

The Regulation has been implemented in all the Member States considered in this work. In the United Kingdom, two separate statutory instruments were made in 1989, one of which extends to Great Britain[41] and the other to Northern Ireland.[42] The complexity of the instrument should be contrasted with the comparative simplicity of the German *EWIV-Aüsführungsgesetz* of 14 April 1988.[43] Implementation took place in France as the result of the law of 13 June 1989,[44] and the Decree of 28 June 1989.[45] In Belgium, it took place through the medium of two implementing laws and one implementing decree.[46] In the Netherlands only one law has been passed for the purpose of implementing the Regulation.[47]

II. The European Company

A. Introductory remarks

After very prolonged discussions of proposals for a European Company (*Societas Europaea*, SE),[48] Council Regulation (EC) No. 2157/2001 on the European Company[49] and Council Directive 2001/86/EC supplementing the Statute for the European Company with regard to the involvement of employees[50] were finally unanimously adopted by the Council on 8 October 2001 on the basis of Article 308 EC, which was formerly Article 235 EC. The constitutional basis of the Directive on employee involvement was thus changed from Article 44(3)(a) EC, which had been controversial. The present basis appears more satisfactory: Parliament withdrew a threat to take proceedings against the Council before the Court of Justice in respect of the alteration in legal basis. It did take such proceedings in relation to the enactment of the

[41] SI 1989 No. 638. [42] SI 1989 No. 191.
[43] *Federal Law Gazette* (BGBl) 1988 I-514; see also BGBl 1989 I-1113.
[44] JORF, 10 June 1989, 7440. [45] *Ibid*., 30 June 1989, 8101.
[46] Law of 12 July 1989, *Moniteur Belge*, 22 August 1989, 14385; Law of 17 July 1989, *Moniteur Belge*, 22 August 1989, 14391; Royal Decree of 27 July 1989, *Moniteur Belge*, 22 August, 14400.
[47] *Staatsblad* 1989, 245.
[48] For a useful history of these proposals, see V. Edwards, *EC Company Law* (Oxford: Clarendon Press, 1999), 399–404. A good account of the new Regulation and Directive is given by E. Werlauff, 'The SE Company' [2003] EBLR 85.
[49] Regulation 2157/2001.
[50] Council Directive 2001/86/EC of 10 November 2001, OJ 2001 L294/22.

European Cooperative Society Regulation and Directive, which were (unsurprisingly) dismissed in a unanimous decision by the European Court of Justice.

Although the Regulation is intended to permit the creating and management of companies having a European dimension, the SE is subject to a mixed legal regime set out in Article 9 of the Regulation consisting in part of the Regulation, and when authorised thereby, by the company's statutes.[51] As far as aspects not covered by the Regulation are concerned, it will be governed by the provisions of law adopted by Member States in implementation of Community measures relating specifically to SEs; the provisions of Member States' laws which would apply to a public limited liability company formed in accordance with the laws of the Member State in which it has its registered office; and the provisions of the statutes, in the same way as a company formed in accordance with the latter. It will be noted that the statutes of the company may apply either because the Regulation expressly says so or because they are the remaining supplementary source of law.

The company must be entered in a register designated by the law of the Member State in which it has its registered office,[52] but this cannot be done until certain requirements relating to employee involvement have been fulfilled.[53] The company's name must be preceded or followed by the acronym SE.[54] It will be treated in every Member State as if it were a public limited liability company formed in accordance with the law of the Member State in which it has its registered office.[55] According to Article 7, the registered office and the head office must be situated in the same state, but this requirement will be reconsidered by the Commission within five years of the entry into force of the Regulation, i.e. by 8 October 2007.[56]

Article 8 contains extremely detailed provisions which are in part intended for the protection of shareholders and creditors concerning the transfer of the registered office from one Member State to another.

[51] According to Art. 6 of Regulation 2157/2001, for the purposes of the Regulation, the statutes of the SE shall mean both the instrument of incorporation and where they are the subject of a separate document, the statutes (or articles) of the company.

[52] Regulation 2157/2001, Art. 12(1). [53] *Ibid.*, Art. 12(1) and (2).

[54] *Ibid.*, Art. 11. [55] *Ibid.*, Art. 10.

[56] *Ibid.*, Art. 69. This requirement may possibly then be considered for amendment or deletion in view of decisions of the ECJ such as Case C-208/00 *Überseering BV* v. *Nordic Construction Company Baumanagement GmbH* [2002] ECR I-9919, which are based directly upon freedom of establishment provided for in Arts. 43 and 48 EC.

These resemble to a considerable extent the corresponding provisions of Council Regulation 2137/85 on the EEIG governing the transfer of the official address of a grouping. The transfer becomes effective when the SE is registered in the register for its new registered office.[57] By Article 8(13), on publication third parties may rely on the new registration. However, until such publication, third parties may continue to rely on the old registered office, unless the SE can prove that they were aware of the new one.

The present Regulation does not contain any provisions on groups of companies, nor does it attempt to define controlled and controlling undertakings, as did Article 6 of the draft Regulation of 1989.[58] A brief account of some important features of the SE Regulation and of Directive 2001/86/EC which supplements it appears below. The Regulation, like the European Cooperative Society Regulation, does not cover such areas as taxation, competition, intellectual property or insolvency. The twentieth recital makes it apparent that in these areas, as well as in other areas not covered by the Regulation, the provisions of the laws of the Member States and Community law shall be applicable. The SE Regulation provides for several different methods forming an SE. According to Article 2(1) public limited liability companies formed under the law of a Member State with registered and head offices within the Community may form an SE by means of a merger, provided that at least two of them are governed by the laws of different Member States. This facility is unfortunately not open to private companies, perhaps because the Third Company Law Directive concerning mergers does not apply to such companies, although similar rules have been applied to mergers in the legislation of certain Member States.

According to Article 2(2), public and private limited liability companies formed under the law of a Member State with registered and head offices within the Community may promote the formation of a holding SE, subject to the proviso that each of at least of them are governed by the

[57] Regulation 2157/2001, Art. 8(10).

[58] Note however, recital 15 in the Preamble, which stipulates that:

> according to the general principles of private international law, where one undertaking controls another governed by a different legal system, its ensuing rights and obligations as regards the protection of shareholders and third parties, are governed by the laws governing the controlled undertaking.

This approach does not seem capable of solving all the problems arising from multinational groups.

law of a different Member State, or has for at least two years had a subsidiary company governed by the law of another Member State, or a branch situated in another Member State. The fulfilment of the latter requirements should not give rise to great difficulties.

Furthermore, Article 2(3) provides that companies and firms within the meaning of Article 48(2) EC and other legal bodies governed by public or private law formed under the law of a Member State with registered or head offices within the Community may form a subsidiary SE by subscribing for its shares, provided that each of at least two of them is governed by the laws of a different Member State, or has for at least two years had a subsidiary company governed by the law of another Member State, or a branch situated in another Member State. The present facility appears open not only to corporate bodies but also to unincorporated partnerships such as those familiar in Germany and Holland. Entities in the same Member State which wish to form a subsidiary SE may form branches in different countries for this purpose. It would seem that the activities of such branches might well be fairly minimal.

Article 3(1) extends the scope of Articles 2(1)–(3). It stipulates that for the purposes of these provisions, an SE shall be regarded as a public limited liability company governed by the laws of the Member State in which it has its registered office. Thus two SEs which fulfil the detailed requirements explained above may merge, or set up a subsidiary, or take part with other companies in such formation.

Article 2(4) provides that a public limited liability company formed under the laws of a Member State having its registered office and head office within the Community may be converted into an SE provided that, for at least two years, it has had a subsidiary company governed by the law of another Member State. The latter provision is apparently designed to prevent too easy conversions of public companies into SEs.

According to Article 3(2), an SE may set up one or more subsidiaries in the form of SEs, which may be single member companies. Any provisions of the law of the Member State where the subsidiary SE has its registered office requiring a public limited liability company to have more than one member is inapplicable to such companies.

The rules governing the different methods of formation of an SE are rather complicated, and perhaps necessarily rather inconsistent with one another. Their somewhat restrictive character has been subject to criticisms in the past. It may well be possible to circumvent certain of them.

A number of detailed rules concerning formation procedures are contained in the Regulation. The relevant rules governing formation by means of a merger resemble those contained in the Third Directive on Mergers[59] and the Tenth Directive on cross-border mergers.[60] Their complexity makes it doubtful whether much practical use will be made of the merger provisions: it is perhaps unfortunate that it is not apparently possible to form an SE by means of a takeover. Articles 32–34 are concerned with the formation of a holding SE, and Articles 35 and 36 with that of a joint subsidiary. These operations will often be carried out as a practical alternative to a formal merger. Article 37 governs the conversion of an existing public company into an SE, which is said not to entail the winding up of the former company or the creation of a new legal person.

As already indicated, an SE acquires legal personality on the date of its registration. According to Article 13, publication of the documents and particulars concerning an SE which must be published under the Regulation must be effected in the manner required by the law of the Member State of the registered office, in accordance with Directive 68/151/EEC. Furthermore, by Article 14(1), notice of the registration of an SE and the deletion of such registration must be published in the Official Journal for information purposes.

B. *Capital, shares and bonds*

The 1989 draft Regulation contained detailed provisions concerning the above matters in Title III thereof. It follows from Article 5 that this is no longer the case. This provision stipulates that apart from the requirements of a minimum capital expressed in euros, matters relating to capital, its maintenance and changes thereto, together with questions governing shares, bonds and similar securities will be determined by the provisions which would apply to a public limited liability company with a registered office in the Member State in which the SE is registered.

C. *Principal organs*

1. The two systems

There is a division of powers between the general meeting, which is required to decide certain items of business, and the bodies responsible for managing the company. Depending on the terms of the statutes, the

[59] Third Council Directive 78/855/EEC of 9 October 1978 based on Art. 54(3)(f) of the Treaty concerning mergers of public limited liability companies, 1978 OJ L295/36.

[60] See OJ 2005 L310/1.

management of the company would either be entrusted to a management organ with a supervisory organ monitoring its activities (two-tier system) or to an administrative organ (one-tier system) depending upon the provisions of the statutes.[61] The two-tier system is dealt with in Articles 39–42, and the one-tier in Articles 43–45. Rules which are common to both systems are contained in Articles 46–51, and the general meeting is dealt with in Articles 52–60.

Where the two-tier system is employed, the management board would be responsible for managing the SE. However, according to Article 39(1), a Member State may provide that a managing director or directors shall be responsible for the current management under the same conditions as for public limited companies which have registered offices within its territories. As in a German public company the members of the management organ may be appointed and removed by the supervisory organ.[62] Nevertheless, a Member State may require or permit the statutes to provide that the member or members of the management organ shall be appointed or removed by the general meeting in accordance with the same conditions as for public limited liability companies that have their registered offices within its territory.[63] It would not be possible for a person to serve on both organs at the same time. Although a member of the supervisory organ could be nominated by that body to act as a member of the management board in the event of a vacancy on that board, his or her functions as a member of the supervisory organ would then be suspended.[64] Where a Member State makes no provision for a two-tier system in relation to public limited liability companies with registered offices on its territory, that state is empowered to adopt appropriate measures in relation to SEs.[65] The similar provisions of Article 43(4) should be noted, which are applicable when a state has no one-tier system.

As in Germany, the supervisory organ has to supervise the management organ, but it may not exercise managerial powers.[66] The members of the supervisory organ are appointed by the general meeting. However,

[61] Regulation 2157/2001, Art. 38. No detailed provisions on the single or two tier board system are contained in the implementing regulation in England and Wales and Scotland (European Public Limited Liability Regulations, SI 2004 No. 2326). See J. Schmidt (2006) 27 Co Law 105 for a discussion of this matter. Spain, which does not provide for a double board system in private or public companies, has however recognized the double board system as an option for the European Company with registered office in Spain, see the Spanish Public Companies Act 1989, Articles 327 and 329 to 336, as amended by Law 19/2005.

[62] Regulation 2157/2001, Art. 39(2). [63] *Ibid.*, Art. 39(2). [64] *Ibid.*, Art. 39(3).

[65] *Ibid.*, Art. 39(5). [66] *Ibid.*, Arts. 39(1), 40(1) and 41(1).

in the case of the first supervisory organ, they may be appointed in the statutes. In addition, the Regulation respects a provision of national law allowing a minority of shareholders, other persons or authorities to appoint some members of the supervisory board. Finally, certain members may have to be appointed in accordance with employee participation arrangements made in accordance with Directive 2001/86/EC.[67]

The management board would be required to report to the supervisory board at least every three months on the progress and foreseeable development of the company's business.[68] Furthermore, it might also require the management organ to provide it with information of any kind needed for the purpose of exercising supervision.[69] In addition, the supervisory organ might undertake or arrange for any investigations necessary for performance of its duties.[70] Each member of the supervisory organ would be entitled to examine all information submitted to him or her.[71]

The one-tier system does not involve the use of a supervisory organ. The management of the company is the task of the administrative organ.[72] As is the case under Article 39(1), when the two-tier system is employed, a managing director or directors may be made responsible for the day-to-day management of the company.[73] The SE's statutes may prescribe the number of members of the administrative organ or the rules governing its determination. A Member State may also stipulate the minimum or maximum number of members.[74] These rules resemble those applicable to the membership of the management board under Article 39(4) when the two-tier system is employed. However, if employee participation takes place in accordance with Directive 2001/86/EC, the administrative organ must consist of at least three members.[75]

The member or members of the administrative board would be appointed by the general meeting. However, in the case of the first organ, they would be appointed by the statutes. Such powers of appointment are without prejudice to any such powers vested in a minority of the shareholders, or under the terms of employee participation agreements made according to Directive 2001/86/EC.[76]

Certain rules which are common to the one-tier and the two-tier systems will be considered in outline only. Members of company organs may be appointed for a period provided for in the statutes not exceeding six years, and subject to any restrictions contained therein, may be

[67] *Ibid.*, Art. 40(2). [68] *Ibid.*, Art. 41(1). [69] *Ibid.*, Art. 41(3). [70] *Ibid.*, Art. 41(4).
[71] *Ibid.*, Art. 41(5). [72] *Ibid.*, Art. 43(1). [73] *Ibid.*, Art. 43(1). [74] *Ibid.*, Art. 43(2).
[75] *Ibid.*, Art. 43(2). [76] *Ibid.*, Art. 42(2), second sentence.

reappointed.[77] According to Article 47(1), an SE's statutes may designate a legal person to be a member of one of its organs, on condition that the law of SE's registered office permits such appointment in relation to public limited liability companies. The legal person is required to designate a natural person to exercise its functions on the board.

An SE's statutes is required by Article 48(1) to list the categories of transactions which require the authorisation of the management organ by the supervisory organ in the two-tier system.[78] This provision further states that a Member State may provide that in the two-tier system, the supervisory organ may itself make certain classes of transactions subject to its authorisation. In addition, Article 48(2) stipulates that a Member State may determine the categories of transactions that must at least be indicated in the statutes of an SE which is registered within its territory.

Article 49 requires the members of an SE's administrative, management or supervisory organs to exercise discretion with regard to confidential information, even when they have ceased to hold office. However, they are permitted to disclose such information when such disclosure is required or permitted under the provisions of national law which apply to public limited liability companies, or is in the public interest. Article 50(1) is concerned with quorums and decision making. Unless the statutes or the Regulation otherwise provides, at least half the members of the administrative, supervisory or management organ must be present or represented to constitute a quorum. Such organs must take their decisions by a majority of the members present or represented. In those cases in which employee participation is provided for in accordance with Directive 2001/86/EC, a Member State can provide that the supervisory organs quorum and decision making process shall be subject to the rules applicable to public limited liability companies governed by the law of the relevant state.[79]

In contrast with earlier draft versions of the Regulation, the question of the liability of members of an SE's management, supervisory or administrative organs for loss or damage suffered by the SE following any breach of their obligations is referred by Article 50(3) to the relevant provisions applicable to public limited liability companies in the state of the registered office. Thus, the controversial provisions formerly included concerning the joint and several liability of the members of

[77] *Ibid.*, Art. 46.
[78] German Public Limited Liability Companies Act, para. 111(4) is in similar terms.
[79] Regulation 2157/2001, Art. 50(3)

such organs no longer exist. The Regulation now contains no provisions concerning a derivative action, and does not say much about minority protection, which may be of considerable practical importance in an SE having few members.

2. General meetings

According to Article 52, the general meeting decides on matters for which it is given it sole responsibility under the Regulation or under the legislation of the Member State in which the SE's registered office is located adopted for the purpose of implementing Directive 2001/86/EC. In addition, it also has the power to decide upon matters for which responsibility is given to the general meeting of a public company governed by the law of the Member State where the registered office of the SE is situated, either by the law of that Member State, or by the SE's statutes in accordance with that law.

Under the Regulation, the general meeting is given sole responsibility for such matters as the transfer of the registered office of the company within the Community,[80] the approval of the draft terms of a merger or the formation of a holding SE,[81] the amendment of the statutes,[82] and the approval of draft terms of conversion of an SE into a public limited liability company.[83] The general meeting will sometimes have sole responsibility for the appointment and removal of the members of the supervisory or administrative organ, but it follows from Articles 40(2) and 43(3) that this will not always be true.

Certain matters which govern the organisation and conduct of meetings and voting procedure thereat are dealt within the Regulation. Insofar as they are not dealt with, Article 53 provides that such matters are governed by the law of the Member State where the SE's registered office is situated governing public limited liability companies.

By Article 54(1) a general meeting must normally be called once every calendar year within six months of the end of the financial year. Article 55 provides that shareholders holding at least 10 per cent of the subscribed capital may request the calling of a general meeting, and draw up the agenda for such a meeting. The statutes, or national legislation may provide for a smaller proportion under the same conditions as are applicable to public limited liability companies in the Member State of the registered office. Article 56 permits shareholders to place additional

[80] *Ibid.*, Arts. 8(4) and 59. [81] *Ibid.*, Arts. 23(1) and 32(6).
[82] *Ibid.*, Art. 59. [83] *Ibid.*, Art. 66(b).

items on the agenda if they hold at least ten per cent of the company's subscribed capital. This proportion may be reduced by the statutes or by the law of the Member State in which the SE's registered office is situated.

Decisions are taken by a majority of the votes validly cast, unless the Regulation or the law applicable to public companies in the Member State of the registered office requires a higher majority.[84] A majority consisting of two-thirds of the votes cast is necessary for the amendment of the statutes, unless the law applicable to public limited liability companies in the Member State of the SE's registered office requires or permits a higher majority.[85] A Member State may however provide that where at least one half of the subscribed capital is represented, a simple majority of the votes cast is adequate.

D. *Annual accounts and consolidated accounts*

Except where the special rules contained in Article 62 concerning SEs which are credit, financial or insurance undertakings are applicable, an SE will be governed by the rules applicable to public limited liability companies under the law of the Member State of the registered office with respect to the publication of its annual and, where appropriate consolidated accounts, including the accompanying annual report and the auditing and publications of such accounts.[86] The Member States have been under an obligation to implement the provisions of the Fourth,[87] Seventh[88] and Eighth Company Law Directives[89] in respect of their annual accounts, consolidated accounts and the audit thereof in their national laws, but there are substantial differences between accounts which have been prepared in accordance with national legislation implementing the Fourth and Seventh Directives in the different Member States. Certain of these differences may be removed as the result of recent Community legislation aimed at modernising and updating accountancy rules.[90]

[84] *Ibid.*, Art. 57. [85] *Ibid.*, Art. 59(1). [86] *Ibid.*, Art. 61. [87] OJ 1978 L222/11.

[88] OJ 1983 L193/1. This Directive and the Fourth Directive on annual accounts were amended by Directive 2001/51 of the European Parliament and Council, OJ 2003 L 179/16.

[89] OJ 1984 L126/20. This latter Directive was repealed by Directive 2006/43 of the European Parliament and Council on the statutory audits of annual accounts and consolidated accounts, (OJ 2006 L 157/87).

[90] Note in particular the IAS Regulation, Regulation (EC) No. 1605/2002, 19 July 2002 on the application of international accounting standards, 2002 OJ L243/1.

As far as an SE which is a credit or financial institution is concerned, the above matters are governed by the rules provided for in the national law of the Member State in which the registered office is situated which implements the provisions of the European Parliament and Council Directive 2000/12/EC. This Directive is a consolidating one, and relates to the taking up and pursuit of the business of credit institutions.[91] Where insurance undertakings are concerned, corresponding reference has to be made to the national law of the Member State where the registered office is located implementing Council Directive 91/674/EEC.[92] This Directive relates to the annual and consolidated accounts of insurance undertakings.

E. Winding up and other insolvency procedures

Insofar as winding up, liquidation, insolvency, cessation of payments and similar procedure, are concerned, an SE will be governed by the legal rules which would apply to a public limited liability company formed in accordance with the law of the Member State in which the registered office is situated, including provisions relating to decision making by the general meeting.[93]

The Member State in which an SE has its registered office is required by Article 64(1) to take appropriate measures to compel the SE to regularise its position when it no longer complies with the requirement contained in Article 7 that the head office and the registered office must be in the same state. Such regularisation might take place by re-establishing the SE's head office in the same state as that of the registered office, or instead by transferring the SE's registered office. The Member State of the SE's registration must put in place the measures necessary to ensure that an SE that fails to regularise its position is liquidated.[94]

The above procedures may not be completed very frequently. This follows from the fact that Article 64(3) stipulates that the Member State in which the SE's registered office is situated shall set up a judicial remedy

[91] Council Directive (EC) 2000/12/EC of 20 March 2000 relating to the taking up and pursuit of the business of credit institutions, 2000 OJ L126/1.

[92] Council Directive (EEC) 91/674/EEC of 19 December 1991 on the annual accounts and consolidated accounts of insurance undertakings, 1991 OJ L374/7. This Directive was amended in 2003: see Directive 2003/51/EC of the European Parliament and of the Council OJ L 178/16.

[93] Regulation 2157/2001, Art. 63. [94] *Ibid.*, Art. 64(2).

with regard to any established infringement of Article 7, which will have a suspensory effect on them.

F. Entry into force

It has already been explained that the Regulation did not enter into force until 8 October 2004. Recital 22 of the Preamble to this Regulation makes it clear that this delay is intended to enable each Member State to incorporate into its national law provisions of Directive 2001/86/EC, and also to set up in advance the appropriate machinery for the formation and operation of SEs with registered offices within its territory, such that the Regulation and Directive can be applied concomitantly.

G. Employee involvement

1. Purpose and definitions

As is clear from the wording of the third recital to its Preamble, Council Directive 2001/86/EC is in part aimed at ensuring that the establishment of an SE does not entail the disappearance or reduction of practices of employee involvement existing within the companies taking part in the formation of an SE. As is implicitly the case with recital 9 of the Preamble to Regulation 2157/2001/EC, recital 4 of the Preamble to Council Directive 2001/86/EC invokes the principle of subsidiarity to justify the enactment of the instrument. The Directive is said in Article 1(1) to cover the involvement of employees in the affairs of SEs. Article 1(2) provides that, to this end, arrangements for the involvement of employees shall be established in every SE according to the negotiating procedure referred to in Articles 3–6, or in the circumstances defined in Article 7 (which is concerned with the enactment and applicability of standard rules), according to the Annex, which contains detailed provisions governing such standard rules.

Article 2 is concerned with definitions. Thus, the phrase 'involvement of employees' is said to mean any mechanism involving information, consultation and participation through which employees, representatives may exercise an influence on decisions to be taken within the company. Furthermore, the phrase 'employees' representatives' is said to mean the employees' representatives provided for by national law or practice, whilst the phrase 'representative body' means the body representative of the employees under the agreements referred to in Article 4 (which are agreements on arrangements for the involvement of employees within the SE) or in accordance with the Annex, with the purpose of informing and consulting the employees of an SE, its subsidiaries and establishments situated within the Community, and where applicable, of exercising participation rights in relation to the SE.

2. Negotiating procedure

The above matter is governed by the somewhat complex provisions of Articles 3–7 of the Directive. Where the management or administrative organs of the companies taking part draw up a plan for the establishment of an SE, they must as soon as possible after the publication of the draft terms of the merger or creating a holding company, or after agreeing a plan to form a subsidiary, or to transform into an SE, take the necessary steps to commence negotiations with the representatives of the companies employees on arrangements for the involvement of employees in the SE.[95] For this purpose, a special negotiating body representing the workers in the participating companies and the concerned subsidiaries or establishments must be set up.[96] The phrase 'concerned subsidiary or establishment' is defined in Article 2(d), and is said to mean subsidiary or establishment of a participating company which is proposed to become a subsidiary or establishment of the SE upon its formation. It should be remembered that it is also necessary to set up a special negotiating body under the European Works Council Directive.

Article 3(2) contains detailed provisions governing the election and appointment of members of the special negotiating body. Its membership will be determined in accordance with proportional criteria relating to the number of employees in the participating companies and the concerned subsidiaries of establishments. Additional membership is provided for where an SE is formed by means of a merger and certain of the participating companies will cease to exist as separate legal entities. By Article 3(3), the special negotiating body together with the participating companies shall determine, by means of written agreement, arrangements for the involvement of employees. Subject to the special rules contained in Article 3(6), which are applicable when it is decided not to open negotiations or to terminate them, the special negotiating body will take decisions by an absolute majority of members, provided that such majority also represents a majority of employees.

95 Council Directive (EC) 86/2001 supplementing the Statute for a European company with regard to the involvement of employees, 2001 OJ L294/22, Art. 3(1).

96 *Ibid.*, Art. 3(2).

However, according to Article 3(4) should the result of the negotiations lead to a reduction in participation rights, a special majority is required to approve it in accordance with the rules mentioned in the following paragraph. Participation is defined in Article 2(k) as the influence of the body representative of the employees and/or the employees; representatives in the affairs of the company by way of the right to elect or appoint some of the members of the company's supervisory or representative organ, or the right to recommend and/or oppose the appointment of some or all of the members of the company's supervisory or administrative organ.

The required special majority is the same as the majority required for the purpose of deciding not to open negotiations to terminate them. It consists of the votes of two-thirds of the special negotiating body representing the votes of at least two-thirds of the employees, including the votes of members representing employees employed in at least two Member States. When an SE to be established by a merger and participation covers at least 25 per cent of the total number of employees of the participating companies, this special majority is necessary. It is also required where an SE is to be formed by means of establishing a holding company or forming a subsidiary, and participation covers at least 50 per cent of the total number of employees involved.[97]

The special negotiating body may require experts of its own choice to assist it with its work: these may, for example, be representatives of appropriate Community level trade union organisations.[98] As already indicated, Article 3(6) provides that the special negotiating body may decide by a special majority not to open negotiations or to terminate them. In such an event, it will decide to rely upon the rules on the information and consultation of employees in force in the Member States in which the SE has employees. In such a event, the standard rules provided for in the Annex are inapplicable, and a new request to reconvene the special negotiating body cannot be made for two years, except where the parties agree to a shorter time period. Article 5(5) of the European Works Council Directive contains a similar provision.

Article 3(7) stipulates that any expenses relating to the functioning of the special negotiating procedure and to negotiations in general shall be borne by the participating companies in order to enable the special negotiating body to perform the task in an appropriate manner. Member States may establish budgetary rules concerning the operation

[97] *Ibid.*, Art. 3(4). [98] *Ibid.*, Art. 3(5).

of the special negotiating body and, are empowered to limit the funding to one expert only. Despite this limitation it would appear that if negotiations are fairly protracted, the costs imposed on the participating companies may be quite considerable, and that this possibility may act as some detriment for companies contemplating the use of the SE. If they do make use of it, there may conceivably be advantages on their agreeing to apply the standard terms considered below.

The competent organs of the participating companies as well as the special negotiating body are required to negotiate in a spirit of cooperation with a view to concluding an agreement on arrangements for employee involvement within the SE.[99] Such an agreement must specify the matters mentioned in Articles 4(2)(a) and (b), which include such items as the scope of the agreement, particulars of arrangements for the information and consultation of employees (including some details regarding any representative body set up for this purpose) and of arrangements for employee participation; and the date of entry into, and the duration of, the agreement. The agreement will not be subject to the standard terms set out in the Annex, unless it provides otherwise.[100] Where an SE is formed by the conversion of an existing public company, it must provide for at least the same level of all elements of employee involvement already existing in that company.[101] This obligation appears to be a somewhat imprecise one, but would entail that where for instance a German AG was converted into an SE, the German rules governing employee participation would still apply.

Negotiations must begin when the special negotiating body is set up, and may continue for six months thereafter; this period may be extended to twelve months by the joint agreement of the negotiating parties.[102] Unless the Directive provides otherwise, the legislation which is applicable to the negotiation procedure is that of the Member State where the registered office of an SE will be located.[103]

3. Standard rules

Article 7 requires Member States to lay down standard rules governing employee involvement which satisfy the provisions set out in the Annex to the Directive. Nevertheless, Article 7(3) provides that such states may stipulate that the standard rules (reference provisions) on participation contained in Part 3 of the Annex shall not apply in the case provided for

[99] *Ibid.*, Art. 4(1). [100] *Ibid.*, Art. 4(3). [101] *Ibid.*, Art. 4(4).
[102] *Ibid.*, Art. 5. [103] *Ibid.*, Art. 6.

in Article 7(2)(b), which relates to participation in SEs established by mergers, and which is explained below. This rule will sometimes permit public companies to evade participation by means of a cross-frontier merger. The standard rules laid down by the legislation enacted by the Member State of the registered office are applicable as from the date of registration of the company, provided that certain rather complex conditions are fulfilled.

These are that the parties so agree, or that by the deadline for the duration of negotiations laid down in Article 5, (i.e. six months, extendable to one year) no agreement has been reached. In the latter event, the competent organ of each of the participating companies must decide to accept the application of the standard rules to the SE and thus to continue with its registration, and the special negotiating body must not have reached a decision under Article 3(6) not to open negotiations or to terminate negotiations already opened and rely on the rules for the information and consultation of employees in the different Member States in which the SE has employees. It would seem often likely to be the case that the detailed requirements mentioned above were not fulfilled. The position regarding the application of the standard rules seems somewhat complex, and may be capable of leading to errors on the part of those who wish to form an SE. This may be particularly the case in relation to their application in the field of employee participation.

Standard rules are set out for employee participation in Part 3 of the Annex. They are, unsurprisingly, only applicable to an SE established by means of conversion if the rules of a Member State relating to employee participation in the administrative or supervisory board apply to the company transformed into an SE. According to Article 7(2)(b), in the case of an SE established by merger, they are applicable, (unless a Member State decides not to apply them), if before registration of the SE, one or more forms of participation applied in one or more of the participating companies covering at least 25 per cent of the total number of employees in all the participating companies, or if the situation is the same apart from the fact that the relevant percentage is less than 25, but the special negotiating body decides on the application of the standard rules.

Where an SE is established by setting up a holding company, or forming a subsidiary, and if before registration of the SE, one or more forms of participation applied in one or more of the participating companies covering at least 50 per cent of the total number of employees in all the participating companies, the standard rules are applicable. They are also applicable where the situation is the same apart from the fact that the forms of participation cover less than 50 per cent of the employees, providing that the special negotiating body so decides. When there is more than one form of employee participation within the different participating companies, the special negotiating body has the task of deciding which form may be used in the SE. Member States may determine the rules in the absence of any decision on the matter for an SE registered in their territory. No time limit is prescribed within which the special negotiating body must take its decisions.

4. Provisions of the Annex (standard rules)

Part I of the Annex governs the composition of the body representative of the employees of the company. This body will consist of employees of the SE and its subsidiaries and establishments elected or appointed from among their number by the employees' representatives, or in the absence of such persons, by the entire body of employees. The election or appointment of members of the representative body is governed by national law. Four years after it is established, it has to decide whether to open negotiations for the conclusion of an arrangement or arrangements for the involvement of employees, or to continue to apply the standard rules. Part 2 of the Annex sets out standard rules for information and consultation. It stipulates that the competence of the representative body shall be limited to questions which concern the SE itself, its subsidiaries and establishments or which exceed the powers of decision makers in a single Member State. The question whether the latter requirements are fulfilled may be difficult to determine, and might even require reference to the ECJ.

Apart from the rules applicable where there are exceptional circumstances, the representative body will have the right to be informed and consulted, and for this purpose will have the right to meet with the competent organ of the SE at least once a year, to consider the progress of the business of the SE and its prospects. In addition, where there are exceptional circumstances which affect the interests of the employees, to a considerable extent, such as relocations, transfers, the closure of establishments or undertakings or collective redundancies, the representative body has the right to be informed and meet with the competent organ of the SE, or any more appropriate of management therein. This provision, contained in Part 2(c) of the Annex can be usefully compared with paragraph 111 of the German Works Councils Act 2000, which has some similar features. Part 2(c) further provides that when the competent organ decides not to act in accordance with the opinion expressed by the representative body, the latter body has the right to a further meeting with it for the purpose of seeking agreement. It is not given any power to veto any proposed decision. The representatives of the employees of the SE and of its subsidiaries and establishments are required by Part 2(e) of the Annex to be informed of the content and outcome of the information and consultation procedure.

As already indicated, Part 3 of the Annex contains standard rules for participation. If an SE is established by the conversion of an existing public limited liability company, and the rules of a Member State relating to employee participation in the administrative or supervisory board applied before registration, all aspects of employee participation continue to apply to the SE.

In other cases of establishing an SE, the standard rules stipulate that the employees of the SE, its subsidiaries and establishments and/or their representative body shall have the right to elect, appoint, recommend or oppose the appointment of a number of members of the administrative or supervisory board of the SE equal to the highest proportion in force in the participating companies before registration of the SE. If none of the participating companies was governed by participation rules before registration of the SE, the latter is not required to set up provisions for employee participation.

5. Miscellaneous provisions

Article 8 of the Directive contains detailed rules requiring Member States to enact rules governing confidentiality and the transmission of information. The first paragraph of this Article stipulates that Member States shall provide that members of the special negotiating body or the representative body, and experts who assist them, are not authorised to reveal any information given to them in confidence. This obligation is applicable to employees' representatives in the context of an information and consultation procedure. The same obligation continues to apply, irrespective of the situation of the persons, even after the expiry of their terms of office. According to Article 8(2), each Member State shall provide in specific cases and under the conditions and limits laid down by national legislation that the supervisory or administrative organ of an SE, or a participating company established in its territory, is not required to transmit information where its nature is such that, according to objective criteria, to do so might seriously harm the functioning of the SE, or the participating company, or its subsidiaries and establishments, or would be prejudicial to it. The present rule somewhat resembles that contained in paragraph 131(3) No. 1 of the German *Aktiengesetz*, although it is necessarily more qualified and thus rather uncertain in its impact.[104] A Member State may make the relevant dispensation subject to prior administrative or judicial authorisation.

Member States are required by Article 8(4) to make provision for administrative or judicial appeal procedures which may be initiated when the supervisory or administrative organ requires confidentiality, or fails to give information.

Article 9 requires the competent organ of the SE and the representative body to cooperate with one another, and requires similar cooperation between the supervisory or administrative organ of the SE and the employees' representatives (i.e. those representatives provided for by national law and/or practice). Article 10 is concerned with the protection of the different categories of employees' representatives to which it relates, i.e. members of the special negotiating body and the representative body provided for by Article 4(2)(b) of the Directive, employees' representatives exercising functions under the information and consultation procedure, as well as the employees' representatives in the supervisory or administrative organs of an SE who are employees of the SE, its subsidiaries or establishments, or a participating company. It provides that in the exercise of their functions, such persons shall enjoy the same protection and guarantees provided for by employees' representatives by the national legislation and/or practice in force in their country of employment. Article 12 requires Member States to ensure compliance with the Directive, and to provide for appropriate measures in the case of non-compliance.

Article 13 is concerned with the relationship between Directive 2001/86/EC and certain other provisions of law. Article 13(1) provides that where an SE is a Community-scale undertaking[105] or the controlling

[104] German Public Limited Liability Companies Act, para. 131(3) No. 1 provides that the management board may refuse to provide information to the extent that providing it is, according to sound business judgment, likely to cause material damage to the company or an affiliated company. According to the German Public Limited Liability Companies Act, para. 132(2) a shareholder who has been denied information may, under certain conditions, appeal to the district court.

[105] A Community-scale undertaking must have more than 1,000 employees in the EEA, and at least two different establishments in two different Member States, each employing at least 150 persons.

undertaking of a Community-scale group of undertakings within the meaning of Directive 94/45/EC or Directive 97/74/EC,[106] the provisions of these Directives and the provisions transposing them into national legislation shall not apply to them or to their subsidiaries. Nevertheless, where the special negotiating body decides in accordance with Article 3 (6) not to open negotiations or to end them, the Directive on the European Works Council, and the provisions transposing into law, shall apply. According to Article 13(3)(a) of the Directive, the latter instrument is said not to prejudice the existing rights to involvement of employees provided for by national legislation and/or practice in the Member States as enjoyed by the employees of the SE and its subsidiaries and establishments, other than participation in the bodies of the SE. Article 13(3)(b) provides that in addition the Directive shall not prejudice the provisions on participation in the bodies laid down by national legislation and/or practice applicable to subsidiaries of the SE.

Article 14 requires the Member States to adopt the laws, regulations and administrative provisions necessary to comply with the Directive no later than 8 October 2004, or to ensure by that date at the latest that management and labour introduce the required provisions by way of agreement, the Member States being obliged to take all necessary steps enabling them at all times to guarantee the results imposed by the Directive. According to Article 15, the review of the procedures for applying the Directive was to take place no later than 8 October 2007. As already indicated, the Directive entered into force on the date of its publication.[107]

H. Concluding remarks

Given the long delay in adopting the European Company Statute, the recent enactment of Regulation (EC) 2157/2001 and Directive 2001/86/EC is a noteworthy achievement. However, despite the manifest labour and effort which was involved in drafting these instruments, and the meticulous attention to detail that they often display, it unfortunately seems possible that the SE may ultimately transpire to be no more

[106] This Directive extended the former one, the European Works Councils Directive, to the United Kingdom.

[107] Directive 86/2001, Art. 16.

successful or widely used than the EEIG. The legal regime governing the SE is extremely complex, at first reading difficult to understand, and frequently makes reference to national law. Indeed, it may not be an exaggeration to say that there are as many different regimes as there are Member States. This plurality may be to some extent regarded as less burdensome than it might be because the enactment of the EC company law directives have led to some degree of harmonisation of the laws of the Member States. Whatever may be the implications of the principle of proportionality, and the somewhat vague one of subsidiarity, the fact remains it will take practitioners, and others some time to adjust themselves to this complex new legal regime. The likelihood that national company law regimes may change may give rise to increased burdens in the future.

The possibility of transferring the registered office of an SE to another Member State is accompanied by the sometimes unwelcome (and perhaps outdated) need to change the central administration to such a state as well. The provisions of the Directive accompanying the Regulation are very complex, and sometimes a little imprecisely drafted. Although a similar situation exists when a European Works Council has to be established, the prospect of fairly protracted and possibly expensive negotiations on employee involvement when an SE is formed may dissuade companies and other legal persons from making use of this entity. It seems unlikely that small and medium-sized companies will make frequent use of it.

The SE will be recognised as a public limited liability company having legal personality in all the Member States. Its use may permit the carrying out of certain operations such as cross-border mergers, and certain other types of operation which have involved very considerable difficulties in the past. It may also make certain types of joint venture easier to carry out, although it remains possible for such operations to be carried out through the medium of contractual arrangements, the licensing of intellectual property rights, or by the use of private companies or limited partnerships, including the German GmbH & CoKG. Cross-border takeovers have become increasingly common in the EC in recent years. The provisions of the Regulation governing the formation of an SE by means of a merger may be too cumbersome to be widely used. However, some German and Scandinavian companies have made use of the SE in recent years. The Nordic banking group Nordea announced plans to transform into an SE, but found difficulties in completing the process owing to regulatory obstacles.

The SE has not been made subject to any particularly favourable fiscal regime.[107A] It seems doubtful whether many public limited liability companies will convert themselves into SEs. The European Company Regulation seems likely to have a modest impact on the development of European Company law.[108] However, the influence of the accompanying Directive may well be less significant because, despite its often careful and elaborate drafting, this instrument contains few provisions which are not inspired by existing ones of national law and Community law. Unlike its forerunner, the draft Directive of 1989, it does not attempt to provide for new models of employee participation which the parties to an agreement between the founders of an SE, and the representatives of the employees of such founders may choose from.

It is possible, though by no means certain, that the adoption of the Regulation and Directive governing the SE and employee involvement therein, may encourage the Commission to consider the introduction of a European Private Company (EPC) which has already been considered and discussed by such authors as Mme Boucourechliev,[109] Messrs. Drury and Hicks.[110]

III. European Cooperative Society

The Commission made proposals for a European Association (EA), European Cooperative Society (ECS) and a European Mutual Society (EMS) in 1991. These proposals were subsequently revised. The EA would not be allowed to distribute profits amongst its members, whilst the EMS would be restricted to certain activities, in particular social and health care and insurance. These proposals for an EA and an EMS eventually failed to be adopted, but these entities are likely to undergo further consideration in the future, where a proposal for a European Foundation may also be suggested.

107A However, Articles 10b–10d of the Merger Tax Directive, OJ 1990 L225/1, as amended, are applicable to the cross-border transfer of the registered office of an SE. An SE (and also a European Cooperative Society) enjoys tax deferrals with a permanent establishment in the Member State from which it is moving.

108 The influence of the Regulation and the Directive which supplements it on employee involvement is to be found in the made for a European Cooperative Society. Certain of the provisions of the Regulation may have some influence on national company law.

109 Note in particular, Boucourechliev (ed), *Propositions pour une société fermée europeènne* (Luxembourg, 1997).

110 These gentlemen were members of a research team attached to the French *Centre de Recerche sur le Droit des Affaires*.

The European Cooperative Society owes its basis to the Regulation and Directive of 22 July 2003, which have been mentioned above.[111] The provisions governing this entity are somewhat more precise than those applicable to the SE. A ECS may be formed in three different ways. A new ECS may be formed by two or more natural persons resident in at least two member states, with or without one or more legal persons of a cooperative nature; or by two or more companies or firms within the meaning of Article 48 EC and also other legal entities governed by the laws of at least two different member states or by members of each of the former groups. Furthermore, an ECS may be formed by a merger between cooperatives governed by the laws of at least two different Member States; or by conversion of a cooperative formed under the law of a Member State which has for at least two years had an establishment or subsidiary governed by the law of another Member State.

An ECS is governed in accordance with Article 8 of the ECS Regulation by a complex hierarchy of sources of law similar to that applicable to the SE under Article 9 of the SE Regulation. This may have the disadvantage of resulting in a number of different types of ECS in the different Member States. By Article 8(2) of the ECS Regulation the minimum capital of an ECS is €30,000. The structure of an ECS is similar in most respects to that of an SE. It must have a general meeting, and may choose between a single or double board system. By Article 59 of the ECS Regulation, the general meeting is in principle governed by the one man–one vote system, but within certain limits. If the national law of the registered office so permits, the statute may make provision for multiple voting rights. The rules governing the general meeting of an ECS are more detailed than those applicable to that of an SE.

According to Article 7 of the ECS Regulation, an ECS may transfer its registered office to another Member State. The relevant procedures contained in Article 7 are similar to that contained in Article 8 of the SE Regulation. The rules governing the drawing up of annual accounts of

[111] See council Regulation 1435/2003 of July 22 2003 on the statute for a European Cooperative Society (SCE) [2003] OJR 207/1 Council Directive 2003/72 of July 22 2003 supplementary to the statute for a European Cooperative Society with regard to the involvement of European [2003] OJL 207/25. Note the useful account of this entity and the SE by J. Schmidt, 'SE and SCE: two new European Company forms – and more to come' (2006) 27 Co Law 99. This article also contains useful comparison of the implementation of the SE Regulation in the United Kingdom and Germany: see pages 104–106.

the ECS are in general those enshrined in the legal provisions in force in the Member State where the ECS has its registered office.

The provisions contained in the Directive on employee involvement which accompanies the ECS statute contains provisions similar to those of the SE Directive, and are of very considerable complexity. They may, for this reason, detract from the usefulness of the ECS.

IV. The European Private Company

As already indicated, the proposal for such an entity, which would be based upon an EC Regulation, emanates largely from individual scholars rather than from the Commission. The supposed advantages of such a company are said to be that it would have the same structure in each Member State, and when business requirements so dictated, it could move from one Member State to another. Although it might be possible to provide that an EPC had a similar structure in each Member State, it would probably prove difficult or impossible to exclude all references to national law, unless the Regulation was extremely detailed.

It has been suggested that a European Private Company (EPC) could be formed as a joint holding company on subsidiary, or by means of a merger, or the conversion of an existing company. It has been suggested by the proponents of the new entity that although the Statute for the European Private Company would have to provide for a complete regulatory infrastructure, the EPC would have a largely contractual basis, and that model statutes might be provided for. The Regulation would, it is contended have to deal with such matters as formation, access thereto, capital, organisation of the internal administrations, shareholders, minority protection and the protection of third parties. Although it has been proposed that reference to national law should be minimised or excluded, it is, as already been emphasised, doubtful whether the latter aim would be achieved. Thus, Article 12 of the draft Regulation presented by a working party to the Commission in 1998[112] provides that reference may be made to the provisions of national company law in the state of the registered office of the EPC when the Regulation makes express reference to it. Article 36 provides that matters relating to insolvency

[112] This working party consisted of members of the staff of CREDA (*Centre de Recherche sur le Droit des Affaires*), CNPF (*Conseil National du Patronat Francais*), together with Mme Boucourechliev, Robert Drury, Dieter Helm and Professor Peter Hommelhoff.

shall be subject to the legal rules applicable to the companies considered equivalent in each Member State. Article 12 also provides that reference should be made to the general principles of the Regulation and the general principles of Community company law and national law where necessary. It would seem that in particular cases, there might be controversy about the implications of such general principles, and references to the European Court of Justice under Article 234 EC might well be necessary. Primacy is given to the provisions of the Regulation and of the statutes, provided these are not inconsistent therewith, in determining what shall be the governing law.

Both individuals and companies (including public limited liability companies) could participate in the formation of an EPC. The latter would have a minimum capital of €25,000, and would enjoy limited liability. It would come into existence as the result of registration in the companies registry of the state where its central administration was situated. Certain of the provisions relating to capital would be of a stringent character. Shares would have to be paid for in full before registration, and evidence of the transfer of contributions in kind would have to be provided before the company could be registered. A valuation of such contributions by a qualified person would have to be included in the company's articles. If the company's net assets fell to below the minimum capital, the shareholders would be required either to wind up the company, or make further contributions to the company, until the capital was restored to its minimum amount.

The founders could make use of what management structure they desired by inserting appropriate provisions in the company's statutes. The latter would set out the rights of the shareholders. Certain matters would be reserved for the latter, for example the approval of the accounts, the apportionment of the profits, and its appointment of the auditors, where necessary. A distinction would be made between the management and the representation of the company similar to that familiar under German law applicable to private companies. The Regulation contains special provisions concerning the liability of the company's officers.

Restrictions on transfer would, as is the case with German private companies, be optional. If there are such restrictions, and if a person desirous of transferring his shares has no real prospect of finding a purchaser, he would be able to claim to have his shares acquired by the other shareholders in accordance with the provisions of the articles. The Regulation also provides that any shareholder may petition the court for the compulsory acquisition of his or her shares in certain specified circumstances. A remedy would also be granted to shareholders who were denied an answer to written questions submitted to company officers.

According to Article 32 of the draft Regulation, the EPC would be subject to the accounting rules applicable in each EC Member State to private companies. Because of the existing disparities between such rules, an EPC which was active in a number of such states might be subjected to a considerable burden.

Rather unsurprisingly, the question of employee participation has given rise to some controversy. The draft Regulation takes the approach that the rules governing disclosure to and the participation of employees should be determined by the law applicable to the registered office of the EPC. This approach if persisted with will lead to a considerable diversity between different jurisdictions, but it may prove difficult to agree upon any other. Accounting law, tax law and insolvency law would probably be governed by the law of the state of registration.

The draft Regulation on the EPC seems carefully conceived, subject to the reservations made above. A simplified version of any such Regulation would probably be made applicable to single member private companies. It is possible that a European Private Company might prove to be of considerable utility, and if the governing regime, does not ultimately transpire to be unduly complex, more popular than the SE. It is to be hoped that the institutions of the Community show themselves willing to give serious attention to the existing proposal. The Commission has proposed, in its Communication entitled *Modernising company law and enhancing corporate governance in the EU* that a feasibility study should be undertaken by it on the possible introduction of a European Private Company Statute, which it is thought would serve the needs of small and medium enterprises active in more than one Member State. The Commission circulated a consultation document on the European Private Company in 2006.[113]

[113] The Law Society expressed doubts about the existence of any demand for such an entity from English lawyers in reply to the Commission 2006 consultation document on the European Private Company.

8

Employee participation

I. Introduction

The involvement of employees by such process as giving information to, or the consultation of such employees or their representatives, and the participation or that of their representatives in decision making, takes place in a number of Member States. The methods and intensity of such participatory processes varies in the different Member States. Thus, in Germany, the representatives of employees have a right to participate in decision making on the supervisory boards of certain types of undertakings.[1] The Dutch system of participation on the supervisory boards of large public and private companies involved a system of cooption, which system of participation has been recently amended, and which differs from that provided for by German law. In Belgium and Spain participation takes place solely through the medium of works councils, whilst in Germany the same enterprise may be governed by the Works Councils Act 1972, as amended, and also be subject to one of the forms of employee participation at board level. Works councils are also provided for by French and Dutch legislation.

In France, the employer (*chef d'entreprise*) is a member of the works council, but the position is different in Germany and the Netherlands. The powers of works councils differ in different countries. Thus mandatory consultation may only be required (if at all) in a limited number of cases in some states while the works council's participation in certain forms of decision making may not exist in certain countries, such as Spain.

In certain countries where there is conflict between the works council and the employer, judicial remedies are available. Thus, in the Netherlands some acts of the management must be preceded by the giving of prior advice by the works council.[2] If the management takes an action contrary to the advice of the works council, the latter may appeal to the Enterprise Chamber of the Court of Appeal of Amsterdam on the limited ground that the management could not possibly have

[1] Note, e.g., the rules contained in the 'Paritative' Codetermination Act of 1976.

[2] *Wet op de ondernemingsraad* (WOR), Art. 25(1).

reached the decisions if it had evaluated the interests involved.[3] Appeals are usually granted on procedural grounds rather than on substantive ones. However, if the Enterprise Chamber sustains a claim, it may grant an injunction requiring the employer to repeal the action wholly or partly, and to reverse any specific effects thereof, regard being paid to the acquired rights of third parties acting in good faith.[4] If an action is taken by the management without seeking the necessary prior consent of the works council, it is treated as being null and void.[5] French law requires the works council to be consulted before certain important decisions are taken by the management, relating, for example, to the reduction in personnel, mergers and the transfer of the undertaking. Failure to carry out such consultations may result in penal sanctions, but the action taken is not affected.[6] Article 8 of the Directive of the Council and European Parliament on establishing a general framework for improving the information and consultation rights of employees provides that Member States shall provide for appropriate measures in the event of non-compliance with the obligations arising from the proposed Directive and adequate penalties which will be applicable in the case of infringement, which will be effective, proportionate and dissuasive.

In addition to the Framework Directive on the information and consultation of employees, certain other Community directives require employees to be informed at a later stage than does this directive of the Council and European Parliament. These include the Directive on the European Works Council,[7] which was implemented in the United Kingdom by the rules on the Transnational Information and Consultation of Employees of 1999,[8] and certain other instruments.[9] Certain Commission proposals concerning employee participation have not yet been enacted. These include the draft Fifth Company Law Directive (which now seems unlikely to be enacted), which is considered in outline in this chapter.

[3] *Ibid.*, Art. 26(4). [4] *Ibid.*, Art. 26(5). [5] *Ibid.*, Art. 27(5).

[6] French Employment Code (*Code du Travail*), Art. L483-1.

[7] Council Directive (EC) 94/45/EC of 22 September 1994 on the establishment of a European Works Council or a procedure in Community-scale undertakings and dealing with market abuse, 1994 OJ L254/16. On which see F. Wooldridge (2005) Co Law 182–4.

[8] SI 1999 No. 3323.

[9] Note, e.g. the Directive on collective redundancies, the consolidated version of which is Council Directive 2001/23/EC of 12 March 2001 on the approximation of the laws of the Member States relating to the safeguarding of employees' rights in the event of transfers of undertakings, businesses or parts of undertakings or businesses, 2001 OJ L82/16, and the Directive on the Protection of employees' rights on the transfer of the undertaking, Directive 77/187/EEC, 1977 OJ L61/26. The latter Directive was amended by the further one.

The first main section of this chapter will deal with national legislation concerning employee participation. This term will occasionally be used in the present chapter to include all forms of employee involvement, i.e. information and consultation as well as participation in the strict sense. The second part of this chapter will deal with certain of the provisions of European law concerning the involvement of employees and their representatives, and with the draft Fifth Company Law Directive.

It will not, however, concern itself with Council Directive 2001/86EC with regard to the involvement of employees which supplements the statute for the European Company, which Regulation was enacted last year. This is because the former instrument is closely connected with the European Company statute, is of a very complex nature, and seems better considered together with that instrument. Such consideration appears in the previous chapter. The provisions of the Tenth Directive on Cross-Border Mergers concerning employee participation are considered in chapter 10, which deals with cross border mergers and acquisitions.

II. The position in the United Kingdom

Owing to the special position enjoyed by the union representatives in the undertaking (shop stewards) who are often empowered to negotiate wages and conditions of employment, there has been little demand for the introduction of works councils under UK law until recently. Their introduction has not been made indispensable by the European Works Councils Directive or by the Council and European Parliament Directive establishing a general framework for informing and consulting employees. Both these instruments give as an alternative to the establishment of a works council that of a procedure for informing and consulting employees. There is no compulsory employee representation on the boards of United Kingdom companies.

III. The position in France

Three separate institutions represent the interests of the employees of an undertaking which will have one or more of these representative bodies depending on the size of the workforce. The relevant representative bodies are the works council, the personnel representatives and the trade union delegation. The latter may sometimes be members of the works council. Collective agreements often create what is called the expression group, which is concerned with the manner of exercise of collective rights of freedom of expression regarding employment and conditions of employment, which is provided for by Article L461-1 of the Employment Code.

In addition, public companies may provide in their statutes that representatives of the employees may sit on the management board.[10]

A. Works council

Works councils first came into existence in France in 1945. According to Article L431-1 of the Employment Code (*Code du Travail*), undertakings of all kinds, including entities carrying on liberal professions and social security bodies (but not certain public administrative bodies) employing at least fifty persons for a period in excess of twelve months, whether consecutively or not during the last three years, must establish a works council (*comité d'entreprise*).[11] Elections take place every two years on the basis of lists of candidates which are submitted by trade unions only and which represent the different categories of employees. The employer (*chef d'entreprise*) or his representative, is a member of the works council, and may take the chair at meetings.[12] As in Germany, a central works council must be established if the undertaking has a number of establishments: this will function in addition to the existing works council. The relevant requirement is contained in Article L439-1 of the Employment Code. A group of undertakings may likewise be required to set up a group works council.

The works council is required to encourage a close relationship between employer and employees, and to act as a medium for communication between them. It has a very important role concerning the provision of information, and has to be consulted when certain significant business decisions are taken.

Article L432-6 of the French Employment Code provides that in the case of companies,[13] two delegates from the works council, one representing the technical and supervisory staff (*agents de maitrise*) and the other manual and clerical staff shall be entitled to attend all meetings of the management or supervisory board in an advisory role. The number of delegates is increased to four in the circumstances mentioned in Article L432-6 of the Employment Code, i.e. where there are three

[10] French Commercial Code, Art. L225-27.

[11] Special rules, which are discussed below, may be applicable where the undertaking employs less than 200 persons: see French Employment Code, Art. L431-1-1.

[12] The works council has trade union representatives among its members.

[13] The French term is '*sociétés*', which includes general and limited partnerships as well as public and private companies.

electoral colleges for personnel representatives. The delegates from the works council are said by paragraph 2 of Article L432-6 of the Employment Code, to be entitled to the same documents as the directors.

According to Article L432-1 of the Employment Code, the works council must be informed of and consulted on, questions of an economic nature concerning the organisation, management and general development of the undertaking, and in particular, on measures of a kind likely to affect the number or structure of the work force. It is also obligatory to consult the works council in good time on proposals to reduce the work force. Furthermore, Article L432-1 also provides that the works council must be informed of and consulted on, modifications of the economic or legal organisation of the undertaking, especially in the event of mergers, and transfers of the control of the company, and on important changes in the structure of the production of the enterprise, as on the acquisition or disposal of subsidiaries and of take-over offers. Article L432-1 further provides that the works council must be informed of and consulted on situations in which the undertaking ceases to be able to pay its debts as they fall due, and in which it becomes subject to a process of judicial reorganisation.

The works council has a right to receive certain documents of an economic and financial nature one month after being elected.[14] According to Article L225-231 of the Commercial Code, the works council may ask the president of the local commercial court, acting in summary proceedings, for the appointment of one or more experts in order to obtain independent advice on any business transactions decided upon by a public company. If the president of the commercial court deems it appropriate to appoint an expert, he determines his powers and remuneration. The expert's report is made available to the works council, the statutory auditors, the public prosecutor and the board of directors or executive board and in companies which appeal to the public for subscribers, the Stock Exchange Authority (*Autorité des marchés financiers*, AMF). In any undertaking, the works committee may require information upon any matter of a kind that might prejudicially affect the business of the company. If no such information is given, or if the replies given indicate that there is cause for concern, the works council must prepare a report which must be communicated to the head of the undertaking (*chef d'entreprise*) and the statutory auditors.[15]

[14] See in particular, Art. L432-4 of the Employment Code.
[15] French Employment Code, Art. L432-5.

B. Personnel representatives

An undertaking with a regular work force of more than ten must have personnel representatives elected by the employees. The personnel representatives' principal function appears to be the presentation of claims on behalf of the employees relating to employment regulations and rules.[16] They are also empowered to communicate the suggestions and observations of the employees on matters within its competence, to the works council.[17] If an undertaking has less than 200 employees, the head of the undertaking may decide, after having consulted the personnel representatives and the works council, that the personnel representatives shall form the employees representatives on the works council.[18] This may of course simplify the formalities with which the employer has to comply. Although the bodies will have a similar composition in the circumstances envisaged they will continue to meet separately.

C. Trade union delegations

Such delegations are selected in enterprises having at least fifty employees. They are established by unions which are considered to be the most representative ones. Union branches of the major unions considered as representative at the national level are irrebuttably presumed to be representative at the level of the establishment or enterprise. The delegations have the task of furthering the interests of trade union members, and they may engage in collective bargaining.

D. Purpose of the different institutions

The purposes of the three different institutions cannot be regarded as necessarily distinct. This is because for example, the works council will sometimes try to coordinate the work of the personnel representatives and the trade union delegates. This is possible because the trade unions have some influence on the composition of the works council, and the chairman thereof may be the head of the undertaking. Where there is a temporary absence of a works council (e.g. because the undertaking has insufficient

[16] *Ibid.*, Art. L422-1.

[17] French Employment Code, Art. L422-2. According to Art. L422-5, if there is no works council the personnel representatives may communicate to the head of the under-taking all suggestions aiming to improvement of the output and organisation of the undertaking.

[18] *Ibid.*, Art. L431-1-1.

employees), then it follows from Article L431-3 of the Employment Code that the personnel representatives perform its economic functions.

E. Employee representatives on the boards of public companies

According to Article L225-27 of the Commercial Code, public companies (*sociétés anonymes*, SAs) may provide in their articles that representatives of the company's employees will be members of its executive board.[19] Such persons may be elected by the personnel of the company alone, or by such personnel and that of its direct and indirect subsidiaries, provided that the registered offices (*sièges sociaux*) of such undertakings are in France. The number of such directors must not be more than four, but may be increased to five in the case of companies whose shares are admitted to dealings on a regulated market.[20] Directors elected by the employees must have a contract of employment with the company, or with one of its French direct or indirect subsidiaries, which commenced more than two years before their nomination.[21] The rule is inapplicable if the company was formed less than two years before their nomination. Employees of the company and, in appropriate cases, of its direct or indirect subsidiaries (whose registered offices are in France) who have been employed by the company more than three months before the date of the election, are eligible to vote. Voting is by secret ballot. The candidates or lists of candidates, may be presented by one or more representative trade unions, or by one-twentieth of the electors, or if the number of employees is more than 2,000 by 100 of them.[22]

The maximum period of office of employee directors is six years, which may be renewed.[23] Employee directors must be shareholders, and they have the same rights, duties and liabilities as other directors. Their office may cease as the result of their dismissal from employment, their resignation, as directors or employees, or their dismissal from office as a director for cause by a decision of the president of the civil court (*tribunal de grande instance*) acting in summary proceedings, on the

[19] If the articles do not contain such a provision, they will require modification by means of an extraordinary resolution of a general meeting of the shareholders.

[20] The number of such directors must not exceed one third of the members of the board and they are not taken into account for the purpose of calculating the maximum number of members of the board.

[21] The nationality requirement for the employing company as set out here, could constitute discrimination in violation of the provisions about free movement in the EC Treaty.

[22] French Commercial Code, Art. L225-28. [23] *Ibid.*, Art. L225-29.

request of the majority the board of directors.[24] The employment agreement can only be terminated at the company's instance if the labour court (*conseil des prud'hommes*) so consents in summary proceedings.[25] It follows from Article L225-30 of the Commercial Code that an employee director cannot at the same time be a trade union delegate, a member of the works council, or a personnel representative.

According to Article L225-79, a company which has the dual board system may include a provision in its articles that representatives of the employees shall be members of the supervisory board. In such an event, it follows from Articles L225-79 and L225-80 of the Commercial Code that most of the provisions explained above relating to employee directors will be applicable to such representatives.

By Article L225-23 of the Commercial Code, one or more employees must be elected as director if the employees' participation in the capital of the company exceeds 3 per cent. They are elected by the general meeting from among those employees who are also shareholders. They are not treated as directors for the purpose of calculating the maximum and minimum number of directors that may serve on the board. A similar rule is, by Article L225-71, made applicable to employees who are members of the supervisory board of a company making use of the dual board system.

IV. The position in Germany

A. Works councils

Works Councils have existed in Germany since the enactment of the *Betriebsrätegesetz* of 1920. They were reintroduced into Germany by the *Betriebsverfassungsgesetz* (Works Councils Act) of 1952, which was extensively amended, especially by the Acts of 1972, and of 2001 when a new Works Councils Act was published.[26] As far as the public sector is concerned special rules are applicable to employee representation. The law changed in 2001 as far as the private sector was concerned, partly to take account of changes in methods of work and technology. Thus

[24] *Ibid.*, Art. L225-32. [25] *Ibid.*, Art. L225-33.

[26] Works councils and employee participation on the supervisory boards of German undertakings are dealt with clearly in chapters 5 and 6 of Weiss and Schmidt, *Labour Law and Industrial Relations in Germany* (The Hague, London: Kluwer Law International, 2000). The full title of the amending Act of 2001 is *Gesetz zur Reform des Betriebsverfassungsgesetzes* BGBl 2001 1.1852.

paragraph 5(1) of the 1972 Act, as mended by the 2001 Act, includes persons working within or outside the establishment or persons using telephonic means of communication. Persons who work from home are also included within the definition of workers, provided that their main activity is for the establishment. According to paragraph 1 of the Works Council Act 1972, as amended, any establishment having more than five employees over the age of eighteen at least three of whom have been employed there for at least six months must establish a works council.[27] The same is true of a common establishment belonging to more than one undertaking which fulfils these requirements.[28]

It is left to the employees of the relevant establishment to decide whether they want to hold an election with regard to membership of the works council. Many small establishments fail to comply with the requirement of the law governing the establishment of a works council. Works councils are separate entities from trade unions, but their members are usually also members of trade unions.[29] If an enterprise has more than one works council, these bodies must form a common works council.[30] If the enterprise is part of a group, a group works council can be formed by resolutions of the individual common works councils, but such bodies (*Konzernbetriebsräte*) do not play a significant role in practice.[31]

The term of office of works council members is four years and they may be reelected.[32] Candidates may be proposed by trade unions which have at least one member in the establishment or by one-twentieth of the employees entitled to vote. This proposal must be signed by at least three persons, which is reduced to two if the enterprise has less than twenty employees.[33] The size of the works council depends on the number of employees in the establishment.[34]

Persons over the age of eighteen who have worked in the establishment for at least six months are eligible for election.[35] This takes place by a system of proportional representation unless only one electoral proposal is made, or the simplified electoral procedure applicable to establishments employing five–fifty persons is used, when a simple majority vote takes place.[36] The works council is required to include

[27] Works Councils Act (*Betriebsverfassungsgesetz*, BetrVG) 1972, as amended, paras. 1(1), 7 and 8.

[28] *Ibid.*, para. 1(1) second sentence. [29] *Ibid.*, para. 2(1) and (2). [30] *Ibid.*, para. 47.

[31] *Ibid.*, para. 54. [32] *Ibid.*, para. 21. [33] *Ibid.*, para. 14(3), (4) and (5).

[34] See Works Councils Act, 1972, as amended, para. 9.

[35] *Ibid.*, paras. 7 and 8. [36] *Ibid.*, paras. 14(2) and 14a.

persons of both sexes and persons from different departments and pursuing different activities in the undertaking.[37] The executive staff, as defined in paragraph 5(3) of the Act can neither participate in the election of works council members, nor may they become members of the works council. This right is reserved for what used to be called manual and white collar workers. An Act of 1989 permits the election of a separate body for executive staff.[38]

As in the Netherlands, works council members are entitled to be released from their duty to work without loss of pay, to the extent necessary for properly carrying out their duties, account being taken of the nature and size of the establishment.[39] In establishments which regularly employ more than 100 persons, the works council must appoint an economic committee,[40] and may appoint other committees and confer specific tasks on them,[41] and also entrust groups of workers with particular tasks.[42]

The works council has a number of rights which extend from a simple right to information and to be consulted to a right of veto and codetermination.[43] The right to codetermination is of much importance in social matters, for example the length of the working day and accidents at work.[44] As far as certain economic matters are concerned (for example a merger or division of the undertaking or an establishment thereof), the rights of the works council to be informed and consulted are vested in the economic committee, by virtue of paragraph 106(2) and (3) of the Act, as amended. There is no right to codetermination concerning such matters. However, the works council has important participatory rights in respect of certain specific economic decisions involving a substantial alteration to the establishment which might cause significant hardship to its workforce, provided that such an establishment employs at least twenty persons.[45] Codetermination is of less significance in personnel matters.

Conflicts which arise between management and the works council may, and in some cases, must be referred to a conciliation board (*Einigungsstelle*).[46] Such a reference may be made where management

[37] *Ibid.*, para. 15.

[38] *Gesetz über Sprecherausschüsse der leitenden Angestellten* (*Artikel 2 des Gesetzes zur Änderung des Betriebsverfassungsgesetzes, über Sprecherausschüsse der leitenden Angestellten und zur Sicherung der Montan-Mitbestimmung*) of 20 December 1988, BGBl I 1988, 2312, 2316.

[39] *Ibid.*, para. 37(2). [40] *Ibid.*, para. 106. [41] *Ibid.*, para. 28. [42] *Ibid.*, para. 28a.

[43] Works Councils Act 1972, as amended, paras. 80(2) and 87.

[44] *Ibid.*, para. 87(1) No. 3 and 7. [45] *Ibid.*, para. 111; see also paras. 112, 112a and 113.

[46] *Ibid.*, para. 76.

and the works council are unable to agree on whether and how measures envisaged by the management in the event of a substantial alteration to the establishment have to be carried out.[47]

B. Functions of the unions

Many works council members also belong to a union. Such union also has a preparatory function, calling a works meeting in an establishment without a works council, which decides whether or not such a council shall be set up. The unions also play a significant role in controlling the works council election procedure, and should legal rules be violated, a union may obtain a consent order nullifying the elections. Furthermore, in large companies, unions frequently have trusted representatives (*Vertrauensleute*) who form a link between the members of the union and its administrators and have an important influence on the activities of the works council.

C. Employee representation on the supervisory board

The supervisory board has considerable powers in German public companies. It thus exercises control over the management board, has an extensive right to information from it, appoints and dismisses the directors, and has important functions in relation to the accounts.[48] Private companies usually do not have supervisory boards, but are permitted by paragraph 52 of the *GmbH Gesetz* to establish one on a voluntary basis.[49] Large private companies which are subject to the codetermination laws mentioned below are required to have a supervisory board; these laws extend rather similar provisions of the laws governing public companies to them. In both public and private companies, the management board or the managers are responsible for both the management and representation of the company.[50] The double board system dates from the nineteenth century.[51]

[47] See e.g., Works Councils Act 1972, as amended, para. 112(4).

[48] German Public Limited Liability Companies Act, paras. 111, 112, 170 and 171.

[49] German Private Limited Liability Companies Act, para. 52(1).

[50] German Public Limited Liability Companies Act, paras. 76(1) and 78; German Private Limited Liability Companies Act, para. 35(1).

[51] For details, see K. J. Hopt and H. Kanda (eds), 'The German Two-Tier Board: Experience, Theories, Reforms', in *Comparative Corporate Governance – The State of the Art and Emerging Research* (Oxford: Clarendon Press, 1998).

D. Codetermination in the coal, iron and steel industry

There are three principal systems of employee codetermination on supervisory boards in Germany. The model used in the coal, iron and steel industries involves the equal representation of shareholders and employees on the supervisory board and the neutral chairperson being elected by the majority vote of the shareholders' and the employees' representatives.[52] The Coal, Iron and Steel Codetermination Act applies to public and private companies and to incorporated cost book companies (*bergrechtlichen Gewerkschaften*), employing more than 1,000 persons.[53] The supervisory board will have at least eleven members, which will be increased to fifteen or twenty-one in very large companies.[54] At least two of the employees' representatives must belong to the workforce of the company.[55] Two out of the three remaining members may, and generally do, belong to unions represented in the enterprise, but the third member may not be a representative of a trade union or have a service agreement with or be an employee of the enterprise, or have significant interests in it.[56] The employee representatives are nominated together. Before such nomination takes place, the unions which are active in the enterprise and their executive organisations must be consulted.[57]

Assuming that the supervisory board has the usual complement of eleven members, proposals regarding the remaining three seats (i.e. those of the remaining two employee representatives and that of the additional member) will be made by the trade unions represented in the undertaking.[58] Nominations will be made by secret ballot and the persons nominated will be elected and confirmed in office by the general meeting, which is bound by the nominations made. The same rule will apply if the number of seats to be filled is more than three.[59] In companies subject to the system of codetermination of the coal, iron and steel industry, the Act of 1951, as amended, provides for employee representation on the executive board in the form of an employee director, responsible for labour and social affairs.[60] Such a director cannot be appointed or dismissed against the majority of the votes of the employee representatives on the supervisory board.[61]

[52] German Coal, Iron and Steel Codetermination Act 1951 as amended, paras. 4 and 8.
[53] *Ibid.*, para. 1 (2). [54] *Ibid.*, paras. 4 and 9. [55] *Ibid.*, para. 6(1). [56] *Ibid.*, para. 4(2).
[57] *Ibid.*, para. 6(1). [58] *Ibid.*, para. 6(3). [59] *Ibid.*, paras. 6(3)–(6) and 9.
[60] *Ibid.*, para. 13(1) sentence 1. [61] *Ibid.*, para. 13(1) sentence 2.

E. Codetermination in certain holding companies

Coal, iron and steel holding companies are subject to the special system of employee codetermination provided for in the *Montan-Mitbestimmungserganzungsgesetz* (MBErgG) of 1956, as amended. According to paragraph 3(2) of this statute, a controlling company is subject to this statute if the controlling and dependent companies' combined turnover (account being taken of the relevant costs of raw and operational materials and of fuel and of services performed by third parties) derived from activities in the coal, iron and steel industries amount to one-fifth of its total turnover, or if at least one-fifth of the employees of the group are employed in the latter industries.[62] The supervisory boards of such holding companies must consist of at least seven representatives of the employees, seven of the shareholders and one additional person. Coal, iron and steel holding companies employing more than 7,000 persons elect the employees' representatives to the supervisory board by an indirect method through the medium of delegates. The rules governing the number of such delegates and their votes contained in paragraph 9 MBErgG have been altered by paragraph 6 of Article 2 of the Act of 18 May 2004.

F. Codetermination under the Works Councils Act 1952

The provisions of the Works Councils Act 1952 remained in force for many years: its scope was limited to public and private companies, limited partnerships with shares, incorporated cost book companies, cooperatives and mutual insurance companies.[63] The relevant entity had to employ at least 500 persons.[64] if it does so, one third of the members of the supervisory board had to be representatives of the employees.[65] Like the *Drittelbeteiligungsgesetz*, which means the 'Third

[62] The previous requirement in para. 3(2) that 2,000 of the employees should be involved in these industries was subject to constitutional review. The German Federal Constitutional Court (BVerfG) ruled on the matter in 1999 (see *Official Journal of the German Federal Constitutional Court* (BVerfGE) 99,367). The Court held that the requirement violated Art. 3(1) of the Federal Constitution, which provide that all people are equal before the law. The requirement as to the number of employees was, according to the Court, capable of including large enterprises which did not carry out sufficiently meaningful activities in the coal, iron and steel industries. The previous para. 3(2) was amended in 2004 to comply with this ruling.

[63] See Works Councils Act (BetrVG) 1952, para. 77.

[64] *Ibid.*, para. 77. [65] *Ibid.*, para. 76(1).

Participation Statute') of 2004, paragraph 76(2) of the Works Councils Act 1952 provided that if one employee representative had to be elected, that person must be in the employ of the company, and that, should it be necessary to appoint two or more representatives, at least two of these must consist of such employees. The employees' representatives were elected by a secret ballot of all the employees of the enterprise over the age of 18.[66] According to paragraph 76(3) of the 1952 Act, nominations had to be made by the employees or the works councils and at least one-tenth of the employees of the enterprise, or at least 100 employees entitled to vote.

G. Codetermination under the Act of 2004

The provisions of the Works Councils Act of 1952 which used to govern this matter have been replaced by those of the Act of 18 May 2004 (*Zweites Gesetz zur Veireinfachung der Wahl der Arbeitnehmervertreter*[67] or more simply, *Drittelbeteiligungsgesetz*, which means the One-Third Participation Statute'). This Act does not only apply to public and private limited liability companies employing between 500–2,000 persons but also companies registered before August 1994 which employ fewer than 500 workers unless they are family companies.[68] It also covers registered cooperative societies and mutual insurance undertakings which have between 500–2,000 members. However the Act is inapplicable to undertakings which in a direct and preponderant sense have political, charitable, educational, scientific or artistic objectives, or which have the purpose of reporting or expressing opinions to which Article 5(1) sentence 2 of the Federal Constitution is applicable.[69] In undertakings subject to the Act, one third of the members of the supervisory board must consist of employees. The rules governing the establishment of the supervisory board are set out in paragraph 4 of Article 1 of the Act. If one or two employees' representatives have to be elected to the board, these must be chosen from the undertaking. If more than two persons have to be elected to the supervisory board, at least two of them must work in the undertaking. The number of members of the supervisory board of a public company depends on its nominal capital, and must be divisible by three, subject to conflicting provisions in other codetermination legislation. Employees' representatives must be at least eighteen years old,

66 *Ibid.*, para. 76(2). 67 BGBl (2004) 1.974.

68 Such companies are companies which have only one member who is a natural person or whose members are related by reason of consanguinity or marriage.

69 See Art. 1, para. 1 of the Act.

and have worked for the undertaking for at least one year. Employment in undertakings which are entitled to participate in the election of employees' representatives on the supervisory board of the relevant undertaking (ie employees of dependant companies within the meaning of paragraph 18(1) AktG) counts towards the relevant period of one year.

According to paragraph 5 of Articles of the Act, the employees' representatives are elected by a simple majority vote which takes place generally in secret and covers the same period of time for which the shareholders' representatives on the supervisory board are elected in accordance with the law or the company's articles. The employees of the undertaking who have reached the age of eighteen are entitled to participate in the ballot. According to paragraph 6 of Article 1, voting takes place on the basis of nominations made by the works council and the employees. Those made by the employees must be made by at least one tenth of those employees entitled to vote, or by 100 such employees.

H. Codetermination under the 1976 Act

The above Act applies to public and private companies, limited partnerships with shares and industrial and trading cooperatives which regularly employ more than 2,000 employees.[70] If an entity of one of the former kinds, is the controlling company in a group, the employees of the subsidiary companies are then taken into account for the purpose of ascertaining whether the Codetermination Act 1976 applies to the latter kind of company.[71] The 1976 Act provides for an equal number of representatives of employers and employees. The actual size of the supervisory board depends on the number of employees.[72] If the board has six or eight employee representatives, two of these seats must be reserved for trade union representatives. If the number of employee representatives on the supervisory board is ten, the number of trade union representatives is increased to three.[73] The remaining seats on the supervisory board are reserved for employees of the enterprise, who for the present purposes, include executive staff defined in the same way as in paragraph 5(3) of the Works Councils Act 1972, as amended. According to paragraph 15(1) of the Codetermination Act, when the employees' representatives are elected by delegates they must include one executive (*leitender Angestellter*).

[70] *Gesetz uber die Mitbestimmung der Arbeitnehmer (Mitbestimmungsgesetz)* of 4 May 1976 (BGBl 1976 1:1153) as amended, para. no. 2.

[71] Paragraph 5(1). [72] Paragraph 7(1). [73] Paragraph 7(2).

The method of election of employee representatives is very complex. It follows from paragraph 9(1) that there are basically two methods of election. If an undertaking employs more than 8,000 persons, the election takes place through the medium of delegates unless the employees who are entitled to vote decide on direct elections. On the other hand, if the undertaking has fewer than 8,000 employees, direct elections take place unless the employees who are entitled to vote decide that it shall take place through the medium of delegates. A vote on the question whether the election is to take place through the medium of a direct vote or through that of delegates must be requested by a motion signed by at least one-twentieth of the workforce of the undertaking. The ballot is secret. The relevant decision can only take place with the participation of at least half the workforce eligible to vote, and by a majority of such votes.

Whether an election is by delegates or is direct, it takes place by a secret vote of all the eligible persons (including the executives) or their delegates).[74] At least one executive must be appointed to the supervisory board. Voting is by a system of proportional representation, unless the representatives are chosen by a majority vote. The latter has to take place if there is only one nomination in which case the number of candidates has to be twice the number of seats vacant for representatives of the workers and the executives on the supervisory board.[75]

The trade union representatives mentioned in paragraph 7 of the 1976 Act are also elected by a system of proportional representation. Unless there is a direct election, there is a common secret ballot of the delegates of the workers and executives.[76] The candidates may be nominated by the trade unions which are represented in the undertaking, and in other undertakings which belong to the same group as a controlling undertaking and which participate in the choice of the members of the latter undertaking's supervisory board. If only one nomination is made, the trade union representatives are chosen by a majority vote rather than by proportional representation; once again, the number of candidates nominated must be twice the number of vacant seats.[77]

[74] Paragraphs 8(1), 15(1) and 18. The choice of the shareholders' representatives is governed by para. 8(1). This text provides that they are chosen by the organ designated by law or the articles of the company, and insofar as the law does not provide otherwise, in accordance with the provisions stipulated in the articles.

[75] Paragraph 15(3).

[76] Paragraph 16(1). The system of proportional representation is used.

[77] Paragraph 16(2).

Most decisions of the supervisory board require a simple majority. However, a two-thirds majority is required in the cases, set out in paragraphs 27 and 29 of the Act. The former paragraph stipulates that the chairperson of the supervisory board is elected by a two-thirds majority of the members. If such a majority cannot be attained, the shareholders' representatives elect the chairperson and the employees' representatives the vice chairperson. This explains why the chairperson is usually a representative of the shareholders, such that the law cannot really be said to have introduced paritative codetermination, because the chairperson has a casting vote if the first vote is tied.[78] This casting vote cannot be exercised by the vice chairperson, but it may be exercised by a member of the supervisory board duly authorised by the chairperson if he or she is unable to attend the meeting.

According to paragraph 31(2) of the Codetermination Act 1976, the appointment of the members of the board of directors requires at least a two thirds majority vote of the members of the supervisory board.

I. Constitutionality of the Codetermination Act 1976

Objections have been made to the system of codetermination introduced by the 1976 Act on the grounds that it may discourage investment, increase the power of trade union officials and result in conflicts at the level of the supervisory board. It has also sometimes been contended that it may go beyond equal or paritative codetermination in its effect. There has also been some doubt about the constitutionality of the Codetermination Act 1976 [79] but this would seem to be of less significance since the Constitutional Court has found the Act to be constitutional in its decision of 1 March 1979.[80] The complaint that the Act was unconstitutional was made on several grounds, the most important of which seems to have been that it violated the guarantee of private property contained in Article 14 of the Federal Constitution and also violated Article 9(3) of that Constitution.

The latter provision stipulates, inter alia, that the right to form associations for the purpose of promoting and enforcing employment and business conditions is guaranteed for everyone and for all associations. It is treated as requiring the strict separation of employers and employees

78 Paragraph 29(2) of the Codetermination Act 1976.

79 See K. Schmidt, *Gesellschaftsrecht* (Cologne: Heymanns, 2002), § 28 III 4b for supporting documents.

80 *Official Journal of the German Federal Constitutional Court* (BverfGE) 50, 290.

in the collective bargaining process.[81] The guarantee of private property was said to be infringed because it was contended that investors could no longer use their invested capital in the way they wished to.

The Constitutional Court rejected the arguments based upon the above provisions and also upon the other constitutional provisions cited by those who made the constitutional complaints. As far as the complaints based upon Article 9(3) were concerned, the Court found that although the Codetermination Act 1976 resulted in the mutual dependence of the shareholders and employees' representatives on the supervisory board, these parties differed from those to a collective agreement which was usually employers' associations and unions. It should be noted that the independence of the parties to collective agreements may arguably be prejudiced by the continuous process of compromise and negotiation which takes place at supervisory board level. The approach taken by the employees' representatives (who will usually be union members) on the supervisory board has clearly had some effect on the employers' associations. The Court did not however think that this pragmatic fact was enough to compromise the independence of the two negotiating parties.

Although private property is guaranteed by the first sentence of Article 14(1) of the Constitution, the second sentence of that provision stipulates that the contents of this right and limitations thereon may be prescribed by law. Article 14(2) stipulates that property involves obligations, and its use should also serve the public good. The Constitutional Court took the view that Article 14(1) protects the substance of property rights, and that limitations thereon must comply with the principle of proportionality. It had no difficulty in finding that the ownership of shares conferred, both as far as the membership rights and the rights to assets it gave rise to were concerned, a kind of indirect ownership arising through the medium of company law. Limitations on such ownership existed insofar as the shareholder was unable to make direct use or dispose of it. The use of such rights of ownership was limited by the principle of majority rule.

The court found that the relevant provisions of the Codetermination Act 1976 were a restriction placed upon the use of property which served the public good. It found that because it followed from paragraphs 27(2) and 29(2) of the Codetermination Act 1976 that the ultimate decisions of the supervisory board remained within the power of the shareholders'

[81] This is called *Tarifautonomie*: see Hesse, *Grungzüge des Verfassungsrechts*, (20th edn., (Müller, 1995), p. 180.

representatives, the property rights of the shareholders were sufficiently guaranteed. The Court also indicated that the Codetermination Act of 1976 did not meaningfully restrict the value of the shares, or the respective yield on them.

The Constitutional Court found that the 1976 Act did not establish a system of paritative codetermination, because of the casting vote of the shareholders' representative on the supervisory board. It also emphasised that there was no form of codetermination in the other principal organs of the company, the management board and the general meeting.

It is not clear from the judgment of the Constitutional Court whether a system of genuinely equal or paritative codetermination at the level of the supervisory board would be constitutional. It will be remembered that it exists both in the legislation of 1951 and 1956 relating respectively to codetermination in coal, iron and steel companies, and coal, iron and steel holding companies. The system of paritative (or quasi-paritative) co-determination introduced by the 1976 Act has undergone considerable criticism in recent years, but it seems doubtful whether it will be abandoned in the immediate future.

V. The position in Italy

Works committees which were regulated by collective agreements rather than by law used to be familiar in Italy. Such committees were elected by all the employees of the plant, (establishment) on the basis of lists put forward by the major trade unions. They are now of little or no importance, having been supplanted by representative organs set up at the level of the establishment in accordance with Title I of Act No. 300 of 20 May 1970 on workers' rights. Such representative bodies have no fixed structure, but must be connected with the most representative unions. These bodies have an exclusive access to collective bargaining, and their officers are granted time off and leave of absence for these activities.

Employee codetermination through the medium of an organ of the company, or through that of works councils, has been resisted by the trade unions in Italy. However, the enactment and implementation of the European Works Councils Directive has had some effect on large Italian undertakings. The implementation of the Framework Directive of 11 March 2002, which is discussed below will also have a significant effect.

VI. The position in Spain

A. *Works councils*

The minimum legal requirements for worker participation are set out under Organic Law 8/80 of 10 March 1980, which relates to works councils, and under Organic Law 11/85 of 5 August 1985, which relates to the representation by trade unions. These requirements are often improved on by the terms of collective agreements. Works councils (*comités de empresa*) are compulsory under the Organic Law of 1980 if the enterprise employs at least fifty employees; these are replaced by personnel representatives (*delegados de empresa*) if it employs less. Companies having more than one works council may elect one common to the company. If the works council is established, but the enterprise consists of part of a group of undertakings, a group works council may be formed by means of a collective agreement. The number of members of the works council depends on the number of employees.

Candidates for the works council may be proposed by trade unions, and also by a minimum number of members of the works council. Elections may be convened by unions which are represented by at least 10 per cent of the workforce of the company. Two electoral groups exist, one being made up of technical and administrative workers, and the other consisting of skilled and unskilled workers. These groups may be supplemented by a third in accordance with the terms of a collective agreement. Voting is direct and secret, and postal voting is permitted. The members of the works council are elected for four years.

The members of the works council are protected in various ways in the performance of their duties; and are entitled to certain facilities such that they may perform them. They are protected against dismissal when they are performing their duties, except in certain special circumstances. Works councils do not enjoy the right of worker participation or codetermination in the strict sense, but they must be informed of and consulted about certain matters. It is thus necessary to inform the works council of the general development of the industrial sector to which the company belongs and its position in relating to sales and productivity. The works council has to be consulted in respect of proposed mergers, takeovers or changes in the legal status of the company, when such transaction would affect the level of employment. It also has to be consulted on certain social policy decisions.

The works council has standing to bring administrative or judicial proceedings in all cases relevant to its powers. It may also participate in the conclusion of collective agreements.

B. Employees' meetings

Employees have the right to hold meetings at the premises where the enterprise is situated, which may discuss any matter relating to working conditions which is placed on their agenda. Decisions are adopted at such meetings by a majority of one-half plus one of the workers employed by the enterprise or at an establishment thereof. Such meetings are presided over by the works council or the personnel representatives.

C. Trade union section

Union sections comprise all the employees of a company who belong to a particular union. Not all union sections have the same rights or powers: these vary according to whether or not the union is the most representative. All employees who belong to a union may establish union sections, hold meetings, and receive information sent to them by the union at the level of the enterprise or establishment. Sections of the most representative union have the right to collective bargaining, and if the workforce is more than 250, to the use of suitable premises for the purpose of carrying out union activities.

If the company or establishment has more than 250 workers, and the union to which the section belongs has obtained more than ten per cent of the votes in the works council election, the union section may be represented by delegates, who have certain special powers.

VII. The position in Belgium

The establishment of a works council (*ondernemingsraad*) in Belgium is governed by Royal Decrees and collective agreements. It is mandatory in undertakings employing an average of at least 100 persons. Furthermore, businesses which established a works council or which were required to do so on the occasion of the previous social election act which usually employ an average of at least fifty persons must also establish a works council. In addition to the works council, a committee on health and safety must be set up if fifty or more persons are employed, and which assumes the functions of the works council if there are on average fewer than 100 employees. Furthermore, trade unions may be represented at the level of the enterprise and may attempt to deal with problems in the field of social policy. The lists of candidates for the works councils are proposed by the trade unions, and must be formulated in such a way as to represent the different types of employees. The employer or his representative have a seat on the works council, which is chaired by or on behalf of the employer.

The employees on the works council are entitled to certain facilities, and their position is protected in some ways. Their contract can only be terminated on limited grounds. The works council has the right to be informed about economic and social circumstances relating to the undertaking, to appoint and dismiss the company's statutory auditors, and to be consulted about some social matters. Its right of codecision or codetermination are limited.

VIII The position in the Netherlands

A. Works councils

The establishment of a works council is compulsory if the enterprise employs fifty or more persons.[82] In smaller enterprises which have more than ten but less than fifty employees, the employees are entitled to hold biennial meetings and to be given information and consulted about major decisions which affect the volume of employment in the enterprise.[83] The members of the works council are elected by and must be employees of the enterprise. Such election is based upon a list of candidates which may be proposed by trade unions having amongst their members' employees in the enterprise, or by the lesser of thirty persons or one third of the number of employees qualified to vote who do not belong to a trade union which has proposed candidates.[84]

The works council consists of at least three members,[85] who are elected for at least three years. As in other jurisdictions (such as Spain), members of the works council are entitled to certain facilities and to receive education and training.[86] Except for serious reasons, an employee who works for the undertaking and who is a member of the works council, or a committee of the works council, or who has a special relationship with it may not be dismissed without the consent of the cantonal division of the District Court.[87] The latter is required to ensure that the reason for the dismissal does not relate to his or her membership of the works council, or to the inclusion of the employee's name in the list of

[82] WOR (*Wet op de Ondernemingsraad*), Art. 2.

[83] *Ibid.*, Art. 35b. The management of enterprises having less than ten employees may set up an optional body for employee representation, which may also be established in enterprises having between ten–fifty employees.

[84] *Ibid.*, Art. 9(2). [85] *Ibid.*, Art. 6(1). [86] *Ibid.*, Arts. 16–18. [87] *Ibid.*, Art. 21.

candidates for election. Employees must not suffer any disadvantage as regards their position in the undertaking as the result of their membership or candidature for membership of the works council or any of its committees.

A company or group which has established two or more works councils must establish a central or group works council.[88] Such a council or group works council deals with matters of common interest in the enterprises involved. In addition to the requirement relating to the central of group works council. If a company or a group of companies has two or more establishments employing at least fifty employees, it is required to set up a joint works council for some or all these establishments if this would further the proper implementation of the Works Councils Act.[89] The distribution of powers between works councils at the different levels has led to conflicts in the past.

The Dutch works council and its committees have extensive powers. The management must supply these bodies with all information necessary for the performance of their duties; this includes financial information and information on economic and social policies.[90] The works council must be consulted on a number of important economic and social decisions, such as the transfer of control over the enterprise or any part thereof, the discontinuance of the activities of the enterprise or a major part thereof, the recruitment or sub contracting of categories of workers, and major measures taken in connection with the preservation of the environment.[91] The categories of measures which cannot be taken without the consent of the works council may be expanded as the result of an agreement between the management and the works council. The works council cannot give its advice until there has been at least one consultative meeting on the relevant matter. If it considers that the company could not reasonably have reached the decision on consideration of the relevant interests, the Enterprise Chamber of the Court of Appeal of Amsterdam may require the employer to wholly or partly retract his decision,[92] subject to the acquired rights of third parties who have acted in good faith.[93]

Certain actions in the social field may not be taken by the management without the prior consent of the works council. These include rules relating to working hours or vacations, rules pertaining to the handling

[88] *Ibid.*, Art. 33. [89] *Ibid.*, Art. 3(1) and (2). [90] *Ibid.*, Art. 31–31c.
[91] See WOR, Art. 25(1) for a complete enumeration of the relevant areas.
[92] WOR, Art. 26(5). [93] *Ibid.*, Art. 26(5).

of complaints and to the position of minors in the enterprise.[94] If the consent of the works council is not given when it so required, any action by the management with respect to the relevant matter is treated as null and void.[95] However the works council does not have to approve matters if and to the extent that such matters as would normally require the consent of the works council are already dealt with in a collective agreement.[96]

B. *Employee participation on the supervisory board*

The Dutch system of appointment to the supervisory boards of 'large' public and private companies, which ensures employee participation on such boards, has already been explained in the chapter on management and control. It was emphasised in that chapter that the general meeting has been given greater powers in this connection by an alteration in the law which took effect in October 2004. However, in large companies the works council has an enhanced right to suggest candidates up to a maximum of one third of the seats on the supervisory board, which nominates the candidates. The actual appointment and in some circumstances the dismissal of the members of the supervisory board, including those suggested by the works council, is a matter for the general meeting. The general meeting is empowered by Articles 2.272a and 2.161a of the Netherlands Civil Code to pass a resolution by an enhanced majority dismissing the members of the supervisory board if it has lost confidence in them.

IX Community law and employee participation

A. *Collective redundancy*

The information and consultation of employee representatives is provided for in directives on collective redundancies,[97] and on the transfer of undertakings.[98] Collective redundancies are treated as occurring when for reasons not related to the individual workers concerned, a certain

[94] For a complete list of the relevant areas, see WOR, Art. 27(1).
[95] WOR, Art. 27(5). [96] *Ibid.*, Art. 27(3).
[97] Council Directive (EC) 98/59/EC, 1998, OJ L225/16.
[98] Council Directive (EC) 2001/23/EC, 2001 OJ L82/16. For the early implementation of the Directive in the Member States, see C. Barnard, *EC Employment Law*, 1st edn (London: Wiley, 1996), p. 354, n. 6.

number of redundancies occur, e.g. over a period of ninety days, at least twenty, irrespective of the number of employees in the establishments in question. The Directive has no application to redundancies resulting from the expiry of fixed-term contracts on the completion of a particular task, nor is it applicable to termination of the employment contracts of persons employed by public administrative bodies.

According to Article 2(1) of the Directive, when an employer is contemplating collective redundancies, he must begin consultations with the employees representatives in good time with a view to reaching an agreement. During the course of the consultations, the employer must supply the worker's representatives with all the relevant information, and must also explain in writing the reason for the projected redundancies, the number of categories of workers to be made redundant, the period over which the redundancies are to take effect, the criteria proposed for the selection of workers for redundancy, and the method of calculating any redundancy payment.[99] A copy of the information relating to the redundancies has to be sent to the competent authority.[100] Employers must send a copy of the notification to the workers' representatives. The proposed redundancies cannot take effect until thirty days after the Article 3(1) notification to the competent authority.[101]

B. *Transfer of undertakings*

The above matter was originally governed by Council Directive 77/187/EEC, which has been subsequently amended and this area has now been codified by Council Directive 2001/23/EC.[102] Article 1(1)(a) of the codifying Directive states that this Directive applies to the transfer of an undertaking, business or part of a business to another employer as the result of a legal transfer or merger.[103] A Member State is permitted by Article 5 to exclude the application of the Directive where the transferor undertaking, business or part of the business is subject to bankruptcy or analogous proceedings instituted with a view to the liquidation of the

99 Collective Redundancies Directive, Art. 2(3).

100 *Ibid.*, Art. 3(1). 101 *Ibid.*, Art. 4(1).

102 The 1977 Directive may be found in OJ 1977 L61/26. The Directive was substantially amended in 1998 and consolidated in 2001, Council Directive (EC) 2001/23/EC, 2001 OJ L82/16.

103 According to Art. 1(1)(b) of the codifying Directive of 2001, a transfer occurs where there is a transfer of an economic entity which retains its identity, meaning an organised grouping of resources which has the objective of pursuing an economic activity, whether or not that activity is central or ancillary.

assets of the transferor. According to certain decisions the European Court of Justice, the decisive criterion for deciding whether there has been a transfer is whether the business retains its identity insofar as it is transferred as a going concern, which may be indicated in particular by the fact that its operation is continued, or renewed by the new employer with the same or similar activities.[104] In the case of a takeover of the shares of a company there is no change in the employer, and thus such an operation does not come within the provisions of the Directive.

The above instrument was designed to ensure that, as far as possible, the employment relationship remains unchanged with the transferee, and that workers are protected against dismissals solely by reason of the transfer.[105]

According to Article 7 of the Directive, both the transferor and the transferee must inform the representatives of their respective employees affected by a transfer in good time of the date or proposed date of the transfer, the reasons for the transfer, the legal, social, and economic implications of the transfer for the employees, and the measures envisaged in relation to them. Employees' representatives have the right to be consulted in good time with a view to seeking their agreement concerning measures in relation to the workforce, such a reduction in their numbers. The representatives are not however, given any right to veto such a measure.

C. *European Works Councils Directive*

The European Works Councils Directive is designed to give adequate information and consultation opportunities to employees affected by corporate decisions taken by a head office or controlling undertaking outside their Member States. It is apparently influenced by the abortive Vredeling proposals for a directive concerning the information and consultation of employees of undertakings having a complex structure.[106] Legislation on the

[104] Note in this sense Case 24/85, *Spijkers* v. *Benedik* [1986] ECR 1119, paras. 11 and 12 and Case 287/86, *Ny Mölle Kro* [1987] ECR 5465, para. 18. See also Case C-13/95, *Suzen* [1997] ECRI-1259, in which the Court took a multi-factor approach to the transfer of an undertaking, holding that the pursuit of similar activities did not necessarily lead to the conclusion that such a transfer had taken place.

[105] See Case 19/83, *Wendelboe* [1985] ECR 457, para. 15, Cases C-132, 138 and 139/91 *Katsikas* [1992] ECR I-6577.

[106] The two Vredeling proposals may be found in OJ C297/3 Bull Supp 3/80 and OJ 1983 OJ C217/3, Bull Supp 2/83. The European Works Council Directive 94/95/EEC may be found in 1994 OJ L254/64. It was amended by Council Directive 97/74/EEC, OJ 1997 L10/22, which extended the former Directive to the United Kingdom.

information consultation and participation of employees was advocated in the non-binding Community Charter of Fundamental Social Rights, adopted at the Strasbourg summit in 1989. The provisions of the Charter clearly influenced the enactment of the European Works Councils Directive. This Directive requires the establishment of a European Works Council, or a procedure for informing and consulting employees in the case of Community scale undertakings or Community scale groups of undertakings[107] having at least 1,000 employees in the Member States and at least two establishments employing 150 workers in each of two Member States. The ambit of the Directive has been extended to Iceland and Norway. It is also applicable where the Community-scale undertakings or groups of undertakings have their headquarters outside the states covered by it, but meet the threshold requirements therein. In the latter types of situation, the central management should designate a representative agent to carry out the responsibilities for creating the European Works Council or information and consultation procedure required by Article 4(1) of the Directive. In the absence of such a representative agent, responsibility falls on the undertaking with the higher number of employees in the Member States.

The Directive contains detailed provisions governing the initial establishment of a special negotiating body which according to Article 5(3) and (6) of the Directive, will be free to determine by written agreement with the central management, the scope, composition, functions and term of office of the European Works Council, or the arrangements for initiating a procedure for informing and consulting employees.

According to Article 6(2) of the Directive, the written agreement is required to determine:

(a) the undertakings belonging to the Community-scale group of undertaking or the establishments of the Community-scale undertaking which are covered by the agreement;
(b) the composition of the European Works Council, the number of members, the allocation of seats, and the terms of office;
(c) the functions of and procedure for informing and consulting the European Works Council;
(d) the venue, frequency and duration of meetings of the European Works Council;

[107] See Council Directive 94/95/EEC, 1994 OJ L254/64, Arts. 2(1)(b) and 3 for the definition of a group of undertakings and a controlling undertaking.

(e) the financial and material resources to be allocated to the European Works Council; and
(f) the duration of the agreement and the procedure for its renegotiation.

If it is impossible for an agreement to be reached after three years of negotiations or if the management fails to begin negotiations within six months of the request being made, or if the central management and the negotiating body so decide, subsidiary requirements which are laid down by the legislation of the state where the central management is situated, which must comply at least with the provisions of the Annex to the Directive, are applicable.[108] The special negotiating body, may decide, by at least two-thirds of the votes, not to open negotiations or terminate such negotiations, in which case the procedure to conclude an agreement will terminate and the Annex is inapplicable.[109]

According to Article 8(1) of the Directive, Member States are required to provide that members of special negotiating bodies or of the European Works Council and any experts who assist them shall not reveal information which has been expressly provided to them in confidence. The position is similar in relation to employees' representatives who have been engaged in any information and consultation procedure. According to Article 8(2), Member States may provide that the central management need not transmit information where this would be seriously harmful to any of the undertakings concerned. Employees' representatives are required by Article 11(4) to have access to administrative or judicial appeal procedures when the management requires confidentiality, or denies access to information.

The Directive confers a measure of employment protection on employees involved in special negotiating bodies, European Works Councils or acting as employees' representatives in the alternative information and consultation procedure. Article 10 thereof provides that such persons must enjoy the same protection and guarantees as are provided for employees representatives under national law, including the payment of wages.

The European Works Councils Directive has had to be implemented in the Member States. In the United Kingdom, such implementation took place by a statutory instrument of 1999,[110] in France, it took place as an amendment to the Employment Code in November 1996;[111] in the

[108] Directive 94/95/EEC, Art. 7. The Directive does not contain any detailed rules determining what constitutes an acceptable information and consultation procedure.
[109] Directive 94/95/EEC, Art. 5(5). [110] SI 1999 No. 3323.
[111] Law No. 96-985 amending Arts. L439-1, and L439-6–L439-24 of the Employment Code.

Netherlands it took place through the Law on the European Works Council (*Wet op de Europese ondernemingsraden*, WOEOR) of 1997.

D. *Directive on a general framework for informing and consulting employees in the EC*

The Directive on the European Works Council has been followed by a Council and Parliament Directive which will require information and consultation with employee representatives at national level on a number of issues affecting workers.[112] The Directive has been the subject of a conciliation procedure between the Council and Parliament which was successfully completed in a short time, and the Directive was finally adopted on 11 March 2002.

The Directive establishes a general framework setting out minimum requirements for the right to information and consultation of employees of undertakings having at least fifty employees in any one Member State, or establishments employing at least twenty employees in any one Member State. According to Article 4 of the Directive, the Member States will be required to determine the practical arrangements for information and consultation in accordance with national law and national industrial relations practice. Information and consultation will cover:

(a) information on the recent and probable development of the undertaking or the establishment's activities and economic situation;
(b) information and consultation on the situation, structure and probable development of employment within the undertaking or establishment, and on any anticipatory measures envisaged, in particular where there is a threat to employment;
(c) information and consultation on decisions likely to lead to substantial changes in work organisation or in contractual relations.

Information must be provided at such time, and in such a way, as will enable employee representatives to conduct an adequate study and, where necessary, prepare for consultation.[113]

[112] 2002 OJ L80/29.

[113] It is of interest to note in the present context that para. 13 of the Preamble to the Common Position adopted by the Council on 23 July 2001, criticises the fact that existing legal frameworks for employee information and consultation at Community and national level adopt an excessively *a posteriori* approach to the process of change.

The Directive contains provisions similar to those of the European Works Councils Directive concerning the disclosure of confidential information. Considerable controversy has arisen about how decisions taken without complying with the proposed obligations of consultation should be treated. The Directive stipulates that Member States shall provide for appropriate measures in the event of non-compliance with it by the employer and by employees' representatives, and for adequate sanctions to be applicable in the event of its infringement of the Directive by such persons. According to Article 8 of the Directive, which is a standard form provision, such sanctions must be effective, proportionate and dissuasive. The Directive does not however provide for circumstances in which a decision taken without consultation will be void and have no effect. However, it would seem that in some circumstances, this gap might be filled by the competent courts.

Article 10 of the Directive contains transitional provisions for Member States in which the date of entry into force of the Directive there is no general, permanent and statutory system of information and consultation of employees, nor any system of employee representation at the workplace enabling employees to be represented for this purpose. The Directive envisages the use of arrangements for information and consultation as an alternative to works councils. The Directive may have a significant effect in countries such as the United Kingdom, Ireland and Italy, where works councils have not developed to any significant effect, as well as in France, Germany, Belgium and the Netherlands, where they have important functions. However, the Directive seems likely to undergo revision in the future, its present requirements appear fairly minimal.

E. Models for employee participation in the draft Fifth Directive

The proposed Fifth Directive on employee participation and company structure appears to have been abandoned. The amended proposal of 1982,[114] suggested four models for employee participation in public companies having more than 1,000 employees. It was subsequently

[114] COM(83) 195 final, 1983 OJ C240/2: see Welch, 'The Fifth Draft Directive – A False Dawn?' (1983) ELRev 83.

amended in certain other respects on three occasions.[115] The models suggested[116] were:

(a) participation through employee representatives at board level, whether the company had a two-tier board or a single board;
(b) participation by means of the appointment of supervisory board members through a system of cooption, the general meeting and the representatives of the employees having the right to object to a candidate;
(c) participation through a body representing the employees which would have the right to be informed and consulted on various matters; and
(d) participation through collective agreements concluded between the company and the trade unions, which would provide for participation in accordance with one of the three foregoing models.

The models suggested are in accordance with national practice and political and ideological attitudes to the question of employee participation. It seems unfortunate that it has proved impossible to adopt the relevant proposals. However, the Commission's Communication on Modernising Company Law and Enhancing Corporate Governance in the EU proposes short term action enhancing corporate governance disclosure requirements. It is possible, but rather unlikely, that such proposals might be followed by substantive proposals governing corporate structure, at some time in the future.

[115] The 1988 amendment was never published, but reference is made to it in certain of the literature, for example Du Plessis and Dine, 'The Fate of the Fifth Draft Directive on Company Law – Accommodation Instead of Harmonisation' (1997) JBL 23. The 1990 amendment, COM(90) 679 final may be found in 1991 OJ C7/4; the 1991 amendment, COM(91) 272. final in 1991 OJ C321/9.

[116] See Art. 4 of the proposed Directive.

9

Groups of companies

I. Introduction

Groups of companies have become increasingly common, and may come into existence as the result of mergers, takeovers and the acquisition of controlling shareholdings. Groups of companies may also be made use of where a large company wishes the different businesses carried on by it to be managed by different companies, in which case each company will normally only be liable for its own transactions. Research, investments, sales and marketing activities are sometimes carried on by subsidiaries. Both large companies, and medium-sized and small companies, sometimes make use of group structures.

The present chapter will be primarily concerned with vertical groups which have a single controlling company which is the controlling company of the various subsidiaries. Horizontal groups occur where legally separate enterprises are subject to common direction, and none of such enterprises controls the others. They usually come about as the result of contractual arrangements, or provisions in the articles of the relevant companies. The existence of a group of companies gives rise to many problems, which arise largely because the interests of the parent company and its creditors, shareholders and employees may be different from those of individual subsidiaries. The question arises whether the interests of the subsidiary may be subordinated by those who manage it to those of the controlling company in any circumstances.

In certain countries, an attempt is made to resolve the problems which arise from the existence of a group of companies by the enactment of a specific body of rules governing the conduct of groups of companies: This approach is taken under German *Konzernrecht*: the relevant rules are contained in paragraphs 15–19 and 291–328 of the German *Aktiengesetz*,[1] insofar as dependent public companies and limited partnerships with shares are concerned. It has been followed in such countries as Brazil,

[1] Note also for accounts of groups the German Company Disclosure Law (*Publizitätsgesetz*) of 15 August 1969 (*Federal Law Gazette* (BGBl) 1969 I 1189 and BGBl 1970 I 1113).

Portugal, Slovenia, Croatia and Taiwan. However, the rules contained in the German *Aktiengesetz* have not worked entirely satisfactorily. A different approach, which has attempted to reconcile the interests of the parent company and its subsidiaries has been taken by the French courts in accordance with the *Rozenblum* doctrine developed by the civil and criminal chambers of the *Cour de Cassation*, which is mentioned below.

II. The preliminary draft Ninth Directive

The preliminary draft Directive on the Conduct of Groups which was influenced by German scholars such as Würdinger and Gleichmann, was eventually withdrawn in 1990: the Commission had been divided about its merits. It was based upon German law and proposals for its reform, and was much criticised, especially one might add by persons who were sometimes, unfamiliar with German *Konzernrecht*.

The provisions of section 4 of the preliminary draft Directive are modelled on those of paragraphs 311–318 of the *Aktiengesetz*, which govern de facto groups, and are indeed to protect, inter alia, subsidiary companies and their creditors and minority shareholders. The latter section would be inapplicable where a control contract or a unilateral declaration under section 6 was made, and the appropriate publication took place. Such a declaration would have an effect comparable to the German procedure called integration. Section 7 of the draft Ninth Directive would require the management body of the subsidiary to prepare a report similar to the German special dependency report on its relationship with its parent undertaking during the previous financial year. This report would be audited by the person responsible for auditing the accounts of the company, and would be made available to every shareholder. The provisions of section 5 of the draft Directive concerning control contracts are very complex, and like those of section 4, are based upon German law. It is unlikely that the provisions on the draft Ninth Directive will be revised. The new initiative taken by a private body, the *Forum Europaeum Konzernrecht*, which is referred to in outline later on, may well have more influence in the future. The recent Commission *Communication on Modernising Company Law* suggests that a proposal for a framework Directive on the implementation of a group policy will be presented by the Commission in the fairly near future. It is envisaged that it will provide for the protection of the interests of a group company's creditors and for the existence of a fair balance of advantage for the company's shareholders. If the proposal is made, it may be modelled on the approach taken in the important French *Rozenblum* decision which is considered below.

III. European Community legislation on groups[2]

Apart from the abortive preliminary draft Ninth Directive there are a number of European Community instruments having an impact on groups of companies. The most important of these is the Seventh Directive on consolidated accounts; certain other Community company law directives contain relevant provisions, which may also be found in certain instruments relating to taxation and mergers.

Article 1 of the Seventh Directive contains six definitions of groups, four of which are based upon legal criteria, and two of which have an economic character. The latter two definitions occur in Article 1(1) of the Directive, which provides that a Member State may require any undertaking governed by its national law to draw up consolidated accounts if that undertakings (a parent undertaking) holds a participating interest (which must be at least 20 per cent of a company's capital) in another undertaking (a subsidiary undertaking) and either (a) it actually exercises a dominant influence over it or (b) it and the subsidiary undertaking are managed on a unified basis by the parent undertaking. The latter two requirements may be found in paragraph 290 of the German Commercial Code. The concepts of 'dominant influence' and unified management have been familiar in Germany, but seem to be of an economic nature. The implementation of the Seventh Directive has had a considerable influence on the laws of certain Member States, particularly in relation to the definition of groups.[3]

The concept of a group is also relevant to certain provisions of the Second and Third Company Law Directives. Thus, Article 10(4) of the Second Directive permits Member States to relax the requirement of

[2] *Forum Europaeum Konzernrecht 'Konzernrecht für Europa'* [1998] ZGR, 672–772; see also: F. Fleischer, *Neue Entwicklungen im englischen Konzernrecht – Vergleichende Notizen im Lichte der Empfehlungen des Forum Europaeum Konzernrecht* [1999] Die AG, pp. 350–62.

[3] Thus, the optional definitions contained in Arts. 1(1)c and 1(2)(a) and (b) have been implemented in the United Kingdom by ss. 258(2)(c) and 258(4) of the UK Companies Act 1985 (replaced by ss. 1162(2)(c) and 1162(3) of the Companies Act 2006). The compulsory definitions, contained in Art. (1)(a), (b) and d(bb) of the Directive are reflected in ss. 1162(2)(a), 1162(2)(b) and 1162(2)(d) of the 2006 Act (previously in ss. 258(2)(a), 258(2)(b) and 258(2)(d) of the 1985 Act).

the valuation of non-cash consideration for shares when 90 per cent of the nominal value or accountable par value is issued to one or more companies for a non-cash consideration, provided that certain conditions are fulfilled. This exception is intended to cover certain inter-group issues and corporate reorganisations. Furthermore, Article 29 of the Third Company Law Directive provides that there is no need for the preparation of management and experts' reports by the appropriate organs of the merging companies where 90 per cent of more of the shares in the company being acquired are held by the acquiring company.

The concept of the group of companies is also of relevance to certain Community legislation on taxation. An example is provided by Council Directive 90/435 on the common system of taxation of parent companies and subsidiaries in different Member States, according to withholding tax is abolished on profit distributions by a company belonging to one Member State to its parent in another Member State.[4]

The Council Regulation 4064/89,[5] as amended by Council Regulation 1310/97[6] constitutes an important means of controlling certain mergers. Article 3(1) stipulates, inter alia, that a concentration shall be deemed to arise where one or more undertakings acquire, whether by purchase of securities or assets; by assets, by contract or any other means, direct or indirect control of the whole or parts of one or more undertakings. The Merger Regulation does not define what is meant by control, but the Commission has held that the acquisition of a 30 per cent holding in a company was enough to give a bidder control, where the other shareholdings were widely dispersed.[7] A further instrument which is of interest because it makes use of the concept of dominant influence is Council Directive 80/723/EEC on the transparency of financial relations between public enterprises and the state.[8] The concept of the group of companies is also of importance in EC banking and insurance law, and is employed in the Works Councils Directive, which was considered in an earlier chapter.

IV. German *Konzernrecht*

Apart from Portugal,[9] Germany and Italy are the only countries in the EC to systematically regulate groups of companies. The Italian rules,

[4] For other examples in the field of taxation, see Dorrensteijn, Kuiper and Morse, *European Corporate Law* (Deventer and Boston: Kluwer, Law and Taxation, 1994), para. 9.27.

[5] 1989 OJ L395/1. [6] 1997 OJ L180/1.

[7] *Arjomari-Prioux/Wiggins Teape* [1991] 4 CMLR 854. [8] 1980 OJ L195/35.

[9] M. Lutter and H. P. Overrath, *Das portugiesische Konzernrecht von 1986* [1991] ZGR, 394–411.

which have only been enacted recently, are apparently influenced by German law. As already indicated, the German law governing groups of companies had a significant influence on the abortive preliminary draft Ninth Company Law Directive. The relevant rules of German law are contained in paragraphs 15–19 and 291–328 of the *Aktiengesetz*,[10] and it is thought appropriate to consider them in outline. The rules only govern groups in which the dependent company is a public company (AG) or a partnership limited by shares (KGaA). However, the controlling enterprise may take any form,[11] and may thus take that of a company, a partnership, a sole trader, a private person or a public authority. If the enterprise is owned by a natural person, the question arises as to whether that person is in a position to exercise significant influence on at least one other company or carries the business on his own.[12]

Although the German law of groups of companies is designed both to provide a framework within which groups can operate effectively, and to protect minority shareholders and creditors, it has been stigmatised for relying too much on a conflict model and on the protection of the subsidiary. Unlike the *Rozenblum* concept[13] of the French *Cour de Cassation*, it has been argued that it is not directed at achieving an even balance between the interests of the individual companies in a group, and the overall interests of the group.[14]

A. Connected companies

German law expressly recognises five different forms of legal association between enterprises which are legally independent.[15] According to the opinion of legal scholars and the relevant case law, these enterprises may take any form and the dependent ones do not need to be public

[10] Note also for conglomerates the German Company Disclosure Law (*Publizitaetsgesetz*) of 15 August 1969 concerning accounting rules.

[11] See BGHZ 69, 334 '*Veba Gelsenberg*'. [12] See BGHZ 115, 187 '*Video*'.

[13] According to this concept, three conditions must be fulfilled before the interests of the subsidiary can be legitimately subordinated: the group structure must be firmly established, a coherent policy must exist for the whole group, and the advantages and disadvantages must be appropriately distributed within the group: see '*Konzernrecht für Europa*', 672, 705–10. The above requirements seem somewhat vague and imprecise, but are further explained in the relevant decisions.

[14] Note in this sense '*Konzernrecht für Europa*', [1998] ZGR 672, p. 710.

[15] German Public Limited Liability Companies Act, paras. 15–19. These provisions do not expressly mention integrated companies, which are governed by paras. 319–327 of the German Public Limited Liability Companies Act.

companies or partnerships, limited by shares, as is the case under paragraphs 291–328 AktG which contain substantive provisions relating to groups of companies.[16] According to paragraph 15 AktG, associated or connected enterprises are defined as legally independent enterprises, one of which holds the majority of the shares or the vote in another, controlling and dependent enterprises, mutually participating companies, members of a group of companies, and parties to an enterprise contract. A dependent or controlled enterprise is a legally independent enterprise over which another enterprise (the controlling enterprise) can exercise decisions influenced by direct or indirect means.[17] An enterprise the majority of whose shares or votes are held by another enterprise is presumed to be dependent on that enterprise.[18] An enterprise may however be treated as a controlling one if it holds less than 50 per cent of the shares in another company if the remainder of the voting rights are widely distributed, and a significant proportion of the shareholders fail to attend general meetings.[19]

If a controlling and one or more dependent undertakings are brought under uniform management, they are treated as forming a group.[20] Companies between which a control contract exists (paragraph 291 AktG), or which are integrated with one another (paragraph 319 AktG), are treated as being under uniform management.[21] A controlling and a dependent enterprise are treated as forming a group.[22] The concepts of uniform, management and controlling and dependent companies are of an economic nature and perhaps somewhat vague. However enterprises would be treated as being under uniform management if the controlling one determined policy guidelines for other enterprises dependent on it.[23]

German groups may be of a contractual or de facto character. A group is a contractual one if a control contract is concluded between the controlling enterprises and other enterprises dependent on it. De facto groups were formerly subdivided into ordinary ones, and qualified ones (*qualifizierte faktische Konzerne*), in which it was not possible to isolate

[16] T. Raiser, *Recht der Kapitalgesellschaften* (Munich: Vahlen, 2001), § 51, paras. 3–10.

[17] German Public Limited Liability Companies Act, para. 17(1). [18] *Ibid*., para. 17(2).

[19] *Official Journal of the German Supreme Court* (BGHZ) 135, 107 '*VEBA/Gelsenberg*'; Raiser, *Recht der Kapitalgesellschaften*, § 51, para. 17.

[20] German Public Limited Liability Companies Act, para. 18(1) sentence 1.

[21] *Ibid*., para. 18(1) sentence 2. [22] *Ibid*., para. 18(1) sentence 3.

[23] U. Hüffer, *Aktiengesetz* (Munich: Beck, 2002), § 17, paras. 1 ff, 24.

particular prejudicial measures taken by the controlling enterprise and to calculate the compensation due in respect of them to the dependent one, in accordance with the usual rules applicable to de facto groups.[24] It was considered that such liability would generally arise where the enterprise which has been prejudicially affected has been closely integrated with the dominant one, which has exercised a long-standing and extensive influence on its management. In such an event, it is frequently hard to separate prejudicial interventions, from one another, and to isolate their detrimental effects. However, it would seem that the concept of de facto group has been abandoned.

The rules contained in the *Aktiengesetz* of 1965 were intended to encourage the use of contractual groups:[25] however, this result has not happened in practice. Paragraph 291 AktG governs control contracts which are usually combined with profit transfer contracts. Special rules protecting creditors and minority shareholders of the dependent company are made applicable to such contracts by paragraphs 300–307 AktG. Paragraph 292 AktG is applicable to a further category of contracts of a mutual nature, in which there is no relationship of subordination between the parties, i.e. profit pooling, partial profit transfer and business leasing contracts. The parties to such contracts are treated as connected companies, but unlike those to control contracts, they are not treated by paragraph 18(1) AktG as giving rise to a group of companies.[26] The special protective provisions contained in paragraphs 302–305 AktG are generally speaking, inapplicable to such contracts, and they do not require further detailed consideration here.[27] Such contracts are treated by commentators as mutual ones, involving performances and counter-performances but (unlike control contracts) having no organisational effects.[28]

The provisions of the AktG governing control contracts are only applicable where the dependent company is an AG. However, certain of them have been applied by way of analogy by the courts where it is a GmbH.[29] This matter is considered below.

[24] See German Public Limited Liability Companies Act, paras. 311–318; see also K. Schmidt, *Gesellschaftsrecht* (Cologne: Heymanns, 2002), § 17 III 2.

[25] Schmidt, *Gesellschaftsrecht*, § 17 IV 1.

[26] Raiser, *Recht der Kapitalgesellschaften*, § 57, para. 2.

[27] An exeption is e.g. 302(2); see Raiser, *Recht der Kapitalgesellschaften* 57, para. 2.

[28] *Ibid.*, § 57, para. 1, 2.

[29] See for more details Schmidt, *Gesellschaftsrecht*, § 17 II 2 and 17 IV.

Enterprise contracts of all kinds are required by paragraph 293(3) AktG to be in writing. They can only become effective with the consent of the general meetings of all the parties to the contract. The relevant resolution giving such consent requires to be passed by a simple majority consisting of at least three-quarters of the share capital represented at the passing of the resolution.[30] The management board of each of the AG or KGaA which are parties to the agreement as required by paragraph 293a AktG to give a comprehensive written report on the agreement. In addition the enterprise agreement is required by paragraph 293b AktG to be accounted by one or more qualified auditors for each contracting party unless all shares of the dependent company are in the hands of the dominant enterprise. The auditors are required by paragraph 293b AktG to make a written report on the agreement. By paragraph 294(2) AktG, the contract becomes effective once it has been registered in the commercial registry of the company's place of registration.

In a contractual group, the parties thereto are expressly permitted by paragraph 308 AktG to give instructions to the dependent company, which may be disadvantageous for the latter, provided they are beneficial to the group or a company within it. According to paragraph 308(2) AktG, the management board is obliged to follow the instructions of the controlling enterprise. It is not entitled to refuse to follow an instruction because, in its opinion, it does not serve the interests of the controlling enterprise or of one of the enterprises within the group, unless it is obvious that it does not serve these interests.[31] It is generally thought that the controlling enterprise may not give instructions to the dependent company which threaten its existence.[32] Furthermore, according to paragraph 309(1) AktG the legal representatives of the controlling enterprise must exercise the degree of care of a careful and conscientious manager when giving instructions. Furthermore, by paragraph 309(2) AktG, if they act in breach of their duties, they are jointly and severally liable for the damages resulting from such breach. In addition, according to paragraph 310 AktG, the members of the management and supervisory boards of the dependent company are also jointly and severally liable in accordance with paragraph 309 AktG if they act in violation of their instructions.

[30] German Public Limited Liability Companies Act, para. 293(2).

[31] *Ibid.*, para. 308(2) sentence 2.

[32] See for more details Raiser, *Recht der Kapitalgesellschaften*, § 54, para. 34.

The instruction right given to the controlling company in a contractual group in Germany only exists in a few other legal systems which recognise such groups, such as that of Brazil. However, whatever the strict rules of company law in particular countries which have no specific regulation of contractual groups providing for an instruction might require, such instructions are often given and followed in group situations in such countries. The general position in relation to them appears to be that the subsidiary's directors are obliged to refuse to obey the instructions of a parent company if carrying them out would give rise to permanent harm to the subsidiary.[33]

According to paragraph 302 AktG, where there is a control contract, the contracting company is required to compensate the dependent one for any annual net loss occurring during the period of the agreement. If a control contract is cancelled or terminated, Article 303 AktG requires the controlling enterprise to provide security to the creditors of the company whose claims arose prior to the registration of the cancellation or termination.

The provisions of paragraphs 304 and 305 AktG are very complex, and suffer from some defects. According to paragraph 304, the minority shareholders in the dependent company must be offered an annual compensation payment. However according to paragraph 305 AktG, if they prefer not to remain in the dependent company, they must be offered the opportunity to withdraw in exchange for adequate compensation or for shares in the controlling company. A cash settlement alone is treated as appropriate where the controlling company is not a public company or a limited partnership with shares, or is governed by a foreign system of law, or is dependent on a third enterprise which is neither a public company nor a limited partnership with shares. Difficulties arise in the method of calculating share exchange ratios, which has to be done in accordance with both paragraphs 304 and 305.[34]

It has been suggested by the *Forum Europaeum Konzernrecht* that control contracts might be replaced by revocable group declarations which would involve management control, compensation of minorities and liability for losses, without, it is said, the loss of independence of the subsidiary company.[35] Such a declaration could be made where the parent company was in a position to change the statutes of the subsidiary,

[33] See Dorrensteijn *et al.*, *European Corporate Law*, para. 9.41, in this context.

[34] See for more details Raiser, *Recht der Kapitalgesellschaften*, § 54, paras. 80–88.

[35] '*Konzernrecht für Europa*', 740–41.

and would usually require the approval of the general meeting of both companies. It may be doubted whether groups dependent on such declarations would be any more popular than are contractual groups in Germany and elsewhere.

B. Integration

A group may be formed by means of the integration of a subsidiary into a principal or parent company which holds 100 per cent of its share capital, in accordance with paragraph 319 AktG. Both companies have to be public companies, as is also the case under paragraph 320 AktG, which is considered below. If all the subsidiary's capital is owned by the parent company, the sole shareholder will resolve on the integration at a general meeting. This resolution will become effective only on consent by the shareholders' meeting of the prospective principal company.[36] According to paragraph 320 AktG, integration may take place when the principal company holds at least 95 per cent of the share capital of the subsidiary. In such an event, a resolution must be biased in favour of such integration by the shareholders' meeting of the subsidiary. Minority shareholders in the latter company may be bought out against adequate compensation.[37]

From an economic point of view, an integrated company functions as a branch of the parent company. The latter may give instructions to it, and is not limited by the requirement applicable to contractual groups that the instructions must further the interests of the group or a member thereof.[38] The parent company may also make use of the profits and assets of the subsidiary.[39] The principal company is liable to the creditors of the integrated company as a joint and several debtor for the obligations of the latter company incurred prior to the entry of the integration into the commercial register. It is also liable for all obligations of the integrated company incurred after the integration.[40] The principal company may be required to provide security for debts occurring before integration provided that the creditors have made application for this purpose within six months of the announcement of the integration.[41] The principal company is also required to make compensation for any

[36] German Public Limited Liability Companies Act, para. 319(2) sentence 1.
[37] *Ibid.*, para. 320b. [38] *Ibid.*, para. 323(1). [39] *Ibid.*, para. 323(2).
[40] *Ibid.*, para. 322(1). [41] *Ibid.*, para. 321(1).

accumulated loss of the integrated company, insofar as such loss exceeds the amount of the capital reserves and the profit reserve.[42]

C. *De facto groups*

As already indicated, de facto groups are much more common in Germany than contractual groups. Such de facto groups, as well as simple dependency relationships, are regulated by paragraphs 311–318 AktG. It is generally agreed that those provisions have a number of defects especially where a group is closely integrated. A number of questions remain to be answered about the exact meaning of the relevant provisions, and their effectiveness is doubted by some commentators.[43]

Paragraph 311(1) provides that if an enterprise[44] exercises control over a German public company in the absence of a control contract, it may not use its influence to cause the dependent company to enter into any transaction detrimental to itself, or to cause it to take or abstain from taking any measure whereby it suffers a disadvantage, unless this detriment or disadvantage is compensated for by equivalent gains or advantages. By paragraph 311(2), the compensation to be provided to the dependent public company must actually be paid during the year in which the disadvantage was incurred, or a binding obligation fixed as to amount and time of payment must be undertaken by the controlling enterprise at the end of that year. If neither of these steps is taken, the controlling enterprise and the members of its management board are jointly and severally liable to the dependent company for the damage suffered by it as the result of their failure to fulfil the obligations imposed on the controlling enterprise in relation to compensation.[45] If the members of the management board and the supervisory board of the dependent company fail to fulfil their obligations in respect of the special dependency report which is described below, this joint and several liability extends to them as well.[46] However, the controlling enterprise and the members of its management board will not incur any liability if the enterprise fails to pay compensation or to grant a vested right to such compensation in the required time, if a conscientious manager of an independent company would have entered into the

[42] *Ibid.*, para. 324(3). [43] See for further details Schmidt, *Gesellschaftsrecht*, § 31 IV 1.
[44] Such an enterprise may take any form whatsoever.
[45] German Public Limited Liability Companies Act, para. 317(1). [46] *Ibid.*, para. 318.

relevant transaction or would have taken or abstained from taking the relevant measure.[47]

The complex provisions of paragraphs 312–315 of the *Aktiengesetz* concerning the special dependency report are also intended to protect the company, its creditors and minority shareholders, but some authorities criticise that they are of limited value only.[48]

The report is intended to make it easier to ascertain whether a dependent enterprise suffered loss as the result of the influence of a controlling one. The management board of the dependent company is required to prepare an annual report (*Abhängigskeitsbericht*) setting out all transactions entered into with the controlling enterprise, or with third parties at the instance of that enterprise, and all other measures taken at its request or in its interest, and the report is requiting to state whether the dependent enterprise has thereby suffered any disadvantage and whether such detriment or disadvantage has been compensated for.[49] If the balance sheet has to be examined by an auditor, the report must be examined by the company's auditor as well.[50] Additionally, it has to be examined by its supervisory board which must then report to the general meeting on the conclusions of the auditors and on its own examination.[51] Should the report contain any reservations or matters for complaint, any shareholder may apply to the court to appoint special examiners to investigate the matter.[52] Unfortunately, employees' representatives and creditors are not entitled to require such an examination.

The provisions of paragraphs 311 and 317 AktG like those of paragraphs 312–315 concerning the special dependency report, have given rise to criticism. Thus, there may be difficulties in calculating loss for the purposes of paragraph 311 AktG, as well as in calculating whether such loss has been compensated for. The relevant time in relation to which the calculation must be made is that when the transaction or measure was entered into, or the measure was abstained from. It may be difficult to determine the effect of long-term supply contracts entered into between parent and subsidiary companies. It may also prove difficult to estimate the loss arising from particular transactions or measures. Special difficulties may arise in relation to measures

[47] *Ibid.*, para. 317(2).

[48] J. Götz, *Der Abhängigkeitsbericht der 100%igen Tochtergesellschaft* [2000] Die AG, p. 499 f.; for another opinion, Schmidt, *Gesellschaftsrecht*, § 31 IV 2c.

[49] German Public Limited Liability Companies Act, para. 312 (1).

[50] *Ibid.*, para. 313. [51] *Ibid.*, para. 314. [52] *Ibid.*, para. 315.

because it is difficult (as is required by paragraph 317(2) AktG, to make a comparison between measures taken or abstained from at the instance of the controlling enterprise with those which would be taken by a hypothetical independent form. Difficulties also arise in respect of transactions between parent and subsidiary companies where the goods sold do not have a market price. Such difficulties may be multiplied where the group operates at a number of different levels, and is of multinational character. It has been contended by Emmerich and Sonnenschein[53] that because the system of compensation for disadvantages provided for by the *Aktiengesetz* cannot be implemented if there is a constant direct influence by the controlling company on the board of management of a dependent company, such a closely integrated de facto group should be regulated by rules similar to those applicable to contractual groups. Unlike the *Rozenblum* doctrine adopted by the French courts, the rules contained in paragraphs 311–318 AktG do not provide any judgment as to whether a group is firmly established and has a coherent policy, although they do provide for the annual balancing of the advantages and disadvantages in a group situation. The application of the *Rozenblum* doctrine permits balancing of advantages and disadvantages over a longer time period. The Belgian,[54] Dutch and French[55] courts have all adopted the view that such a balance should remain reasonable.

There is nothing in the laws of the latter three states corresponding to the special dependency report. It has been considered unfortunate by some commentators that this report is not made available to shareholders. In the past, at least, it has proved difficult for researchers to obtain a specimen copy. It has also been contended that the auditors of the dependent enterprise will often owe their appointment to the controlling enterprise, and will sometimes fail to take an independent critical attitude. Furthermore, the auditors are required to evaluate economic matters, and it may be that their education does not always fully equip them to do so. Where the controlling enterprise is a foreign one, it may be difficult to obtain the necessary information from it. Obtaining adequate information often proves difficult in groups.

[53] *Konzernrecht*, 2nd edn (Munich: Beck, 1977), p. 217.

[54] For references to relevant Belgian cases, see the Forum Europaeum Konzernrecht, '*Konzernrecht für Europa*', (1988) 27 ZGR 689, p 672, 740-1, fn. 186. The English translation, Forum Europaeum Corporate Group Law, 'Corporate Group Law for Europe', is published in 1 EBOR (2000) 165.

[55] For references to relevant French decisions, see '*Konzernrecht für Europa*', pp. 740–41, fns. 184 and 188.

D. *Contractual groups involving private companies*

Such groups are commonly found in practice, and their legality is no longer in question,[56] but if a GmbH enters into a control contract with a controlling enterprise, or a profit transfer contract with such an enterprise, it is not clear what kind of majority is required for the GmbH's consent to such a contract. Some authorities have argued that unanimous consent of the shareholders in general meeting is necessary, whilst others have argued in favour of the same majority as that required for the alteration of the statutes, i.e. three-quarters of the votes cast at a general meeting.[57] The contract must be drawn up as a formal deed and be duly registered.[58] When a GmbH is the dependent party to a control contract, the controlling enterprise may issue instructions to it, which may be disadvantageous to it, provided they serve the interests of the controlling enterprise or other enterprises in the same group, and is also required to compensate any annual net loss suffered by the dependent company. The provisions of paragraphs 304 and 305 AktG, which have been considered above, may be applicable to the minority shareholders in such a dependent GmbH by way of analogy.[59]

GmbHs are more likely to be dependent companies in an ordinary de facto group than in a contractual group. This is because, in a GmbH, the shareholder(s) have the power of giving instructions to the managers in accordance with paragraph 37(1) GmbHG; a control contract is not necessary for this purpose. Such instructions may also be provided for in the company's articles. A further reason for using GmbH as a dependent company is that multiple voting rights can be exercised in a GmbH.[60]

1. De facto groups in which a GmbH is the dependent company

An ordinary de facto group, which is usually based upon shareholdings, voting rights and special provisions in the statutes, must be distinguished from a qualified de facto group insofar as, in the former type of group, it is possible to isolate individual transactions or measures and to estimate the amount of loss and damage resulting from them: this is not possible

[56] Note in this context *Official Journal of the German Supreme Court* (BGHZ), 105, 324 '*Supermarkt*' and BGH, GmbHR 92, 253 '*Siemens*'.

[57] See Schmidt, *Gesellschaftsrecht*, § 38 III 2a for supporting documents.

[58] BGHZ 105, 324 '*Supermarkt*'; see also Schmidt, *Gesellschaftsrecht*, § 38 III 2b.

[59] See for details about the discussion Schmidt, *Gesellschaftsrecht* , § 39 III 3a.

[60] Raiser, *Recht der Kapitalgesellschaften*, § 33 para. 48.

in qualified de facto groups. The ordinary de facto group differs from a dependency relationship insofar as the dependent company is placed under the uniform management of the controlling undertaking in such a group. The rules relating to dependency relationships and ordinary de facto groups contained in paragraphs 311–318 AktG, which are applicable when public companies are dependent companies, are inapplicable by way of analogy to a GmbH, because there are significant differences between these categories of companies.[61]

When a GmbH is a dependent company or a subsidiary in an ordinary de facto group, it is now generally thought that a controlling undertaking which holds shares in it has an enhanced duty of good faith in its relationship with the GmbH and its shareholders. It is forbidden from exercising any detrimental influences on the company unless all its shareholders agree[62] and there is no violation of the rules governing the maintenance of the company's capital contained in paragraph 30(1) GmbHG. Thus the controlling enterprise must not give prejudicial instructions to the shareholders of the dependent company, or misappropriate its corporate opportunities. If the controlling company breaches its duties, every minority shareholder in the dependent company has an action for default (*Unterlassungsklage*) against both the controlling and dependent companies. The controlling enterprises incur liability towards the dependent company if the former company violates its duties thereto. The minority shareholders may enforce the company's claim, provided the general meeting so resolves. Unsatisfied creditors of the dependent company may attach their claims for compensation in accordance with paragraphs 829 and 835 of the Civil Procedure Code without any need for such a meeting.

The complex rules contained in paragraphs 32a and 32b GmbHG which permit loans from shareholders granted at any time when the company is in need of capital to be treated in an a similar way to capital in the bankruptcy of the company, will sometimes be applicable when a GmbH is a dependent company in a de facto group. These rules are likely to be repealed in the near future. The provisions of paragraphs 51a and 51b concerning the shareholders' right to obtain information may also be applicable to the above-mentioned situation. Shareholders in a dependent

[61] Note Schmidt, *Gesellschaftsrecht*, § 39 I 2b; Raiser, *Recht der Kapitalgesellschaften*, § 53 paras. 7 and 46.

[62] BGHZ 65, 15 *ITT*; BGHZ 80,69 '*Süssen*'; BGHZ 89, 162 '*Hermann.Ogilvy*'; BGHZ 95, 330 '*Autokran*'.

GmbH may have the right to avoid resolutions passed by the general meeting of the company on the grounds set out in paragraph 243 AktG, which is applicable by way of analogy. They may have the right to withdraw from the company when there are important grounds for so doing, for example where they did not consent to the establishment of the dependency relationship.[63]

2. Qualified de facto groups

The concept of the qualified de facto group was formerly used in the case of closely integrated groups involving private companies (GmbHs). According to this concept, liability in a qualified *de facto* group depended on the application of the presumption that the lasting and comprehensive exercise of controlling influence by the controlling undertaking gave rise to the conclusion that insufficient attention was paid to the affairs of the dependent private company. In *TBB*[64] the German Supreme Court restricted a cause of action analogous to that permitted by paragraphs 302 and 303 AktG against the controlling shareholder of a company in such a closely integrated group, who was also a director of the company. In the *TBB* case, the Court held that, contrary to what it had said in its earlier judgment in the case of *Video*,[65] the lasting and comprehensive exercise of controlling influence by the controlling undertaking did not give rise to the presumption that insufficient attention was paid to the affairs of the dependent company. The plaintiff was required to particularise and give evidence of facts leading to the conclusion that the management of the company, in pursuing the interests of the group, had done harm to the interests of the company in a manner which was not susceptible to compensation by isolating individual transactions. However, a reduction in the burden of proof in particularising and giving evidence of relevant matters placed on the plaintiff would occur to the extent that the controlling undertaking, and not the plaintiff, was aware of the relevant facts and did not properly explain them. The Supreme Court emphasised in *TBB* that a controlling undertaking might avoid liability under paragraphs 302 and 303 AktG if the dependent companies used proper accounting methods.[66] Liability in the qualified *de facto*

[63] Raiser, *Recht der Kapitalgesellschaften*, § 52 para. 19. See also HGB, para. 118.
[64] BGHZ 122, 123.
[65] BGHZ 115, 187. The earlier cases in which the concept of the qualified *de facto* group was used, were BGHZ 93, 330 *Autokran* and BGHZ 107, 7 *Trefbau*.
[66] See for more details Schmidt, *Gesellschaftsrecht*, § 39 III 4.

group situation remedied the sacrifice of the interests of the dependent company by defective or improper management of a group.

3. The new concept of liability for causing insolvency

A new cause of action resulting in unlimited liability for a German private company's director was established in the German Supreme Court in *Bremer Vulkan*,[67] the decision in which has been followed in a number of subsequent cases.[68] In *Bremer Vulkan* the court held that the protection of a dependent GmbH against the wrongful acts of its shareholder should not take place in accordance with the analogous application of the rules contained in paragraphs 291–310 AktGG applicable to contractual groups, or those contained in paragraphs 311–317 applicable to de facto groups in which the dependent company was an AG. It should instead take place in accordance with other legal rules governing the maintenance of capital,[69] and the safeguarding of the company's continued existence (*Bestandsschutz*), which required proper consideration to be given to the affairs of the company.

The court found that no such consideration was given in a situation in which a company was rendered incapable of paying its debts because of the activities of its sole shareholder. The court also held that of the sole shareholder induced a dependent GmbH to place its funds in the central treasury of a group dominated by the shareholder, it was under an obligation to ensure that when disbursements were made from the funds adequate consideration should be given to the company's capacity to fulfil its obligations and continue in being. Failure to comply with this obligation should result in criminal liability for breach of trust. The Court did not accept a claim for causing insolvency in *Bremer Vulkan*.

A comprehensive justification of the new liability concept was given by the German *Bundesgerichtshof* in its decision in *KBV*,[70] in which the claim for causing insolvency was accepted. The Court found that the basic and indispensable precondition for the principle of limited liability provided for in paragraph 13(2) GmbH was the preservation of the company's assets for the preferential satisfaction of its creditors during the whole period of the company's existence. The company may not have a right to its continuance, but its termination must take

[67] BGHZ 149, 10. See F. Wooldridge, 'Controlling shareholders' liabilities in German private companies' (2005) 26 Co Law 285, and M. Shillig, 'The development of a new concept of creditor protection for German GmbHs' (2006) 27 Co Law 348.

[68] Which are to be considered in the text below.

[69] See paras. 30 and 31 GmbHG.

[70] BGHZ 151, 181.

place in an ordered procedure which guarantees the preferential availability of the property of the company for the satisfaction of its creditors.

The *Bundesgerichtshof* clarified the concept of liability for causing insolvency in two decisions in 2004. In the first of these two decisions, *Autohändler*,[71] the court held that an indirect shareholder who itself owned the shares in a private company which held all the shares in another such company which became insolvent might be held liable for causing insolvency if he transferred all the latter company's assets to himself or to another company in which he was a shareholder without giving adequate consideration to the company. A further precondition for imposing unlimited liability was the impossibility of being compensated by avoiding identifiable individual transactions. Furthermore, the court held that the shareholder could limit his liability if he could show by comparing the actual situation of the company with the hypothetical situation which should have resulted had the shareholder acted appropriately, it could be shown that the company had only suffered a small loss.

The court also considered the liability of an indirect shareholder in *Unterschlagung*[72] in 2004. In that case the court held that the concept of liability for causing insolvency was not based upon mismanagement but required a deliberate deprivation of the company's assets for non-operation purposes. It also found that the interference should be with assets which are actually available for the satisfaction of the unsecured creditors, in order to incur liability for causing insolvency.

It appears that, according to the relevant cases, there are two positive conditions for imposing liability for causing the company's insolvency, and one negative condition. The two positive requirements are that the shareholders must deprive the company of its assets without full consideration, and that such deprivation must inhibit the company's ability to pay its debts. The negative one is that the unlimited liability is only incurred if the loss cannot be fully compensated in accordance with paragraphs 30 and 31 GmbHG[73] or if the shareholder is unable to

[71] BGH II ZR 206/02 (*Autohändler*) [2005] ZIP 117.
[72] BGH II ZR 256/02 (*Unterschlagung*) [2005] ZIP 250.
[73] Paragraph 30(1) GmbHG provides that assets necessary to maintain the capital of a GmbH must not be distributed to its shareholders. According to para. 31(2) GmbHG, such distributions must be returned to the company.

demonstrate that, if he had acted lawfully, the company would not have become insolvent.

When a claim for causing insolvency is brought, this may result in the unlimited liability of those shareholders who consented to the interference with the company's assets. In insolvency proceedings, the claim must be brought by liquidators, but if insolvency proceedings are not initiated or are closed, every creditor may pursue his outstanding claims against the shareholder if execution against the company proves fruitless.[74]

It is thought that the concept of a qualified *de fact* group will no longer be employed by German courts. However, the rules set out in TBB,[75] concerning the burden of proof which have been explained above still appear to be valid. The plaintiff is thus requested to show a prejudicial interference with the company's assets by the shareholder. The onus is placed upon the latter to show that the loss caused by his actions did not occasion or contribute towards the downfall of the company, or that compensation may take place by avoiding specific transactions and that such compensation is appropriate.[76]

German law relating to the recently established concept of unlimited shareholder liability for causing the insolvency of a private company ('*Existenzvernichtungshaftung*') underwent some revision as the result of an important judgment of the Federal Supreme Court (BGH) of 16 July 2007 (II ZR 3/04, *Trihotel*). Such shareholder liability would in principle only be towards the company itself, and not towards its creditors. It will be based upon Article 826 of the German Civil Code (BGB), which imposes dialectal liability for damage caused intentionally, and in violation of good moral behaviour. It will constitute 'eine besondere Fallgruppe der sittenwidrigen vorsätzlichen Schädigung'. The requirement mentioned in certain earlier cases that unlimited shareholder liability is only incurred if the loss cannot be fully recovered under Article 31 and 30 GmbHG will no longer be applicable. ('§ 826 BGB sind gegenüber Erstattungsansprüchen aus §§ 31, 30 GmbHG nicht subsidiär Schadensersatzansprüche aus Existenzvernichtungshaftung gemäß § 826 BGB sind gegenüber Erstattungsansprüchen aus §§ 31, 30 GmbHG nicht subsidiär.')

[74] This was decided in *KBV*, BGHZ 151, 181. See Shillig, 'The development of a new concept', 351 fn. 351.

[75] Shillig, 'The development of a new concept', 350.

[76] *Ibid*, p. 350.

V. The new provisions of Italian law concerning groups of companies

The above provisions are contained in Chapter IX of Title V of Book V of the Civil Code, which relates to companies which are subject to the direction and control of their activities by another company or business entity. They attempt the systematic regulation of group relationships, and for this reason are considered separately before the definition of controlled and associated companies under Italian law receives detailed consideration. The relevant provisions of Italian law considered below are in certain respects less restrictive than the corresponding ones of German law.[77]

The requisite direction and coordination is presumed to exist when the requirements of Article 2497 *sexies* of the Civil Code are fulfilled, i.e. when the parent company is required to include the subsidiary company in consolidated accounts, or when the former company exercises control in the sense meant by Article 2359 of the Civil Code. According to this provision, such control is deemed to exist when the controlling company holds the majority of votes at the ordinary general meeting of the controlled company, or can exercise a dominant influence at such a meeting, or is in a position of control owing to certain contractual bonds with the controlled company. Furthermore, Article 2497 *septies* provides that the provisions of Chapter IX of Title V of Book V of the Civil Code apply to the exercise of activities of direction and coordination based upon a contract with the subsidiary company, or on a clause in its articles.[78] The new provisions of the Civil Code do not contain any formal definition of groups of companies, but like former versions of the Code, define certain related concepts.

The new legislation does not exhaustively define how the direction and coordination of activities may come about, and relies partly on presumptions. According to Article 2497(1), a company or entity which exercises an activity of direction and coordination in another company and which acts against the entrepreneurial interests of that company, or otherwise in violation of the principles of correct company and entrepreneurial management,[79] is directly responsible to the members of

[77] The Italian courts have not developed any concept comparable to that of the qualified *de facto* group.

[78] It appears somewhat controversial whether contractual groups are generally recognised in the Italian legal order: see D. Santosuosso, *Il nuovo diritto societario* (D&G *diritto e guistizia supp. al Fasi*), p. 118.

[79] These concepts are undefined. It is not clear what is meant by entrepreneurial interest.

the subsidiary company for any resulting loss of income or loss of the value of their shares. Problems of causation may arise in proving such losses, and perhaps a diminution in the value of shares. Article 2497(1) also makes the directing and coordinating company liable to the creditors of the subsidiary company for damage caused to the integrity of the assets of the company. The granting of such direct rights of action may be controversial. There are certain parallels for a direct action by creditors in German law.[80]

According to Article 2497(2) of the Italian Civil Code, persons who have taken part in wrongful acts which have damaged the subsidiary incur joint liability with the parent company for damages suffered by it. Persons who consciously benefit from such acts are also liable within the limits of the advantages obtained by them. Members and creditors are only allowed to take action against the parent company or entity if they cannot obtain satisfaction from the subsidiary, which is subject to its control and coordination. The provisions of Article 2497(4) are applicable to the situation in which the subsidiary company which is subject to the direction and coordination of its activities by another company or entity is bankrupt, in compulsory administrative liquidation or extraordinary administration (*liquidation coatta amministrativa o amministrazione straordinaria*). In such an event, the action which belongs to the creditors of the subsidiary is brought on their behalf by the administrator (*curatore*) or by the liquidating or extraordinary administration committee (*commissario liquidatore o commissario straordinario*).

Article 2497 *bis* contains important publicity provisions. The subsidiary company must indicate its subjection to the direction and coordination of another company in its transactions and correspondence, and must also indicate such subjection in a special section of the Register of Enterprises: the parent company must also appear in this section.

Directors who fail to comply with the above requirements, or who maintain a record indicating that the subjection already indicated exists when in fact it has ended, are responsible for the damage caused to members or to third parties by reason of their failure to be aware of the relevant facts. The fourth paragraph of Article 2497 *bis* provides that the subsidiary company must insert a summary account of the essential

[80] A direct action is given to the creditors of integrated companies within the meaning of paras. 319, 320 and 322 of the German Public Limited Liability Companies Act. Such integration is only possible when the parent company owns 95 per cent of the share capital of the subsidiary.

particulars contained in the last balance sheet of the parent company in an appropriate part of its notes on its accounts (*nota integrativa*). The final paragraph of Article 2497 *bis* provides that the directors of the subsidiary company must include in their annual report details of its relationships with the parent company, and with other companies subject to the latter's direction and coordination. The report must also contain details as to how the relationship with the parent company has affected the exercise of the subsidiary's business, and its results.

Furthermore, Article 2497 *ter* provides that any decision of the subsidiary company which has been affected by the influence of the parent company shall be explained in detail, and reasons given for it. According to Article 2497 *ter*, such decisions would have to be mentioned in the annual report required by Article 2428.

The provisions of Article 2497 *quater*, which provides for a right of withdrawal from a subsidiary company under certain circumstances, may be found controversial in certain other jurisdictions. This right is given to shareholders in the subsidiary company under three circumstances. The first of these is where the company has converted itself into a company of another type and this involves a change in its purpose; and where it has changed the provisions of its objects concerning the carrying on of business activities in a way that alters the economic and assets position of the subsidiary company in a perceptible and direct manner. The second of these is where a member of the subsidiary company has obtained a judgment from a court pronouncing that the parent company has exercised its rights of direction and coordination in a manner which results in liability under Article 2497. Finally, the third situation in which withdrawal is possible is when the activity of direction and coordination begins and ends; such withdrawal is not possible where the subsidiary company is a public one which is listed on a regulated market.

If a subsidiary company makes loans to the parent company which is responsible for the direction and coordination of its activities or to another company subject to direction and coordination of its activities by the same parent company, the provisions of Article 2467 governing loans by shareholders to a private company are made applicable to such loans by Article 2497 *quinquies* of the Civil Code. The provision on loans by shareholders, which may suffer from drafting difficulties, stipulates that:

> the repayment of loans from shareholders (*finanzimenti di soci*) to the company is postponed until other creditors are satisfied, and if such a loan

> is repaid by the company within one year before the commencement of bankruptcy, the payment must be restored to the company
>
> For the purposes of the previous paragraph, loans from shareholders mean loans, in whatever form granted, made at a time at which regard being paid to the type of activity carried on by the company, they result in an excessive disequilibrium between debts in comparison with the net assets, or at which the situation of the company is such that the reasonable approach would have been to make a contribution for shares.

The requirement of reasonability is likely to give rise to some difficulties. There are somewhat similar provisions in paragraphs 32a and 32b of the German *GmbH Gesetz*, which are likely to be repealed. The Italian provisions are likely to require further elucidation by the courts.

It is interesting to compare the Italian willingness to legislate in the field of groups of companies with the reluctance so far displayed in this matter of the United Kingdom to do so. The Italian provisions appear to some extent influenced by German law: the German concept of *einheitliche Leitung* or uniform management used in paragraph 18(1) of the German *Aktiengesetz* appears to resemble the Italian concept of *esercita l'attivata di direzione e coordinamente* (exercise of the activities of direction and coordination). The recent Commission Communication on Modernising Company Law suggests that a proposal for a Framework Directive on the implementation of a group policy may be presented in the near future, which will provide for the protection of the interests of a group company's creditors and for the existence of a fair balance of advantage for such a company's creditors. The Italian legislation attempts to achieve these aims, and it remains to be seen to what extent they will be achieved, and to what extent further legislation might be necessary for such achievement. The relevant legislation is somewhat complex and certain at least of its provisions would seem to be of most use to more sophisticated members and creditors: other such persons may well remain unaware of the opportunities given to them by them, or lack sufficient confidence to invoke them.

VI. Definition of groups of companies and related concepts

A. The position in the United Kingdom

General definitions of a 'subsidiary', 'holding company', 'parent company' and 'wholly owned subsidiary' appear in sections 1159 and 1162 of the Companies Act 2006. Additional provisions relating to the meaning of a subsidiary are contained in Schedule 6 to the Act. Schedule 7 includes supplementary provisions concerning parent and subsidiary undertakings. The 2006 Act does not give a general definition of a group, but section 1161(5) defines a group undertaking. The 2006 Act does not define the concept of a 'participating interest', which is used in the Fourth Company Law Directive, or that of a 'significant shareholding'.

It follows from section 1159 of the Companies Act 2006 that a company is treated as being a subsidiary company of another company, its holding company, if that company controls it in any of four ways, namely:

(a) holds a majority of the voting rights in it;
(b) is a member of it and has the right to appoint or remove a majority of its board of directors; or
(c) is a member of it and controls it alone, pursuant to an agreement with other shareholders and members, a majority of the voting rights in it; or
(d) is a subsidiary of a company which is itself a subsidiary of that other company.

The general definitions contained in sections 1159 and 1162 (parent and subsidiary undertakings) are supplemented by Schedules 6 and 7. Thus, for example, voting rights in a company are defined in paragraph 2 of both schedules, as the rights conferred on shareholders in respect of their shares, or in the case of companies not having a share capital, on the members, to vote at general meetings of the company on all or on substantially all matters. Rights which are only exercisable in limited circumstances, only have to be taken in account when the circumstances have arisen and for so long as they continue to obtain, or when the circumstances are within the control of the person having the rights. The reference to the right to appoint or remove a majority of the board in sections 1159 and 1162 is said in Schedules 6 and 7 paragraph 3(1) to be to the right to appoint or remove directors holding the majority of the voting rights on all or substantially all matters. The holding company's power to appoint or remove may be based upon voting power at general meetings, provisions of the memorandum and articles of the subsidiary, or of a contract between the holding company and the subsidiary.

The Companies Act 2006, unlike the predecessors, does not contain any definitions of parent and subsidiary companies for the purpose of group accounts. However, section 405 permit subsidiary undertakings to be excluded from consolidation in certain circumstances.

B. The position in France

There is no general definition of groups of companies under French law, but there are general ones of subsidiaries, participations and control. According to Article L233-1 of the new Commercial Code, when one company holds more than one-half of the capital of another company, the latter may be said to be its subsidiary. When a company holds between 10 and 50 per cent of the capital of another company, it is treated as having a participation therein.[81] Furthermore, by Article L233-3-(1) of the new Commercial Code, a company is treated as controlling another in the following circumstances. These are where:

(a) it directly or indirectly holds a fraction of the latter company's capital conferring on it the majority of votes at general meetings of the company;
(b) it possesses the majority of the voting rights in the company by virtue of an agreement concluded with the other shareholders which is not contrary to the company's interests;
(c) when it has the de facto power, by exercising the votes it disposes of, of determining the results of the vote at general meetings of the company.

    A company is presumed to have such a power if it directly or indirectly disposes of more than 40 per cent of the voting rights in another company, and no other company directly or indirectly holds a larger percentage of such shares.

Exclusive control is said to exist in different circumstances in Article L233-16 of the Commercial Code, which implements many of the requirements of Article 1 of the Seventh Directive in France. This provision also contains a definition of joint control and significant influence. The former is said to be the division of control over a common enterprise between a limited number of persons in such a way that decisions with respect to the enterprise result from their common agreement. A significant influence over the management and financial policy of an enterprise is presumed to exist when a company directly or indirectly holds at least 20 per cent of the voting rights in that enterprise.

[81] French Commercial Code, Art. L233-2.

C. The position in Germany

The use of the concept of the group and related concepts in Germany has been thoroughly discussed above. It has been suggested that the relevant German legal provisions are probably not suitable for general transplantation elsewhere.

Paragraph 290 of the German Commercial Code contains certain definitions of groups for the purpose of imposing the obligation to prepare consolidated accounts and a consolidated annual report on the situation of the group on the parent or controlling company. The obligation exists where there is a vertical group in which the controlling undertaking is a capital company (i.e. an A.G., GmbH or KGaA) having its registered office in Germany, and which has one or more dependent undertakings under its uniform management, provided that the controlling company has a participating interest in such undertakings. A similar obligation is placed on a capital company having its registered office in Germany which has the majority of the voting rights in another undertaking; or which is a member of another undertaking and which has the right to appoint or dismiss the majority of the members of its management or supervisory board; or which has the right, to exercise a dominant influence on another undertaking pursuant to a control contract, or by reason of a provision in its statutes. Thus, the requirement to produce consolidated accounts depends not only upon the application of the German concept of uniform management, but also upon that of the Anglo-Saxon concept of control.

D. The position in Italy

As already indicated there appears to be no definition of a group of Companies under Italian law However, Article 2359(1) of the Italian Civil Code defines controlled and associated companies. This provision stipulates that there are three categories of controlled companies. These are:

(i) companies in which another company holds the majority of votes that can be exercised at the ordinary shareholders' meeting;
(ii) companies in which another company has sufficient votes to exercise a dominant influence at the ordinary shareholders' meeting; and
(iii) companies which are under the dominant influence of another company by reason of particular contractual arrangements with it.

Article 2359 also provides that companies are considered as associated where one of them can exercise a significant influence on another. This influence is presumed to occur whenever one company can exercise at least one-fifth the votes, at an ordinary shareholders' meeting of another company. This requirement is reduced to at least one tenth of the votes if the company has shares listed on the stock exchange.

The criteria for treatment as controlled enterprises in the case of the imposition of the requirement to draw up consolidated accounts on controlling companies and certain other entities which is imposed by Article 25 of Legislative Decree No. 127 of April 9, 1991 are different from those employed in Article 2359(1) of the Civil Code. Article 26 of the Decree requires that for the purpose of consolidated accounts, controlled enterprises do not only include the first two categories of enterprises mentioned in Article 2359(1), but in addition two further categories of enterprises. These include:

(i) enterprises over which another enterprise has the right, by virtue of a contract, or a clause in the articles, to exercise a dominating influence, when applicable law permits such contracts or clauses; and
(ii) enterprises in which a shareholder pursuant to an agreement with other shareholders, controls by himself a majority of voting rights.

A similar definition of a controlled enterprise is employed in Article 93 of Decree No. 58 of 24 February 1998 (which contains rules governing financial intermediaries). Article 93 is applicable to Italian or foreign companies where shares are quoted on a regulated market.

E. The position in Spain

Spanish law now contains a concept of group of companies in Article 42 of the Commercial Code.[82] The reform of Article 42 by Law 16/2007 has moved from the concept of a group as a decision making unit to focus on the control a company has, direct or indirectly, over other companies. Article 42 concerns accounting and determines when a company must present consolidated accounts. However, this article establishes a general legal concept of group of companies, and other legislation makes reference to it. Such reference is made in Article 10(2) of the LSRL, permitting a private limited liability company to grant credits, loans, guarantees or other financial assistance to companies in the same group; in Article 87

[82] This Article has been amended by Law 16/2007. Spanish law did not previously contain an entirely clear concept of groups. This was much criticised, see for instance F. Vicent Chuliá, *Introducción al Derecho Mercantil*, 14th edn (Valencia: Tirant lo Blanch, 2001), p. 579.

of the LSA, on restrictions on the purchase by public companies of their own shares or the purchase of the shares of the parent company by a subsidiary; and, finally, in Article 4 of Law 24/1988 on the securities market, as amended by Law 47/2007.

According to Article 42 of the Commercial Code, a group of companies exists when a company possesses or can possess, direct or indirectly, the control over another company or other companies. Such control exists when:

(a) the dominant company holds the majority of the voting rights;
(b) the dominant company has the power to appoint or remove the majority of the directors;
(c) the dominant company may have the majority of the voting rights as a result of agreements with third parties;
(d) the dominant company had nominated with its votes the majority of the directors who were in charge at the moment of consolidated accounts must be prepared and who have served during the two previous financial years.

There were previously two principal definitions of a group of companies under Spanish law, but further definitions existed for fiscal and other purposes. The definition contained in Article 42 of the Commercial Code, which resulted from the Spanish implementation of the accounting directives, has had its influence elsewhere, for example in Article 10(2) of the LSRL and in Article 87 of the LSA, which is concerned with restrictions on the purchase of shares in such companies. According to Article 42 of the Commercial Code, companies are deemed to form part of the same group when any one company (the controlling company) meets certain criteria with respect to another company. These are that it possesses the majority of the voting rights; or has the power to appoint or remove the majority of the directors; or indirectly, by reason of agreements with other shareholders, commands a majority of the voting rights; or actually appoints, in certain circumstances, a majority of the directors by its sole vote even though it (the controlling company) does not by itself directly or indirectly hold a majority of the voting rights.[83] Article 87 of the LSA

[83] Before the 2007 reform, Article 42 of the Commercial Code gave rise to uncertainties. It apparently applied to the majority of members of the board who are serving when the consolidated accounts must be prepared, and who have served during the two previous financial years: see Seventh Directive, Art. 1(1)(d)(aa) and Dorresteijn *et al.*, *European Corporate Law*, para. 9.34.

on public companies' purchase of own shares, providing, inter alia, that a company is presumed to be is controlling one if its relationship to the acquiring company falls within the categories then enumerated in Article 82 of the Commercial Code.[84]

The second principal definition of a group of companies was contained in Article 4 of Law 24/1988 of 28 July 1988 on the securities market, apparently influenced both by the concept of control and the German one of the *de facto* group. This provision stipulated that for the purposes of the Act, entities which constituted a decision making unit because one of them controls or can control, directly or indirectly the decisions of the others, were deemed to belong to the same group. It also contained provisions stipulating when control was deemed to exist. The concept of a group as a decision making unit was developed by academic writers and by the Spanish courts. There were some unclear features in this method of defining a group: it was uncertain what was meant by a decision making unit and (as is the case with the term enterprise, used in German legislation) what is meant by an entity.[85] Although the concept of a group of companies (as opposed to that of a controlling company) was not defined in Spanish company legislation before the reform of Article 42 of the Commercial Code by Law 16/2007, it was already used, for instance in the 1995 law governing private companies (LSRL). Paragraph 10(1) of LSRL permits a limited liability company to grant credits, loans, guarantees or other financial assistance to companies in the same group. The lack of an entirely consistent or systematic regulation of groups of companies in Spain was deplored by academic commentators, and there was strong support for reform which eventually took place in 2007.[86]

F. The position in Belgium

Belgian company law does not contain any definition of a group of companies. Such a definition exists for the purposes of tax law. However, it contains definitions of control, common control and of a parent company and a subsidiary. According to Article 5(1) of the Companies Code of 7 May 1999, control is defined as the power to

[84] This article was included in the Spanish law in implementation of the accounting Directives: see Dorresteijn *et al.*, *European Corporate Law*, paras. 9–31.

[85] Note in this sense, Dorresteijn *et al.*, *European Corporate Law*, paras. 9.34.

[86] Vicent Chuliá, *Introducción al Derecho Mercantil*, p. 579.

exercise a decisive influence on the appointment of the majority of the directors or managers, or on the orientation of the company's policy. It follows from Article 6 of the Code, that a company which exercises such control is a parent company, and a company subject to it is a subsidiary. According to Article 7(1), powers held indirectly through the medium of a subsidiary are treated in the same way as powers held directly for the purposes of determining whether control exists.

Control may be according to law, or of a de facto character. The only difference between the two situations is that in the former case, it is irrebuttably presumed to exist in accordance with Article 5(2) of the Code, which enumerates five cases in which such an irrebuttable presumption arises. These are:

(a) where it results from the holding of the majority of the votes attached to all the shares or rights issued by the company in question;
(b) when a member has the right to appoint or dismiss the majority of the company's directors or managers;
(c) when a member has a right to control the company by reason of the provisions of its articles, or agreements concluded with it;
(d) when a member disposes of the majority of the voting rights attached to all the shares or rights issued by the company as the result of agreements with other members thereof; and
(e) in the event of common control.

Article 5(3) of the Code provides that de facto control may arise from other circumstances. A member is presumed, subject to proof to the contrary, to dispose of such control over a company if at the last two general meetings of the company, he has exercised the majority of the votes attached to the securities represented at these meetings. In a large company, de facto control may arise from a minority shareholding if sufficient persons abstain from voting.

According to Articles 109 and 110 of the Companies Code, Belgian parent companies will be required to establish consolidated accounts in respect of subsidiary enterprises which they control or control jointly, unless they fall within one of the exemptions from consolidation contained in Articles 112 and 113. Subsidiary enterprises include:

(a) Belgian or foreign subsidiary companies;
(b) economic interest groupings having their registered office in Belgium or elsewhere; and

(c) organisations governed by Belgian or foreign law, whether of a public character or not, and whether or not their object is the making of profits, which, whether or not this is by reason of the tasks entrusted to them by their statutes, carry on a commercial, financial or industrial objective.

The definition of subsidiary enterprises seems to be a largely descriptive one, which does not make it entirely clear how it will be possible to determine whether an enterprise is a subsidiary one, unless this is a company.

Associated companies are defined in Article 12 of the Companies Code. Consortia are dealt with by Article 10(1) of the Companies Code. They are said to exist when one company and one or more companies governed by Belgian or foreign law are centrally directed without being subsidiaries of one another or of another company.[87] Article 13 of the Companies Code defines what is meant by a participation, which was formerly only defined under accounting law. Subject to proof to the contrary, a participation is presumed to exist in the event of a direct or indirect holding[88] of 10 per cent of more of the company's capital, or of a class of shares therein. A participation is also deemed to exist, subject to proof to the contrary, when the disposal of the shares or the exercise of the rights appertaining thereto are subject to contractual arrangements or unilateral commitments to which the company has subscribed.

It will be noted that the definition of a subsidiary company in Belgian company law is the same for accounting as for other purposes. The definition of a subsidiary company is based on what are generally speaking precise concepts.

G. *The position in the Netherlands*

The definitions of subsidiaries, groups and participations under Dutch company law are contained in Articles 24a–24d of Book II of the Civil

[87] The consolidation of accounts by consortia is dealt with by Art. 111 of the Belgian Companies Code. These accounts must include the companies forming the consortium and their subsidiary enterprises.

[88] I.e. through a subsidiary. Participation is more generally defined in Art. 13 of the Belgian Companies Code as existing when companies have shareholdings in others which are intended through the establishment of a durable and specific link with such companies, to exercise influence on the orientation of the management thereof.

Code. They apply generally to all legal persons but not to Dutch partnerships, and were incorporated in the Code as the result of the implementation of the Fourth and Seventh Directives. Thus the definition of subsidiaries applies for the purpose of consolidated accounts as well as for other purposes.

A subsidiary is defined in Article 24a-1 as a legal person in which a parent company may exercise more than half of all the voting rights at a general meeting, of the shareholders, or can appoint or dismiss more than one-half of the management or supervisory board, on the assumption that all the votes are cast. The parents rights may be exercised alone or jointly with subsidiaries, and may originate from a shareholders agreement. A general or limited partnership in which a company or one or more of its subsidiaries has unlimited liability towards creditors is deemed to be a subsidiary of such a company.[89]

A group is defined in Article 24b of Book II as an economic unit in which legal persons and partnerships are united in one organisation. The definition is of an economic nature, and uses a concept apparently similar but clearly not identical with the German one of unified management, i.e. being united in one organisation. Majority control is apparently sufficient for this to exist.

According to Article 24c of Book II, a participation exists where a legal person or a partnership has for its own account, either directly or through one or more subsidiaries, a capital contribution in another company with the object of a long-term relationship with that company in furtherance of its own business activities. Contributions consisting of one-fifth or more of the issued capital create the rebuttable presumption of a participation. A company participates in a partnership if it or its subsidiary is, as a partner, fully liable to its creditors or has as its objective a long term relationship with that partnership in furtherance of its own business activities.

It has been found necessary to define the phrase 'dependent company' for the purpose of the provisions relating to large public and private companies. Such a company is defined in a rather similar way to a subsidiary, as a legal person in which the company or any of its dependent companies, solely or jointly, and on their own account, contributes at least half the share capital.[90]

[89] Dutch Civil Code Book 2, Art. 24a-1. [90] *Ibid.*, Arts. 2.152 and 2.262.

VII. Group liability

Subsidiaries are often used for the purpose of limiting liability. Under English law, the directors of a parent company owe no duties to its subsidiaries,[91] and those of a subsidiary of a company owe no duties to the parent company.[92] It is possible for group liability to be voluntarily assumed. This takes place under a control contract, and would take place under the type of revocable declaration envisaged by the proposals of *Forum Europaeum Konzernrecht*,[93] and under the very guarded proposals contained in chapter 10 of DTI's Consultative Document, *Modern Company Law For a Competitive Economy: Completing the Structure*, which proposes an elective group regime for wholly owned subsidiaries, having the effect of exempting such subsidiaries from the preparation of annual accounts and audit.[94] The Consultative Document does not tackle the question of group liability in a detailed manner or positive sense. The caution of the approach is paralleled by the similar caution displayed by the English courts when asked to open the corporate veil. The whole matter of group liability appears to need thorough re-examination in the United Kingdom.

The voluntary assumption of group liability through a system of cross-guarantees is familiar in all the Member States considered in this work. Under such a system, the parent and all the subsidiaries in the group may assume liability for each others and the whole group indebtedness. Such cross-guarantees may have a prejudicial affect on the subsidiaries themselves, and on their minority shareholders.

In all the Member States in question, the courts will sometimes open the corporate veil with the consequence that a parent undertaking will be responsible for the subsidiary's debts. The veil of incorporation is commonly opened in US jurisdictions. However, the English Courts should

[91] *Lindgren* v. *L and P Estates Ltd* [1968] Ch 572. [92] *Bell* v. *Lever Bros* [1932] AC 161.

[93] '*Konzernrecht für Europa*' [1998] ZGR 672, 740–42. Such a declaration would have rather similar consequences to the conclusion of a control contract, except insofar as the rights of creditors were concerned.

[94] Such an exemption is possible under s. 57 of the Fourth Company Law Directive, as amended by the Seventh Company Law Directive. One of the conditions of such an exemption is that the parent company guarantees the subsidiaries' debts.

The Steering Group's proposals were abandoned in the final Report. They are somewhat timid, and would have done little to help the contract and tort creditors of subsidiary companies. Note in this context, A. J. Boyle, 'The Company Law Review and Group Liability' (2002) 23 Co Law 35.

a reluctance to open the corporate veil in *Adams* v. *Cape Industries*,[95] but indicated that this might be done where a subsidiary was formed for an improper motive. Opening the corporate veil would seem to be more readily admitted in France and Spain than in the United Kingdom: however, in Spain it does not always lead to the parent company being made liable for the subsidiary company's debts. In France a parent company may become liable for its subsidiary's debts, or the liquidation of one of these companies may be extended to the other where the assets of these two companies have been commingled,[96] or where the subsidiary's legal personality is of a fictitious character,[97] or where the parent and subsidiary company have appeared to outsiders to form a single legal entity.[98]

The veil will be lifted where the assets and affairs of the parent and subsidiary have been commingled, and for other reasons (for example because the subsidiary is being used to perpetrate a fraud) in other jurisdictions. In Spain, a parent company may be made liable for the subsidiary's debts where the latter is under capitalised. Much has been made of the concept of undercapitalisation by certain US jurisdictions. The concept of capitalisation by means of loans is of importance in the law governing German private companies,[99] and could be invoked in the group context in order to make a parent enterprise contribute to its subsidiary's debts in bankruptcy. However, it has never been used for this purpose in the United Kingdom.

A parent company's liability for its subsidiary debts may be based upon such familiar concepts as agency or tort in most of the Member States. In the United Kingdom case of *Cape Industries*, the Appeal Court confirmed the possibility that a subsidiary might be treated as the agent of its holding company. A Dutch parent company which acts as a director of its subsidiary may be held liable in tort towards the subsidiary's creditors by reason of a breach of duty of care towards them, if it permitted the subsidiary to incur debts when it was aware that the claims of the creditors of the subsidiary would remain unsatisfied.[100]

95 [1990] Ch 433.

96 See the judgment of the Supreme Court (*Cour de Cassation*) in *Société Immobilière et Financière du Parc* v. *Bitsch*, Gaz Pal 1958/1, 150; *Revue Trimestrielle du droit commercial* 1958, note by Houin.

97 See *Pilon* v. *SA Phillipe Pain et Vermorel*, Pares, 12 November 1962, RD 1962, 648 (note by Verdier) for a case in which this conclusion was reached.

98 See *Société Lambourn* v. *Varounis*, Req 20, November 1922 DS-1926, 1-305.

99 German Private Limited Liability Companies Act, paras. 32a and 32b. These provisions are likely to be repealed.

100 Judgment of 19 February 1988, HR 1988, NJ No. 487.

Furthermore, if a parent company has involved itself to a considerable extent in its subsidiary's affairs without having proper regard to the interests of the creditors, it may incur tortious liability even if it is not a director of the subsidiary.[101] The Dutch case law on the liability of parent companies towards the creditors of their subsidiaries is complex, and is also based upon the analogical application of general rules of civil law, in areas either than tort, including rules governing non-contractual promises, the Paulian action and accounting standards.

In Germany, it follows from ITT and a number of subsequent cases that a controlling undertaking which holds shares in a dependent GmbH has an enhanced duty of good faith in all its relationships with the GmbH and its shareholders. It may not exercise any detrimental influence on that company unless all the shareholders agree thereto,[102] and there is no violation of the rules concerning the maintenance of capital. Thus, the controlling company must not give prejudicial instructions to the shareholders of the dependent company, or misappropriate its corporate opportunities. If the controlling company violates its duties, every minority shareholder in the dependent company has an action for discontinuance (*Unterlassungsklage*) against both the controlling and dependent companies. Furthermore, the controlling company incurs liability to the dependent company if the former violates its duties thereto. The minority shareholders may enforce the company's claim. Furthermore, the unsatisfied creditors of the dependent company may attach their claims for compensation against the controlling company in accordance with paragraphs 829 and 835 of the Civil Procedure Code.

Group liability may arise under English law where the parent company has been required to pay a contribution equal to the whole or part of a subsidiary company's debts in its liquidation because the parent company has taken part in the management with the intention of defrauding creditors, or the creditors of another person, or for any other fraudulent purpose,[103] or because the parent company has acted as the shadow director of its subsidiary and has been guilty of wrongful trading.[104]

[101] The action is brought for abuse of power by the controlling shareholder of the company. There are a number of relevant decisions': see, e.g. judgment of 18 November 1994, HR 1995, NJ No. 170.

[102] BGHZ 65, 15 '*ITT*'; BGHZ 80, 69 '*Süssen*'; BGHZ 89, 162 '*Hermann/Ogilvy*'; BGHZ 95, 130 '*Autokran*'.

[103] Insolvency Act 1986, s. 213(1) and (2).

[104] *Ibid.*, ss. 214(1), (2), (3) and (7).

A person who was a director or shadow director[105] of a company and who some time before the commencement of the winding knew or ought to have concluded that the company would go into insolvent liquidation, and who failed to take every step which would have minimised potential loss to the creditors which he ought to have done, may be ordered by the court on the application of the liquidator, to make such contributions to the assets of the company as it deems fit. The onus is placed on the director to prove that he did not either negligently fail to recognise that the company would go into insolvent liquidation or endeavour to take steps which would have minimised the losses of the creditors. The liability which is imposed on shadow directors by section 214 of the Insolvency Act 1986 is rather similar to that imposed on the *diregeant de fait* in accordance with the *action en comblement du passif* under Article 180 of the French law of 5 January 1985 and under Articles 265 and 530 of the Belgian Companies Code of 1999.[106] This action arises in the event of insolvent liquidation, and penalises misconduct by the management which has given rise to the insolvency of the company, and which is thus in part responsible for the deficit. The culpable wrong does not consist in delaying a winding up which is inevitable, as under English law,[107] but is rather the directors' failure to perform the duties which require to be performed in the interests of the company. However, account may be taken of the directors conduct after the financial crisis has arisen, and before the onset of the liquidation proceedings.

A parent company in a group which exercises power over the decisions of a subsidiary and over its commercial and financial activities to such an extent as to reduce the management of the subsidiary to the role of merely carrying out the instructions of the parent company may be

[105] Companies Act 1985, s. 741(2), where a shadow director (which may include a parent company) is defined as any person in accordance with those directions or instructions the directors are a accustomed to act: see *Hydrodam (Corby) Ltd* [1994] 2 BCLC 180.

[106] Note also the liability imposed on de facto directors of a Netherlands private or public company whose bankruptcy (liquidation) is to a significant extent caused by apparent negligence on the part of the management board within the three year period prior to the bankruptcy, by Book 2, Arts. 138 and 248 of the Netherlands Civil Code.

[107] Directors may become personally liable to creditors under German law for delaying winding up, *Konkursverschleppung*), but it appears that the English provisions have a greater effect than the German provisions, as they take affect at an earlier stage in the descent towards insolvency. Note in this context, the Forum Europaeum Konzernrecht, '*Konzernrecht für Europa*', (1988) 27 ZGR 689, p 754. The English translation, Forum Europaeum Corporate Group Law, 'Corporate Group Law for Europe', is published in 1 EBOR (2000) 165.

treated as a *dirigeant de fait* under French and Belgian law. There is a similarity between these criteria and those which apply to an English shadow director. The concept of a shadow director is not completely unfamiliar to German and Spanish law.

The *Forum Europaeum Konzernrecht* made two proposals concerning the liability of the parent company in the event of its subsidiary being unable to escape winding up by means of its own resources. The first of these is closely related to English, French and Belgian law, and would provide that in the above circumstances, the parent company would be obliged to carry out a fundamental restructuring or initiate the winding-up procedure. If it failed to do so, the parent company would be liable to the subsidiary company in liquidation for the losses caused to all creditors by the said acts. In such an event, it would be presumed that the parent knew or ought to have known that the subsidiary company had arrived at a crisis point. The second proposal, is exactly the same as the first one, except insofar as it is contingent on the parent company having instructed the management of a subsidiary to act in accordance with a commercial policy in the interests of the group. This proposal, which is said to be based upon the *Rozenblum* concept of the group, would lead to the relevant liabilities being imposed in only limited circumstances.

A. *Special provisions protecting creditors*

In addition to the rules governing liability which have been described above, the United Kingdom insolvency laws often contain provisions protecting creditors which may be of relevance to creditors of subsidiaries. Thus, for example the Insolvency Act 1986 contains provisions governing transactions at an undervalue and preferences which may be used for the purpose of impugning certain transactions between a subsidiary and a parent company. The relevant provisions have a less far-reaching effect than the proposals of the Cork Committee that, on the winding up of a company, those of its liabilities whether secured or unsecured which are owed to connected persons or companies, and which appear to the court to form part of the long term capital structure of the company, should be deferred to the claims of other creditors. There appears to be considerable merit in this recommendation,[108] but far reaching, UK legislation governing the liabilities of a parent company seems unlikely in the near future.

[108] The Cork Report (Report of the Insolvency Law Review Committee) (1982 Cmnd 8558), para. 1936.

Where a subsidiary company is the subject of an administration order or goes into liquidation, the administrator or liquidator is empowered by section 238(2) of the Insolvency Act 1986, to make application to the court to set aside a transaction as a transaction at an undervalue or a preference. A transaction at an undervalue is defined in rather broad terms in section 238(4). By section 238(5), the court may not make an order setting aside a transaction at an undervalue if it is satisfied that the company entered into it in good faith, and for the purpose of carrying on its business and that at the time it did so, there were reasonable grounds for thinking that the transaction would benefit the company. The provisions of section 239(1)–(3) governing preferences, resemble those of section 238(1)–(3) governing transactions. Preferences are also rather broadly defined in section 239(1) of the Insolvency Act 1986.

In cases in which the transaction at an undervalue is with a person connected with the company at a time in the period of two years ending with the onset of insolvency, the transaction is presumed (in accordance with the provisions of section 240(2)) either to have been at a time when the company was unable to pay its debts within the meaning of section 123 of the Insolvency Act 1986, or at a time when it became so incapable by reason of the transfer. Parent and subsidiary companies are treated as connected persons within the meaning of sections 219 and 435 of the Insolvency Act 1986. The effect of section 240(2) is to cast the burden on the parent of proving that the subsidiary was solvent at the time of the transaction. When the subsidiary is alleged to have given a preference to its parent company, a similar onus will be placed on the parent company to show that the subsidiary lacked any intention to prefer.

B. Minority shareholder protection

The detailed rules of the Member States considered in the present work are quite complex, and only a brief outline of them can be attempted. As is the case with the rules contained in sections 994–995 of the Companies Act 2006 concerning unfairly prejudicial conduct, or those available in most Member States permitting shareholders to challenge company resolutions on certain grounds, such rules are not necessarily applicable only to the group situation.

Most textwriters correctly state that one of the principal problems minority shareholders in a group of companies experience is lack of information about the management.[109] In Germany, the shareholders

[109] Note in this context, Dorresteijn *et al.*, *European Corporate Law*, para. 9.49.

in a private company have the right to be informed about the affairs of the company by the managers, and are also permitted to examine the company's books and records. Such information and examination may be refused if there is reason to believe that the shareholder intends to use it for purposes foreign to those of the company, and may thus cause it or a connected company, significant harm. The general meeting has to decide whether such information shall be refused, and its decision may be challenged by the relevant shareholders in the competent court.[110]

Shareholders in German public companies are entitled to be given information about the affairs of their company by the management board insofar as such information is necessary to permit a proper evaluation of items on the agenda of a general meeting. This duty to provide information extends to the company's legal and business relations with any commercial enterprise. The grounds for refusing information are much wider than in the case of private companies. In other jurisdictions, the right to receive information is generally conferred upon the general meeting rather than individual shareholders, and a certain percentage of the shareholders are given the right to call a general meeting.

Thus for example, under Article 2367 of the Italian Civil Code the holders of one-tenth of the company's share capital or the lesser amount provided for in the articles may require the directors to convene a general meeting, and may specify the items to be included on the agenda. The required percentage is lower in other jurisdictions: thus in the German AG the holders of 5 per cent or such lower percentage as may be specified in the articles [111] may call a special shareholders meeting.[112] The required percentage is 10 per cent in the case of a German GmbH,[113] which is the same as that required in the Netherlands[114] and the United Kingdom.[115] The required percentage in France was reduced to 5 pct in 2001.[116]

Other minority remedies exist in the jurisdictions considered in the present book, for example the special investigation of companies, which is considered in detail in chapter V of the report of the *Forum Europaeum*

[110] German Private Limited Liability Companies Act, paras. 51a and 51b.
[111] *Ibid.*, para. 122(1) and (2). [112] *Ibid.*, para. 122(1). [113] *Ibid.*, para. 50(1).
[114] Dutch Civil Code Book 2, Arts. 110–112 and 220–222. An order of the President of the competent District Court is necessary. Arts. 220 and 221 will be revised if the reform proposals governing the BV are adopted.
[115] Companies Act 2006, ss 303 *et seq.*
[116] French Commercial Code, Art. L-225-103-II. This rule only applies to public companies.

Konzernrecht, and which takes place in such countries as Germany, France, Belgium, the United Kingdom and the Netherlands. The special investigation of German public companies in governed by paragraphs 142–146 of the *Aktiengesetz*; special examiners are appointed either by the general meeting by a simple majority, or on the application of a minority holding 10 per cent of the nominal capital or shares having a total value of at least €1 million. In France, special investigations are possible both in the SA and the SARL, and may be required by a majority holding at least 10 per cent of the nominal capital: this amount is reduced to 5 per cent in the case of quoted companies.[117] In Belgium, a special investigation by experts can be required by the holders of shares carrying at least 1 per cent of the voting rights or representing an amount of at least €1,250,000.[118] Investigations by inspectors in the United Kingdom are governed by sections 431–453 of the Companies Act 1985, whilst in the Netherlands, special investigations are covered by Articles 344–359 of Book II of the Dutch Civil Code. As in the United Kingdom they may be applicable to public or private companies. In some states the special investigation is envisaged as extending throughout the group.

A successful special investigation may form the basis for a court claim, and sometimes prove an effective way of detecting and punishing those responsible for corporate misconduct. It may however prove expensive and lengthy and come too late to help minority shareholders. Nevertheless, the *Forum Europaeum Konzernrecht* took a favourable view of such investigations, which they thought should be permitted (as is the case in some Member States) to extend group wide.

Minority shareholders in a subsidiary company may receive protection under certain general principles of law, for example the principle of the equal treatment of shareholders (which is required by Article 42 of the Second Company Law Directive), or that of the fiduciary duties owed by shareholders (including controlling ones) to one another and to their company under German law.[119] Although English law, unlike German law, does not appear to recognise that controlling shareholders have any fiduciary duties towards other shareholders or their company, if shareholders who control the votes which may be exercised at a general

[117] French Commercial Code, Arts. L223-37 and L225-231.

[118] *Ibid.*, Arts. 168 and 169. These rules apply both to public and private companies.

[119] This principle was first recognised as applicable in partnerships and private companies, and has recently been extended to public companies: see BGHZ 103,184 '*Linotype*', and BGHZ 129, 136 '*Girmes*'.

meeting procure the passing of a resolution which is oppressive or unfairly prejudicial to minority shareholders, the court will set it aside. Rather similar remedies are available in other jurisdictions.[120]

The right to buy out a residual minority of shareholders and a right of withdrawal of such minorities exists in a number of jurisdictions. The former right may be applicable both to public and private companies, or simply to public or listed public companies.

The right to buy shares belonging to a minority, or a minority's right to be bought out must be distinguished from the rights to forfeit shares or expel shareholders for serious reasons which exists in certain jurisdictions, for example Belgium.[121] The relevant rights must also be distinguished from rights which may arise, especially under German law, when a fundamental change takes place in a parent-subsidiary relationships.[122] The right to buy out a residual minority exists under UK law, as well as under the law in the Netherlands, Belgium, France and Italy. In the United Kingdom and Italy, such a right of exclusion follows a take over bid: a shareholder who holds 90 per cent of the share capital as the result of a public bid can buy out the minority in accordance with the provisions of section 479 of the Companies Act 2006. In Italy, according to Article 111 of the Law of 24 February 1998 concerning financial intermediaries, an offeror who after a takeover bid holds 98 per cent or more of the shares of a listed public company, may buy out the minority within a certain period. In the Netherlands, in both public and private companies,[123] a majority shareholder holding 95 per cent of the share capital may demand and enforce the transfer of the remaining shares for cash, the amount being determined by three independent experts. This

[120] For a brief account of the annulment of resolutions of the board of directors and general meeting in France on the ground of abuse of voting rights, see Le Gall, *French Company Law*, 2nd edn. (London: Longman, 1992), pp. 132–8.

[121] The exclusion of shareholders is permitted under Arts. 334–339 (private companies) and Arts. 636–641 (public companies which do not invite public investment) of the Belgian Companies Code. In such companies shareholders holding together 30 per cent of the shares may for good reasons require that other shareholders transfer their shares to them.

[122] Thus, paras. 305 and 306 German Public Companies Act contain provisions concerning the payment of compensation for the acquisition of shares, and confer jurisdiction on the district court when disputes occur concerning such compensation. They are applicable when a control or profit transfer contract is concluded. According to para. 320b German Public Companies Act, the former shareholders of an integrated company are also entitled to compensation.

[123] See Dutch Civil Code Book II, Arts. 92a and 201a.

right requires that a group relationship is involved or that a public take overbid is made.

In Belgium, the shareholders of a public company which is listed or which offers its share for public subscription, who hold at least 95 per cent of the voting rights can exclude the minority.[124] In France, shareholders of a listed company holding 5 per cent or less of the shares of a listed company are required to withdraw on being requested to do so by shareholders holding at least 95 per cent of the voting rights.[125]

Minority shareholders also have a right to withdraw in certain jurisdictions, which is generally related to requirements concerning the making of a mandatory offer, and which are now regulated by the Takeover Directive. These jurisdictions include the United Kingdom, France, Italy and Belgium (when public companies are concerned). In the United Kingdom where at least 90 per cent of the voting share capital of a company has been acquired as the result of a takeover bid, the holder of any voting shares to which the offer relates who has not accepted the offer may require the offeror to acquire these shares.[126] In France, every shareholder in a listed public company may require the *Autorité des marchés financiers* to compel majority shareholders with at least 95 per cent of the voting rights to make an *offre publique de retrait* for all the remaining shares.[127] In Italy, a person (or persons) who comes to hold more than 90 per cent of the shares of a listed public company, must make a public offer to acquire the residue thereof at a price fixed by CONSOB.[128] An extensive right of withdrawal for serious reasons (*pour juste motifs*) is available in Belgium in accordance with Articles 340, 341, 635, 642 and 643 of the Companies Code 1999, which are applicable to private companies and to public companies which do not invite public subscriptions. The relevant right is not contingent on any minimum shareholding of the applicant or respondent. It is questionable whether such an extensive right of withdrawal would be generally acceptable. However, as the *Forum Europaeum Konzernrecht* contended,[129] there might be room for European regulation of a right of exclusion at a certain threshold of shareholding, which might be

[124] Belgian Companies Code 1999, Art. 513.

[125] *Règlement générale du Conseil des marchés financiers*, Arts. 236-3 *et seq.*

[126] Companies Act 2006, ss 983–985 ('sell-out' right). The 'squeeze-out' right is regulated by ss 979–982.

[127] *Règlement général de l'Autorité des Marchés* Arts. 236-1 *et seq.*

[128] Italian Law No 58 of 24 February 1998, Art. 108.

[129] '*Konzernrecht für Europa*', 672, 738–9.

considered as justified in view of any requirements that may be imposed regarding mandatory offers. The granting of the right of withdrawal independently of any regime governing mandatory offers would seem likely to improve minority protection but might prove burdensome for public companies.[130] Such a right of withdrawal is not provided for by Article 16 of the Thirteenth Directive on Takeovers, which provides for a right of sell-out and for a right of squeeze-out in Article 15. The right of withdrawal was not recognised in all the Member States.

Article 5 of the Thirteenth Directive provides for a mandatory offer, but does not specify the percentage of voting rights above which control can be deemed to have been acquired. The adoption of this provision was preceded by considerable controversy.

The requirement of a mandatory bid seems worthy of general adoption. It exists under United Kingdom,[131] French,[132] Belgian[133] Italian[134] and Spanish law,[135] and under the laws of the other EU Member States, but the relevant thresholds differ in these countries. And there are too many exceptions to the requirement of a mandatory bid in the Member States.

Groups of companies give rise to a number of difficult problems, which would seem to require a number of different solutions. It is unlikely that the conservative attitude to these questions which was adopted in the United Kingdom Act of 2006 can be maintained indefinitely.

130 Note in this context the view taken by '*Konzernrecht für Europa*', 672, 739. This body takes the view that the right of withdrawal might be restricted to listed companies. It is noteworthy, however, that in Germany it is available to members of private companies and partnerships.

131 Rule 9 of the Takeover Code requires an existing offer to be extended to the remaining shareholders where any person acquires shares carrying 30 per cent or more of the voting rights in the company.

132 *Règlement général AMF*, Arts. 234-2 ff. The supervisory authority has power to grant exemption from the mandatory bid obligation, for example where there are changes of control within the same corporate group.

133 See Belgian Royal Decree of 8 November 1989, Art. 41.

134 See Art. 106 and subsequent articles of the Italian Law of 24 February 1998.

135 See Spanish Securities Markets Act of 28 July 1988, Art. 60, and Royal Decree 432/2003 of 11 April 2003.

10

Cross-border mergers and acquisitions

I. Introduction

The present chapter will concentrate on cross-border mergers, which are the subject matter of the Tenth Directive[1] which has to be implemented in the Member States, and takeovers, which are governed by the Thirteenth Directive on Takeovers,[2] the transposition date for which expired on 20 May 2006. Cross-border cooperation may be occasioned by economic factors, and take a number of different forms, for example through the medium of contracts, partnerships, European economic interest groupings, or through the grant of intellectual property rights. It may also take place through the medium of joint ventures, which may be subject to Article 81 EC and to the Merger Regulation.[3] Such joint ventures may take the form of a contractual partnership or a European Economic Interest Grouping. These forms of cooperation between different enterprises are clearly distinct from mergers and takeovers. Mergers involve the assets and liabilities of an acquired company being transferred to the acquiring company. They may take place by means of acquisitions or through the medium of the formation of a new company. Takeovers involve the acquisition by a company (the bidder) of sufficient shares in another company (the target) to result in the purchaser obtaining control over the other company.

This is also the case with cooperation between companies. Mergers may be motivated by a number of economic considerations, they may also be motivated by a desire to reduce liability to transactions. Although takeovers have frequently taken place in the United Kingdom in recent years, the type of merger transaction provided for by the Third Company Law Directive

[1] Council Directive 2005/56/EC of 26 October 2005 on cross-border mergers of limited liability companies, OJ 2005 L310/1. The DTI launched a consultation on the implementation of this Directive on 5 March 2005.

[2] Directive 2004/25/EC of the European Parliament and the Council of 21 April 2004 on takeover bids, OJ 2004 L142/12.

[3] Council Regulation (EC) 139/2004 of 20 January 2004 on the control of concentration between undertakings OJ 2004 L24/1.

and by section 427A of the Companies Act 2985 (which will be replaced by sections 904–918 of the Companies Act 2006) has not been used in the United Kingdom. This is because section 427A did not apply if the consideration given included something other than shares or cash, or if the company subject to the proposed compromise or arrangement was being wound up. The same is true of the provisions of sections 914–918 of the Companies Act 2006; it follows from section 900 of the latter Act that it will be possible to avoid sections 904–918 by carrying out transactions which will have a similar affect to a Third Directive merger.

The test immediately below deals with the new Cross-Border Mergers Directive. This Directive may have only a limited effect as far as UK companies wishing to merge with companies in other Member States are concerned. If they can secure the necessary agreement, there are considerable advantages in an agreed takeover as it may be easier to get rid of dissenting minorities. The remainder of this text largely concerns takeovers, and places special emphasis on certain aspects of the Takeovers Directive (Thirteenth Company Law Directive) and its implementation in the Member States.

II. Cross-border mergers

A. *Influence of the Third Directive*

Domestic mergers of public limited liability companies are governed by the Third Company Law Directive,[4] which has been implemented in all the Member States. Such mergers can be carried out by means of acquisition or by the formation of a new company. The effect of such a merger is to effect a transfer of assets and liabilities with implied continuity of ownership. The consideration for the transfer consists of shares together with, if thought necessary, a cash balancing item issued and paid to the shareholders of the absorbed companies by the transferee or absorbing company.[5] The shareholders of the company or companies which have been dissolved, become shareholders in the resulting company. The Third Directive provides for certain mechanisms to achieve this result which have been adopted for the purposes of the Cross-Border Mergers (or Tenth) Directive. The latter Directive enables two or more limited

4 Note in this sense, Professor J. Rickford, 'The Proposed Tenth Company Law Directive on Cross-Border Mergers and its Impact in the United Kingdom' (2005) 16 EBLR 1393, 1595–6 and 1410.

5 Rickford, 'The Proposed Tenth Company Law Directive' 1395.

liability companies to engage in trans-frontier mergers of the type envisaged in the Third Directive. It appears that the resulting company may be incorporated in a member state different from those of the participating companies, this seem to follow from Article 8(2) of the Directive which relates to experts' reports.

B. *History and legal basis*

The Tenth Directive was preceded by a draft Convention based upon Article 220 EC (now Article 293 EC, which failed to be adopted because of disagreements, especially concerning employee participation. It seems clear from the European Court's judgment in *SEVIC Systems AG* v. *Amtsgericht Neuwied*[6] that participation is an international merger may be regarded as an exercise of the right of freedom of establishment. The Cross-Border Merger Directive was based upon Article 44 EC. Paragraph 1 of this article provides that in order to attain freedom of establishment as regards a particular activity the Council, acting in accordance with the procedure refined to in Article 251, and after consulting the Economic and Social Committees shall act by means of directives.

C. *Advantages over the European Company Statute*

The Tenth Directive appears to have certain advantages over the European Company Statute as a method of merging companies across frontiers. Thus it is applicable to mergers involving private companies, unlike the European Companies Statute. The rules which it contains governing employee participation are more liberal than these contained in the Employees Involvement Directive which accompanied the European Company Statute in some respects. In addition the company resulting from a Tenth Directive Merger will be a company subject to a national system of law, whilst a European Company resulting from a merger will have a complex legal regime, which may give rise to uncertainties.

D. *Scope*

There are some uncertainties as to the precise ambit of the Directive according to Article 1, it is applicable to mergers of limited liability companies formed in accordance with the laws of a Member State and

[6] Case 411/03, L.

having their registered office, central administration or principal place of business within the community, provided that at least two of them are governed by the laws of different Member States. The latter article obviously permits letter box companies having their principal place of business in a state not belonging to the EU to take advantage of the Directive.

Limited liability companies are said in Article 2(1)(a) of the Directive to be companies as referred to in Article 1 of Directive 68/151/EEC, i.e. public and private limited companies in the Member States. However the second category of company covered in accordance with Article 2(1)(b), is hard to comprehend. This is said to be a company with a share capital and having legal personality, possessing separate assets which alone serve to cover its debts, and subject under the national law governing it to conditions concerning guarantees such as those provided for by the First Directive for the protection of members and others.[7]

According to Article 4(J)(a), cross-border mergers shall only be possible between types of companies which can merge according to the national law of the relevant Member States. This would seem to mean that all the states involved in the merger must permit mergers of the specified kind.

E. Cash and shares components of merger consideration

The rules contained in Article (2)(a)–(b) and Article 3(1) define the permissible cash component in the merger consideration. The first two texts adopt the same approach as does Article 4(1) of the Third Directive, thus requiring that any balancing cash component of the consideration shall not exceed 10 per cent of the total nominal value of the shares in the case of a merger by absorption, and of the new company's shares to the case of a merger taking place by the formation of such a company. However, Article 3(1) of the Cross-Border Mergers Directive provides that the cash component may exceed 10 per cent of the aggregate nominal value or par value of the shares or securities representing the capital of the resulting company provided that the law of at least one of the Member States concerned so permits. Article 3(1) does not appear to be well drafted. At first reading, the use of the word 'securities' gives the

[7] See the discussion of this matter in Rickford, 'The Proposed Tenth Company Law Directive', 1401–2. The author does not reach any conclusions about what type of entity is envisaged.

impression that bonds or securities might form part of the relevant consideration. This does not seem to be the case because such instruments will not have a nominal or par value.

F. Relevance of national law

According to Article 4(1)(b) of the Directive a company taking part in a cross-border merger shall comply with the provisions and formalities of the national law to which it is subject. Article 4(2) makes it clear that such provisions and formalities include the decision making process. As the Third Directive had been implemented in all the Member States, this rule will entail that general meetings of any public companies involved in the merger other than a public company which has been newly formed for the purpose of the merger, have to approve its draft terms and any subsequent alterations to the company's statutes either by at least two-thirds of the notes attaching either to the shares or to the subscribed capital represented, or by a simple majority of such votes when at least half of the subscribed capital is represented.[8] A Member State is given an option by Articles 8 and 27 of the Third Directive not to require a general meeting of the acquired company, provided that the provisions of the Directive concerning minority protection are complied with.[9] This rule is inapplicable where the merger takes place through the medium of the formation of a new company. There is no requirement of a qualified majority vote at the general meeting or a private company which has to approve the draft terms of a merger. However, it follows from Article 6 of the Tenth Directive that a decision[resolution] of a general meeting of such a company is required.

G. Requirements governing formation and disclosure

Article 5 of the Tenth Directive like the corresponding Article 5 of the Third Directive and Article 70 of the European Company Statutes, requires the boards of the merging companies to draw up common draft terms of the merger.[10] Article 6 provides for the publication of

[8] Third Directive, Art. 7(1)(3), Member States were given an option to choose between the two alternatives.

[9] *Ibid.*, Arts. 8(c), 25(c) and 27(c). One or more shareholders of the acquiring company or the company being divided holding a minimum percentage to be fixed at not more than 5 per cent of the subscribed capital must be entitled to require that a general meeting is called.

[10] There are many similarities between the relevant provisions of these three instruments.

common draft terms; Article 7 provides for a report on the merger by the management or administrative organ; and Article 8 provides for a report by an independent expert.[11]

H. Location of the registered office: the real seat doctrine

The draft terms of the merger are required to contain particulars of the form, name and registered office of the merging companies. According to the Commission's Explanatory Memorandum, the place where the registered office is situated determines which law will be applicable to the new company, which is an important item of information as far as interested parties including creditors are concerned. The question arises as to what constraints, if any, may be imposed on the place of the head office (which may well be that of the real seat from which central control is exercised), when the real seat doctrine is applied to the resulting company, or to one of the other companies participating in the merger.[12] If the decision of the European Court in the *Daily Mail* case is still regarded as good law, the view might be taken that the resulting company could not move its real seat to another Member State. A similar view might well be taken where one of the other participating companies has its real seat in a Member State adopting the real seat doctrine. There is some doubt as to whether the European Court would overrule *Daily Mail.* However, the approach taken in this case seems illogical, and contrary to much of the European Court's jurisprudence on the free movement of goods and persons. It also appears to be the case that participation in an international merger must be regarded as an exercise of the right of free movement, and cannot be referred by national laws restricting this right.[13]

I. Independent expert reports

According to Article 8(1) of the Tenth Directive an independent expert's report is required for each participating company. However, a combined report may be given by experts appointed for that purpose by any one of the regulatory authorities at the joint request of the participating

[11] Article 9 of the Third Directive is similar to Art. 7 of the Tenth Directive and Art. 10 of the Third Directive resembles Art. 8 of the Tenth Directive.

[12] This matter is dealt with in detail by Rickford 'The Proposed Tenth Company Law Directive', 1450–8 in which four paradigmatic situations are considered.

[13] Note in this context Case C-411/03 *Sevic Systems AG* v. *Amtsgericht Neuwied* [2005] ECR I-10805; [2006] 1 CMLR 45; [2006] 4 All ER 1072.

companies.[14] Article 8(4) provides that in the somewhat unlikely event of the agreement of all the members or the companies involved in the cross-border mergers there is no need for an expert's report. This provision is likely, if at all, to be useful to small and medium-sized companies. The Explanatory Memorandum expressed the view that cross-border mergers would be particularly useful for such companies. It is thought likely that larger companies may well avail themselves of the mechanism provided by the Tenth Directive which is more flexible in some respects than the European Company Statute.

J. The protection of shareholders and creditors

Article 4(2) of the Directive makes it clear that participating companies are subject to their domestic law relating to the protection of creditors, shareholders and debenture holders. It also stipulates that such protection has to take into account the nature of the merger, thereby indicating that additional protection may be provided for. However, it appears from recital 3 of the Preamble to the Directive that any restrictions of freedom of movement or the free movement of capital would require justification in accordance with the principles set out in case law of the European Court of Justice.

K. Opposition on public policy grounds

According to Article 4(1)(b) of the Tenth Directive, the laws of a Member State enabling its national authorities to oppose a given merger on grounds of public interest shall also be applied to a cross-border merger where at least one of the merging companies is subject to the law of the member state. This text makes it clear that only the same rules as were applicable to internal mergers are applicable. However, it appears to be the case that the public interest ground may be invoked against any of the companies involved.

L. Scrutiny and publicity

The provisions of Articles 10 and 11 of the Tenth Directive relating to scrutiny and publicity of the merger are similar to those contained in Articles 25 and 26 of the European Company Statute, which are

[14] Tenth Directive, Art. 8(2).

applicable when an SE is formed by means of a merger. The decision-making process of participating companies are supervised by the designated court, notary, or other authority of their member state.[15] Such authorities are required by Article 10(2) of the Tenth Directive to issue certificates pertaining to the proper completion of pre-merger acts and formalities without delay. Article 10(3) makes provision for the amendment of share exchange ratios or a procedure to compensate minority shareholders without preventing the registration of the cross-border merger. In this respect it resembles Article 25(3) of the European Company Statute. According to Article 11(1), the designated authority for the completion of the merger and, where appropriate, for the formation of the new company is that of the Member State of the resulting company. This authority is required by Article 11(2) to check that the merging companies have approved the common draft terms in the same terms, and that the provisions for employee participation have been determined in accordance with Article 16[16] (which makes detailed reference to the Employee Involvement Directive). The registration of the merger is governed by Article 13. The first paragraph of that article provides that the laws of each of the Member States to whose jurisdiction the merging companies were subject shall determine the arrangements for publicising completion of the cross-border merger in the public register in which each of the companies is required to file documents.

M. Consequences of the merger

The consequences of the merger are set out in Article 14, which is similar to Article 19 of the Third Directive. All the assets and liabilities of the relevant companies are transferred to the acquiring company or new company; the members of the companies being acquired for the new company. The companies being acquired or the merging companies cease to exist. Provisions are made in Article 14(3) for the carrying out of special transfer formalities by the company resulting from the cross-border merger and for the preservation of rights arising from contracts of employment. Earlier versions of the Directive contained provisions regarding the nullity of a merger, but no such provisions are included in the final version of this instrument.

[15] Cross-Border Mergers Directive, Art. 10(1).

[16] Cf. Art. 26(3) of the European Company Statute.

N. Employee participation

1. Introductory remarks

The provisions concerning employee participation contained in the Cross-Border Mergers Directive are of considerable complexity and involve a considerable amount of cross-referencing to the Employee Involvement Directive 2001/86 of 8 October 2001. Although the relevant provisions of the Cross-Border Mergers Directive differ from those of the Employee Involvement Directive in certain respects, they place considerable emphasis on the negotiation procedure provided for in that Directive. The view has been taken that certain of these differences constitute improvements on the regime applicable to the European Company (SE) under the Employee Involvement Directive.[17] Thus, Article 16(4)(a) of the Cross-Border Mergers Directive enables the relevant organs of the merging companies to choose to be directly subject to the standard rules on employee involvement without any process of negotiation. In addition, Article 16(4)(c) gives Member States the choice to reduce the effect of a participation regime to one-third where as the result of the merger a higher level of participation (e.g. parity under the German Codtermination Act 1976 would be applied to a single-tier board. The Cross-Border Mergers Directive unlike the Employee Involvement Directive, contains no provisions relating to an information and consultation procedure, and is solely concerned with employee involvement. There are some other differences between the two Directives, some of which are mentioned below. The provisions of Article 16 represent a necessary compromise between the different employee participation regimes in the Member States.

2. The legal regime applicable to employee participation

By Article 16(1) of the Cross-Border Mergers Directive, without prejudice to Article 16(2), the company resulting from the cross-border merger shall be subject to the rules in force concerning employee participation, if any, in the Member State in which it has its registered office.

This general rule does not apply where one of the three exceptions set out in Article 16(2) applies, in which case the detailed regime set out in the Directive governs the situation. These exceptions are:

[17] Note in this context M. Pannier, 'The EU Cross-Border Merger Directive – A New Dimension for the Employee Participation and Company Restructuring' (2005) 16 EBLR 1424 at 1435-b.

(1) where at least one of the merging companies has more than 500 employees within the six months prior to the publication of the draft terms of the merger, and is subject to an employee participation scheme; or
(2) where the national law applicable to the company resulting from the merger does not provide for at least the same level of employee participation as operated in each of the relevant mergers measured by reference to the proportion of employee representatives among the members of the administrative or supervisory organ, or their committees, or the management group which covers the profit units of the company subject to employee representation; or
(3) where such law does not provide for employers of establishments of the company resulting from the merger that are situated in other Member States, the same entitlement to exercise participation rights as those enjoyed by those employees employed in the Member State where the company resulting from the cross-border merger has its registered office.

At first sight, there appears to be an overlap between conditions (1) and (2), condition (2) is obviously intended to maintain participation standards. As is pointed out by Pannier,[18] companies resulting from a merger under the Directive can never escape employee participation when it operates in any of the merging companies, irrespective of condition (1). However, it seems that condition (1) applies to the case in which the resulting company would be governed by the law applying the highest level of participation in the merging companies. The level of participation for certain of the workforce would be increased. However, the relevant parties may apply the negotiation procedure referred to in Article 16(3)(c) and (d) of the Tenth Directive in order to reduce the level of employee participation. Condition (1) makes such negotiations possible where the rights of employees are not at risk, and gives the management an opportunity to reduce the level of participation, even when the standard rules are applicable.

The third provision, Article 16(2)(c), governs the situation where a member state such as Germany does not provide for employee participation for employees situated in another Member State. Such exclusions may well be contrary to general rules of Community law governing the movement of workers. It appears to follow from Article 16(2)(b) that the levels of employee participation in the organs of the merging companies

[18] 'The EU Cross-Border Mergers Directive', 1437.

and their committees must be compared for the purpose of determining the highest level of participation.

3. The process of negotiation

As is the case with an SE, a cross-border merger will generally require employee participation to be dealt with either by a process of negotiation, or through the medium of the standard rules contained in point (b) of the Annex to the Employee Involvement Directive, which is made applicable to companies resulting from cross-border mergers by Article 16(3)(b) of the Cross-Border Mergers Directive. Like the creation of an SE, a cross-border merger may not be registered unless an agreement or agreements for employee participation has been concluded or if such an agreement has not been concluded within the prescribed period of six or twelve months from the establishment of the special negotiating body, the competent organs of each of the participating companies decide upon the application of the standard rules for participation. This conclusion follows from Article 16(3) of the Cross-Border Mergers Directive, which makes reference to Article 12(2) of the SE Regulation.

Negotiations which take place may end with an agreement on employee participation, which may increase or reduce participation rights. The standard rules procedure may be applicable if the negotiations do not succeed,[19] or if the relevant organs of the participating companies opt directly for the application of the standard rules on employee involvement without any prior negotiation process,[20] or of the special negotiating body and the managerial organs of the participating companies so agree.[21] The application of the standard rules is dependent on the attainment of a 33⅓ per cent threshold in respect of the number of employees in the merging companies who have rights of participation. As is the case with an SE, the negotiation process entails the setting up of a special negotiating body. Such a body will contain in respect of a particular Member State, one seat per portion of employees employed in that state which equals 10 per cent of a fraction thereof, of the number of employees employed by the participating companies and concerned subsidiaries in all the Member States considered together.[22]

[19] Article 16(3)(e) of the Tenth Directive, which makes reference to Art. 7(1) of the Employee Involvement Directive.

[20] *Ibid.*, Art. 16(4)(a).

[21] *Ibid.*, Art. 16(3)(e), *ibid.*, together with Art. 7 (1) of the Employee Involvement Directive.

[22] *Ibid.*, Art. 16(3)(a), together with Art. (3)(a)(i) of the Employee Involvement Directive.

The negotiation process may be expensive and somewhat protracted, but it is necessary to use it in order to increase or reduce participation rights. If such rights are to be reduced it follows from Article 3(4), paragraph 1 and first indent of the Employee Implement Directives to which Article 16(3)(a) of the Cross-Border Mergers Directive makes reference, that the special negotiating body has to act by a qualified majority in certain circumstances. It normally takes decisions by an absolute majority of its members, provided that such a majority represents an absolute majority of its employees. It has to abide by a qualified majority to reduce participation rights. Such a majority represents the votes of two-thirds of the members of the special negotiating body representing two-thirds of the employees, and must include the votes of members representing employees employed in at least two different Member States. This qualified majority is only required to reduce participation rights if at least 25 per cent of the total number of employees of the participating companies have such rights.

In addition a special negotiating body may, according to Article 16(4)(b) of the Cross-Border Mergers Directive, acting by the same qualified majority as that mentioned above, decide not to open negotiations or to terminate negotiations already opened, and rely on the rules on participation which are in force in the Member State where the registered office of the company resulting from the merger will be situated. This option is not available in accordance with the procedure applicable to the state.

4. The standard rules

The above rules are in essence higher proportion rules. Member States are requested to lay down standard rules on employee participation which must satisfy the requirements laid down in Part 3 of the Annex to the Employee Involvement Directive, which is concerned with such rules. The standard rules provide that where an SE is established other than by transformation, the employees of that company and its subsidiaries and establishments shall have the right to elect, appoint, recommend or oppose the appointment of a member or members of the administrative or supervisory body of the SE equal to the highest proportion in force in the participating companies concerned before the registration of the SE. This provision is applicable to a cross-border merger. It should be noted that the 25 per cent limit which should be obtained in respect of the total member of employees in all the participating companies for the standard rules to be mandatory applicable to an SE is increased to 33⅓ per cent in the case of a cross-border merger by

Article 16(3)(e) of the Cross-Border Mergers Directive. However, as is also the case with the SE, the special negotiating body may decide that the standard rules shall be applicable if the required percentage of the workforce is not attained. This proposition follows from Article 16(3)(e) of the Tenth Directive, which makes reference to Article7(2)(b) of the Employee Involvement Directive.

It will be noted from the above paragraph that the threshold for the standard rules apply, namely 33⅓ per cent is different from that applicable to the procedure for the agreed reduction of participation rights, which requires a qualified majority if more than 25 per cent of the workforce had rights of participation.[23]

The provisions of Article 16(4)(e) of the Cross-Border Mergers Directive find no parallel in anything in the Employee Involvement Directive. The latter test permits Member States to limit the proportion of employee representatives in the administrative organs of companies resulting from the merger where, after prior negotiations, standard rules apply. However, if in one of the merging companies, employee representatives constituted at least one-third of either the administrative or supervisory organ, the level of such representation in the administrative organ may not be reduced below one-third.

As already indicated, the provisions of the Tenth Directive concerning employee participation are more flexible than those of the European Involvement Directive. The use of the special negotiation procedures provided for by the Directive, as well as the possible use of experts during the course of such procedures may, however, prove costly to merging companies.

5. Employees' rights other than those of participation

The twelfth recital in the Preamble to the Cross-Border Mergers Directive provides that such rights should remain subject to the national provision referred to in the relevant Council Directive. These are Council Directive 98/59/E on collective redundancies,[24] Council Directive 2001/23/EC on the safeguarding of employees rights in the event of transfers of undertakings, businesses or parts of undertakings or businesses,[25]

[23] See M. Pannier, 'The EU Cross-Border Mergers Directive', at 440, where it is suggested that there is an ambiguity in this procedure.

[24] OJ C 1999 L225/16.

[25] OJ 2001 L82/16. The question has arisen in the relevant cases as to what kind of transaction constitutes the transfer of an undertaking. It seems clear that any type of merger transaction may constitute such a transfer.

Directive 2002/14/EC on the European Parliament and the Council establishing a general framework for informing and consulting employees in the European Community[26] and Council Directive 94/45/EC on the establishment of a European Works Council.[27]

O. *Concluding remarks on the Tenth Directive*

As has been pointed out above, the Cross-Border Mergers Directive appears to create a more satisfactory regime for cross-border mergers than does the European Company Statute. Takeovers enjoy tax advantages over the use of an SE effecting a merger as a method of effecting a cross-border merger under the Tenth Directive: merging companies are subject to transfer taxes on assets which are inapplicable in the case of a takeover. It is thought that agreed takeovers may prove to be more popular than Tenth Directive Mergers, especially where United Kingdom or Irish companies which wish to acquire companies in other Member States are concerned. However, British companies wishing to merge with companies in other Member States may sometimes find it necessary to make use of the new procedure.

A DTI consultation on the implementation of the Cross-Border Mergers Directive was launched in March 2007. According to Article 19 of the Directive, Member States are required to bring into force the laws, regulations and administrative provisions necessary to comply with the Directive by 15 December 2007.

III. Takeovers

A. *Introductory remarks*

Takeovers are often thought of as producing economic benefits, especially by means of replacing less productive or efficient management by more efficient managers. The mere threat of a takeover bid is said to be a spur to efficiency. However, there is room for doubt whether takeovers always have beneficial effects. Public takeover bids have been subject to regulation in the Member States to provide for disclosure, transparency and a satisfactory procedure such that the shareholders can decide on the merits of the bid. In the past, self regulation has been predominant in the

[26] OJ 2002 L80/29.
[27] OJ 1994 L754/64 as amended by Directive 97/74/EC, OJ 1998 L10/2.

Member States in this area, and has involved enforcement by the national stock exchange or another non governmental body. The City Code on Takeovers and Mergers is the oldest example of such self-regulation, and dates from 1968. However, the Panel will be in a different position following the implementation of the Thirteenth Directive on Takeovers in the United Kingdom.[28] Takeovers have been subject for some time to statutory regulation in Belgium, Germany, France and Spain. The tendency to such regulation will increase as the result of the implementation of the requirements of the Thirteenth Directive, which is intended to be one of the most important instruments of economic reform furthering European competitiveness.

Barriers to takeover bids of various kinds are common in the Member States. These include the use of voteless shares or shares having multiple voting rights, the consideration of all voting rights in a special class of shares (e.g. the priority shares familiar in the Netherlands, or the use of pyramidical ownership structures as in Italy. In addition to these legal barriers to bids, de facto barriers exist in some countries, for example the strong position of the banks in relation to the control of German listed companies. Hostile takeovers have become a frequent phenomenon in the United Kingdom; the position has been different in Germany, where there have been certain legal and factual barriers to hostile bids. The United Kingdom City Code has severely restricted certain defences. Thus, General Principle 7 provides that at no time after a bona fide offer has been communicated to the Board of the offeree company, or after the board of the offeree company has reason to believe that a bona fide offer might become imminent, may any action be taken by the board of the offeree company in relation to the affairs of the company without the approval of the shareholders in general meeting, which should effectively result in any bona fide offer being frustrated, or in the shareholders being denied the opportunity to decide on its merits. Furthermore, rule 21 of the Code provides that during the course of an offer, or even before the board has reason to believe that a bona fide offer might be imminent, the board must not without the approval of a general meeting, take any steps to increase the share capital, sell, dispose, or

[28] Section 943 of the Companies Act 2006 provides that the Takeover Panel must make rules giving effect to Arts. 3(1), 4(2), 5, 6(1)–6(3), 7–9 and 13 of the Takeovers Directive, and may make other provisions for or in connection with the regulation of takeover bids.

acquire assets of a material amount, or enter into contracts other than in the ordinary course of business.

The regulation of takeover bids in different Member States deal with similar issues relating to the conduct of the bid, such as pre-bid obligations, disclosure of the details of the bid, rules prescribing the period for acceptance of the bid, and obligations which have to be complied with after the offer has expired, for example, communication of certain particulars to the supervisory authority. Mandatory bids are provided for in all the countries included in the Commission Staff Working Document Report on the implementation of the Directive on takeover bids, published in 2007.[29]

The mandatory bid rule provides that if a person acquires control over a company, he or she is obliged to make a full takeover bid for all the remaining securities of the company at an equitable price. The thresholds for control vary in the different Member States.

B. The Thirteenth Directive on Takeovers

1. Introduction

The above Directive of the European Parliament and Council was adopted in 2004. It was the result of nearly twenty years of work. The Commission's proposal of October 2002[30] adopted nine months after the Winter Group had reported was revised by the compromise solution adopted by the Council and Parliament and which forged the basis of the new Directive. This compromise retained the disclosure obligation proposed in the Winter Reports. Article 10 of the Directive provides for a far-reaching and extensive disclosure of information on certain matters which may constitute or involve control mechanisms such as pyramidical structures, cross shareholdings and the existence of shareholders with special control rights. Such information has to be published in the company's annual report. The compromise provided for board neutrality in Article 9 and for a breakthrough provision in Article 11. However, it made the adoption of these two articles optional for Member States. When Member States opt out of either or both of these articles, the compromise required such states to allow companies established in accordance with their law, to opt back in again. It also provided for the controversial reciprocity provision now contained in Article 12(3),

[29] SEC (2007) 268. [30] OJ 2003 C45/1.

according to which Member States are allowed to exempt companies which apply the rules contained in Article 9(2) and (3) and/or Article 11 from applying Article 9(2) and (3) and/or Article 11 if they become the subject of an offer launched by a company which does not apply the same articles as they do. These options have given rise to considerable criticism, but were necessary for the purpose of achieving agreement on the neutrality and breakthrough provisions in the Council.

Articles 9 and 11 must be regarded as two of the most important features of the Directive. The Commission's original proposal included both types of defences for the purpose of creating a level playing field between states. It was intended to create favourable conditions for the emergence of a European market for corporate control, and significant rights for shareholders including minority shareholders. The existence of the abovementioned options has resulted in the fact that the Directive is very unlikely to create a level playing field. The report of the Commission[31] correctly makes it clear that the reciprocity option contained in Article 13(3) gives management additional powers to take frustrating action and makes it easier for companies to disapply the board neutrality or the breakthrough rule.[32]

2. Implementation in the Member States

When the Commission Staff Working Document was published in February 2007, seven Member States had transposed the Directive or adopted necessary framework rules. However, only Austria, Denmark, France, Hungary, Luxembourg and the United Kingdom met the deadline for implementation. In the United Kingdom, interim regulations were provided by the Takeover Directive (Interim Implementation) Regulations 2006, which had effect until the relevant provisions of Part 18 of the Companies Act 2006 came into force in April 2007. The interim regulations could not make provisions for the adoption of amendments to the Takeover Code as far as they referred to matters contained in the Takeover Directive. This was because Schedule 2, paragraph 1 of the European Communities Act 1973 excludes the power to legislate by means of orders, rules, regulations and other subordinate instrument, for the purpose of implementing any community obligation. The Takeover Panel thus could not make or alter rules which would have a

[31] SEC (2007) 268.

[32] This rule is criticised by J. Rickford in his comprehensive article, 'The Emerging European Takeover Law From A British Perspective' (2004) 15 EBLR 1379.

statutory effect. This position will be different now that section 943 of the Companies Act has come into effect.

3. Board neutrality and the breakthrough rule

The board neutrality rule relates to post-bid defences, whilst the breakthrough rule neutralises certain pre-bid as well as post-bid defences, including share transfer restrictions in the company's articles and shares with multiple voting rights. The board neutrality rule set out to Article 9(2) provides that during the bid period, the board of the offeree company must obtain the prior authorisation of the general meeting of shareholders before taking any action which may lead to the frustration of any bid. Furthermore, Article 9(3) provides that as regards decisions taken before the board of the offeree company receives information about the decision to make the bid, which are not fully implemented, the general meeting of shareholders shall approve or confirm any decision which does not form part of the normal course of the company's business and the implementation of which may result in the frustration of the bid. Article 3 of the Directive contains a number of general principles one of which is that the board of the offeree company must act in the interests of the company as a whole and must not deny the holders of the securities the opportunity to decide upon the merit of the bid.

The breakthrough rule makes restrictions on share transfers during the bid period set out in Article 7(1), which is not less than two weeks or more than ten weeks from the publication of the offer document inoperable. Restrictions on voting rights shall not have effect at the general meeting of shareholders which decides on any defensive measures in accordance with Article 9. Multiple voting securities only carry one vote each at the general meeting of shareholders which decides on such defensive measures. According to Article 11(4), where following a bid, the offeror holds 75 or more per cent of the capital carrying voting rights, no restrictions on the transfer of securities or on voting rights, nor any extraordinary rights of shareholders concerning the appointment or removal of board members provided for the articles of the offeree company shall apply. Multiple-vote securities shall carry only one vote each at the first general meeting of shareholders following the closure of the bid, called by the offeror in order to amend the articles or to remove or appoint board members.

The breakthrough rule has been criticised on the ground that it only covers certain defences, and is thus apparently inapplicable to non-voting shares as also to preference shares, in accordance with Article 11(6).

The definition of the threshold contained in Article 11(4) has also been said to lack clarity, and the implementation of the provisions for compensation breakthrough contained in Article 11(5) have also justifiably been used to give rise to difficulties.[33]

As already indicated, Article 12 of the Directive subjects the board's neutrality and breakthrough rules to complex optional arrangements. If a Member State fails to make these rules obligatory it must give companies the opportunity of applying the rules on a voluntary basis. The decision on voluntary application of the rules has to be adopted by the general meeting in accordance with the rules applicable to the amendment of the article and may be reversed in the same way. The final compromise contained the reciprocity exception which has already been explained above. The use of this exception has to be authorised by the relevant Member State, and by the general meeting of the shareholders of the offeree company. The latter authorisation must according to Article 12(5) be granted not earlier than eighteen months before the bid was made public in accordance with Article 6(1), which contains detailed rules governing information concerning bids. The use of this reciprocity exception is likely to discourage the emergence of an active takeover member in the EU.

4. Implementation of the board neutrality and breakthrough rules

Eighteen of the twenty-five Member States researched in the Commission Staff Working Document have imposed or are expected to impose the board neutrality rule,[34] which was not implemented in any of the Member States except one. However, in five of the states, the reciprocity exception has been introduced. In the majority of these five Member States, shareholders are required to give prior authorisation to the management every eighteen months to apply takeover defences in a reciprocity situation. Reciprocity is thought likely to increase the likelihood of potential abuse by the management to the detriment of shareholders in these Member States. It has also been contended that the reciprocity exception may be contrary to fundamental rules or Community law governing freedom of establishment and the free movement of capital.[35]

[33] See Rickford 'The Emerging European Takeover Law', 1379, at 1394.

[34] For the position in Germany, see paras. 33 and 33a of the Takeover Act 2002, as amended by the Act of 2006 implementing the Thirteenth Directive.

[35] See Rickford, 'The Emerging European Takeover Law', 1402.

Whatever the merits of the breakthrough rule, it is only expected to be implemented on a mandatory basis in the Baltic States. Some countries such as France and Italy have operated a partial version of it. The voluntary application of the breakthrough rule is made dependent on the grant of the option by a member state, and a decision of the company. However, it appears to have been made conditional on other factors in certain Member States, for example, Austria requires the approval of a person holding the right to appoint members of the supervisory board. The relevant UK rules relating to opting in and out are contained in section 966 of the Companies Act 2006. This text provides that a company may opt in by special resolution if three conditions are met. The company must have voting shares admitted to trading on a registered market. Its articles must either contain no restrictions such as those which are mentioned in Article 11 of the Takeover Directive, or if they do provide that they shall not apply at a time or in circumstances in which they would be disapplied by this article. Furthermore, they must not contain any provisions which would be incompatible with Article 11.

Section 966 does not contain any provision relating to multiple voting rights. It is presumably intended that such rights can only be excluded in conformity with the relevant provisions of Article 11(2)(4) or by Takeover Directive if they have been modified in accordance with the provisions of section 630(2) of the Companies Act with such an effect. Opting in to the breakthrough rule is made impossible where shares concerning special rights in the company are held by a minister, or a nominee of a minister, or any other person acting on behalf of a minister; or a company directly or indirectly controlled by a minister; and as such rights are excusable by or on behalf of a minister under any enactment. The enactment of the latter rules appears to conform with Article 11(7) of the Directive. Article 966(5) provides that a company may revoke an opting-in resolution by means of a further special resolution. Such action is compatible with the Directive.

Section 968(2) of the Companies Act 2006 governs the effect of opting-in on certain contractual restrictions, and is in apparent conformity with the requirements of the Directive. The question of compensation which is a difficult one, forms the subject matter of section 968(6) of the Companies Act. Section 969(1) governs the power of an offeree to require a general meeting to be held when a takeover bid is made for an opted-in company; it appears to conform with the requirements of Article 11(4) of the Directive. However, the use of the phrase 75 per cent of the capital carrying voting rights in Article 11(4) is somewhat ambiguous. The requirement in it is treated in section 969(1) of the Companies Act 2006 as being satisfied where the offeror holds no less than 75 per cent of all the voting shares in the company.

The United Kingdom has not implemented the reciprocity rule in relation to the breakthrough procedure although a number of other Member States have done so. As already suggested, the rule seems likely to have as its predominant effect an increase in the powers of managements to take frustrating action.

5. The right of squeeze-out

The above procedure, is provided for by Article 15 of the Takeover Directive which permits a bidder who has acquired a very significant part of the share capital (90 per cent of the capital carrying voting rights and 90 per cent of the voting rights) to acquire the remaining shares.[36] Like the neutrality rule and the breakthrough procedure, it is intended to facilitate takeover bids. A squeeze-out procedure was already provided for in a number of Member States, for example in paragraphs 327a–327f of the German *Aktiengesetz*. Takeover squeeze-out procedures have been introduced for the first time in a number of Member States including Greece, Spain, Luxembourg, Malta, Slovenia and Slovakia. The use of the procedure enables a bidder to finalise a takeover, indeed may render a takeover bid more attractive. In the United Kingdom, it is provided for in the somewhat detailed provisions of section 979 of the Companies Act 2006. According to paragraph 2 of this section, if the offeror has by virtue of the offer acquired or unconditionally contracted to acquire not less than 90 per cent in value of the shares to which an offer relates, and where the shares are voting shares not less than 90 per cent of the voting rights carried by those shares, he may give notice to the holder of any shares to which the offer relates which he has not acquired or unconditionally contracted to acquire that he wishes to acquire those shares. The 90 per cent threshold of capital and voting rights is common in many Member States. The Takeover Directive also offers certain guarantees to minority shareholders which are mentioned below.

[36] Member States may set a higher threshold which may not be higher than 95 per cent of the capital carrying voting rights and 95 per cent of the voting rights. The new German provisions governing the squeeze out and sell out procedures contained in paras. 39a and 39c of the Takeover Act 2002 as amended in 2006 are conditional on the holding by the bidder of share capital carrying at least 95 per cent of the voting rights.

6. The Mandatory bid rule

This rule, which has been explained above, appears to be familiar in all the Member States but, as already pointed out the relevant control thresholds vary from 25 per cent of the voting rights in Hungary (provided that no other shareholder holds more than 10 per cent of the voting rights in the company) to 66 per cent in Poland. The most common control threshold is 30 per cent, as in the United Kingdom. The rule is protective of minority shareholders by granting them the right to sell their shares in the event of a change of control, as well as the advantage of the premium paid for the controlling block. Article 5 of the Takeover Directive, which makes provision for the mandatory bid rule contains a rule in paragraph 6 thereof which provides for further instruments to protect the interest of the holders of securities insofar as these instruments do not hinder the normal course of the bid. The precise effect of the provision does not seem entirely clear. Member States have frequently derogated from the Directive's provisions in order to maintain their exceptions from the mandatory bid rule. Certain of these exceptions have been rather far-reaching, and, as is the case with paragraph 37 of the German Takeover Act of 2002, are applicable by the supervisory authority.[37] The relevant exemption appears to be of a rather broad character.

7. Sell-out rights

The above right is provided for in Article 16 of the Takeover Directive, and provides minority shareholders with a right corresponding to the squeeze-out right; it protects minority shareholders from abuse by a majority shareholder of his dominant position. A sell-out is available to such shareholders when following a bid made to all the offeror's shareholders, the offeror holds securities representing not less than 90 per cent of the capital carrying voting rights and 90 per cent of the voting rights in the offeree company. Once again, Member States may set a higher threshold which may not be higher than 95 per cent of the capital carrying voting rights and 95 per cent of the voting rights. Member States must ensure that the shares are bought at a fair price. The sell-out

[37] This paragraph stipulates that the supervisory authority may release the offeror from the obligation to publish and submit a mandatory takeover bid where this seems justified having regard to the interests of the offeror and the shareholders at the target company, the way in which control was obtained, the shareholder structure in the companies, the actual possibility of acquiring control or the need that the percentage of shares in the target company is reduced below the control threshold after the acquisition of control.

right is provided for in the detailed provisions of sections 983–985 of the United Kingdom Companies Act 2006, but it existed before the enactment of the Act. The provisions formally applicable were those of sections 430A–430C of the Companies Act 2006. Such a right was not provided for in a number of countries, including Germany, Austria, Spain and the Netherlands when the Takeover Directive was enacted.

8. Some other provisions of the Takeover Directive

Article 3 sets out a number of general principles which are to be complied with by Member States. Five of these principles are also to be found in the City Code. It has been suggested by Professor Rickford that some changes may have to be made in the existing Code to fit in with the general principles in the Directive.[38] Article 4, which is of a rather complex nature, is concerned with the supervisory authority and the applicable laws. The effect of Article 4(2)(e) will be to extend the jurisdiction of the Takeover Panel which will have to make rules giving effect to Article 4(2) of the Directive.[39] The subject matters of Articles 6 and 7 are information concerning takeovers and time related for acceptance. These matters are generally dealt with in the takeover rules of the Member States, which are likely however to require some modifications. Disclosure of the bid and all information concerning it are dealt with in Article 8. Member States are required by Article 8(1) to ensure that a bid is made public in such a way as to ensure market transparency and integrity for the securities of the offeree company, of the offeror and any other company affected by the bid, in particular in order to prevent the dissemination of false or misleading information.

9. Information for and consultation of employees' representatives

The above matter is dealt with in Article 14 of the Takeover Directive, which provides that this instrument shall be without prejudice to the rules relating to information and consultation of representatives of and, if Member States so provide co-determination with the employers of the offeror and offeree company governed by the relevant national provisions and in particular those adopted pursuant to Directives 94/45/EC (European Works Council Directive), 98/59EC (collective redundancies), 2001/86/EC (Employee Involvement Directive) and 2002/14/EC

[38] 'The Emerging European Takeover Law', 1410–11.

[39] Companies Act 2006, s. 943(1), see also Rickford's discussion of dual jurisdiction cases, above, 1417–18.

(Directive establishing a general framework for informing and consulting employees in the EC). In addition, the board or the offeree company is required to draw up a document giving its opinion on the bid, and its view on the effect of the implementation of the bid on all the company's interests including employees, and on the offerors' strategic plans for the company, and their likely impact on employment. This document must be communicated to the employees' representatives or where there are no such representatives to the employees themselves. Where the board of the offeree company receives in good time a separate opinion from the representatives of its employees on the effects of the bid on employment, this opinion must be appended to the document.

10. Sanctions

Article 17 is concerned with sanctions which, in the customary language used in Community instruments, are required to be effective, proportionate and dissuasive. The Takeover Panel may impose a number of sanctions ranging from reprimand to making a reference for cold-shouldering action to the Financial Services Authority. However, the principal statutory sanction in the United Kingdom is contained in section 143 of the Financial Services and Markets Act 2000, which permits the Financial Services Authority on the request of the panel to sanction market professionals. Such a sanction may involve the loss of the licence to trade.

According to Article 4(5) of the Takeover Directive, the supervisory authorities should be vested with all the powers necessary for the purpose of carrying out their duties, including that of ensuring that the parties to a bid comply with the rules made or introduced pursuant to the Directive. It does not appear that there is any objection to using combined supervisory authorities for the purposes of Section 143, i.e. the Panel and the Financial Services Authority.

11. Concluding remarks

The Takeover Directive has some positive features, for example the provisions of Articles governing the disclosure of defences and the general principles contained in Article 3. However, the use of the options permitting Member States not to apply the neutrality or breakthrough rule, and of the provision for reciprocity in Article 12(3) has done little to encourage the belief that the Directive has created a market for corporate control in the European Union. The Commission has stated its intention to clearly monitor the way in which the Directive's rules are applied and work in practice. It will analyse the reasons why Member States are so reluctant to endorse the fundamental rules of the Directive. The Commission has added[40] that in the light of the evaluation, the revision of the Directive scheduled for 2011[41] may if necessary be brought forward. It seems somewhat doubtful whether this will happen in practice.

[40] Commission Staff Working Document, SEC (2007), 268.
[41] See Art. 20 of the Directive.

11

Investor protection

I. Introduction

Member States of the European Union have followed very different models for investor protection. The extent to which company legislation provides protection for investors in shares and bonds, and for minority shareholders, has varied considerably. The regulatory regimes dealing with the control of the prospectus, with financial reporting and with different aspects of the primary markets (new issues) and secondary markets (trading in shares and bonds and related derivatives) has varied even more.[1] The distinction between what is considered to belong to company law and to market regulation is also drawn differently. All Member States have seen a strengthening of the regulatory protection of investors, whatever their starting point. There has been a considerable convergence in the level and form of investor protection. European Union Law has played an important part in this, and the regulatory regime is now based on a set of directives. As discussed in previous chapters, minority shareholders' rights and the liability of directors is not yet harmonised in the way financial reporting and the further regulatory regime are. The present chapter will be concerned most principally with Directive 2003/6/EC of the European Parliament and the Council on insider dealing and market abuse.[2] The Directive has amended and extended the previous rules of Community law relating to insider dealing, and also covers market manipulation, as defined in Article 1(2). The new rules on insider dealing are similar to those

[1] The differences between the highly developed systems of the United Kingdom and France and more minimalist one in Germany and the smaller countries of the present study, also to some extent reflect the different relative roles of capital markets and banks and other credit institutions.

[2] Directive 2003/6/EC of the European Parliament and of the Council of 28 January 2003 on Insider Dealing and Market Manipulation (Market Abuse), 2003 OJ L96/16. This chapter will not deal with the EU directives on the stock exchanges or with the rules governing the offering of securities to the public. The rules governing takeover bids which were considered above in Chapter 10 are also relevant to investor protection.

contained in the 1989 Directive in many ways. Those on market manipulation are influenced by the United Kingdom Market Code, and the new regulatory regime is influenced by the situation in the more sophisticated financial markets. The complexity has posed a challenge for the implementation in the less developed financial markets in the Member States. [3]

Insider dealing has been usually understood to mean transactions in shares and other transferable securities by persons who by reason of their position are in possession of price sensitive information which has not been made public and who take advantage of their position by acquiring or disposition of such securities.[4] Transactions by persons who take corresponding advantage after directly or indirectly receiving price sensitive information from such persons, have also been classified as insider dealing.

Insider dealing was first dealt with in Europe, in contrast to the United States, by self-regulation which has certain inadequacies. The first country in Europe to introduce statutory regulation of such dealing was France, initially by Ordinance 67-833 of 1967. It is now regulated by Article L465-1 of the *Code Monétaire et Financier* which provides for penal sanctions and by Articles 622-1 and 622-2 of the *Règlement Général de L'Autorité des Marchés Financiers* in that country.[5] Other Member States have introduced statutory rules governing insider dealing including the United Kingdom, Belgium, the Netherlands, Spain and Germany. The introduction of such rules was made necessary by the enactment of Council Directive EEC/89/842 coordinating regulation on insider dealing in 1989.[6] This Directive was a minimum standards directive which emphasised the need for the smooth operation of the market in its Preamble. The last country to implement it was Germany in 1994. As in the United Kingdom and France, the German legislation made insider dealing a criminal offence.

[3] As will be discussed at the end of this chapter, also certain of the more economically developed Member States of the EU did not bring the Market Abuse Directive and its technical implementing instruments into force by the required time (October 2004). The European Commission brought infringement procedures under Art. 226 EC for failure to transpose the Directive and implementing instruments against a majority of Member States, including the United Kingdom and France.

[4] Note in this sense K. Hopt and E. Wymeersch, *European Insider Dealing* (London: Butterworths, 1991), p. v.

[5] Market manipulation is now dealt with in France by Arts. 633-1–633-4 of the *Règlement Général*, which transposed certain of the provisions of the Market Abuse Directive.

[6] OJ 1989 L334/30.

It is noteworthy that economists have sometimes contended that insider dealing may have beneficial effects.[7] Legislation imposing criminal penalties on insider dealing has been justified in recent years on the basis of the need to protect the market on which securities are quoted, rather than on the basis of the need to impose criminal penalties for the violation of the fiduciary duties of directors and others towards the company. Thus, Recital 15 of the Preamble to the Market Abuse Directive provides that insider dealing and market manipulation prevents full and proper market transparency, which is a prerequisite of trading for all economic actors in an integrated financial market.

Article 20 of the Market Abuse Directive repeals the earlier Directive of 1989 governing insider dealing. As already indicated, the Market Abuse Directive is concerned both with insider dealing and market manipulation, which are defined in Article 1, paragraphs 1 and 2. The Financial Services Action Plan, published by the Commission in 1999, emphasised the need for a directive on market manipulation to supplement the existing one on insider dealing. The new Directive makes use of the Lamfalussy procedure, which has sometimes been criticised by the European Parliament, according to which Framework Directives may be supplemented by implementing rules made by the Commission in accordance with the comitology procedure where implementation is thought to give rise to technical questions. The Market Abuse Directive was itself made under the co-decision procedure provided for by Article 251 EC. This complex procedure gives a fundamentally important role to the European Parliament, and its use may result in delays. A number of implementing measures have been adopted by the Commission after consulting the Committee on European Securities Regulation (CESR), which is made up of representatives of the national supervisory authorities.[8] These measures include the Commission Directive 2004/72/EC on accepted market practices, the definition of inside information in relation to derivatives or commodities, the drawing up of lists of insiders, the notification of managers' transactions and the notification of suspicious transactions; Commission Directive 2005/125 on the definition of insider information and market manipulation, as well as on the mandatory disclosure of market information; a directive on the fair presentation

[7] The view has been advocated that such dealing is a victimless crime, which may increase market efficiency. Insider trading may theoretically lead to information being reflected more rapidly in the market prices than if trading is restricted to reflect only information that is available to the whole market.

[8] CESR was established by Commission Decision 2001/527/EC of 6 June 2001, OJ L191/43.

of investment recommendations and the disclosure of conflicts of interest;[9] and a regulation on the safe harbour attached to certain share buy-back programmes and stabilisation schemes.[10]

The Lamfalussy procedure includes two further levels of law making, namely securing the uniform implementation of EU law, and ensuring its proper enforcement.

Originally the Commission envisaged only a directive on market manipulation to supplement the Insider Dealing Directive of 1989, but it came to the conclusion that a more comprehensive instrument was necessary. This approach may have been influenced by the enactment of the Financial Services and Markets Act 2000 in the UK, section 11 of this Act employs the concept of market abuse, which embraces insider dealing and market manipulation. The purpose[11] of the Act was to introduce an administrative regime to supplement the original regime already applicable to insider dealing in the United Kingdom.

The Market Abuse Directive deals with three related matters, insider dealing, disclosure and market manipulation. It covers financial instruments which are traded on a regulated market. The kinds of financial instrument are set out in Article 1(3) of the Directive which covers all types of securities, such as equities, debts, options and derivatives on commodities. A regulated market is defined in Article 1(4) of the Market Abuse Directive which refers to Article 7(13) of the Investment Services Directive of 1992, which provides that Member States shall list their regulated markets. As was the case with Article 2(4) of the Insider Dealing Directive of 1989, Article 7 of the Market Abuse Directive contains an exemption for transactions carried out in pursuit of monetary exchange rate or public debt management policy by a Member State, by the European System of Central Banks and national central banks or any other officially designated body.

II. Insider dealing

In the United States, the prohibition of insider dealing has been developed by the courts relying on the provision on fraud contained in section 10(b)

[9] Commission Directive 2005/125 of 22 December 2003 implements the provisions of Art. 6(3) of the Market Abuse Directive.

[10] The Exemptions Regulation, Commission Regulation EC 2273/2003.

[11] Note in this context, the comprehensive article by Professor J. L. Hansen, 'MAD in a Hurry: The Swift and Promising Adoption of the EU Market Abuse Directive' (2004) 15 EBLR 183–221.

of the Securities Exchange Act 1934 and SEC Rule 10b-5 made thereunder. However, it seems that the recent European approach has not been so much based upon the abuse of information by insiders, but rather on the need to prevent distortions in the market from being caused by trading on information concerning financial instruments which has not been made public.[12] Even though this may be the case, the Market Abuse Directive makes use of the term 'inside' information, although it seems clear from Article 2(1) of the Directive that such information may be possessed by persons who are not necessarily in a fiduciary position, for example persons who obtain the information by virtue of their holding of capital of the issuer, or by reason of their criminal activities.[13]

Article 1(1) of the Directive provides that 'inside information' shall be information of a precise nature which has not been made public relating, directly or indirectly, to one or more issuers of financial instruments, or to one or more financial instruments and which, if it were made public, would be likely to have a significant effect on the prices of those financial instruments, or on the prices of related derivative financial instruments.[14] It also stipulates that in relation to derivatives on commodities, inside information shall mean information of a precise nature which has not been made public relating directly or indirectly to one or more such derivatives, and which users of markets on which such derivatives are traded would expect to receive in accordance with accepted market practices on those markets.

The test of whether information is public is one of availability. Thus, Recital 31 of the Preamble to the Directive states that research and estimates derived from publicly available data should not be regarded as inside information. The fact that data are publicly available does not, of course, entail that both parties to a transaction have an equal capacity to obtain access to it.

The categories of insiders mentioned in Article 2(1) of Directive 2003/6/EC are similar to those included in the Insider Dealing Directive of

[12] The sixteenth paragraph of the Preamble mentions information which could have a significant effect on the evolution and formation of the prices of a regulated market as such. Note in the present context, Hansen, 'MAD in a hurry', 192–4.

[13] See Recital 17 of the Preamble to the Market Abuse Directive, which indicates that inside information may result from the preparation or execution of criminal activities, which could have a significant effect on the prices of one or more financial instruments or on price information in the regulated market as such.

[14] As already indicated, the phrase 'financial instrument' is given a very wide definition in the Directive.

1989. The 1989 Directive distinguished between primary and secondary outsiders: the second category were persons who received information from primary outsiders. The 2003 Directive also makes a distinction between categories of insiders mentioned in Article 2 and those mentioned in Article 4, who are persons possessing information which they know or ought to have known that it is insider information. The language of Article 4 makes clear that such persons do not need to have received the information from a primary insider within Article 2.

Article 2 of the Insider Dealing Directive of 1989 prohibited any person who possessed inside information from taking advantage of it with full knowledge of the facts. This requirement is absent from the Market Abuse Directive of 2003. However, this matter may not be of much significance because it will still be necessary to prove that a primary insider is in possession of the relevant information when the transaction took place, and it follows from the definition of inside information in Article 1(1) of the 2003 Directive that the information would have to be unavailable to the public and price sensitive. If criminal liability were imposed, these factors would be relevant to the *mens rea* of the defendant.[15]

III. Disclosure

Article 6(1) of the Market Abuse Directive requires Member States to ensure that the issuer of financial instruments informs the public as soon as possible of all inside information which directly concern the issuers. Article 6(1) of the Market Abuse Directive (much in the same way as did Article 7 of the 1989 Directive) places an emphasis on the need for the disclosure of inside information by the issuers of tradable securities and financial instruments in certain circumstances. Disclosure has been said to be a prophylactic against insider dealing, in the European context this is formulated by K. Hopt.[16]

The method by which disclosure is performed has been addressed in Commission Directive 2003/124 as regards the definition and public disclosure of inside information and the definition of market manipulation

[15] See P. K. Jain 'Significance of *mens rea* in insider trading' (2004) 25 Co Law 134 and Hansen, 'MAD in a hurry', 198. Criminal liability for insider trading was imposed in the UK by the Criminal Justice Act 1993, provided that the defendant has received information from an inside source.

[16] K. J. Hopt and E. Wymeersch, *European Insider Trading*, p. 148.

(the Definition and Disclosure Directive).[17] The Definition and Disclosure Directive provides that Member States have an option to provide an officially appointed mechanism for this purpose. In addition, Article 6(1), paragraph 2 of the Market Abuse Directive provides that Member States should ensure that issuers, for an appropriate period, post on their internet sites, all inside information that they are required to disclose publicly.

The temporary suspension of disclosure is justified under Article 6(2) of the Market Abuse Directive. The first sentence of this text provides that an issuer may under his own responsibility delay disclosure of inside information such as not to prejudice legitimate interests. This scope of Article 6(2) of the Market Abuse Directive has been particularised in Article 3 of the Definition and Disclosure Directive. There may be constricting considerations to bear in mind when determining when disclosure should be made. It follows from Article 6(3) of the Market Abuse Directive that when disclosure has been made to a third party in the normal exercise of his or her profession, employment or duties, complete and effective public disclosure should be made of the information. The Directive specifies that this disclosure should be made simultaneously in the case of an intentional disclosure and promptly in the case of a non-intentional disclosure. It adds that 'the provisions of the first sub-paragraph shall not apply if the person receiving the information owes a duty of confidentiality, regardless of whether such duty is based on a law, on regulations, on articles of association or on a contract'. This is linked to the next requirement, that 'Member States shall require that issuers, or persons acting on their behalf or for their account, draw up a list of those persons working for them, under a contract of employment or otherwise, who have access to inside information. Issuers and persons acting on their behalf or for their account shall regularly update this list and transmit it to the competent authority whenever the latter requests it.'

Article 6(2) further provides that disclosure may be delayed provided that such omission to disclose would not be likely to mislead the public and provided that the issuer is able to ensure the confidentiality of the

[17] Commission Directive 2003/124/EC of 22 December 2003 implementing Directive 2003/6/EC as regards the definition and public disclosure of inside information and the definition of market manipulation, OJ L339/, 70. Other Lamfalussy Level 2 instruments include Commission Directive 2003/125 concerning the fair presentation of investment recommendations and the disclosure of conflicts of interest, OJ L339/73, and Commission Regulation 2273/2003, OJ L336/33. Level 3 guidance is provided by the Committee of European Securities Regulators (CESR), in a document of 11 May 2005.

information. Such justified delay could occur in the context of takeover or merger negotiations, or when the issuer is in serious financial difficulties.[18] It should be noted that where disclosure can be delayed, the rules governing insider dealing are still applicable.

The former Insider Dealing Directive of 1989 contained two precautionary measures which were designed to reduce the risk of insider dealing. The first one of these was contained in Article 3(a) which required Member States to prohibit primary insiders from disclosing that information to any third party unless such disclosure was made in the normal course or the exercise of his or her employment, profession or duties. The exemption contained in Article 3(a) was an extensive one, but it was intended to deal with the fact that inter-company cooperation is widespread, as also is access to information via the internet. The prohibition was a wide one; it will catch an insider even if he or she is unaware that the information disclosed is inside information and he or she has no reasonable cause to believe that it will be used.[19]

Furthermore, Article 3(b) of the Insider Dealing Directive of 1989 prohibited primary insiders from recommending or procuring a third party on the basis of inside information to acquire or dispose of securities. It does not appear necessary that the person giving the option should be aware that the information on the basis of which he makes his or her own recommendation is inside information.[20]

The two preventative measures contained in the Insider Dealing Directive of 1989 have been retained with the same wording in Article 3(a) and (b) of the Market Abuse Directive of 2003. Article 6(3) of the Market Abuse Directive contains a prohibition on selective disclosure. Thus when such disclosure is made in accordance with the exemptions contained in Article 3(a), Article 6(3), paragraph 1 requires that a public disclosure

[18] Note on this, J. L. Hansen, 'MAD in a hurry', 202–3. The situation when the company is in serious financial difficulties is dealt with in Art. 3(1)(9), para. 2 of the Definition and Disclosure Directive. The exemption provides that the financial position of the issuer should be in great and imminent danger, and that disclosure would seriously jeopardise the interests of the shareholders by undermining the conclusion of speedy negotiations.

[19] Note in this sense, V. Edwards, *EC Company Law* (Oxford: Oxford University Press, 1999), p. 327.

[20] As pointed out by Edwards, *EC Company Law*, p. 327, the prohibition is not relaxed when the recommending or procuring takes place in the normal course of the person's employment, profession or business. Directors of an offeror company may be prevented from recommending their company to bid, and directors of the target company from recommending their shareholders to accept the offer.

should be made. However, this is not necessary if the recipient is required to respect the confidentiality of the inside information.[21]

Article 6(9) of the Market Abuse Directive provides that Member States shall require that any persons professionally arranging transactions in financial instruments who reasonably suspect that a transaction might constitute insider dealing or market manipulation shall notify the competent authority without delay. It should be noted that this obligation falls on stock exchanges and financial intermediaries and not on managers, lawyers or accountants who receive notice of lawful transactions.[22]

IV. Market manipulation

Market manipulation is defined in paragraphs (a) to (c) of Article 1(2) of the Market Abuse Directive, which also contains one example of each of the types of market manipulation mentioned in these paragraphs. Market manipulation does not only include misinformation, but also interference with market mechanisms by abusing a dominant position. Market manipulation of both kinds is prohibited by Article 5 of the Market Abuse Directive.

The different forms of market manipulation covered by Article 1(2) of the Directive include verbal misinformation, non-verbal misinformation, and the abuse of a dominant position. Verbal misinformation is dealt with in Article 1(2)(c) which mentions the dissemination of information through the media, including the internet or by any other means which gives or is likely to give, misleading signals as to the financial instrument, where the person who disseminated the information know, or ought to have known, that it was false or misleading. Non-verbal information is dealt with in Article 1(2)(a), paragraph 1 and Article 1(2)(b), which respectively mention transactions or orders to trade which give or are likely to give false or misleading signals as to the supply or demand for or price of financial instruments, or which employs fictitious devices or any other form of deception or contrivance. Abuse of a dominant position is treated in Article 1(2)(a), paragraph 2 as transactions or orders to trade which secure, by a person, or persons acting in collaboration, the price of one or several financial instruments

[21] See Art. 6(3) para. 2.

[22] See U. Noack and W. Zetsche, 'Corporate Governance Reform in Germany' (2005) 16 EBLR 818.

at an abnormal or artificial level. Whether or not behaviour is considered to constitute such abuse, depends on market conditions.

A defence is offered to market manipulation in Article 1(2)(a) where the person who entered into the transactions or issued the orders to trade establishes that his reasons for so doing are legitimate and that these transactions or orders to trade conform to accepted market practices on the regulated market concerned. Verbal dissemination of misinformation has to be considered against the background of the right to freedom of speech, which is recognised in human rights instruments, and which appears of special significance to the media. Journalists may legitimately claim the right to publish material which may be controversial in a system with a free press, and critical and investigative journalism is playing an increasing role in the financial markets. According to Recital 22 to the Preamble of the Market Abuse Directive, Member States are free to choose the most appropriate way to regulate persons producing or disseminating research concerning financial instruments or issuers of financial instruments or persons producing or disseminating other information recommending or suggesting investment strategy, including appropriate mechanisms for self-regulation. The Investment Recommendations Directive[23] takes account of the need for the regulation of journalists. Furthermore, Recital 44 of the Market Abuse Directive mentions the Charter of Fundamental Rights of the EU and the European Convention on Human Rights, and requires that the Directive does not in any way prevent Member States applying their constitutional rules relating to the freedom of the press and freedom of expression in the media.

The first of the examples of market manipulation given in Article 1(2)[24] is of an abuse of dominant position. The abuse takes place when there is conduct by a person, or persons acting in collaboration, to secure a dominant position over the supply of or demand for a financial instrument which has the effect of fixing, directly or indirectly, purchase or sale prices or creating other unfair trading conditions. The example of non-verbal communication consists of the buying or selling of financial instruments at the close of the market with the effect of misleading

[23] Commission Directive 2003/125/EC of 22 December 2003 implementing Directive 2003/6/EC as regards the fair presentation of investment recommendations and the disclosure of conflicts of interest, OJ L339/73–7.

[24] After the general definitions offered in (a)–(c), the Directive offers examples which are introduced in this way: 'In particular, the following instances are derived from the core definition given in points (a), (b) and (c) above.'

investors acting on the basis of closing prices. The example of verbal misinformation consists of taking advantage of occasional or regular access to the traditional or electronic media by voicing an opinion about a financial instrument (or indirectly about its issuer) while having previously taken positions on that financial instrument and profiting subsequently from the impact of the opinions voiced on the price of that instrument, without having simultaneously disclosed that conflict of interest to the public in a proper and effective way.

The last part of paragraph 1(2) states that the definitions of market manipulation shall be adapted so as to ensure that new patterns of activity that in practice constitute market manipulation can be included.

V. Standard of communication

According to Article 6(5) of the Market Abuse Directive, Member States are required to ensure that the disseminators of communications take reasonable care to ensure that information is fairly represented, and disclose their interest or indicate conflicts of interest concerning the financial instruments to which that information relates.

Because of the particular consideration given to the media, the Investment Recommendations Directive[25] has taken a restrictive view of the concept of investment recommendations insofar as they would expressly or implicitly indicate an investment strategy.[26] Distinct advice is classified as implicit recommendations whilst reference to a price target or otherwise constitutes implicit recommendation. Such implicit recommendations would mainly be given by natural or legal persons active on the financial services industry, and arguably not by journalists.

Part II of the Investment Recommendations Directive governs the production of information whilst Part III governs those who disseminate it. Those who produce recommendations must identify themselves and their regulatory body,[27] and take care that facts are differentiated from interpretation and that their sources are reliable.[28] They must also be able to substantiate recommendations made at the request of the authorities.[29]

[25] Directive 2003/125/EC, OJ/L339, 73–7.

[26] J. L. Hansen, 'MAD in a Hurry', 208–9, contending that if journalists have investments of their own, they might be guilty of market manipulation within Art. 5.

[27] Investment Recommendations Directive, Art. 2(1) and (2).

[28] *Ibid.*, Art. 3(1). [29] *Ibid.*, Art. 3(3).

Certain recommendations are made subject to more stringent requirements and are applicable to financial analysts and investment firms. Such persons and firms are required to give particulars of all substantial sources, and disclose whether their recommendation has been given to or amended by the issuer. Particulars must also be given of the bases of valuation and be dated. Mention must also be made as to whether the recommendation differs from other ones made on the same subject within the past twelve months.[30] Disclosure must be made of all economic engagements which may be expected to impair objectivity. The remuneration of natural persons making the recommendation must be disclosed, as also whether they have any connections with investment banking or have received or bought shares from the issuer prior to a public offering of securities.[31] Disclosure must also be made on a quarterly basis by the financial professionals of the proportion of recommendations falling within particular categories, such as to buy, hold or sell.[32] The disclosure requirements are intended to give particulars of all relevant factors which may have given rise to the suspicion of lack of impartiality had they not been provided.

Those who disseminate recommendations made by others are required to identify themselves by Article 7 of the Investment Recommendations Directive. Persons who make significant changes to a recommendation made by others are bound by the rules governing producers of information.[33] Nevertheless, only professionals such as investment firms, have to comply with all the rules which apply to producers, which include the disclosure of possible conflicts of interest.[34] If a disseminator merely summarises information which others have produced, it is enough to make sure that such summary is not misleading. The source of information should be disclosed in order that members of the public may reach their own conclusions.[35]

VI. Safe harbour

Two safe harbours exists in accordance with Article 8 of the Investment Recommendations Directive: one of these is for trading in own shares in buy-back programmes, whilst the other is for stabilisation of a financial

[30] *Ibid.*, Art. 4(1). [31] *Ibid.*, Art. 6(3). [32] *Ibid.*, Art. 6(4).
[33] *Ibid.*, Art. 8, which makes reference to Arts. 2–5.
[34] *Ibid.*, Art. 9. [35] *Ibid.*, Art. 8(4).

instrument. The Commission has enacted a Safe Harbour Regulation[36] as it was required to do by Article 8 of the Investment Recommendations Directive.

If a company issuing shares which are publicly traded, trades in its own shares, it will be in possession of certain information about itself and its financial situation, certain of which may be unavailable to the public even if the company is bound by a continuous disclosure obligation.[37] The company's dealings in own shares is likely on this ground to contravene the ban on insider dealing. Furthermore, there is a possibility that the directors and senior officers of the company may be able to manipulate the market. A company acquisition of its own shares is at present subject to the safeguards contained in Article 19 of the Second Company Law Directive, the modernisation of the regime contained in this Directive has been recommended by the Commission,[38] but no revision of the Directive with this aim has yet taken place. At present, a public company may only acquire its own shares if the shareholders have so resolved in general meeting, the acquisition has not exceeded 10 per cent of the company's share capital; the funds used must come out of assets available for distribution, and only fully paid up shares may be acquired. It has frequently been contended that if a company is permitted to trade in its own shares, this may be beneficial to the company in some circumstances. In the past, some Member States have forbidden companies to trade in their own shares, but this approach has generally been abandoned in recent years.[39]

Article 8 of the Market Abuse Directive gives a safe harbour to a company that buys back its own shares in the context of implementing measures contained in the implementation measure, is inapplicable in certain other situations, for example where a company wishes to sell its own shares after having acquired them, or to acquire debt securities. The Safe Harbour Regulation permits the acquisition of shares for the purpose of reducing the company's capital, or meeting the requirements of

[36] Commission Regulation (EC) 2273/2003 implementing Directive 2003/6/EC as regards exemptions for buy-back programmes and stabilisation of financial instruments, 23 December 2003, OJ L336/33.

[37] See Art. 6(2) of the Market Abuse Directive.

[38] See the European Commission's Action Plan, *Modernising Company Law and Enhancing Corporate. Governance in the European Union – A Plan to Move Forward*, COM (2003) 284 final of 21 May 2003. See however the reforms that were implemented by Directive 2006/68/EC of 6 September 2006 amending Council Directive 77/91/EEC as regards the formation of public limited liability companies and the maintenance and alteration of their capital.

[39] See, e.g. the detailed rules contained in paras. 71–71e of the German *Aktiengesetz* concerning the acquisition by a company of its own shares, and related matters.

convertible debt instruments, or selling as an incentive scheme for employees.[40] The acquisition must be regulated by a programme, which must conform with the requirements of the Second Company Law Directive, and it must not begin until the programme has been published.

The safe harbour programme for share purchases is subject to these restrictions. The issuer is not permitted to sell its own shares during the existence of the programme.[41] Furthermore, it may not buy or sell when it has decided to postpone publication of inside information under Article 6(2) of the Market Abuse Directive. The rule is designed to prevent any infringement of the prohibition of insider trading. Finally, the issuer is only permitted to trade within closed periods, as prescribed by national law.[42]

These restrictions are inapplicable if the programme is managed by an investment undertaking which acts independently of the issuer, or if the intended transactions are set out in advance in the programme and free from the discretion of the issuer.[43] In such cases the trading in shares takes place independently from the control of the management of the issuer.

Financial institutions such as investment firms or banks are not subject to the restrictions of the availability of safe harbour for the purchase of shares contained in Articles 6(1)(a)–6(1)(e) of the Safe Harbour Regulation subject to the proviso that certain safeguards are provided to ensure that the inside information that such undertakings may have about the issuers as the result of their activities is unavailable to other persons working for the same undertaking.[44] These information barriers are familiarly called Chinese walls, and may sometimes prove to be ineffective.

The Market Abuse Directive contains a safe harbour for stabilisation in Article 8. Such stabilisation has to conform with certain requirements set out in the Safe Harbour Regulation, relating to such matters as disclosure before and after the stabilisation periods and time limits for that period. The purpose of stabilisation is to maintain the initial offer price, and combat pressures exerted by speculators.

VII. Preventive measures

The Market Abuse Directive requires participants in the market[45] to establish certain means of control to contribute to market integrity.

[40] See Art. 3 of the Safe Harbour Regulation. [41] Safe Harbour Regulation, Art. 6(1)(a).
[42] *Ibid.*, Art. 6(1)(b). [43] *Ibid.*, Art. 6(3). [44] *Ibid.*, Art. 6(2) and (3).
[45] Recital 24 of the Preamble to the Market Abuse Directive calls such participants 'professional economic actors'.

Recital 24 provides that such measures could include the creation of 'grey lists', the application of 'window trading' to sensitive categories of persons, the application of internal codes of conduct, and the establishment of Chinese walls. A 'grey list' consists of a list of companies the services of which a company's employees are required not to trade in whilst they are on the list. The phrase 'window trading' applies to a rule in a company governing when it is permissible to trade in particular securities. Codes of conduct consist of the rules made by self-regulatory bodies and the issuers' own rules governing the treatment of inside information. Chinese walls are intended to prevent employees who are empowered to engage in trading from obtaining information from other departments of the company. At the present, the above categories of measures are recommended while certain other types of preventative measures are made mandatory by the Market Abuse Directive. Thus the third paragraph of Article 6(3) provides that issuers or persons acting on their behalf or for their accounts, draw up a list of those persons working for them under a contract of employment who have access to the inside information. This list is intended to deter insider dealing, and must be distinguished from the list of persons discharging managerial responsibilities provided for by Article 6(4), which provision requires such persons to disclose managerial transactions in the shares of the issuer or in derivatives or other financial instruments linked to them. This list is intended as a preventative measure against market abuse.[46]

Disclosure may be used to prevent and deter market manipulation practices; this is recognised in Article 6(6) of the Market Abuse Directive. It provides that Member States should ensure that market operators adopt structural provisions to achieve these goals. Such disclosure is required under Article 4(4) of the Safe Harbour Regulation. This provision stipulates that the issuer must give publicity to share buy-backs which take place in conformity with the programme.

VIII. Supervisory authority and sanctions

Article 11 of the Market Abuse Directive provides that without prejudice to the competences of judicial authorities, each Member State shall designate a single administrative authority competent to ensure that the provisions adopted pursuant to the Directive are applied. It is

[46] This is recognised in Recital 26 to the Preamble of the Market Abuse Directive.

thought that a variety of competent authorities in a Member State may create confusion.[47]

According to Article 12(1) of the Market Abuse Directive, the competent authority shall be given all supervisory and investigative powers that are necessary for the exercise of its functions. It may exercise such powers directly, or in collaboration with other authorities or with the market undertakings, or under the responsibility by delegation to such authorities or to the market undertakings, or by application to the competent judicial authorities. The powers of the competent authority are set out in Article 12(2), and are of an extensive nature, including access to documents, the right to demand information from any person, the freezing of assets, carrying out on-site inspections, and the ability to require the cessation of any practice which is contrary to the provisions adopted in the implementation of the Directive. The authorities would, of course, have to be in conformity with European Human Rights Law.

By Article 13, the obligation of professional secrecy applies to all persons who work for the competent authority, or for any other authority or market undertaking to whom the competent authority has delegated its powers. Furthermore, Article 14(1) provides for administrative measures to be taken or administrative measure imposed which shall ensure effective, proportionate and dissuasive enforcement. The Market Abuse Directive does not explain what are meant by administrative sanctions.

IX. Implementation in the Member States

The Market Abuse Directive and the implementing instruments which followed its adoption have endeavoured to achieve a considerable degree of harmonisation of national law regarding market abuse and disclosure. It appears to have been influenced by the situation in the more sophisticated financial markets, and the complexity has posed a challenge for implementation in the less developed financial markets in the Member States. However, also certain of the more economically developed Member

[47] This is stated in Recital 36 to the Preamble to the Market Abuse Directive. This Recital also provides that such an authority should be of an administrative nature, guaranteeing its independence of economic actors and avoiding conflicts of interest. The Committee on Economic and Monetary Affairs of the European Parliament recommended that in accordance with national law, Member States shall ensure the appropriate financing of such an authority in its amendments to Recital 36, which were adopted. The authority should assume at least final responsibility for supervising compliance with the provisions adopted pursuant to this Directive, as well as international collaboration.

States of the EU have not managed to bring the Market Abuse Directive and its technical implementing instruments into force by the required time (which was 12 October 2004). The European Commission brought infringement procedures under Article 226 EC for failure to transpose the Directive and implementing instruments, against sixteen Member States, including the United Kingdom, France, Spain, Sweden, Belgium and the Netherlands. Several of the countries, including the United Kingdom, have subsequent to the institution of these proceedings implemented the requirements of the Directive satisfactorily.

X. Implementation in the United Kingdom

The implementation of the Market Abuse Directive in the United Kingdom was the subject of a joint consultation by the Financial Services Authority (FSA) and the Treasury (Ministry of Finance) which took place in 2004. Although the regime governing market abuse under the Financial Services and Markets Act 2000 was generally similar to that provided for in the Market Abuse Directive and the secondary legislation which complements certain of its provisions, there were some differences between these regimes.[48]

The Financial Services and Markets Act 2000 (Market Abuse) Regulation 2005[49] makes changes both to Part 8 of the Financial Services and Markets Act 2000 and to the Prescribed Markets and Qualified Investments Order of 2001.[50] Section 118 of the Financial Services and Markets Act, as amended by Schedule 2 to the Market Abuse Regulations of 2005, uses the term 'market abuse' to denote both insider dealing and market manipulation. The relevant subsections deal with seven types of behaviour. 'Inside information' is defined in section 118C of the amended Financial Services and Markets Act 2000. This definition appears to comply with the requirements of the Market Abuse Directive.

The new section 118B of the Financial Services and Markets Act deals with five categories of insiders: managers and shareholders, employees and professional advisers, and persons who have obtained information by other means. The latter category of persons must know, or could reasonably be expected to know, that the information is inside information.

[48] For a helpful account of these differences, see 'Implementation of Directive requires changes to the UK market abuse regime' (2004) 25 Co Law 279–80.

[49] SI 2005 No. 381. [50] SI 2001 No. 996.

The prohibition of market manipulation contained in new sections 118(5)–(7) follow the requirements of the Directive. However, the prohibition contained in new section 118(8) appears to have been based upon the definition of market abuse contained in former sections 118(2)(b) and (c) of the Financial Services and Markets Act 2000.

Article 10(1) of the Market Abuse Directive requires each Member State to apply the prohibitions and requirements provided for in the Directive to actions carried out on its territory or abroad concerning financial instruments which are admitted to trading on a regulated market situated or operating within the its territory or for which a request for admission to trading on suck a market has been made. Formerly, in the United Kingdom, only behaviour in relation to investments specified for the purposes of section 22 of the Financial Services and Markets Act 2000 used to be covered by the market abuse regime. The position has been altered by regulation. Section 10(2) of the Market Abuse Regulations of 2005, which amends the Prescribed Markets and Qualifying Instruments Order of 2001 so as to extend the scope of the markets to which certain provisions of Part 8 of the Financial Services and Markets Act 2000 applies to regulated markets.

By Article 10(2) of the Markets Abuse Directive, each Member State must apply the prohibitions and requirements provided for in the Directive to actions carried out on its territory concerning financial instruments that are admitted to trading on a regulated market in a Member State or for which a request for admission for trading on such market has been made. The scope of the qualifying instruments is, according to Article 10(2) of the United Kingdom Market Abuse Regulations of 2005, extended to include all financial instruments within the meaning of Article 1(3) of the Market Abuse Directive, which includes financial instruments admitted to a regulated market in a Member State.

Amendments to the Listing Rules have been made to take account of the disclosure provisions in the Market Abuse Directive. The Listing Rules used only to cover issuers whose securities were admitted to the official list. However, the Market Abuse Directive has a wider ambit; it follows from Article 10 that it is applicable to all issuers whose securities are admitted to trading (or for which a request for such admission has been made) on a regulated market in a Member State. Schedule 1 to the Market Abuse Regulations of 2005 amends Part 6 of the Financial Services and Markets Act 2000, and prescribes (in the new section 96A) what the rules concerning financial instruments admitted to trading (or for which a request for such admission has been made) on a regulated market in the United Kingdom must contain.

Schedule 1 also makes amendments to section 91 of the Financial Services and Markets Act 2000, which is concerned with penalties for the breach of the Listing Rules, so as to extend the range of persons or entities liable to sanctions for infractions of the rules.

XI. Implementation in Germany

The German *Anlegerschutzverbesserungsgesetz* of 2004[51] attempts to secure increased transparency and imposes civil and criminal liability for misconduct on securities market actors. Article 1 of this law is chiefly concerned with the implementation of the Market Abuse Directive and the implementing measures defining details of it.[52] German law has had to change to accommodate the continuous disclosure requirement relating to inside information which is contained in Article 6(1) of the Market Abuse Directive. This has required alterations in the German *Wertpapierhandelsgesetz* (the Securities Trading Law). The implementation of Article 6(9) of the Market Abuse Directive, which has been called the European whistle-blowing provisions, entrusts that financial intermediaries and stock exchanges will be required to inform the *Bundesaufsichtsamt für Finanzdienstleistungen* (the Federal Agency for Financial Services) of any fact which gives rise to the assumption that a transaction constitutes insider dealing or market manipulation.[53]

The German provisions on market manipulation which were enacted in the *Viertes Finanzförderungsgesetz* of 2002 (the Fourth Law on the Improvement of the Financial Markets)[54] have undergone some changes. The finding of market manipulation will no longer require acts in bad faith.[55] The specific actions which constitute market manipulation have been set out in an order made by the Federal Ministry of Finance. Furthermore, the *Bundesaufsichtsamt für Finanzdienstleistungen* will be enabled to interpret and define provisions of European and German securities law. The changes in German law have been thought to be

[51] BGBl 2004, 2630. The title may be translated as Law on the Improvement of Investor Protection.

[52] See U. Noak and S. Zetzsche, 'Corporate Governance Reform in Germany' (2006) 16 EBLR 1033, at 1047 and 1048 for a brief account of the implementation of relevant instruments in Germany.

[53] See paras. 10 and 14 of the *Wertpapierhandelsgesetz*. [54] BGBl 1 (2002) 201.

[55] See para. 20a(1) of the *Wertpapierhandelsgesetz*.

justified by Article 12 of the Market Abuse Directive which provides that the competent authority shall be given all the supervisory powers necessary for the exercise of its functions.[56] The power to cooperate with competent authorities in other Member States, which is provided for by Article 16 of the Market Abuse Directive, is given by paragraph 36 of the *Wertpapierhandelsgesetz*.

[56] The extended powers given to the *Bundesaufsichtsamt für Finanzdienstleistungen* has been criticised as contrary to German constitutional law, see Noak and Zetzsche, 'Corporate Governance Reforms', 1048–9.

INDEX

abuse of dominant position, 525–6
accounts
  See also specific countries and entities
  directives, 24–5
  disclosure, 265
  diversity of practices, 37
  merger accounting, 44–5
  special purpose vehicles, 25
  standards, 24–5, 33
  UK-Irish practices, 44
acquisition of own shares. *See* **purchase of own shares**
agencies, freedom of establishment, 7n, 10–11
audits
  directives, 25
  effectiveness, 265
Australia, objects clauses, 57n
Austria
  implementation of Takeover Directive, 507, 510
  partnerships, 144
  takeovers, sell-out right, 513

Belgian private companies (SPRLs) (BVPAs)
  See also **Belgium**
  bonds, 125–6, 261–3
    transfer, 126–7
  capital
    contributions in kind, 125
    increases, 222–4
    minimum, 90, 125
    payment for shares, 125
    payment on incorporation, 91
    preference shares, 187–8
    purchase of own shares, 241–4
    reductions, 225–6
    share transfers, restrictions, 109, 126–7
    shareholder liabilities, insolvency, 125
    shares, 125
    single-member companies, 42, 124–5
  directors
    appointments, 367
    conflicts of interest, 367
    powers, 367
  financial assistance for purchase of shares, prohibition, 246
  financial plans, 125
  incorporation, 90–1
  insolvency, 127–8
  management, 127–8, 367–8
  minority protection
    derivative actions, 368
    withdrawal rights, 489
  overview, 124–8
Belgian public companies (SAs) (NVs)
  accounts, approval, 365–6
  auditors
    discharge from responsibility, 366
    reports, 363
  bonds, 261–3
    convertible bonds, 263
    preferential rights, 263
  capital increases, 222–4
    bonds and, 263
    extraordinary general meetings, 366
  capital reductions, 225–6, 366

directors
  appointments, 361
  delegation powers, 362
  discharge from responsibility, 366
  effect of decisions, 362
  insolvency of companies, 365
  liabilities, 362–5
  numbers, 361
  powers, 361–2
  terms of office, 361
equity securities
  founders' shares, 186
  preference shares, 188–9
financial assistance for purchase of shares, 246
general meetings, 365–7
  approval of accounts, 365–6
  convening, 365
  discharge of directors' liabilities, 363
  extraordinary meetings, 366–7
  notices, 365
  powers, 365
  quorums, 366
  voting rights, 367
group companies, liabilities, 363–4
incorporation, 90–2
management, 361–7
market abuse
  implementation of Directive, 532
  insider dealing regulation, 517
minority protection, 363–4
  listed companies, 489
  mandatory bids, 490
  withdrawal rights, 489
purchase of own shares, 241–4
takeovers, regulation, 505
terminology, 104

Belgium
bonds, 261–3
  bondholders' meetings, 262–3
  lottery bonds, 261
  registration, 261
capital increases, 222–4
  authorisation, 222–3
  contributions in kind, 223, 224
  deeds, 223
  payments, 224
  pre-emption rights, 223–4
capital reductions, 192, 225–6
  amendment of articles, 225
  protection of creditors, 225–6
  purchase of own shares and, 242
company law
  influences, 50
  reform, 90
EEIGs, implementation of EC Regulation, 391
employee participation, 437–8
  information and consultation, 446
  works councils, 417, 437–8
equity securities, 186–9
  actions de jouissance, 242
  certificates, 186–7
  convertible bonds, 186
  preference shares, 186, 187–9
  private companies, 187–8
  public companies, 188–9
financial assistance for purchase of shares, 246
group companies, 460, 476–8
  group liability, 484
incorporation, 90–2
  pre-incorporation liabilities, 92
management, 361–8
  private companies, 127–8, 367–8
  public companies, 361–7
  shadow directors, 483, 484
minority protection
  listed companies, 489
  mandatory bids, 490
  private companies, 368, 489
  public companies, 363–4, 489–90
  purchase of shares, 488
  special investigations, 487
  withdrawal rights, 489
partnerships
  civil partnerships, 132
  deeds, 151
  general partnerships, 134, 150–1
  legal personality, 131, 134, 135, 151
  liabilities, 151, 158
  limited partnerships, 134, 157–8
  limited partnerships with shares (SCAs), 107, 109
  silent partnerships, 134

Belgium (cont.)
privatisations, 15–16
purchase of own shares, 241–4
limits, 243, 244
no reduction of capital, 242
price, 242
registration of companies, 91–2
boards, structures, 45–6
bonds
Belgium, 261–3
France, 250–3
Germany, 252–6
Italy, 256–9
Netherlands, 264
perpetual subordinated bonds, 248
priority ranking, 248
Spain, 259–61
United Kingdom, 249–50
Boucourechliev, Jeanne, 412
Boyle, Alan, 51
branches
disclosure requirements, 25–6
freedom of establishment, 7n, 10–11
Brazil, group companies, 47, 448, 456

Cadbury Report, 266
Capital
See also **purchase of own shares**
debt securities. *See* **loan capital**
EC Treaty and capital markets, 8
equity. *See* **equity securities**
free movement
case law, 14–20
direct effect, 20
golden shares, 15–20
harmonisation, 37–9, 104
increase and reduction, 192
Belgium, 222–6
France, 196–202
Germany, 202–11
Italy, 211–18
Netherlands, 226–30
Spain, 218–22
United Kingdom, 192–5
pre-emption rights, 37, 38–9
public companies, 52, 104
Chinese walls, 529, 530
civil law systems, influence, 43–4
collective redundancies, EC employee participation, 440–1
comitology, 6
communication standards, 526–7
companies, EC definition, 7n
Company Law Review Steering Group
alternative dispute resolution, 111
company formation, 55
constructive notice, 59n
deemed contracts, 58
electronic voting, 278
financial assistance for acquisition of shares, 110, 247
migration of companies, 60–1
objects clauses, 57n
comparative law, 2, 41–51
conflicts of interest, 43
constructive notice, 58–9
Contact Committees, 37
contracts, applicable law, 48
Convention on Mutual Recognition of Companies and Legal Persons, 9–10
Cork Report, 484
Corporate Law Group for Europe, proposal for, 32
Croatia, 47, 448
cross-border mergers
3rd Company Directive, 492–3
implementation, 495
10th Company Directive, 491
advantages over SE Statute, 493, 504
assessment, 504
implementation, 504
legal basis, 493
origins, 493
scope, 493–4
accounting, 44–5
cash and shares, 494–5
creditor protection, 497
effects, 498
employee participation, 498, 499–504
legal regime, 499–501
negotiations, 499, 501–2
standard rules, 499, 501, 502–3
employee rights, 503–4

formation, 495–6
freedom of establishment, 11–12
general meetings, 495
independent expert reports, 496–7
managers' reports, 496
meaning, 491
meaning of concentration, 451
national law, relevance, 495
public policy opposition, 497
publicity, 498
real seat doctrine, 496
registered offices, location, 496
scrutiny, 497–8
shareholder protection, 497

cross-border takeovers
13th Company Directive, 491
adoption, 506
assessment, 514–15
criticism, 507
implementation, 505, 507–8, 509–11
negotiations, 26–7, 506
origins, 506–7
overview, 507–15
revision, 515
board neutrality, 506, 507, 508–11
implementation, 509–11
breakthrough rule, 508–11
implementation, 509–11
defences, 507, 508–11
employee consultation, 513–14
information disclosure, 506, 513
mandatory bids, 512
meaning, 491
minority shareholders, 507
sell-out rights, 512–13
overview, 504–15
principles, 513
reciprocity exception, 507, 509
sanctions, 514
share transfer restrictions, 508
squeeze-out right, 511, 512
supervisory authorities, 513
voting rights restrictions, 508

Dailly, Senator, 166
Deakin, S., 34
debt securities. *See* **loan capital**

Denmark
implementation of Takeover Directive, 507
incorporation theory, 35
single-member companies, 42

derivatives, 520
directors. *See* **management**
Drury, Robert, 41, 129–30, 412

Emmerich, Volker, 460
employee participation
Belgium, 437–8
cross-border mergers, 498, 499–504
cross-border takeovers, 513–14
definitions, 402–3
diversity, 417–18
EC law, 440–7
collective redundancies, 440–1
draft 5th Directive, 446–7
information and consultation, 445–6
transfers of undertakings, 441–2
works council, 442–5
EPCs, 416
European Charter of Fundamental Social Rights, 443
European Companies, 402–8
European Cooperative Societies, 414
failure to harmonise, 104
Framework Directive, 418
France, 419–24
Germany, 424–35
Italy, 435
meaning, 419
Netherlands, 438–40
proposed harmonisation, 29, 32, 45–6
Spain, 418, 436–7
United Kingdom, 419

equity securities
2nd Company Directive, 169
acquisition of own shares. *See* **purchase of own shares**
Belgium, 186–9
debt securities and, 169, 248–9
diversity, 168
France, 171–5
Germany, 175–9

equity securities (cont.)
impact of directives, 20–1
Italy, 180–5
Netherlands, 189–91
preference shares, 169
Spain, 185–6
terminology, 168
transfers, 104
United Kingdom, 170–1
establishment. *See* **freedom of establishment**
European Associations, 412
European Charter of Fundamental Rights, 525
European Charter of Fundamental Social Rights, 443
European Community
Committee on European Securities Regulation, 518
competition law
EEIG exemptions, 379
joint ventures, 491
definition of companies, 7n
ECSs. *See* **European Cooperative Societies**
EEIGs. *See* **European Economic Interest Groupings**
employee participation, 440–7
collective redundancies, 440–1
draft 5th Directive, 446–7
information and consultation, 445–6
transfer of undertakings, 441–2
works councils, 47, 442–5
EPCs. *See* **European Private Companies**
financial assistance for purchase of shares, 246
Financial Services Action Plan, 518
group companies
Commission Communication, 470
consultation, 5–6
draft 9th Directive, 32–3, 47–8, 449–50
harmonisation. *See* **harmonisation of company law**
insider dealing. *See* **insider dealing**
Lamfalussy procedure, 6, 518, 519
market abuse. *See* **market abuse**
mergers. *See* **cross-border mergers**
partnerships and, 99
purchase of own shares, 38
SEs. *See* **European Companies**
takeovers. *See* **cross-border takeovers**
European Companies (SEs)
10th Company Directive and, 493
accounts, 400–1
credit institutions, 401
insurance companies, 401
assessment, 410–12
confidential information, 398
employee participation
1989 draft directive, 412
2001 legislation, 402–10
appeal procedures, 409
categories of representatives, 409
confidentiality, 408
definitions, 402–3
information rights, 408
miscellaneous provisions, 408–10
negotiations, 403–5
standard rules, 405–8, 502
subsidiarity, 402
equity capital, 395
formation
conversion of public companies, 394, 395, 412
mergers, 393, 394–5, 404, 411
public notices, 395
restrictive rules, 394
general meetings, 399–400
calling, 399
majorities, 400
role, 399
insolvency, 401–2
joint ventures, 411
legal personality, 395, 411
legal regime, 392, 393, 411
managing structures, 395–9
decision making, 398
liabilities, 398–9
one-tier system, 397–8
quorums, 398
two-tier system, 396–8
nature, 9

public and private companies, 393–4
registration, 392, 395
Regulation
entry into force, 402
origins, 391
status, 394
subsidiaries, 394
transfer of registered offices
complexity, 411
decision makers, 399
protection of shareholders, 392–3
European Convention on Human rights, 525
European Cooperative Societies (ECSs)
accounts, 413–14
employee involvement, 414
formation, 413
general meetings, 413
minimum capital, 413
origin, 413
overview, 412–14
structure, 413
voting rights, 413
European Economic Interest Groupings (EEIGs)
activities, 378
contributions, 385
decision making, 384
EC competition law exemption, 379
formation, 381–2
contracts, 381–2, 390
public notices, 382–3
registration, 381, 382
French model, 167, 377
joint ventures, 491
legal personality, 379, 382
management, 384–5
liabilities, 385
members, 377–8
death, 387
expulsion, 387
insolvency, 387
liabilities, 386–7
numbers, 381
partnerships, 381
withdrawal, 387
mixed legal regime, 378, 389–90
nature, 9
objectives, 378–9
official addresses, 378
legal regime, 390
transfer, 383
overview, 377–91
participations
assignment, 385
use as securities, 386
profits, 380
prohibitions, 380–1
loans to directors, 380
management powers, 380
multiple membershisps, 381
property transfers, 380
shares, 380
registered offices, 377–8
Regulation, implementation, 379, 391
structure, 384–5
uses, 379
winding up, 387–9
European Mutual Societies, 412
European Parliament
blocking powers, 8
European Companies and, 391–2
European Cooperative Society and, 392
Lamfalussy procedure and, 518
rejection of 13th Directive, 26–7
European Private Companies (EPCs)
accounting rules, 416
advantage, 414
assessment, 416
compulsory purchase of shares, 415–16
consultation document, 416
employee participation, 416
formation, 414, 415
future, 412
information to shareholders, 416
insolvency, 414–15
legal regime, 414–15
management structures, 415
minimum capital, 415
model articles, 129–130
overview, 414–16
proposals, 4, 129–130, 414–16
registration, 415
transfers, 415

financial assistance for purchase of shares, 246–8
Financial Services Authority, 268, 514, 532
Finland, 35
formation of companies
Belgium, 90–2
documentation, 52
fees, 35
France, 61–7
Germany, 67–78
incorporation theory, 29, 34–5, 48
Italy, 78–83
Netherlands, 92–8
public companies, objects clauses, 56–7
real seat theory, 29–30, 35, 48, 378, 496
registration, 52
Spain, 83–9
United Kingdom, 53–61
Forum Europaeum Konzernrecht
group liability, 484
minority shareholders, 486–7, 489–90
proposal for a Corporate Law Group for Europe, 32–3
revocable group declarations, 456–7, 480
France
bonds, 250–3
bearer bonds, 252
bondholders' meetings, 252–3
pre-emptive rights, 252
private companies, 251–2
zero coupon bonds, 252
capital increase, 195–9
contributions in kind, 196
private companies, 195–6
public companies, 196–9
capital reduction, 192, 200–2
private companies, 200
capital requirements, 62, 64
civil v commercial law, 61
commercial courts, 100
EEIGs, implementation of EC Regulation, 391
employee participation
collective agreements, 419–20
information and consultation, 446
institutions, 419–20, 422–3
model, 46, 417
overview, 419–24
personnel representatives, 419, 422
public companies, 423–4
trade union delegations, 419, 422
works councils, 418, 419, 420–1
equity securities, 171–5
actions de jouissance, 172–3, 233
capital securities, 171
categories, 173
conversion rights, 173, 174–5
diversity, 168
loan securities, 171–2
ordinary shares, 173
preference shares, 169, 171–2, 173–4
private companies, 172–3
public companies, 171–2
terminology, 168n, 172n
tracking shares, 340
voting rights, 340
formation of companies, 61–7
articles, 62, 64–6
capital statements, 65
extraits kbis, 67
payment for shares, 63
private companies, 62–4
public companies, 64–7
registration, 63–4, 66–7
group companies, 472
definition of parent companies, 45
group liability, 481, 484
Rozenblum doctrine, 449, 452, 460
groupements d'intérêt economique, 103, 107, 166–7
model for EEIG, 167, 377
legal personality, 63
management of companies, 283–97
directors' liabilities, 293–5
first meetings, 66
private companies, 115, 283–6
public companies, 286–95
shadow directors, 483, 484
simplified share companies (SAs), 106, 287

Marin Report, 50
minority protection, 487
  listed companies, 489
  mandatory bids, 490
  purchase of shares, 488
  withdrawal rights, 489
organs of companies, 39
participation certificates, 248–9
partnerships
  accounts, 140
  annual general meetings, 139
  civil partnerships, 61, 131
  de facto partnerships, 61
  death of partners, 140–1
  dismissal of partners, 138–9
  distribution of profits, 140
  general partnerships, 137–41
  insolvency of partners, 140
  legal personality, 131, 133, 135, 138
  limited partnerships, 102, 153–4
  registration, 138
  silent partnerships, 132–3
  terminology, 61
perpetual subordinated bonds, 248
private companies. *See* **French private companies**
privatisations, 15, 16
public companies. *See* **French public companies**
purchase of own shares, 233–5
  employee shares, 234
  private companies, prohibition, 200, 233
  public offers, 234
real seat theory, 35
registered offices, significance, 65
sociétés en commandite par actions (SCAs), 52, 99, 103, 105, 107–8, 165
sociétés en commandite simples à responsabilité limitée, 103, 156
  advantages, 162–4
  disadvantages, 164
  overview, 159–60, 162–6
sociétés par actions simplifiées (SASs), 99
  co-operative ventures, 106–7
  management, 106, 287
  nature, 107
  one-person companies (SASUs), 107
  overview, 105–7
terminology, *sociétés*, 61
works councils, 418, 419, 420–1
  attendance at board meetings, 420–1
  consultation, 421
  elections, 420
  expert advice, 421
  implementation of Directive, 444
  information, 420, 421
  origins, 420
  requirement, 420
free movement
  capital, 14–20
    direct effect, 20
    golden shares, 14–20
  establishment, 8, 10–14, 96–8
  public interest exception, 12
  public security exception, 18
  Treaty provisions, 7–10
freedom of establishment
  ECJ case law, 11–14
  freedom to leave, 13–14
  principle, 8, 10–14
  pro-forma companies in Netherlands, 96–8
  Treaty provisions, 8, 10
freedom of speech, 525
French private companies (SARLs)
  See also **France**
  accounts
    approval, 284–5
    auditors' reports, 285
  auditors, 115
  bonds, 250–1
  capital
    increases, 195–6
    reductions, 200
    requirements, 62
  equity securities, 172–3
    payment for shares, 63
    shares, 112–13
  formation, 62–4
    amendment of articles, 286
  general meetings, 115, 286

French private companies (SARLs) (cont.)
resolutions, ordinary and extraordinary, 286
voting rights, 286
managers, 115, 283–6
1st managers, 283
control, 284–5
duties and powers, 283–4
information to members, 285–6
loans from companies, 284
removal, 283
scope of actions, 283–4
service contracts, 283, 284
single-member companies, 284
minority protection, investigations, 487
nationality, alteration, 286
origins, 112
overview, 111–15
purchase of own shares, 200, 233
registration, 63–4
rigidities, 106
share transfers, restrictions, 109, 113–15
shareholders, information and consultation, 285–6
single-member companies (EURLs), 42, 62, 112
service contracts, 284
French public companies (SAs)
See also **France**
bonds, 251
bearer bonds, 252
capital increase, 196–9
contributions in kind, 199
quoted companies, 198
shareholders' preferential rights, 198–9
capital reduction, 200–2
annual general meetings, 201–2
protection of creditors, 201
capital statements, 65
directors
agreements with companies, 293–4
company loans to, 293
derivative actions against, 295
liabilities, 293–5
negligence, 295
dual boards
executive boards, 290–2
supervisory boards, 292–3
system, 290–3
employee participation, 420, 423–4
elections, 423
numbers, 423
single boards, 288
supervisory boards, 292, 424
terms of office, 423–4
equity securities, 171–2
executive boards, 290–2
appointments, 291, 293
number of members, 291
powers, 291–2
quarterly reports, 292
formation, 64–7
articles, 64–6
general meetings, 295–7
extraordinary meetings, 296
quorums, 296
resolutions, 296
voting rights, 296
insider dealing regulation, 517
management, 286–95
board functions, 287
board structures, 286–95
directors' liabilities, 293–5
dual board system, 290–3
single-boards, 286–90
market abuse, implementation of Directive, 532
minority protection, 296–7
derivative actions, 295
listed companies, 489
mandatory bids, 490
special investigations, 487
special meetings, 486
withdrawal rights, 489
purchase of own shares, 233–5
employee shares, 234
limits, 234
public offers, 233–4
registration, 66–7
rigidities, 106
shareholders, 295–7
abuse of powers, 297
rights, 297

single boards, 286–90
1st directors, 287
censors, 288
chairpersons, 289–90
dismissals, 288
employee representatives, 288
executive officers, 290
functions, 289
managing directors, 290
maximum directorships, 288–90
numbers, 287
remuneration, 288, 290
shareholdings, 287
terms of office, 288
ultra vires transactions, 289
supervisory boards
annual reports, 293
call for meetings, 296
chairpersons, 292
control powers, 292–3
employee representatives, 292
functions, 292
takeovers
implementation of Directive, 507, 510
regulation, 505
terminology, 103
Fritz Thyssen Stiftung, 32n

German private companies (GmbHs)
See also **Germany**
agents, 305
bonds, 252–3
capital increases, 202–5
contribution in kind, 202–3
conversion of loans, 254
powers, 306
preferential rights, 204–5
capital reductions, 207–9
capital-replacing loans, 208–9
powers, 306
capital requirements, 67–8, 117
distributions to shareholders, 208n
employee participation, 117–18, 298, 299
equity securities, 175–6
share transfers, 109, 118
shareholder liability, 118–19
shares, 117
formation, 67–70
articles, 67
names, 67
payment of cash contributions, 68, 69
pre-registration liabilities, 53, 70–2
registered offices, 67
registration, 68–9
general meetings, 305–7
functions, 305
voting rights, 306
group companies, 461–6
contractual groups, 461
de facto groups, 461–4, 466
group liability, 482
information rights, 462
liability for insolvency, 464–6, 483n
loans from shareholders, 462, 481
minority protection, 461, 462–3, 482, 487
legal personality, 116
legislation, 116–17
analogy, 116–17
management, 117–18, 297–307
advisory boards, 305
managers, 299–303
appointment, 299–300
ban on loans to, 301
capacity, 299–300
criminal liabilities, 302
dismissal, 300
duties, 301–2
insolvency trading, 302–3, 483n
liabilities, 301–3
powers, 301
Prokuristen, 301, 303
minority protection, 486
group companies, 461, 462–3, 482, 487
information, 486
origins, 115–16
overview, 115–19
purchase of own shares, 235
restricted businesses, 116

German private companies (cont.)
single-member companies, 42, 116
formation, 70
payment of contributions, 68
Prokuristen, 301
registration, 70
resolutions, 306
supervisory boards, 298–9
confidentiality, 298
criticism, 298
dismissal of managers, 300
employee participation, 427
employees, 298, 299
functions, 303–5
membership, 298–9
trade union representation, 299
German public companies (AGs)
See also **Germany**
accounts, approval, 315
articles, 73–4
auditors
1st appointments, 74
special auditors, 75
boards, 1st appointments, 74
bonds, 253–6
conversion rights, 254–6
participation rights, 254–5
securities, 255
capital increase, 205–7
conditional increases, 206
contributions in kind, 205
from company reserves, 206–7
maximum authorised, 206
pre-emptive rights, 205–6
preference shares, 205
registration, 206
capital reduction, 209–11
compulsory purchase of own shares, 211
ordinary reduction, 209–10
protection of creditors, 210
simplified reduction, 210–11
comparative law, 49
employee participation, small companies, 307
equity securities, 175, 176–9
complexity, 169
cumulative preference shares, 316
preference shares, 176–9
voting rights, 316–
financial assistance for purchase of shares, prohibition, 246
formation, 72–7
capital statements, 73
minimum capital, 73
minimum number of members, 72
names, 73
objects clauses, 73
payment of contributions, 75
pre-registration liabilities, 77–8
registered offices, 73
registration, 76
general meetings, 314–18
appointment of examiners, 319–20
calling, 314
capital losses, 309
dividend decisions, 314–15
financial reports, 313, 314
functions, 314
necessity, 309–10
notices, 315–16
records of resolutions, 317–18
voting rights, 315, 316–17
group companies, 451–66
contractual groups, 453–7
de facto groups, 453, 458–60, 461–4, 466
group liability, 482
involving private companies, 461–67
minority protection, 487
insider dealing regulation, 517
legal personality, 76
management boards, 307–20
appointments, 307–8
business letters, 308–9
calling general meetings, 309–10
capacity, 308
competing activities, 309
confidentiality, 311
dismissals, 308
dual board system, 307, 311
functions, 307

liabilities, 310–11
loans to, 309
Prokuristen, 308, 309
remuneration, 309
standard of care, 310
market abuse, implementation of Directive, 534–5
minority protection, 318–20
appointment of examiners, 319–20
derivative actions, 318–19
group companies, 456–7, 487
information, 486
special investigations, 487
purchase of own shares, 230, 235–6
shareholders' information rights, 316, 318
single-member companies, 77
supervisory boards, 311–13
annual financial reporting, 313
capacity, 311
dismissals, 312
employee participation, 427
important consents, 312–13
liabilities, 313
limits on directorships, 312
membership numbers, 311
standard of care, 313
terms of office, 311–12
takeovers
banks' powers, 505
barriers, 505
mandatory bids, 512
regulation, 505
sell-out right, 513
squeeze-out right, 511
terminology, 103
validity of transactions, 77

Germany
analogies, use of, 41, 116–17, 203
bonds, 252–6
conversion rights, 254–6
private companies, 252–3
public companies, 253–6
capital increase, 202–7
contributions in kind, 202–3, 205
preferential rights, 204–5
private companies, 202–5
public companies, 205–7
capital reduction, 207–11
private companies, 207–9
public companies, 209–11
capital requirements
private companies, 67–8
public companies, 73
car sector, 19–20
commercial courts, 100
company law influences, 49–50
EEIGs, 379
implementation of EC Regulation, 391
employee participation
1952 Works Council Act, 429–30
1976 Act, 431–5
2004 Act, 430–1
coal, iron and steel industry, 428–9
compulsory nature, 307
EEIGs and, 379
foreign employees, 500
holding companies, 429
information and consultation, 446
model, 45, 46
overview, 424–35
structures, 417
supervisory boards, 427
trade unions, 427, 432
works councils, 424–7
equity securities, 175–9
conversion of loan capital, 254
preference shares, 176–9
private companies, 175–6
public companies, 169, 175, 176–9
silent partnerships, 254
terminology, 168n
financial assistance for purchase of shares, 246
formation of companies, 67–78
pre-registration liabilities, 53, 70–2, 77–8
private companies, 67–70
public companies, 72–7
single-member companies, 70, 77
GmbH & Co. KG, 102, 116, 155–6
advantages, 162–4
disadvantages, 164
forms, 160–1

Germany (cont.)
overview, 159–65
protection of creditors, 164
protection of limited partners, 164–5
uses, 160
GmbH & Co. KGaA, 103, 107, 108, 156, 165–6
group companies, 473
accounts, 473
capital companies, 473
connected companies, 452–7
contractual groups, 453, 454–7
de facto groups, 453–4, 458–60, 461–4, 466
definition of parent companies, 45
group liability, 482
integration, 457–8
Konzernrecht, 448–9, 451–66
liabilities, 455
liability for insolvency, 464–6, 483n
minority shareholders, 456–7, 462–3, 488
model, 448–9, 452, 456, 470, 476
private companies involved, 461–6
profit pooling, 454
proposed 9th Directive, 32, 47
standard of care, 455
influence of legal system, 43, 47–8
management, 297–320
private companies, 297–307
public companies, 307–20
shadow directors, 484
two-tier boards, 45, 298, 427
mergers, harmonisation negotiations, 26
minority protection, 486, 487
group companies, 488
organs of companies, 39
partnerships
authority of partners, 142–3
civil partnerships, 101, 131, 141
commercial undertakings, 141–2
dismissal of partners, 144, 146
EEIG membership, 381
general partnerships, 101, 141–4
Gesellschaften bürgerlichen Rechts (GbRs), 131–2
Kommanditgesellschaften, 154–6
Kommanditgesellschaften auf Aktien, 52, 99
legal personality, 101, 132, 142
liabilities, 142, 143–4
liberal professions, 144, 146
limited partnerships, 101, 102, 103, 144, 153, 154–6
limited partnerships with shares, 107, 108
management, 142
offene Handelsgesellschaften, 141–4
Partnershaftgesellschaften, 99, 100, 101, 132, 144–6
registration, 142, 155
silent partnerships, 133–4, 254
tax transparency, 130
public companies. *See* **German public companies**
purchase of own shares, 235–6
private companies, 235
public companies, 230, 235–6
taxation of companies, 102–3
transfer of real seat of companies, 30
validity of transactions, 42, 77
workers, definition, 425
works councils, 424–7
conciliation procedure, 426–7
economic committees, 426
elections, 425–6
gender equality, 426
origins, 424
requirement, 425
rights, 426
Gleichmann, K., 47, 449
golden shares, 14–20
Greece
partnerships, legal personality, 135
single-member companies, 42n
group companies
Belgium, 476–8
definition of parent companies, 45
EC law, 5–6, 32–3, 47–8, 449–50, 470
failure to harmonise, 104
France, 472

Germany, 448–9, 451–66, 473
group liability, 480–90
corporate veil, 480–1
horizontal groups, 448
importance of concept, 451
issues, 448
Italy, 451–2, 467–70, 473–4
minority shareholders, 485–90
Netherlands, 478–9
protection of creditors, 484–5
Spain, 474–6
United Kingdom, 470–1
uses, 448
vertical groups, 448

Hampel Report, 266
harmonisation of company law
comparative law and, 42–9
Contact Committees, 37
directives, 20–8
draft legislation, 28–33
failure to implement, 40
implementation choices, 36–7
liquidations, 33
methodological problems, 33–40
model laws, 36
petrification of law, 37–9
reflexive harmonisation, 34
regulatory competition or, 33–5
salami implementation, 40
Treaty competence, 7–10
Hicks, Andrew, 129–30, 412
Higgs Report, 266, 268
High Level Group of Company Experts
acquisition of own shares, 38
cross-border mergers, 26
draft 5th Directive, 29
draft 14th Directive, 31
establishment, 27
European Private Company, 4
group companies, 5–6, 32–3
misleading statements, 47
reform of 2nd Company Directive, 3, 23
remuneration disclosure, 47
takeover bids, 26n, 27
valuation of non-cash contributions, 44
Winter Report, 27, 506
wrongful trading, 47
Hommelhoff, Peter, 129–30
Hopt, K.J., 521
Hungary, takeovers, 512

Iceland, works councils, 443
incorporation. *See* **formation of companies**
incorporation theory, 29, 34–5, 48
insider dealing
beneficial effects, 518
criminalisation, 518, 521
derivatives on commodities, 520
disclosures
confidentiality, 522–3
delay, 522–3
inside information, 521–4
methods, 521–2
professional obligations, 524, 530
selective disclosure, 523–4
to third parties, 523
Market Abuse Directive, 516–17, 520–6
meaning, 517, 520–1
mens rea, 521
national regulation, 517
preventive measures, 529–30
primary and secondary outsiders, 521
self-regulation, 517
transparency and, 518
International Accounting Standards, 25
investor protection
Chinese walls, 529, 530
codes of conduct, 530
diversity, 516
insider dealing. *See* **insider dealing**
market abuse. *See* **market abuse**
Ireland
cross-border mergers, 504
employee participation, 446
floating charges, 258
incorporation theory, 35
influence of legal system, 44
partnerships, 101
single-member companies, 42n

Italian private companies (SRLs)
See also **Italy**
accounts, 351
auditors, 83, 122
bonds, 256
committees of auditors, 348–9
control, definition, 239
debt securities, 122
directors, 347–8
conflicts of interest, 348
liabilities, 348
powers of representation, 347–8
written records, 347
distribution of profits, 351
equity securities, 180–5
capital increase, 211–14
capital reduction, 211–12, 214–18
share transfers, 83, 120–1
shares, 119–20
formation, 82–3
capital requirements, 82, 119
deeds of incorporation, 83
payment for shares, 83, 119
general meetings, 346, 349–50
calling, 350
proxies, 350
management, 122, 346–52
origins, 119
overview, 119–22
purchase of own shares, 237–9
shareholders
annulment of decisions, 350–1
decisions, 349–51
minority rights, 351–2
withdrawal rights, 121, 351–2
single-member companies, 42n, 121
Italian public companies (SpAs)
See also **Italy**
accounts, 343–5
approval, 331
auditing, 325, 344–5
external auditors, 325
financial reports, 344
inspection rights, 344
venture capital, 325, 331
bonds, 257–9
bondholders' meetings, 258–9
categories, 259
convertible bonds, 259
fixed-rate, 259
limits, 257–8
securities, 258
subordinated bonds, 257
capital increase, 211–14
preferential rights, 213
capital reduction, 211–12, 214–18
bonds and, 257, 259
chairmen, 321
committees of auditors, 320, 324–30
calling general meetings, 334
challenging shareholder agreements, 341–2
court interventions, 326–7
directors' reports to, 329
dismissals, 328
disqualifications, 325, 328
duties, 326, 328–9
investigations, 334
numbers, 324–5
powers, 329–30
quoted companies, 327–30
reporting irregularities, 328–9
reports to courts, 330
reports to general meetings, 326, 330
terms of office, 325
unquoted companies, 324–7
control, definition, 239
directors
appointment, 321
breach of duties, 323–4
capacity, 321
competing activities, 323
conflicts of interest, 323
court interventions, 326–7
delegation of powers, 321–2
derivative actions, 324
duties, 322–3
fraud, 324
liabilities, 322–4
negligence, 324
quorums, 321
removal, 321
remuneration, 322
reports to auditors, 329
scope of powers, 322

dividends, 345
dualistic system, 330–1
equity securities, 180–5
  savings shares, 339–40
  tracking shares, 340
executive boards, 330
  appointments, 331
formation, 78–82
  documents, 78–80, 83
  incorporation by public subscription, 79, 80–1
  minimum capital, 79
  payment for shares, 81
  pre-registration liabilities, 82
  registration, 81–2
  simultaneous incorporation, 79–80
general meetings, 332–43
  annual general meetings, 332–3
  annulment of resolutions, 342
  auditors' reports, 326, 330
  calling, 333–4
  extraordinary general meetings, 332, 333
  majorities, 337–8
  necessity, 327
  notices, 334–5, 338
  notification of agreements, 340–2
  proxies, 335–7
  quorums, 337–9
  voting rights, 339–40
  withdrawal rights, 342–3
legal personality, 82
listed companies
  accounts, 344
  calling general meetings, 333–4
  challenging accounts, 345
  Code of Corporate Governance, 320
  committees of auditors, 327–30
  derivative actions, 346
  Internal Code Committees, 320
  minority protection, 489
  Remuneration Committees, 320
  remuneration of directors, 320, 322
  withdrawal rights, 343
management, 320–46
  audit committees, 331–2
  dual or single boards, 321
  dualistic system, 320, 330–1
  traditional model, 321–4
  unitary board system, 331–2
minority protection, 345–6
  derivative actions, 345–6
  listed companies, 489
  mandatory bids, 490
  withdrawal rights, 342–3, 489
prospectuses, 80–1
  amendments, 80–1
purchase of own shares, 237–9
registered offices, transfer abroad, 342
shareholders, information rights, 335
società in accomandita per azioni, 52
supervisory boards, 330–1
  challenging shareholder agreements, 341–2
  numbers, 331
  powers, 331
takeovers
  barriers, 505
  implementation of Directive, 510
terminology, 103
Italy
accounts, group companies, 468–9
auditors, 1st auditors, 80
bonds, 256–9
  private companies, 256
  public companies, 257–9
capital increase, 211–14
  authorisation, 212
  bonus shares, 213
  contributions in kind, 212
  from reserves, 213
  registration, 214
capital reduction, 211–12, 214–18
  circumstances, 215
  court orders, 217
  expulsion of members, 217–18
  losses, 216
  methods, 215
capital requirements
  private companies, 82
  public companies, 79
collective agreements, 435
control of companies, definition, 239
EEIGs, 379
employee participation, 435, 446

Italy (cont.)
energy privatisations, 19
equity securities, 180–5
bearer shares, 183
classes of shares, 182
employees, 184
enjoyment shares, 183–4
preferences, 180–1, 182–3
formation of companies, 78–83
incorporation documents, 78–80, 119
private companies, 82–3
public companies, 78–82
group companies, 451–2, 467–70, 473–4
accounts, 468–9
annual reports, 469
connected companies, 467–8
definition of parent companies, 45
German model, 470
liabilities, 468
loans to parent companies, 469–70
public notices, 468
withdrawal rights, 469
management, 320–52
1st directors, 80
private companies, 346–52
public companies, 320–46
minority protection, 486
mandatory bids, 490
private companies, 351–2
public companies, 342–3, 345–6, 489, 490
purchase of shares, 488
withdrawal rights, 489
partnerships
agreements, 147
civil partnerships, 131, 132, 146
death of partners, 148
dismissal of partners, 148
general partnerships, 146–8
insolvency, 148
lack of legal personality, 147
liabilities, 147
limited partnerships, 102, 146, 147, 156–7
registration, 146–7
società semplice, 132, 146
terminology, 61, 146
personalised companies, 120
private companies. *See* **Italian private companies**
public companies. *See* **Italian public companies**
purchase of own shares, 237–9
limits, 238
terminology, *società*, 61

journalism, 525, 526

Kronstein, Professor, 49–50

Lamfalussy procedure, 6, 518, 519
Law Society, 37
legal personality
See also specific countries
cross-border recognition, 9
EEIGs, 379, 382
European Companies, 395, 411
partnerships, 101–2, 131
public and private companies, 101
liquidations, draft directive, 33
loan capital
Belgium, 261–3
bonds, 248
equity securities and, 169, 248–9
France, 250–3
Germany, 252–6
harmonisation issues, 37–8
Italy, 256–9
Netherlands, 264
priority ranking, 248
Spain, 259–61
United Kingdom, 249–50
Lohne, K.H., 130
Luxembourg, 42n, 507

management
Belgium, 361–8
corporate control market, 266
delegation, 265
EEIGs, 384–5
EPCs, 415
European Companies, 395–401
France, 283–97

Germany, 297–320
inefficiency, market mechanism, 266
Italy, 320–52
legal controls, 265
liability of directors, failure to harmonise, 516
national diversities, 266
Netherlands, 368–76
remuneration of directors, proposals, 47
Spain, 352–60
United Kingdom, 267–83
market abuse
Chinese walls, 529, 530
codes of conduct, 530
Directive, 516–17
co-decision procedure, 518
exceptions, 519
implementation, 531–5
scope, 519
disclosure, 521–4
insider dealing. *See* **insider dealing**
market manipulation, 521–2, 524–6
preventive measures, 529–30
safe harbour, 527–9
sanctions, 531
standards of communication, 526–7
supervisory authorities, 530–1
trading in own shares, 527–9
market manipulation
abuse of dominant position, 525–5
defences, 525
definition, 521–2, 524, 526
forms, 524–5
journalists and, 525
media
market manipulation and, 525, 526
standards of communication, 526–7
mergers. *See* **cross-border mergers**
Mestmäcker, Ernst-Joachim, 50
minority shareholders
See also specific countries
national regulation, 104
proposed harmonisation, 48–9, 516
mutual recognition of companies, 9, 11
Netherlands
accounts, 371–2
adoption, 373
European cooperative societies, 376
pro-forma foreign companies, 96
auditors' reports, 373
bonds, 264
capital increases, 226–8
authorisation, 226–7
employee shares, 228
pre-emptive rights, 227–8
capital reductions, 228–30
authorisation, 228
limits, 229
protection of creditors, 229
redemption and purchase of shares, 192, 229–30
registration, 228–9
capital requirements
contributions in kind, 94
payment on formation, 93–4
pro-forma foreign companies, 96, 97
directors
appointments, 369
conflicts of interests, 372
de facto directors, 483n
functions, 371–2
insolvency of companies, 372
liabilities, 372
standard of care, 372
EEIGs, implementation of EC Regulation, 391
employee participation, 438–40
information and consultation, 446
model, 45, 46
structures, 417–18
supervisory boards, 440
works councils, 438–40
equity securities, 189–91
preference shares, 190–1
priority shares, 191
vesting in foundations, 189–90, 191
vesting in trust companies, 189–90
warrants, 191
European cooperative societies, 376
management, 376
transfer of registered offices, 376

Netherlands (cont.)
executive boards, functions, 368–9
financial assistance for purchase of shares, 192, 246–7, 248
formation of companies, 92–8
pre-incorporation liabilities, 94–5
private companies, 128
pro-forma foreign companies, 95–8
registration, 94
general meetings, 373–4
notices, 373–4
powers, 370, 373
role, 373
group companies, 460, 478–9
definition of dependent company, 479
definition of group, 479
definition of subsidiary, 479
group liability, 481–2
works councils, 439
incorporation theory, 35
large companies, 369–71
definition, 191n, 369–70
foreign control, 371
priority shares, 191
supervisory boards, 369, 370–1
works councils, 370
loan capital, 264
management, 368–76
European companies, 376
large companies, 369–71
structures, 368–9
minority shareholders
compulsory sale of shares, 375, 488
investigations, 487
judicial protection, 374
priority shares, 191
purchase of shares, 488
rights, 374–6
special meetings, 486
voiding decisions, 374
organs of companies, 39
partnerships
authority of partners, 152
categories, 101
deeds, 151
EEIG membership, 381
general partnerships, 134, 151–2
law reform, 151, 152
legal personality, 101–2, 151, 152, 159
liabilities, 152
limited partnerships, 151, 159
limited partnerships with shares, 107
names, 151
public partnerships, 151
registration, 151
silent partnerships, 134
private companies. *See* **Netherlands BVs**
privatisation of telecommunications, 19
pro-forma foreign companies, 95–8
free establishment, 96–8
public companies. *See* **Netherlands NVs**
purchase of own shares, 244–6
authorisation, 245
circular ownerships, 245–6
limits, 244
repurchase, 245
shares of parent companies, 246
single-member companies, 42
supervisory boards
employee participation, 440
functions, 369
large companies, 369, 370–1
works councils, 438–40
approval of decisions, 371
consultation, 439
dismissal of representatives, 438–9
elections, 438
group companies, 439
implementation of Directive, 445
large companies, 370
mandatory consents, 439–40
powers, 439
requirement, 438
Netherlands BVs
acquisition of own shares, 129
capital increases, 226–8
financial assistance for purchase of shares, 246–7

formation, 92–8, 128
loans, 129
management, 368–76
minimum capital, 129
minority shareholders, compulsory sale of shares, 375, 488
names, 93
overview, 128–9
purchase of own shares, 244–6
share transfers, 128–9
Netherlands NVs
acquisition of own shares, 129
capital increases, 226–8
equity securities, 189–91
warrants, 191
financial assistance for purchase of shares, 246–7
formation, 92–8
insider dealing regulation, 517
loans, 129
management, 368–76
market abuse, implementation of Directive, 532
minimum capital, 92–3
minority shareholders, compulsory sale of shares, 488
names, 93
purchase of own shares, 244–6
takeovers
priority shares, 505
sell-out right, 513
terminology, 104
New Zealand, 57n
Nordea, 411
Norway, 135, 443

Ommerschlage, Professor Van, 47
organs of companies, concept, 39–40

Pannier, M., 500
parent companies, definitions, 45
partnerships
civil partnerships, 100–1, 131–2
civil v commercial, 100–1
EC law and, 99
forms, 130–67
general partnerships, 135–52
harmonisation, 21
hybrid forms, 103, 159–67
joint and several liability, 131
joint ventures, 491
legal personality, 101–2, 131
limited partnerships, 102, 152–9
limited partnerships with shares, 107–9
personal element, 130–1
silent partnerships, 132–4
tax advantages, 130
Poland, takeovers, 512
Portugal
group companies, 47, 449
privatisations, 15, 16–17
single-member companies, 42n
private companies
Belgium, 124–8
Europe-wide use, 109
European Private Companies (EPCs), 4, 129–130
France, 111–15
Germany, 115–19
Italy, 119–22
Netherlands, 128–9
Spain, 122–4
United Kingdom, 109–11
uses, 109
privatisations, 15–20
proportionality
company regulation, 12
free movement restrictions, 18n
harmonisation and, 36
public companies
See also specific countries
capital requirements, 52, 104
hybrid forms, 99
limited partnerships with shares, 107–9
mergers. *See* **cross-border mergers**
national similarities, 104
overview, 103–4
proposed 5th Directive, 28–9
share capital, 2nd Company Directive, 169
share transfers, 104
terminology, 103–4
trading in own shares, 527–9
use, 104

public interest exceptions, 12
public security exceptions, 18
purchase of own shares
Belgium, 241–4
EC law, 38
France, 233–5
Germany, 235–6
Italy, 237–9
Netherlands, 129, 244–6
Spain, 239–41
United Kingdom, 230–3

real seat theory, 29–30, 35, 48, 378, 496
registered offices
See also specific countries
EEIGs, 377–8
incorporation theory, 29, 34–5, 48
transfers, 30
European Companies, 392–3, 399, 411
proposed 14th Directive, 30–2, 35, 56, 60
registration, requirement, 52
regulatory competition
Delaware, 95
harmonisation or, 33–5
Rickford, J., 513
Rodière, René, 37–8

Schmitthof, Clive, 43
Scotland, partnerships, 135–6, 137, 153
shareholder rights, draft 5th Directive, 29
shares. *See* **equity securities**
single-member companies
See also specific countries
availability, 42
SLIM Group, 3, 21–2, 38
Slovenia, 47, 448
SMEs, directives, 24
Sonnenschein, Jürgen, 460
Spain
bonds, 259–61
capital increases, 218–20
amendment of articles, 219
pre-emptive rights, 219
private companies, 218–19
public companies, 220
registration, 219
capital reductions, 220–2
amendment of articles, 221
registration, 221
capital requirements, private companies, 85
EEIGs, transfer of official addresses, 383
employee participation, 436–7
employees' meetings, 437
trade unions, 436, 437
works councils, 417, 436
equity securities, 185–6
non-voting shares, 185–6
private companies, 185
public companies, 185
terminology, 168n
formation of companies, 83–9
private companies, 83–5
public companies, 87–9
single-member companies, 85–6
group companies, 474–6
group liability, 481
limited partnerships with shares (SCAs), 108–9
management, 352–60
private companies, 123, 352–6
public companies, 357–60
shadow directors, 484
minority protection
mandatory bids, 490
private companies, 123–4
partnerships
agreements, 148–9
civil partnerships, 100, 132
distribution of profits, 149–50
general partnerships, 148–50
legal personality, 131, 149
limited partnerships, 157
limited partnerships with shares, 157
management, 150
names, 149
powers of representation, 150
payment of contributions, 85
private companies. *See* **Spanish private companies**

privatisations, 17, 18
public companies. *See* **Spanish public companies**
purchase of own shares, 239–41
circumstances, 240
limits, 240
SLNEs, 124, 354
Spanish private companies (SLs)
accounts, 353
bonds, prohibition, 259–60
capital
purchase of own shares, 239–41
reductions, 220–2
requirements, 85, 122
share transfers, 122–3
capital increases, 218–19
amendment of articles, 219
pre-emptive rights, 219
public offers, 220
registration, 219
conflicts of interest, 124, 355
directors
appointments, 352
capacity, 353
challenging resolutions, 354, 356
confidentiality, 353
executive directors, 353
liabilities, 354
non-compete obligation, 353
numbers, 352
powers of representation, 353
removal, 352
remuneration, 353
standard of care, 353
equity securities, 185
general meetings, 354–6
conflicts of interests, 355
convening, 355
information rights, 355
location, 355
majorities, 356
notices, 355
proxies, 355
role, 352, 354
void resolutions, 354, 356
incorporation, 83–5
articles, 87
deeds, 84–5
pre-incorporation liabilities, 86
registration, 85
simplification of procedures, 86–7
single-member companies, 85–6
legal personality, 85
management, 123, 352–6
minority protection, 123–4
overview, 122–4
single-member companies, 42n, 85–6
sociedad limitada de nueva empresa (SLNE), 124
number of members, 354
restricted activities, 354
Spanish public companies (SAs)
bonds, 260–1
authorisation, 260
certificates, 260
convertible bonds, 260–1
limits, 260
ministerial consent, 260
capital
equity securities, 185
increases, 220
purchase of own shares, 239–41
reductions, 220–2
directors
appointments, 357
delegation of powers, 357–8
dismissal, 357
liabilities, 358
listed companies, 360
powers of representation, 358
remuneration, 357
general meetings, 358–60
calling, 358–9
challenging resolutions, 360
notices, 359
quorums, 359
voting rights, 359
incorporation, 87–9
articles, 87–8
names, 88
non-cash contributions, 89
objects clauses, 88
pre-incorporation liabilities, 89
insider dealing regulation, 517
listed companies

Spanish public companies (SAs) (cont.)
committees of auditors, 360
corporate governance statements, 360
management, 357–60
market abuse, implementation of Directive, 532
minority protection, mandatory bids, 490
takeovers
regulation, 505
sell-out right, 513
terminology, 103–4
special purpose vehicles, 25
stock exchanges, regulation, 265
subsidiaries
freedom of establishment, 7n, 10–11
proposed 9th Directive, 32–3
subsidiarity
employee participation, 402
harmonisation and, 36
Sunday trading, 17n
supervisory authorities, 513, 530–1
Sweden
incorporation theory, 35
market abuse, implementation of Directive, 532
partnerships, legal personality, 135

Taiwan, 448
takeovers
See also **cross-border takeovers**
benefits, 504
national regulation, 504–6
taxation
discrimination, 10
proposed harmonisation, 48
transfer of undertakings, EC law, 441–2

UK directors
appointment
1st directors, 268
life appointments, 268
common law, 267
conflicts of interests, 273–4
law reform, 51
definition, 267
disqualifications, 269
duties, 271–5
breaches, 276
fiduciary duties, 271–3
insolvency, 269
loans to, 274
loss of office, payments, 274
meetings, quorums, 270
negligence, 274–5
non-executive directors
Higgs Report, 266, 268
negligence, 275
reviews, 266–7
powers, 269–2
property transactions with, 274
remuneration, 268–9
retirement, 268
rotation, 268, 269
shadow directors
definition, 273
group liability, 482, 483
shareholdings, 268
two-tier boards, opposition, 45
ultra vires actions, 272
unauthorised profits, 272–3
wrongful trading, 274, 482
UK private companies
See also **United Kingdom**
alternative dispute resolution, 111
annual accounts, 110
auditors' reports, 110
capital, 53
increase, 193
purchase of own shares, 230–3
reduction, 194–5
financial assistance for acquisition of shares, 110
general meetings, 110, 275, 277
limited by guarantee, 110
nature of entity, 109–11
share transfers, 109, 110–11
single-member companies, 42n, 111
voting rights, 278
UK public companies
See also **United Kingdom**
capital
increase, 193
purchase of own shares, 230–3
reduction, 194–5

formation, 54–5
  objects clauses, 56–7
general meetings, 110, 275–8
insider dealing regulation, 517
listed companies
  Combined Code, 265–6, 267
  Listing Rules, 533
market abuse
  concept, 519, 532
  implementation of Directive, 532–4
  Listing Rules, 533
  Market Code, 517
  penalties, 534
mergers, 44n, 491–2, 504
minority protection
  mandatory bids, 490
  withdrawal rights, 489
takeovers
  breakthrough rule, 510–11
  City Code, 268, 505–6, 513
  hostile takeovers, 505
  implementation of Directive, 507–8, 510–11
  mandatory bids, 512
  principles, 513
  sanctions, 514
  squeeze-out right, 511
  Takeover Panel, 513, 514

United Kingdom
2nd Directive, implementation, 44
agents, 60
book debts, 250
capital increase, 192–3
capital reduction, 194–5
  purchase of own shares and, 232
capital requirements
  authorised share capital, 192
  contracts with shareholders, 58
  non-cash considerations, 44, 55
  payment for shares, 54–5
  private companies, 53
  statements, 54, 57
civil law systems and, 44
company law influences, 49–50
company law reform
  See also **Company Law Review Steering Group**
  comparative law, 50–1
  Strategic framework, 50–1
constructive notice, 58–9
directors. *See* **UK directors**
EEIGs
  implementation of EC Regulation, 379, 391
  liabilities of members, 386
  negotiations, 380
  savings banks, 381
  territorial units, 382
  transfer of official addresses, 383
  winding up, 388–9
employee participation, 419
  information and consultation, 446
  reluctance, 47
equity securities, 170–1
  debentures, 171
  debt securities, 171
  impact of directives, 21
  pre-emption rights, 193
  preference shares, 169, 170–1, 179
  redeemable shares, 171
  redemption and purchase of shares, 195
  terminology, 168
financial assistance for purchase of shares, 192, 246, 247
Financial Services Authority, 268, 514, 532
formation of companies, 53–61
  articles of association, 55, 57–8
  capital statements, 54
  certificates of incorporation, 53, 54
  constructive notice, 58–9
  legal personality, 58
  memoranda, 55–7
  migration, 60–1
  objects clauses, 57

United Kingdom (cont.)
overview, 53–61
payment for shares, 54–5
pre-incorporation contracts, 59–60
process, 53–4
public companies, 54–5
public v private, 53
registration, 53–4
general meetings, 275–8
electronic voting, 278
notice, 277
quorums, 277
requests, 276–7
voting rights, 278
good faith transactions, 59
group companies, 470–1
future, 490
group liability, 480–1, 482
minority protection, 487–8
protection of creditors, 484–5
incorporation theory, 34–5
influence of legal systems, 44
legal personality, 58
loan capital, 249–50
debentures, 249–50
fixed charges, 250
floating charges, 250
securities, 249–50
management, 267–83
articles, 267–8
directors. *See* **UK directors**
general meetings, 275–8
minority protection, 278–83
public and private companies, 267
reviews, 266–7
mergers
accounting, 44n
cross-border, 504
practice, 491–2
minority protection, 278–83, 485
derivative actions, 278–80
fraud on minority, 278
group companies, 487–8
investigations, 487
law reform, 282
mandatory bids, 490
personal actions, 281
purchase of shares, 488
special meetings, 486
unfair prejudice, 281–3
winding up petitions, 281
withdrawal rights, 489
partnerships
agency, 136
EEIG membership, 381
general partnerships, 135–7
importance, 130
lack of legal personality, 135, 136, 137
law reform, 136–7, 152–3
liabilities, 136, 137
limited liability partnerships, 102
limited partnerships, 102, 152–3
partner numbers, 101
property, 136
termination, 135
privatisations, 17–18
purchase of own shares, 171, 230–3
capital redemption reserve, 232
court powers, 233
market purchases, 231–2
off-market purchases, 231
public notices, 233
upper limits, 230
receivables, 250
registered offices, transfers, 56
Sunday trading, 17n
ultra vires transactions, 56
works councils, 47, 419, 444
United States
13th Directive and, 27
company law influences, 49–50
Delaware, 34, 95
directors' functions, 270
group liability, 480
insider dealing, 517, 519–20
leveraged buy-outs, 248
limited liability partnerships, 102
model laws, 36
regulatory competition, 34
subordinated bonds, 257
tracking shares, 340

undercapitalisation concept, 481
Uniform Commercial
Code, 34

Vredeling, Henk, 442

Werlauff, E., 7n
Winter Report, 27, 506
works councils
See also **employee participation**
Directive
contents, 442–4
implementation, 444–5
scope, 47
transfer of registered
offices, 411
Vredeling proposals, 442
Würdinger, Professor, 47, 449

Xuereb, Peter, 41

Lightning Source UK Ltd.
Milton Keynes UK
UKOW041900021212

203064UK00001B/36/P

9 781107 407640